Modern Architecture Through Case Studies

Peter Blundell Jones

Architectural Press

OXFORD AMSTERDAM BOSTON LONDON NEW YORK PARIS
SAN DIEGO SAN FRANCISCO SINGAPORE SYDNEY TOKYO

Architectural Press
An imprint of Elsevier Science
Linacre House, Jordan Hill, Oxford OX2 8DP
225 Wildwood Avenue, Woburn MA 01801-2041

First published 2002

British Library Cataloguing in Publication Data
Blundell Jones, Peter
Modern Architecture Through Case Studies
1 Architecture, Modern, 'Case Studies', 20th Century
I. Title
724.6

Library of Congress Cataloguing in Publication Data
A catalogue record for this book is available from the Library of Congress

ISBN 0 7506 3805 2

For information on all Architectural Press publications
visit our website at WWW.architecturalpress.com

Contents

Acknowledgements

Friends and colleagues have long urged me to write a general book on the Modern Movement, but I was put off by the way architects I was well-informed about were served by such histories. I preferred to dig deeper, even if this meant a narrower territory. Monographs on Scharoun and Häring were the initial vehicles. Critiques for *The Architectural Review* under Peter Davey honed my pen and broadened my views: a history article for the *AR* written on Scharoun's centenary became the basis for Chapter 13 of this book. An additional catalyst was the *Masters of Building* series run by *Architects Journal.* Edited by Dan Cruickshank under the leadership of Peter Carolin, this bold series looking at buildings in unprecedented detail proved surprisingly popular among practitioners.The high point for me was a multiple edition on the work of Asplund, which funded a trip to Sweden. The resulting pieces on the Gothenburg Lawcourts became the basis for Chapter 11. Chapter 16 also began life with the *AJ*, part of a Kahn special issue launched by editor Stephen Greenberg. Chapter 15 on Lewerentz's St Peter's Church derives likewise from an article published both in Anthony Tischhauser's *Archithese* and Giancarlo De Carlo's *Spazio e Societa*, but the inspirational visit took place on the *AJ* Asplund trip. The foundations for other chapters were laid in lectures given at conferences and to undergraduates at the Universities of Cambridge, South Bank and Sheffield where I was sequentially employed. Sometimes these were connected with model-building programmes, notably at Sheffield for the Scharoun and Häring Exhibitions. Besides revealing the project concerned in three dimensions, the questions of interpretation raised by modelling invariably extended my understanding, and I thank the students for their patient work.

This book is part of an academic discourse, and without being able to pinpoint precisely who and when, or making too a long list while still omitting some, I gratefully acknowledge that exchanges with colleagues and students at the institutions to which I belonged have contributed much to the development of my understanding, as have discussions with many contemporary architects about whose work I have written.

In immediate connection with the book I thank Michael Spens for promoting it with the publisher and Neil Warnock-Smith for offering the contract. Colin St John (Sandy) Wilson, who has provided support and inspiration over the years, read the typescript and gave the benefit of his advice. Alan Williams read it for errors and inconsistencies hopefully since corrected. David Wild has graced it with one of his ironic collages, adding a touch of the surreal. John Sergeant gave advice on the Wright chapter and provided drawings and photographs: Jan Woudstra, Olga Popovic, and Björn Linn gave advice on other chapters. For use of drawings I thank Elias Cornell, Otto Graf, Jürgen Joedicke, Gerhard & Karin Kirsch, Dirk Lohan, Richard MacCormac, Helge Pitz & Winfried Brenne, the Scheper Family, Curt Siegel and Maritz Vandenberg. For use of illustrative material I thank the following institutions: Akademie der Künste Berlin, Alvar Aalto Foundation Helsinki, Architekturmuseet Stockholm, Bauhaus-Archiv Berlin, Beeldrecht Foundation Amsterdam, Centro Studi Giuseppe Terragni Como, Centro Studi Pier Luigi Nervi Parma, Fondation Le Corbusier Paris, Frank Lloyd Wright Foundation, Getty Research Institute, IISH Amsterdam, Kunstbibliothek Berlin, Landesmedienzentrum Baden-Württemberg, Louis I. Kahn Collection Pennsylvania, Netherlands Architecture Institute Rotterdam, MIT Press, Öffentliche Kunstsammlung Basel, Princeton University Press, and Stadtarchiv Stuttgart. Peter Lathey contributed model photographs and made most of the scans. Taewoong Kang cleaned some of them electronically. Doreen Spurr helped with administration and Melvyn Broady with production. At Architectural Press I thank editorial staff Katherine MacInnes, Alison Yates Sue Hamilton and Pauline Sones. Finally, I must acknowledge the considerable support of the University of Sheffield School of Architecture, especially of my fellow professors Jeremy Till and Bryan Lawson.

Peter Blundell Jones, Sheffield, November 2001

Introduction

This book is an attempt to look again at the Modern Movement in architecture and to reframe it according to broader criteria. The first histories of the Movement described a revolution of which they were still a part, and which they sought to perpetuate and to justify. Nikolaus Pevsner, author of *Pioneers of Modern Design*, was the main importer into Britain of the Movement's German core soon after it began. Sigfried Giedion, author of *Space, Time and Architecture*, was the secretary of the Congresses of Modern Architecture and a key advocate for Le Corbusier's ideas. Henry Russell Hitchcock and the young Philip Johnson, organisers of the exhibition *The International Style* in New York in 1932 and authors of the eponymous book/catalogue, were the main importers of European Modernism to the United States. All these commentators had axes to grind and necessarily told partial stories to further their cause. Inevitably they reduced and simplified, selected and interpreted. They were so successful in their efforts to produce a convincing picture that their word was taken as law by a couple of generations, their principles adopted in the education of architects internationally for decades.

Although the ideology propagated by them fell out of favour in the 1970s, the interpretation they presented has remained stubbornly persistent, for Post-modernists did them the honour of rejecting 'The Modernist Project' precisely on their terms, taking their story largely as read. And although progress has been made towards a more balanced view by rehabilitating some forgotten figures, architects such as Mies and Le Corbusier have retained the dominant roles first ascribed to them, even growing in mythical status through the weight of attention from historians. In comparison talented and once influential architects like Bruno Taut and Erich Mendelsohn, to cite but two examples, have been largely left out in the cold.[1]

In proclaiming their new orthodoxy, the first historians of the movement set narrow limits and cut off historical roots. Instead, this study celebrates the Movement's depth and complexity, stressing not so much its common aims as its exploratory spirit and the resultant creative diversity. It also attempts to get close to the buildings, for too many past histories, in concentrating on styles and periods and general cultural history, have touched on buildings only in passing. Typically, they display a single image to make a simple point.[2] Instead, this study takes as case-studies fifteen buildings by fifteen architects, some well-known, others less so. Former heretics stand alongside mainstream heroes, all given equal billing. Perhaps the lesser-known were no less gifted and are no less valuable as examples.

Why case-studies?

The case study approach is partly the result of misgivings, through years of teaching architectural history, about the possibility of ever writing a comprehensive modernist history that will stand scrutiny. As Lytton Strachey wrote in the preface to *Eminent Victorians*; recent history is difficult because *'we know too much about it'*.[3] To avoid being submerged by the abundance and complexity of material, Strachey advocated that one should; *'row out over that great ocean of material, and lower down into it, here and there, a little bucket, which will bring up into the light of day some characteristic specimen.'*[4] Looking at a small sample in detail, one can feel more confident of getting at least something right than when building an edifice of theory that might crumble into a thousand pieces in the face of contradictory evidence. In comparison with a grand theory, the case-study is not so irrevocably won or lost: it provides possible evidence for other versions, and there is always the opportunity of adding further studies to make a progressive investigation.

Inspiration for a case-study approach came also from a discipline acutely concerned about the dangers of imposing narratives on the lives of others: social anthropology. In the essay, *Found in translation*, Clifford Geertz indicated how to live with the vertigo of relativity, for if cultural interpretation is always 'translation' involving some loss of meaning, all is not lost: much is also 'found'.[5] This hopeful stance gently reminds us not to despair in the absence of firm truths but to make the best of it. History, like anthropology, is the creation of narrative to make sense of events, and it too involves trading in versions. Geertz has also reported a *'move away from a laws and instances view of things to a cases and interpretations one'*.[6] If such a move is taking place, it surely reflects the doubts we share at the turn of the millennium about the powers of science to solve humanity's problems, let alone to define the nature of things. It shows our distrust of intellectual shortcuts and easy solutions, above all of a narrow Positivism.

General laws may well be implied by the narrative of a case-study and are perhaps never avoided, but starting with the case rather than the laws at least assures dialogue with the material. To be specific, it involves investigating the physical and cultural context of each building, and even if one is trying to discover general rules or principles behind it, this is perhaps better than bending the work to fit the rules.

All the architects whose work is considered in this book were born between 1860 and 1910 and are now dead:[7] the last of the works considered date from the 1960s. Much has been built since by younger generations, and there have been both stylistic changes and technical advances, so why concern ourselves with this historical work rather than with production closer to our own time?

For three main reasons:

- First, the changes brought about in the 1920s amounted to the greatest revolution architecture has ever known, and much innovation took place in an extraordinarily short time. The implications of the new possibilities were so well understood by the pioneers that many technical advances since achieved can be considered but footnotes to the earlier work.
- Second, we are still unavoidably obsessed with unfolding modernity, and the main so-called movement to have occurred since, Post-modernism, still defines itself only in relation to that which it tried to replace.
- Third, if, as many Post-modernists claim, Modernism's *tabula rasa* was the cause of our cultural impoverishment, this suggests an urgent reconnection with history, and surely we need to reconnect where the break took place, in the 1920s. This is all the more reason why that period requires careful study.

Sequence of the book

The book opens with a study of the Weissenhof housing development at Stuttgart of 1926-7. This propaganda exercise by the Deutsche Werkbund has often been taken as the moment of establishment of the International Modern Movement as well as the birthplace of the so-called International Style.[8] The flat roofs, cubic look and lack of ornament of its buildings gave an intentional impression of solidarity and unity, which must have been all the more impressive when all the architecture surrounding and elsewhere was traditional and decorated. However, the consistency was not as great as it seemed, for under the visible surface lay many different architectures based on contrasting principles. Some designs were site-specific, others repeatable and intended for universal application. Some houses, like those of Gropius, stressed the discipline of construction to the point of complete dependence, while others, like that of Scharoun, ignored it cavalierly in favour of a concentration on spatial and relational issues. Even the design of the initial layout shows a conflict in concept between Mies and his partner in the early planning stages, Hugo Häring. Including buildings by several architects considered later, the chapter on Weissenhof is used to set the scene and to introduce some of the main ideas about diversity within the Modern Movement. There follow a series of case-studies of single buildings taken in chronological sequence:

- **Hugo Häring**, father of Organic Architecture in Germany, believed that for each site and programme some form is implied which it is the architect's task to discover. His Garkau Farm, near Lübeck, of 1923-5 (Chapter 2) is a key work of Functionalism, its hierarchy of forms suggested by agricultural processes. At the same time Häring also sought to allow structure and construction a rhetorical role. The freshness of the Garkau buildings was undoubtedly due to the novelty of this approach. Häring was the most articulate theorist among German Modernists and he later became the mentor of the better-known Hans Scharoun, whose work is considered in Chapter 13.

- Though also professing functionalist concerns, **Walter Gropius** was more interested in the so-called machine aesthetic and in repeatable forms derived from the production process. He was the Head of the famous Bauhaus school during its formative period, so the new buildings marking the school's move to Dessau in 1925 (Chapter 3) can be understood both as icons of the new architecture and as the seat of a key institution. Hannes Meyer's influential theoretical programme for a scientific architecture was also launched there in 1928.

• Zonnestraal Sanatorium, Hilversum, of 1926 by **Jan Duiker** (Chapter 4) epitomises the conjunction of a white and airy architecture with health and hygiene. At the same time it is a key work of expressed engineering in concrete exploiting the new separation of skin and bones, of glass envelope and concrete skeleton.

• In Germany the most abundant modernist work of the 1920s took the form of social housing, and **Bruno Taut** was a key figure in Berlin, producing numerous high-quality housing estates. His Waldsiedlung development at Onkel Toms Hütte (Chapter 5) demonstrates his site-planning skills as well as his efforts to produce the most economical, efficient and repeatable house-types. His inventive use of sometimes startling colour schemes to cheer up cheap and plain building went largely unrecorded in the era of black and white photography, and was for a long time overlooked.

• Though later much forgotten, **Erich Mendelsohn** was the best known and most successful of Berlin Modernists in the late 1920s, with the largest office and most important jobs. He invented influential prototypes for commercial buildings such as factories, shops and the cinema. The Schocken department store in Stuttgart of 1927 (Chapter 6), the best of a series built across Germany, shows Mendelsohn's interest in reflecting the dynamism of the modern city, and in exploiting steel frame and electric light. That this building was also cleverly integrated into its urban context has often been overlooked.

• **Le Corbusier's** Villa Savoye at Poissy of 1929, (Chapter 7) has long been considered a key work of Modernism, and shows its author at his most lyrical. Set on an open meadow, it epitomises the idealism of the free-standing object-building and marks the culmination of Le Corbusier's enormously influential first period. Looking to the background, Villa Savoye exemplifies particularly well the abstraction carried over from the Purist movement in painting, of which Le Corbusier was a leading light, and it provides an eloquent vehicle for examining how he put his theories into practice.

• A generation younger than most of the other pioneers, the Fin **Alvar Aalto** (b.1898) made his international reputation somewhat later. Even so, early works like the Paimio Sanatorium and Viipuri Library 1927-35 (Chapter 8) were of crucial importance in the development of International Modernism, particularly its Scandinavian branch. Not only were Aalto's treatment of lighting and acoustics as generating elements of pioneering significance: the long gestation of the Viipuri design through several versions also provides a fascinating glimpse of his struggle to overcome the constraints of tradition.

• The Italian Engineer **Pier Luigi Nervi** made his remarkable sports halls and aircraft hangars (Chapter 9) by exploiting new construction methods and new means of calculation. Certainly this was a case of 'form follows structure' and was most convincing when large spans were required. It also produced forms of great elegance which seem close to nature in their underlying logic.

• Another Italian, **Giuseppe Terragni**, was the master of composition within a structural frame and the most sophisticated exponent of Italian Rationalism. Although in Germany Modernism was suppressed under Hitler, the Italian Fascists embraced it as progressive, and Terragni's masterpiece (Chapter 10) was the Fascist headquarters in Como completed in 1936. Inevitably it raises the difficult question of when and how architecture reflects political ideas.

• Though not completed until 1937, the Gothenburg Law Courts extension (Chapter 11) was the result of a competition won by **Gunnar Asplund** in 1913. The design went through numerous versions, the architect trying a whole series of plan and elevation ideas while checking and rechecking the relation with the context, and the brilliant final solution contains elements from every stage of this process. The drawings document one of the most remarkable design narratives of the century, showing development from tradition to modernity within the same project. By the same token, it is a complete denial of Modernism's supposed *tabula rasa*. This masterpiece by Sweden's leading

Modernist is one of the greatest 20th century examples of how to set a new building in studied contrast with an older one.

• No history of 20th century architecture could reasonably omit the highly influential **Frank Lloyd Wright**, who exerted an early and decisive influence on Europe with his prairie houses, and also imported ideas from Japan. His worklist reveals quite a different pattern from those of European contemporaries, for the bulk of it was not public and urban but domestic, reflecting his own special suburban ideal, his dream of Usonia. The building chosen for scrutiny (Chapter 12) is one of his so-called Usonian houses from the late 1930s, finding Wright at the height of his powers. The interlocking and intersecting spaces, all based on a strict module which also governs the construction, shows extraordinary mastery and assurance.

• **Hans Scharoun** (1893-1972) was one of the younger architects included at Weissenhof, and had only just made his name in Weimar Germany when Hitler came to power. He remained in that country to re-emerge as one of the leading figures of the post-war scene, completing his masterpiece the Berlin Philharmonie concert hall in 1963. Here the audience surround the orchestra in a space of unrivalled complexity, promoting the sense of a shared social event in an unexpectedly powerful way. Chapter 13 examines not this hall but an unbuilt forerunner, the National Theatre Mannheim Project of 1953, in which many of the ideas sustaining the hall were first explored. It shows better than the hall Scharoun's contextual intentions, while it also marks the emergence of his concept for the aperspective auditorium.

• The other famous entry to the Mannheim Theatre Competition was by **Ludwig Mies van der Rohe**, who in contrast to the specificity of Scharoun's approach pushed to an extreme the notion of the universal flexible building. In his later work this became enmeshed with his desire to reinterpret the classical monument, following in the path of Schinkel. The result was the Neue Nationalgalerie (Chapter 14), which stands adjacent to Scharoun's Philharmonie in Berlin's Kulturforum. Foursquare on eight columns and built of steel and glass with a stone-clad base, it recreated for the 20th century the eternal promise of the classical temple.

• The New Brutalism refers to a reawakening of interest during the post-war period in materials and textures. Supposedly inspired by Le Corbusier's use of *béton brut* at his Unité d'habitation at Marseilles, it marked a complete swing away from the white abstraction of pre-war Modernism. But the story was of course not so simple. Modernists like Häring and Mendelsohn had been interested in expressing materials from the beginning, while others like Asplund and Aalto did so also by the mid 1930s. In his last work and masterpiece the church of St Peter at Klippan of 1963 (Chapter 15), **Sigurd Lewerentz**, contemporary and for a long time partner of Gunnar Asplund, indulged the raw and the rough to an unprecedented degree. This modest building questions basic assumptions about processes and finishes, about the nature of brickwork and the detailing of window frames. It also provides a powerful brooding space for worship, a man-made cave, as if returning Christianity to the catacombs.

• The last and latest completed building studied is **Louis Kahn's** Kimbell museum at Fort Worth completed in 1972 (Chapter 16). Like most Kahn buildings it makes architecture out of the ordering of services into served and serving bays, while an extraordinary system of concrete vaults and metal reflectors throws natural light onto the paintings at just the right intensity. With its central axis, the plan is almost classical, reflecting Kahn's Beaux Arts training, and the repeated module is almost too strict, yet he makes use of every cunning variation to differentiate the spaces and orientate the visitor. Materials are expressed and subtly differentiated, the detailing impeccable. This building reaches the heights of sophistication in many ways, providing an apt termination for the series of studies.

The **Conclusion** recapitulates the main arguments and ties up some loose ends. It also makes some observations about our current architectural predicament.

Readers should not assume that I consider the architects included the only ones of their time worthy of consideration: Adolf Loos, Gerrit Rietveld, Konstantin Melnikov, Berthold Lubetkin, Jean Prouvé, Rudolf Schindler and others would certainly have merited inclusion had space allowed. The choice was intended to produce a lively balance of interests.

Bibliographical references

Books consulted and quoted from are listed alphabetically in the bibliography on pages 246-249.

References in the endnotes (as below) give the author, date and if relevant the page numbers. When an author published two or more items in a single year, a bracketed number (1) (2) etc. is added in both places.

Notes

1. Amazon lists for July 2001 revealed 256 items for Le Corbusier and 109 for Mies, but only 20 for Mendelsohn and 17 for Taut. Furthermore, among the Mendelsohn and Taut volumes cited, only six of the former and one of the latter were in print and readily available.

2. Most general histories can afford only one image of each building - no plan, no context - and refer briefly only to the special aspect of its architecture that concerns their argument. Pevsner's *Pioneers* (Pevsner 1960) is typical. This is not to deny the considerable difficulty of illustrating buildings adequately in print, even given the required number of pages.

3. Strachey, Lytton *Eminent Victorians*, Penguin, Harmondsworth 1948, p. 6.

4. Ibid.

5. Clifford Geertz, *Found in Translation*, included in Geertz 1983, pp. 36-54.

6. Ibid p. 19.

7. They are also white and male, from bourgeois western society etc. I am well aware that here I am only modifying the existing history of heroes, whose structure and basis is questionable. Buildings can equally be read as the more general product of society, in terms of typologies etc. and such readings provide both a valuable alternative view and a corrective to narratives purely about creative individuals. Even so, bodies of work by particular artists do make readily definable subject areas, and the reader readily identifies with them by imagining him/herself in that position.

I regret the absence of women architects in the book but feel that it would not have helped to elevate a token figure for the sake of a balance that even then would have remained lopsided. Women are of course no less capable than men, and attempts have been made to rehabilitate such talented figures as Eileen Gray and Lillly Reich, but unfortunately there is not much extant work as they were not able to build much. Women now find some success in a still male-dominated profession, but it was difficult, if not impossible, in the early 20th century for them to reach the status needed to command the huge budgets required for buildings. Unlike literature or painting, architecture is not an art that one can pursue effectively on one's own, except in drawings - and then it becomes almost another medium. Built architecture requires not only talent but credibility, good political circumstances, windows of opportunity, and even then considerable luck. Indeed, the careers of most of the architects described in these pages were full of disappointments and unrealised projects. What is more, experience of building tends to extend the sensibilities of architects, changing the nature of their production, so there is no knowing how a talent might have developed given more opportunity for realisation.

8. Philip Johnson wrote in 1947 that the Weissenhofsiedlung was *'the most important group of buildings in the history of modern architecture',* and that it demonstrated how the various tendencies had *'merged into single stream',* quoted in Pommer & Otto 1991, p. 2.

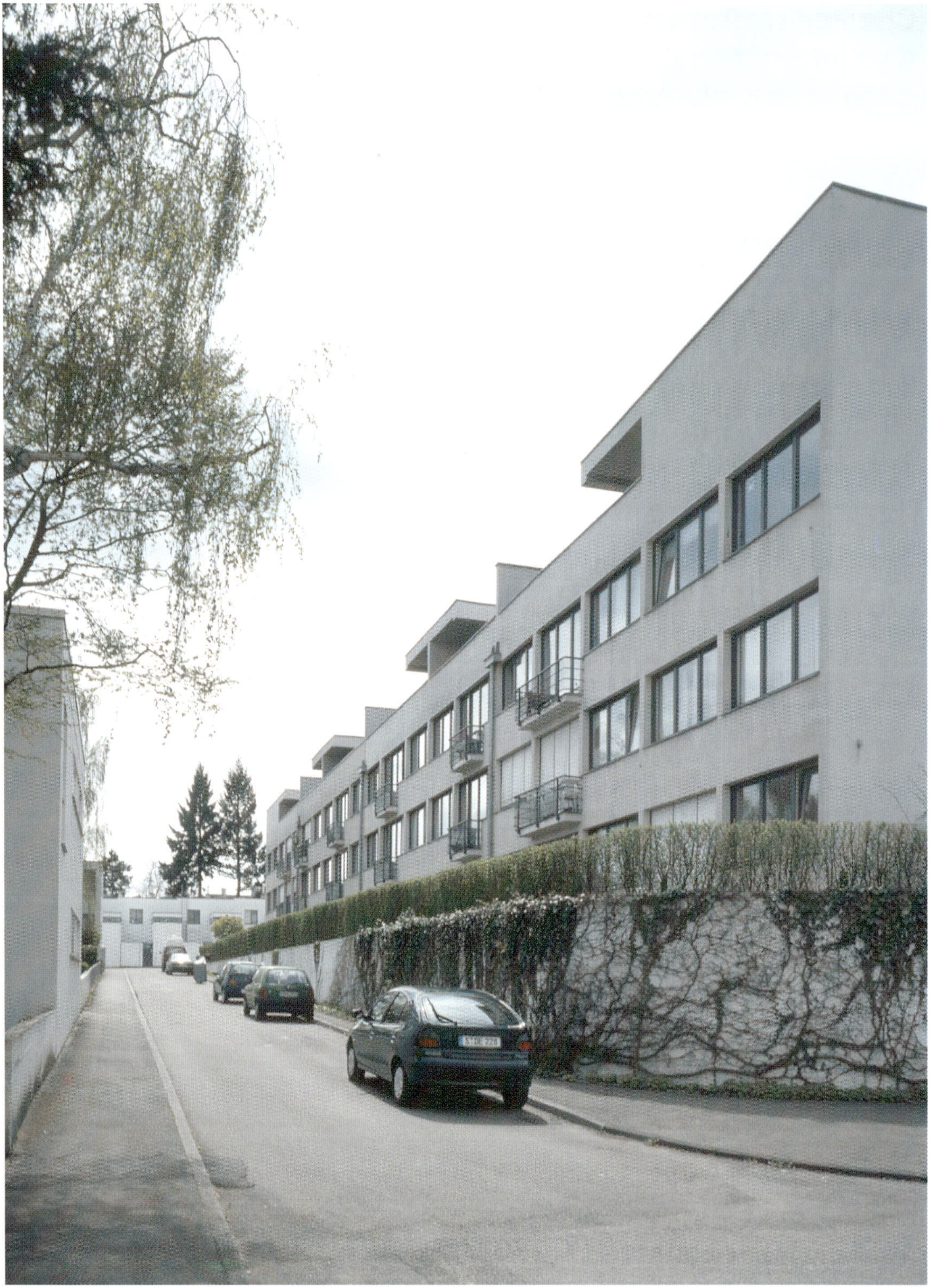

Chapter 1. The Weissenhof Experiment, 1927: One International Style or sixteen different architectures?

The Weissenhofsiedlung was a model housing development built on a hill above Stuttgart in 1926-7 as part of an exhibition entitled *Die Wohnung*. It marked the recovery of the German economy after the economic chaos of the early 1920s and expressed the progressive optimism of the Weimar Republic. The inclusion of leading architects from France, Holland, Belgium and Austria showed the solidarity of Modernists across Europe, a solidarity that gave rise a year later to the founding of CIAM, the International Congresses of Modern Architecture. It also showed Germany's will to be part of Europe and the world at a time when the 'war to end wars' had made international co-operation a progressive ideal as well as a moral duty. Organised by the Deutsche Werkbund (German Arts and Crafts Society), which had been founded in 1907, the exhibition was planned under the artistic direction of Ludwig Mies van der Rohe, a bold choice as he was known mainly for unbuilt projects. It was funded by the city on the basis that the houses and flats would be rented after the show was over. Although it was supposed to be a demonstration of social housing, the site and budget restricted many architects to building a single unit, and most produced work closer to bourgeois villas than houses for the working class. Many had a maid's room, one even a garage.[1]

Mies lived in Berlin, where along with Hugo Häring he founded an organisation of modernist architects called 'The Ring', and Ring architects dominated the show.[2] There were struggles about money which was always short, and there was opposition from conservatively-minded architects in Stuttgart who resented the imposition of foreign ideas and foreign architects on their city. There were also struggles in getting the housing built, for it had to be done in a short time, without much opportunity for supervision from the more distantly located architects. The choice of materials and techniques was in a few cases ideologically vital, but in others it was more economic and pragmatic. The building site was controlled by the Stuttgart architect Richard Döcker who also designed two of the houses. The budget was tight and he had a hard time getting information from the other architects including even Mies, so he had to take many design decisions in haste himself.

1. (opposite) Weissenhof Estate today, with Mies's block to right and Oud's houses at the end.
2. Late 1920s view from north-east corner, Scharoun's house in foreground, Max Taut's with rounded corner, Mies's block crowns hill.

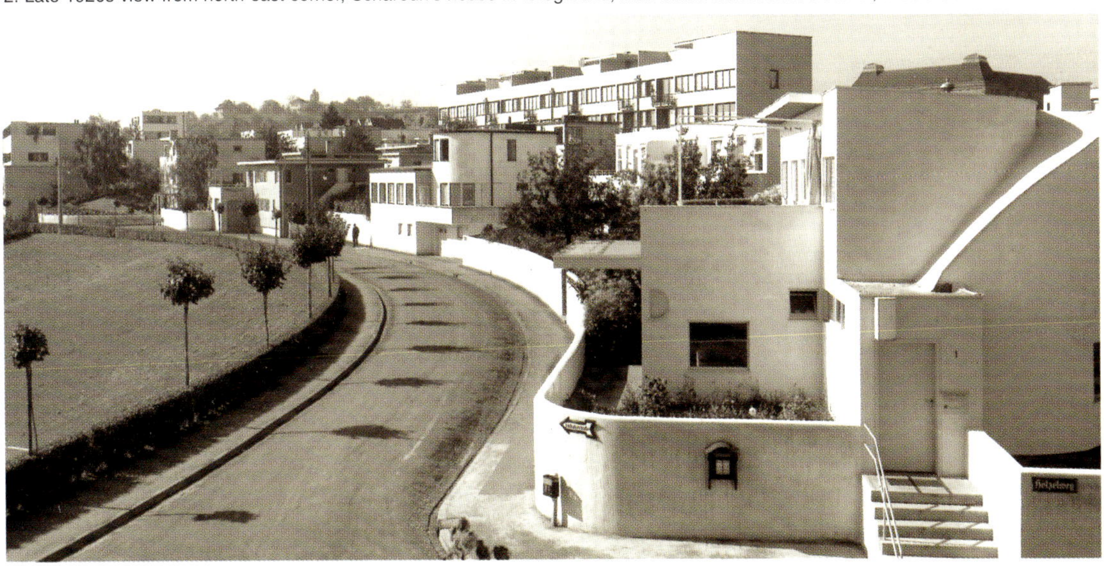

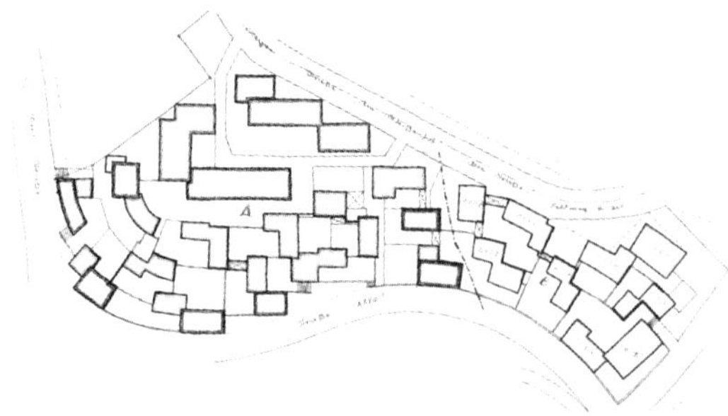

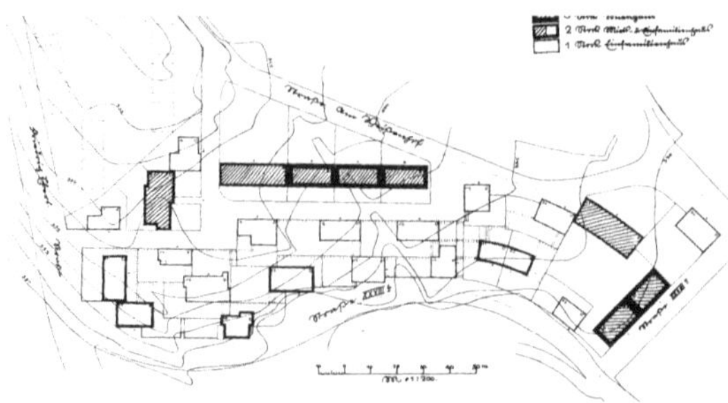

3. (above left) First site plan, probably by Häring, following contours and with linked buildings.
4. (above right) Mies's revised site plan with separate buildings.
6, 7. (opposite) The *Siedlung* today after restoration, Mies's block and Scharoun's house.
5. (below) Site plan as built. Architects as follows:

1. Mies	9. Schneck
2. Oud	10. Bourgeois
3. Le Corbusier	11. Stam
4. Gropius	12. Scharoun
5. Bruno Taut	13. Rading
6. Max Taut	14. Döcker
7. Hilberseimer	15. Behrens
8. Poelzig	16. Frank

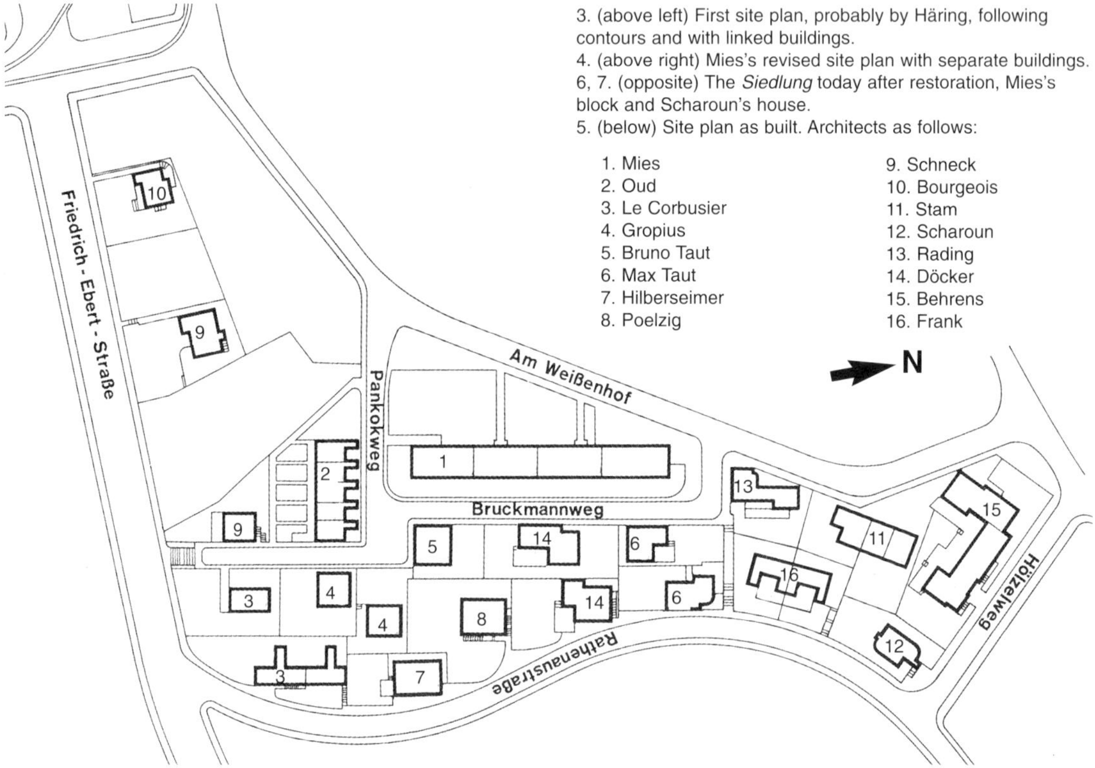

The site was an east-facing hillside overlooking the city, with rounded contours and a considerable slope. As it was a group project largely involving Ring architects, and as Mies shared an office with Ring secretary Hugo Häring, the two collaborated on initial decisions about the choice of architects and the design of the site plan.[3]

The earliest preserved plan drawing, probably by Häring,[4] shows a curved arrangement of interlocking courtyard houses which follow the contours linked by common retaining and party walls. A large block at the top - to be Mies's in the final plan - forms a kind of *Stadtkrone*,[5] and unlike the arrangement built, no building stands alone. This plan was criticised in Stuttgart as unworkable, and Mies revised it through several versions in which the buildings gradually became more separated.

Even so, the pattern of retaining walls and steps remained, and the linked pairs of houses by Max Taut and Döcker were already prefigured. Häring was unhappy with the change, and also quarrelled with Mies over the issue of architects' fees, as a result of which both he and Erich Mendelsohn withdrew their participation. Häring commented later that Mies had *'left everything to the other architects'*.[6] He thought Mies had thrown up the chance for a truly integrated site-plan, and set the course instead for the dominance of buildings conceived as free-standing objects.

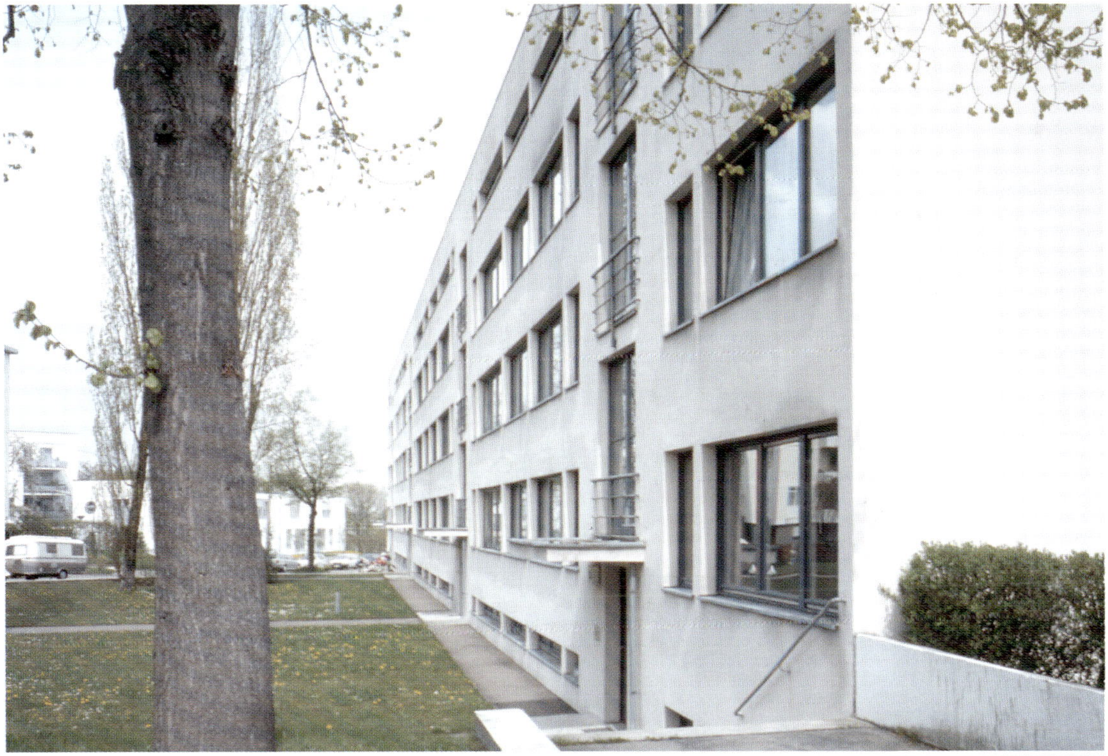

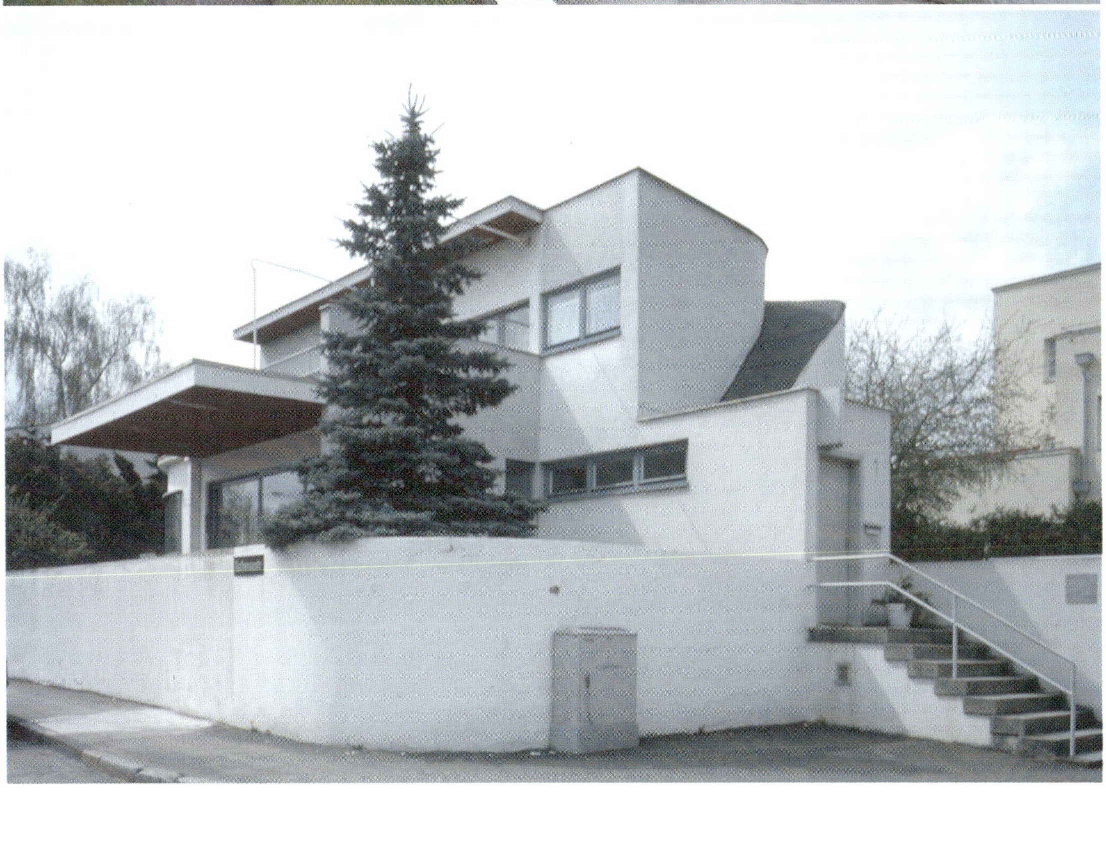

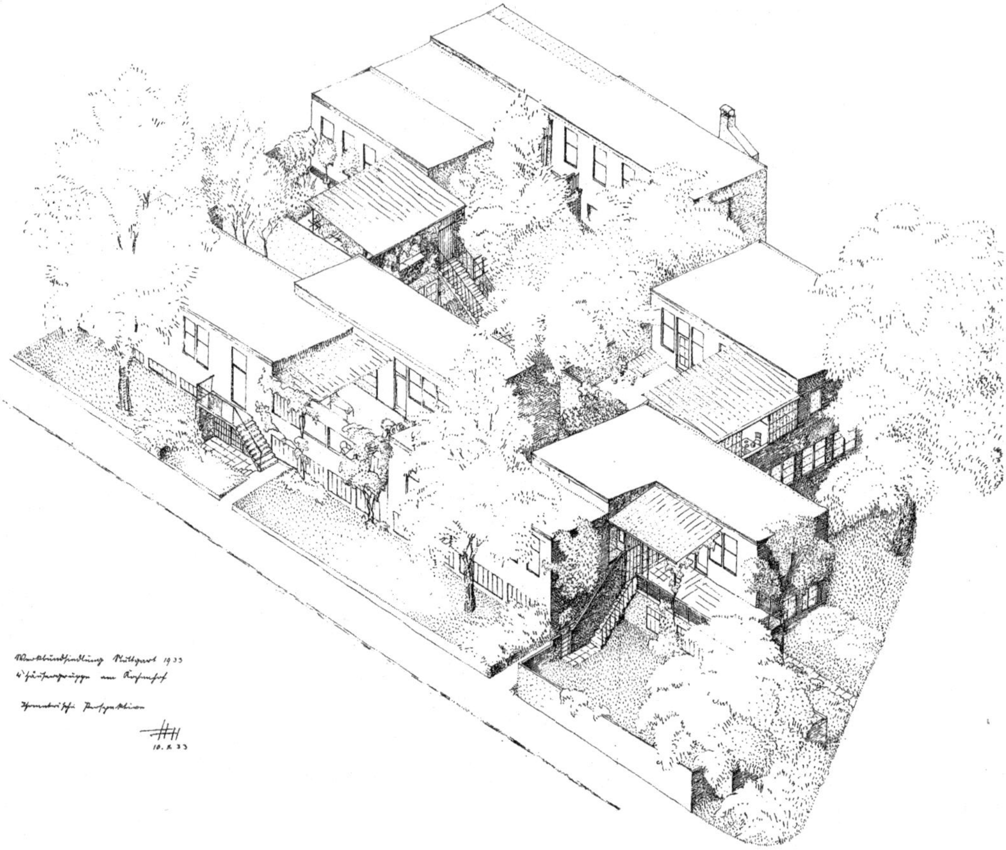

8. Hugo Häring, group of houses intended for the Kochenhofsiedlung 1933-4, an extension to the Weissenhof exploiting timber construction. After the rise of Hitler the project was removed from the Modernists and put in the hands of Paul Schmitthenner.

Häring

If he ever got as far as designing it, no drawing for Häring's housing group at Weissenhof has survived, but a later proposal for such a group of houses, at the proposed Kochenhofsiedlung[7] nearby, indicates his intentions. The houses are all different and irregularly grouped around a series of courts which serve as outdoor rooms. Habitability is all, the design being worked from the inside out starting with the consideration of spaces and their uses, but also accepting the discipline of timber frame construction. In this design as in others by him of the same period, Häring deliberately eschewed the monument and work of art in favour of a domestic world in which people could find a place and feel at home.[8]

The marginal role of Häring at Weissenhof would hardly be worth remarking were he not the spokesman for a significant ideological position opposed to that of Mies, a position shared with other Weissenhof architects such as Scharoun, Rading, Poelzig and Döcker.

While Mies always interested himself in general types and universal architectural solutions, Häring believed that every building should be specific to its purpose and context, gaining its form and identity from the role in life that it serves. He was in many ways the most committed and consistent proponent of Functionalism, while Mies by contrast pursued a form of Rationalism.[9] Thus Häring's houses for Kochenhof respond to site boundaries and levels, and each house is differently planned from the next. Theoretically, he could work across a site the size of Weissenhof with varying programmes for different families, attending in each case to whatever was different or unique to produce an endlessly changing fabric. We shall investigate Häring's approach further in Chapter 2.

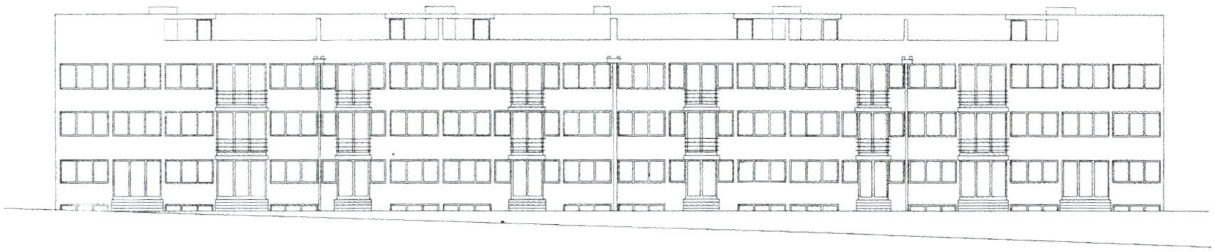

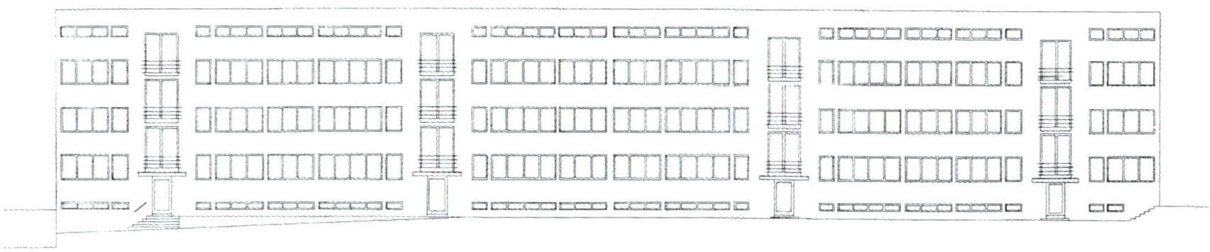

9. (top) Mies's three storey block of flats, south-east elevation facing garden and valley view. 10. (above) North-west elevation facing street. 11. (below) Upper floor plan with typically varied flat layouts: flats are of two sizes reached by shared staircases.
12. (bottom) Façade garden side, close-up.

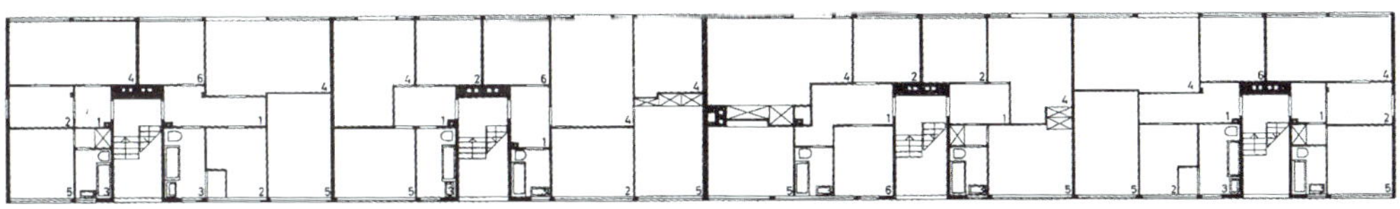

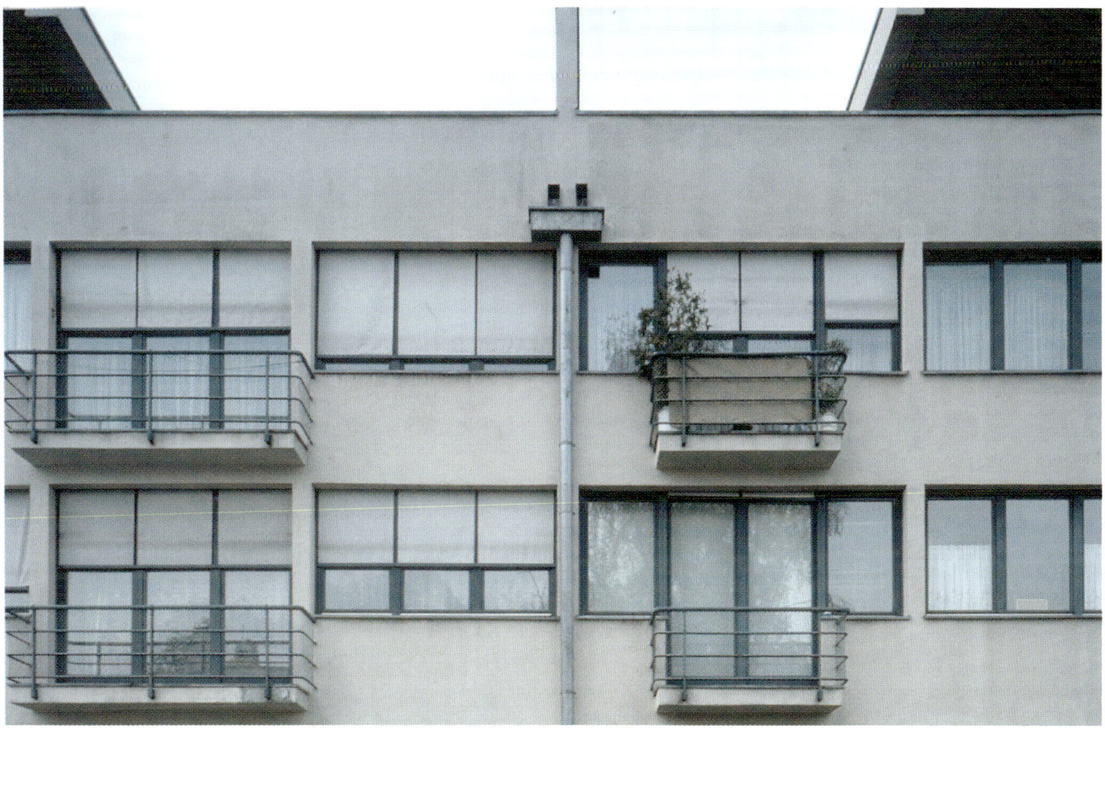

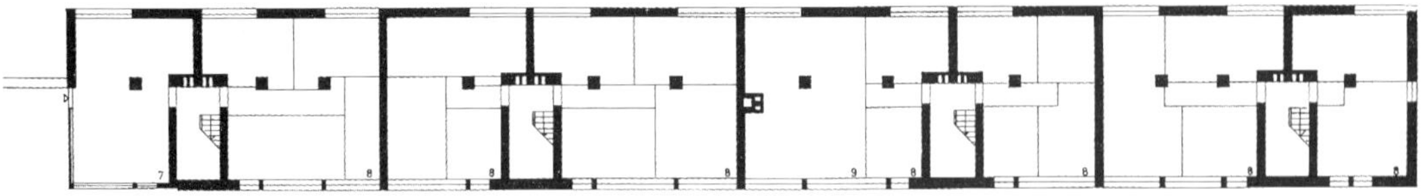

13. Mies block: plan showing the essential structural arrangement.

Mies

Mies took the opposite attitude. His block of 24 flats crowning Weissenhof was designed from the start to be flexible, lending itself to a number of suggested partitioning arrangements and yet others that the tenants might later discover. In execution he was happy to let the interiors be decked out by other designers,[10] and indeed this tested the system. But it also allowed Mies to concentrate on reducing his block to the minimum framework necessary: the open box with columns but without partitions except the party-walls. It was divided into flats of two standard sizes paired around four staircases. Since he did not know how rooms might be placed, all windows were of the same type and in a standard order, indeed in groups of three and four they determine the frame spacings, the window module becoming the module of the whole. So locked into the system, there was no question of them expressing the uses of the interior, of differentiating between a living room and a bedroom as Häring and some others would have done. Even kitchens and bathrooms varied in size and layout, though always set next to the stair walls for access to services. Mies repeated the same conditions from floor to floor, flats at ground level being identical to those at first and second floors except that garden steps replaced the balcony in front of the identical glazed doors.

The small degree of variation available to Mies in the facades was used in a masterly way: front was differentiated from back with entrance and stair windows, a changing rhythm was produced by alternating the sizes of flats, and the roofline to rear was broken by alternating attic service rooms with partly-roofed terraces. Simple and elegant, the building's reduced form was skillfully proportioned. By restricting his palette and concentrating hard on detail, Mies makes a few crucial decisions pay off. The building cannot be accused of ignoring its site, for it crowns the *Siedlung* convincingly, and Mies does just enough to tie it in with retaining walls and steps. Yet there is nothing in the design to make it belong essentially to that street, or for that matter to Stuttgart rather than to Rome or Stockholm. It was certainly understood at the time as a universal proposition, a design repeatable in serried ranks and extendible to any length - and this was also what the City had asked for. Mies saw it as a prototype, and his comments about rationality and machine production suggest he would have been happy had it been taken up.[11] But as built, it profits from being unique, and from being the right size. This is a paradox haunting Mies's whole career and those of many followers: repetition devalues.

Like many colleagues at Weissenhof, Mies was an avid reader of Henry Ford's recently published autobiography and an enthusiast for mass-production.[12] These architects understood the economies of the production line, and considered its application to the building site inevitable, so as Lucien Kroll has shrewdly pointed out, they had imitated by hand the kinds of forms that they thought the machine might later bring.[13] Traditional joiners in small workshops made endless identical windows which could equally easily all have been different, and old-fashioned brickwork was concealed with render and paint to give it a seamless surface. This was the 'machine aesthetic' that made buildings look like ships - an obvious model in terms of size and technical efficiency.

Gropius

Mies's block was built around a steel frame, but the wall construction in brickwork and render followed traditional practice. Of all the Weissenhof architects only Walter Gropius went substantially further with mass-production. He devised a pair of two-storey houses using a dry panel system with a steel skeleton of small sections placed at one metre

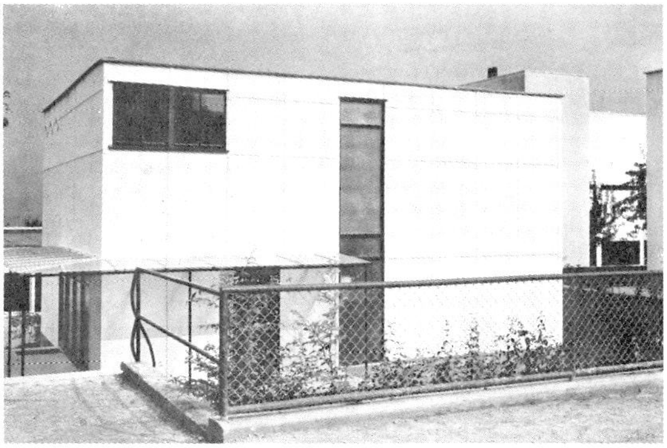

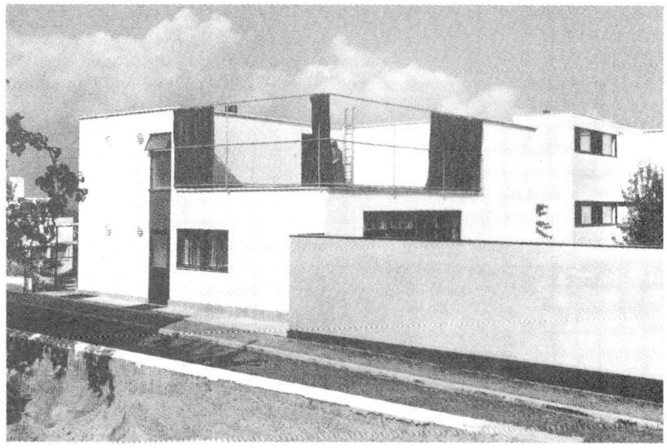

intervals, and a single central column in the almost square plan. In the end only the smaller of the houses was built according to the system, and it clearly displayed the panel joints both inside and out, the larger house being conventionally constructed. Nonetheless, both obeyed the same planning discipline: a strict 1.06 metre grid conforming to the same standard panel size and the same standard-width doors and windows. This was supposed to minimise building time and site work, transferring it to the more secure and predictable conditions of the factory.[14]

Looked at closely, Gropius's plans are not very efficient, for internal partitioning only allows rooms in multiples of one metre, so that lavatory and stair, for example, both have to be one metre wide when they could be narrower - Le Corbusier's main corridor was only 70 cm. Gropius would have argued that any inefficiency in terms of space is counteracted by economy of construction, and in 1927 it seemed likely he would be right, but this promise was not fulfiled. Even in the period 1945-60, with system building pursued at the largest scale and with the longest series, it did not prove cheaper than traditional building methods.[15] Meanwhile the price paid in terms of architectural quality was high. The Gropius houses have an austere elegance, but show almost no relation to place or site, and not much variation from room to room - always the same kind of window, the same rectangular space with the same rhythmic joints. The thought of meeting them in serried ranks in one city after another, of visiting the same kind of room in different houses if not different cities, is not inspiring, and Gropius's claim a few years later that we need not fear standardisation because *'repetition of the same thing for the same purpose exercises a settling and civilising influence on men's minds'* [16] hardly bears repetition 65 years later without irony.

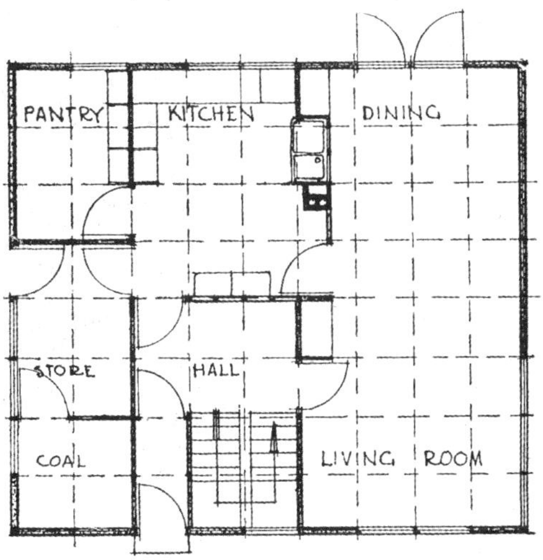

14. (above left) House no. 17, entrance side: visible cover-strips show the prefabrication module.
15. (above right) House no. 16, street side: this one was constructed more conventionally though it followed the same planning principles.

16. (left) Plan of house no. 17, showing dominance of the metre grid required for the dry panel construction.
17. (below) Detail of the outside wall showing the z-shaped steel sections, cork insulation and eternit sheets on timber battens.

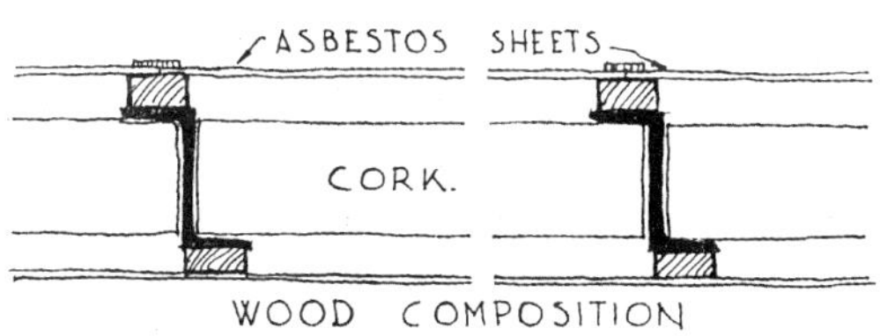

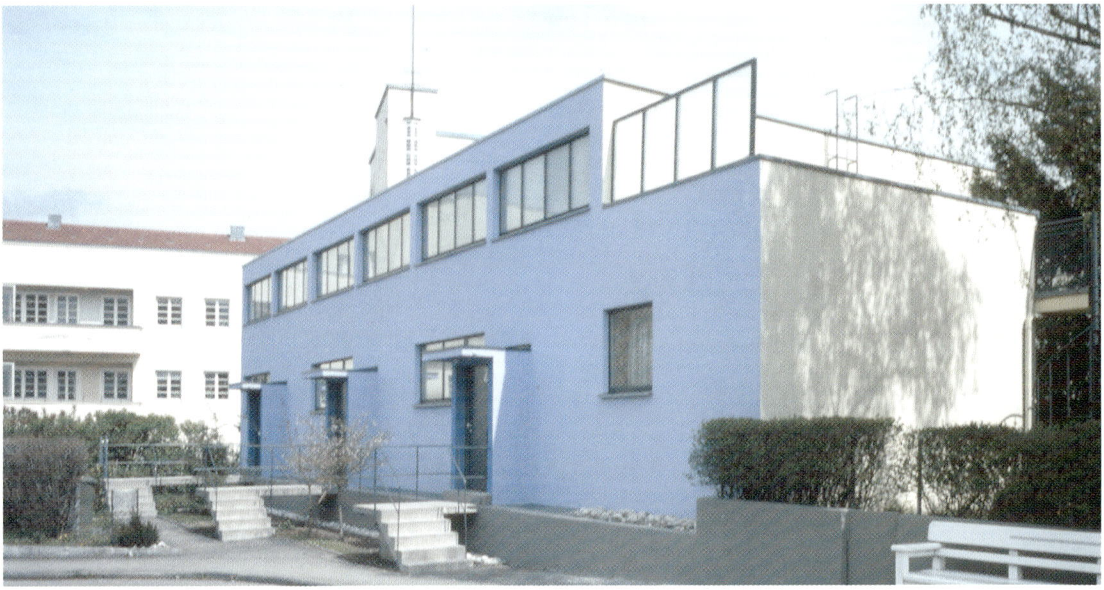

Stam

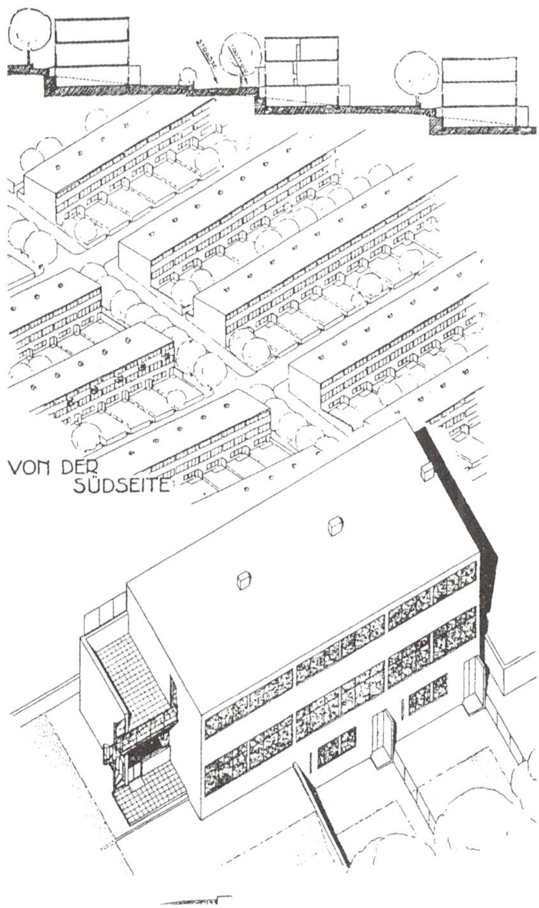

Although Gropius was the only architect at Weissenhof to devise a completely prefabricated construction prototype, several others were interested in the rationality of mass-production and its implications for housing at a large scale. The young Dutchman Mart Stam contributed a row of four very simple terrace houses on a strictly modular plan. Frame construction was intended, but they were built largely of blockwork for economic reasons.[17] The rationale of the system is nonetheless apparent: the plan of each house is bifurcated, the six-metre frontage divided into two three-metre strips by a line of steel columns and the partition between bedrooms. The stair goes into one half, the kitchen and bathroom into the other, and the division is also clear in both façades, making the garden-side readable as six dwellings rather than three. The planning is a bit schematic, and was criticised at the time both for its lack of privacy and for the astonishing windowless children's bedroom. Although he adapted the houses to the site by creating a variant end house with a spiral stair from the terrace, the real intention of the design is seen in an ideal drawing placing row upon row. Once again this might be Stuttgart, Rotterdam or anywhere. Stam's houses may look commonplace today, but the wide windows on the garden side were an impressive novelty at the time, while the rhythm of porches on the more closed public side did help create a traditional street frontage.

Schneck

Similar to both Gropius and Stam's houses in some ways, and again driven by the idea rather than the reality of prefabrication, were the two houses of Adolf-Gustav Schneck, a progressive and respected Stuttgart architect who was also known as a furniture designer. He had made earlier projects for the city on land adjacent to that allotted for the exhibition, and was finally able to build there both a house for himself and a model house for repetition.[18] Drawings setting them in rows of various kinds make the intention clear. Schneck sought to produce a clear and economical two-storey rectangular volume which could be subdivided in many different ways, even allowing varying positions for the stair. The key idea was a spine wall placed just off centre which divided the house into two structural spans not quite equal in width.[19] The rooms were relatively generous in size, allowing flexibility in the placing of furniture. As with Mies and Gropius a 'loose-fit' policy was intended to leave room for variation within a standard form, but as with Stam the form anticipated machine production rather than engaging it directly.

18. (opposite top) Stam's terrace houses restored, street side.
19. (left) Drawing by Stam showing intended mass-replication: top, ideal spacing on a slope; middle, the houses in serried ranks; bottom, the houses as built at Weissenhof.

20, 21. (below) Stam house plans.

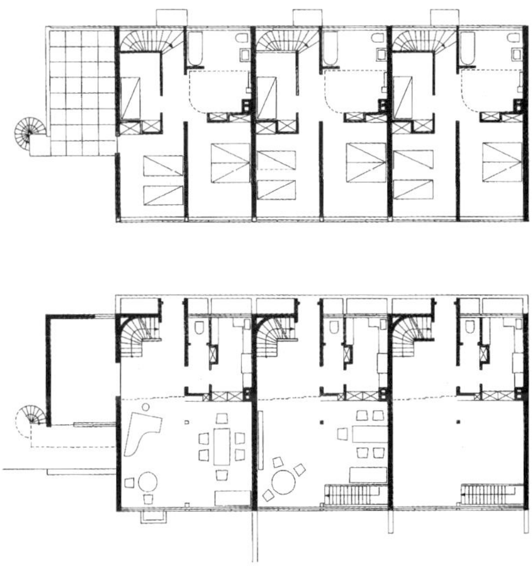

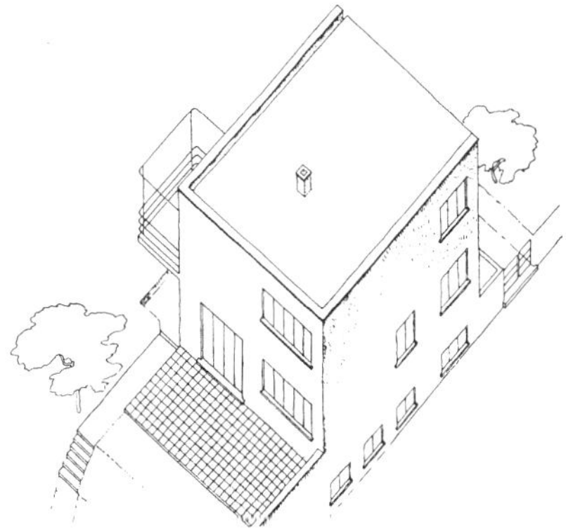

22. (above) Schneck, house no. 11 at Weissenhof, axonometric projection.

23. (right and below) Schneck house plans, first and ground floor.

24. (bottom) Schneck, plans for mass-produced houses.

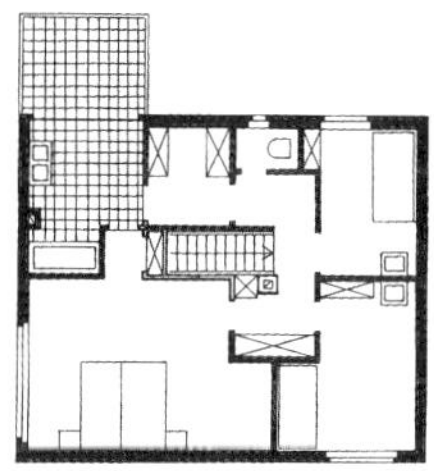

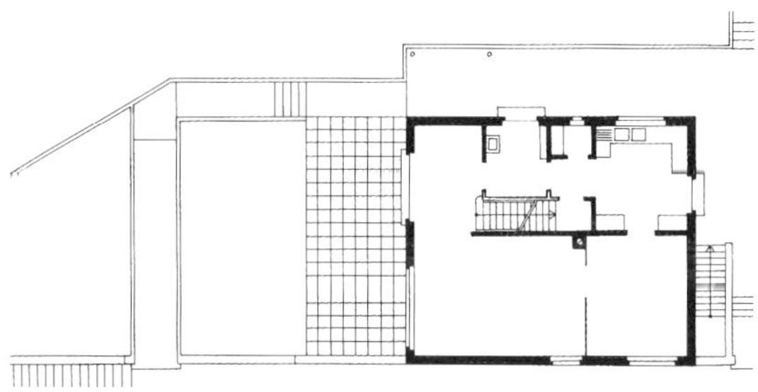

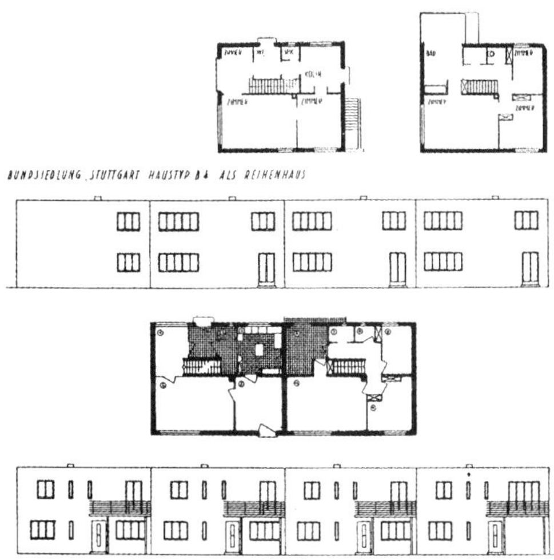

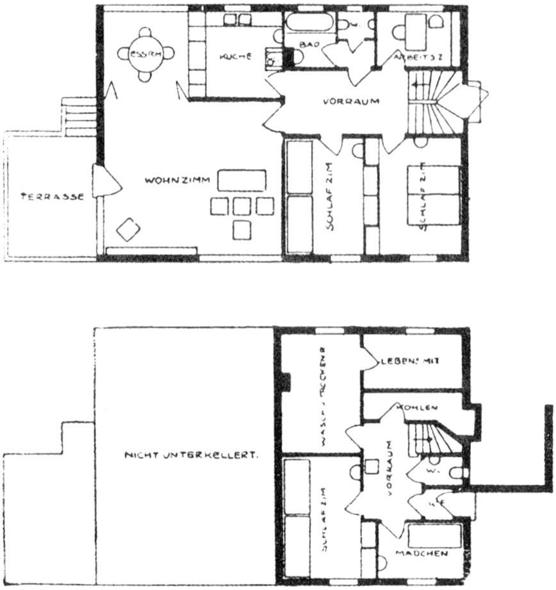

25. Hilberseimer house plans.

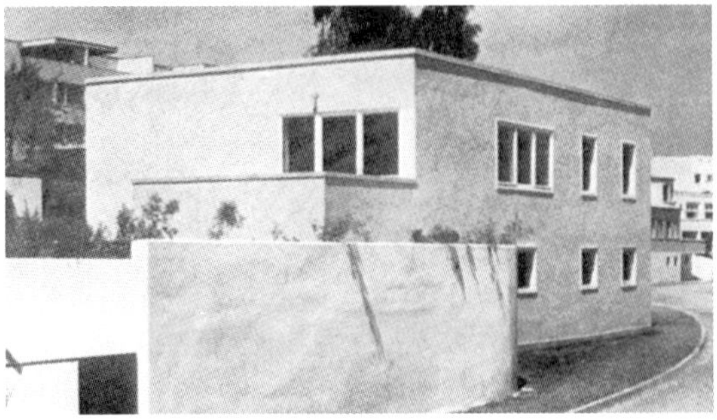

26. Hilberseimer house from street (later destroyed).
29. (bottom) Interior of living room.

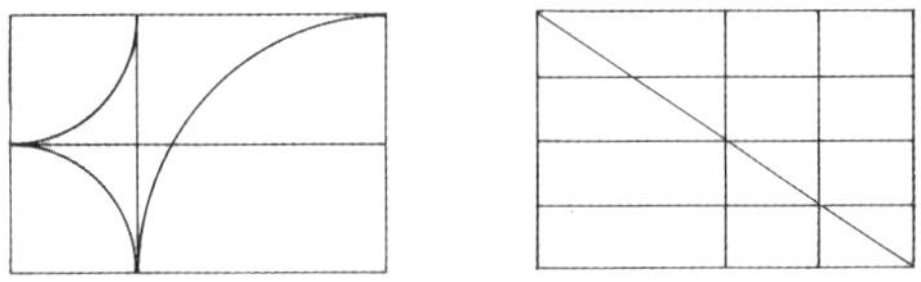

27, 28. Author's diagrams to show geometry of plan: basic figure is a 2x3 rectangle subdivided by halving.

Hilberseimer

Carrying on with the theme of rational systems, one of the most curious designs is by Ludwig Hilberseimer, who was given a lower edge site for a single house. At first sight he seems hardly to have exploited it, for although he copes with the level-change, the spaces and overall form are remarkably bland. The original construction intended was the steel frame system used by Gropius, but delivery problems precipitated a change to the Feifel Zickzack timber system - rather like scaled-up corrugated cardboard. With render outside and plaster within, this could have been any material. Hilberseimer had been careful in detailing the windows, but in the hurry to get the house constructed on time standard ones were adopted, and the intended glazed corner of the living room was lost. The spatial as well as the tectonic intentions were thus compromised, obscuring Hilberseimer's design intentions. The essential rationale is best seen in the plan, based on a module that can be doubled and halved, so that it could theoretically be used for houses and flats of various different sizes which then interlock to produce a piece of city. This might be neither terrace nor block, but more like a stack of dominoes. Even the stair takes a standardised minimal form as a generalised idea about vertical access. In the built version it unexpectedly sets the main entry onto too small a half-landing.

Friend to both Mies and Häring, Hilberseimer was the acknowledged expert at calculating arrangements and densities, and he never shrank from showing the ruthless logic of the system. His book *Gross-stadt Architektur* of 1924 showed what a rationally-planned city would look like and proved remarkably prophetic, albeit in a negative way.[20] His house at Weissenhof must thus be understood less as an opportunity to show what can be done with a small villa on a specific site (as with Scharoun, Rading or Poelzig described later), than as a test-fragment for a much larger ideal system.

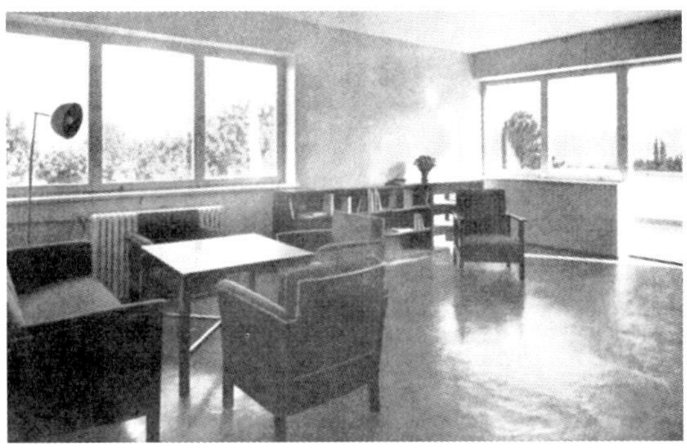

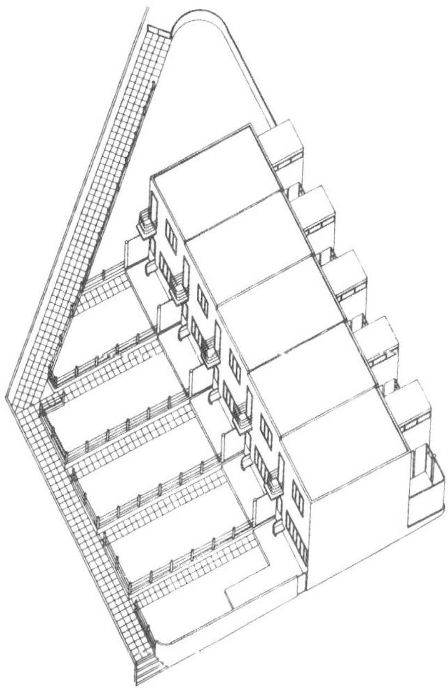

30. (above) Axonometric projection of Oud's row of houses.

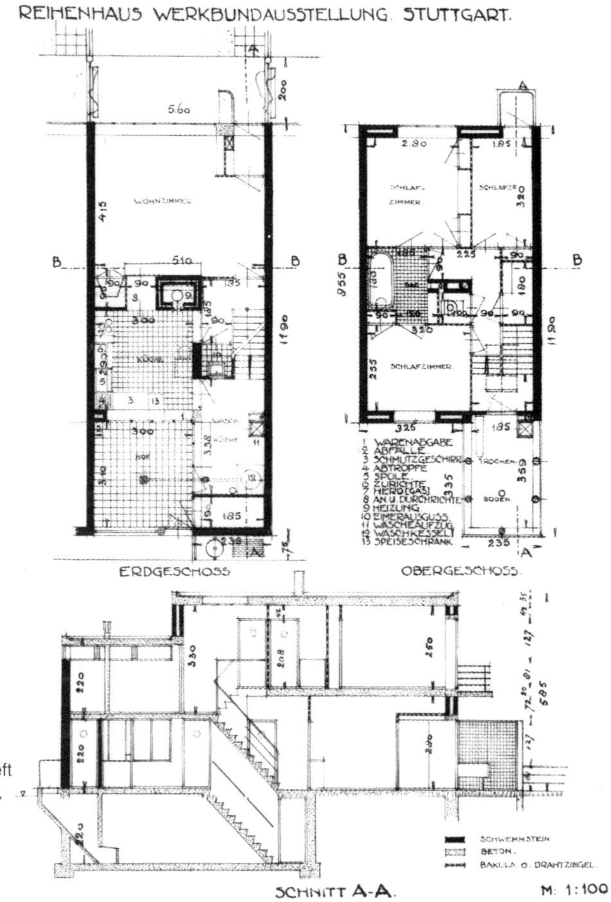

31. (right) Oud's plan and section drawings: ground plan is to left and first floor to right, garden side is top and street side bottom.

Oud

The houses of Jacobus Johannes Pieter Oud, the second Dutch architect at Weissenhof, are also repeated standard types but taking the more traditional form of a terrace. The Dutch economy had not suffered like the German, modernist architects got major jobs much earlier, and Oud had already built several large housing schemes in Rotterdam where he was City Architect. He thus had much greater practical experience than his German colleagues, and had already made his experiments with housing form. With its limited budget, he took Weissenhof as an opportunity to refine a familiar type, making the most generous-seeming house within limited economical means. He definitely had mass-production in mind, as a plan with row upon row demonstrates, and he used a standard casement window, bracketing them together in groups of two, three and six.

The two-storey houses are of traditional plan with a narrow outshot on the street side enclosing a small yard. As a basic plan-form this is traditional, much used in the nineteenth century, for the main body of a house needed daylight from both sides, so the plan could be extended only at half width. In Oud's houses the outshot contains laundry and drying-room - no electric tumble-dryers then - articulated as a sort of service tower. Minimal in height as well as floor area, and with clerestory vents as the only visible fenestration, it presents itself as a kind of houselet, setting an intimate scale for the approach side. At the same time it defines a neat, almost square kitchen yard as a visual and practical extension of the kitchen, its 3 metre width contrasting with the 5.6 metre plot width found in the wider south-facing living room and garden. A novel feature was an electric gate to the yard controlled from within the kitchen. The threshold on the garden side was achieved with a band of paving contained by a projecting trellis and column, a projecting seat to the right of the door, and a balcony to the smaller bedroom above, which also sheltered the door below.

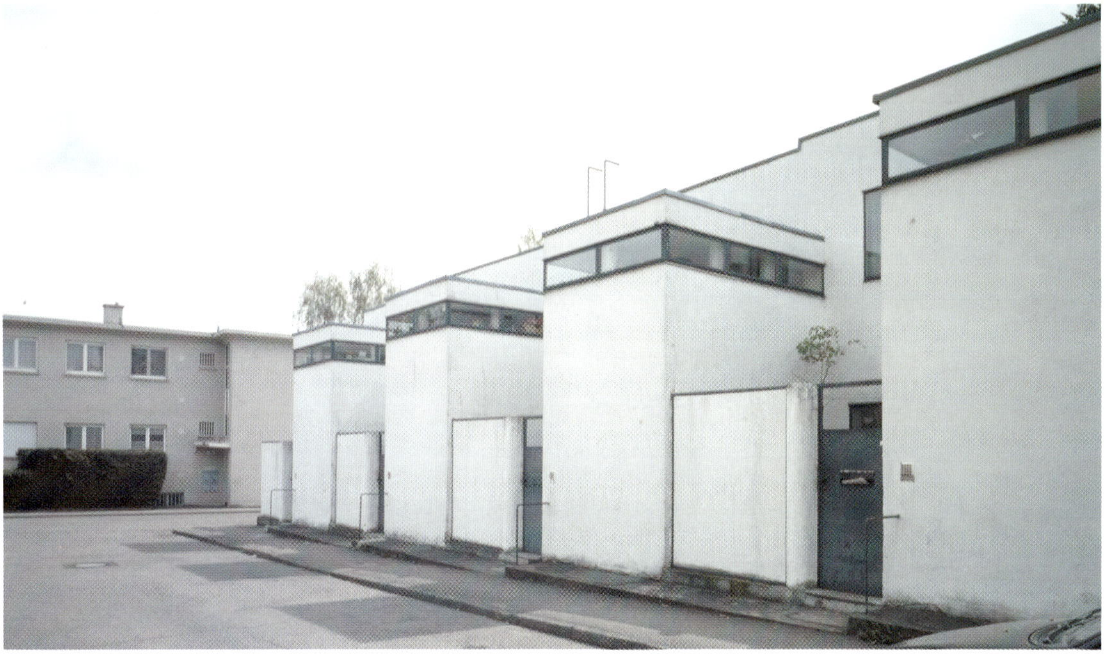

Oud's main effort went into planning the interior to produce the most efficient house within the smallest possible volume. Wherever possible cupboards were built-in, precluding the need for free-standing furniture and making the spaces unexpectedly generous for their size. Circulation was reduced to the bare minimum, and the stair raised to maximum pitch and divided to keep it short. The concrete slab spanning between party walls allowed upper partitions to run free of lower, so only the flue from the central stove was taken vertically through, and room sizes could be adjusted to the last centimetre. The kitchen with its integrated worktops was in the vanguard of development, ahead of the famous 'Frankfurt kitchen'.[21] Construction was in rendered block and concrete slab, with some of the best detailing seen at the exhibition. That Oud's houses have always been among the most photographed parts of Weissenhof testifies to his compositional skill, yet their real virtues lie in their habitability, due partly to planning skill, partly to experience of the dense fabric in old Dutch merchant cities.[22]

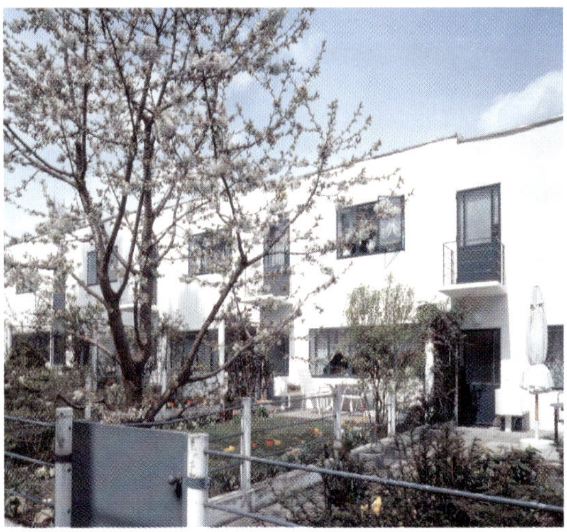

32. (top) Oud's houses, street side with small yards.
33. (below left) Garden side after restoration.
34. (below) Site plans showing the houses as deployed at Weissenhof (left) and as repeated in rows for more general use.

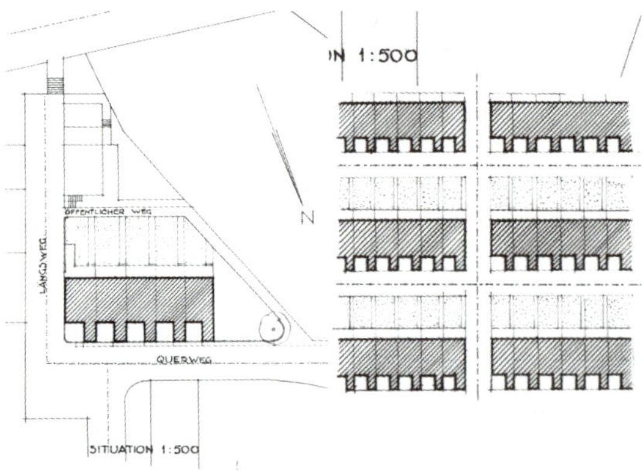

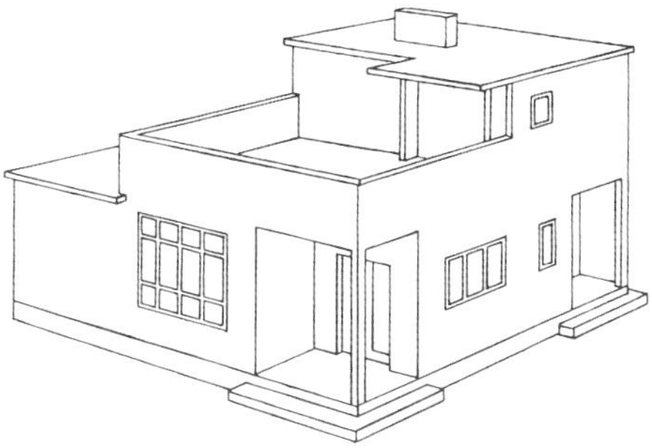

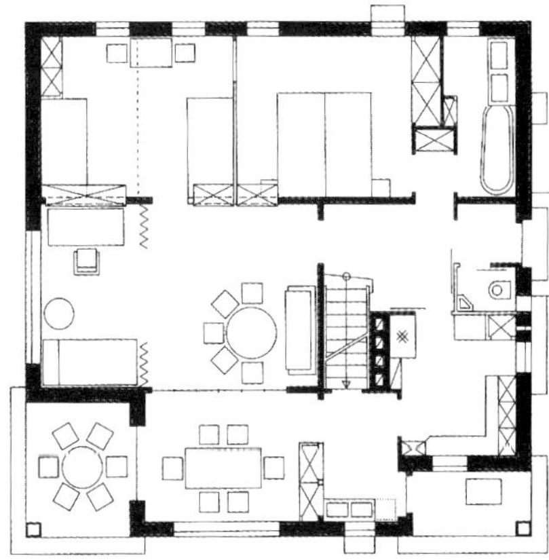

35. Bruno Taut, projection of house as seen from garden side.
36. (right) Plan of the house: main entrance is mid right, service entrance at the north-facing corner. The upper floor contained maid's room and laundry room.

Bruno Taut

The other highly experienced housing architect at Weissenhof, a friend of Oud's, was Bruno Taut. Though famous as the leader of the Expressionists and writer of Utopian books just after the First World War,[23] he had by this time become Chief Architect at the GEHAG building society in Berlin.[24] Between 1925 and 1931 he was responsible in that city for the construction of around 12,000 dwellings of exemplary quality, mainly flats.[25] He was one of the last architects invited to take part at Weissenhof, and produced a design more or less overnight. It was based on his general experience and definitely intended as a repeatable type.

Although he had been taught by and worked with the contextual master Theodor Fischer[26] and was normally sensitive to the placing of buildings, the house is disappointing in its relationship to the site, which he probably had not visited, and which was the smallest of the whole Siedlung. Sitting opposite Mies's block at the end of Bruckmannweg, it had its entrances, logically enough, on the west side, while its private garden lay to east and north, with a roofed terrace for outdoor dining at the corner. Taut strengthened the entry and answered the massing of Mies's block with a little tower, which also provided access to a sun-terrace behind. The unconvincing aspect of his design was that the south-facing bedroom windows opened onto the public street. As a type, it would have presumably been repeated in north-south rows with western entry and garden to the three other sides.

In tune with the prevalent Functionalism and Taut's experience of housing the masses, the main virtue of the building lies in its internal planning, honed down, like Oud's houses, to the last centimetre. Storage is everywhere built in, and almost every piece of available wallspace serves some cunning purpose. The general pattern is that service rooms to the north-west and bedrooms to the south create an L, embracing the square of living rooms to north-east. This presents the option of an open plan, for the central sitting area could be divided from the dining-space with a folding glazed screen, and from the study/bedroom by a concertina wall. There was also provision to divide the children's bedroom. Great attention was given to the planning of the kitchen with its separate servery and roofed porch, and it was linked closely to storage rooms in the cellar. The upstairs rooms were also for housework, to be used for drying the washing, sewing, and a potential maid's room. Taut had dedicated his book *Die neue Wohnung* to women (Taut 1924), and constantly stressed what was needed for the easy running of a household. If it was too early for a general emancipation, Taut tried at least to make the housewife's life easier with a clearer, more compact, more efficient organisation.

Taut had no great interest in how the building was constructed and did not supervise it,[27] so the use of a steel frame was merely expedient - not polemical as with Gropius - and it was made invisible, the wall surfaces rendered and painted both inside and out in the normal way. The paint, however, was crucial. Taut was always interested in colour, and had the house painted externally and internally in vibrant shades of red, blue, green and yellow, making it highly controversial: Le Corbusier even remarked that Taut must be colour-blind. On another occasion the Mies block, seen in the evening sun reflected by Taut's red west wall, was

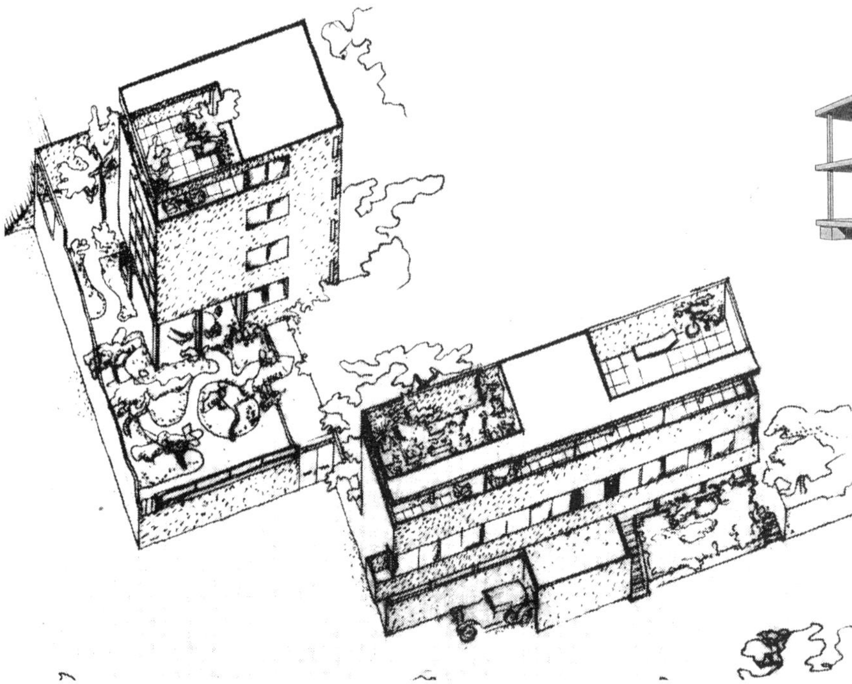

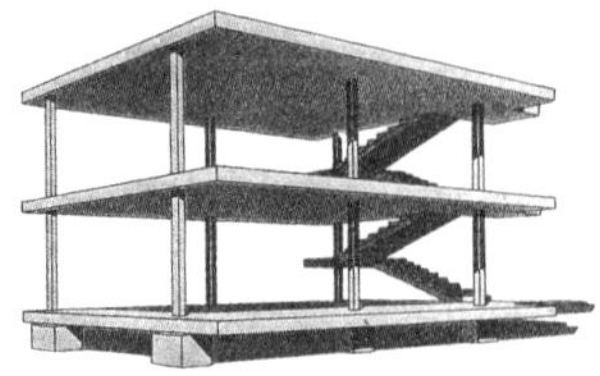

37. Le Corbusier's own axonometric projection of his two buildings at Weissenhof, with the single villa top left and double house middle front.
38. (top right) Le Corbusier's famous diagram of the proposed 'Domino' system.

thought to be on fire.[28] We know that Taut took great care to supervise colour mixing in Berlin,[29] and could not control it here, so perhaps the effect backfired, but it is now hard to know, for in the age of black and white photography it was not recorded, and the building has been destroyed. Recently restored Taut colour schemes elsewhere are, however, a revelation.[30] Not only did he use the brightest of colours; he also contrasted different parts of door and window frames with complimentary colours, producing striking and beautiful effects. More will be said of Taut's colour theories and space-planning in Chapter 5.

Le Corbusier

With the possible exception of Mies's block, Le Corbusier's houses are the best-known works at Weissenhof, and certainly the most photographed. They marked a significant advance in his reputation. In terms of housing experience he was far behind Oud and Taut, but he had great plastic skill and his houses were both photogenic and spatially exciting, arguably more suited for exhibition than habitation. As author of *Vers une Architecture* (Le Corbusier 1923/1927) he was also a great polemicist, backing up his inventions with emotionally persuasive if not always consistent theory. He used Weissenhof as a chance to exemplify his five points of the new architecture: *pilotis* (columns), roof-gardens, the free plan, the free façade and the horizontal window. The list can be counted off on the fingers of one hand and was an easy way to expand a single point first made with the famous Domino drawing (above).

The replacement of traditional load-bearing wall by a column and slab system meant that both partition walls and façades could be non-structural and freely placed. The façade could be omitted, revealing a columned space (*pilotis*), or it could be made as a lightweight curtain of material with openings any shape one wanted. As a horizontal slab rather than a cap, the roof could become habitable space, replacing the ground that the building covered. By 1927 these implications of the new structural system were certainly well-known, but it was the genius of Le Corbusier to dramatise them visually and make them into a programme.

It is hard in most frame buildings to know what is load-bearing and what is not, since it is easiest to make the walls follow and complete the frame. Le Corbusier did the opposite, contrasting his regular grid of columns with partition walls in snaking curves, wrapping around baths and lavatories or running diagonally across a space. He also often

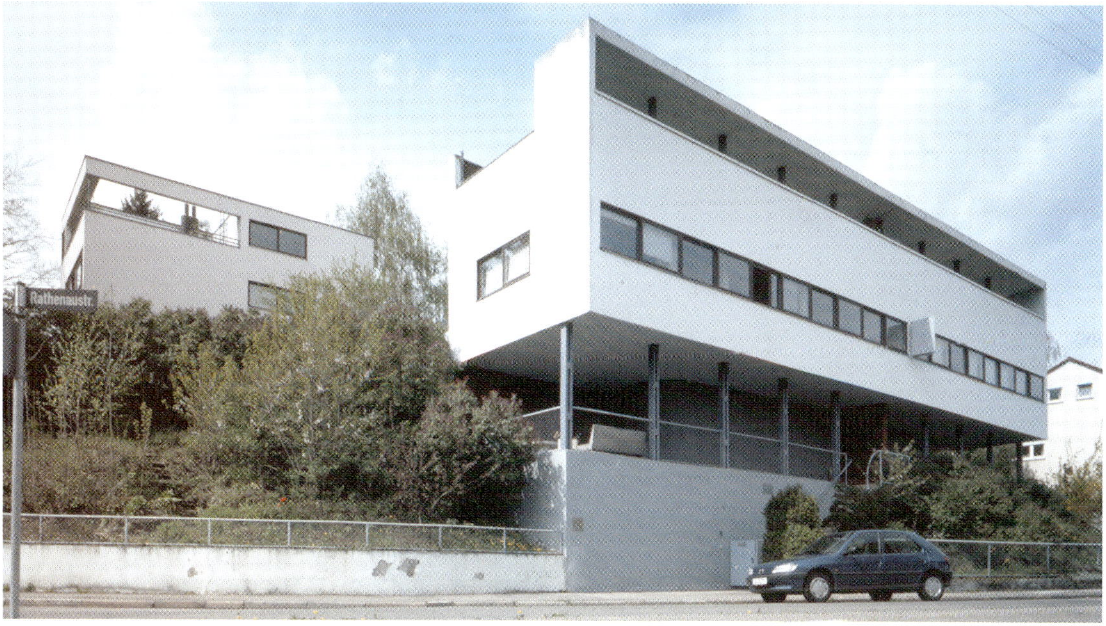

39. (above) Both buildings seen from the street, post-restoration.

40. (below left) Single villa, space between *pilotis* and free wall at ground floor level.

41. (below) Single villa seen from its entrance gate on the west side.

kept such partitions short of the ceiling, further stressing their independence. In his facade treatment too, he sought the maximum contrast with tradition, for in loadbearing walls openings were vertical to minimise the span of the arch or lintel: now they could be horizontal, stretching right across the façade. This allowed panoramic views at eye-level, which could be framed like a picture, a practice continued for purely visual reasons on the roof terraces.

Le Corbusier contributed two buildings to Weissenhof, and again they were in studied contrast. The single tower-like villa stands in the middle of its plot, carried on *pilotis* at ground level, and irregular rounded walls show a 'free' enfolding of entrance and service elements. *Pilotis* give way

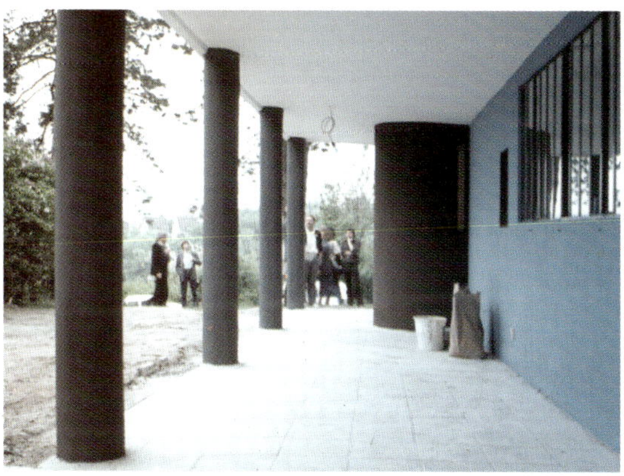

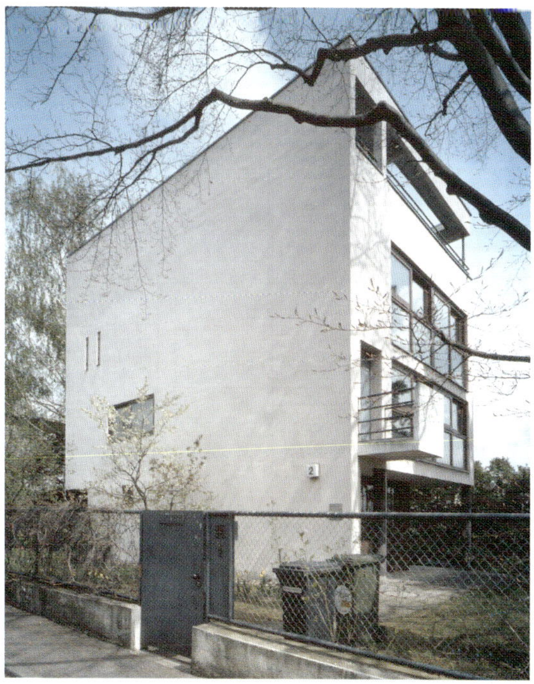

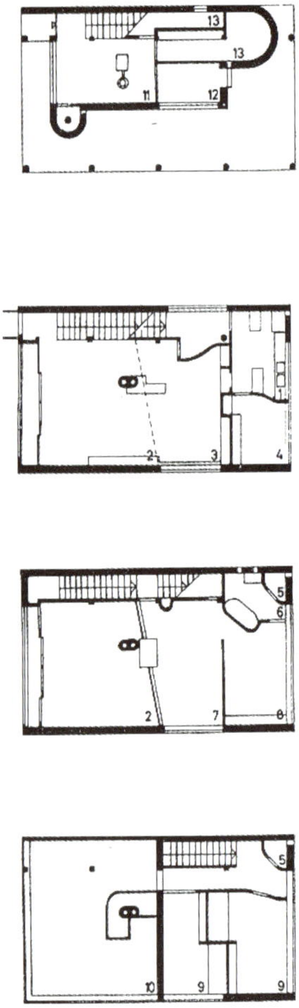

42. (above) Plans of the single villa, ground at top.
43. (below) Single villa south elevation.

44. (top right) Double villa from street.
45. (right) Double villa half plans: clockwise from top - roof, entry level and main floor.

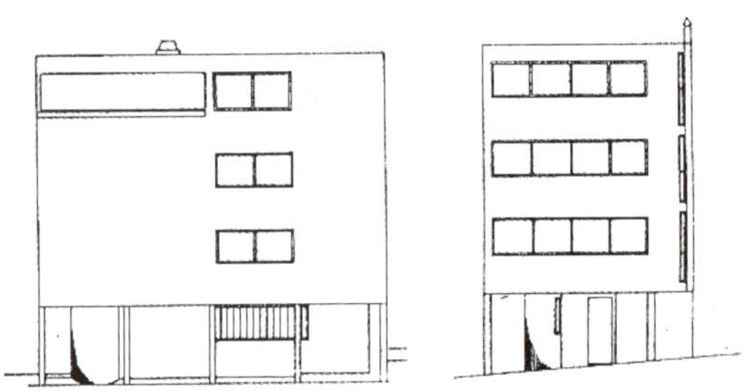

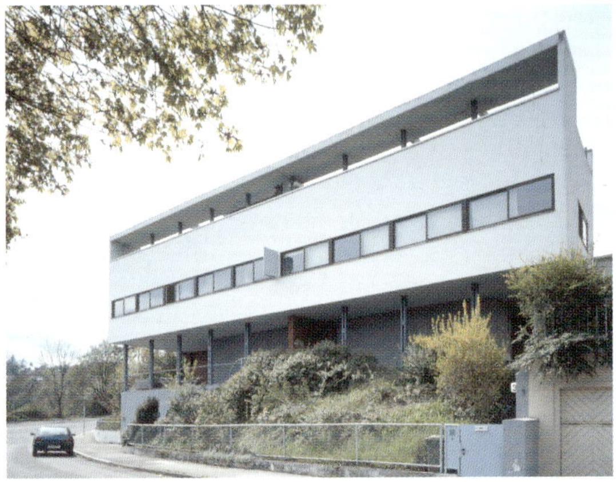

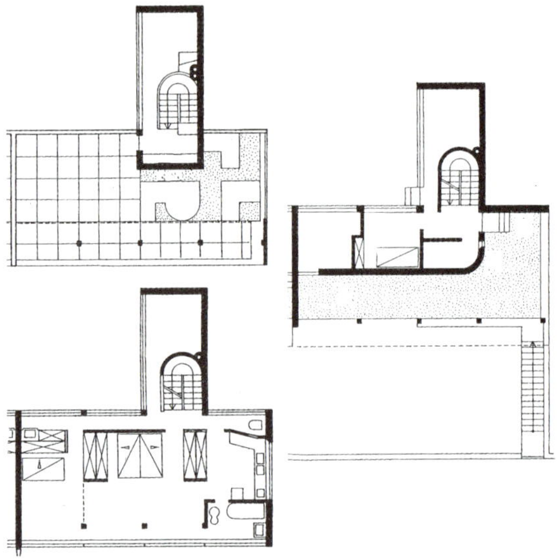

on the west side to a solid wall which the main stair follows, dramatising the ascent. Turning through a small vestibule, the visitor enters a studio-like double height living room with south-facing window, also double-height, and made as a *Blumenfenster*[31] with space for plants. The cut back second floor is like a balcony, but with its edge angled in plan, again to make the point that this is a 'free' element playing against the geometric system. The north end of the plan has kitchen and maid's room at first floor and principal bedroom at second. The stair again follows the wall, repeating that below and running right on up to the top of the house, the third floor being half bedrooms, half roof terrace. Partitions curl in response to sanitary ware or circulation flow lines at each level: yet more 'free' elements.

The formal invention and the architectural drama of Le Corbusier's *promenade architecturale* are impressive, but the lack of visual and acoustic privacy would make it hard for more than a couple to live there.[32] In comparison with other houses at Weissenhof the isolation of house from garden seems perverse, while the presence of the garden makes the roof terrace almost superfluous.

Did Le Corbusier have repetition in mind? It certainly makes a better exhibition piece solo, particularly in contrast with the double-villa which he built next door. This is already on a linear plan, with the implication that it could be extended indefinitely if the end windows were removed. One façade would be continuous, the other punctuated rhythmically with stair towers, one per dwelling. Placed as it is, however, Le Corbusier's double villa definitely profits from its cliff-like site, the stairs rising even to *pilotis* level. From there one passes under the building into a group of service rooms as with the single villa, but the dog-leg stairs project behind within a small volume used at ground level for service, at first floor level as a parlour, and at roof level as the master's study.

Apart from a narrow train-like corridor[33] and a bathroom and kitchen at the end, the main floor is presented as a single partitionable space with built-in storage. Le Corbusier intended to show a simpler, more direct form of life stripped of clutter and sentimentality, no longer wasting space on rooms used only half the time; or building, heating and cleaning large spaces to be occupied by inefficient and decorative furniture. His double-villa proved highly controversial, and critics claimed it must be for a new kind of rootless urban intellectual: *'It is not everybody's wish only to have a temporary bed-station at night, and by day to box it away... Many want a closed bedroom in which they not only rest and dream, but make love, conceive, give birth, and die.'*[34]

Le Corbusier claimed to be able to make the partitions soundproof, but they did not meet the windows, and some crucial ones were omitted, so the whole arrangement could be criticised on grounds of habitability. The horizontal window runs the length of the double façade, even necessitating a projecting external screen for privacy between the two dwellings: Le Corbusier could scarcely have dramatised this visual slot more. Again there is a roof terrace above.

Much more will be said about Le Corbusier in Chapter 7, which deals with his masterpiece, the

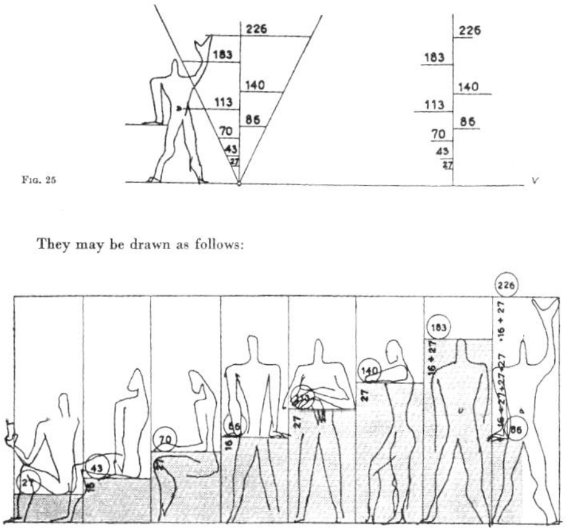

46. Le Corbusier's 'Modulor', a proportion system based on the golden section which he published in the late 1940s. These drawings from the book show the Modulor scale against the human body and defining a convenient set of heights for various activities.

Villa Savoye, but we should note here his strong faith in the virtues of pure geometric solids such as the cube, the sphere and the cylinder; his classically-based belief in proportional systems which led to the development of his own proportioning system, The Modulor, based on the golden mean; and his constant search for regulating lines, in paintings, façades, and even in site-plans. Le Corbusier believed that he had discovered a set of rules for a plastic language of universal aesthetic validity based on pure forms and primary colours.[35]

To make its abstract visual qualities stronger, he suppressed not only aspects of the programme but the very materiality of building, covering up the texture and the handwork of the masonry process under a smooth coat of render, and painting it in artificial colours - pink, blue and chocolate brown in the case of the single villa. As far as possible he removed cills, drips and cornices, even that hitherto dominant architectural feature the roof - everything to differentiate his work from traditional building - and he inverted floors from their socially expected positions. His work was excitingly novel, seductive and enjoyed a great following. Many thought his houses the most beautiful of the *Siedlung*,[36] but his opponents accused him of formalism, of making architectural sculpture at the expense of everyday needs.[37] Architects like Oud and Taut could claim - with some justification - that this work was not about the housing question.[38]

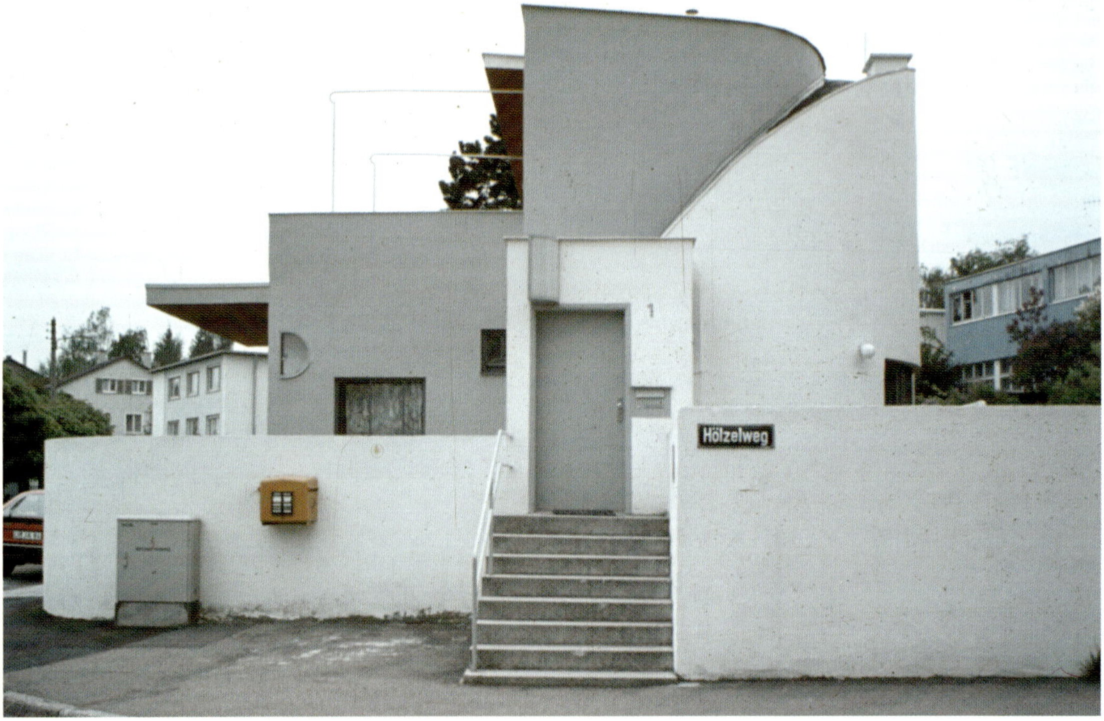

Scharoun

If Hans Scharoun possessed one of the greatest spatial imaginations in 20th century architecture, it has little in common with that of Le Corbusier and is not very evident in his single Weissenhof house. Born in 1893, he was one of the youngest architects invited, and though he had already built housing of a traditional kind, he was best known for the fantastic drawings and watercolours produced in the Expressionist period (see p.189) and for his extraordinary free-form competition projects. In 1927 he was still finding his way, and had yet to discover the manipulations of space produced by departing from the right-angle that are the hallmark of the later work (discussed in Chapter 13). His struggles at Weissenhof show, however, that he was already primarily interested in space, not form, and in relationships rather than construction. Unlike Le Corbusier, he had little interest in geometric primary figures, harmonic proportions or regulating lines: indeed he felt traditional axial planning methods as a straitjacket and longed to be free. *'Why does everything have to be straight?'* he once complained to the critic Adolf Behne.[39] The essence of Scharoun's planning method was infinite adjustability, so that appropriate relationships of parts could be discovered, not forced into a predetermined geometric scheme.

For revealing Scharoun's intentions, earlier designs for the house are better than the final building, for his ambitions far outstripped the budget, and the design passed through three reducing versions before reaching its final form. The first, and in many ways the richest, was intensely site specific, for Scharoun tried to exploit not only the corner position of his site but also the

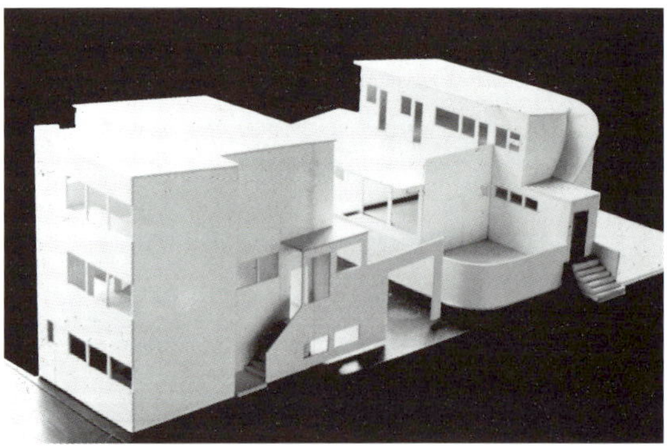

47. (opposite) Entrance to Scharoun's house with its tower-like corner.
48. (opposite bottom) Models of second and fourth versions, both seen from the crucial corner. The earlier is more tower-like.

This page: drawings of Scharoun's first design for the house which was rejected on grounds of cost.
49. (right) South-east elevation of first version.
50. (middle right) First floor plan of first version.
51. (bottom right) Ground floor plan of first version imposed on the original garden plan.

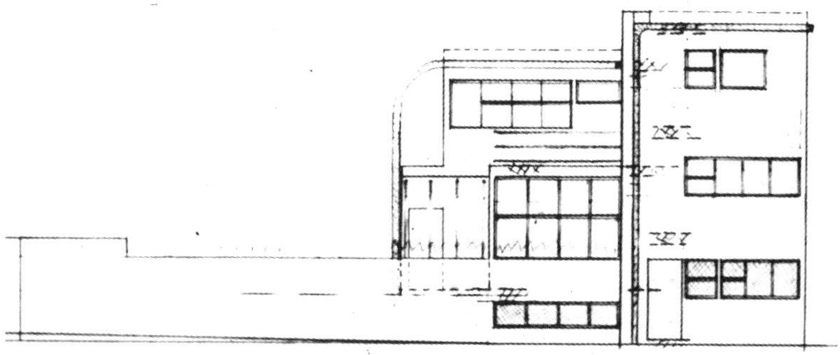

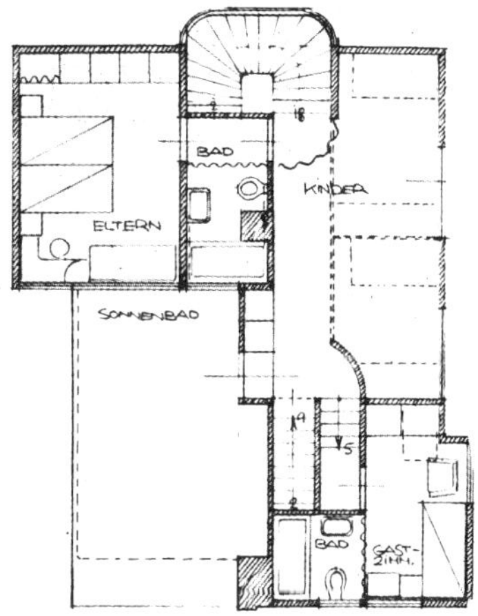

changing levels. He planned a wall around north and east sides which was also the wall to the whole *Siedlung*, and he placed a tower at the corner as if on a town-wall. This tower had three low storeys while the building behind had two taller ones, linking at half-levels. He sought to make the whole site space into a complex of indoor and outdoor rooms, dividing the garden with fences and hedges into no less than eleven function-specific places including a pool, a pond, exercise area and children's playspace, as well as garden areas.

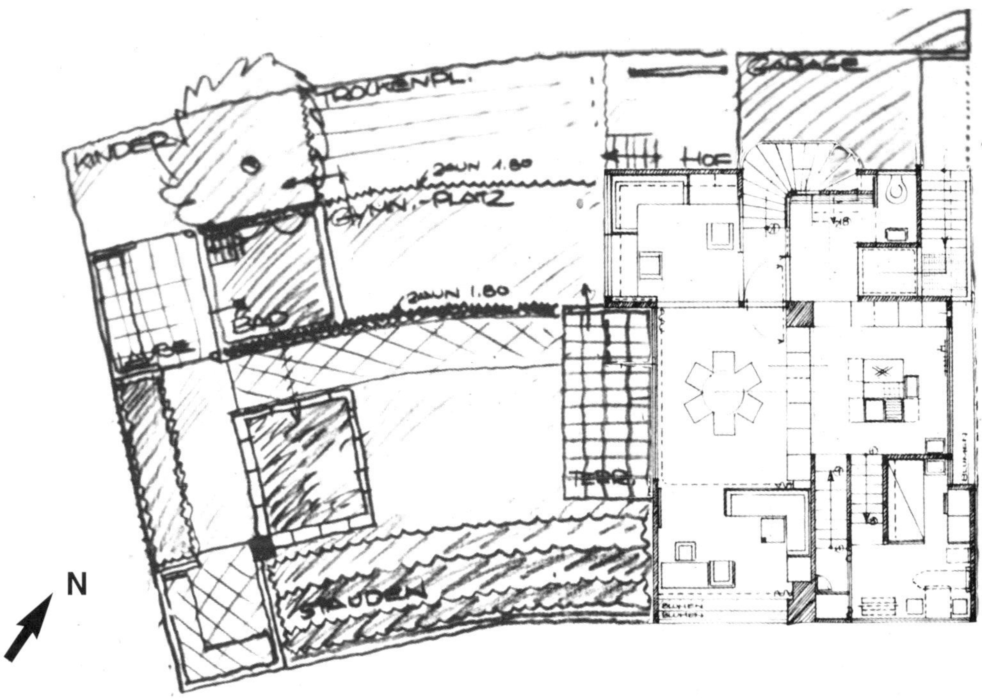

52. (below) Ground plan of second version. Apart from a reduction in area, the main difference is the omission of the stair at the northern corner. Now that the family must use the stair in the corner tower, it is made to interlock vertically with the service stair, so the two outer flights in this plan link the same levels.

53. (right) Ground plan of third version. The tower has gone, replaced by a garden court, and the main theme is now the axis linking street-entrance and garden.

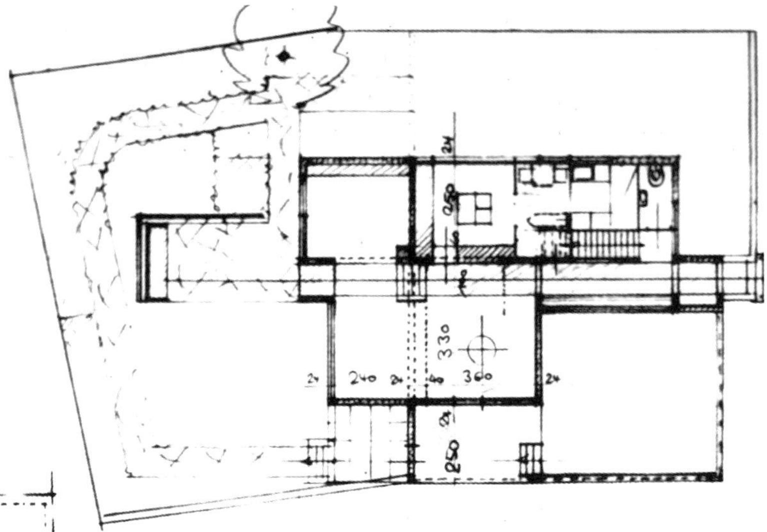

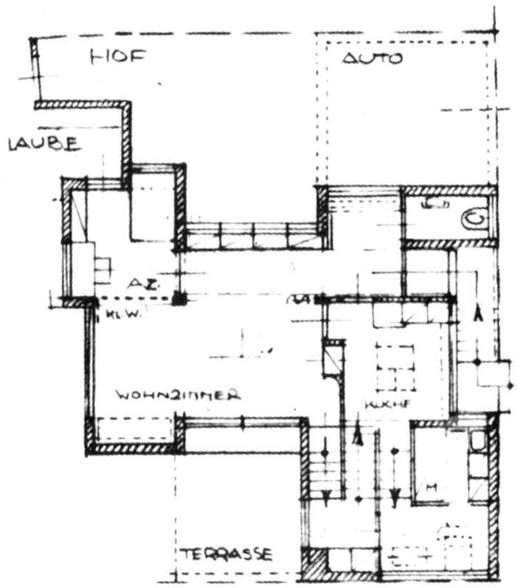

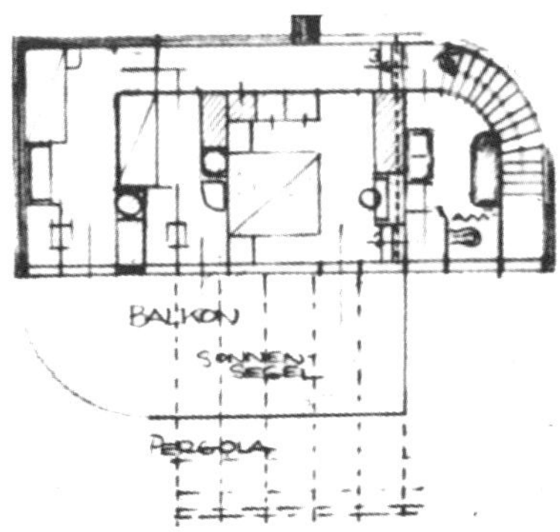

54. (middle right) First floor plan of fourth version, largely as built. The bedrooms open onto a wide terrace for sun and view served by a corridor to the rear. In a late design move, Scharoun articulated the staircase with curved wall and spiralling roof.

55. (right) Ground floor plan of final version, largely as built. The axis, terminating in an intended pond and sitting place, delimits living rooms from service rooms, but living, dining and study are one continuous space divided by a small level change and built-in sofa. The curve, introduced for the stair on the north, is counterpointed by a curved bay window facing south.

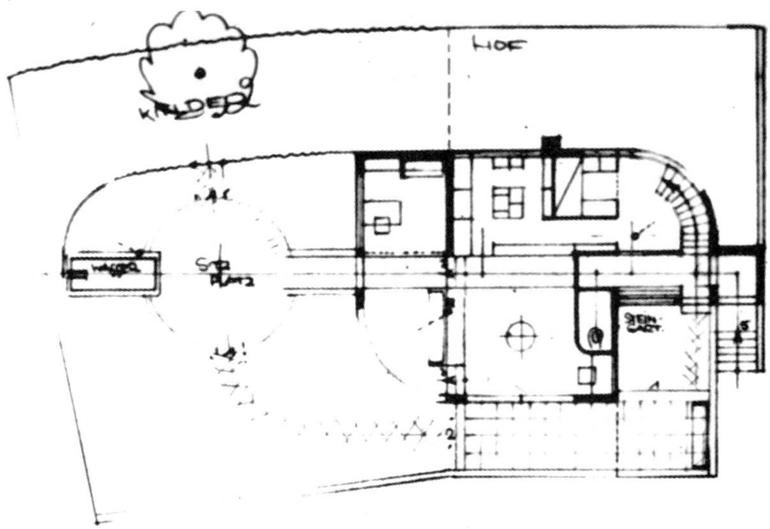

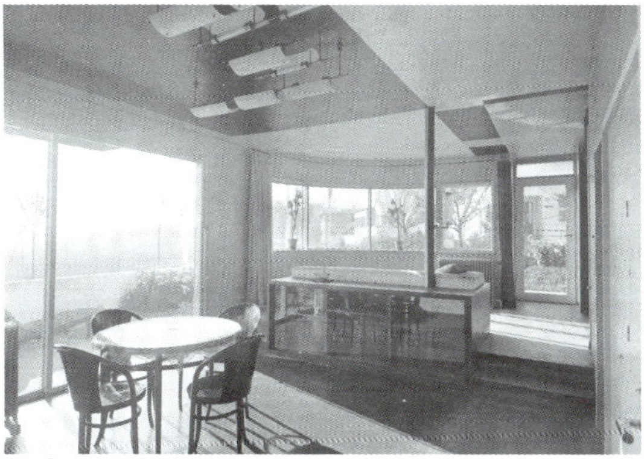

56. Open-plan living-dining room with level change and built-in sofa, period photograph.

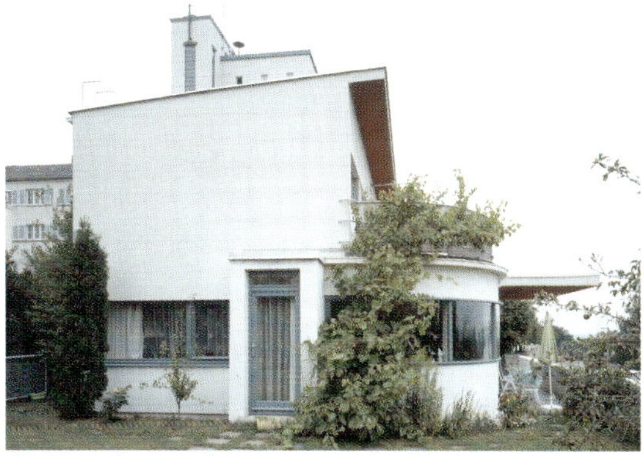

57. House from garden, post-restoration. The intended sitting place to terminate the axis was never executed.

Outdoor rooms were linked to indoor ones by doors and windows of every size and height, so that for example one could stand in the living-dining room and look out south-westward to the terrace through full-height glass doors, south-eastward to the distant view through a double-skin *Blumenfenster*[40] or more intimately westward into the exercise area via a casement over the study desk. The house had two staircases, one to north-west linking the main rooms, the other to south-east with an entrance to the street. Here the maid could come and go independently, gaining discreet access to every part of the house.

This plan must be inhabited in the imagination for its rich sequences of spaces to be appreciated. If the elevation is uninspiring, it is because it reflects working from the inside out rather than vice versa. Structure is unclear, and lack of a column under the southern corner of the main bedroom suggests a cavalier attitude.

The second version reduced the floor area and eliminated the north-west stair. Instead, the south-east stair was elaborated to maintain its privacy, gaining duplicated outer flights: one for the maid, the other for the family. The elevation improved, revealing Scharoun's skill at resolving and integrating the myriad elements produced in the 'explosion' of the first scheme. Sadly, this version was still too large: the original drawings are covered in area calculations.

In the third version the idea of the corner tower was abandoned in favour of a linear design strung along an axis from street entrance to garden, terminating in a paved terrace and seat. This was refined in the fourth and final version. The stepped section follows the contours and exploits the view to the valley. On the ground floor, living rooms lie to left of the axis, service rooms to right and bedrooms above. The most visible changes were the two rounded corners, one south-facing opposite the built-in sofa of the living room, the other to north containing the rounded stair which reconciles the shift in axis between the passages at the two levels. This rounded corner with its spiral roof was the most controversial feature of the house and criticised as 'Expressionist', but it accurately articulates what is going on inside. With its vertical emphasis, it also returned to the end elevation some sense of the lost tower from the first and second versions.

This evolution demonstrates what Scharoun was about. Completely ignoring the drive for a standard and repeatable type, he concentrated on his corner site, devising a complex programme of rooms and spaces. The living rooms were open-plan for dynamic views but divided into dedicated areas by furniture and level changes, and spaces flowed from inside to out and back. Clearly a bourgeois villa, his first version even boasted a garage, while the maid was not merely present but required complex spatial tricks to preserve privacy. Construction was denied a driving role, but the flat roofs and general abstraction of materials and textures allowed Scharoun freedom in his spatial experiments. He was not trying to develop a plastic language with implicit rules like Le Corbusier. Contradicting Gropius too, he was prepared to make each window in the house different to perform and express its particular purpose. Scharoun was quite explicit about this: he had no objection to industrial products, being prepared to use mass-produced door knobs, light-switches, even doors and windows, but this did not necessitate standardising the whole building.[41]

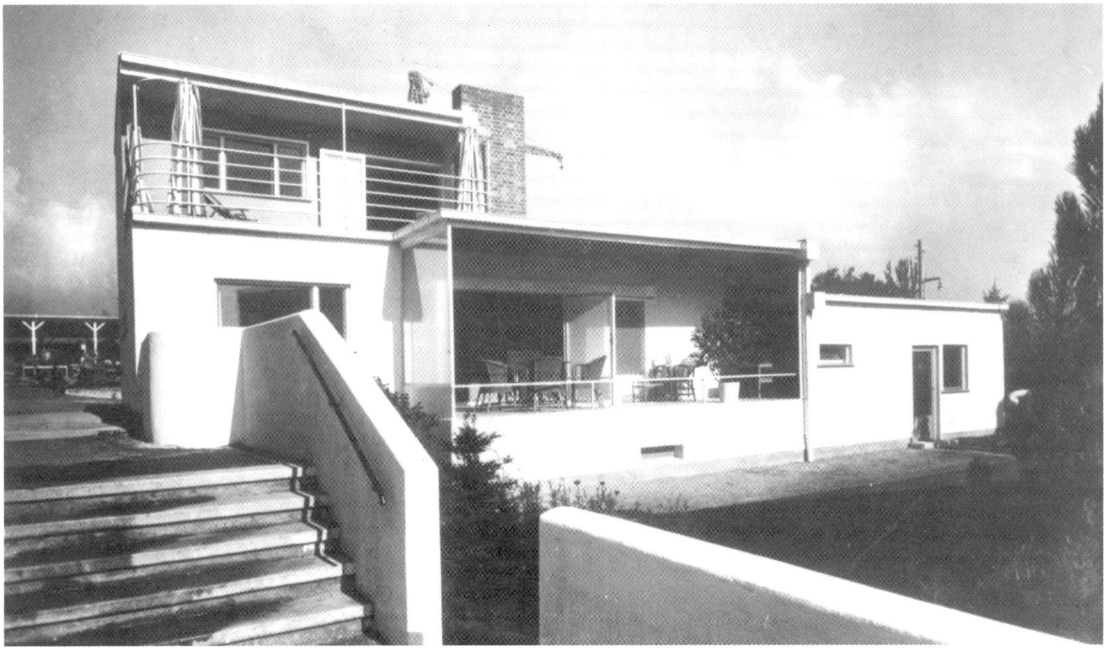

58. Rading house from the south-west as seen at the exhibition: it was destroyed in the war.

Rading

Although largely forgotten today, Adolf Rading (1888-1957) was a significant figure in German Modernism of the 1920s, grouped on equal terms with Scharoun and Häring by the leading critic Adolf Behne, who considered him a similar talent.[42] He was a close colleague of Scharoun at the Staatliche Akademie für Kunst und Kunstgewerbe at Breslau[43] and for a time the two shared an office, so there was much exchange of ideas. Writing in 1929, Rading claimed that *'New Building... is not the cliché invented by followers-on and clever commentators, then used to discredit us.... Its signature is not the white-painted cigar box with cut holes and horizontal divisions.... "New" Building is an ethos... a resonance with the spiritual tendencies of the time... We no longer compose façades as a disengaged abstract activity: rather we pursue the engaged, organic product growing in its own time.'*[44] Scharoun recognised Rading as a significant intellectual force who had: *'...a clarifying effect in architectural theory and practice... He had special insight into the connection between the functional and the formal, and how to translate insights gained from life into spatial and technical entities.'*[45]

Thus it is hardly surprising to find in Rading's house similar concerns to those in Scharoun's. It too is site-specific, placed at the top of the *Siedlung*

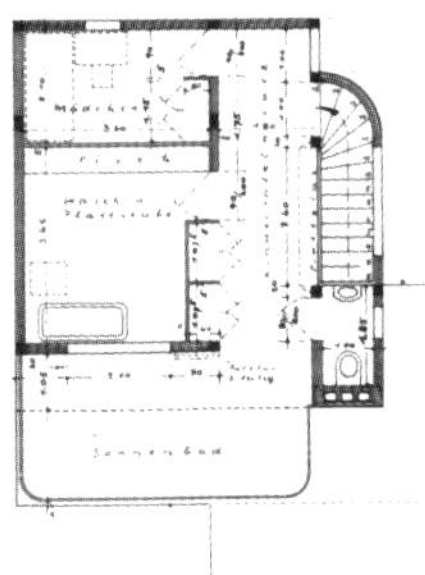

59. (left) Upper floor plan with maid's room and laundry room.

60. (below) Main floor plan with open-plan living rooms to left and lower bedroom area to right.

61. (opposite top) East elevation.
62, 63. (opposite middle) Views of the open-plan living area.

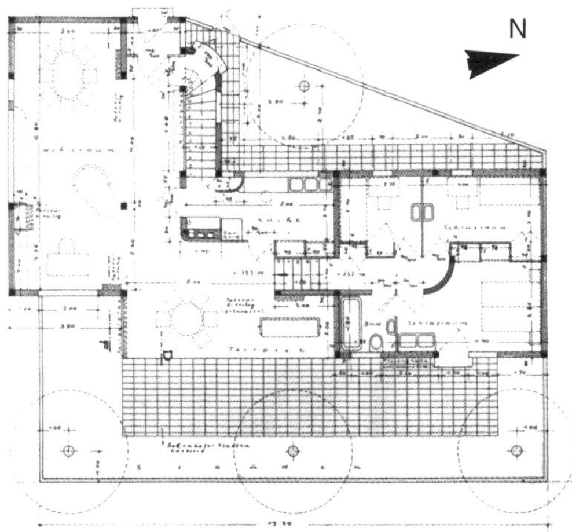

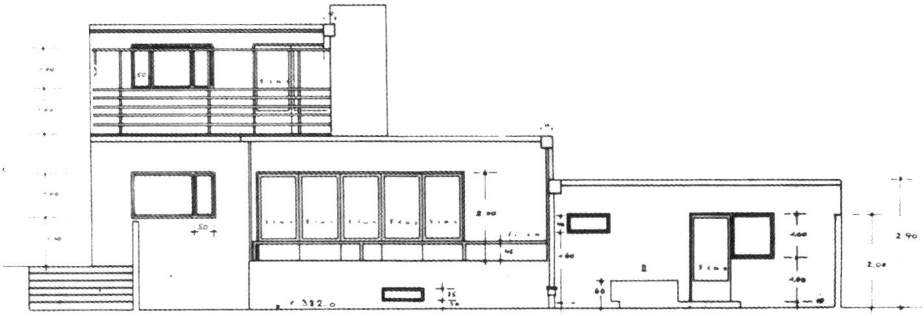

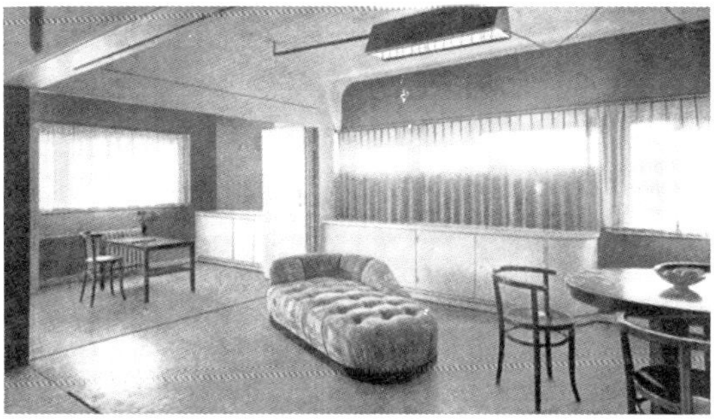

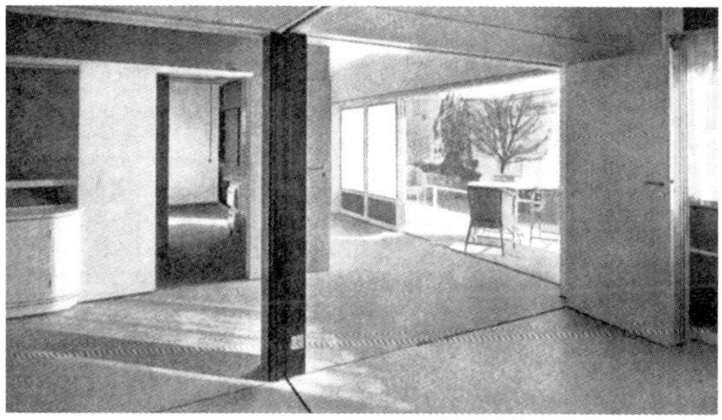

immediately to the right of Mies's block. Accepting the alignment set by Mies and followed by all surrounding buildings, it also needed to respond to the skewed west wall along the street Am Weissenhof behind. The result is an L-shaped house stacked up to create a tower-like corner opposite Mies's block. The living rooms are in the corner, with maid's room and laundry in the tower above, while family bedrooms occupy the tail of the L in a distinct block at a lower level. This allows the master bedroom to open directly onto the lower-lying east-facing garden, while living rooms look into it only from a wide, sheltered balcony-like terrace. The stair down to the bedroom wing helps differentiate the two territories internally in accordance with the contemporary tendency to create distinct functional zones.[46]

The main entrance on the north-west corner of the tower leads straight through the living spaces on axis toward the long view framed by the terrace. The stair placed next to it is articulated in a curved corner just like Scharoun's, but without its daring spiral top. This curve helps animate the triangular yard, which also distances the kitchen and lesser bedrooms from the street. Set in the curve at ground level is a special service entrance which allows independent access to the cellar. Steps repeat the same direction above, linking kitchen to laundry and maid's room, so she could come and go without disturbing the family.

As with Scharoun's house, the living rooms were open-planned, but to a greater degree. Extensive folding partitions allowed the choice of three separate rooms or a single space nine metres long with even longer oblique views. The kitchen could serve either the main living-space to south or a table on the terrace to east for frequent use in the summer. With doors to the terrace open, what was merely a glazed passage past the kitchen would become a major room. At the end of an article on his house, Rading commented: *'All in all, the essential things for me were the liberation of the plan and the new connection between house and garden, and I think this was important for all the houses. We hope that our efforts will have some influence.'*[47]

Like Scharoun's house, Rading's is so site-bound that its repetition would be senseless, but a rearrangement of the same parts in response to another site is not unthinkable. It would be wrong to claim that Rading or Scharoun were always opposed to the repeatable type, for both produced type-designs in parallel with their more site-specific works:[48] but in practice they gave priority to the question of specificity, feeling strongly the need for a building to belong to a particular place.

Frank

The Viennese Josef Frank was another gifted architect who deserves to be better known, the key Austrian figure of the period. Born in 1885, he was of the same generation as the other Modernists and an inheritor of Adolf Loos's ideas. An articulate theorist, he became the Austrian representative of CIAM and also a member of the Deutsche Werkbund. In 1932 he organised the Vienna Werkbund Exhibition, a follow-up to Weissenhof and also a criticism of it.[49] His built work was mainly housing and private houses, relatively modest in scope. Unlike Germany and Holland, there was no boom period in Austrian architecture in the late 1920s, for the old heart of the lost empire was slow to regenerate its economy. Most talented architects emigrated, especially in the 1930s with the build up of Fascism. Frank went to Sweden in 1934, where he became the leading designer for Svengst Tenn, a progressive furniture firm which still sells his elegant chairs, tables and fabrics. Except for fleeting visits, he never returned to his native Vienna. He died in 1967.

Like Häring, Scharoun and Rading, Frank was a functionalist of the organic persuasion. In other words he was primarily interested in the requirements of dwelling and the provision of suitable spaces and furnishing, rather than in the manipulation of form. His architectural sensibility was rooted in the small scale, moving from furniture to the question of furnishing and the nature of rooms. Following Loos, he was suspicious of style as an applied 'look', which he saw as an attempt to short-cut processes of cultural evolution that were social, not individual, in nature. It was not necessary to reinvent or standardise furniture which had already evolved according to its own logic, he claimed, nor was it desirable to impose stylistic consistency between pieces:

'If one forms a sitting area in the wrong way, it matters not if the furniture is Baroque or steel-tube. Both are quite unmodern. Modern is only what gives us perfect freedom, which means we must also reject every kind of personal room-architecture.'[50]

In contrast with more puritanical contemporaries, Frank also understood the need for people to personalise their homes with possessions carrying memories:

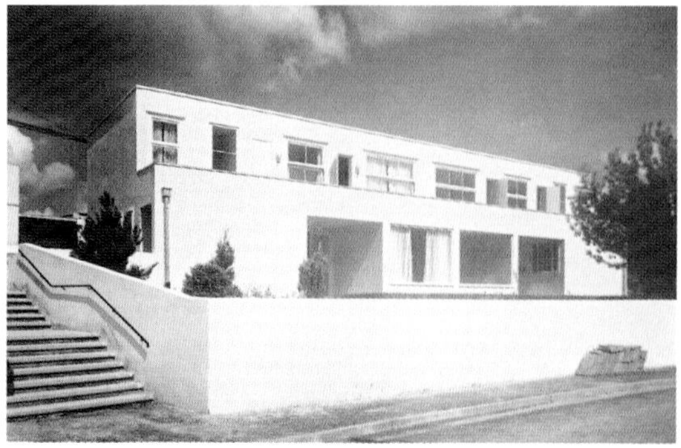

64. Josef Frank, pair of houses, street view.

68. (opposite top) Frank's houses today.

65. (below) Ground floor plan.
key: 1 living room, 2 kitchen, 3 porch, 4 maid's room, 5 semi-enclosed outdoor room.

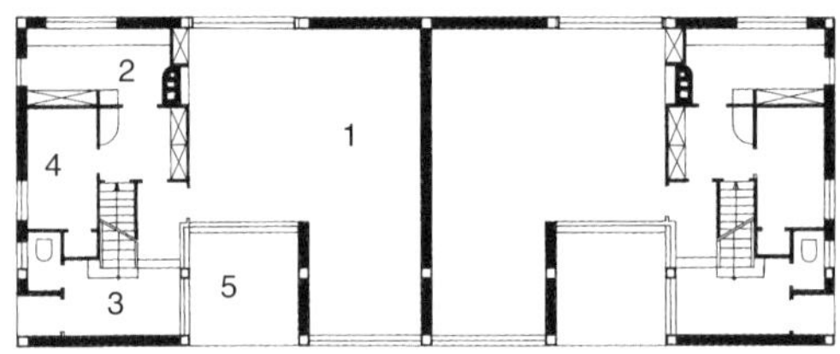

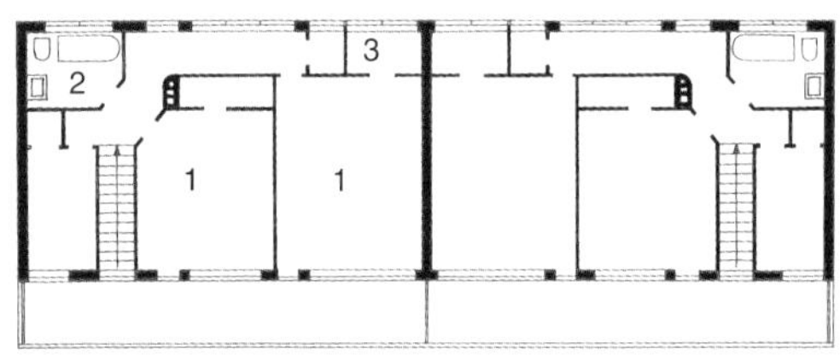

66. (above) First floor plan.
key: 1 bedroom, 2 bathroom, 3 wardrobe.

67. (bottom) Elevation of south side which faces valley and view.

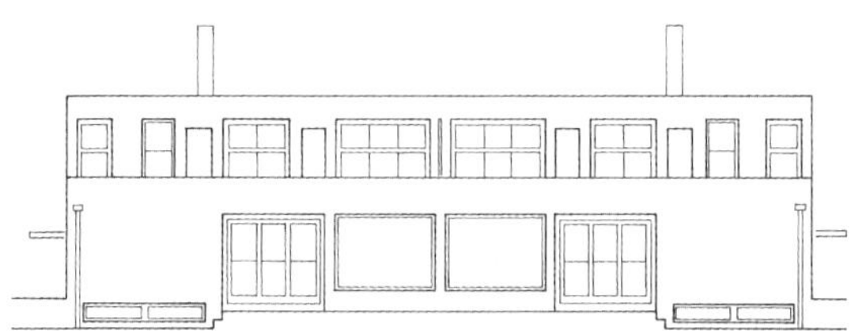

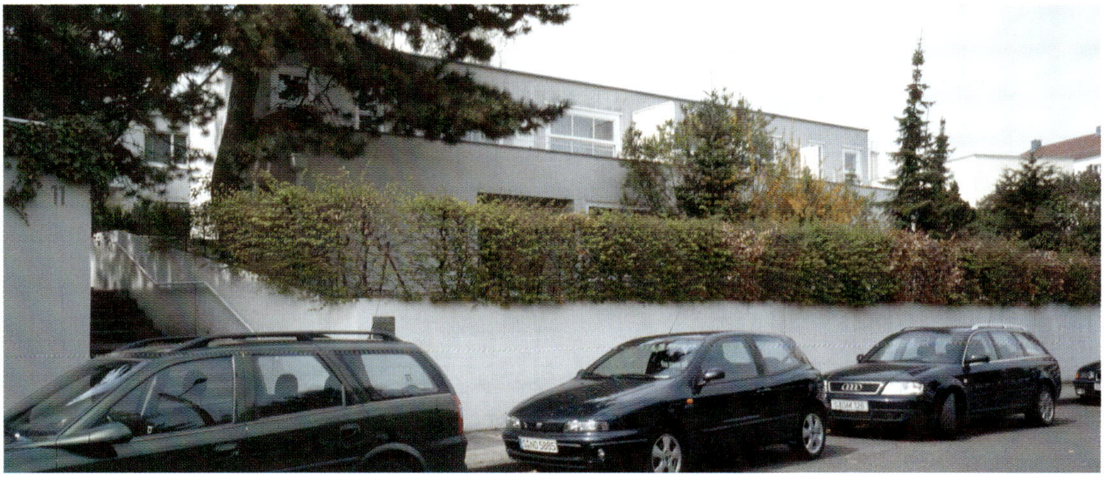

'As in the course of life a variety of views, experiences and objects are collected together, so the dwelling must allow the possibility to absorb them all; therefore a unity or consistency in colour, harmony or style, even the modern one, must be avoided. The dwelling is no art work, and it has no duty to irritate, which indeed would be the opposite of its purpose. Excessive unity and lack of decoration make it unrestful.' [51]

The relation between rooms, or rather spaces dedicated to particular uses, was also a great fascination for Frank. In his essay, *The house as street and square*[52] he suggested a parallel between the house and the spaces of the city. The house should have static and dynamic spaces, he claimed, and experience of route is of great importance. The visitor must be guided imperceptibly, without having to seek the way or being forced along it, and the route should unfold as a progression, never turning back on itself:

'The rules for the good house as ideal do not change in essence even if they are always being reinterpreted. How does one step into the garden? How does the way to the front door present itself? What form does a vestibule take? How does one get from the vestibule via the cloakroom to the living room? How does the sitting area relate to door and windows? Many such questions must be answered, out of which the house arises. This is modern architecture.' [53]

These statements help in understanding Frank's Weissenhof houses. A symmetrical pair, they occupy the lower edge site next to the corner house by Scharoun. Their stepped-form follows the contour, enjoying the view across the valley from a generous bedroom terrace. Most of the the ground level change is taken up in the retaining wall to the street, which is rendered and painted to seem continuous with the house. The house-type is essentially repeatable in parallel rows, though gaps would be needed between pairs to allow for the side entrances. Windows show no standardisation, they are diverse in form to create different inside/outside relationships. Large picture windows in continuous plate glass serve the living room while smaller ones subdivided with glazing bars protect the bedrooms, and still finer panes protect living areas from the vestibule. Different again are the horizontal strips which light the cellar and first-floor corridor. As with Scharoun and Rading's houses, a separate domain of service is created, with maid's room next to the kitchen and servery, and steps down to basement laundry. The stair to first-floor runs on top, starting with a kind of entrance platform next to the main door, whose raised level creates space for the basement clerestory.

The larger part of the ground floor plan is given to a generous living-dining room nearly eight metres in length with picture windows looking out both ways, but set in different bays. Its L-shaped form suggests the combination of three sub-spaces: a dining area by the kitchen looking to both back and front, a projecting bay on the other side focusing on the valley view, and a solid corner which during the exhibition held a grand piano. The L-shape surrounds an external room between vestibule and living room which is named on the plan *Hof*, meaning yard or court. Protected on both sides by walls and above by the floor to the terrace, it provides a sheltered space for sitting out, as in Rading's house, and is also well related to the kitchen for dining. Through it is the only way out to the front garden, and when not in use, it frames the view from the dining area. Small-paned windows allow a restricted view into it from the vestibule, so it is a crucial spatial filter.

Bearing in mind Frank's statements about spatial progressions, we should look at approach and entry. The modest front door is at the corner, with steps up and a protective low wall dividing approach path from garden. One enters a generous vestibule with a solid wall to right and the main stair arriving to left. Looking up the stair, one would see the upper passage veering right, and light entering from the clerestory. Ahead is a partial view through small-paned windows into the *Hof*, and as one turns left after the stair this becomes a diagonal glimpse of the dining space via two glass layers. Two steps down, a right turn leads via a glass door into the living room. Here is the centre of the house with views out both sides. It must be crossed to discover the delights of the sitting bay beyond. This is elaborate for such a small and simple house. The bedrooms above are rather generous in comparison to most at Weissenhof, and have substantial built-in storage. The skewed passage at the top of the stairs indicates the rightward direction of the main bedrooms, while the corner bathroom with its efficient plan presents itself to visitors at the top of the stairs.

With the two houses seen together, the symmetry gives the building a stronger formal presence, its more visually open middle flanked by solider ends. Entry from the sides makes the twin dwellings feel more independent, but the continuity of gardens and terrace, left entirely open for the exhibition, might stretch neighbourliness a bit far.

Döcker

Richard Döcker (1894-1968) was one of the younger Modernists and a contemporary of Hans Scharoun. By the late 1920s he had become the leading Modernist in Stuttgart, and the sole Ring member from that region. His best work was a hospital at Waiblingen of 1928, but he also built houses and some progressive housing schemes.

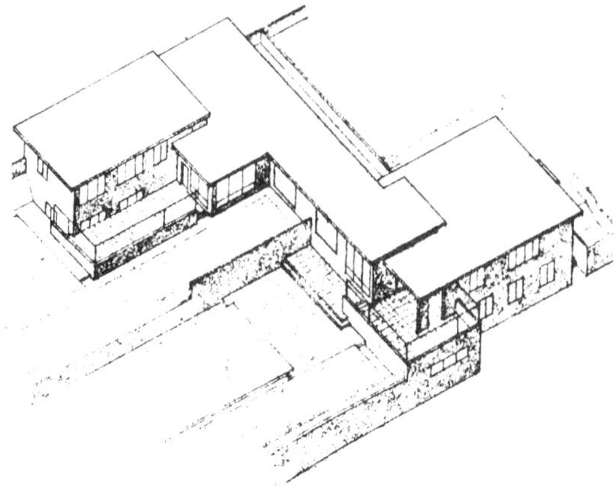

69. Richard Döcker. Linked house running from street to street as initially intended.

70. (below) Upper floor plan of the lower placed house.

71. (bottom) Lower floor plan of same house, with bedrooms and service rooms.

72. (opposite top) The pair of houses from the upper street.

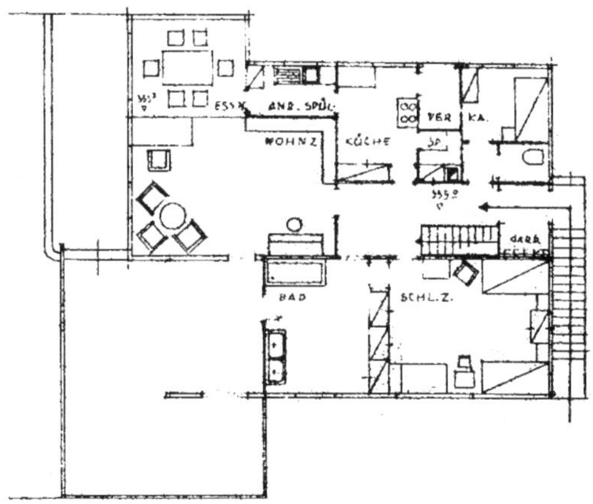

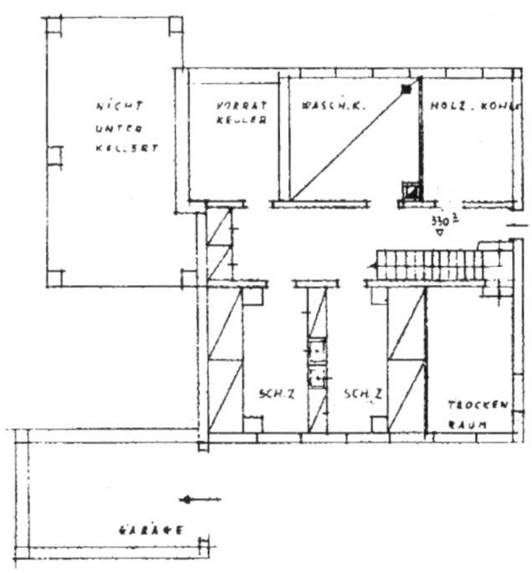

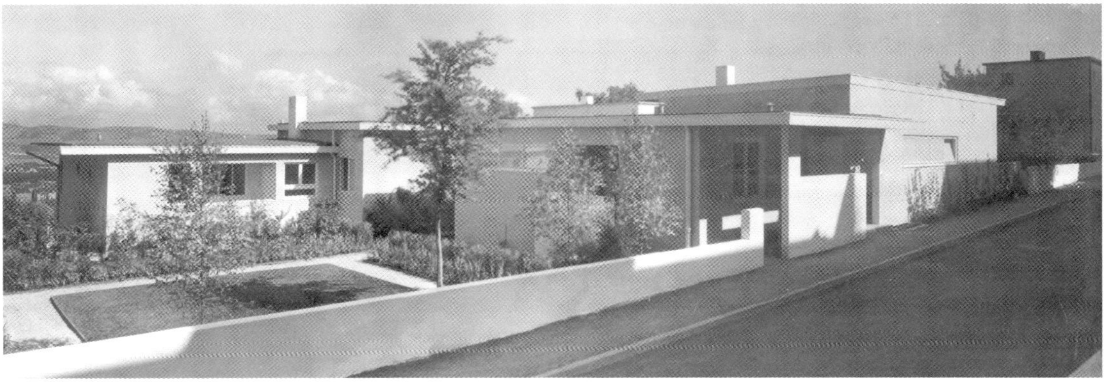

Being on the spot, it fell to him to supervise almost the whole Weissenhof site, a tough job in view of the experimental nature of the project and the short time for construction.[54] In design philosophy, Döcker veered to the organic side. He admired Frank Lloyd Wright, whose influence is clear in the Weissenhof houses, and he shared Häring's conviction that a building should be shaped by purpose and content:

'*House and man are a unity, the relationship between people forms the being of building.... The connections set up between house and man are the being and meaning of building. From these opposed demands and duties, and the tension and movement between them, arise the body and form of the building, its* Gestaltung. *Thus architecture becomes* Gestaltung *and reality.... Building is the fulfilment of the demands of life, it is an organic body... function is form, feeling becomes organism. House, man, sun and landscape come together in a complex of relationships.*'[55]

Döcker's houses occupied a site in the middle of the development, running between Bruckmannweg and Rathenaustrasse, absorbing a level change of around five metres. One house starts on the top street, the other at the bottom, and they move towards each other, stepping in stages and terracing the garden into carefully landscaped outdoor rooms. In the initial design the two met at a party wall, united by a central piece of roof, together enclosing a shared piece of south-facing garden; but after cost-cutting they became independent. Even so, they remained site-bound, coming closer than any other project to Häring's initial concept of interlocking courts. Coherence was given to the stepping volumes by stressing the overhanging roofs, which from some angles appear Wrightian. The upper house's bedroom block lines the top street, raised half a storey for privacy with cellar rooms beneath. The street side is passage, leaving good views and east orientation for the bedrooms. North of the entrance is the maid's room and kitchen with service yard, kept at street level but with the roof lower than the bedroom wing. From the vestibule you would descend half a storey to the living room and its garden terrace to south, the dining area being a raised gallery at the north end. The roof-plane of kitchen and entrance is maintained while the floor drops, giving the living room the necessary increased height. The highest roof of the lower house reaches the same level, and was to run through, covering an additional room in the upper house intended as a study.

The lower house uses a step in the retaining wall to Rathenau Strasse to create a garage, raising the sun-bathing terrace above for privacy. Just above ground level minor bedrooms line the street, enjoying eastern orientation, with cellar rooms behind. But the main life of the house occurs a storey up, approached by an outside stair to north. The master bedroom occupies the east side, kitchen and maid's room the west, with living-dining and a big terrace to south. The curious placing of large bathroom next to terrace reflects the intention that both be used for gymnastic exercises, popular in a period dedicated to health and hygiene.

These houses were among the most generous at Weissenhof, with some of the most convincing garden spaces. They were cheaply built using the same experimental timber Zickzack system as the Hilberseimer house. It did not prove very durable. Döcker was limited by its spanning capability from being more radical in opening his garden façades, but he produced much house for the money.

Max Taut

Max (1884-1967) was younger brother of the more famous Bruno and took a junior role in the Expressionist movement led by his brother,[56] but in the 1920s when he began to get opportunities to build - notably offices for various trade-unions - he proved himself a substantial architect in his own right. He was known by colleagues and students as a *Baumeister* - a master of building, because he was a pioneer in construction and interested in the question of how to express it. His headquarters for the German Book Printers Union of 1924-6 was sophisticated not only in its differentiation of wall and frame, but in the careful articulation and layering of its façades. Not for Max Taut the ubiquitous and abstract render that became the hallmark of Modernism: he preferred to show how things were made, relishing the colour and texture of materials. It is not surprising, then, that his two Weissenhof houses were the most textured, covered in a cladding of glazed panels that acknowledged the frame and revealed its rhythm. Taut's interest in constructive means was accompanied by a belief in the virtues of fast construction avoiding wet-trades, both for urgent projects and to reduce interest charges.

Building next to Döcker, Taut's site also stretched from Rathenaustrasse to Bruckmannweg, and he placed one house at the top and one at the bottom. Treated as separate buildings, they took opposite corners to allow both the valley view. The upper house was the simpler, with two identical

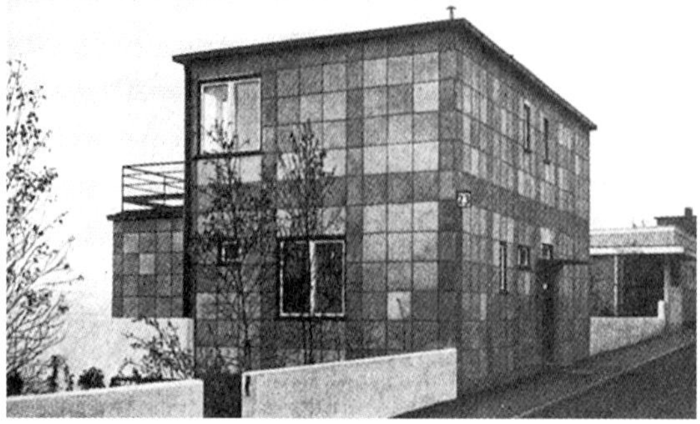

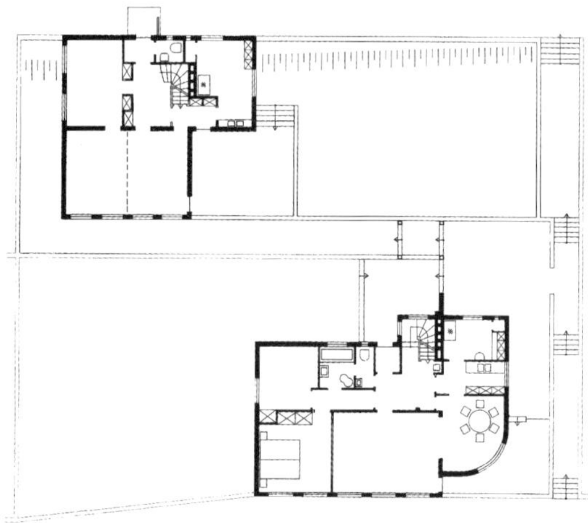

73. (top) Max Taut, upper house seen from street with expressed framing.

74. (above) Main plans of both houses.

75. Lower house with its rounded dining corner.

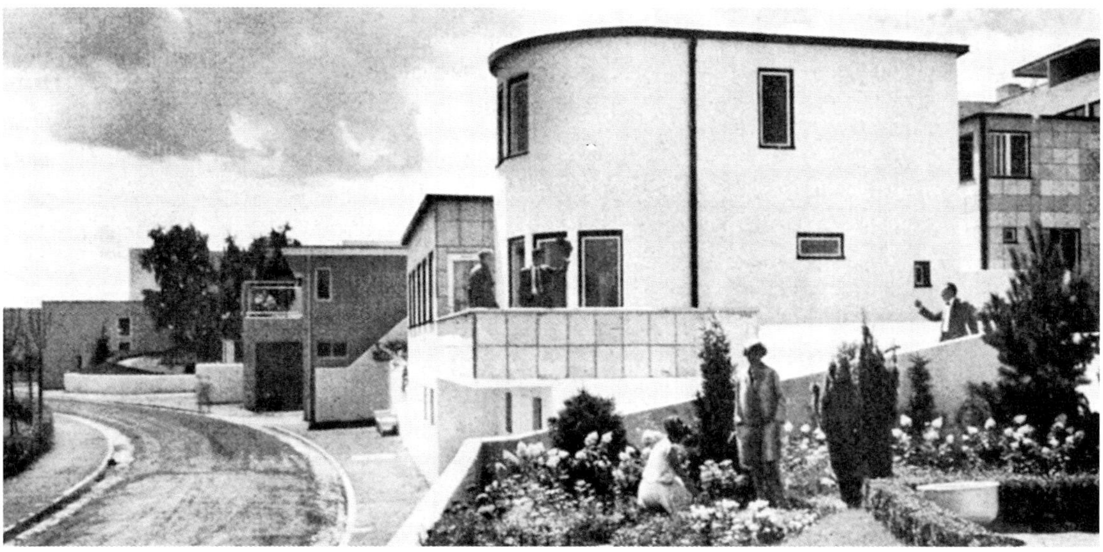

spans and a clear framing rhythm. The block on the street housed entrance, kitchen and study at ground level with bedrooms above; the single storey element adjacent provided living rooms and sun terrace. The lower house sat by an alleyway linking the two streets, the corner marked by a half-round tower. The main entrance was from behind, via a small court protected by a pergola. The main block of the house contained living rooms to front looking east across the valley, and bedrooms looking south to the garden. The tower element contained kitchen, dining and stair, presumably with service rooms in the upper floor, as in the houses by Taut's brother Bruno and Adolf Rading.

Although photographs show a constructive rhythm dominating the upper house, involving frame, cladding panels and windows, it is evidently not the same system and dimension as used in the other, so perhaps Taut was experimenting with different arrangements. Also not clear from published material is the construction of the curved wall in the lower house. Taut used rendered surfaces, it seems, both to provide a contrast with the texture of the panelled walls, and to allow some relaxation from the strictness of their insistent rhythm. He was not prepared to give construction as much priority as Gropius, indeed his houses can be seen as a compromise between system building and response to the site.

Bourgeois

The site taken by Belgian architect Victor Bourgeois was originally intended for Adolf Loos and would presumably have been a demonstration of *Raumplan*,[57] but Loos had made enemies in Stuttgart with his outspokenly critical stance, while there was also political pressure for a Belgian representative.[58] It seems that Bourgeois (1897-1962), already known for the Cité Moderne outside Brussels, was recommended by his teacher Henry van de Velde. He was one of the youngest architects commissioned, and due to the late invitation had little time. His house is interesting mainly for its attempt to escape a still pressing convention. It seems to have started life as a conventional and symmetrical classical villa plan with a central wide bay and two narrower side ones. In the first version the central axis is stressed by the aligned main entrance and paired garden steps, though admittedly the left wing is pulled forward and the living room opened up by omitting a wall and creating a void by the stair. In the developed version the void goes - presumably for economy - and asymmetry increases. Bourgeois tries to redirect the entrance route - now from the south - with steps leading around to the north door. With hindsight this house is an odd hybrid, almost like a conversion, showing little concern for the site. Conventionally load-bearing in construction, it also

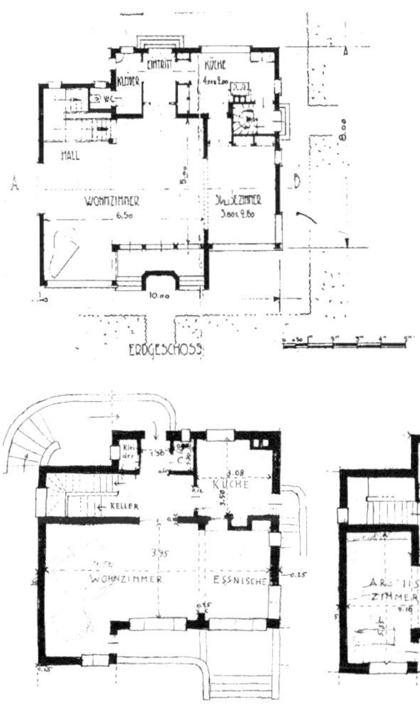

76. (left) Victor Bourgeois house plans, ground floor of first version and beneath ground floor (left) and first floor plans of built version.

77. (below) The house from the south side.

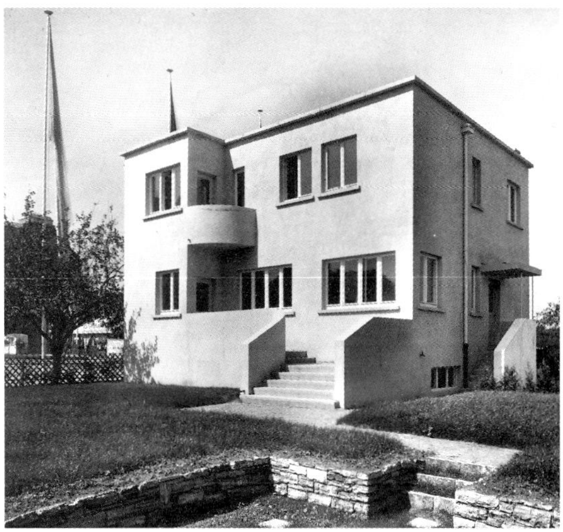

unnecessarily obeys the shape needed for a pitched roof. Such modernist freedom as Bourgeois achieves occurs by erosion of the initial *parti*, rather than by starting from a new principle.

Two major architects of the previous generation were invited to build at Weissenhof, and both quite late in the day.[59] Hans Poelzig (1869-1936) was given a single house on the lower side between Hilberseimer and Max Taut; Peter Behrens (1868-1940) took the large site at the north end formerly intended for Häring. Both were in their late fifties and had done their pioneering work in the early years of the century, and neither felt at home with the emerging architectural language, though Poelzig's design is arguably the less conservative of the two.

Poelzig

Poelzig's can be placed among houses at the *Siedlung* that are unique, and respond closely to the given site, like those of Scharoun, Rading and Döcker. Like other work by Poelzig it is thoughtful, conceived from the inside out, and as a result somewhat elusive in style. The garden-plan is the first clue to its rationale, with specialised outdoor rooms for children's play, for growing vegetables, sitting in the sun or the shade, etc. Poelzig pushes his house to the northern boundary to create a large flat space to south, then sets up his main floor as a continuation of this garden plateau. The one-storey drop in ground level is absorbed in a partial basement containing cellars, laundry and maid's room, while outside stairs rise on both north and east sides, hugging the flank walls of the house and tying it into the hill. The eastward step in the site corner where it adjoins Hilberseimer's house is resolved with a quadrant-shaped wall and conical bank. The upper floor is also pulled back to the northern edge to create a south-facing balcony and sun-bathing area, making the building impressively tower-like at the corner. The asymmetry of the situation is a gift lovingly received.

A pupil of Poelzig in the 1920s, Julius Posener stressed how undoctrinaire this architect was, how uninterested in style *per se*:

'He never spoke of what architecture might need at a particular time, even less of what architecture is. He talked about the position of the dining area in relation to the kitchen, about comfortable and uncomfortable staircases, about the structure of

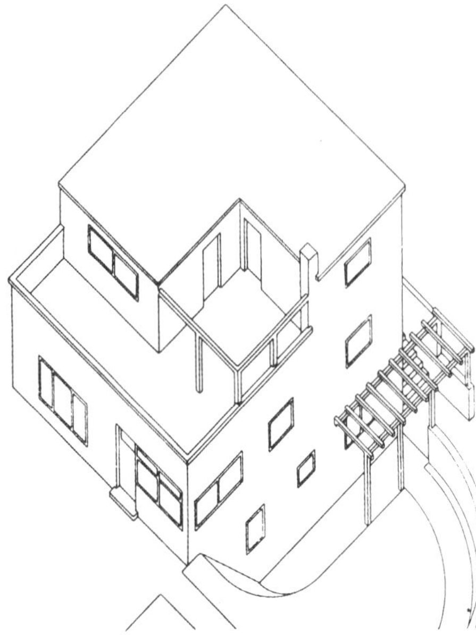

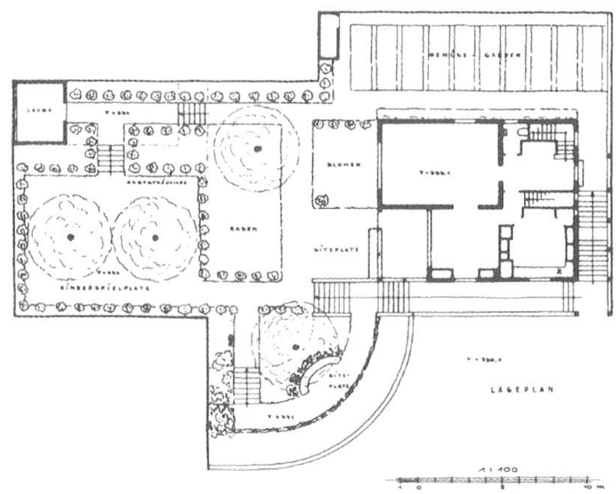

78. (top) Hans Poelzig, axonometric of house showing exploitation of site level change.

79. (above) Garden plan with house plan incorporated showing intended progression of spaces.

80. (below) House as seen from the street.

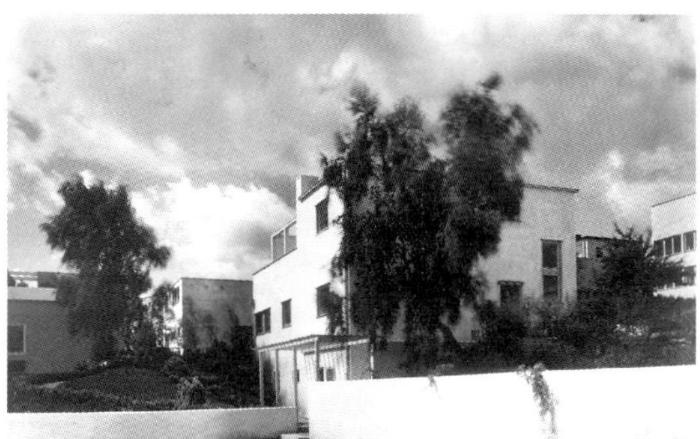

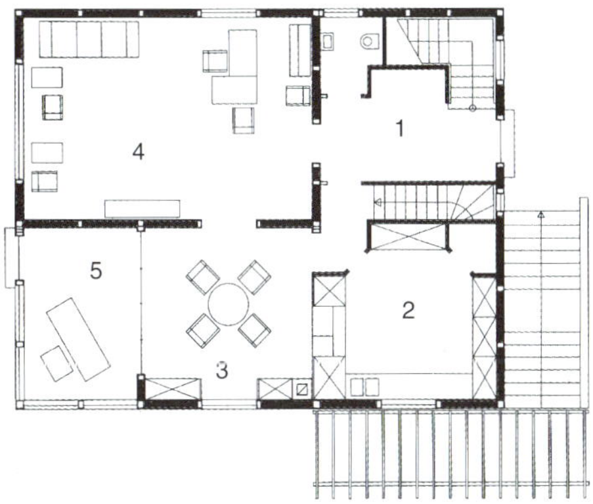

81. Poelzig house, main floor plan showing framing system: 1 entrance hall, 2 kitchen, 3 dining room, 4 living room, 5 sunroom.

82. (below right) Peter Behrens's block of flats from the north.

roofs with large spans, about how different spaces with different functions could be made to relate to each other.' [60]

The plans are deceptively simple, and must be inhabited in the imagination for their virtues to be understood. Visitors arrive at a pair of gates covered by a pergola marking the threshold to the site. Passing through, they take the broad stair ahead which was meant to be roofed, turning left at the top into the front door. They see nothing of the garden save the edge of the vegetable plot. Entering, they discover a generous vestibule with tall stairwell lit by two vertical windows. Taking the obvious door on axis with the entrance, they progress to the main living room, and through its picture window see the garden beyond. The dining room lies on the cross axis, its table aligned with windows on both east and west facades. Moving that way, they catch the east view out across the city. Turning south again, glass doors open to a corner sun-room, which leads in turn to an outside sitting place. Paths invite exploration of the garden.

For the family there are generous bedrooms and bathroom upstairs, with a framed terrace for sunbathing. Rooms are flexibly square with built-in cupboards. The basement contains the usual laundry, heating and maid's room, with independent door to the street. The service stair emerges discreetly in the generously-sized kitchen out of the thickness of the wall.

Construction was timber frame clad on the outside with Fornitram, an early form of woodwool slab. At first Poelzig planned to use a coated version which could remain exposed to display the joints, but in the event they were rendered and painted grey. There was some dry construction of the inner skin and ceilings with exposed battens. The house was simply and elegantly furnished, but with a strong and controversial colour scheme.

Behrens

Peter Behrens's block of 12 flats took up the large site at the north corner of the *Siedlung*. In many ways the most conventional building, it had conventional rooms and solid masonry walls punctuated by relatively small window holes, and nothing in the way of flowing space. Behrens claimed to offer a new form of block providing open terraces to all flats for health reasons, and he stacked up flats to allow the roof of one to become a terrace for the next,[61] but this can be only a small part of the story. His driving concern seems to have been formal: he wanted to explore the new kind of asymmetrical composition that had arrived under the influence of Frank Lloyd Wright, taken up by Dutch architects such as Dudok, or closer to home by Erich Mendelsohn. At the same time, he wanted to explore how flats of a more or less standard type might be repeated as a theme and variations. Nor did he neglect the site, for the building masses into a tower on the corner and enfolds a kind of

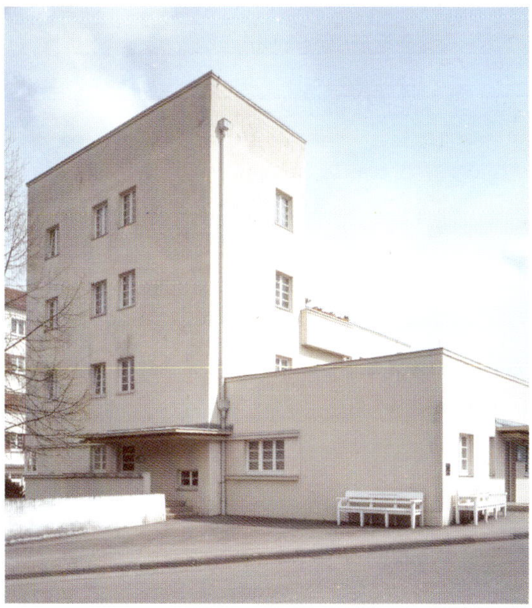

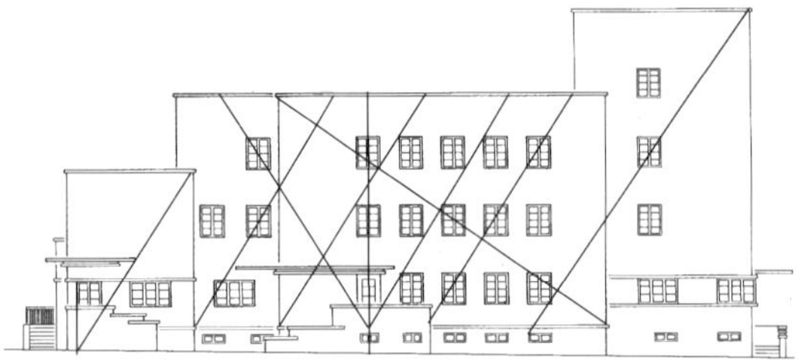

83. Behrens block of flats, north-east elevation, with diagonal lines to indicate proportion system (applied by the author).

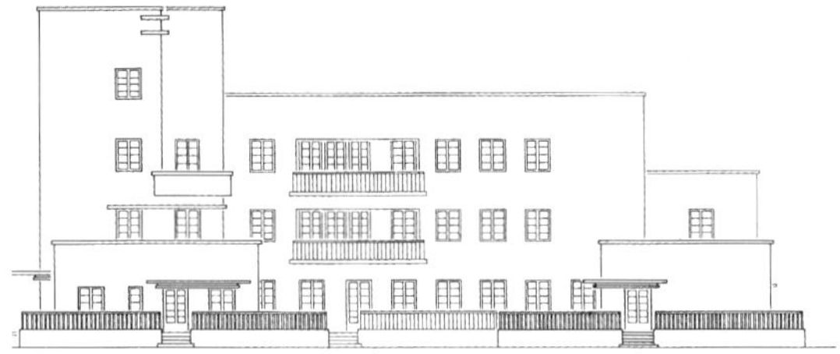

84. Behrens block of flats, south-west elevation.

entrance court facing south. There he levelled off the ground to make a base for the building, while on other sides the walls rose out of the sloping ground. To re-assert his horizon line, Behrens added string courses, horizontal projecting canopies, and walls with horizontal parapets. He even gave ground-floor flats three-light and corner windows instead of the standard two-light ones, purely for the sake of the façade composition.

Composition was his game. Fifteen years earlier he had been a keen Classicist, a great admirer of Schinkel, and deeply interested in proportional systems.[62] A little analysis shows that this interest persisted, even if in asymmetrical form, for both plans and elevations turn out to be full of parallel diagonals. These reflect the method established by August Thiersch in his *Handbuch der Architektur* of 1883: Thiersch's son Paul had worked for Behrens. When diagonals concur, it means that the rectangles which they cross share the same proportion, even without a significant size relationship. It is therefore a quick way to check for proportional harmony, or to impose it. Examination of Behrens's plans suggests as a repeated base figure a single flat plan just over 12 x 8 metres, precisely proportioned in the ratio three to two. When variously turned, doubled and overlapped, it seems to produce most of the key dimensions of the plan. The same figure works in the elevations, its resonant diagonals showing this to be a three-dimensional compositional system.

Whatever one's feeling about its aesthetic efficacy, this kind of concern was not pursued without a price. Obviously room dimensions follow the system, rather than precise functional planning of the kind pursued by Oud and Bruno Taut, necessitating a looser fit and larger rooms. Behrens was not much interested in the minutiae of domestic life, and was criticised for creating kitchens where the stove was overshadowed by the cook. Further, an aesthetically based manipulation of forms on paper with overlaps and intersections makes more sense than on the building site. So while it might seem to suggest a form of rational

85. Behrens block of flats, ground floor plan with diagonal lines to indicate proportion system (applied by the author). The angles are the same as in the elevation above.

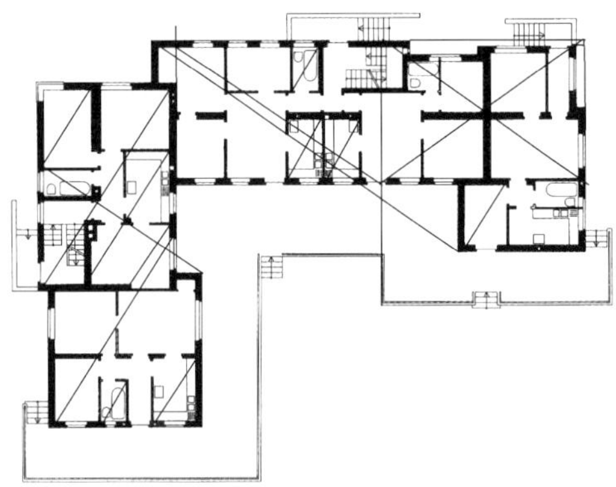

86. Behrens block of flats, second floor plan. Behrens was concerned that for health reasons every flat should have a balcony or a roof terrace.

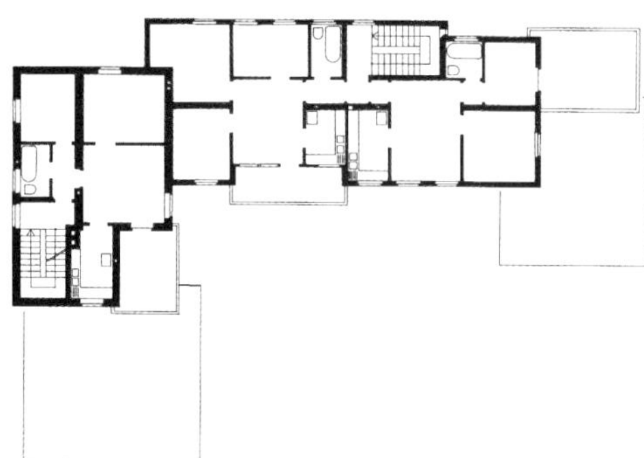

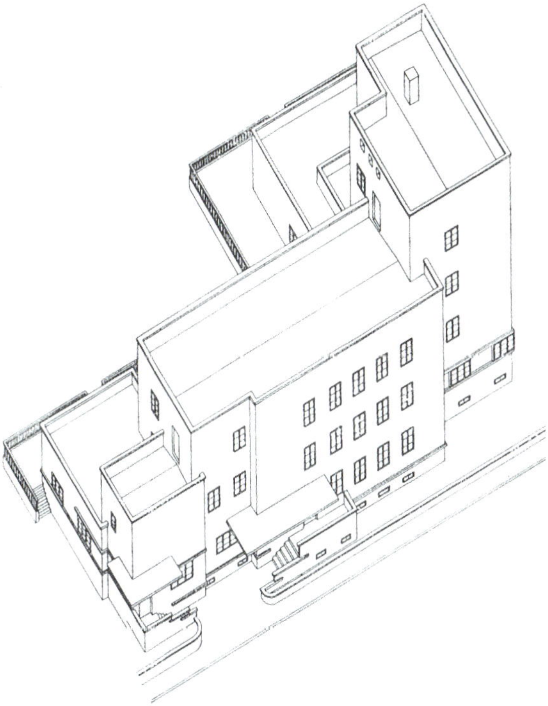

87. Behrens block of flats, axonometric projection.

88. Entrance side of the flats today.

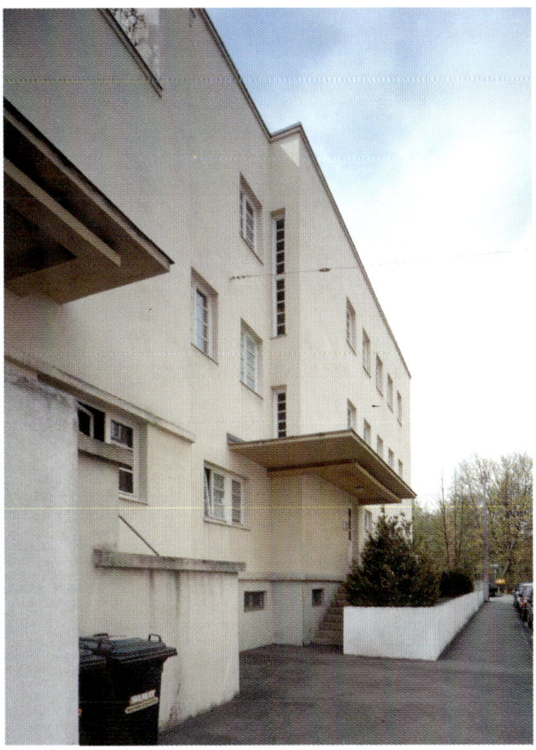

coordination, it would not lend itself to system-building. It rather depended on traditional craftsmanship with which Behrens was familiar. His aesthetic system thus has nothing in common with his ex-assistant Gropius's efforts nearby, even if Gropius had also experimented with proportion, and even if the two architects shared a common neoclassical heritage.

Conclusion

The first visitors to Weissenhof were struck by the departure from tradition. It looked radically new and radically different, for at that time nearly all new buildings in every European city were still covered in sculptural ornament based on some variant of a historical style. Load-bearing wall construction was the norm, with visible pitched roofs, cornices, string courses, rustication, and other academically defined elements which dominated the curricula of architectural schools. Plans were set up on axes according to the Beaux Arts method, assuming that the building would take a symmetrical form with a central entrance.

The social revolution that accompanied the end of the First World War in German-speaking countries had made a break with these conventions thinkable, and for the first time buildings other than factories could be left unadorned, but it took nearly a decade of experiments before the recognisable and consistent modern architecture later to be called 'The International Style' could emerge. It is hard to imagine how, in the absence of this modernist orthodoxy, buildings of the early 1920s like Mendelsohn's Einstein Tower (p.100), Häring's Garkau farm (p. 49-55), Le Corbusier's Ozenfant Studio or a project such as Mies's Friedrichstrasse tower (p. 204) would have appeared. Isolated oddities, they were rare experiments involving not so much a search for new forms as for new principles and methods, and they all looked different. Who could say which was right? The change at Weissenhof was the sudden apparent consistency. Considering the varied underlying ideas described above, it was to some extent illusory, but it was intended and understood to be of value at the time. It was even deliberately imposed, for Mies had made flat roofs compulsory. Its value lay in the strong impression of solidarity that it created.

The idea of establishing a style was anathema both to Mies and Häring, but the foundation of the

Berlin Ring around 1923-4 had been motivated precisely by a need for solidarity. The Ring's work had been not just to promote the new architecture in print and exhibitions, but to displace the conservative City Architect who prevented Modernists getting jobs and building permissions, and in this they were successful.[63] That this power of consensus should also appear visually at Weissenhof was perhaps inevitable. It put the new architecture on the map and helped make it respectable, but it also paved the way for its reduction into a repetitive formula. In Germany the rich mix of ideas and directions might have continued, had not the Wall Street crash two years later precipitated an economic depression to slow down building and help bring Hitler to power, and had not the Nazis then outlawed Modernism. But success in the outside world was different. It was bound to depend on the printed page, on reports, printed drawings and photographs; mainly on the medium of the architectural book and magazine. That the new plain cubic style lent itself well to this medium was surely no accident, but it forced an emphasis on visible form at the expense of response to context, habitability, and other issues. The selective powers of the medium are exemplified today particularly by the absence of colour, for black and white photographs engendered the myth of 'The White Architecture'. Photography concealed the fact that Bruno Taut was not the only one to experiment with strong colour: the Mies block was pink, the Stam houses a vivid blue, the Behrens ochre yellow, and the Corbusier double houses blue and green, just to name a few, and these colours were only the ones on the outside.

The image of the new architecture travelled the world. The transfer to foreign shores was bound to be reductive, but the effect was worse when commentators from the host country provided the interpretation. With the exhibition *The International Style* and the eponymous catalogue, Henry Russell Hitchcock and Philip Johnson transplanted the flower of Architectural Modernism to New York and the English-speaking world just as it was killed at home by the Nazis. They turned the visual consistency of Weissenhof into a formal doctrine, identifying stylistic characteristics and making high-handed judgements about composition and fenestration.[64] Oddnesses and inconsistencies were rejected as heresies. They made light of the earnest functionalist arguments promoted by German Modernists, even calling their International Style 'post-functionalist'.[65] They largely disregarded the European Modernists' serious social programme, which in Germany had produced the bulk of the work.[66] Their focus of interest was purely aesthetic.

But with 'International', Hitchcock and Johnson chose the right word. Pan-European authorship at Weissenhof added to the impression of solidarity, for it suggested that 'the new building' as the Germans called it, rose above petty narrow-mindedness and local squabbles. Internationalism, according to Hannes Meyer in his Bauhaus manifesto, was the privilege of the period.[67] It reflected the use of standard forms, methods, and materials, *'which know no native country'*[68], as well as the Marxist brotherhood of man.

Since Nationalism had produced the Great War, Internationalism was full of virtue:[69] it named the anthem of the left, to be sung by anti-fascists in the Spanish Civil War. Almost contemporary with Weissenhof were key modernist projects for the League of Nations Building in Geneva by Hannes Meyer (p. 47) and Le Corbusier, and though both were unsuccessful, Corbusier later played a major role in the United Nations building in New York. The Nationalist dictatorships of Hitler and Mussolini only strengthened Internationalism as the humane and enlightened opposition, adding to its moral authority. This has made the case for regionalism difficult to re-establish ever since.

Architectural Internationalism led inevitably to the pursuit of ideas, types, or forms, that could be applied worldwide, ignoring differences of climate and culture. It therefore became allied with universalism: that is with the pursuit of the universal as opposed to the specific. The technical justification was the inevitable arrival of mass-production, then seen in terms of Ford and of F.W. Taylor's 'scientific management'.[70] The cultural justification was the brotherhood of man supported by the new scientific view of the world. Not only was science solving all kinds of practical problems: it was banishing ignorance and superstition along with disease, and past architectural styles could certainly be seen as superstition, if not disease.[71] The truth was an objective material reality defined by scientific laws, to which Logical Positivism gave philosophical backing, dismissing every kind of metaphysical speculation as nonsense.[72] Objectivity (*Sachlichkeit*) became a key word, applied equally to architecture and painting. It might refer to the 'objective' and 'scientific' design process, as opposed to a 'subjective' or intuitive one: hence Pevsner's favourite polarity between Functionalism and Expressionism. It might equally refer to the object-like nature of the building or to the cool geometric pattern of an abstract painting, done as perfectly and mechanically as possible: it might even refer to the fact of its abstract as opposed to representational nature.[73] In both realms it meant the clean, pure, starkly defined image, the art-object as independent totality. 'Objective' named both a philosophical and an aesthetic stance, and if in the early days it identified only a few ideal islands in a sea of outmoded convention, they could be seen as harbingers of a brave new world for all: this was the heady promise of the modernist revolution.

'Form follows function', 'truth to materials', 'mechanisation takes command': these are the slogans of the high-modernist period, and it is easy with hindsight to see how this constellation of thoughts could seem so compelling and self-evident: but things were neither so simple nor so neat. The attempt to reduce architecture to an objective quantifiable basis, most clearly expressed by Meyer at the Bauhaus, was doomed, after decades of struggle, to failure. The functionalist design philosophy, given lip-service by so many, proved a chimera, for it involved contradictions from the start.[74] The appropriate use of materials turned out to be equally difficult, and fraught with problems of interpretation.[75] The promised economies of the production line never arrived, and attempts to define a universal aesthetic formula equally applicable to Laplanders and Papuans also failed.[76] Attempts across the globe to reorganise cities rationally in line with the technical demands of modern life through zoning are mostly now regretted, even if they were to some extent inevitable. The modernist credo, in short, led to dismay and disappointment, and to recriminations from those who, in a bid to escape its influence, called themselves Post-modernists. But the problem lay not so much in the social and technical changes that had taken place as in the way they had been interpreted. The modernist credo was too full of shortcuts, and we need now to abandon these in favour of the longer - and more difficult - way round.

Although the Weissenhofsiedlung was acknowledged as a historical milestone, relatively little serious research on it was undertaken until the 1980s when Karin Kirsch started work on her standard monograph (Kirsch 1987). It had been denigrated by the Nazis and bombed in the war, and even houses that survived suffered numerous unsympathetic changes, so before the restorations started in the 1980s it was difficult to get much sense of the original achievement. Why was there so little interest? Perhaps because the *Siedlung* was seen only as background evidence for a set of ideas completely taken for granted and already supposedly improved upon; perhaps also because Orthodox Modernism was uninterested in history, even its own history. There was also the idea, much encouraged by leading historians, that the only buildings worth looking at were the works of Le Corbusier and Mies, who were seen as the principal and exclusive innovators. Architects like Rading, Poelzig and Frank, if known at all, were second-raters consigned to the dustbin of history. Few thought that they might also have had interesting ideas.

I called this chapter *The Weissenhof Experiment* in a bid to reopen its experimental nature and show the rich mix of ideas behind it. Many of these ideas are familiar, and architects are still juggling with them, so a clarification of their ancestry should be helpful. In following chapters some of the ideas will be pursued further and yet others proposed, through more detailed case studies. They tell a story of unprecedented change, of the opening up of new opportunities but also the imposition of new duties. The changing natures of knowledge and society made both inevitable.

Notes

1. There are two monographs on the Weissenhofsiedlung: Kirsch 1987/1989 and Pommer & Otto 1991. The earlier, German edition of Kirsch was consulted, and page numbers may not accord with the translated edition.

2. For story of the Ring, see Blundell Jones 1999, pp. 99-102.

3. Ibid pp. 102-104.

4. Häring claimed: *'I had done all the preliminary work for Stuttgart'*: ibid p. 103.

5. Literally 'City-crown' and the title of a book by Bruno Taut, see Pehnt 1973, p. 79 and Nerdinger 1988, p. 93.

6. Blundell Jones 1999, p.103.

7. Ibid. pp.104-106.

8. Ibid. pp.117-125.

9. Adolf Behne's distinction, see Behne 1964.

10. On Mies interiors, see Kirsch 1987, pp. 69-89.

11. Mies 1924: *'I consider the industrialisation of building methods the key problem of the day. Once we succeed in this, our social, economic, technical and even artistic problems will be easy to solve...All parts will be made in the factory and the work of the site will consist only of assemblage...I am convinced that traditional methods of construction will disappear.'* from Blake 1960, p. 38.

12. See for example Neumeyer 1991.

13. See Kroll 1986, p.10.
14. See Herbert 1984.
15. Experience of the Hertfordshire schools and CLASP systems with long series was that serial production did not prove cheaper than traditional construction: see Saint 1987.
16. Gropius 1935, p. 27.
17. Time and costs were pressing, and Döcker was left to supervise the whole site and deal with all the practical problems. It seems to have been his decision to change the nature of the construction for economic reasons. Gropius was able to retain personal supervision of his site, one reason why he was able to experiment more successfully with construction than the others. On Stam's construction see Kirsch 1987, pp.176-180.
18. For the whole background story see Kirsch 1987, pp.105-111.
19. Though less apparently 'rational' than Stam's halved plan, this asymmetry allows more variation in room layout, which could make it functionally more efficient.
20. Häring commented on Hilberseimer's Utopian city plans in a substantial article: see Blundell Jones 1999, pp.110-112.
21. The 'Frankfurt kitchen' designed by Margarete Schütte-Lihotsky for mass Housing in that city under city architect Ernst May was mass-produced in large numbers and became the prototype for the modern fitted kitchen.
22. Herman Hertzberger made this point very convincingly in a lecture about Rietveld's Schröder house and in his book: Hertzberger 1991, pp. 218-9.
23. See Pehnt 1973, pp. 73-84.
24. Gemeinnützige Heimstätten Spar- und Bau-Aktiengesellschaft founded April 1924, see Speidel 1994, p. 209.
25. Ibid. p. 236.
26. See Nerdinger 1988, pp. 86-95.
27. See Kirsch 1987, pp.144-149.
28. On reactions to Taut's colour scheme see Kirsch 1987, pp.147-149.
29. With many projects on the go, he often left the general supervision entirely to subordinates and only visited the building at the end, in order to supervise colour mixing. See Speidel 1994, p. 210.
30. Several of the colour schemes for Taut's Berlin work have been restored by Winfried Brenne: see Pitz & Brenne 1980.
31. Literally 'flower-window', a space between two glass skins used as a greenhouse.
32. After the restoration in 1984 an elderly couple refused it but it was later rented to an artist: see Kirsch 1987 p.130.
33. So described by Le Corbusier, a mere 70 cm wide, see Kirsch 1989, p.126.
34. Edgar Wedepohl, 1927, quoted in Kirsch 1987 p.128; my translation.
35. Le Corbusier & Ozenfant, *Purism* included in Herbert 1964.
36. See for example Konrad Düssel, quot. Kirsch 1987, p.130.
37. Particularly strong opposition came from the Czech critic Karel Teige as well as from Hannes Meyer and Hugo Häring. On Teige see George Baird in Oppositions 4, 1974, pp. 80-81.
38. Only two years later, Taut wrote rather perceptively:- *'In all estimation of Le Corbusier there lies his great weakness, that he is not only architect but also abstract painter, and therefore mixes up the problems of building with those of studio painting, even those of a purely practical or constructive nature. This division between studio and the people it must have been, which led Lenin in his time to a dialectical rejection of Russian abstract painting. The Mexican Diego Rivera was perhaps the only one to achieve, in his paintings for ministerial buildings in Mexico, a connection between the people and high quality (art)'.* Taut 1929 p. 58, my translation.
39. Letter from Behne to Scharoun reproduced in Wendschuh 1993, p. 74.
40. See note 31.
41. For more on Scharoun's Weissenhof house and for further illustrations, see Blundell Jones 1993 (2) & 1995, pp. 46-56.
42. Behne 1964.
43. Akademie der Künste 1965.
44. From a lecture by Rading given in 1929 and reported in Pfankuch 1970, p. 7.
45. For Scharoun on Rading, see introduction to Pfankuch 1970.
46. For a clear example see Scharoun's model house at Liegnitz, Blundell Jones 1995, p. 56.
47. Rading in Die Form, vol 9, 1927, pp. 287-289, reprinted in Pfankuch 1970, p. 48.
48. Rading's design for a block of flats at the Breslau Werkbund Exhibition was a repeatable type-design although Scharoun's was site-specific.
49. In a counter-demonstration against the formalism of the new architecture, Frank invited architects not involved at Stuttgart: Lurçat (France) but not Le Corbusier, Rietveld (Holland) but not Oud or Stam, Häring (Germany) but not Mies or Gropius.
50. Quoted from Frank: *Die Grosstadtwohnung unserer Zeit,* 1927, reprinted in Spalt & Czech 1981 pp. 31-33; my translation.
51. *Die Moderne Einrichtung des Wohnhauses,* ibid, p. 84.
52. *Das Haus als Weg und Platz*, ibid, p36.
53. Ibid.
54. For the difficulties experienced by Döcker, see Kirsch 1989, essays on individual buildings. For problems in the construction of Mies's block see Kirsch 1989 pp. 48-55.
55. Döcker, 1923, quoted in Mehlau-Wiebking 1989 pp. 67-68.
56. In architecture the Utopian tendency recorded in drawings and texts just after the First World War, in which Bruno Taut was the leading figure. The best general source is Pehnt 1973.
57. Loos's term for his way of designing houses as progressions of interior volumes, see Risselada 1988.
58. Kirsch 1987, pp. 100-104.
59. They were both brought in late, in November 1926, though both had been on earlier lists, see Kirsch 1989, p.150.
60. Posener 1992, p. xiii.
61. The aim was healthy housing to avoid the scourge of tuberculosis which was rife in Europe at the time, see Chapter 4. Behrens's intentions are well described in Kirsch 1987, pp.185-6.
62. Key works of his neoclassical period were German Embassy, St Petersburg, 1910-11 and Wiegand house of 1911-13, for a famous archaeologist. For further information on Behrens see Anderson 2000.
63. Blundell Jones 1999, pp. 99-101.
64. See Hitchcock & Johnson 1932.
65. Ibid p.14, on Functionalism pp. 35-39.
66. The great social housing programmes of Berlin, Frankfurt and other German cities made up the bulk of Modernist work in terms of sheer built floor area.
67. *Building* 1927, reprinted in Conrads 1970 pp.118-120 with translation.
68. Ibid
69. See for example H.G.Wells's novel *The War in the Air.*
70. Frederick W. Taylor was pioneer of time and motion studies and author of *The Principles of Scientific Management.*
71. The famous example is Adolf Loos's essay *Ornament and crime*, (in English in Conrads 1970 pp.19-24) but see also Pevsner 1960 pp.17, 42-46.
72. The classic text in the English-speaking world was A.J. Ayer, *Language Truth and Logic.*
73. Adolf Behne, writing in 1923, saw it in these terms: *'it is not the limited, emotional, human will that decides and plans the work, but the will of objectivity, of purpose, of the material seeking its own realisation - the human being is merely the medium through which this takes place'.* Behne 1964, author's translation.
74. Behne also saw a significant distinction between Rationalism and Functionalism as early as 1923: Behne 1964 (1926). On the dating see the introduction to the 1964 re-edition.
75. Kenneth Frampton considers at length the differences between tectonic fact and tectonic fiction in Frampton 1995.
76. Precisely the peoples cited by Le Corbusier and Ozenfant in their essay *Purism.*

Chapter 2. Hugo Häring: Garkau Farm 1922-5

The phrase 'Form follows function', coined by Louis Sullivan in Chicago, resounds through the literature of the Modern Movement, and in many places the word 'Functionalism' even became synonymous with Modernism,[1] yet although many architects paid lip-service to the idea, few really followed it through. Looking at their buildings, 'Form follows Geometry' 'Form follows Construction', or 'Form follows Assembly' (for example Gropius's Weissenhof house) would often be more appropriate designations. Mies even positively avoided direct response to function in the interests of flexibility, rational construction and general types.

Even on those occasions when architects took the activity to be housed as a generating principle, the effect could be rather extreme and one-sided, as for example in Johannes Duiker's open-air school (fig. 1) which is described by its architect not so much in terms of its educational programme but as a machine for sunning children,[2] or in Konstantin Melnikov's 'laboratory of sleep' (fig. 2) of 1929 where apart from a symmetrical division of the sexes, the main physical effect of the programme on the design seems to have been a sloping floor, merely to eliminate the need for pillows. The intended 'blissful slumber' was in fact meant to be produced not so much by the architecture as by environmental controls, 'salubrious scents' and pleasant sounds.[3] Hannes Meyer too attempted to justify his League of Nations competition entry (fig. 3) on a purely functional basis, but his technical arguments about lighting and acoustics were too ill-founded to be credible, while he contradicted himself about his symbolic intentions.[4] Among those who seriously tried to develop a Functionalist position, Hugo Häring was therefore perhaps the most consistent and the most articulate, and it helped that he was also trying consciously to throw off the shackles of 'geometry' and rational planning procedures inherited from the Classical Tradition.

1. (below) Jan Duiker, Open-air school, Amsterdam 1928.
2. (bottom) Konstantin Melnikov, laboratory of sleep project, 1929, (from Starr 1978, p178).

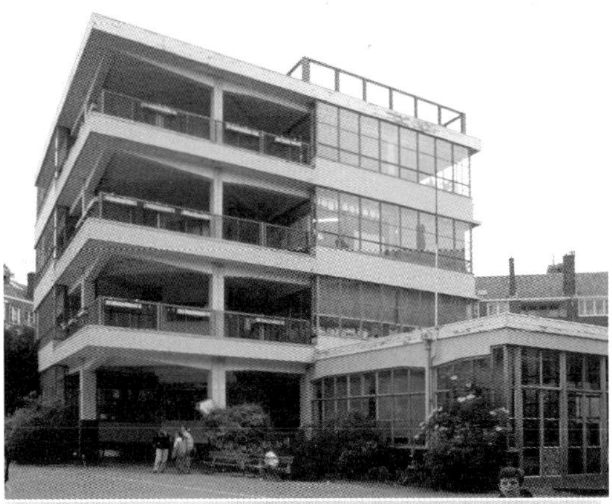

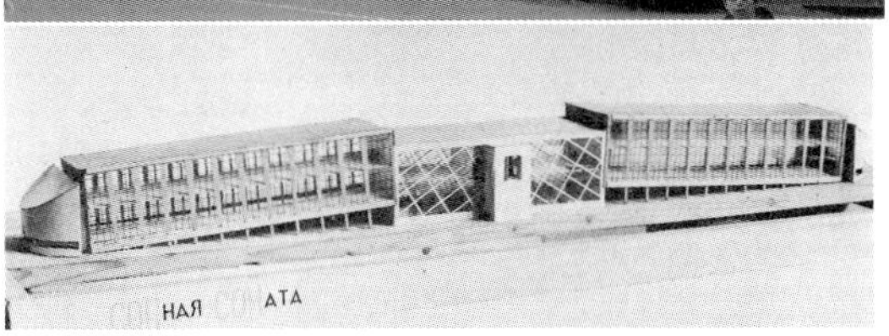

3. Hannes Meyer, competition design for the League of Nations Building, 1927.

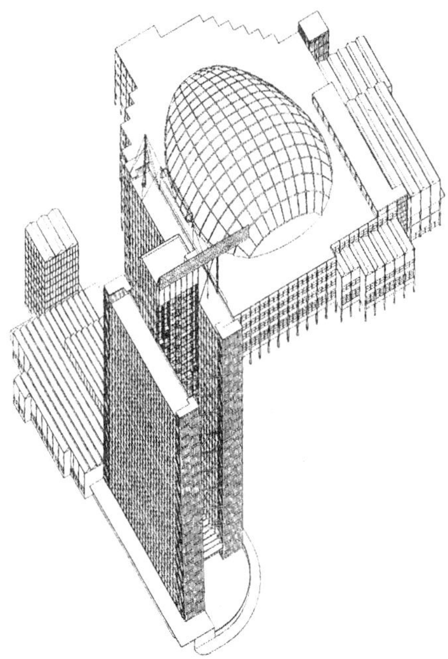

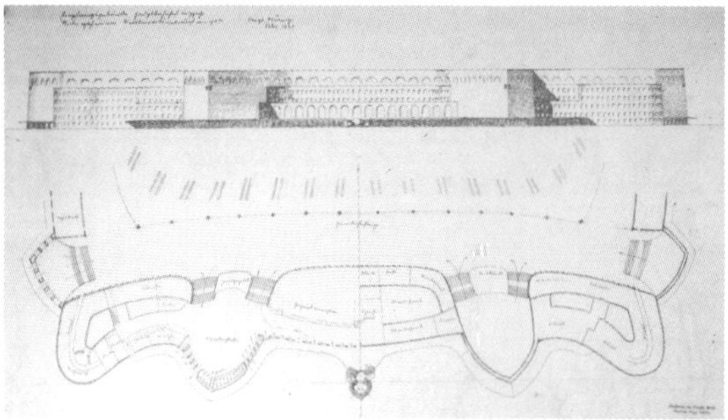

4. Hugo Häring, Design for a railway station, 1921, taking circulation flow as main cue.
5. Competition entry for Berlin Friedrichstrasse skyscraper, 1921; note motto at the bottom - *Funktionale Form.*

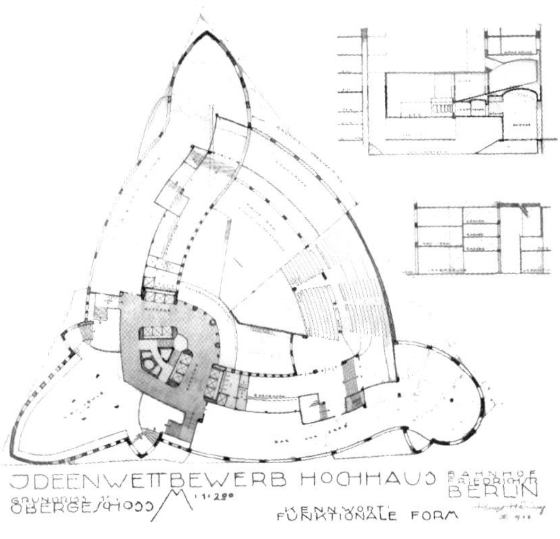

6. (below) Plan for a villa, 1923; north is up.

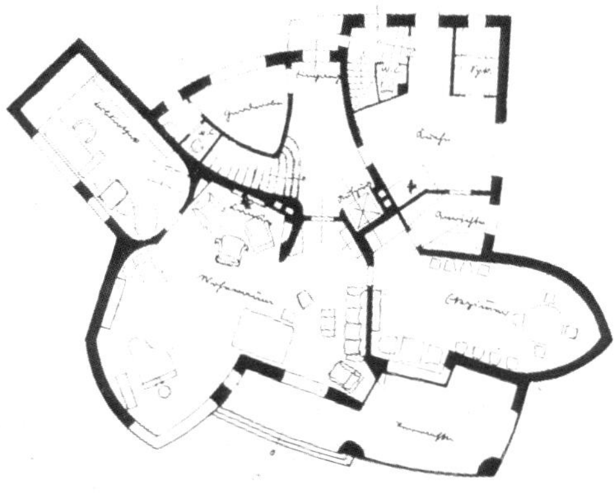

In the early 1920s Häring was already experimenting with a railway station shaped by the flowing crowds of travellers (fig. 4) and he submitted a design for an office block shaped in a similar way to a competition in 1922 under the motto *Funktionale Form* (fig. 5). He also tried to plan houses around orientation and furniture arrangements (fig. 6), again partly shaped in response to movement flow. But the key work in which he put his ideas to the test was a group of farm buildings near Lübeck in northern Germany conceived between 1922 and 1925. He justified the cowshed in the year of its completion with a published essay which is the most comprehensive account of a piece of functional planning in that period,[5] part of which will be quoted in due course. It was a special moment in Häring's career, for he had been radically revising his ideas about architecture but due to the catastrophic economic conditions following the First World War and the punitive Treaty of Versailles had been unable to put them into practice.

Garkau farm gave him his first chance to realise something in the new manner, and as a building dedicated to a clearly defined practical process, it was ideally suited to an experiment in Functionalism. The client Otto Birtner was a progressive farmer interested in the most modern labour-saving methods, and the building was taken very seriously in agricultural as well as architectural circles, being visited in its early years by farmers as well as by architects.

Garkau Barn

Häring planned a whole farm including a new farmhouse (fig. 12), but only the barn, cowshed and a series of implement sheds were built. We shall concern ourselves here with the barn and the cowshed. The barn is interesting mainly for its lamella roof (fig. 9). This form of construction, known since the eighteenth century, saw a revival of interest in the early 1920s.[6] A series of short timbers is nailed together in an interlocking form to make a curved shell, which forms the shape of a gothic arch by taking up the line of structural thrust. The advantage for a barn is complete avoidance of trusses which would interrupt the space, for only short ties are needed at the apex, and the whole volume can therefore be used for storage of winter hay. For Häring the appeal of this form as the *Leistungsform* (form-of-performance) is that it promised the optimum capacity, much better than traditional barns nearby. But at the same time the

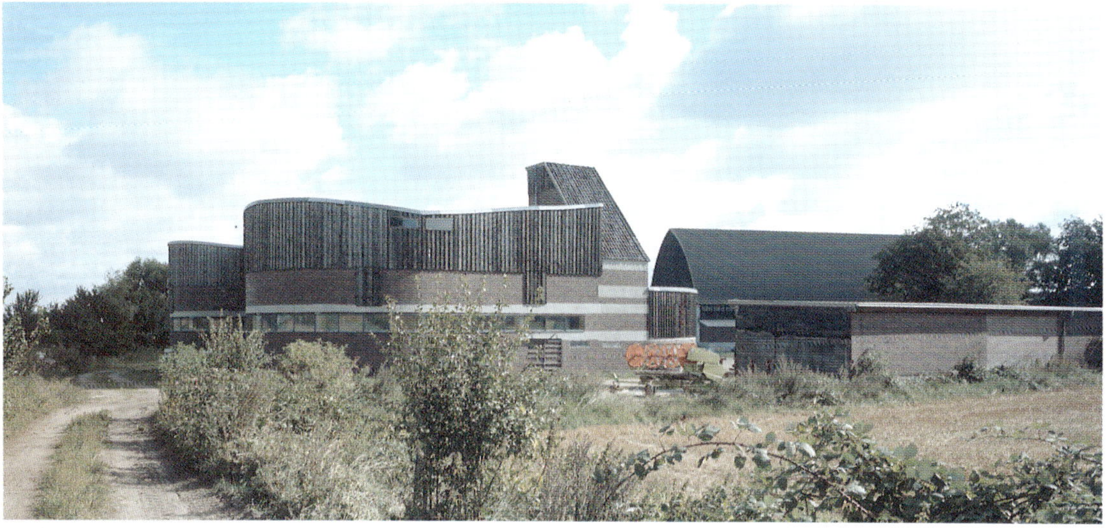

7. Farm from the west along the secondary approach, with lake behind, cowshed centre left, barn behind right.

8. North-west side of cowshed with hayloft above. Foreground projection is calf-house.

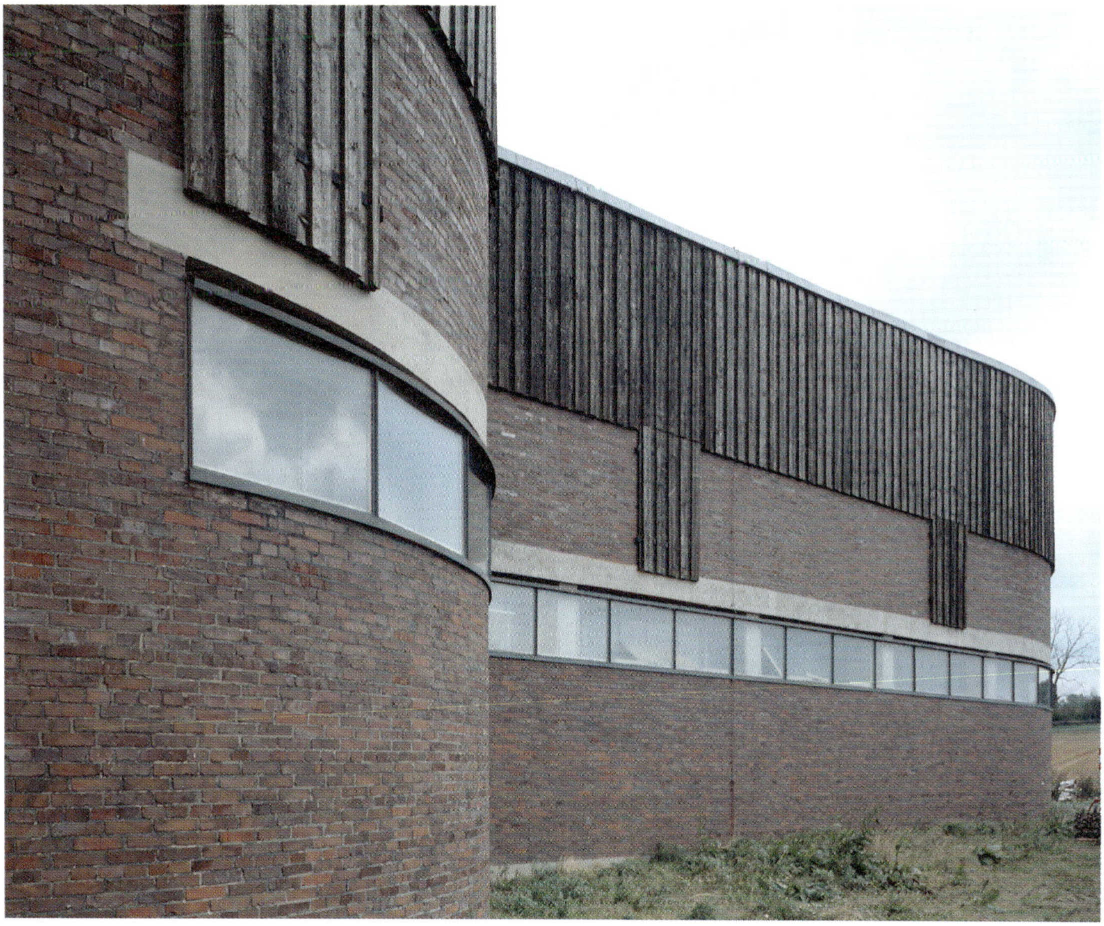

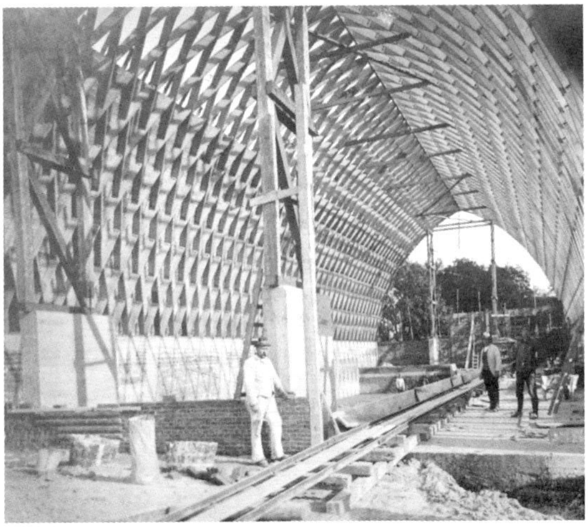

9. Garkau barn under construction, showing the lamella roof.

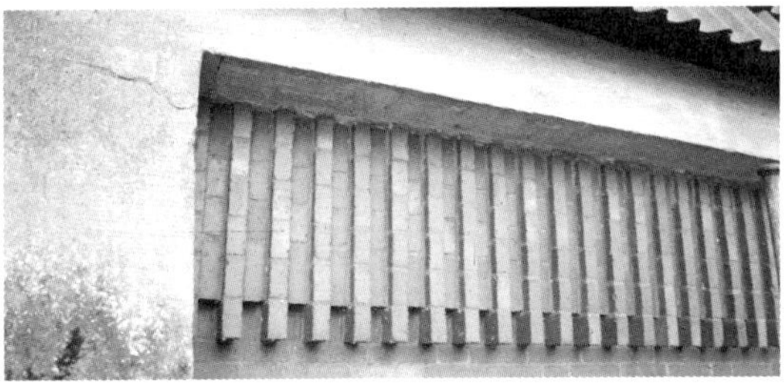

10. Detail of barn corner; with frame and brick corbelling.

11. (below) Barn end.

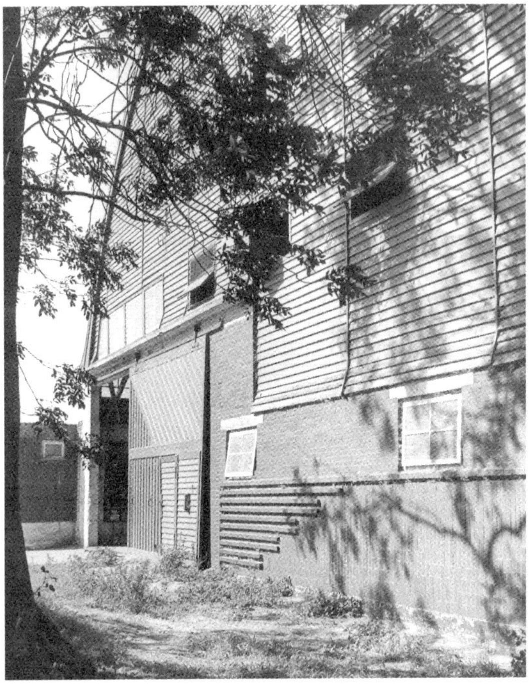

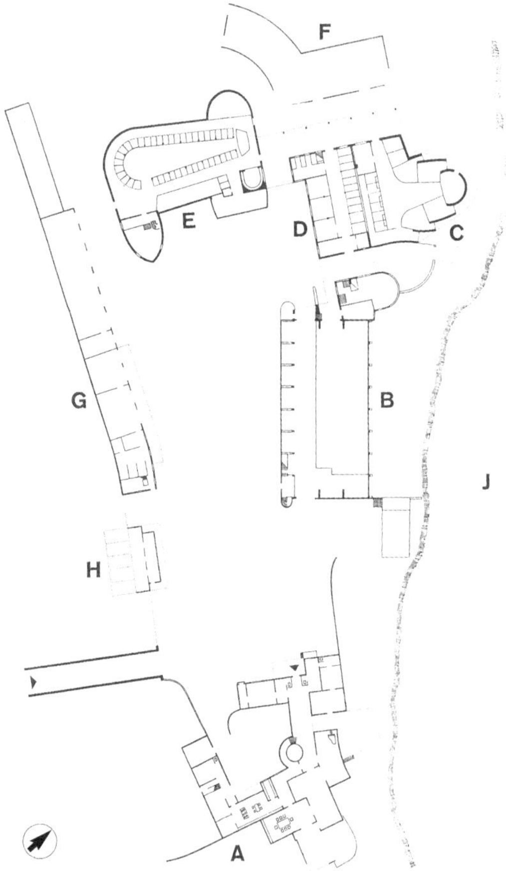

12. Site plan of whole farm as planned by Häring. A farmhouse; B barn; C pigsty; D stable; E cowshed; F dungheap; G cart sheds; H henhouse; J Pönitzer See (a lake). Only B, E and G were built in 1924-5, but there were various projects for the house, A, and a detailed proposal for the pigsty/stable block C/D in 1926.

13. (below) Detail showing brick courses used as doorstop on barn end.

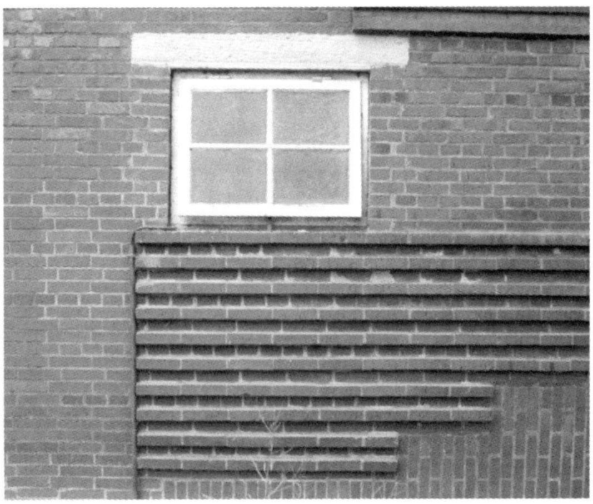

shape was directly derived from structural logic. For an architect who believed that *'we must call on things and let them unfold their own forms... (we must) search for shapes rather than impose them, discover forms rather than construct them'* [7], the discipline of the lamella roof proved a welcome gift.

Also evident in the Garkau barn is a strong expression of construction, differentiating as clearly as possible between the materials used and the contrasting ways in which they work. In principle this can be seen as homage to local vernacular traditions still visible in the beautiful farm buildings found in open-air museums like that at Cloppenburg (fig. 14), but Häring also used new methods and new materials. The rigid base for the barn was formed in reinforced concrete, for example, (fig. 10) just like the skeleton of the cowshed discussed below.

Much more obvious in external views are the linear patterns made by brickwork and timber boarding (fig. 11). Bricks are not laid in normal stretcher-bond, but in a great variety of different ways. On the corner stair to the basement, for example, (fig. 7) they run upright in soldier courses to take the curve of the spiral stair within. Along the north side they corbel out alternately under the frame (fig. 10). On the barn-end alternate courses project out of the wall to make a stop for the sliding barn door (fig. 13). A similar principle applies to the woodwork. The barn ends are clad with horizontal

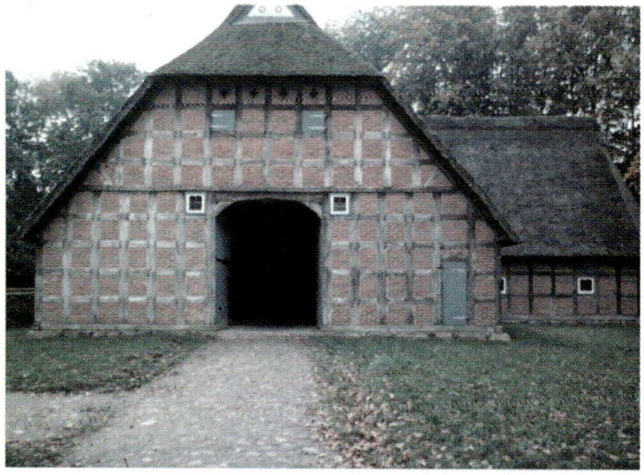

14. Main barn of the Hofanlage Hoffmann at the Cloppenburg Open-air museum near Bremen, North Germany, c.1760.

15. Model by Alan Williams and Rachel Hain of Garkau farm including the unbuilt pigsty/stable block designed in 1926.

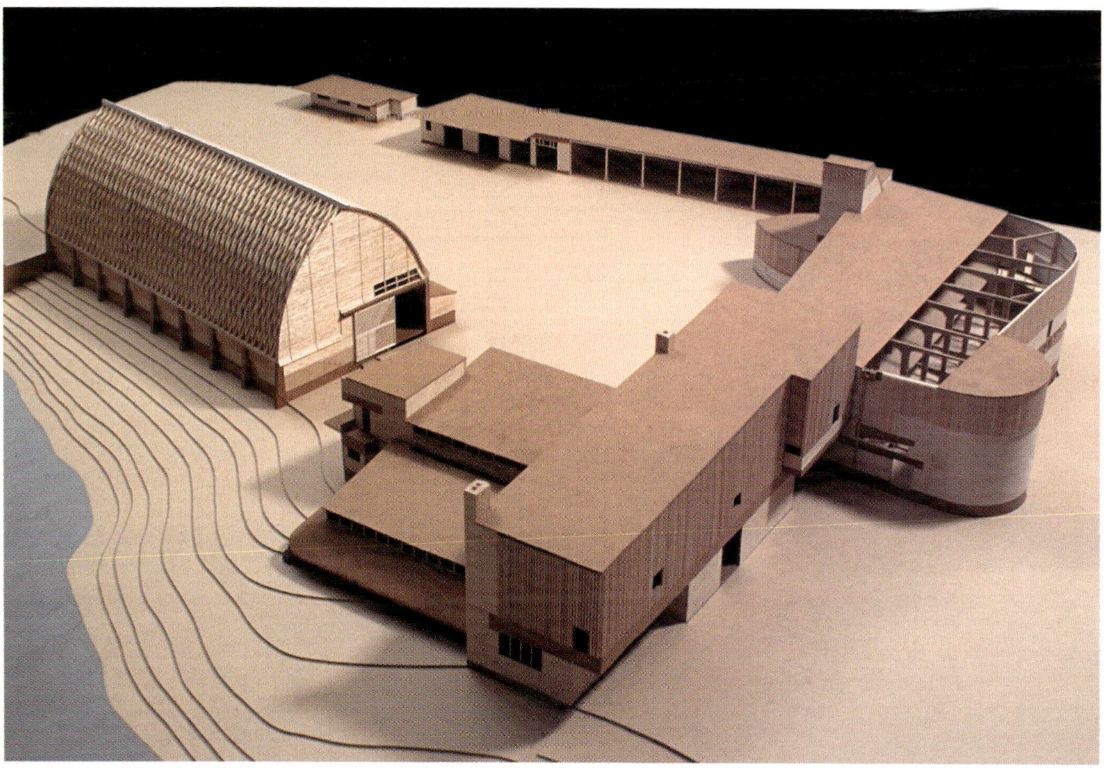

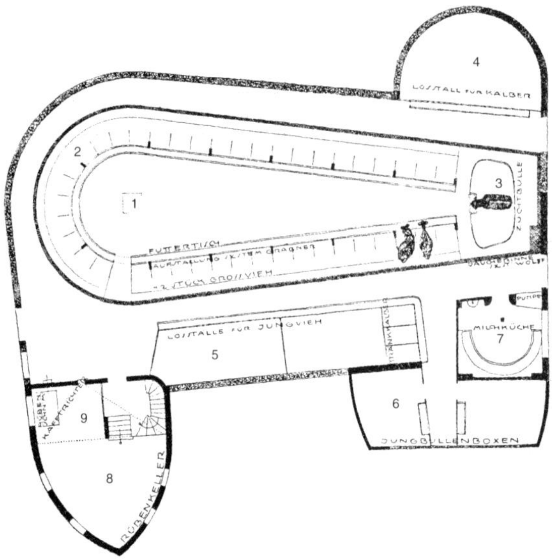

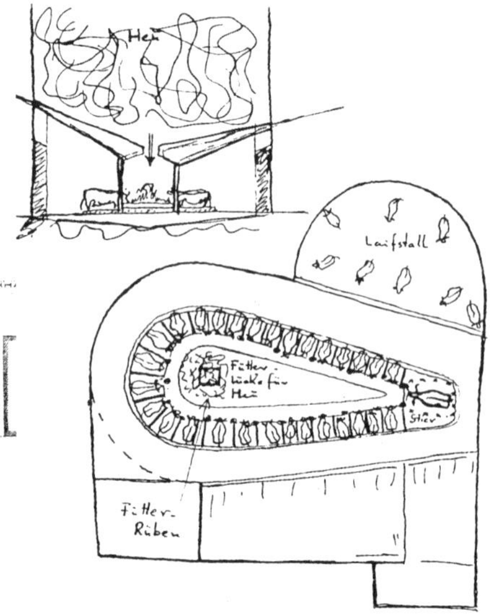

16. (above left) Häring's original published plan.
Key:

1. trapdoor for hay	2. cowstalls	3. bull
4. calves	5. heifers	6. bullocks
7. dairy	8. root cellar	9. silo

17. (above) Häring's rough sketch of plan and section, c.1950.

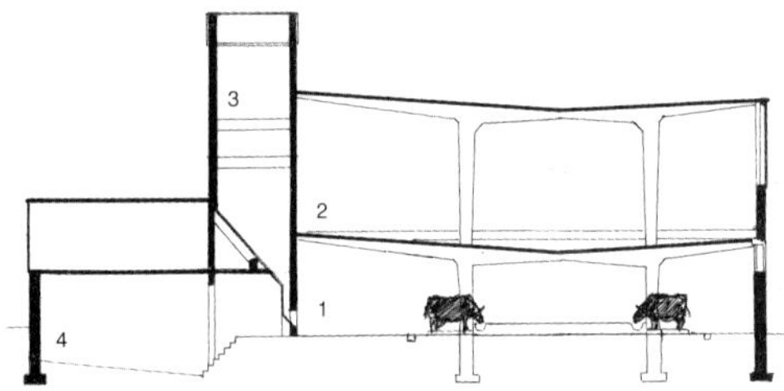

18. (left) Section. Key:
1. cowshed
2. hayloft
3. silo
4. root cellar

weatherboards jointed at the vertical trusses. On the cowshed, though, the timber siding must turn corners in plan, so runs vertically, the outer timbers acting as cover plates over the gaps in the inner ones (fig. 8). Sliding doors need a frame and diagonal bracing. The big ones on the barn ends make the most of this with boarding running in three directions - horizontally, vertically and diagonally (figs 11, 19).

This might be regarded as 'good practice' but from a pragmatic point of view it is exaggerated, pushed beyond necessity into the realm of play.[8] Häring sought more than practical efficiency and a rational process: his interest centred rather on finding an identity for the building through examining its nature. His philosophy demanded that style arise out of the circumstances rather than being imposed as a preconception. It was his process of working from inside out, from principle towards form, that gave Garkau its unprecedented image.

Garkau Cowshed

The cowshed is the most celebrated part of Garkau, and is where form follows function most revealingly. It is easiest to start with the section (fig. 18). The silo tower to left has an inverted pyramid base which guides silage to the trap door in the cowshed, so it flows by gravity. The adjacent root cellar's floor slopes down from the outer side where roots are tipped, towards the middle where they are collected. In the main part of the building, cows stabled on the ground floor face each other across a slightly raised central feed floor on which hay is distributed. The hay comes from a hayloft above, dropped through a trapdoor at the centre of the round end of the plan. The concrete column and slab skeleton allows the outside wall to be treated as infill, so a strip of horizontal clerestory windows is introduced along most of the perimeter. The glass is next to the ceiling to maximise daylight provision. The double glazed windows are sealed, for ventilation takes place through separate vents placed just above them. In his description of 1925, Häring claims that the slope of the ceiling was intended to conduct the rising warm breath of the cattle to the vents, thus minimising spread of disease due to the cattle rebreathing each other's breath.[9] The same slope above in the hayloft floor facilitates movement of hay towards the central trap. The sectional profile is repeated for the roof slab, so rainwater runs in towards the centre and down the axis towards the pointed end of the pear where it is collected in a single downpipe. The combination of three functional advantages in a single form demonstrates a significant aspect of Häring's method: usually one function is not strong or definitive enough to determine one form, but a coincidence of functions working together can suggest a form unique in satisfying them all. This could be called coincidental design.

The principle also applies to the pear-shaped plan. It has a strong central axis, the stabling of the cows and bull intended as the defining event in a building with lesser peripheral elements also dedicated to specific functions. The entrance and exit for cattle are at the pointed end, so in wandering through, the beasts turn around the curved end. The dung channel behind their stalls follows the same pattern, becoming a single unbroken run, a point emphasised in Häring's description. At the same time fodder arriving from the hayloft is deposited at the centre of the round edge where most space is needed, and the feed-floor tapers in sympathy with the diminishing quantity of fodder passed down.

We know Häring was interested in this kind of flow pattern as a formative idea from his experimental station design of 1921 with tapering platforms, and his Friedrichstrasse office block of 1922 with tapering corridors (figs 4 &5). The curved corners on the outside of the cowshed were designed with turning carts in mind, following flow patterns generated within the farmyard.[10]

Whatever the validity of the above arguments, neither is really a clincher for the pear-shaped plan. In his description of 1925 Häring added that the oblique placing of the cattle was intended to reduce the chance of them breathing on one another, but the argument is hardly credible, for one end would be much better in this respect than the other. The real reason for the shape he chose to underplay, but it emerged in a later interview. Asked about the building in the early 1950s, Häring claimed that he had asked his farmer client how cows would eat when left to their own devices, and the answer was that they gather around their food in a circle.[11] A circle of 42 cows leaves too much space in the middle, argued Häring, so the shape would have to become an oval - but then of course there was the question of accommodating the bull. In his statement of 1925 Häring had stated somewhat laconically that '*the single bull, father of the herd, stands freely in a loose box*'; but the position of the bull must be recognised as the defining gesture of the whole plan. Occupying the central axis at the pointed end, he takes pride of place, facing his 42 wives. As father of the herd he embodies its genetic identity and is also the largest and most valuable animal. In Häring's philosophy it was necessary to find a place appropriate to his role, and it would scarcely have been adequate to give him a normal stall alongside the cows, even if in many modern farms he is housed in this way.

The importance of the bull's position is reinforced by the axial symmetry of the stall layout, the spine and ribs of the structural frame, and the flowing route between the symmetrically placed doors. That the peripheral adjuncts to the plan also defer to the central axis is clear from their rounded or pointed shapes, all of which open towards the central axis. Each of these parts has its own *raison d' être*. The semicircle to south-west is for calves, made without corners according to Häring because they fight and trap one another. The built-in room to north-west is the dairy, the semicircular trough around its edge filled with water to cool the standing milk churns. Behind this lies the house for bullocks, separated from the main part of the building so not to challenge their father's supremacy. In the middle of the north side within the main space are stalls for heifers, virgin cows on the margin like spectators to their parents' lives. The food storage silo and root-cellar to north east have already been mentioned. They open onto a large corner area where fodder can be collected and prepared for distribution. The farmer and labourers' work is efficiently concentrated along the north side of the plan, and they have good visual control of the stock thanks to strong daylight and the possibility of inspection both from the centre and periphery, another point made in Häring's early account.

As with the barn, the construction of the cowshed is made explicit, with strong contrast between natural concrete frame, brick infill and timber

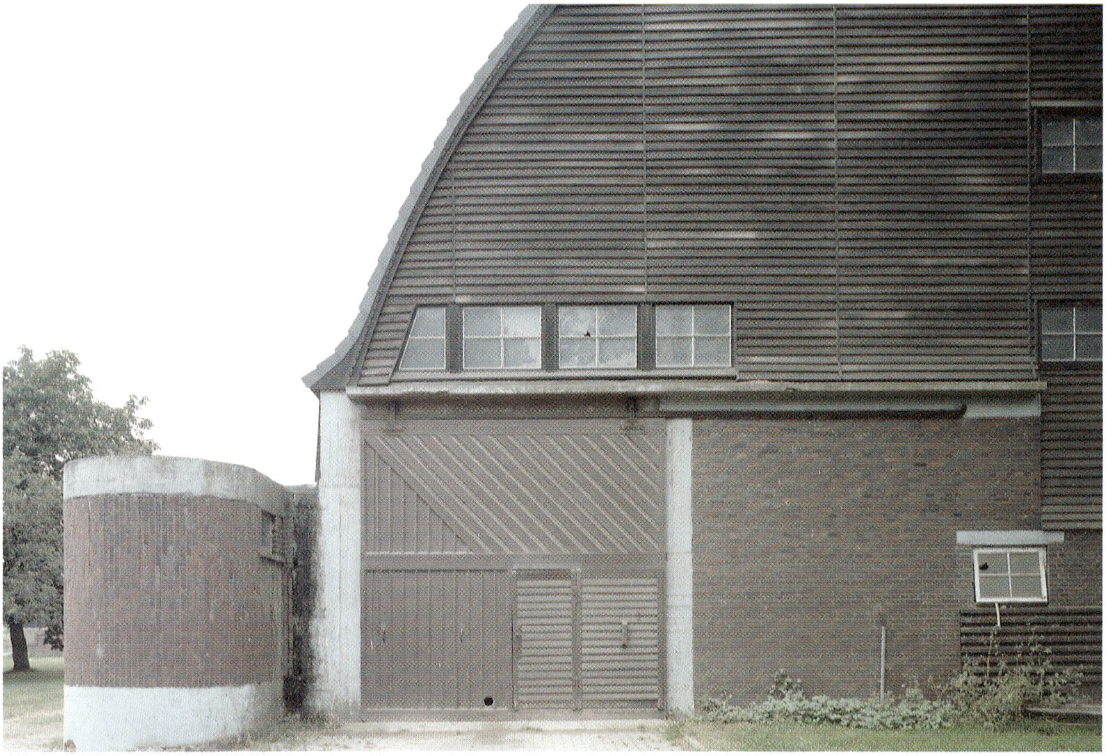

19. Barn end showing sliding door and projecting basement stair.
20. (below) Rear end of cowshed, with projecting courses to fend off passing carts.

21. (opposite) Cowshed from south-east with projecting silo and root cellar.

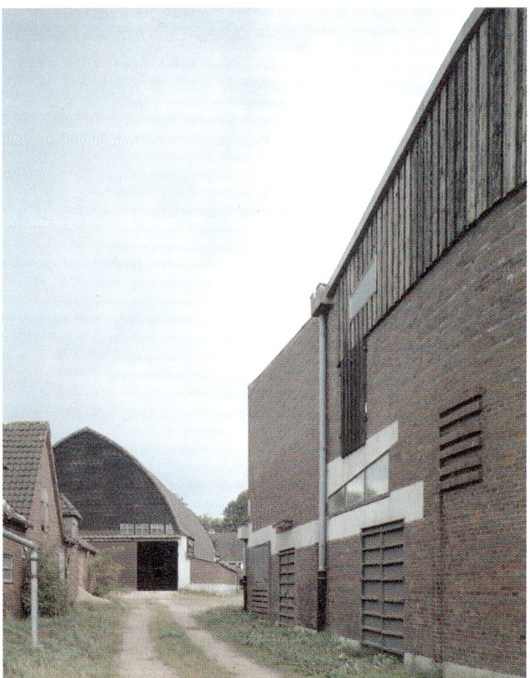

boarding which was left unpainted, weathering to silver-grey. Brick bonding patterns are again evident, especially projecting horizontal courses intended as rubbing strips for unloading carts and vertical ones forming stops for sliding doors or protective niches for open hinged doors (figs 19, 20).

Again this treatment goes beyond the merely practical to reflect the kind of play with technique that one finds in traditional vernacular buildings of North Germany (fig. 14). Decoration is hardly the right word, for the visual effect draws attention to the nature of materials and the way they are assembled, so is neither just 'drawn' nor primarily pictorial. Louis Kahn's definition of ornament as 'the adoration of the joint' would be more apposite, for the textured treatment enhances one's appreciation of the building's substance. We shall revisit this approach in different forms in considering the dramatically raw St Peter's Church, Klippan, by Lewerentz (Chapter 15) and the Kimbell Museum by Kahn, who famously spoke of *'asking a brick what it wants to be'* (Chapter 16).

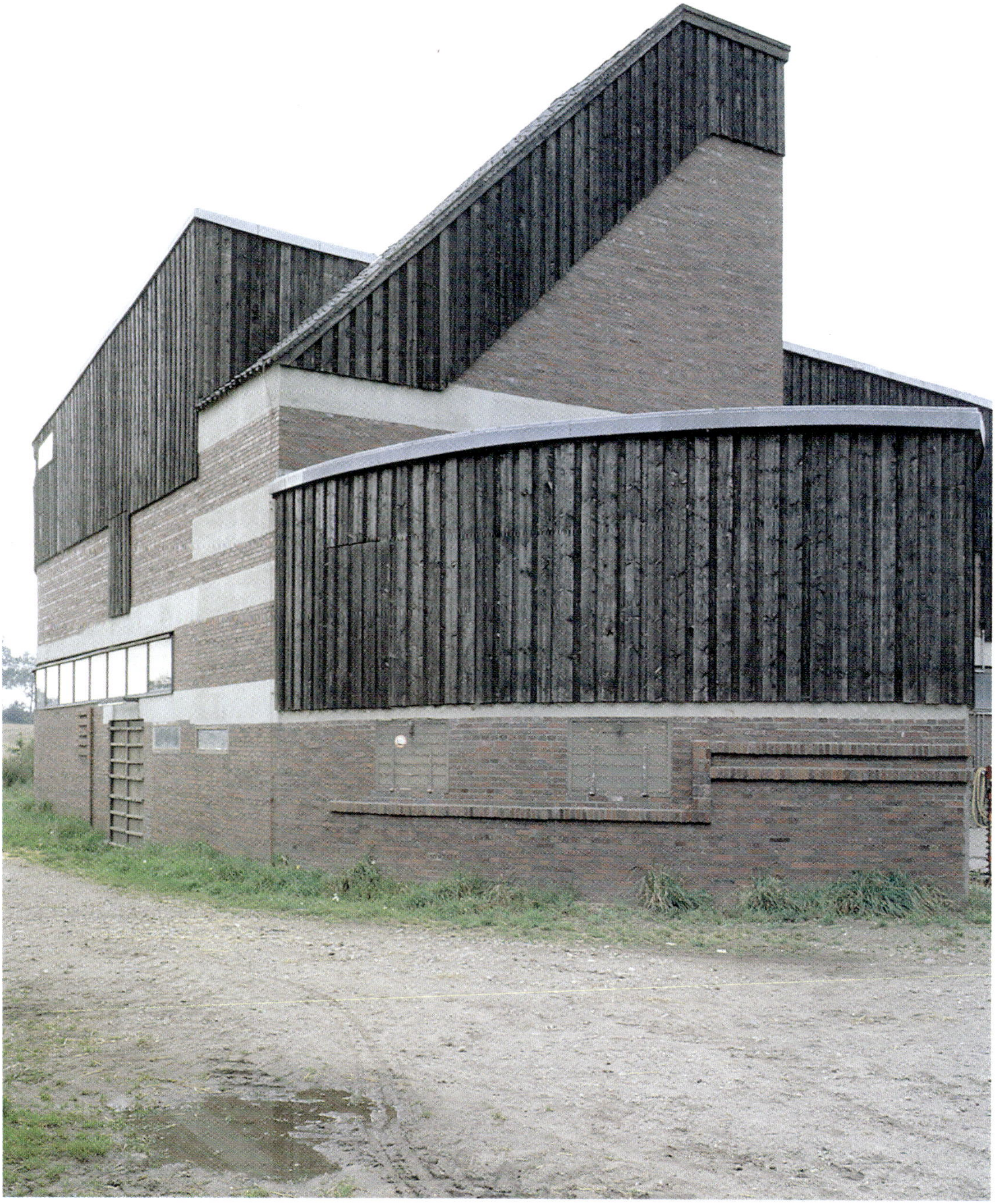

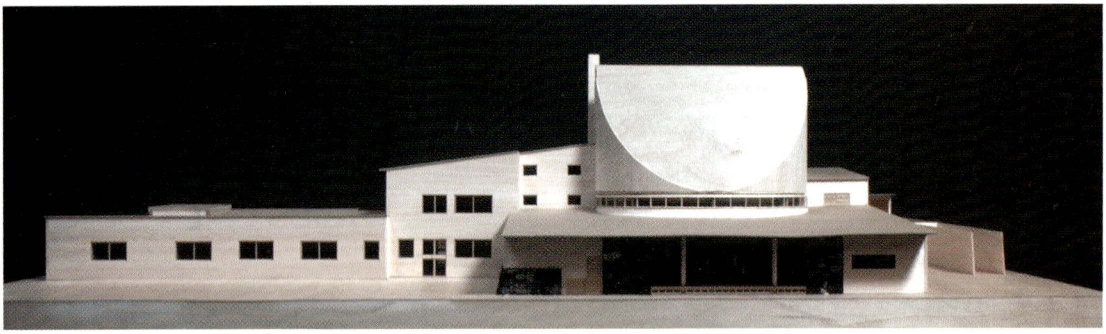

22. Model of Häring's farm project of 1943 by James Potter.

23. (below) Plan of the proposed farm.

Function, Expression and Embodiment

That Häring was concerned with more than mere practical efficiency is clear: his most important theoretical essay, published as Garkau was completed, is not about function *per se* but about the relation between function and expression. Häring is not interested in personal expression: indeed he explicitly denies this as the architect's goal.[12] He is concerned rather with the expression of the task. He thinks that buildings can (and should) be shaped by the needs which they are destined to serve, that in doing so they will gain appropriate expression; an appropriate identity: *'we attempt not to allow our attitudes towards function to conflict with our needs for expression, but to keep them side by side. We try to relate our ideas about expression to life, creation, movement and nature; for in our creation of functional forms we follow the path of nature'.*[13] But how does this 'expression' take place and how is it to be read? This is a more complex and multi-faceted issue than it first appears.

Considering Garkau cowshed, we might begin by noticing the peripheral parts. Calf house, bullock house, silo and root cellar are all separately projecting limbs tacked on to the main body. It could be considered a group of buildings rather than just one, and the projecting parts not only have different characters in accordance with their uses; they also have a hierarchical relationship with the whole. As the main vertical element, for example, the silo is particularly strong, its top and

Key.

1. cowshed
2. calves
3. horses
4. straw barn
5. silo
6. foals
7. dairy
8. potato cellar
9. laundry
10. pigsty
11. piglets
12. farmhouse
13. old people's flat
14. vegetable garden
15. henhouse
16. workshop
17. garage
18. machine sheds
19. covered area

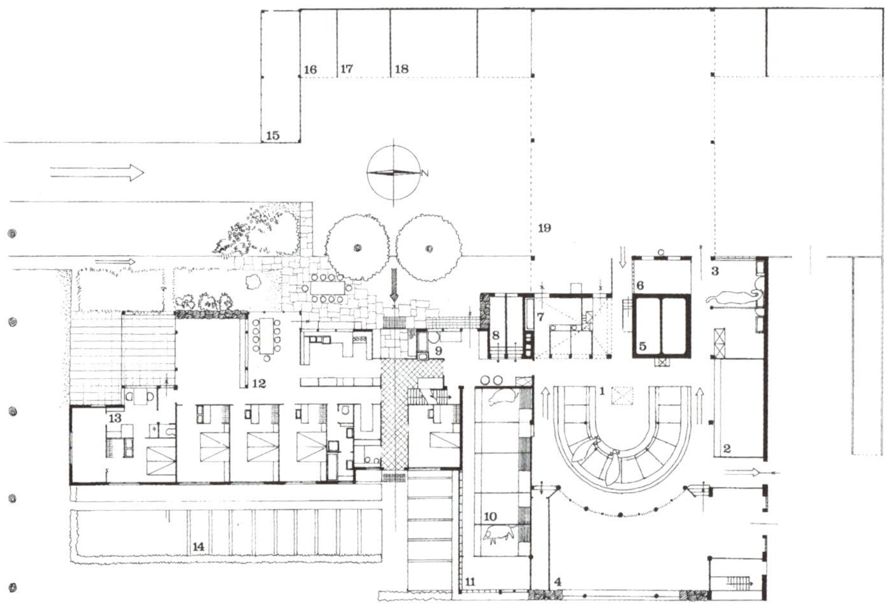

base shaped in accordance with the flow of material. The torso also has its parts - principally the stalls for cows and bull - and these have to be in the right relationship. The standard rectangular shed housing most modern farms cannot allow this, for its form, rhythm and dimensions are determined by the construction system, which therefore also dominates in terms of expression. Typically it is also an open-ended system allowing the choice of as few or as many standard bays as necessary, extendible later by adding more. Häring's pear-shaped plan has a frame and a bay system, but since it rotates at one end and tapers to the other, each bay is different. The bays together form a figure that completes itself: a whole *Gestalt*, not a repetitive system. The ends are treated in contrasting ways, and each brings the complex to a conclusion. Häring admitted that it was built for 42 cows and one bull, and that with more or less animals another arrangement would be needed. True to his word, he planned a smaller farm (unbuilt) in 1943 with 12 cows and no bull in a horseshoe-shaped formation (figs 22, 23).[14]

This practice of articulating parts was probably inherited from the Gothic Revival which strongly influenced Häring as a student.[15] In a famous passage in the treatise *True Principles of Pointed or Christian Architecture*, the movement's leading English theorist Augustus Pugin stated that *'...the external and internal appearance of an edifice should be illustrative of, and in accordance with, the purpose for which it is destined'*.[16] He illustrated this with the example of Magdalen College Oxford (fig. 24), describing the clear and hierarchical articulation of parts, from the dominant chapel through the prominent gatehouse and refectory down to the single rooms, which he claimed could be distinguished by the rhythm of their windows and chimneys. Pugin contrasted this with 'modern collegiate buildings' in 19th century neoclassical mould (fig. 23), claiming that everything is concealed within ...*'one uniform mass, unbroken either in outline or in face, undistinguishable from other large buildings which surround it'*.[17]

He argues, therefore, not only that the parts of a building should make legible the differing internal uses: as a consequence the building as a whole declares its purpose, and one building type differentiates itself from another. But with Magdalen College, as with Garkau, one can legitimately ask who might be able to read the content of the building on the outside, and how. In either case it would be difficult for someone who had not entered it or a similar building to do so, and as James Gowan once wryly remarked, if making such a sign were really the aim it would be easier and less ambiguous simply to write the uses in big letters on the outside walls.[18] The comedy of this suggestion shows, of course, that signage is not really the point, and it pinpoints the way in which buildings are not texts. Certainly buildings can have symbolic features to be read and can even be symbols in themselves, but they are also inhabited and gain meaning through use. We understand them in daily life not merely by observing them externally, but through and through, inside and out. We also get to know how inside relates to outside - which windows look out to where, for example. The layouts of buildings define social institutions: at a most obvious level they divide up territories in terms of genders and classes of people, but they also create orders of privacy and privilege which everyone can recognise.[19] Where you are often denotes *who* you are, and how you should relate to other people. A particularly clear example is the law-court, where the judge sits on axis in the highest seat, the

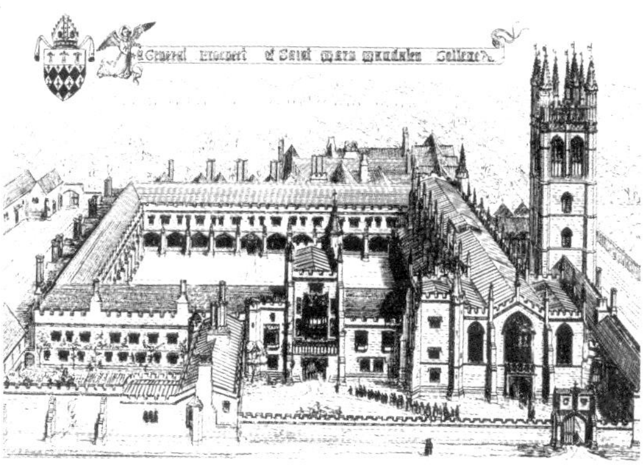

24. (left) Drawing from Pugin's book *True Principles* showing Magdalen College Oxford as an inspiring example of Gothic practice, all its parts meaningfully articulated.

25. This is contrasted with the satirical sketch below of a 'modern collegiate building', in which, Pugin claims, 'everything is concealed behind one monotonous front'.

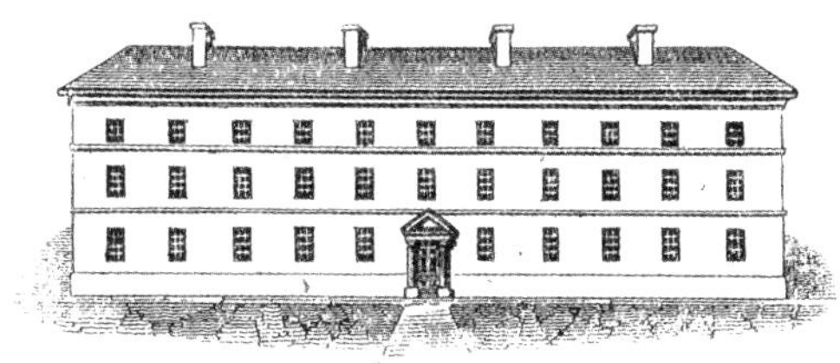

prisoner is in the dock, lawyers do battle in the well off the court, and spectators look on from massed ranks of seats opposite. The organisation of the space helps to empower or to intimidate the participants, and so substantiates the legal process. The arrangement does not merely represent or symbolise the social order, it embodies it when in use and also exemplifies it - stands as a sample of that order.[20]

Pugin's collegiate example derives from a long monastic tradition in which church, cloister, refectory, chapter house, dorter etc. had shapes and places in strict accordance with the Rule of St Benedict and successive rules. The defined territories gave physical expression to the activities of monastic life, and without them it could hardly take place. When we visit a monastery, though, nothing forces us to pray in the church or to discuss community policy in the chapter house. For buildings to work, there must be complicity between people's ideas and the spaces they inhabit: the pattern of ritual and belief has to mesh with the spatial order.[21] This is not special to the monastery, but equally true of the hospital and its operating theatres where entry is just as restricted, special uniforms are also worn, both roles and space being tightly defined.

Returning to Garkau cowshed, the relationship of cows and bull might be considered to be symbolically displayed in the building, even in the round and pointed ends of the plan, but this would be legible only to the initiated and to passing airline pilots. The organisation is surely of more significance to the farmer and his assistants, who daily witness and participate in the building's order. The bull is the farmer's most valuable animal and he represents the genetic identity of the herd, so it is only appropriate that he should be given pride of place - it would be inappropriate to stick him in an identical stall alongside the cows. Similarly, the efficient organisation of the building in accordance with the daily rituals of feeding, milking, cleansing etc. would be a confirmation of the order of work, a sense of getting things shipshape.[22]

The study of traditional farms suggests that the kind of spatial ordering sought by Häring was in fact widely pursued: layouts give hierarchical status to family members, to the various kinds of animals from the essential horses down to the humble bees in the orchard. Different processes give rise to different types of building, and gender roles are spatially defined. In pre-industrial times a farmer's wealth was indicated by the size of the barn in which winter fodder was stored, and even the size of the dung heap was an index of status, reflecting the number of cattle.[23] When people were able to build for themselves using well-established local traditions, their buildings tended more or less automatically to represent their beliefs and values and to embody their social order. The anthropological record is full of examples from all over the globe, all the richer in pre-literate societies because of the more essential mnemonic role served by buildings. In the transmission of myth, for example, elements of a house could serve complex and varied roles in depicting the ancestors and the cosmos, as visual examples close at hand when explaining the order of things to children.[24]

In modern industrialised society architecture has lost much of this role, while it has also been overtaken by other forces. There is now such a long chain of specialists and bureaucrats intervening between inhabitants and their buildings, that most of us have little say in our environment and feel powerless to change it. Häring's battle against the domination of architecture by 'geometry', and his call for a return to allowing things to find their own shapes, seems to have been based on an intuitive understanding of how buildings were made before the task was overtaken by the academic tradition of Architecture. His tirades against geometry and proportion systems were aimed not just at contemporaries - like Gropius at Weissenhof who was prepared to let construction take over, or like Le Corbusier who believed in the magic of proportion systems - but at the whole rationalist tradition stretching back to Durand, with his sterile categories and universal types.[25] Häring's call for a responsive architecture was in essence a plea for architecture to be reconnected with life. This was implicitly a much broader and more tenable concept of Functionalism than the notorious programme of systematic measurement and analysis proposed by Hannes Meyer in his manifesto *bauen* at the Bauhaus.[26]

Garkau as exemplar for the Organic

Garkau farm outlived its usefulness and has become an architectural monument.[27] Its importance today rests not on the passing innovations it introduced to farming practice, but on the approach it demonstrated, both in terms of articulated organisation and expressed construction. It seemed to prove that the nature of a building could be

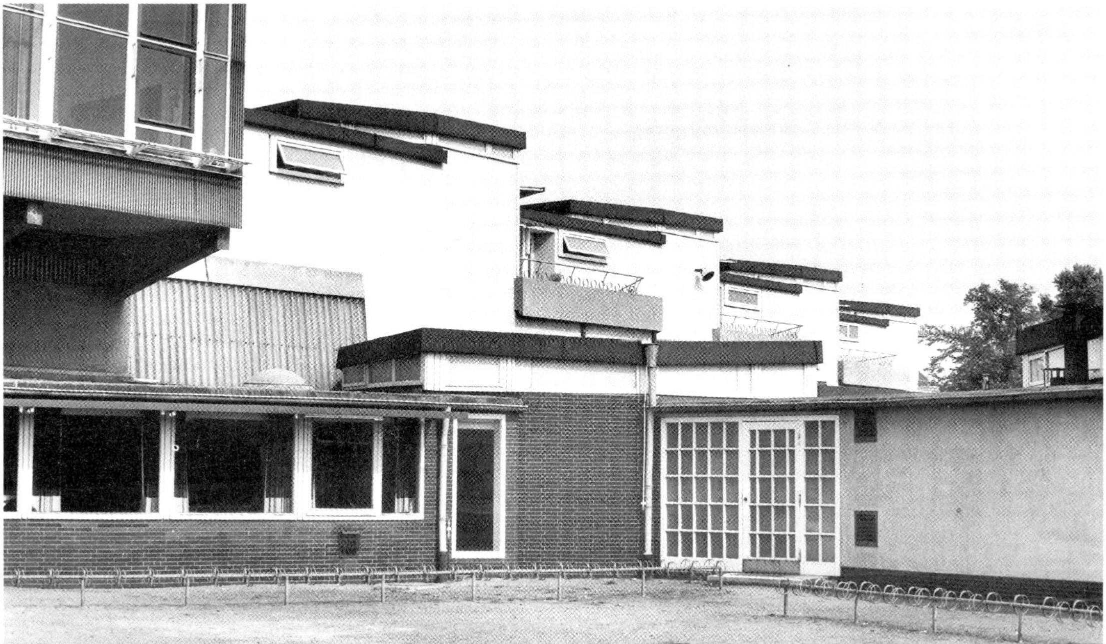

26. Geschwister Scholl school, Lünen, by Hans Scharoun, 1958-62, upper classrooms as seen from playground.

27. (right) Hugo Häring, outline of a school on a neighbourhood plan of c.1949. No more detailed version exists.

28. (bolow) Geschwister Scholl school, Lunen, plan. Assembly hall, lecture rooms, music room and differentiated classroom groups are clearly articulated.

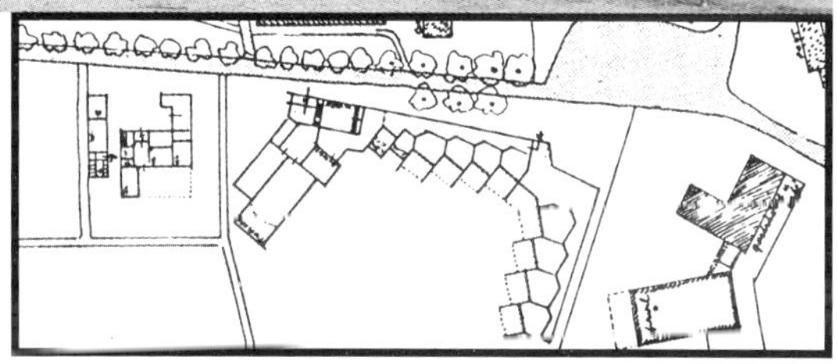

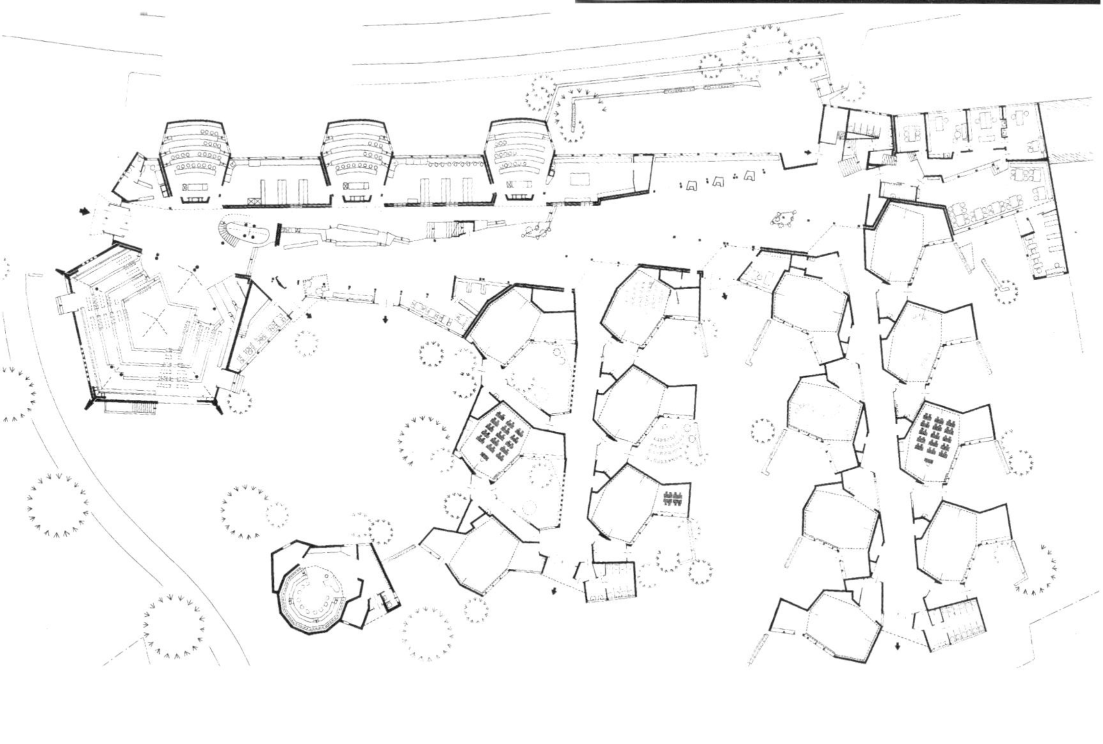

interpreted out of the conditions that it was intended to serve. The appropriate articulation of elements became a primary concern of the Organic Tradition and persists today in the work of architects such as Günter Behnisch and some members of the New Graz Architecture.[28] It was developed in a particularly strong and consistent way in the 1950s by Hans Scharoun, close friend and follower of Häring, so we end this chapter with a key example of how the idea grew.

Scharoun's first chance to build a secondary school came in 1958 with the Geschwister Scholl school for girls at Lünen in Westphalia, completed in 1962. As is evident from a glance at the plan (fig. 28), he articulated all the elements of the programme in a forceful and consistent way. Most important were the classes, built as separate pavilions and designed as a group of rooms comprising main classroom, teaching annexe, external teaching space and entrance lobby. Scharoun called this group *Klassenwohnung* (classroom-flat) as it was meant to become the second home for the child. The *Klassenwohnungen* were strung out along corridors, their distinctive butterfly roofs recognisable externally like separate houses in a village. Other parts were equally strongly articulated: the projecting science lecture theatres and preparation laboratories between, the great polygonal assembly hall, the first-floor art room with its great northlight window and the intended music room at the end of one classroom group. Binding all these parts together is a great internal street which is also used by the pupils as a break hall. In contrast with the more definite and finite shapes of the classrooms and assembly hall, this has a complex amorphous shape determined by the outsides of other elements and by the flow patterns between them. In its very shape it declares its transitional nature. Scharoun managed to make a legible sequence of territories and to make the scale of the institution more intimate. As a celebratory 25th anniversary booklet makes clear, the school buildings were enjoyed by staff and pupils alike, and used mainly with a good understanding of the original intentions, even though the curriculum changed and the school became co-educational.[29] More will be said of Scharoun's work in Chapter 13.

Notes

1. For example in Sweden, where it was the general name given to the new architecture around 1930.
2. See Duiker's own text published in English in Forum no 1, 1962.
3. See Starr 1978, pp.178/179.
4. The arguments are reported in Schnaidt 1965, pp. 25, 32. The acoustic claims ignore the question of reflections, disastrous in an egg-shaped hall; the daylighting arguments ignore the fact that higher storeys receive more light; Meyer denies all symbolism, then claims the transparency represents honest dealings.
5. *Funktionelles Bauen: Gut Garkau/ das Viehhaus*, published in *Die Form* vol. 1, October 1925, pp. 16-17, and reprinted in Joedicke/Lauterbach 1965, p. 17. A complete translation is included in Blundell Jones 1999, p. 59.
6. A short article in *Wasmuths Monatshefte*, vol. IX, 1924-5, pp. 71-72, attributes the origin of the lamella roof to Philibert de l'Orme, claiming it was adopted by Berlin architects including David Gilly around 1800. The six illustrated examples include two barns, one with a clear span of 26 metres, and also the model of a church by Otto Bartning.
7. From Häring's key essay, *Wege zur Form* (Approaches to Form) first published in Die Form vol. 1, October 1925, pp. 3-5, and reprinted in Joedicke/Lauterbach 1965, pp. 13/14, my translation. For a fuller account of the content of this essay and more detail on Garkau farm, see Blundell Jones 1999, Chapters 6 and 8.
8. In the sense of 'Homo Ludens', see Huizinga 1949.
9. See note 5 above.
10. This is discussed in more detail in Blundell Jones 1999, Chapter 6.
11. The interview with Häring in April 1952 was published in German in Baukunst und Werkform vol. 5, 1952.
12. The essay *Wege zur Form* ends as follows: *'It is not our task to give form to* [gestalten] *our own individuality, but to the individuality of things. Their expression should be at one with their being.'*
13. Extract from *Wege zur Form*.
14. My traced copies of the drawings were printed in *The Architectural Review*, June 1985 and can also be found in Blundell Jones 1999, pp.158-159.
15. See Blundell Jones 1999, p.15.
16. Pugin 1853, pp. 35-36.
17. Ibid, pp. 45-46.
18. A memorable moment in a tutorial at the Architectural Association in 1972.
19. For a general study on space and power, see Markus 1993.
20. For a definition of exemplification see Goodman 1976.
21. The anthropologist Pierre Bourdieu calls this the 'Habitus', see Bourdieu 1977.
22. W. R. Lethaby used this word in a discussion of precisely the same issue, see *Towns to live in* in Lethaby 1922, pp. 22-34.
23. For a rich and well-described example see the Alsace volume of *L'architecture rurale francaise*, listed as Denis 1978.
24. For a sophisticated example of how buildings can support mythical systems see Stephen Hugh-Jones's chapter on the Tukanoan Maloca in Hugh-Jones & Carsten 1995.
25. Immortalised in his famous book *Précis des lecons d'Architecture données à l'Ecole Royale Polytechnique*, (Durand 1985).
26. As expressed in his manifesto *Bauen*, see Conrads 1970, pp.117-120. For further discussion of the contrasting positions of Häring and Meyer, see Blundell Jones 1999, pp. 79-82.
27. It was restored in the 1970s by the Lübeck architect Eberhard Zell and listed as a historic monument. The interior was lost due to conversion to a pigsty, but soon pigs too became uneconomical.
28. See Blundell Jones 1998 and Blundell Jones 2000.
29. For further information see Blundell Jones 1995, pp. 136-151 and p. 220.

Chapter 3. Walter Gropius: Bauhaus Building, Dessau 1925-6

Ever since its opening in December 1926, six months before that of the Weissenhofsiedlung, the Bauhaus building at Dessau has been one of the main icons of architectural Modernism. It was long seen as the crowning achievement of Gropius's architectural career, as well as embodying the legendary institution at the heart of modernist activity which became the model for art and architecture schools throughout the world.[1] In his American years, Gropius was a hugely effective self-publicist, but both he and his Bauhaus were already central to the myth of Modernism as purveyed by Nikolaus Pevsner and Sigfried Giedion, the high priests of the modernist cult. Pevsner singled out Gropius as the figurehead for the whole movement,[2] while Giedion took the Bauhaus building as a primary example for his new space-time sensibility.[3] Because of the great and immediate publicity, the buildings also undoubtedly had a powerful influence in establishing what came to be known as The International Style, particularly as the first Bauhaus book by Gropius was entitled *Internationale Architektur.*[4] At the zenith of the school's reputation in the 1960s, a Bauhaus Exhibition catalogue could even claim: *'to write about architecture and the bauhaus would be to write a history of the memorable ten years before hitler'* as though nothing else had happened in art and architecture in Germany at that time.[5]

Yet despite all this, among leading Modernists, Gropius is the one who has suffered most in the historical revisions since 1970. Le Corbusier had a bumpy ride due to his city planning theories and his influence on mass housing, but he was rescued and re-canonised to become 'Architect of the Century' on his centenary in 1987.[6] Following the reconstruction of the Barcelona Pavilion in the 1980s the greatness of Mies was also re-established, and Minimalism gives his work a new resonance. But the feeling that Gropius - as a designing architect at least - had been overrated, has persisted. The uninspired nature of his American work with TAC (The Architects' Collaborative) has not helped, while the precise authorship of even the most famous German works has long been in question. Gropius's inability to draw,[7] and his consequent reliance on the creative contribution of others, must have helped impel him towards the role of convener, spokesman, talent-spotter, leader and critic that made the Bauhaus so successful, but it also left a gap between Gropius and his architecture. Developed by assistants largely to oral instructions, it required from Gropius the clarity of intention and rational refinement that remain among its most persistent virtues, but at the same time it lacked the intuitive link between hand and eye usually expected of great architects. During the period between 1930 and 1970 when the Rationalist Bauhaus ideology was presumed valid, displacement of the personal touch in favour of rational method seemed a worthwhile sacrifice, even a noble one: as Nikolaus Pevsner put it:-

'The glass walls are now clear, the steel frame is hard, and its expression discourages all other-worldly speculation. It is the creative energy of this world in which we live and work and which we want to master, a world of science and technology, of speed and danger, of hard struggles and no personal security, that is glorified in Gropius's architecture.' [8]

As we have seen with Gropius's houses at the Weissenhofsiedlung, the replacement of personal space- or form-making by a systematic order seemed a necessary and even inevitable change.

1. Walter Gropius, house 17 at the Weissenhofsiedlung, 1927.

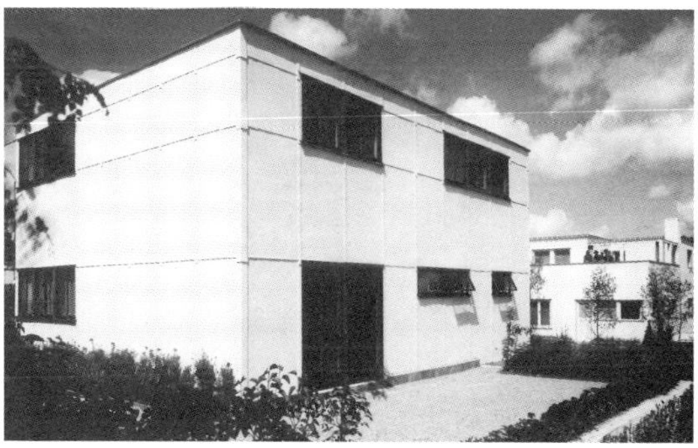

Once orthodox Modernism had fallen from grace and its methods were exposed as ineffective, however, the sacrifice just seemed empty.

It is hard now to imagine nearly a century later how revolutionary the Bauhaus buildings must have seemed when newly complete, when Modernism as an orthodoxy was yet to be established. Their pristine purity and cubic whiteness seemed to express the very essence of the 'New Objectivity', apparently supported by a design philosophy based on analysis, measurement and calculation. The legitimacy of the method seemed self-evident and went unquestioned, while the image of the building was supremely effective. It lent itself to propagation in print, for not only are the perspectives produced by a rising-front camera from its strictly orthogonal forms highly effective: the transparency of the corners and the daring cantilever of the upper floors over the basement are also easily captured, even dramatised in photographs. The colouring in black, white and shades of grey perfectly suited the black and white prints of the time, whose contrast could be adjusted for optimum effect. If the building was not consciously designed for photography, Gropius and his assistants at least had an instinctive feeling for the effect. It helped that leading photographers worked at the Bauhaus, especially Lucia Moholy. For visitors actually on the spot, there was also the rational expressed construction of the building: the regularly spaced concrete frame set back from the facade with its tapered cantilevers indicating the growing load; the richly detailed plate-glass and steel workshop facades with their multiple opening lights linked by bicycle chains; the clear and straightforward spatial organisation. If it seemed like a factory, this only helped to emphasise both the importance of machine-produced components in the philosophy of the Bauhaus, and the major role of workshops in the curriculum. Factories were efficient and modern: as a building type that had remained relatively free of the applied iconography previously understood to be the very essence of architecture, they had played an innocently progressive role. As the sites of mass-production for technological wonders like cars, aeroplanes, and electrical goods, they also represented an exciting brave new world. Henry Ford's autobiography was popular reading among architects at the time.[9]

With hindsight, the object-like status of the Bauhaus buildings and their seeming flotation above a featureless piece of ground, prefigure the difficulty with selfish objects negating their contexts that haunted the whole later movement, contributing to its downfall.[10] But in 1926 their isolation

2. (below) Bauhaus Dessau, view of classroom block from beneath bridge.
3. (opposite top) Perspective of the complex as seen from the south-east drawn by Hinnerk Scheper 1926: © Scheper Family Berlin.
4. (opposite) Workshop block (right), bridge and classroom block, (post-restoration photographs).

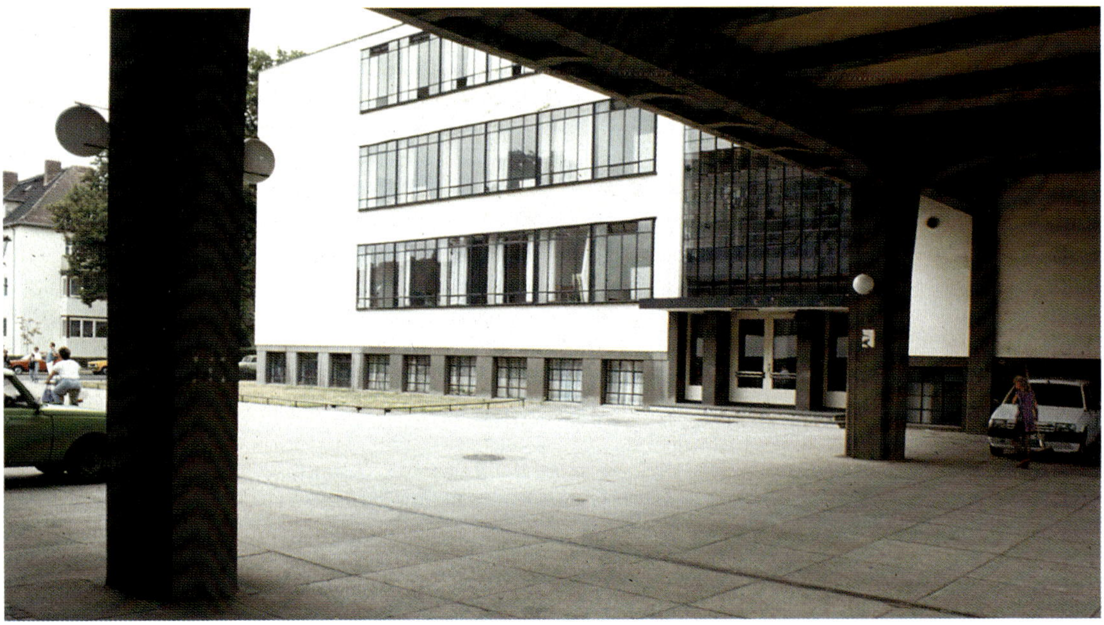

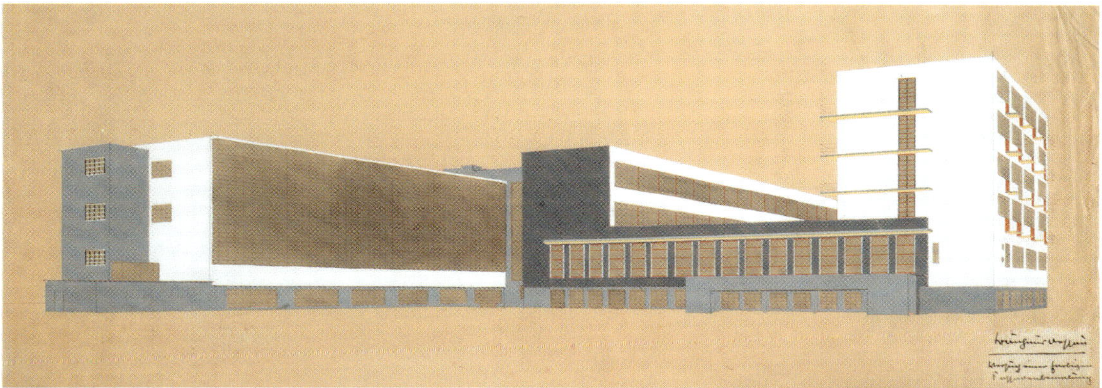

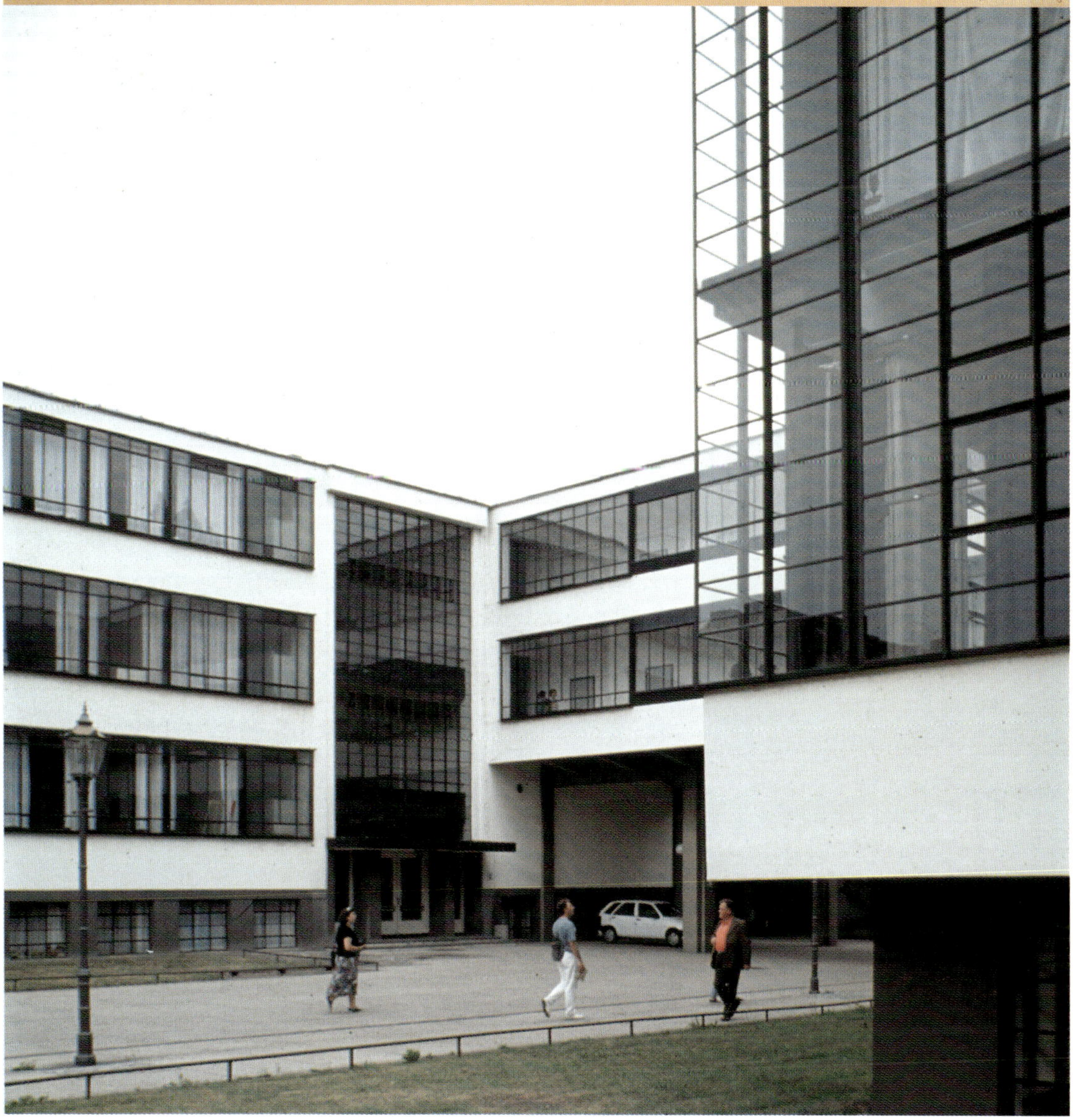

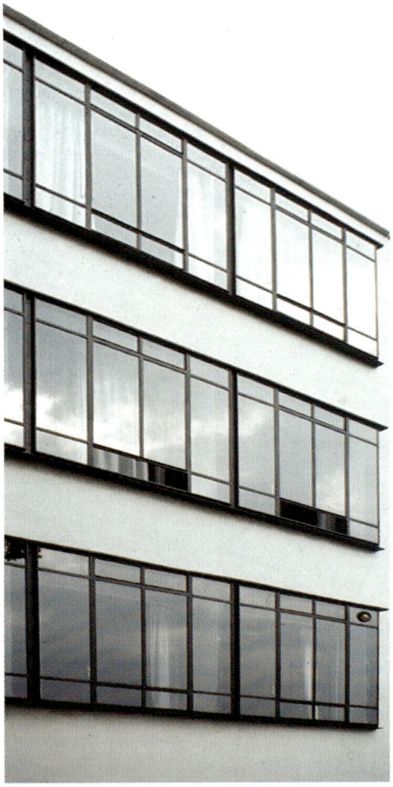

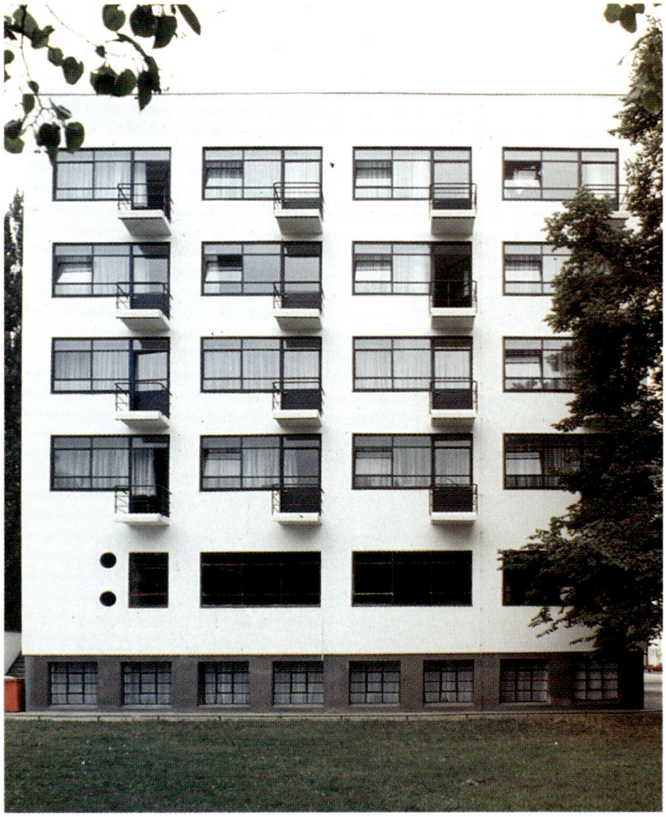

5. (above) Classroom block glazing.

6. (above right) Residential block, east elevation.

7. (below) Walter Gropius, Törten housing, Dessau, on prefabricated system.

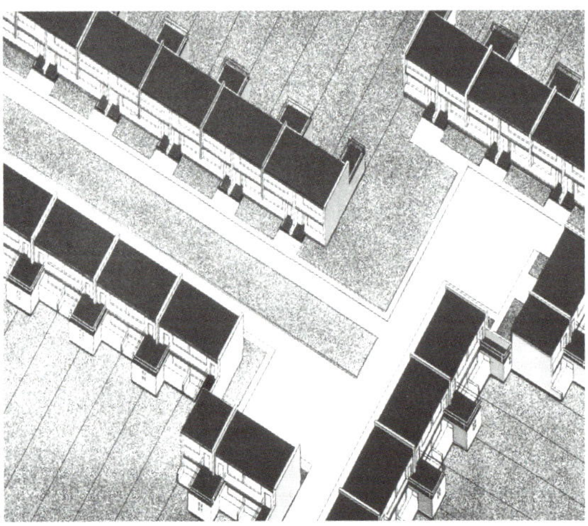

just made the Bauhaus buildings seem clearer and more special. The cutting-off was surely deliberate, for the context did not seem to matter. More important was the invigorating effect of Gropius's reduction to essentials, his rejection of everything superfluous, his wiping of the slate clean. The cleanness, the clarity, the idea that 'nothing is needed more than this' was shocking but also deeply liberating, especially as the visual and spatial effect seemed to justify Gropius's scientific design approach as an escape from historical mush. *Quod erat demonstrandum*, people thought; 'this is the way forward!' There was as yet no architecture department in the school, and Hannes Meyer's positivistic programme, which was later taken to represent it, had yet to be published;[11] but certainly the building was intended to exemplify the design ethos of the institution.

Quite apart from the effect on the public and the outside world, the effect on staff and students must have been profound. The move from Weimar to Dessau allowed the institution to redefine itself, sloughing off the skin of Expressionist mysticism it had embraced in the early 1920s in exchange for an increasing commitment to the 'New Objectivity'.[12] The curriculum entailed the same kind of return to first principles seen in the buildings. The construction of new premises gave Gropius the chance to shape the Bauhaus's physical and symbolic territory according to his own vision, and through building the masters' houses also, he subtly kept his grip even on their domestic lives.[13] Dessau City Council gave him commissions for other buildings, notably the Törten housing estate - a brave experiment in prefabrication - and the Dessau Employment Office. Thus did Gropius's empire spread, all these buildings conceived and drawn within his private architectural office at the Bauhaus building. It has been suggested that he left the school in 1928 partly because this local work had dried up and he felt the need to seek further commissions in Berlin.[14] For an architect, the realisation of ideas in built work is both a confirmation of validity and proof of his or her effective power.

Siting and organisation

The Bauhaus buildings were constructed on an open flat site south of the city near the railway station. There were some bourgeois villas in the vicinity, but laid out at low density to leave a dominant impression of field and forest. A major road provided the west boundary of the site, and an access road had already been planned to cross it from west to east, though no tarmac was actually laid until the buildings were complete. Gropius had sufficient land to plan a sports field to the south side, and he pulled his group of buildings back from the main road. From the beginning they were intended to stand as pristine objects.

There were three main building blocks and two subordinate linking ones. Running parallel to the road and most exposed to public gaze lay the all-important workshop block with its three-storey glass façade. Further north, on the other side of the access road, was placed the classroom block of the Technical College, initially a separate institution that shared the Bauhaus site. The third part was a six-storey residential block containing 28 studios, which Gropius placed behind the workshop block, linked to it by a single-storey wing. Though subordinate to the other parts in height and external expression, this low wing contained the Bauhaus's social facilities: the theatre, stage and canteen.

The workshop and classroom blocks were linked by the final element of the composition: a wing on stilts bridging the site access road, and containing two storeys of offices. Gropius's own rooms as director were placed at its centre, alongside his architectural office. At either end of the bridge was an entrance and staircase, designed as a symmetrical pair. Floors on both sides were set at half levels, allowing clerestory lighting to the basements, raising the main floor (as a *piano nobile* with the theatre, etc.), and giving each entrance lobby equal access to two floors. The buildings were constructed on regular concrete frames with masonry infill, which was rendered over and painted white or grey. Spans and column rhythms were allowed to change between blocks, but remained rigidly systematic within each one, the beams being constantly revealed in the ceilings, their edge cantilevers dramatised by a tapering form. Because of the strong constructive discipline of the frame, the design as a whole remains somewhat dumb in plan. Its brilliance lies in the way this plan is subsequently transformed in the

8. Section running east-west; residential block to left, workshop block right, and theatre/canteen between. Large multi-pane windows towards the right back onto the staircase.

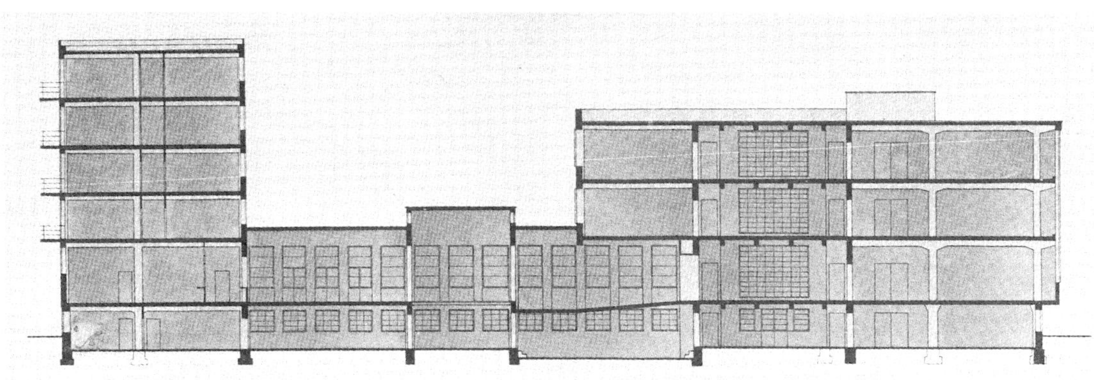

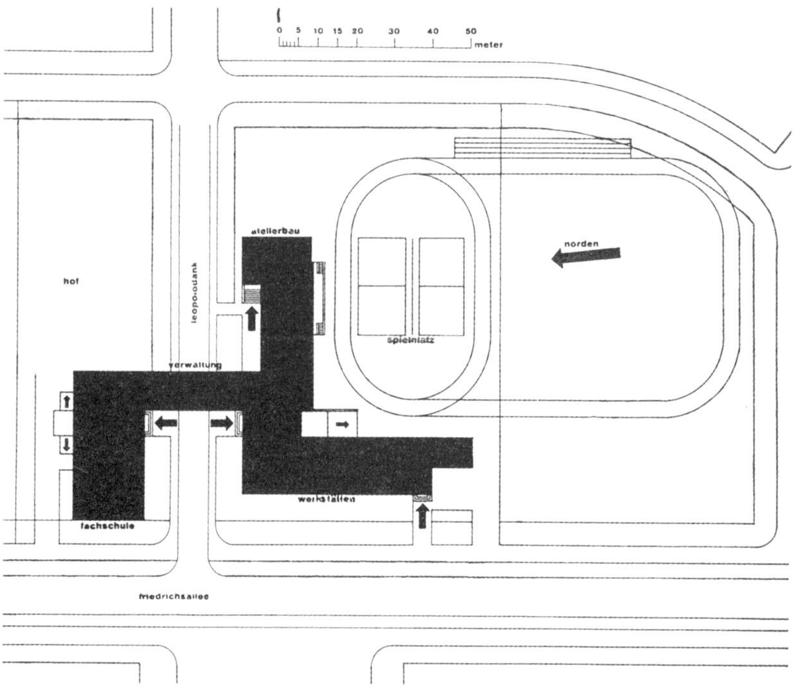

9. (left) Site plan, city centre is to right and south, main road runs through at bottom. The street running vertically which the buildings bridge over did not exist but was on the local plan. Gropius enfolded the sports field to south with workshop and link wings.

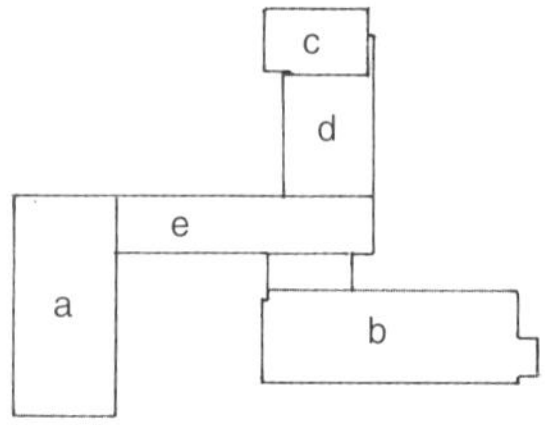

10. Block plan: a, classroom block; b, workshop block; c, residential block; d, link block with theatre/ canteen; e, bridge block.

11. (below) Aerial photograph of the Bauhaus when newly completed showing its comparative isolation.

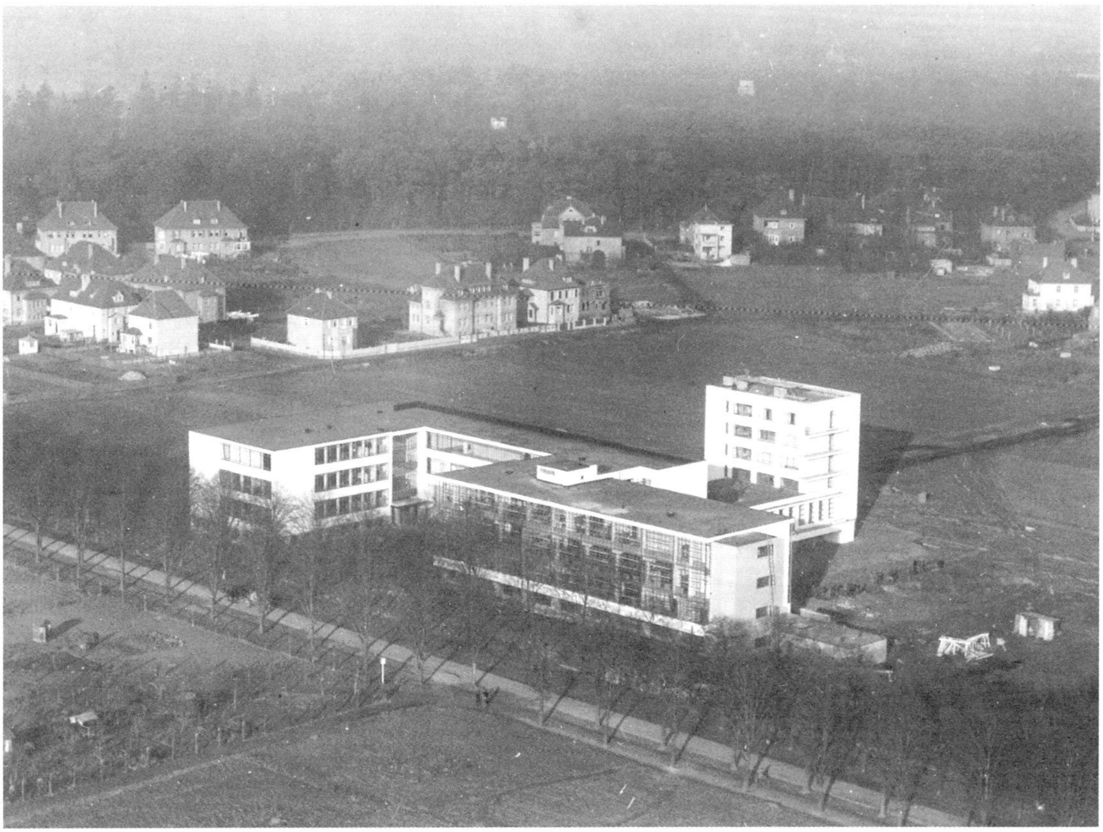

Key:
1. Workshop
2. Weaving workshop
3. Instructor's office
4. Cloakroom
5. Classroom
6. Secretary
7. Administration
8. Director's office
9. Reception room
10. Library
11. Studio

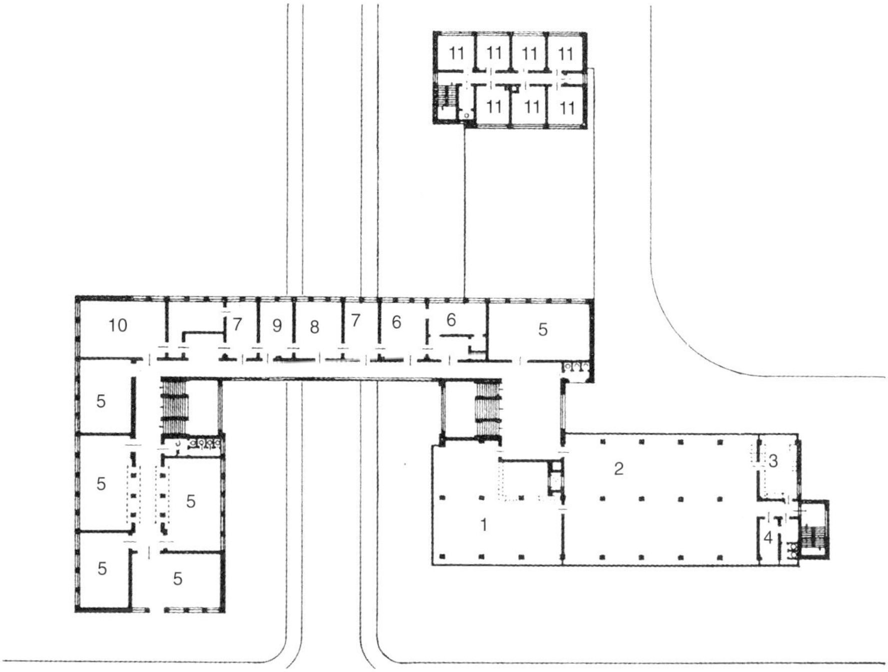

12. (above) First floor plan.

13. (below) Ground floor plan.

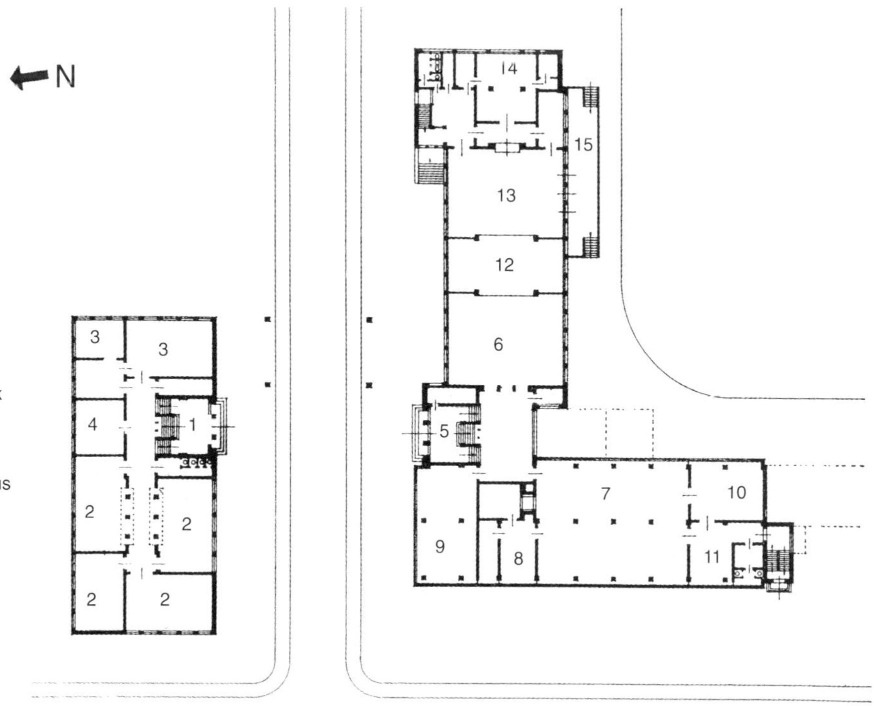

Key:

1. Entry to classroom block
2. Classroom
3. Laboratory
4. Storeroom
5. Main entrance to Bauhaus
6. Auditorium
7. Carpentry shop
8. Instructor's office
9. Exhibition room
10. Machine shop
11. Paint shop
12. Stage
13. Cafeteria
14. Kitchen
15. Terrace

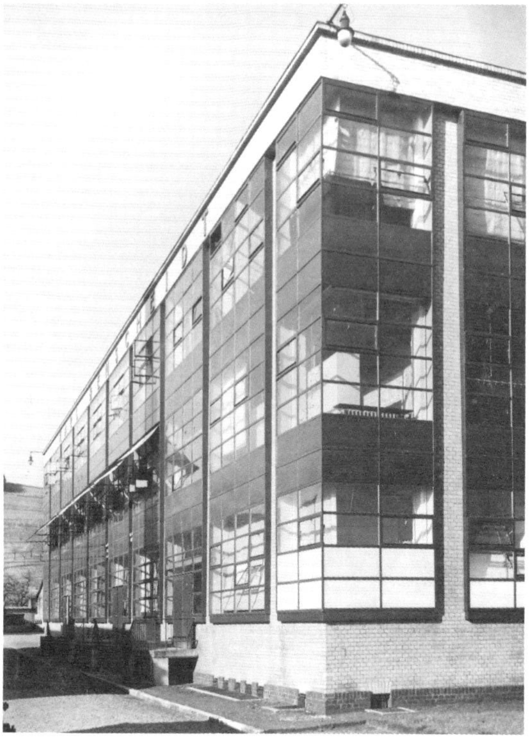

14. Fagus shoe-last factory, Alfeld an der Leine, 1913.
15. (below) Gropius and Meyer, model factory, Werkbund Exhibition, Cologne 1914.

three-dimensional composition, produced by varied massing, alternation of scale, contrasting fenestration and balcony treatments, and dramatic expression of the frame behind the glazing. The most prominent building in the group is the fully glazed workshop block, which presents its long west side to the road. The combination of three storeys in a single vertical element has much the same effect as a giant column order, such as that used by Gropius's mentor Peter Behrens at the German Embassy in St Petersburg. When he worked as assistant to Behrens from 1908-1911, Gropius imbibed both Behrens's Neoclassicism and its Schinkelesque derivation, while he also shared his mentor's predilection for pure geometric forms and proportion systems. Certainly Gropius knew Behrens's industrial work, but by the time the famous AEG Turbine hall was complete, Gropius had already overtaken it with a more progressive work of his own, the Fagus shoe-last factory in Alfeld an der Leine.

On leaving Behrens's office, Gropius set up in partnership with Adolf Meyer, a brilliant draughtsman but a somewhat shy and retiring person, who had also worked for Behrens. Gropius was the public face, and with his aristocratic background sought jobs through family connections. The factory at Alfeld had been planned by another architect and was under way, but Gropius managed to persuade the owner that it needed a new and progressive image. Gropius and Meyer restyled the façade of the office block and in so doing invented the curtain wall. They had to accept the existing plan and the intended framing system, but they clad it in a new way. Not only did the glazing span three storeys, it also left a fully glazed corner.

Although the Fagus factory has often been interpreted as a piece of sheer constructive logic, there are tricks in the detailing that must have been difficult to achieve and indicate a classical pedigree. The brick piers between glazing elements taper back, for example, to become more obviously 'negative', while the glazing panels step forward to gain some thickness, meeting the entablature in the same plane, almost as if they

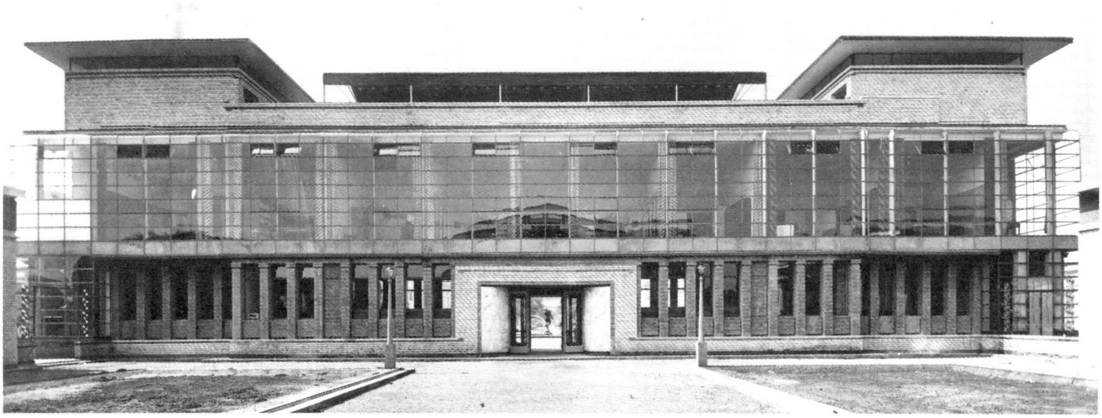

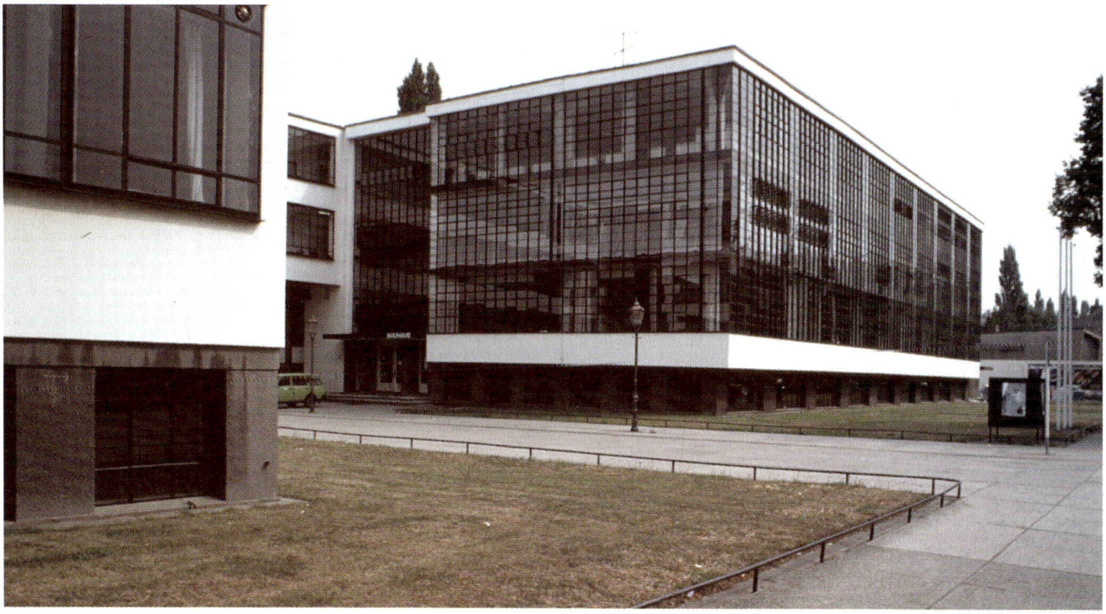

16. Bauhaus Dessau, workshop block seen from main road, post-restoration photo.

hang from it. There was no attempt here to express the content of the building, or even to differentiate the stairs from the office floors. It is a classical and largely symmetrical giant-order composition conceived from without.

Gropius and Meyer's other early masterpiece, the office building for the Werkbund exhibition at Cologne of 1914, also used glass in a novel way and boasted completely glazed stair towers. The architects were able to determine the general plan this time, but made it straightforwardly classical with a strongly emphasised central axis running through to the court behind. The façades even show the remnants of columns on both sides. Only as it gains three dimensions does the building come alive, and again there is subtle interplay between brickwork and glass skin, in the layering of the façade. The floating roofplates acknowledge Frank Lloyd Wright, whose Wasmuth portfolio of 1910 was well known to Gropius and Meyer,[15] but persistent fragments of reduced Egyptian decoration also show that emancipation from applied iconography had not yet quite arrived.

Consistent in many ways with the later Bauhaus, these examples indicate the areas where the decisive skills of Gropius and Meyer lay: in the control of massing and the layering of the façade. The workshop at the Bauhaus is an obvious descendent of the Fagus factory even in the way it runs three storeys together, but the glass façade is brought further forward by cantilevering the floors beyond the frame, and the whole glazed box floats dramatically over the basement, the effect increased by its white paint in opposition to the basement's grey. Much has been made by historians of its transparency, but it is actually rather less transparent than the rear part of the Werkbund building, and the thought of it in modern frameless glazing does not inspire. Gropius evidently wanted the steel cage and the machinery of the opening lights to have a strong physical presence, for he could have chosen larger sheets of glass. The contrast in scale between the different glazing elements is very important to the overall effect. A detail which completely gives the game away is the step in both plan and section to the front glazing of the bridge, a visual refinement that articulates nothing internal whatsoever.

The articulation of parts

Because of the prevalence of functional explanations in 1926 and the supposed reliance on objectivity, much was made by the architects and their interpreters of the way the accommodation is articulated in blocks. Certainly the workshops are glazed like a factory hall, the classroom block is identifiable through its horizontal strips of glazing, and the residential block can be identified by its

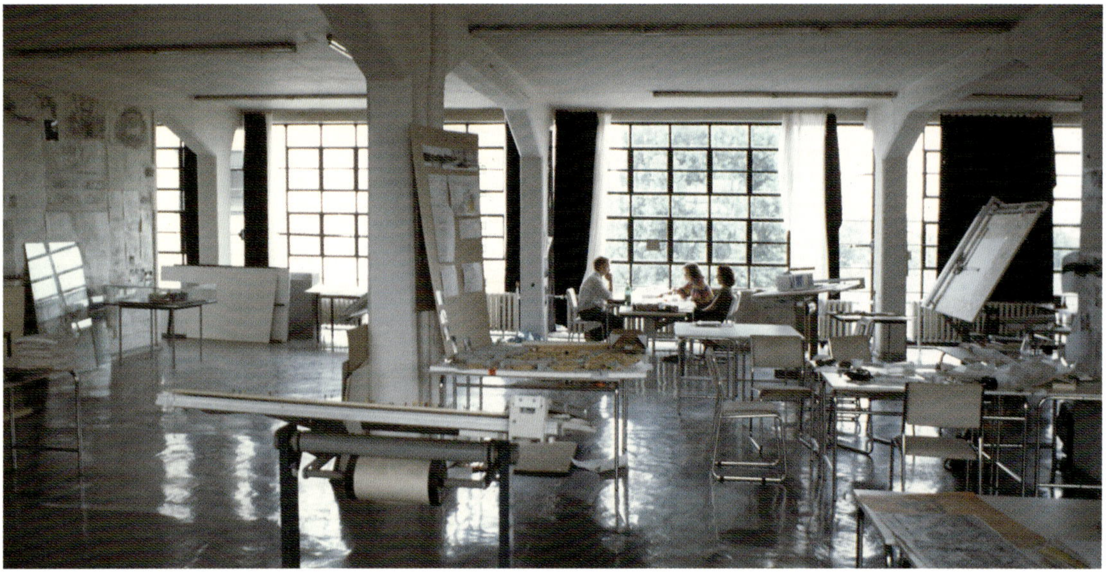

17. One of the workshops, showing frame and glazing, post-restoration photo.

separate windows and balconies. Beyond this basic differentiation, however, the building is very generalised and dominated, like Gropius's Weissenhof houses, by its construction grid. Nothing declares the identity of the weaving workshop on the first floor, for example, or differentiates it from the adjacent foundation workshop or the other specialist workshops above and below. Similarly the offices and classrooms lie behind undifferentiated horizontal glazing which hides the intervening partitions. Even the corner library at first floor north-east is treated as a completely standard room, unrecognisable from without. The circulation elements are not consistently expressed either: much is made of the main stairs, but the staircase on the south end is completely suppressed behind the wall which bears the title 'Bauhaus', and so also is the main stair of the residential block. The side balconies on the south of the latter seem to be present more for compositional effect than for everyday use. Most surprising of all is the lack of any articulation for the main social meeting places - the theatre and canteen. Even the stage occurs behind a blanked-off section of the continuing window band! Little comparison can thus be made with the determined functional articulation of Hugo Häring discussed in the previous chapter, which sought a hierarchical display of elements; or that of Hans Scharoun at the Weissenhof and later. The difference is also evident in Gropius's laconic plan. For the organic architects the ground plan was the driving figure: in Gropius's work it takes a muter, normalised form.

Oddly, one of the things most strongly articulated by Gropius is the bridge. It suggests that the two institutions are divided and then linked, notably by his controlling office at its very centre. In comparison with traditional buildings this is an odd thing to do, because entrances normally address a space of arrival, a *cour d'honneur*, rather than being on the way to somewhere else. The road had no prior use or existence, so could presumably have been sited elsewhere, and in any case there was space enough to avoid having to make the link.

We must conclude that Gropius very much wanted it, perhaps for a dynamic effect he had noticed at busy factories where density had made such elements obligatory, perhaps as part of the general obsession in the 1920s with the dynamics of vehicular movement: we shall encounter this again in the works of Le Corbusier and Mendelsohn. Far from underplaying it, Gropius made the bridge the centrepiece of the most classical part of his composition, for when seen on the axis of the road, it is fully symmetrical with the paired entrances. This conventional perspective view is not touted in the histories, and it does not sit well with Giedion's space-time claims.

Spatially, Gropius's building offers relatively less than most others in this book. The internal

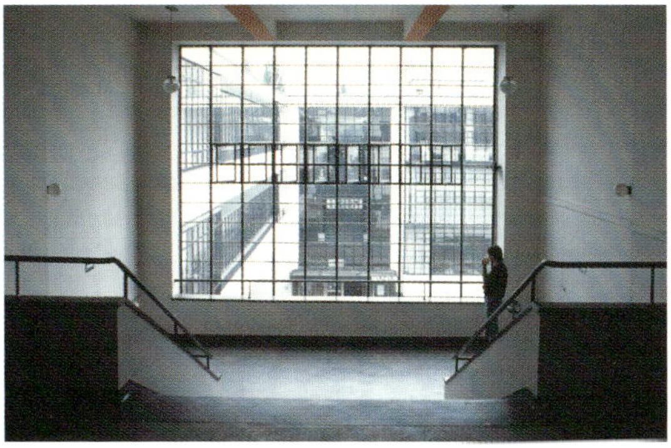

18. Top floor of main stair, classroom block. The bridge can be seen to left and the workshop block to right.

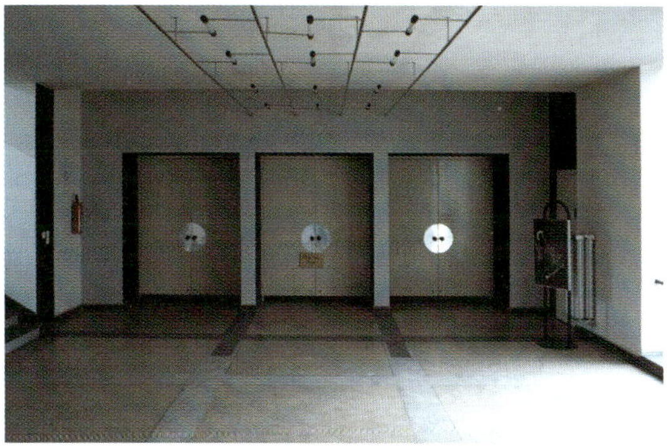

19. Entrance doors to theatre, with main stair to left. The symmetry of such views reflects a classical heritage.

rooms are relatively orthodox and their progression pretty straightforward. The individual elements are mainly box-like and their faces largely symmetrical, so the powerful and photogenic asymmetry on which the whole effect depends is achieved with just a few deft moves, by turning one block's front to engage the side of the next, disengaging one block from another with the stair, pulling the horizontal ranks of glazing from one volume to the next to link them, etc. It is significant that among the most published photographs of the institution are aerial ones that show the whole three-dimensional composition, while the almost contemporary masters' houses designed in Gropius's office are most effectively presented in a similar view produced by axonometric projection.

After three quarters of a century of asymmetrical building, it is hard to recognise how revolutionary these 'few deft moves' could be, but the break from classically inspired symmetry was a consuming theme of the mid 1920s,[16] and Gropius's breaks were all the more influential for their relative simplicity and consequent clarity. It must be admitted too, that the changes in apparent scale contrived through the combination or separation of storeys and by subtle contrasts in the rhythm of the glazing mullions, are masterly.

Hannes Meyer and the quantitative method

If before 1926 and the move to Dessau the Bauhaus had sometimes been too pluralist and even mystical, so that with its new building and revised courses it seemed more harmoniously to come together, the new conformity before long went too far. Gropius invited Hannes Meyer to run the newly founded architecture department in 1927, presumably with approval of his reputation and views, then on Gropius's departure in 1928, Meyer took over the whole institution. With the zeal of a young missionary, he imposed his reductive marxist view, causing some important staff members, among them Oskar Schlemmer, to leave.[17] Meyer's stance is immortalised in his statement *'bauen'* (building) published as the manifesto for his new 'improved' Bauhaus.[18] Dismissing art and composition as superstitious nonsense, Meyer declares that the basis of building is *'function times economy'*. He lists the building materials to be used, and names twelve functions to be considered in designing a dwelling. These, he claims, are the only ones worthy of consideration, and he goes on to advocate a scientific design method based on quantitative criteria. Everything is to be measured and calculated: exposure to the sun, the temperature of the soil etc. Meyer instructs us to *'draw the function diagram for the father, the mother, the child, the postman, the washerwoman etc.'* His proposal has remained a landmark in modernist architectural theory, tacitly, if not explicitly, associated with Bauhaus products, and often assumed to be the Bauhaus's underlying method. It has spread across the world in many guises and still recurs in new forms.[19] It fails because only some things in architecture are readily measured, and unmeasurables therefore tend to get excluded. Clearly it is easier to deal quantitatively with how much hot water comes out of the taps than to assess the value of a view from a window, let alone having a method to calculate the relative priority of hot water and views. This is not to deny the usefulness of measurement, but rather to caution against the assumption of being able to measure everything, to quantify all value judgements involved in design. Finally, it must be admitted that neither the Bauhaus building nor the vast majority of objects and designs emerging from the school were the outcome of the systematic design process proposed by Hannes Meyer. Belief in his design philosophy as the Bauhaus's ideological motive force was largely a retrospective simplification.

Conclusion

The Bauhaus buildings became such an icon with modernist historians because they so neatly combined the prime modernist institution with an exemplary piece of modernist architecture, giving large-scale expression to what quickly became seen as the Bauhaus ideology. For those who wished to see it that way, this architecture fulfiled the promise of being rational and functional, and the aesthetic effect, which can still be felt, could be taken as proof of their thesis. But we now know that it was no simple outcome of a rational design procedure. Undoubtedly well-composed, the group of buildings cleverly combines Gropius's and his assistants' simple straightforward planning with a sense of proportion, balance and colour indebted both to classical roots and to the contemporary art world. The latter was richly represented within the Bauhaus, and the apparent 'fit' of the buildings with the paintings of Kandinsky and Albers, the typography of Bayer, the furniture of Breuer and countless other Bauhaus products is visually compelling, if hard to define precisely. Functionalist and rationalist arguments provided a convenient alibi and gave substance to the curriculum, while the terse, reductive quality of Gropius's architecture seemed also to support the arguments. Perhaps, too, Gropius's fame rests on his arrival on the scene at the moment when his skill at boiling things down to essentials was most relevant. But the reality finally eluded rational and functional definition. As Hugo Häring never tired of pointing out, the prevalent tendency towards simple geometric forms was by no means synonymous with functionalism, and even tended to oppose or displace it. From the beginning various modernist architects accused and counter-accused each other of formalism, and their accusations were seldom completely without foundation.[20]

Notes

1. For a good general introduction to the Bauhaus as an institution see Whitford 1984.
2. See Pevsner 1936/1960.
3. See Giedion 1941.
4. Established by Hitchcock & Johnson with the MOMA exhibition, New York, of 1932, see Hitchcock 1932.
5. See Bauhaus 50th anniversary exhibition catalogue, Stedelijk Museum Amsterdam 1968/9 p.145.
6. The title of a major exhibition at the Hayward Gallery in London, see Raeburn 1987.
7. From the beginning Gropius felt unable to draw, and was therefore reliant on a series of assistants. Adolf Meyer played a strong role in the Fagus and Werkbund buildings, but left just before the Bauhaus project, which was carried through by Fieger, Neufert and others. In England Maxwell Fry was the partner, and in the early American Years the role fell to Marcel Breuer. See *Walter Gropius as a Design Architect* in Nerdinger 1985, pp. 29-31.
8. In the conclusion to his later edition of *Pioneers*, published in 1960, and the quotation continues: *'and as long as this is the world and these are its ambitions and problems, the style of Gropius and the other pioneers will be valid.'* Pevsner 1960, p. 217.
9. As reported by Neumeyer in the case of Mies, see Neumeyer 1991.
10. See for example Rowe 1978.
11. See Hannes Meyer *'bauen'* 1928, reprinted and translated in Conrads 1970 pp.117-120.
12. For a concise version of the Bauhaus's ideological development see Whitford 1984.
13. *'...when the masters' houses were being built there was constant conflict between Gropius, who had very clear ideas about the design of the houses, and the masters' wives, who often bombarded the architect with their personal requests. Ise Gropius was often called upon to smooth things out, supporting her husband uncompromisingly.... Gropius carried his concept through unwaveringly, paying no attention to the many requests that were put to him',* Marie Neumüllers in Bauhaus Dessau Foundation 1998, p.104.
14. See Klaus von Beyme's essay in ibid, p. 96.
15. Nerdinger 1985, p.11.
16. Erich Mendelsohn was an early pioneer in the break from symmetry, with works such as the Weichmann shop, Gleiwitz, of 1922 and the Villa Sternefeld, Berlin of 1923. Hugo Häring shows it very clearly with his Germania Club project of 1923 and his Secession competition design of 1926, both drawn in contrasting symmetrical and asymmetrical versions. Hans Scharoun also experimented with asymmetry throughout the 1920s.
17. Schlemmer in Bauhaus Dessau Foundation 1998.
18. Conrads 1970, pp.117-120.
19. Yona Friedman *Toward a scientific architecture* MIT Press 1972.
20. An ideological conflict between Gropius's Rationalism and Häring and Scharoun's Functionalism was already evident as early as 1923, when Gropius decided to eliminate the work of these colleagues from an exhibition at the Weimar Bauhaus, see Blundell Jones 1999, p. 38. A similar conflict developed later between Le Corbusier and Karel Teige, reported by George Baird in *Oppositions* no. 4, 1974, pp. 80-81.

Chapter 4. Jan Duiker: Zonnestraal Sanatorium, Hilversum 1926

'When the dawn of an enlightened view breaks through the dark chaos around us; when we can enjoy the fruits of the new prosperity and the benefits of serial production; when we recognise how to elevate ourselves spiritually to the state of "observed contemplation" that the development of "objectivity" offers - then we will see before us this perfect building, flooded with light and sun, unthinkable before the "age of steel". It means a new freedom for humanity.' Jan Duiker, c. 1933[1]

Of all building types, none was more perfectly suited in its ideology and imagery to the Modern Movement than the hospital. Representing the victory of science over the invasive and chaotic forces of nature, the modernist hospital not only promised literal functional efficiency but also a powerful symbolic purity. And among hospitals as a general type, the tuberculosis sanatorium had an even greater significance, for in the days before antibiotics, tuberculosis was the major killer of young and healthy people in their teens and twenties. In large cities there were epidemics. For example, in Budapest between 1911 and 1922, the disease killed more than 70% of the girls who died between ten and fifteen and 28% of boys.[2] A respiratory illness, it spread through inhalation of infected droplets from the breath of others, and was thus associated with closeness and overcrowding. The symptoms of coughing and spluttering also linked it with the dirty and polluted air of cities still poisoned by the smog of burning solid fuel, and such atmospheres certainly exacerbated it. Thus tuberculosis came to represent the evils of disease-ridden industrial cities that had grown up in the Nineteenth Century. Modernists sought in contrast a 'dissolution of the cities' [3] or at least a spreading out of their contents in 'garden city' form. In contrast with the darkness and smog there were to be sunlight and air, buildings widely spaced, lifted off the ground to float in the air, exposed to the sun. The belief in the benefits of fresh air and exercise

1. Zonnestraal Sanatorium complex, projection, north is right.

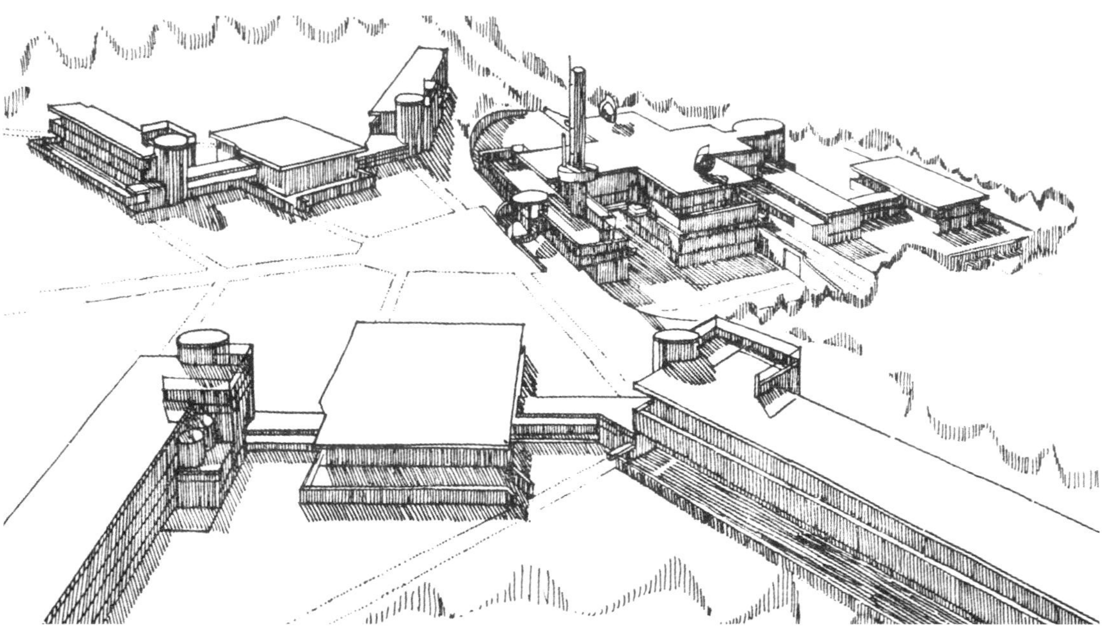

was widespread, but here again the tuberculosis sanatorium was something special, because it provided the most literal proof in the fight against chaos and disease. The tuberculous bacillus can be killed by sunlight, so solar exposure has a direct curative effect. For functionally-minded architects this provided the perfect justification for making buildings like greenhouses, exploiting the new wonder material glass, and getting people out of buildings onto open terraces.

In hospital buildings, real and symbolic purity are inseparably mixed. Once the role of pathogenic organisms in disease was understood, regimes of strict cleanliness were instituted, and this continues as a dominant design consideration today. In operating theatres and intensive care units particularly, there must be thorough cleansing and purification, not only ensuring that instruments are fully sterilised, but that the room is kept clean and under positive pressure to prevent germ-laden air from entering. All people admitted must don protective overalls to contain any dirt that they might bring from the outside world, and in the process they adopt a uniform and become institutionalised. The patients too are stripped of their everyday clothes and dressed in hospital uniform, again ostensibly in the name of physical hygiene, but also to powerful symbolic effect. All objects introduced and used in sterile areas must be cleaned and be cleanable, without crevices where pathogens could lurk. Smooth white surfaces and shiny stainless steel equipment and furniture imply that they are clean and pure, even if a microscopic examination would reveal organisms still present and that cleaning can never be thorough enough. For some viral infections, even the most stringent sterilisation of instruments is not safe.

Whatever the truth of the matter, the new architecture of the 1920s was justified to its public on the basis of being scientific and functionally efficient. For reasons given in earlier chapters, its architects wanted to declare their separation from the past and often, like Gropius, from the local context also. The hospital as an institution needs similarly to set itself apart from the everyday world for the sake of hygiene, and it came to revel in the detached condition offered by a modernist building. Medical regimes demand powerful ordering of both time and space not only for the sake of safety, but also for the sake of social discipline which needs symbolic reinforcement. A strict timetable is imposed, social roles are tightly defined, and there is strict regulation of territories: of who, under what conditions, is allowed to enter where. The architecture is expected to create the special controlled environment where a person is transformed into a patient, a body to be manipulated. In the operating theatre he or she is rendered helpless, their bodies invaded to an extent unimaginable in everyday life: indeed the violence done would in any other context be a criminal act. It is vital therefore that people trust doctors and understand where they are and why, and for this reason a purified and highly structured environment is reassuring. It affirms the power of science and rationality to regain control and to define the order of the world. The hospital has become in consequence one of the most ritualistic spaces of modern life.[4] In its strict timetable, hierarchy of roles linked to uniforms and a clear spatial definition, it might even be compared with a medieval monastery. When in his comedy film *Mon Oncle*, Jacques Tati presented the domestic kitchen as a kind of dentist's surgery, he was satirising the way the cold scientific functionalism of the Modern Movement can destroy the cosiness of domesticity, but through contrast he revealed at the same time just where this kind of Modernism was most wholly appropriate.

Jan Duiker's background in Dutch Modernism

The Dutch economy suffered less than the German after the First World War, so there was much more building in The Netherlands prior to 1925. Modernists therefore gained earlier opportunities to put their ideas into practice. Hence the maturity of experience seen in J. J. P Oud's Weissenhof house (p. 21-2), for as City Architect of Rotterdam he had built enormous housing estates as early as 1920. Cool Rotterdam was counter-balanced by romantic Amsterdam and the bricky Arts & Crafts approach of de Klerk and J. F. Staal. Added to this lively scene was the art movement De Stijl founded in 1917, a major force in the abstraction of architecture which proved internationally influential. Oud was involved, but the central architect of the movement was Gerrit Rietveld (1888-1964), whose planar furniture and Schröder House of 1923 epitomise it. Two further ingredients of the Dutch scene may be noted: the work of Berlage from the previous generation, whose structural rationalism - seen at Amsterdam Stock-exchange (fig. 4) - grew from the Neo-gothic and the theory of Viollet-le-Duc, and the pervasive influence of Frank Lloyd Wright following his Wasmuth publication of 1910.

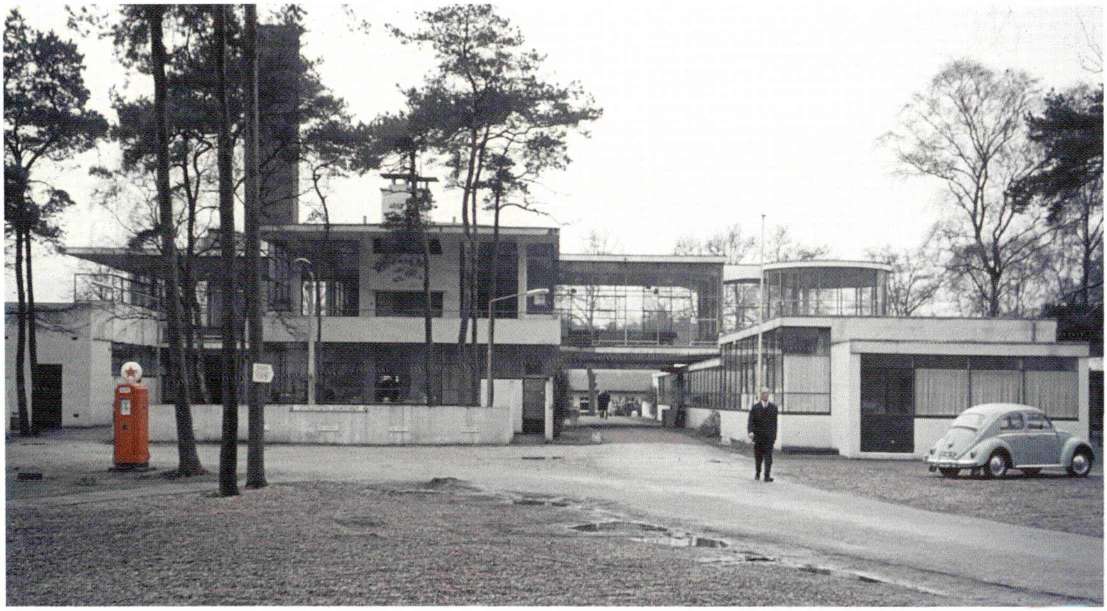

2. Zonnestraal Sanatorium central building from the east, with the drive running through. 1960s photograph by David Wild.

3. Central building from the west, looking into the southern drive-through. This is a rare early case of a building entry sequence geared to vehicles rather than pedestrians, and the unification of the three linear wings through the imposition of the cross-shaped upper floor helps dramatise it.

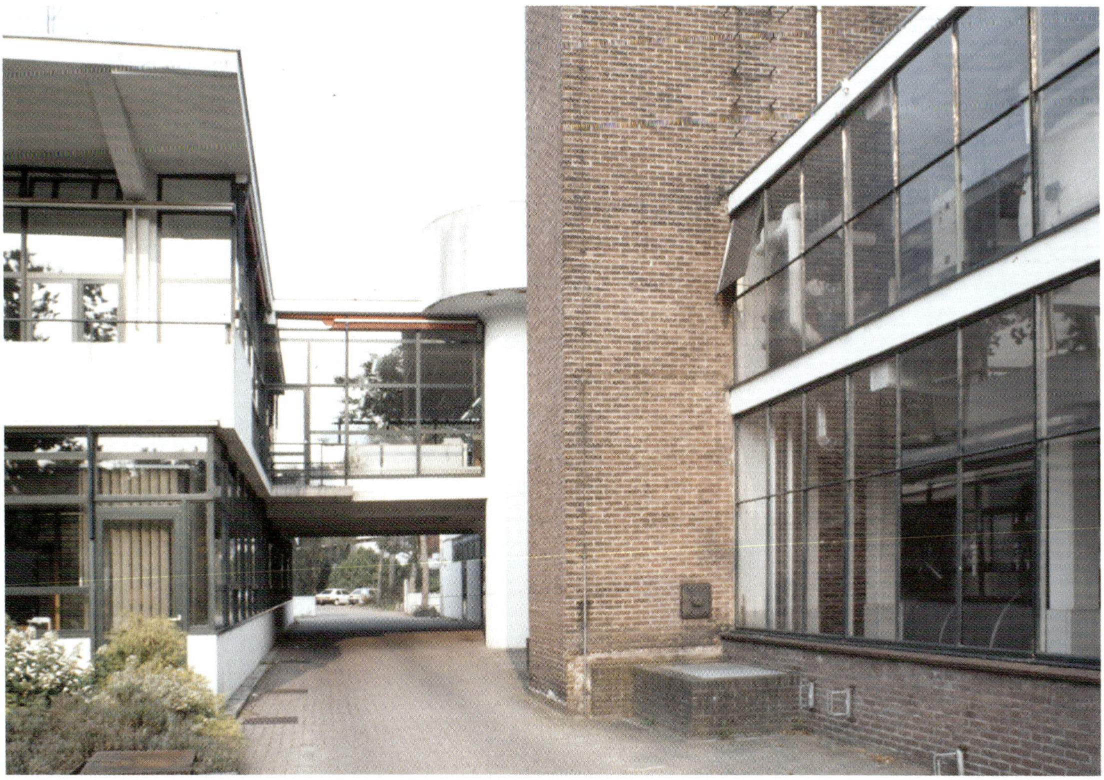

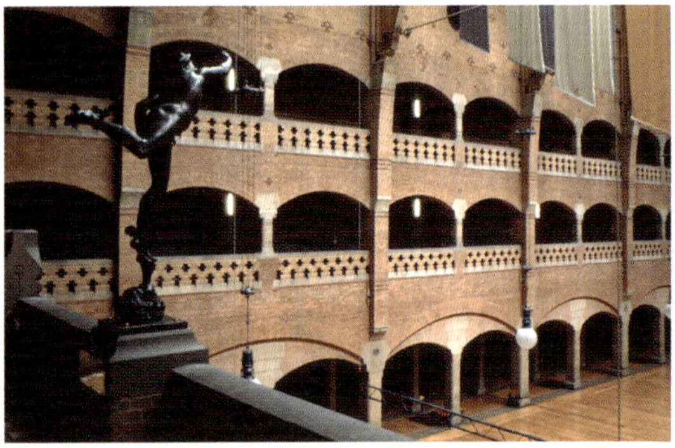

4. Hendrik Berlage, Stock Exchange Amsterdam, interior hall.

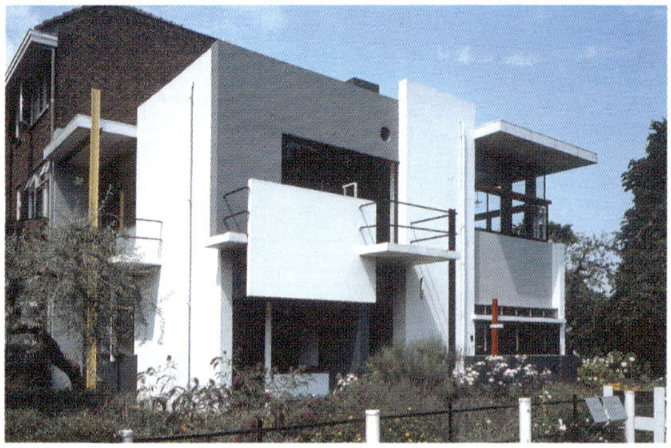

5. Gerrit Rietveld, Schröder House, Utrecht, 1924.

Born in 1890, Duiker was Oud's precise contemporary, but he found his voice as an architect slightly later, working in partnership with Bernard Bijvoet. Both studied at Delft Polytechnic, and their early work followed the Amsterdam brick tradition while also showing a debt to Wright. They demonstrated from early on a readiness to exploit the asymmetrical shapes of irregular sites, accommodating and enjoying the necessary shifts of angle. For example, in the first version of the Scheveningen Technical College 1921, the asymmetrical side became the main front. This taste for irregularity suggests a sympathy for the neo-gothic or Arts & Crafts models rather than neoclassical ones. Duiker and Bijvoet also showed an early concern with social problems and with 'hygiene', a favourite term in Duiker's later writings.

The essential breakthrough to the mature work came with the abandonment of loadbearing brickwork in favour of the frame, which occurred around 1923-4 and involved the help of the engineer Jan Gerko Wiebenga (1886-1974). Some of the later frames were in steel (Cineac cinema, Gooiland Hotel) and some even in timber, but the definitive ones were in reinforced concrete. Interest in the potential of the frame is clear from a patent concrete housing system initiated in 1923, but the key building to demonstrate the arrival of the new vocabulary was the laundry at Diemen (fig. 7). This was the immediate precursor to Zonnestraal and for the same clients, Koperen Stelen Fonds (the Diamond Workers' Union).[5] It was set up not just to clean the overalls of the workers but to recover from them valuable diamond dust for resale, thus paying for the workers' welfare support, which included the sanatorium. The starkly utilitarian three-storey structure housed a great coal-fired boiler and various washing and drying machines. Boiler and wash-tubs were accentuated in vertical glazed projections, while the flue and drying vents also lent themselves to clear functional articulation, but the real breakthrough was the liberation of the skin due to the framed structure. Glazing was added in continuous horizontal bands with trans-

6. Duiker and Bijvoet, Technical College, Scheveningen 1921.

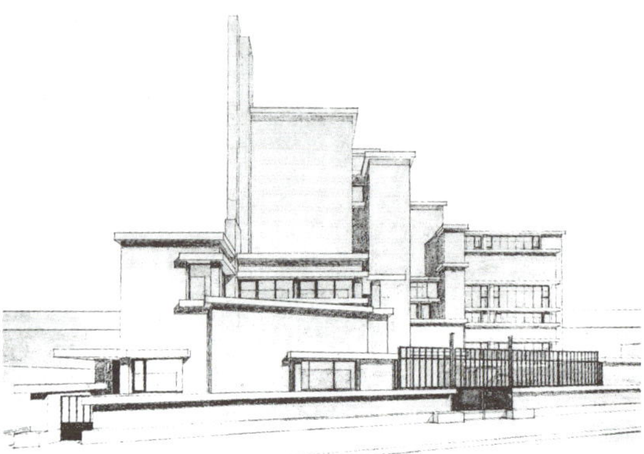

7. Duiker and Bijvoet, laundry, Diemen, 1924-5.

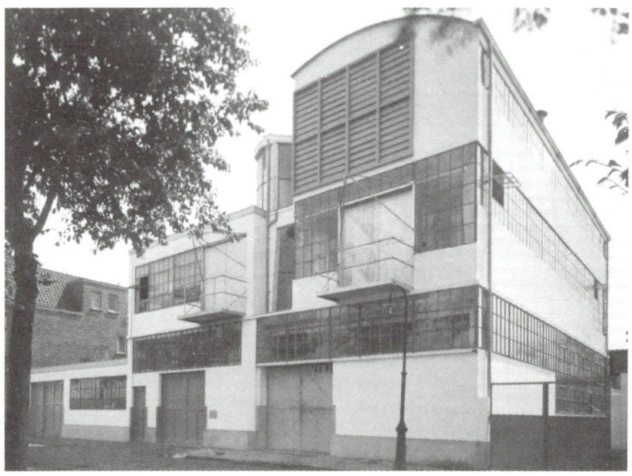

parent corners, and the cill line was allowed to rise and fall depending on the light required. In its initial form this transparent box predated Gropius's Bauhaus workshop by nearly two years.[6]

The Diamond Workers' Union and Zonnestraal
Duiker's principal works date from between 1924 and his early death in 1935, at the age of almost 45. Zonnestraal Sanatorium, the largest complex of buildings ever executed by him, falls right across this period. Founded in 1905, the Diamond Workers' Union was dedicated to the welfare of Dutch diamond workers. In 1919, for the use of convalescents from tuberculosis, it purchased a country estate in Hilversum with an existing villa. Much more accommodation was needed, and Duiker and Bijvoet were recommended as architects by Berlage. They started with small works such as pigsties, for not until the mid 1920s was there money enough to begin building the sanatorium proper. It was designed in 1924-5 and opened for use in 1928. Further buildings were constructed until 1932, and yet more - though less notable - in the late 1930s by Bijvoet alone following Duiker's death.

The starting point for the complex seems to have been a clearing in the landscape running south-south-east, which became the central axis. Approached from the north, all the buildings were laid out to open towards the sun, the headquarters block placed centrally at the back with symmetrically paired groups of pavilions to either side of the open axis. Half the group was able to face directly south, the other half south-east, generating a 45° shift in every pavilion pair. The choice of angle may have reflected the prevailing wisdom in the late 1920s that optimum orientation lay slightly east of south, as it allows more early heat from the morning sun,[7] but the angle shift also meant that each pavilion as well as the main building would have a long uninterrupted clear space in front. The angular plan allowed an escape from conventional neoclassical rigidity, while it also evokes the 'butterfly plans' of Edwardian Arts & Crafts architects such as Prior and Lutyens. These were known and imitated by architects of the Amsterdam School, but Duiker was already on his own trajectory, perhaps dimly aware of the even more dramatic effects to be obtained with his open-air school a couple of years later (fig.1, p. 47). Here the angle shifts and diagonal axes are exploited to even greater effect, dissolving corners and making

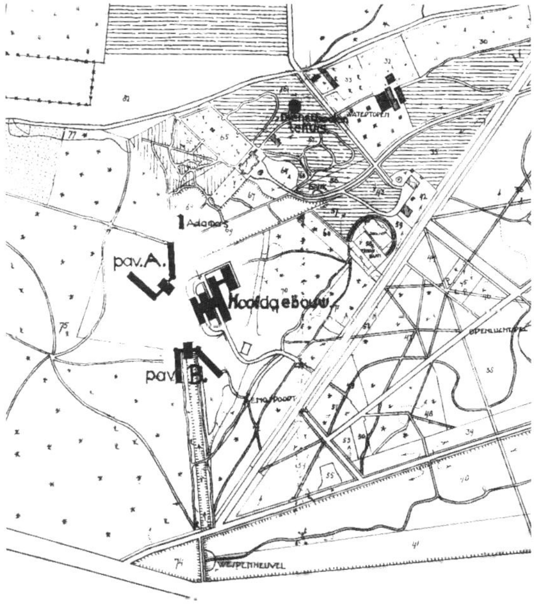

8. Zonnestraal, part of a context plan showing location, north is right.

9. General site plan showing relation of central building to treatment pavilions, with four pavilion groups as originally envisaged.

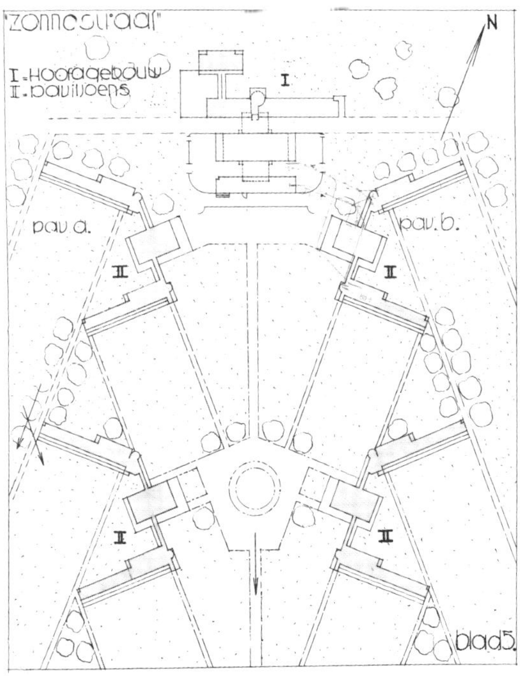

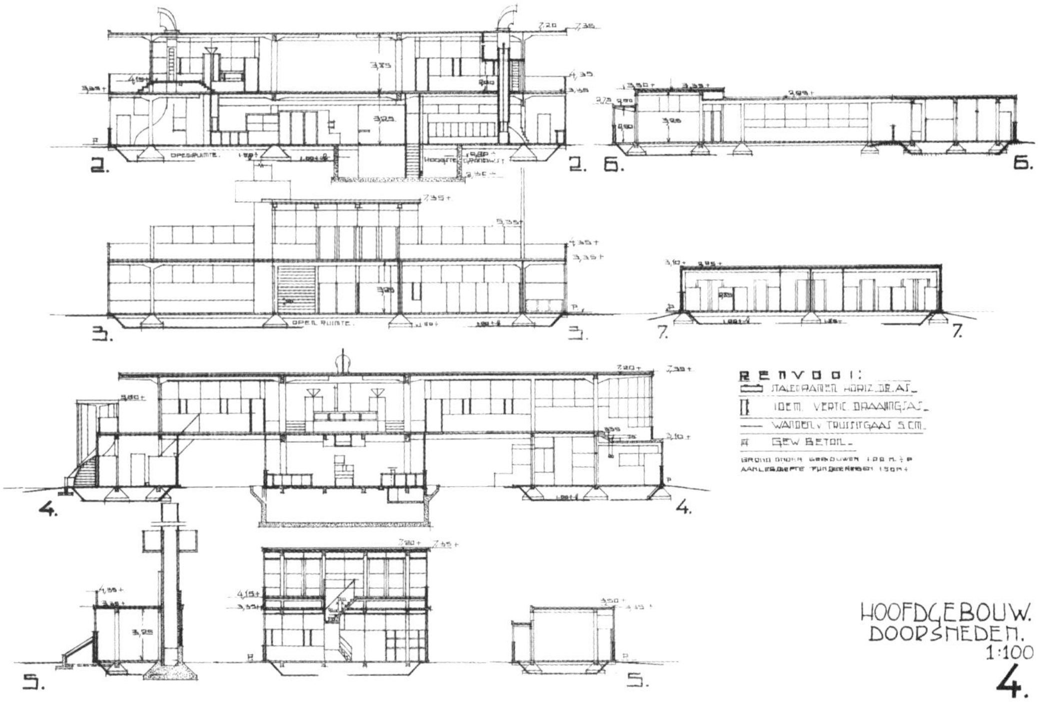

the building seem more insubstantial than ever. Arts & Crafts architects would have been amazed by this transformation, even disturbed.

Thanks to the freedom of its concrete frame structure, the headquarters building at Zonnestraal has an unprecedented form. Its ground floor has three separate east-west running tracts, but these are linked at first floor level by a great cruciform structure bridging the gaps between them. The ground floor tracts, reading from south to north, contain boiler plus bath house, the main kitchen serving meals to the floor above, and offices for doctors and administrators, along with the main entrance. Beyond to north, a shorter fourth east-west tract serves as infirmary for patients in need of special care. Connected by a glazed link, this was placed close to the doctors. The large cruciform structure at first floor is the main dining and social room, a great platform glazed on every side to look out across the landscape. Its effect was heightened by cantilevered roof projections which provide shelter for external terraces to south, east and west sides. Its height, transparency and biaxial symmetry make it the intended climax of the whole complex, the centralised layout reinforced by a raised skylight and four principal supporting columns. It was entered from the centre of its north bay via a glazed and externally articulated spiral stair rising from the ground-floor entrance, but it was also linked to the rest of the complex by a straight stair to south, where the roof of the bath and boiler house provides the most generous terrace. Food arrived from below in two lifts set in the cross's western bay. These formed the flanks of a raised area which could be used as a stage for a band, and from which speeches could be made.

People arrived at the headquarters building by car, driving through the northernmost of the gaps between the three ground-floor tracts. Passengers would disembark from vehicles under the shelter of the north bay of the cruciform upper floor. The dramatised path of the car - chauffeur-driven, not parked - can equally be seen in Duiker's first design for the open-air school. It was a common theme of the period, shared by the Bauhaus building (Chapter 3), Le Corbusier's Villa Savoye (Chapter 7), and more abstractly but just as essentially Erich Mendelsohn's urban work (Chapter 6). A second vehicular road running in the other gap between ground floor tracts was dedicated to service deliveries.

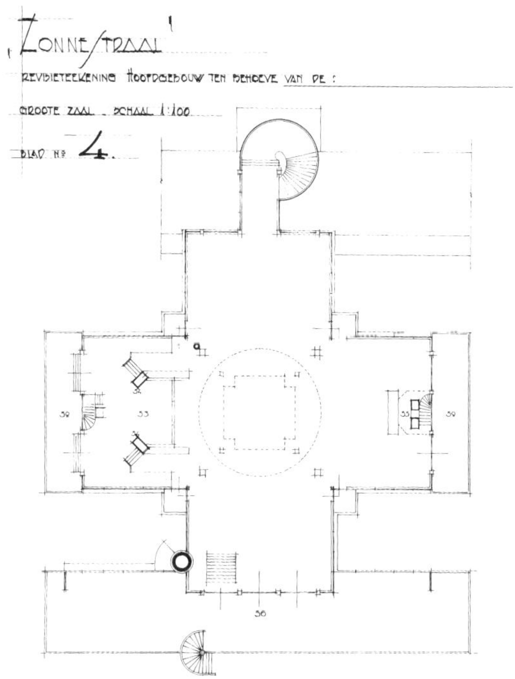

10. (opposite) Zonnestraal main building, sections. Numbers refer to references in plan here below. Section 2 (top) runs west-east through the central wing, while sections 4 & 5 (bottom) run south-north showing gaps for the passage of vehicles.

11. (above right) Plan of upper floor with cruciform social/dining room. Main entrance is by spiral stair at top.

12. (below) Main floor plan showing the four wings divided by two passages for vehicles.

Key:
1. main entrance
2. administration
3. consulting rooms
4. acute ward
5. kitchens
6. bathrooms
7. heating plant
8. main chimney

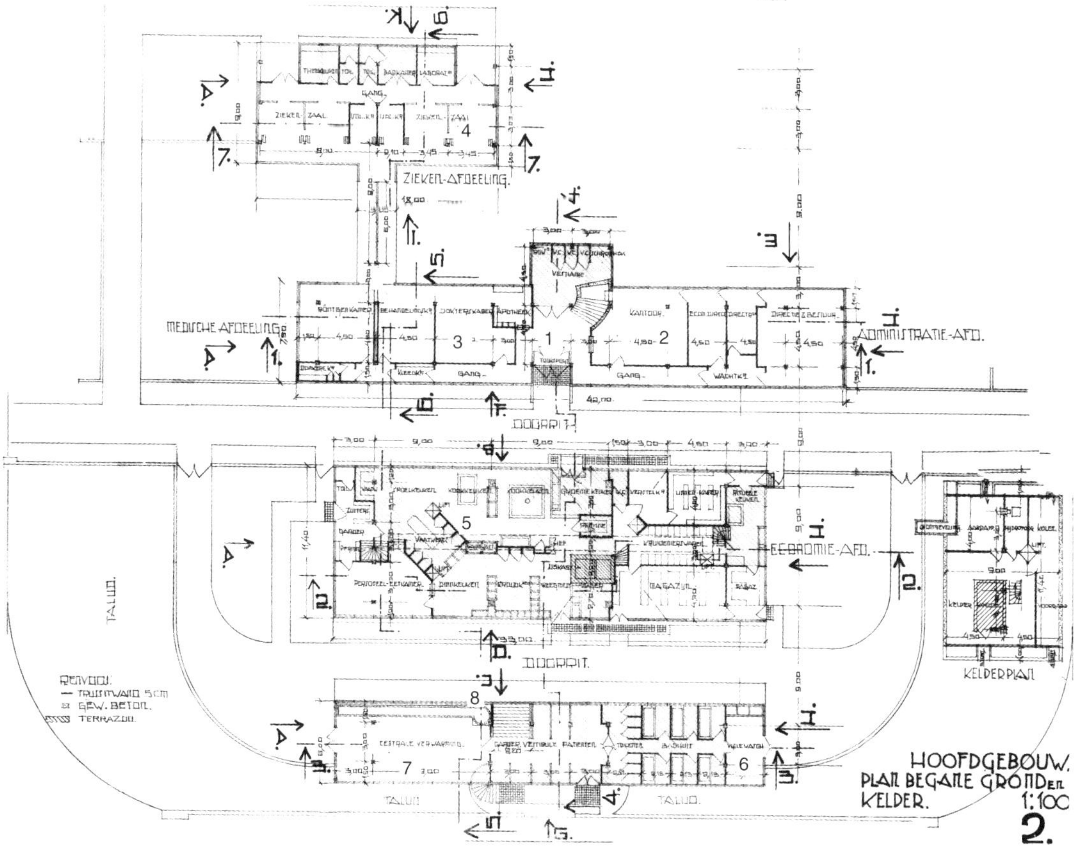

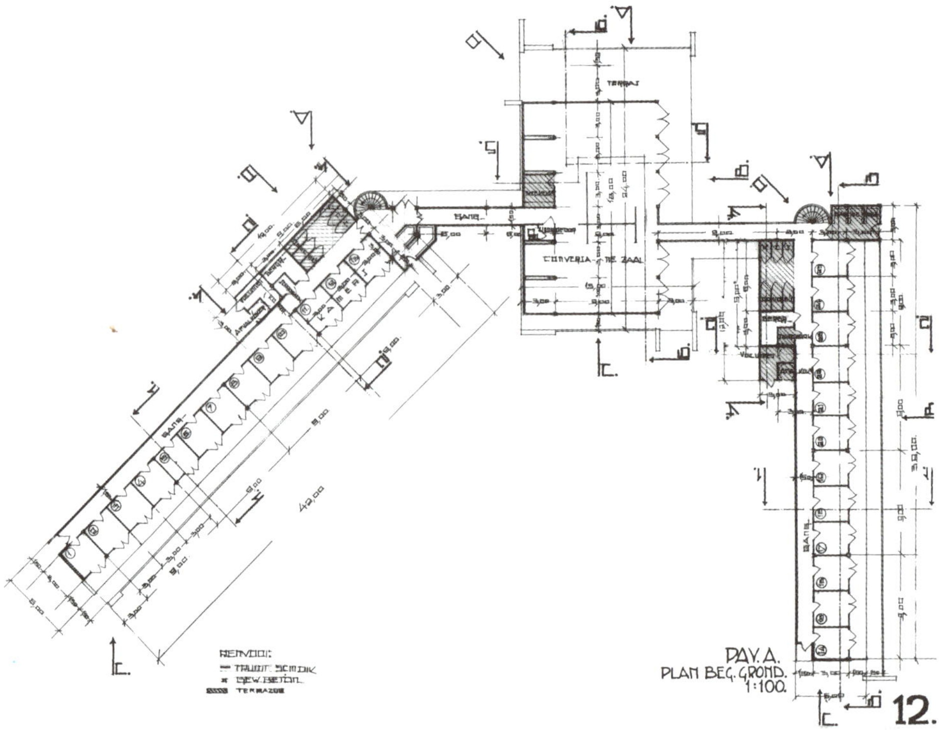

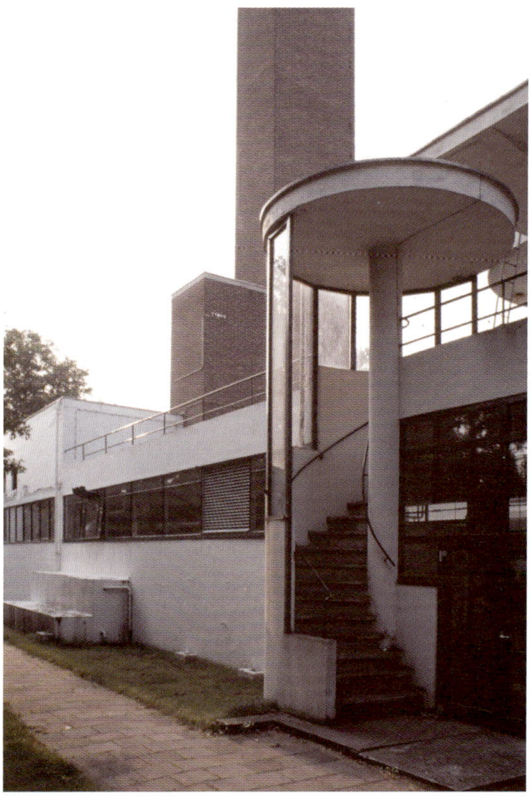

13. (above) Plan of two bedroom wings linked by a dayroom.

14. (left) The semi-enclosed stair forms the knuckle.

15. (below) Projection showing the concrete structure.

16. (opposite) Plans and elevations of the patient wing showing the two floors of sun-absorbing bedrooms with bathrooms behind.

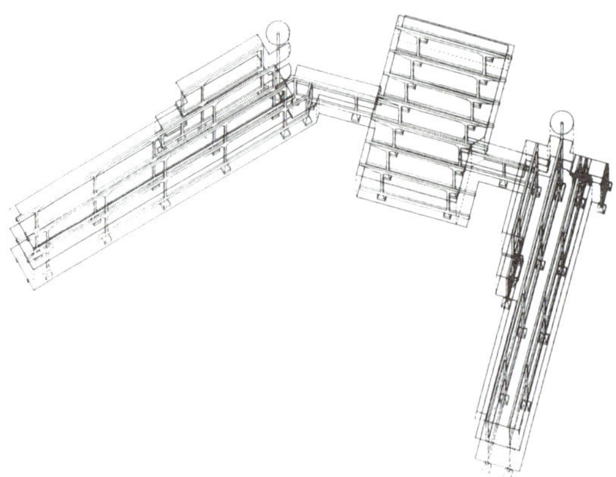

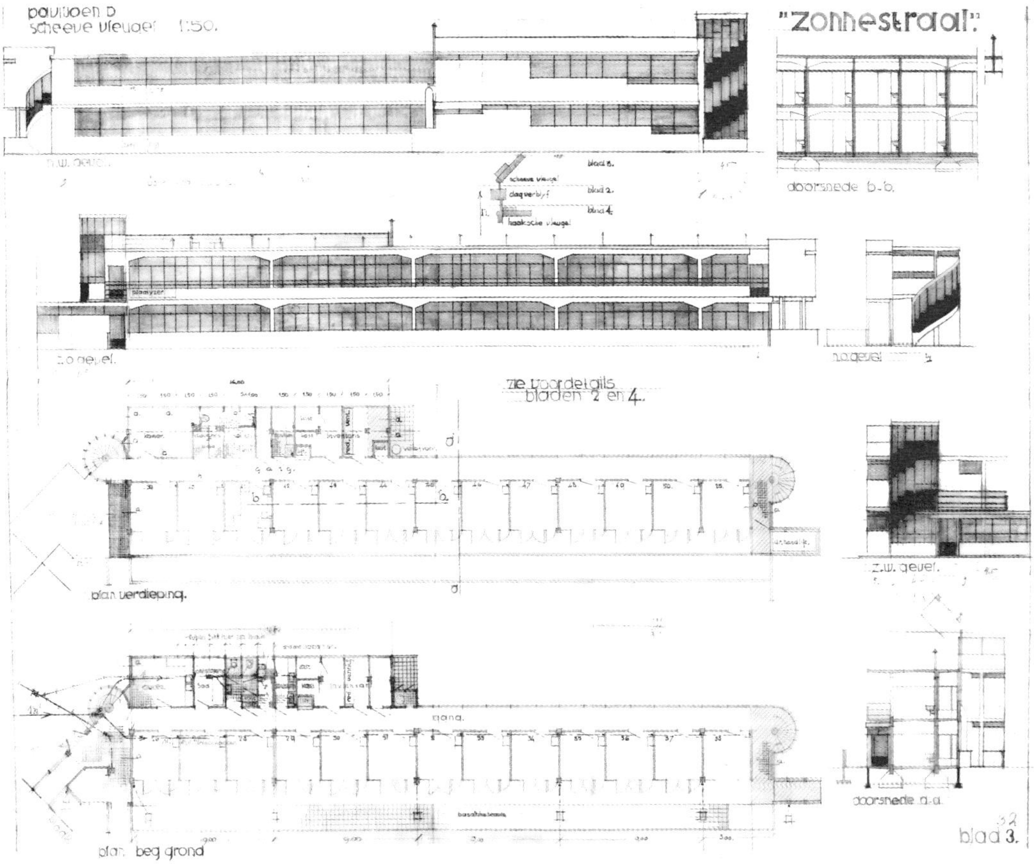

The patient wings

Accommodation for convalescing patients was spread out across the site in a series of pavilions to make the most of the fresh air and sun, the rooms arranged in linear tracts so that every one had southern or south-south-eastern orientation, access being gained by single-loaded corridor on the north side. Every room had a sheltered balcony and a glazed façade with double doors, so that beds could be brought outside. This arrangement allowed a range of possibilities between full enclosure and full exposure to sun and air. There was also a roof terrace provided with a glazed windbreak, accessible via the main stair. Each wing of two floors with 12 or 13 rooms had a range of bathrooms and WCs tacked on the back and a spiral stair at the entry end to link the floors vertically, which also formed a hinge for the changing angle of the plan. Pairs of wings set 45° apart shared a common social room set between them, a diminutive version of the main cruciform one. The division of the accommodation cut down the apparent size of the crowd and created an easily appreciable social grouping. A patient would typically find himself sharing a floor with 11 others in a wing of 24, part of a pavilion group housing 50, and of a whole patient population numbering 200. All who were sufficiently well would make their way to the headquarters building for meals, passing through the open air.

Skin and bones

Seventy-five years later, with framed buildings the norm and frameless glazing in widespread use, it is difficult to imagine just how revolutionary Duiker's group of buildings must have seemed. There was nothing anywhere so light and airy, for nobody had yet exploited the concrete frame to such transparent effect. But the spans and areas of glass are not in themselves the point: it was Duiker's knowing treatment of the contrast between two kinds of construction - concrete skeleton and glass

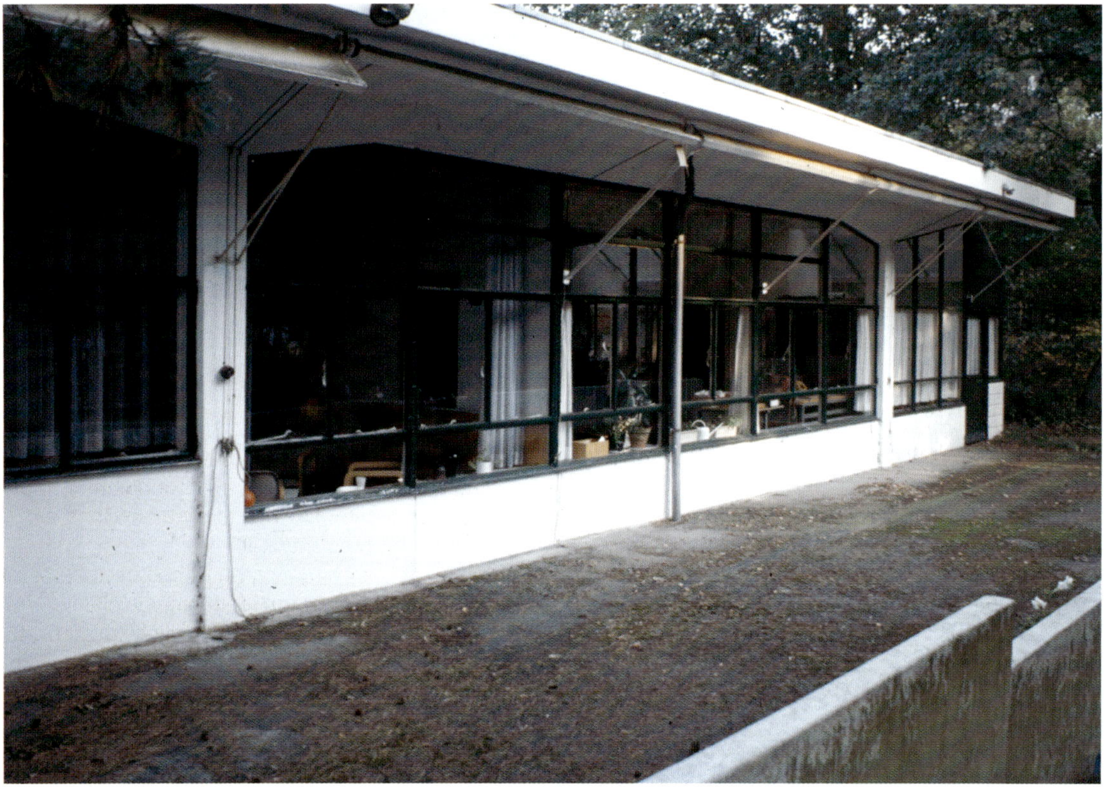

17. Part of a surviving bedroom wing, with the terrace where patients were brought into the open air.

skin - that opened a new chapter in the history of architecture. Photographs of the building under construction are particularly revealing, for they show that the empty frame was no dumb system, and that the concrete bones and glass skin complimented each other perfectly. Perhaps unintentionally, the raw construction had become an object for aesthetic contemplation even before it was rendered and painted over for the sake of monolithic whiteness.[8]

Most of the construction was based on a 3 metre grid, with major spans of 9 metres, but played out as a theme and variations. Concrete cantilevers of 1.5 and 3 metres occur throughout, sometimes meeting a glass screen wall to enclose a corridor, sometimes left external as a shading device, the tapered supports expressing a diminishing load. Angled corners cast between columns and beams, to protect against shear, both identify the span and accentuate the point of support. Special corners and ends, even whole spiral stairs with circular caps, were cast in, and balcony parapets became edge beams. All this was certainly not done in the most straightforward way: spans in the sleeping pavilions were taken along rather than across the building, for example, with columns at 9 metre intervals, even though room width is only 3 metres (figs 16, 17). Perhaps Duiker thought he was allowing for flexibility, but this measure also greatly improves the visual rhythm of the building, helping to relate the sleeping cell visually to the rest of the complex.

The bare skeleton seems to anticipate its cladding. Applied as a membrane with the most minimal steel framing, the glass sometimes runs along the building's edge, sometimes on an inner line of support, at times transparent and at other times reflective. It tends to expose the ceiling line continuously, proving that the wall is never load-bearing, but it drops down progressively from clerestory height to full glazing according to the requirements of light and privacy. At the same time it steps in and out in plan, making its own corners and working its way around beams. Opening lights of different sizes and types further enrich the changing rhythm. The vocabulary was extended at the later Open-air School (fig.1, p. 47) where the skin steps across the frame mid-span, glass-to-glass corners are inverted, and the spatial ambiguity of the axes set at 45° is played to the limit of its potential.

Zonnestraal as a modernist icon

Duiker and Bijvoet were undoubtedly influenced by the various currents, local and international, that swept Dutch architecture in the 1920s, including De Stijl. But they had also shown strong social commitment, dedicating themselves to improving housing conditions for those *'at the bottom of the social ladder'* [9], and as with other Modernists this impelled them towards a functionalist position. By the end of the decade they had aligned themselves decisively with the groups Opbouw and De 8, to the extent that Duiker became editor of the two groups' combined magazine *De 8 en Opbouw* from 1932-34. The stance was typically functionalist and anti-aesthetic. *'De 8 asserts that it is quite possible to build beautifully, but for the time being it would be better to build something ugly and functional, than to erect "façade architecture" to front inferior floor plans.'* [10]

Ugly and functional! The search for a new direction meant abandoning prejudices and pre-conceptions about appearance; instead trying to concentrate on generative principles. Duiker did of course care about how his buildings looked - he evidently cared very much - but he did not wish to prejudge them in terms of style and appearance. They would look like what they had to become as the logical result of the design process, and this would be something entirely new. He held apparently similar views to Hugo Häring (Chapter 2), who explicitly saw design as a voyage of discovery, as opposed to a bestowal of forms. Duiker also considered economy of material an important principle, bringing its own defining discipline, but operating at a 'spiritual' level:

'Is not in the end inspiration the basic impulse, not only in technique, but also in the sciences, in every cultural expression, in everything which may operate, in every natural phenomenon? However, the development of this impulse is only of cultural value if the law of economy follows suit. Nature in itself is the manifestation of this cosmic law, because the body in free fall - or the light beam, the explosion, the star on its course, the tension of a building - all follow the shortest way even though there are infinitely more possibilities.... And those who follow the history of technique, of building construction or of some parallel speciality, see that this development not only occurs according to the same law, but also suffers the same initial rejection as culturally unimportant.... Advance is purely a matter of reducing material: thinner columns, larger spans.' [11]

Evidently captivated by the lightness and efficiency of concrete frame construction, Duiker was at the same time obsessed with the health-giving potential of light and air. His description of his Open-air school dwells on the health benefits of solar exposure, with hardly a mention of education. Yet clearly he was also interested in the idea of articulating the programme. At Zonnestraal the social groups are housed in separate pavilions and the mother building has its ground-floor wings dedicated to specific functions. All comes together in the first-floor cruciform room, the social room where everyone meets, which is both elevated in section and central in the organisation of the plan. Also strongly articulated are the various staircases, whose spiral forms are enjoyed as a formal presence while they also work as hinges in the plan. All this is closer in spirit to the ruthless functional articulation of Häring than to the vague and incomplete articulation at Gropius's Bauhaus, tempered by the 'aesthetic' of abstract composition.

As part of Duiker's desire to lay naked the workings of the whole institution, the flue from the boiler house is proudly displayed, with the main circular water tank cantilevered around it. With flat roofs these servicing elements were less easy to hide, but Duiker never wanted to hide them - he went to the opposite extreme. Even the vents on the side roofs of the mother building were allowed to stand proud. All this marks the beginning of an effort to make architecture out of services, a crucial 20th century development. Factories and machines had provided interesting models, but usually without conscious intention, and for purely utilitarian reasons. Ships were also an important source, and contemporary commentators drew parallels between Duiker and Bijvoet's architecture and contemporary steamers.[12] The architects were flattered.

Before his untimely death in 1935, Duiker moved forward with the Open-air school, Cineac cinema and Gooiland hotel. The latter was completed by Bijvoet, who also famously worked with Pierre Chareau on the latter's masterpiece, the Maison de Verre in Paris.[13] But though evidently a good collaborator, Bijvoet seems to have been unable to initiate masterpieces himself, and his late additions to Zonnestraal are disappointing.

Zonnestraal enjoyed a significant role in the development of Modernism. Its most important contemporary influence was on Alvar Aalto, who visited Hilversum in 1928, presumably saw the sanatorium, and possibly met Duiker, while he was planning his own tuberculosis sanatorium at Paimio. Opinions differ on the extent of Aalto's borrowings,[14] but elements at Paimio such as the delicate cantilevered structure, and the prominent flue with its concentric water tank, suggest direct adoption, while even the pivotal use of staircases follows Duiker's practice. This influence is important, not only because Paimio became a more widely known and influential example for later Modernism, but also because it represented a great advance for Aalto, Duiker's junior by eight years. Paimio turned into a key work for the beginning of Aalto's maturity, marking a radical redefinition of his architecture. Zonnestraal has also influenced later generations of architects concerned with lightness and transparency. It was an acknowledged source for Günter Behnisch, for example.[15]

Serving their original purpose, the Zonnestraal buildings had a relatively short life. A decade later, the discovery of antibiotics brought an effective cure for tuberculosis, and enthusiasm for exposing patients to sunlight and air waned. Since its time, the grip of the technical and scientific view on hospital design has remained and increased, but the control of environmental conditions was found to be more easily accomplished by mechanical means. As quantitative standards were established, variations in weather and solar heating came to be regarded as negative and intrusive forces to be banished, rather than positive and health-bringing ones to be sought. Finally it has even become necessary to prove that giving patients a view out has a beneficial effect on their recovery.[16]

As might be expected, the Zonnestraal buildings suffered technical problems of heating, cooling and water penetration, but we must remember in mitigation that Duiker and Bijvoet were taking a step into the unknown and stretching building technology to the limit. The concrete was daringly thin with floors of only 8 cm, and the steel window frames were painted rather than galvanised. By the 1960s the buildings were in dreadful condition, and though the mother building has been restored, parts of the complex have been allowed to remain in a ruinous state. Following the original construction phase, also, piecemeal additions and alterations were made without regard for the initial site strategy, and the original landscape concept was not respected, so it is impossible to experience the complex today as it was intended, unlike the beautifully restored Bauhaus. Yet today, ironically, the technology finally exists to make such buildings weatherproof, and to limit the solar overheating and winter heat loss which made them so impractical. The spatial effects so long admired can now be freely pursued without their former price.

Notes

1. Quoted in Zoetbrood 1984 p.10, translation by Jan Woudstra and the author.

2. See Kirsch 1989, p.186.

3. *Die Auflösung der Städte* was the title of a book by Bruno Taut published in 1920, see next chapter.

4. For theory about pollution see Douglas 1966.

5. The name of the organisation in Dutch refers to its initial source of funding, the recycling of the copper components used to hold diamonds during processing, which had previously been thrown away.

6. Two further floors were quickly added by Duiker, the foundations having been calculated for the extra load. The building was demolished during the Second World War, see Molema 1989, pp. 58-9.

7. See for example *der grundriss errechnet sich aus folgenden faktoren*, teaching material by Hannes Meyer at the Bauhaus, reproduced in Bauhaus catalogue 1968, p. 78.

8. In view of Duiker's anti-aesthetic stance, I do not suggest that he intended this, but it is an outcome of the process. The design and casting of a concrete skeleton as a stage of the building process certainly requires that it be considered as an entity, and like any other task this can be done clumsily or elegantly, developing its own rules and therefore its own aesthetic potential. I am suggesting that the admiration of concrete *'Rohbau'* advances with Duiker.

9. Molema 1989, p.11.

10. Ibid, pp. 13/14.

11. Jan Duiker c. 1932 quoted in Zoetbrood 1984 p. 9, translation by Jan Woudstra and the author.

12. For example, an article about Zonnestraal in *Zentralblatt der Bauverwaltung*, no 49, 1929, p.165, quoted in German in Zoetbrood 1984, p. 10.

13. Bijvoet was officially in partnership with Duiker from 1919 until 1925. He then moved to Paris and worked with Chareau until 1932 (Zoetbrood 1984, p.11).

14. Pearson made the strongest and most detailed case (1978), but Schildt (1986, p. 56) and Weston (1995, p. 54) consider it overstated, since an earlier Aalto design before the presumed visit included certain key features.

15. It emerges visibly in work done around 1970, such as the Rothenburg sports hall, and has continued ever since, acknowledged many times verbally and in print by Behnisch himself. See Blundell Jones 2000, pp. 15, 63.

16. Work by R. S. Ulrich published in Science 1998, 224: pp. 420-421, under the title *View through a window may influence recovery from surgery*. This and similar research is discussed by Bryan Lawson in *Room for improvement*, *Health Service Journal* 20 January 2000, pp. 24-27.

Chapter 5. Bruno Taut: Housing, Berlin-Zehnlendorf 1926

Of all the architects in this book, Bruno Taut has been the most neglected in the English-speaking world, despite having played a major role in the modernist revolution as convener and commentator, having enjoyed one of the most influential architectural jobs in Weimar Berlin, and having produced a good deal of significant work.[1] Three reasons can be suggested. The first is his prominence in the Expressionist Movement, which the first modernist historians, Pevsner and Giedion, regarded as a retrograde tendency.[2] Later historians have pointed out how deeply indebted the 'New Architecture' was to the complex Expressionist phase which left no German Modernist untouched,[3] but even so, much of the prejudice against 'Expressionism' has remained, perhaps because it reflects the underlying polarity between objective and subjective that was the cornerstone of modernist mythology.[4] The second reason for Taut's neglect was his commitment of creative energy during his most successful career phase to social housing. Although central to the development of the Modern Movement and quantitatively the most representative form of modernist work in Weimar Germany, it lost all support at home in 1933,[5] and was not readily re-applicable in the English-speaking world, especially the United States.[6] The third reason was Taut's early death in 1938, after five difficult years of exile which doubtless took their toll. With his housing work crippled by world recession in 1931, he had gone to Moscow in search of new opportunities which he never found, and had to flee the Nazis on his return. He spent a couple of years in Japan, studying and writing about Japanese culture but without commissions,[7] then was invited in 1936 to post-revolutionary Turkey. There he was honoured, built schools and a university, but only two years later asthma got the better of him. Death not only deprived him of a post-war career, but silenced him as spokesman for his times, a role well exploited in late years by his old rival Gropius. The comparison is apposite, for the two men were equally prominent as leaders of the Expressionist phase and went on to head the two institutions in which the new architecture for the new society was most conspicuously seen: the Bauhaus and the leading Berlin building society GEHAG.[8]

Early life

As his story is not well known, the circumstances of Taut's career must be outlined. Born in 1880 in provincial East Prussia, his family was constantly in financial difficulties, which according to his biographer gave him a permanent sympathy for the poor and disadvantaged.[9] After attending the local

1. Bruno Taut, design for the Folkwang school, 1920.

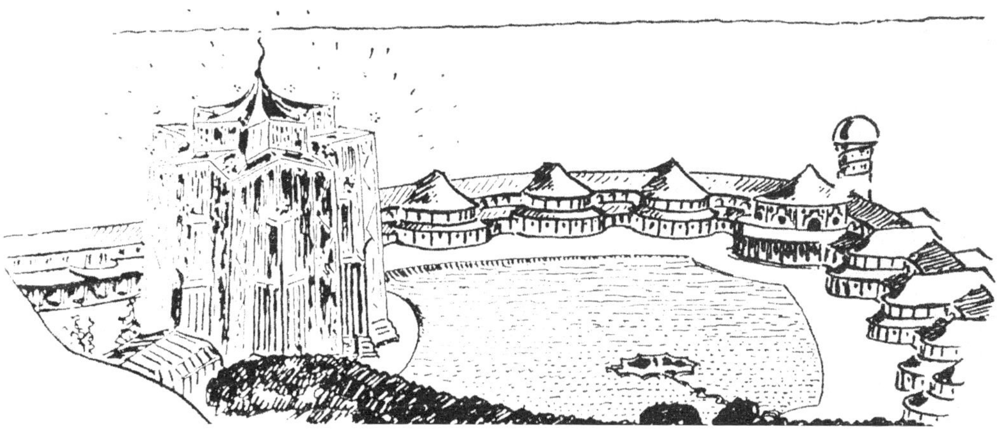

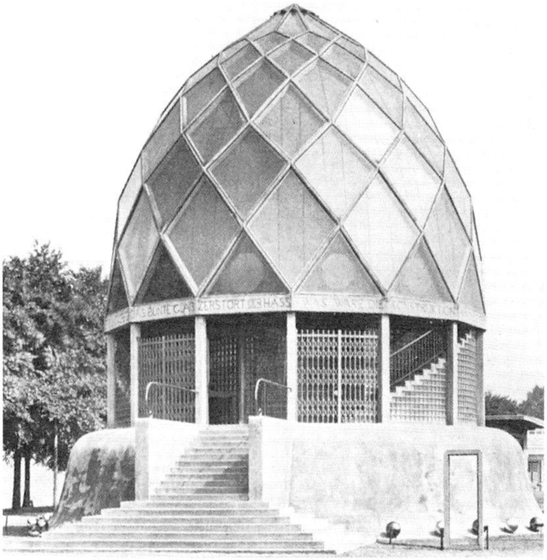

2. Glass Pavilion, Werkbund Exhibition Cologne, 1914.

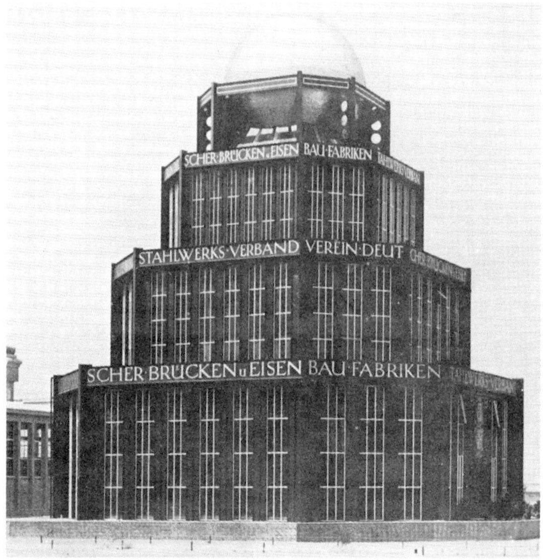

3. Iron Pavilion, Exhibition Leipzig, 1913.

grammar school, he studied building construction while working as an apprentice mason. In 1903, at the age of 23, he gained a place in the Berlin office of Bruno Möhring. He was there only a year, but became involved with the Chorin Circle, a group of writers and intellectuals including the painter Max Beckmann and the critic-to-be Adolf Behne, later to be his supporter and ally.[10] When Möhring's work dried up, Taut moved on to the office of Theodor Fischer in Stuttgart where he spent four years, an encounter of crucial importance for his later work. The South-German master was at the height of his powers. He had risen to fame as leader of the newly-formed planning office for the extension of Munich in 1893, where he put into practice ideas derived from the Austrian planning theorist Camillo Sitte.[11] The starting point was *genius loci*: In his layouts, Fischer rejected the imposition of grids and other abstract geometric figures in favour of working with the shapes and patterns given by lanes, contours and field boundaries. Hierarchical order was given to the streets by grading building heights, and public buildings were placed strategically at nodes or intersections. When it came to designing individual buildings, the contextual aspects were given first priority, which included studying the local styles. This was no question of simple imitation or whimsical eclecticism, but of absorbing the local vernacular and taking it further. Fischer was the teacher not only of Bruno Taut, but also of Hugo Häring (Chapter 2) and Erich Mendelsohn (Chapter 6). Sigurd Lewerentz (Chapter 15) also worked for him briefly. All were left with a deep appreciation of place and a sense of the need to work in specific response to the situation.[12]

The Expressionist phase

When Taut wanted to set up on his own, Fischer gave him jobs. In 1909 he started an office in Berlin with Franz Hoffmann. He became increasingly confident and politically involved, joining the Deutsche Werkbund and also the German Garden City Society. Through the latter, he gained connections with a building society in Berlin-Grünau which gave him his first large housing job at Falkenberg. The simple pitched-roof terrace houses look conventional apart from their strong colouring, but they were designed in close consultation with the inhabitants. Taut relished this participative work and saw Falkenberg as the foundation for all his later housing.[13]

In the same period he discovered a talent as propagandist and convener, joining a progressive circle of artists and writers that met at Herwarth Walden's gallery 'Der Sturm'. They included his friend Adolf Behne, Walter Gropius, Thomas and Heinrich Mann, the playwrights Wedekind and Strindberg, and the novelist Döblin. Walden also started a magazine in which Taut published his first articles. As an architect, Taut became known for a series of exhibition pavilions. These started with a

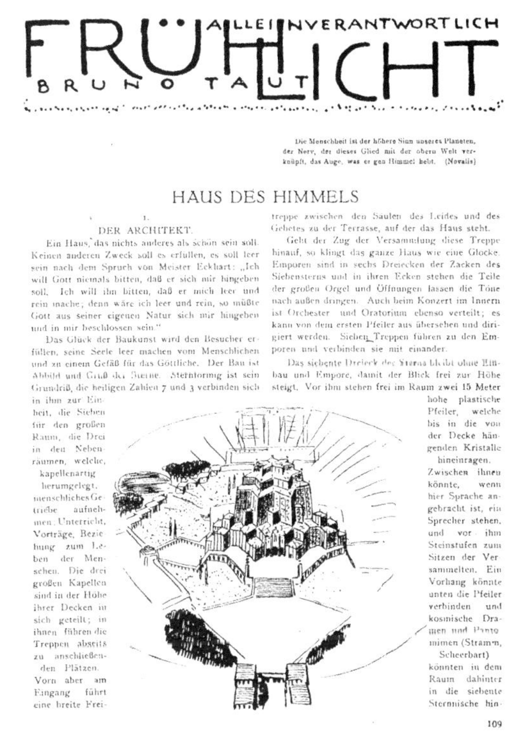

FRÜHLICHT

ALLEIN VERANTWORTLICH BRUNO TAUT

Die Menschheit ist der höhere Sinn unseres Planeten, der Nerv, der dieses Glied mit der obern Welt verknüpft, das Auge, was er gen Himmel hebt. (Novalis)

HAUS DES HIMMELS

1.

DER ARCHITEKT.

Ein Haus, das nichts anderes als schön sein soll. Keinen anderen Zweck soll es erfüllen, es soll leer sein nach dem Spruch von Meister Eckhart: „Ich will Gott niemals bitten, daß er sich mir hingeben soll. Ich will ihn bitten, daß er mich leer und rein mache; denn wäre ich leer und rein, so müßte Gott aus seiner eigenen Natur sich mir hingeben und in mir beschlossen sein."

Das Glück der Baukunst wird den Besucher erfüllen, seine Seele leer machen vom Menschlichen und zu einem Gefäß für das Göttliche. Der Bau ist Abbild und Gruß der Sterne. Sternförmig ist sein Grundriß, die heiligen Zahlen 7 und 3 verbinden sich in ihm zur Einheit, die Sieben für den großen Raum, die Drei in den Nebenräumen, welche, kapellenartig herumgelegt, menschliches Getriebe aufnehmen: Unterricht, Vorträge, Beziehung zum Leben der Menschen. Die drei großen Kapellen sind in der Höhe ihrer Decken in sich geteilt; in ihnen führen die Treppen abseits zu anschließenden Plätzen. Vorn aber am Eingang führt eine breite Freitreppe zwischen den Säulen des Leides und des Gebetes zu der Terrasse, auf der das Haus steht.

Geht der Zug der Versammlung diese Treppe hinauf, so klingt das ganze Haus wie eine Glocke. Emporen sind in sechs Dreiecken der Zacken des Siebensterns und in ihren Ecken stehen die Teile der großen Orgel und Öffnungen lassen die Töne nach außen dringen. Auch beim Konzert im Innern ist Orchester und Oratorium ebenso verteilt; es kann von dem ersten Pfeiler aus übersehen und dirigiert werden. Sieben Treppen führen zu den Emporen und verbinden sie mit einander.

Das siebente Dreieck des Sterns bleibt ohne Einbau und Empore, damit der Blick frei zur Höhe steigt. Vor ihm stehen frei im Raum zwei 15 Meter hohe plastische Pfeiler, welche bis in die von der Decke hängenden Kristalle hineinragen. Zwischen ihnen könnte, wenn hier Sprache angebracht ist, ein Sprecher stehen, und vor ihm Steinstufen zum Sitzen der Versammelten. Ein Vorhang könnte unten die Pfeiler verbinden und kosmische Dramen und Pantomimen (Stramm, Scheerbart) könnten in dem Raum dahinter in die siebente Sternnische hin-

109

4. Opening page of Taut's Magazine Frühlicht, with his design for a crystalline 'House of Heaven'

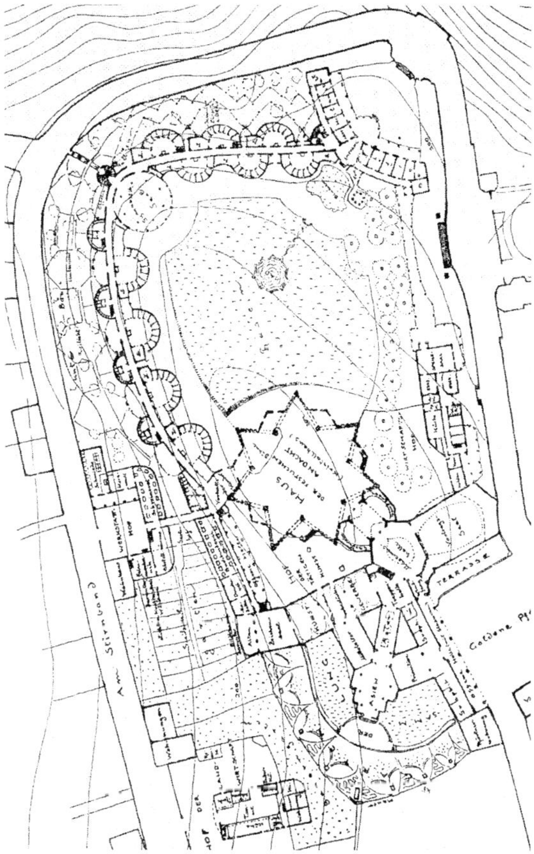

5. (right) Plan of the Folkwang school ,1920.

successful competition entry for the Iron Pavilion in Leipzig of 1913 (fig. 3), a centralised octagonal steel-framed building terminating in a golden sphere. More successful still was the Glass Pavilion at the Werkbund Exhibition in Cologne of 1914 (fig. 2), a double-skinned pointed dome in which Taut tried to use glass in every possible way - as roof, walls, even stair treads - and in every colour. He saw glass not only in technical terms as the ubiquitous building material it has since become, but also as harbinger of a new spiritual enlightenment: the transparent, honest durable, pure, bringer of light.[14] He was encouraged in this by his friend the poet Paul Scheerbart, author of the book *Glasarchitektur*, whose aphorism *'Das bunte Glas zerstört den Hass'* (coloured glass destroys hatred) was inscribed over the pavilion door.[15] The Falkenberg housing and Glass Pavilion show two sides of the 34 year old Taut: on one hand the committed socialist and pioneer of participation who wanted to see architecture as an expression of community and to play down the role of architect as author; on the other the visionary leader using architecture as propaganda to inspire and inflame. Not only were the iron and glass pavilions pioneering in their geometric simplicity and lack of dependence on historical styles; they also showed a theatrical ability to manipulate space and scale.

A convinced pacifist, Taut completed military service in the First World War as building supervisor to a gunpowder factory. He wrote an anti-war manifesto, and when the war was over became a leading figure in the Work Council for the Arts, a left-wing group dedicated to the formation of a new society after the November Revolution. They sought unification of the arts under the umbrella of a glorious new architecture, assuming that the new society would call on them for its buildings and public settings.[16] In the absence of building opportunities, the years 1918-21 were dedicated to manifestoes, visionary sketches and publications. Taut published three books of visionary drawings: *Die Stadtkrone* (The City Crown), *Die Auflösung der Städte* (Dissolution of the cities) and *Alpine*

Architektur, and also some issues of a magazine *Frühlicht* (Dawn). He started a chain correspondence including photostatted sketches with a group of architect friends which he called the *Gläserne Kette* (Glass Chain).[17] The project by Taut that came nearest to construction was the Folkwang School designed for Karl Osthaus at Hohenhagen (figs. 1,5). Had the funds been found to realise this attempt at the 'crystal cathedral', it might have changed the history of Modern Architecture, but the opportunities that eventually came were more pragmatic, appealing to Taut's social and participative side. In 1921, thanks to the votes of workers, Taut gained the post of City Architect at Magdeburg. He made bold proposals but could realise little, and had to content himself mainly by instituting a repainting programme for city facades in strong colours. Again the intention was architecture as propaganda: to cheer people up, make things happen, inspire economic regeneration. Without colour photography, the effect went largely unrecorded, as did the colour schemes of Taut's later housing, restored in recent years only with difficulty and painstaking research.[18]

The Berlin *Siedlungen*

Frustrated by the lack of realisations, Taut leapt at the offer in 1924 to become chief architect for the left-wing Berlin building society GEHAG. With the help of Martin Wagner, who was about to become Berlin City Architect, he instigated and supervised the construction of around 12,000 dwellings before he left the post in 1932. Writing of his experiences later, Taut stressed the teamwork and the value of learning from experience, honing designs for maximum efficiency in space provision and economical construction. There was already an enormous load of bureaucratic criteria to be met: four stages of building control, two of aesthetic control, and in all more than 30 regulators that a project had to pass. The building society leaders were progressive and supportive, but in the early years the conservative city authorities nearly brought works to a halt over the 'outrage' of plain façades and flat roofs. Taut had personally to mollify the retired city architect Ludwig Hoffmann, to get the first part of the Britz scheme through in 1925, and he and Wagner even faced arrest.[19] Even after their victory had paved the way for the cheaper flat roofs, the *Dächerkrieg* (roof war) continued, the traditionalists taking over again when the Nazis came to power.[20]

A pioneer in planning economical dwellings, Taut had written a detailed book on the subject before he arrived at GEHAG. *Die neue Wohnung* (The New Dwelling) of 1924 was dedicated to women in general, inviting them to take a creative role in reorganising their homes to avoid the drudgery of excessive housework. Not surprisingly for the time, Taut begins by condemning the cluttered sentimental furnishing of the 19th century, which he wants cleared away in favour of directness and simplicity, but the argument is made with subtlety, including a historical survey to show that beautiful rooms have been simple and well-coordinated, from 15th century Venice to Japan. They did not need to become empty exhibitions like the traditional front room, which was used only for special occasions. After detailed sections on furnishing and furniture, including room designs by Taut himself, he sums up characteristically:

'What all these examples, and also the old ones, showed, was that a good room does not present itself like a picture, that all its relationships, even that with the sun, first take on meaning when it has us in its embrace, and we really need to be in the room itself to appreciate it, feeling the extent to which it inspires and relaxes us. So we arrive at a paradox: the better the room seems in a picture, taken as it were through a hole in the wall, the more questionable is the room itself, for a good room without inhabitants is nothing and "empty" It is made "full" and given meaning by the act of habitation.'[21]

Taut also gives advice at a more practical level, providing examples of traditional dwelling plans compared with new improved versions. The traditional plan (fig. 6) gave pride of place to the *kalte Pracht* (cold splendour) of the formal front room, with everyday life crammed into the adjacent living/dining room which is supplied with food from the kitchen opposite. Circulation routes (shown as dotted lines) are long and tortuous, and large free-standing cupboards absorb valuable space. There are three heating stoves besides that used for cooking, and jug-filled washstands serve each bedroom. The improved version (fig. 7) has a larger living/dining space linked straight to the well-planned kitchen, and built-in furniture including double-sided cupboards between kitchen and dining. The washstands are abandoned in favour of double bathroom basins with running water, and

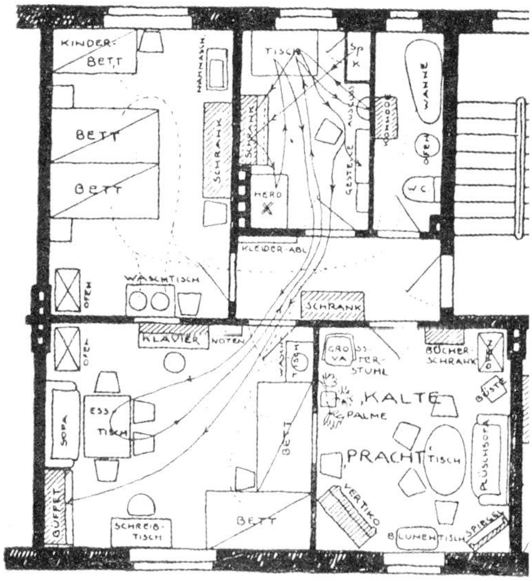

6. Plan of a 'typical flat' from Taut's book *Die neue Wohnung*, 1924, showing circulation problems.

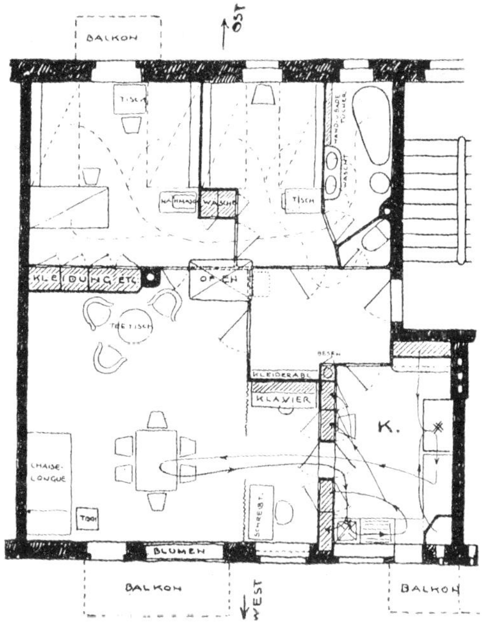

7. Taut's improved version.

there is a separate WC. A central heating stove is shared between rooms; there are folding beds, added balconies, and a double-glazed flower-window in place of the potted palm. The plan dimensions look the same, and the frontage is unchanged, but Taut was able to squeeze the width of the block, reducing floor area and building costs by 5%. In the following pages Taut undertakes the same kind of exercise for his own terrace houses at Falkenberg of 1914, showing how tighter planning and built-in furnishings here too produce a radical reduction of area (figs. 8, 9). He acknowledged a debt to Dutch architects, but much of it was new in Germany, predating by years The New Frankfurt, the Frankfurt kitchen and the CIAM conference on the *Existenzminimum*.[22]

8. (below left) Ground and first floor plans of Taut's terrace houses at Falkenberg.

9. Taut's improved more economical version of 1924.

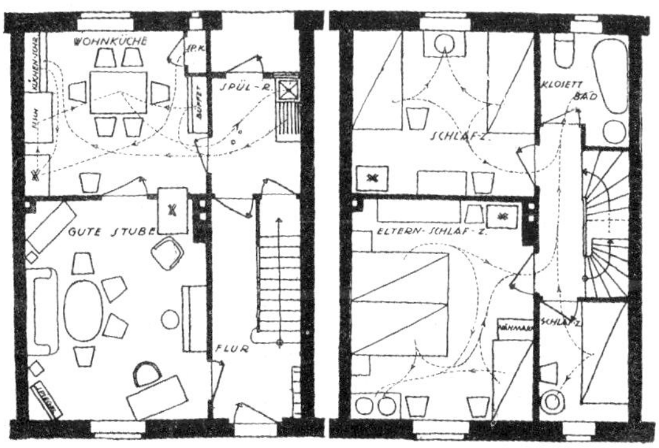

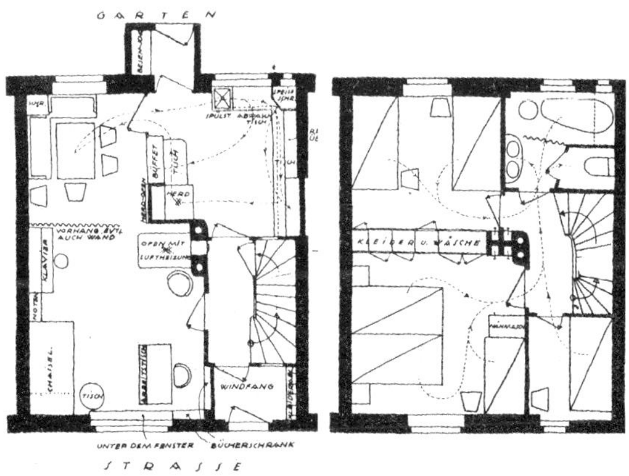

Making a community

If rethinking the dwelling constituted one end of the problem, the other was the question how a *Siedlung* might make sense as a community. Taut had long belonged to the Garden City Society, and the garden city ideal was widespread, along with belief in the virtues of sunlight and air as described in the previous chapter, but Taut's decentralised developments were always also intended to have a community centre or *Stadtkrone*, as seen in his visionary drawings. Not just a Tautian invention of the utopian phase, this *Stadtkrone* further reflected two interests of his teacher Fischer: on one hand the landmark building which takes possession of a place, on the other the community hall or *Volkshaus* which brings the community together.[23]

Taut's *Stadtkrone* idea was most effectively realised at the Horseshoe Estate in Britz, so-called because of the horseshoe-shaped space on which it was centred. This was a formal park with pond and pedestrian path surrounded by a curved block of housing. The flat end of the horseshoe was left open with a great flight of steps to form an entrance. To either side, Taut set blocks containing shops, restaurant and other community facilities, thus giving the large estate both a physical and a social centre. For 'rationalist' architects such as Gropius, there seemed no reason to break away from the serried ranks of *Zeilenbau* development, identical houses in identical rows at the optimum orientation, revealing only the sheer logic of the method. But Taut had already understood the numbing effects of repetition and the consequent problems of scale, which he sought to avoid. He criticised his opponents for being so one-dimensional:

'One of the foremost fashionable theories of that time was Zeilenbau. *It was not really new: people merely rediscovered the benefits of getting sun into a dwelling. But having rediscovered it, these people insisted that all houses without exception be lined up in parallel rows with north-south orientation like lines on a notepad or soldiers on parade, regardless of whether the site was a hillside, a natural basin with a pond like the Horseshoe at Britz, a stand of trees, a hollow or river-bed, an existing road or whatever. Only the sun, which in Germany shines on average one day in three, existed for these people, not the wind nor the rain. Some medical experts claimed the course from east to west was the optimum, so one side of the house*

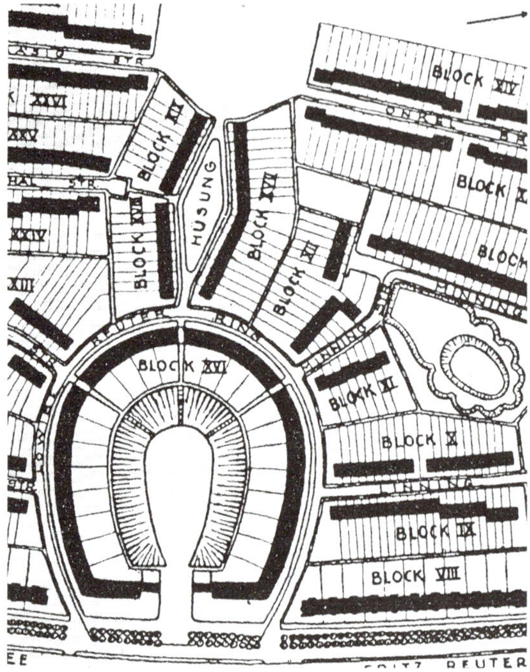

10. Part of the site plan for the Hufeisensiedlung (Horseshoe Estate), at Berlin-Britz 1930. The central horseshoe figure surrounded an existing pond.

11. (below) Part of the wall of housing around the central horseshoe, showing three storeys of flats and the private gardens between building and public path.

12. (opposite top) General site plan of Taut's *Waldsiedlung* at Onkel Toms Hütte, Berlin Zehlendorf 1926, with the curved U-Bahn running across the middle. Streets at south end had terrace houses by Häring and Salvisberg, the rest was by Taut.

13. (opposite bottom) Detailed plan of northern part showing varied building and facade types (from Pitz & Brenne 1980).

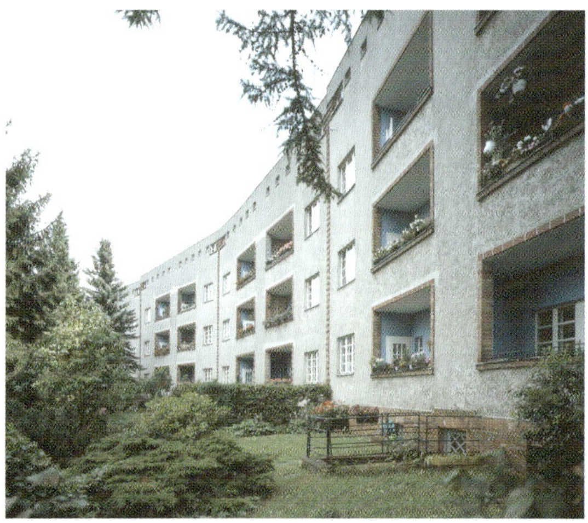

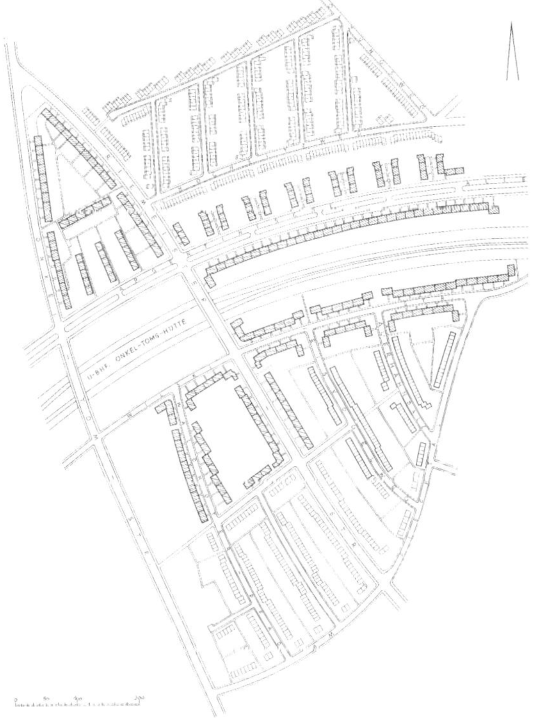

must face directly south. Others held that a slight deviation from full south was better. Those like us who built continuously, and who observed one fashionable theory give way to another, recognised that each theory may have some truth, but not the whole truth. In GEHAG we certainly used Zeilenbau, *but at the same time in the same housing scheme we also had normal border development along the roads. Our buildings were never intended as experiments to test a theory: rather they had to be liveable and comfortable in their grouping and in their courts, streets and squares.'*[24]

Taut mentions almost in passing here qualities of landscape and context that no disciple of Fischer could ignore. The terrain as found was always an essential inspiration. Earlier in the same essay, he discusses the landscape in Zehlendorf where the *Waldsiedlung* was to be built:

'A beautiful woodland area was to be built upon. When this became known the locals started to object: "they're going to put ugly modern boxes with flat roofs in our beautiful wood". How could we convince the public and officials that woods and nature can harmonise not only with pitched roofs but also with flat ones? The special beauty of that wood lay in the fact that between the usual rows of pines beautiful mature birches had grown up.

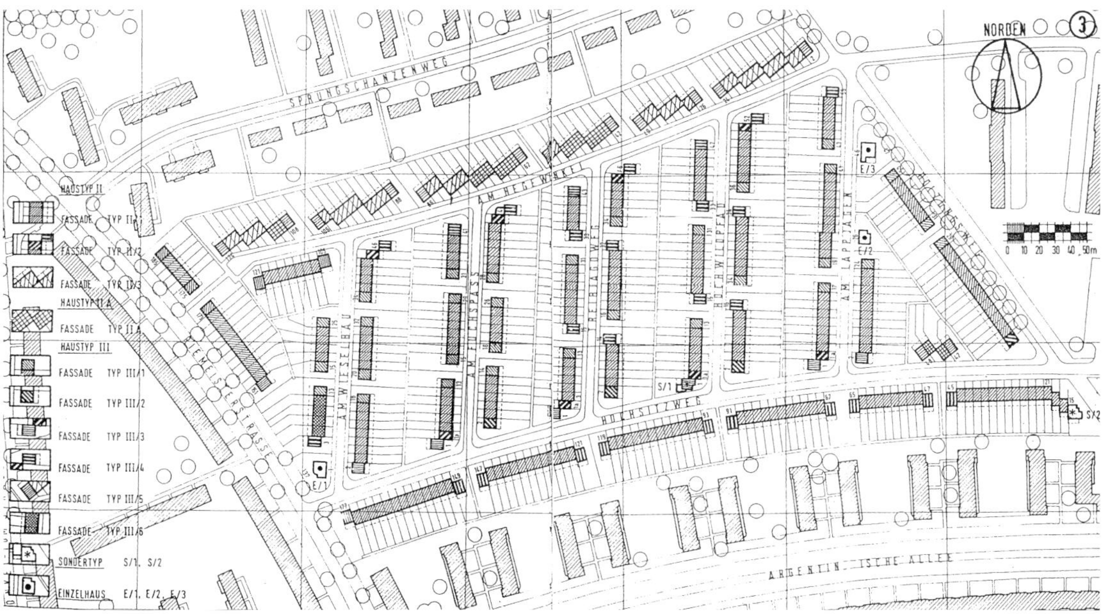

We organised the plan so that none of these birches would have to be cut, but when we delivered our plan to the local authority, an official revealed that the longest and most beautiful line of birches had to be cut as they stood in the path of the projected main road. Nothing could be done: the road crossing had been set out and a trench made for the rainwater drain. Without knowing it this official had helped us. Even before building the wood could not be saved; it had long ago been sold for the purpose, before our building society inherited it. We became the saviours of the beautiful wood from the local authority, finding support from the Greater Berlin authority and the government. So we came to be trusted when we showed that flat roofs would leave the crowns of the trees visible, while pitched ones would conceal them. The development was realised ...and soon found recognition even among our former critics.' [25]

Waldsiedlung in detail

To see in more detail how Taut worked, we shall look at a part of the *Waldsiedlung* at Onkel Toms Hütte completed in 1929 consisting of 416 houses on a series of streets to the north of Argentinische Allee (fig. 13).[26] Part of a larger development plan, it contains no shops or other community facilities like the Horseshoe of Britz: they are placed instead on the main streets nearby and around the U-Bahn station. The area considered is a residential backwater consisting entirely of small family houses with gardens. The houses are three-storey terrace types with flat roof and cellar, a 5 metre frontage (large variants 6.25 m) and 8.5 metres deep. The apparent simplicity of the basic house-plan (fig. 19) is deceptive, for every centimetre is made to count. Planned as tightly as possible, the stair shrinks as storey height reduces. Bathroom and first floor landing are as tight as possible. The remaining space divides into a large and a small room - living and kitchen on ground floor, large and small bedroom on first, another large bedroom and attic on second. Kinked to produce niches for furniture and shelves, the partition wall also swallows flues and service ducts. Great attention is given to threshold conditions front and back, the porch typically raised two or three steps for privacy from the street, while the rear has a paved veranda one step above garden level. The provision of flank walls, glazed roof and paved floor make this veranda almost an extra room. The change in scale of the house between two-room front and the one-room rear sets the basis of the façade treatment.

14. Typical side-street of terrace houses, with green façades facing east (left) and red façades west.
15. (opposite top) Block of flats on the main street on the west (left) of the detailed site plan.
16. (opposite bottom) Typical terrace houses with original colours restored.

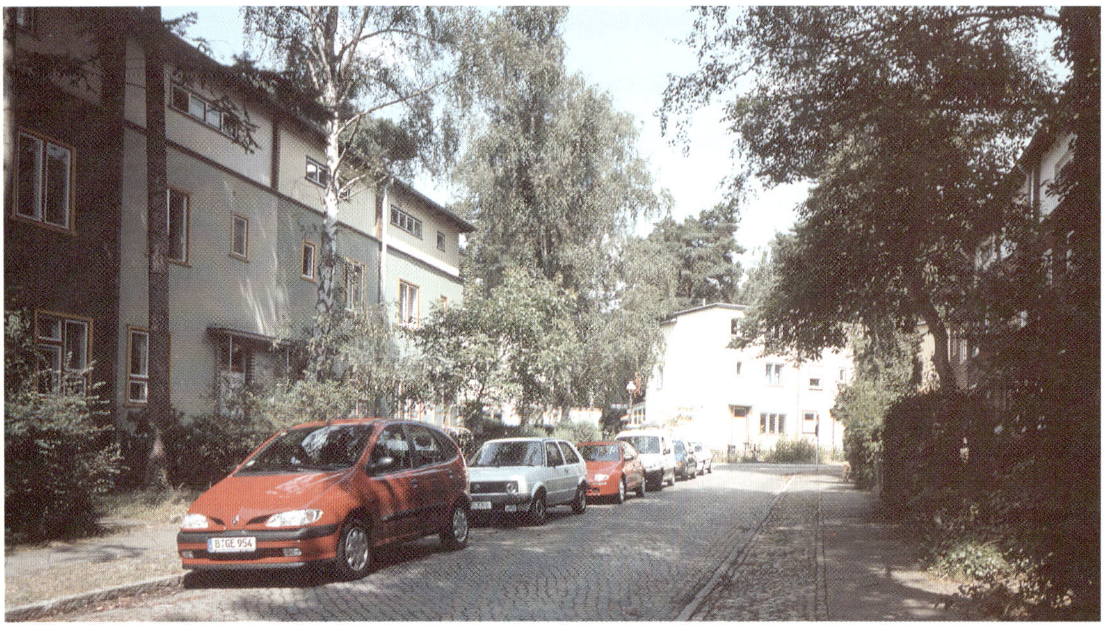

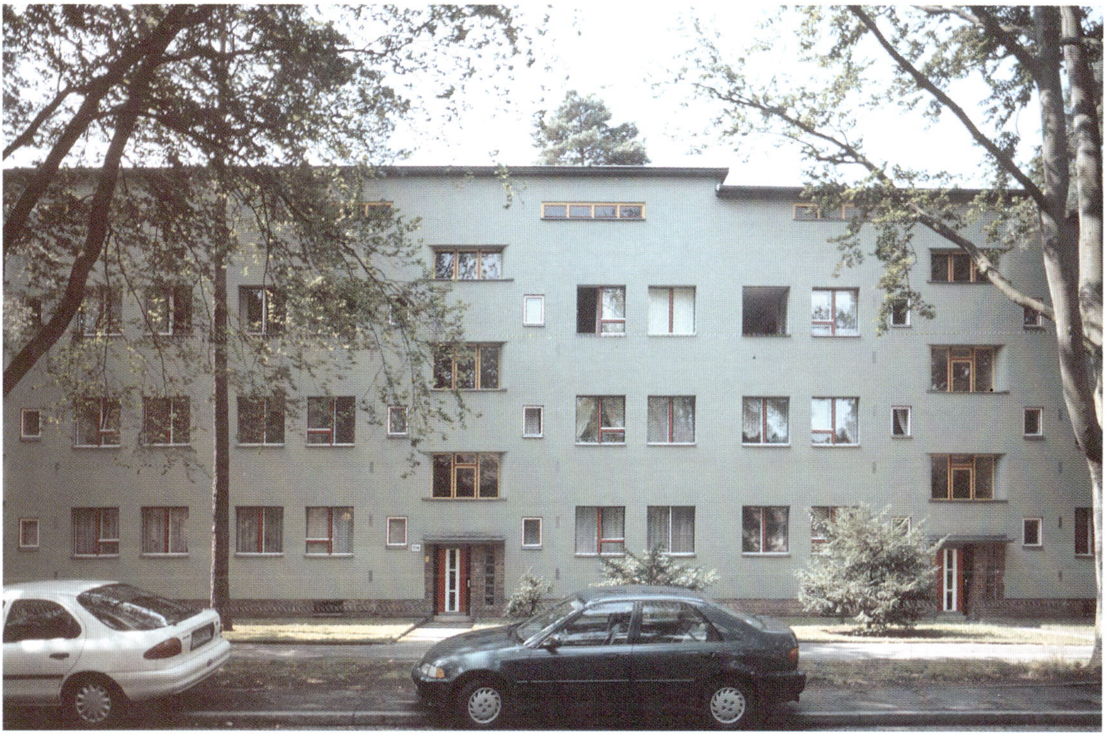

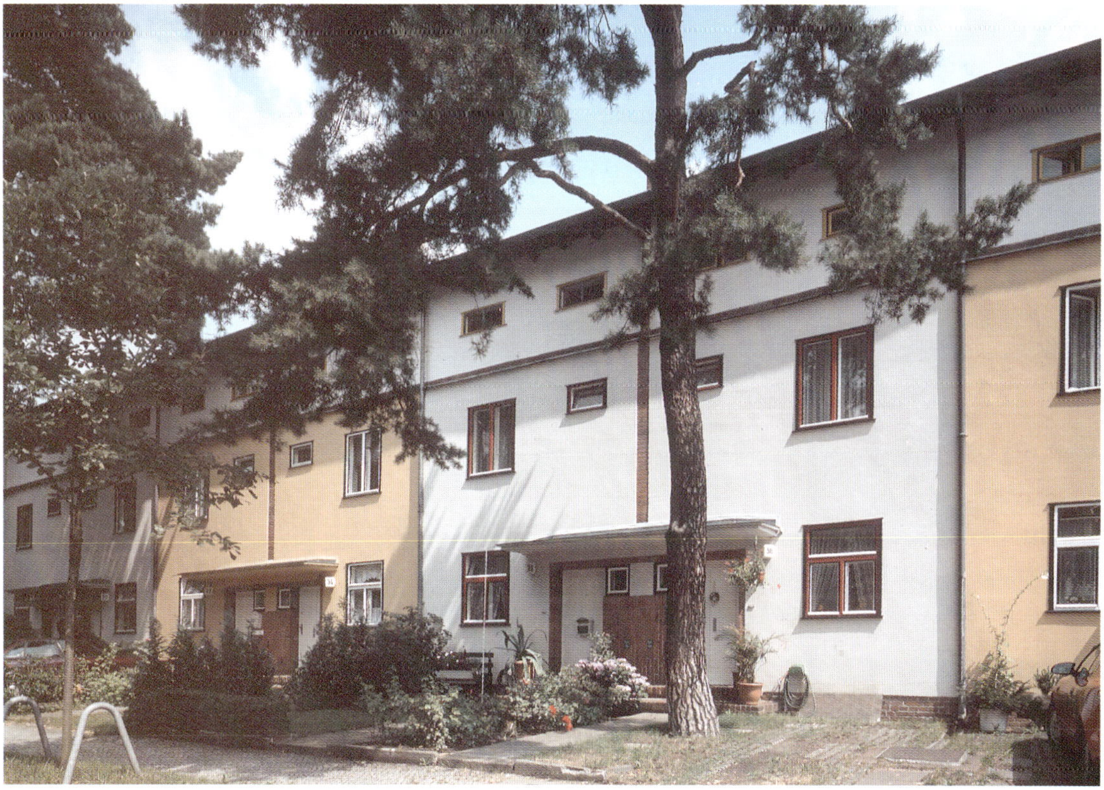

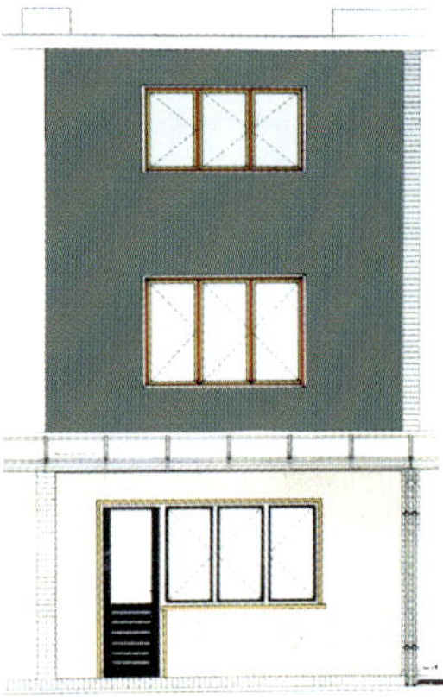

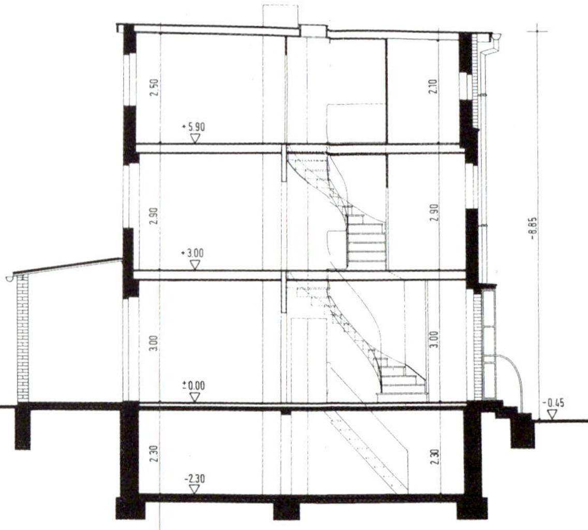

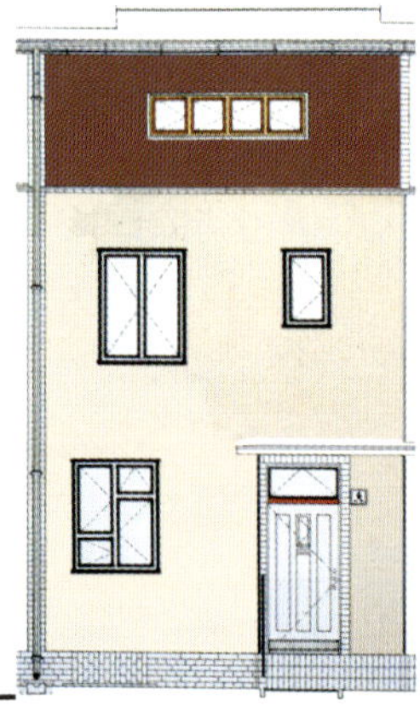

17. (top left) Rear façade with centralised windows and glazed porch, upper floors dark and ground floor white to enhance effect of light.

18. (top middle) Section of house, street side is to right.

19. (bottom) Plans of cellar, ground, first and second floors starting left. Street side is bottom.

Key:
1. cellar
2. laundry
3. kitchen
4. living/dining
5. bedroom
6. bathroom
7. attic

20. (above right) Street façade with asymmetrical fenestration, door paired with neighbour and attic storey picked out with a change of colour and small window. Party wall lines are marked alternately by rainwater pipe and projecting brick course.

21. (opposite) A typical house restored to its original colours. The minor variations in relation to the façade drawing above are typical of the small changes introduced by Taut as the scheme was built.

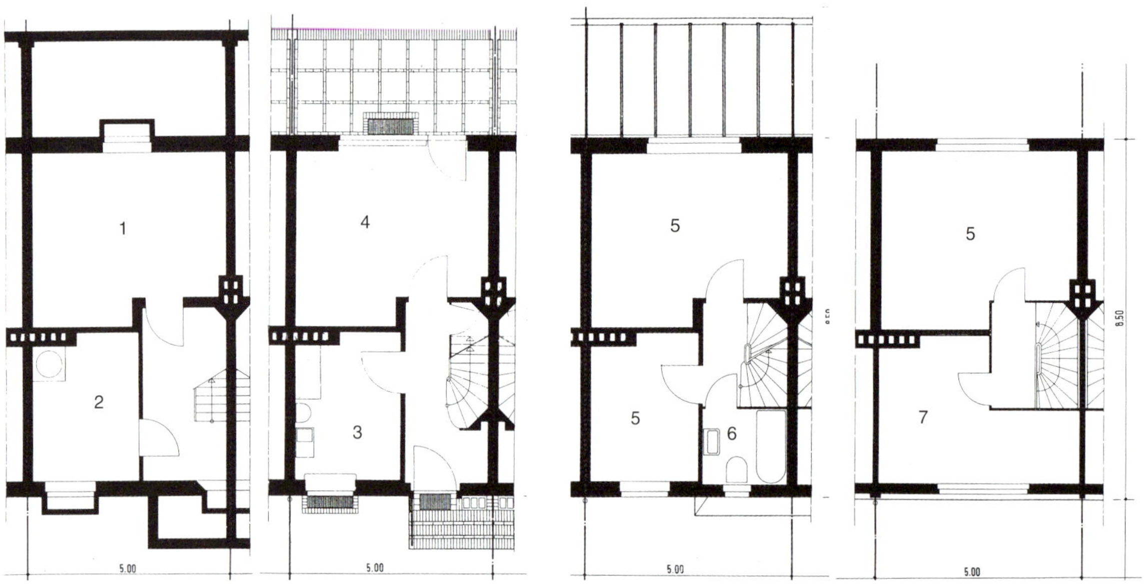

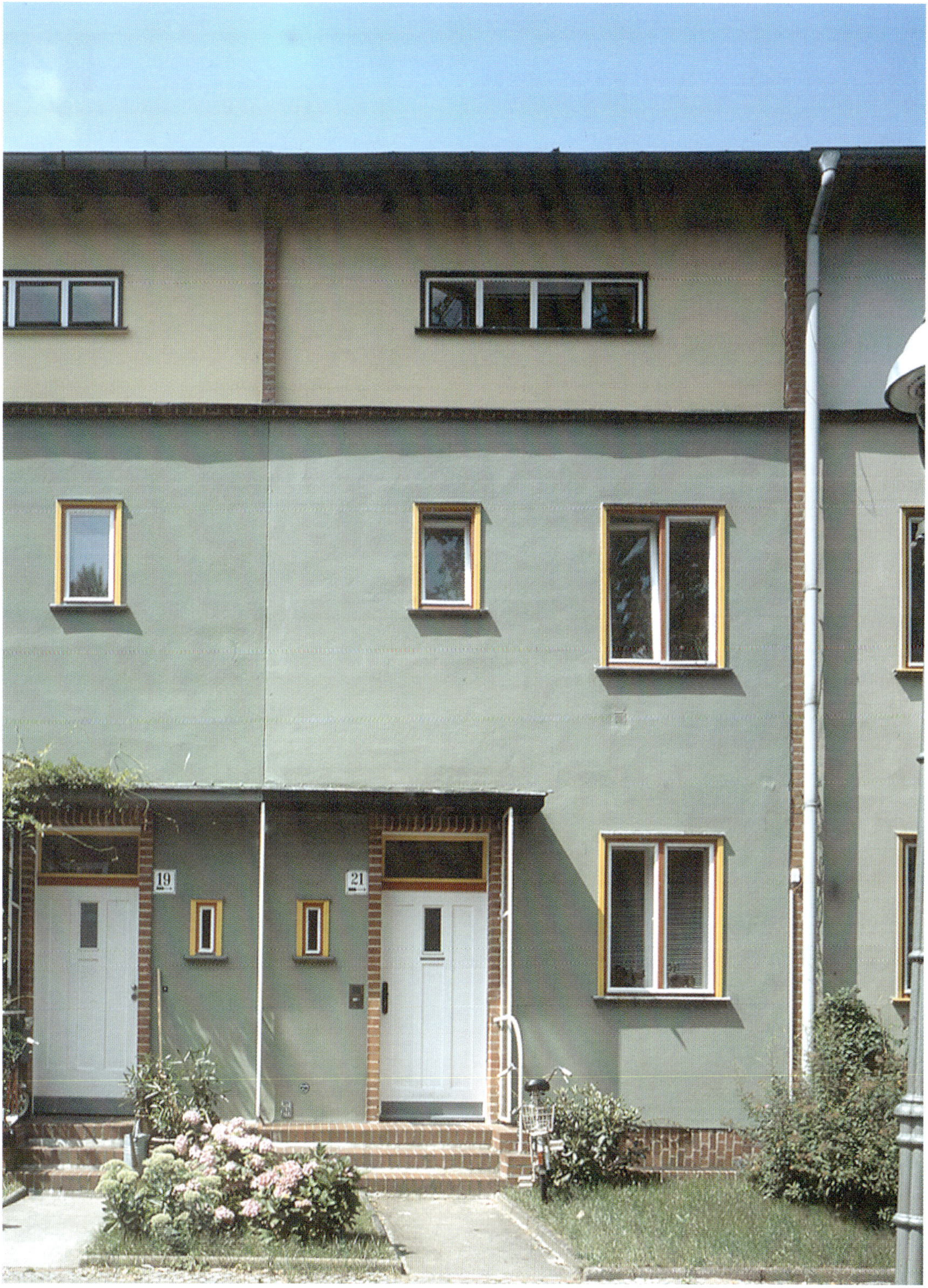
19
21

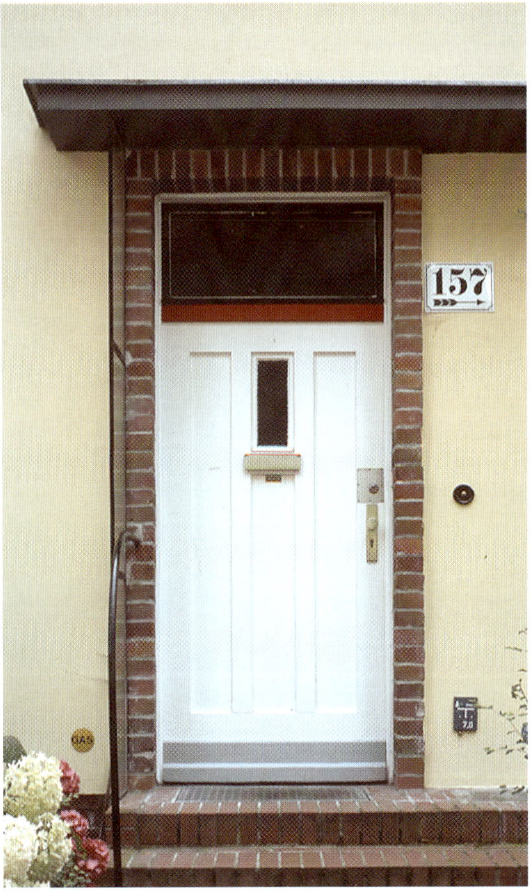

22. Typical entrance with brick surround, steps and canopy.

Façades

Large rooms have large windows with three vertical lights, small rooms smaller ones of two lights or one. Bathrooms have small single lights for privacy, attics the smallest lights of all, if sometimes aligned in a row. Tiny windows set in brickwork between the front doors of some houses (fig. 21) help light the vestibule as well as making the scale more intimate - the porch becomes almost an aedicule. Generally speaking, the plan arrangement does reveal itself externally. Full-width rooms with centrally-placed windows give a larger scale and looser rhythm to the garden side, the apparent height of the block being reduced visually by the projecting glazed roof of the veranda. On the front the scale is reduced by the smaller windows, while the attic storey is differentiated by a step-back the depth of one brick and a radical change of colour. The effect is of a two storey building with an added mansard-like roof storey. Kitchen and bedroom windows, though identical in size, are not vertically aligned. This is partly to distance the kitchen window from the door, partly to illuminate the long side-wall with sink and stove. A series of further effects arises through the left/right handing of houses in the row. In plan this allows their flues and ducts to combine, and places bathroom by bathroom, kitchen by kitchen. In elevation it has little effect on the garden side but enormous impact on the street, most obviously through the sharing of entrance steps and porches. It is possible to read a pair of houses as a single body with central entrance, a reading enhanced in places by colouring the houses in pairs (fig.16). But it is also possible to pair them the other way, centring on the field of wall between the doors. This ambiguity adds visual interest and is kept alive throughout the *Siedlung* by alternating the treatment of the vertical line at party walls. If one shows a 225 mm strip of exposed brickwork, the next has a simple groove scored in the render, the third again brick. The effect of the groove is sometimes strengthened by the rainwater pipe, which again occurs on alternate wall-lines.

Limited and careful use of good brickwork proved a surprisingly effective way to generate an impression of quality. Most of the structure could be roughly built of cheap brick and rendered over, but the courses of wall meeting the ground as base, the entrance steps and door surrounds, suddenly show the solidity and texture of good quality brick. It is made three-dimensional by mere centimetres of projection beyond the wall surface. The same principle applies to the brick strips delimiting storeys or marking party walls and other such things. Paving the veranda floor with squares of brick filled out in concrete was at once clever, attractive and economical.

Theme and variations

Of crucial importance to the overall effect is the variation of house types. The estate is entirely composed of terrace houses, but with variations depending on orientation and juxtaposition. Pitz and Brenne's analysis identifies six main plan types plus three types of free-standing special. The basic site layout (fig.13) acknowledges the gently curving road grid by following it with two curved east-west streets, then creates five short linking streets which run precisely north-south. Houses lining these streets have façades facing east and west, street-front looking to street-front and garden to garden, the long thin gardens being divided by a narrow access path. The street bordering the south edge of the development is built only on its south side, its houses' street façades facing north and their gardens south. The street bordering the northern edge, in contrast, has houses in staggered groups: these turn their garden faces north-west to avoid pure north. Nowhere are houses allowed to make oppressively long rows. Instead, they break into groups of a dozen or so, with tower-like end houses stepped forward or back (made tower-like not by adding a storey but by omitting the step and colour change between middle and top floors). Visual openings occur opposite the ends of north-south streets, and special single houses, some free-standing, occupy street corners and odd spaces. Trees were preserved wherever possible, and changes in ground level allow houses to step or entrance heights to vary along the street. As a result of these measures every street and corner has a unique character, but construction remained manageable on an essentially repetitive system.

Colour

The ubiquitous render was always meant to be coloured as in all Taut's Berlin housing, and at Onkel Tom he instituted one of his most sophisticated colour schemes. The strong reds, blues, greens, and yellows are certainly a surprise in comparison with the chromatic neutrality of most buildings, but the great revelation for first-time visitors to Taut's *Siedlung* is the extraordinary effect of contrasting colours on the window frames. They stand slightly proud of the wall with an outer frame covering the junction with the render, and Taut ordered that the three frames - outer cover, main fixed frame and opening light - should be painted differently. These were typically white/red/yellow or yellow/black/white, and in the lighter façades even black/white/black. The effect is extraordinarily powerful, turning the window into a graphic device and creating harmonies with the dominant colour on the large area of render. Taut had various theories to support his colour policy. In the east-west streets he sought to match the cool morning light with green and the warm evening light with red, while north-facing façades were brightened up with yellow and end walls treated in a contrasting blue. Furthermore, Taut claimed that the use of dark colours on the garden sides of the terrace made the wall recede and the space seem larger. Making the colour of the wall within the glazed veranda lighter than that of the wall above would make the veranda space seem relatively brighter. Without the availability of colour photography, Taut's experiments were only recorded with great difficulty, and within a few years the results were repressed by the buildings being painted over. Only recently, with the work of architects such as Günter Behnisch, has the astounding effect of such strong colour been explored again.[27]

Conclusion: visions or buildings?

Bruno Taut was by nature a 'boundless idealist', always eager to adopt a social cause,[28] and his career was much shaped by political events. His most significant jobs were due to his known left-wing stance and trades-union connections. Although changing in style and detail, the driving idea behind his work was always 'a new architecture for a new society', whether it took the form of the drawn and written visions and fantasies with which he impelled the Expressionist Movement of 1918 - 1920 or the built housing schemes a decade later. Although the visions could suggest the reshaping of a whole landscape and even an architecture of the stars, there were also semi-realistic projects like the Folkwang school.

It is clear from what he built before 1914 that Taut was no innocent who changed his tune when he discovered the realities of the building site: the visionary drawings and the buildings, though interrelated, served different purposes. The former, drawn for his books and circulated as part of the Glass Chain correspondence, are at once icons of hope and vehicles for exploring a new world. Made at a time of physical and economic hardship, with great political changes afoot and with no possibility of professional engagement, they confirm the victory of the spirit and share the Utopia to come. They must have been deeply reassuring to Taut's circle of friends, spurring them on to dream and speculate in turn. The new architecture would come about in tandem with the new society: it had to be different from what had gone before, both technologically and socially, but what would it be like? Nobody knew. The sketches were necessarily tentative: they could only hint at possibilities, clear the air of preconceptions. When real opportunities arrived, conditions were more sober, the new society realisable only within technical, economic and bureaucratic limits. The product was no longer an image to inspire friends, allies and clients, no longer a page in a personal scrapbook, but an inhabited place. For Taut and others of his generation like Hans Scharoun, the essential reality of architecture lay in social relationships rather than aesthetic experience by proxy in drawings or photographs.

Notes

1. There is still no comprehensive monograph on Taut available in the English language, as neither Junghanns 1970 nor Speidel 1995 has yet been translated, nor has the highly informative Akademie der Künste catalogue of 1980. This is not to denigrate Iain Boyd Whyte's important monograph on Taut and Activism of 1982, but his book is limited in time span, concentrates on social and political aspects rather than the architectural work, and does not concern the Berlin *Siedlungen*.
2. There was a prevailing tendency among 20th century historians to see Taut, Scharoun and even Häring as persistent representatives of Expressionism while playing down the influence of the Expressionist phase on Gropius and Mies, who had apparently rejected this heresy. For Pevsner, Expressionism was *'the craving of architects for individual expression, the craving of the public for the surprising and the fantastic, and for an escape out of reality into a fairy world'* Pevsner 1960, p. 217.
3. For example, Whyte 1982, p. 223.
4. It should scarcely be necessary to argue now that the association of Expressionism with subjectivity and the later New Architecture with objectivity is an oversimplification so far from the truth as to be obstructive. Readers will gather from other chapters why I consider the claims to scientific objectivity made on behalf of Gropius no more sustainable than the claims that architects like Taut and Scharoun were just indulging personal whims. Not only were both of the latter politically committed, seeing their work as an expression of society: it was also received as such.
5. The left-wing building societies that built and maintained such housing during the Weimar period were immediately disbanded by the Nazis, and the housing blocks themselves condemned as 'un-German' or as examples of 'culture-bolshevism'. The well-organised maintenance stopped, colour schemes were gradually painted over, the example suppressed. Nazi mass housing went back to pitched roofs, grey walls and enforced rustic homeliness. For further reading see Lane 1968.
6. There were of course numerous public housing schemes based on Modernist examples built in England and the USA after 1945, but by then a more limited modernist ideology was established and Taut's work was largely forgotten.
7. For an account of Taut's Japanese years see Speidel 1995, pp. 270-273.
8. GEHAG, Gemeinnützige Heimstätten- Spar- und Bau-Aktiengesellschaft.
9. Kurt Junghanns in Akademie de Künste 1980, p. 7.
10. Whyte 1982, p. 7, Akademie de Künste 1980, p.152.
11. Sitte published *Der Städte-Bau nach seinen künstlerischen Grundsätzen* (Town-planning according to its artistic principles) in Vienna in 1889. For an English version see Collins 1965. Taut knew of Sitte's theories before he came to Fischer, from lectures by Goecke in Berlin (Junghanns in Akademie der Künste 1980, pp. 7-14).
12. The best German source on Fischer is Winfried Nerdinger's monograph (Nerdinger 1988). The only accounts I know in English are Nerdinger's article in *The Architectural Review* November 1986, pp. 61-65, and my own Masters of Building article in *Architects Journal* of 12th April 1989, pp. 38-55.
13. Taut *Siedlungsmemoiren*, Akademie der Künste 1980 p. 204.
14. On the mythology of crystal see Pehnt 1970, pp.73-80.
15. Unfortunately after the exhibition the pavilion was destroyed, blown up by the army to reduce demolition costs. It was however reconstructed as a scale model and extensively photographed for a Berlin exhibition, see Thiekötter 1994.
16. There is no room here for a detailed exposition of the Expressionist movement and its very complicated roots. The best general source is Pehnt 1970, and for further detail on the cultural background Whyte 1982.
17. The correspondence is available in translation, see Whyte 1985.
18. See Pitz & Brenne 1980, pp.158-165, also Brenne *Die intelligente Farbe - Mit Farben bauen* in Speidel 1995, pp. 228-231.
19. Taut *Siedlungsmemoiren*, Akademie der Künste 1980 pp. 204-211.
20. The rival GAGFAH building society built a pitched roof development right next to the Onkel Tom Siedlung called Im Fischtal with houses by a more conservative faction of architects, notably Paul Schmitthenner, who was to enjoy a prominent role under the Nazis. See Posener 1992, pp.172, 238-240.
21. Taut 1924 pp. 53-55, my translation.
22. For a good summary of The New Frankfurt see Bullock 1978.
23. While Taut was still working for him, Fischer wrote a prescription of what such a community hall might be, entitled *'What I would like to build'*. The concept was to some extent realised in his Pfullinger Hallen and Cornelianum at Worms. See Nerdinger 1988.
24. Taut *Siedlungsmemoiren* (1936) Akademie der Künste 1980 p. 209, my translation.
25. Ibid. p. 206.
26. The raw material for the analysis that follows was derived from Pitz & Brenne 1980, also the source for many of the illustrations. Winfried Brenne has been responsible for many restorations of Taut housing.
27. Perhaps Günter Behnisch is an obvious example for me as I have visited and written about many of his buildings (Blundell Jones 2000), but I can report that he and his colleagues have been much taken up with the question of colour in the last ten years, collaborating with artists, and that the work is unthinkable without it. Behnisch has published a book *On colour*, Gerd Hatje, 1993.
28. Kurt Junghanns in Akademie de Künste 1980, p. 7.

Chapter 6. Erich Mendelsohn: Schocken Department Store, Stuttgart 1927

Erich Mendelsohn was another German Modernist who has received less attention than his due. Although not as neglected in the English-speaking world as Bruno Taut, his career was broken by the same historical circumstances, his reputation damaged by the same kind of historical misinterpretation. Mendelsohn first made his name with a series of distinctive sketches drawn during the First World War and exhibited in the Paul Cassirer Gallery, Berlin, in 1919. He was lucky enough around the same time to gain the prestigious commission for the Einstein Tower in Potsdam when, due to economic collapse, almost no architectural work was to be had. This became the best-known built work of the Expressionist phase in German Architecture and launched Mendelsohn on a meteoric rise to fame. By 1924 he had built enough for *Wasmuths Monatshefte*, the leading Berlin architecture monthly, to publish a 67 page retrospective, something granted to no other Modernist at that time.[1] By 1930 he had the largest office and most prestigious jobs of any German Modernist, was seen as a technical pioneer, and in Germany at least had become a leading figure. He also invented internationally influential models for two evolving building types: the department store and the cinema. But Mendelsohn was a Jew and so were most of his clients. This not only meant he was obliged to leave Germany in 1933 and start again: it also contributed to the destruction of many of his buildings, including the one studied in this chapter. A handful of works were destroyed for ideological reasons by the Nazis,[2] others were bombed, but some of the most important survived the war only to be demolished in the 1950s. Columbus Haus on Potsdamerplatz in the East sector of Berlin was demolished after riot damage in 1953. The Schocken store in Stuttgart survived the war and there was protest when plans for demolition were lodged in the 1950s, but to no avail. The Schocken family and the ethos of their business were long gone. The new owners, Merkur, wanted to update, and took as their architect Egon Eiermann, a leading figure of the time. He should have known better, for he did not produce an inspiring replacement.[3] Industrial and commercial premises certainly date more quickly than other building types and tend in general to be short-lived, but the impression remains that Mendelsohn's oeuvre in Germany has not been loved.

As for the architect, in 1933 he sought new fields in which to work. He came to Britain, won the competition for the De la Warr Pavilion in Bexhill with Serge Chermayeff and built a couple of houses, but did not gain further commissions. He worked to more effect in Palestine, producing a hospital, a bank and a couple of good houses, but again he was dissatisfied, and though a committed Zionist, found the political atmosphere oppressive. With war spreading he moved on to the United States in 1941. There he built a house, a clinic and most importantly a series of synagogues, the best being that at Cleveland, Ohio. But he made little impact on the American scene, and certainly nothing to compare with Mies or Gropius. Deprived of his Berlin context, his network of cultured and sympathetic clients, his assistants, engineers and technologists, he was unable to innovate as he had in Germany. His struggles seem to have contributed to an early death from cancer in 1953.

1. Mendelsohn sketch for a film studio, 1914.

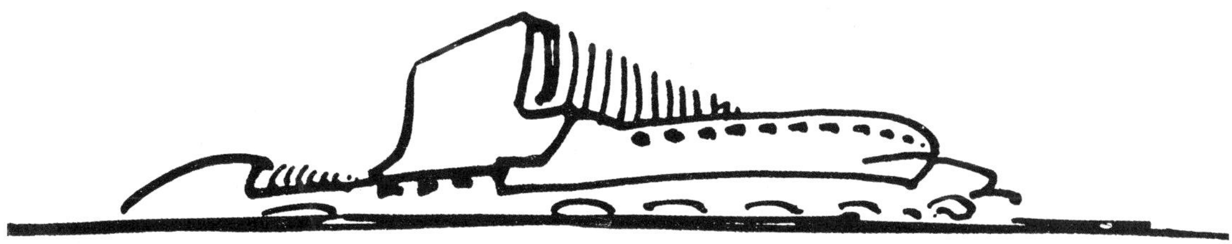

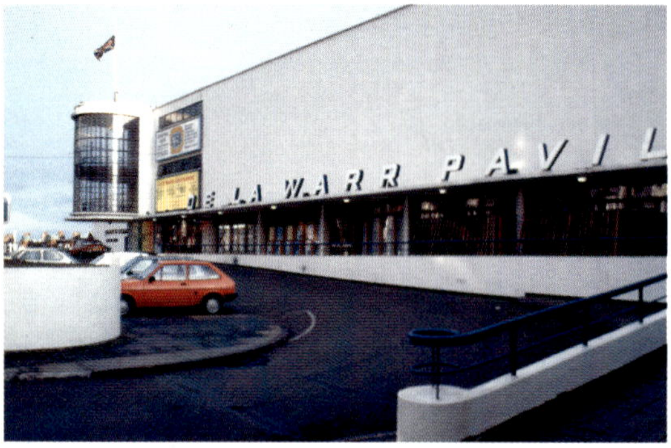

2. Mendelsohn and Chermayeff, De la Warr Pavilion, Bexhill 1934-35.

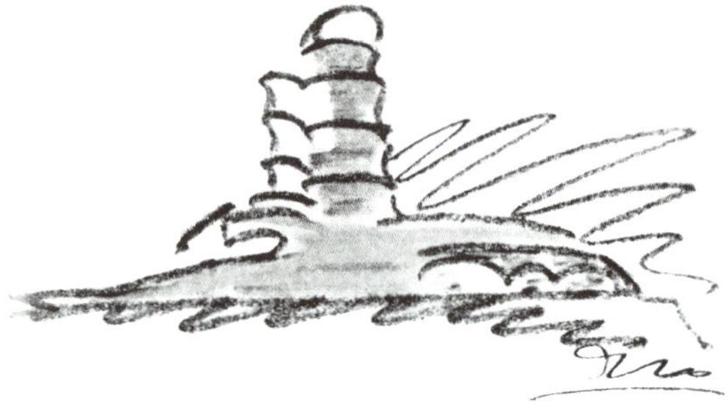

3. Einstein tower, preparatory sketch 1919.

Ideologically Mendelsohn suffered, like Taut, from the after-effects of being a prominent figure in the Expressionist period. The Einstein Tower, which brought him early success and seemed excitingly dynamic when completed, looked dated by the end of the decade. His interest in curves and flowing forms, however much functionally based, was interpreted in the era of 'objectivity' as wilful and subjective. As with Taut, Häring and Scharoun, the use of a broader formal vocabulary including skews and curves opposed the aesthetic conformity that grew with the declaration of the 'International Style'. Mendelsohn's sketches too proved a liability: his ability to evoke the idea for a building in a few lines, while thrillingly prophetic in 1919, could also provoke the mistaken assumption that this simple gesture was the whole story. As we shall see, the sketches have a complex relation to the built work, and often the best ones came after rather than before construction. They are very limited as representations of the buildings, for Mendelsohn was a skilled three-dimensional planner who worked his buildings through and through, interested in context, structural framing, spatial sequence, the signalling role of façades, technical detail and much else besides. From a 21st Century perspective, his work is no less 'objective', hard-headed or functionalist than that of any other Modernist: indeed, his building process was quick and efficient, and in purely pragmatic terms his works could be called more successful than those of Le Corbusier, his precise contemporary and the subject of the next chapter.

Early career

Mendelsohn was born in 1887 in remote Allenstein, East Prussia. After dabbling in economics,[4] he went to study architecture in Berlin in 1908, then moved to Munich in 1910, where he was taught by Theodor Fischer, whose significance was discussed in the last chapter (p. 86).[5] Like Taut, he learned from Fischer the importance of responding to context and of taking a creative attitude to irregularities, both of which are evident throughout the later work. Munich was a major artistic centre, and there Mendelsohn had contact with the Blaue

4. Einstein tower, Potsdam near Berlin, 1920.

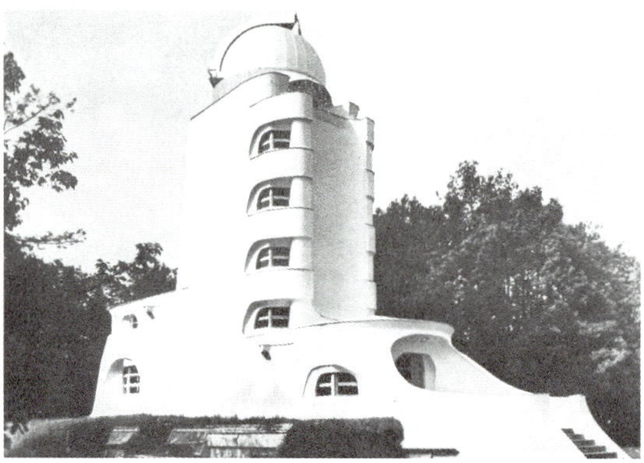

5. Henry van de Velde, Werkbund Theatre Cologne 1914.

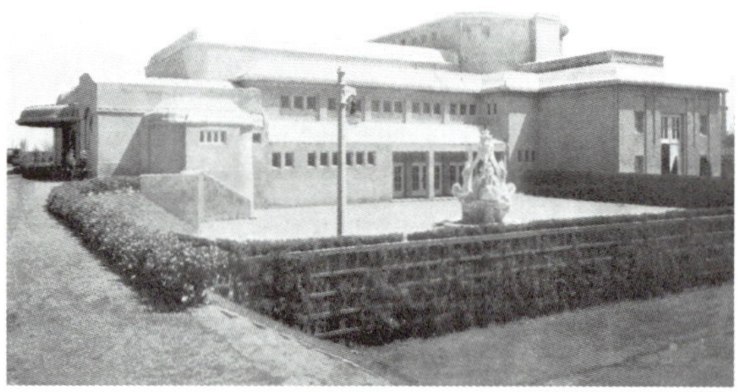

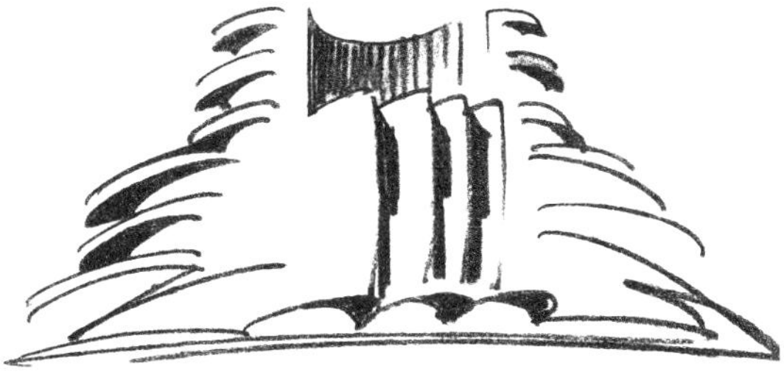

6. Sketch inspired by Bach Toccata in C major, 1920.

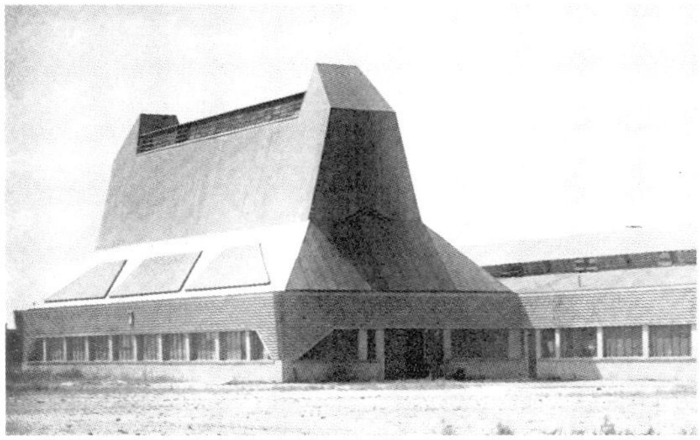

7. Hat factory, Luckenwalde 1921-23.

Reiter painters led by Kandinsky, originator of the first abstract painting and author of *Concerning the Spiritual in Art*. Perhaps this encouraged his interest in the power of line and in blocks of colour. At the same time he became involved with Expressionist theatre, probably meeting its visiting genius Max Reinhardt.[6] The simple forms, strong lighting effects and emphasis on exaggerated gesture - again linear, and dynamic - left their mark. Very much parallel and 'in the air' at the time also was Italian Futurism, which sought to celebrate the dynamism of modern life by depicting arrested movement in paintings and sculptures.

Setting up in practice in 1912 without any commissions to build, Mendelsohn spent the next two years designing theatre sets, posters and programmes. This honed his skills with graphic effects, with strong and simple forms, something he also recognised in Jugendstil and Art Nouveau works of ten years earlier. Among the buildings he most admired at the outset of his career was the Model Theatre for the Werkbund Exhibition in Cologne of 1914 by Henry van de Velde, whose simple flowing forms seemed to point the way to a new architecture in reinforced concrete. Van de Velde's work also tacitly carried the theoretical burden of late 19th century German aesthetic theory, particularly the empathy theory of Wilhelm Worringer, whose brilliant thesis *Abstraktion und Einfühlung* (Abstraction and Empathy), differentiated between two kinds of aesthetic goal. Worringer claimed that the desire for abstraction answered a need for refuge from the chaos of a changing world through the eternal verity of geometry, while the desire for empathy led people to enjoy movements of the eye which harmonised with their own bodily movements.[7] The history of art supposedly alternated between these tendencies, but abstraction was primitive and empathy humanistic. Crucial to our story is that both tendencies sought meaning in abstract form and line as opposed to the figurative display or associative symbolism of traditional ornament, which prior to the First World War was assumed to be compulsory. Mendelsohn's reductive sketches concentrated on just this kind of form and line, and also on rhythm, in which he saw parallels with music. He was an accomplished musician and his wife Luise was a semi-professional cellist. Parallels were widely seen at the time between music and abstract art, and some of Mendelsohn's sketches were even inspired by listening to particular works.

Along with their concentration on abstract line and massing, Mendelsohn's sketches were also intended as an exploration of how the new architecture would reflect the new spirit of society. He meant the Einstein Tower, for example, to show the implications of general relativity, of which he had more than a lay understanding.[8] He also sought to show the essence of new technologies such as the openness of steel frame and the fluidity of concrete. Until he began to build there was no feedback from the building site to correct his sense of constructive logic, and he was deeply disappointed when shuttering difficulties and concrete prices forced completion of the Einstein tower in stuccoed brickwork. Once the dialogue with the building process began, however, Mendelsohn responded quickly and inventively. The Luckenwalde Hat Factory of 1921-3 shows contrast of frame and infill, its façades revelling in the horizontality of brickwork exaggerated with projecting courses, its sections dominated by the structurally efficient shapes of concrete portal

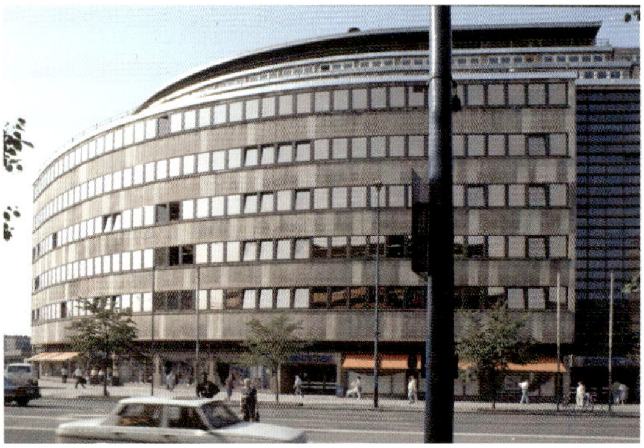

8. Schocken store Chemnitz, 1930, modern photo with thickened glazing mullions.

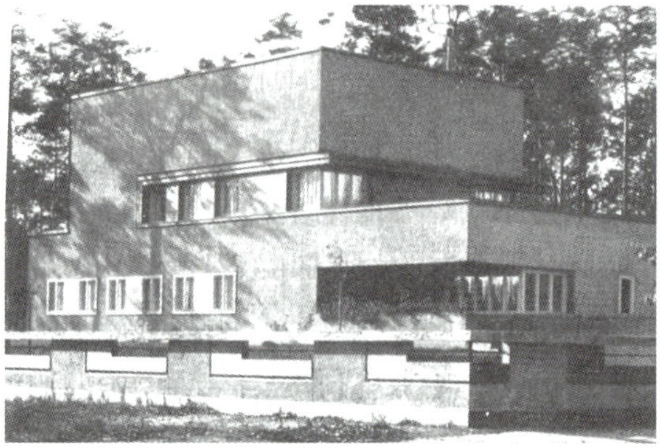

9. Villa Sternefeld Berlin 1923-4, view from street.

frames and the functional profiles of ventilation stacks. His grasp of the creative possibilities in material and detailing was equally evident later in the progression of Schocken store façades, culminating in the light, linear and much-imitated Chemnitz version of 1930.[9]

The early 1920s

It is hard to imagine the contemporary impact of the sketches or the Einstein Tower in their freedom from historical precedent. Ahead of the game, Mendelsohn went on to produce a series of innovative works between 1920 and 1924 which established his modus operandi and set the tone for his new architecture. These works are as notable for their horizontal emphasis in elevation as for their skilled, often asymmetrical plans. The corner reconstruction of the *Berliner Tageblatt* newspaper building in Berlin introduced Mendelsohn's dynamic urban planning, supposedly a celebration of the movement of passing traffic:

'the building is not a disinterested spectator of the rushing cars and of the advancing and receding flow of traffic; rather, it has become an absorbing, cooperating element of the motion. The building both visibly encompasses in its overall expression the high speed of traffic, where the tendency towards motion is raised to an extreme, and at the same time the balance of the forces soothes the frenetic pace of the street and of the passers-by'.[10]

The Herpich store of 1924 also in Berlin, gave drama to the street not only with its extraordinarily extensive glazing and apparently unsupported ground floor, but also with its sophisticated electric lighting at night. The double house on Karolingerplatz played with a diagonal axis in plan, avoiding a traditional layout. The Villa Sternefeld of 1923-4 showed a prowess in asymmetrical composition learned from Frank Lloyd Wright (whom Mendelsohn visited in the USA in 1924) and from parallel developments in Holland which he also knew. It is worth examining briefly to show how plan related to volume at this stage. As a general principle, Mendelsohn would make the top floor a regular figure, adding more and more parts to it

10. Villa Sternefeld, ground floor, first floor and second floor plans, from bottom to top. North is left.

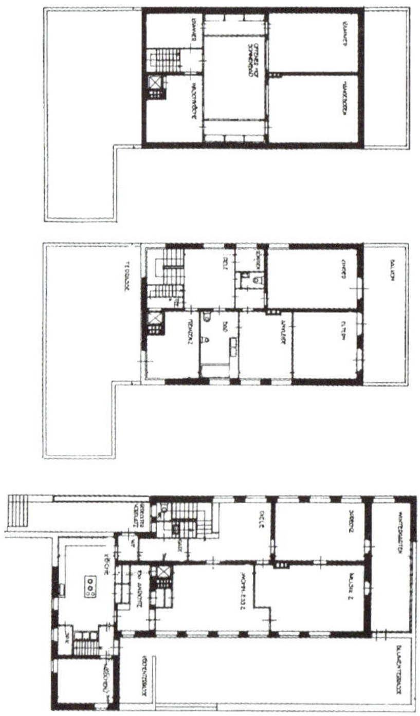

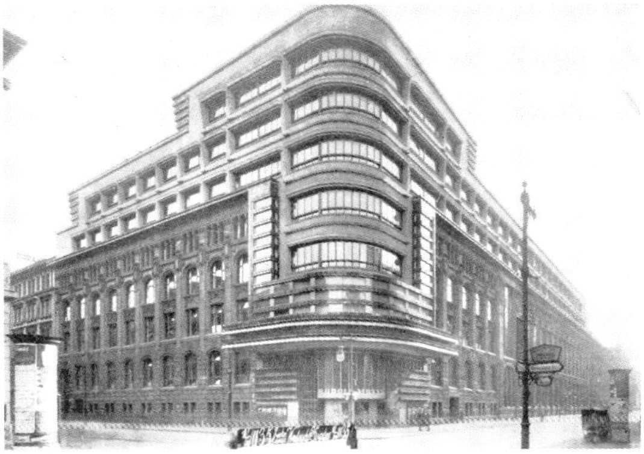

11. *Berliner Tageblatt* newspaper building, Berlin 1921-23.

asymmetrically until the building met the ground by engaging the particularities of the site. Reading the Sternefeld plans from top to bottom, the inward-looking top floor with its central sunbathing court is a pure rectangle symmetrically laid out. The shape is repeated on the floor below, but with the rooms extraverted instead of introverted, and fed by the corner stair. Terraces added to south - for the main bedrooms - and north prepare for the larger volume below, the north one extended westward to create an L-shaped enclosure for the west-facing terrace. The principal living rooms of the main floor open onto this terrace and enjoy a westward view of the garden beyond, while the entrance arrives at the north-east corner up a progression of steps, by-passing the kitchen and maid's room which occupy the north front.

Movement is highly important: the right turn on entry is followed by a left into the vestibule, then right for the living rooms or left for the main stair. It winds up anti-clockwise in the corner of the house, the upper landing dramatising the corner view back out. The site is a north-eastern corner between the avenue Heerstrasse, one of the main western roads out of Berlin, and a side street. A change in site level prompted the high-ground floor entry, and it is typical of Mendelsohn that the garden wall was treated as an integral part of the house.[11] The massing is tower-like in celebration of the corner, yet the corner breaks for the entrance: this is the main idea. Inside all rooms are orthogonal, as is the whole building, and visual axes are exploited, yet there is no hint of classical symmetry. The internal experience of progression is tied to the three-dimensional external form, the two being developed in tandem. Similar principles apply to the Schocken stores, but the story is more complex.

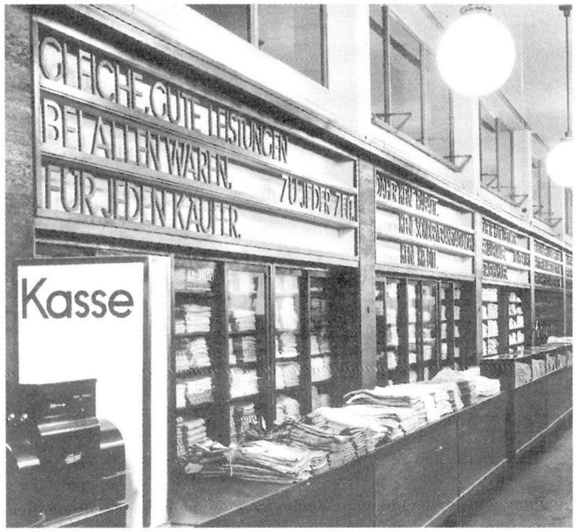

12. Schocken store Stuttgart, interior showing plain treatment and open display of goods.

Schocken and a new concept for the department store

The Schocken department stores started shortly after the turn of the century in the city of Zwickau, expanding rapidly to ten branches by 1914. When German economic recovery allowed a further spate of growth from the mid to late 1920s the chain expanded again, and Mendelsohn was adopted as architect for the more prestigious stores, starting with a conversion at Nuremberg then going on to build anew at Stuttgart and Chemnitz. He was recommended to Salman Schocken, creator of the chain, by Kurt Blumenfeld, President of the German Zionist Organisation. The two men soon established an understanding, for Schocken had felt the need for an image for his expanding operation which Mendelsohn knew how to supply. They had a somewhat quarrelsome interaction, for Mendelsohn refused to compromise his ideas and like many clients Schocken wanted the work faster and cheaper, but the collaboration was effective, for both insisted on a good product.[12]

The Schocken brand was about quality and value for money, and took pride in being functional and direct rather than creating a decadent atmosphere of fantasy like earlier palaces of consumption. Mendelsohn's first job, the Nuremberg conversion of 1926, was as spartan as the factory it was partly intended to represent, attention being turned to the goods which were laid out on counters for customers to view and to handle, an experience commonplace in our supermarket age, but then almost unknown.

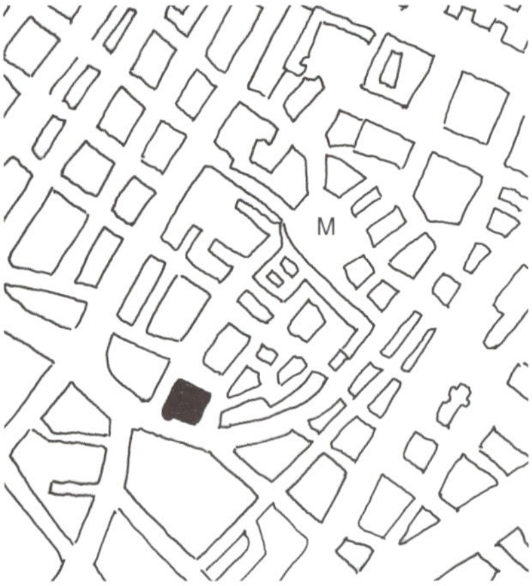

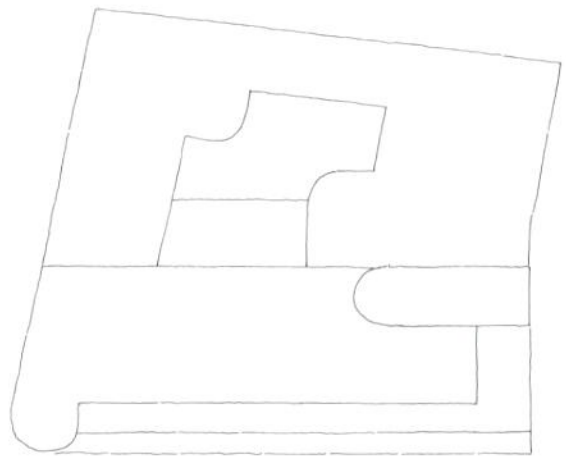

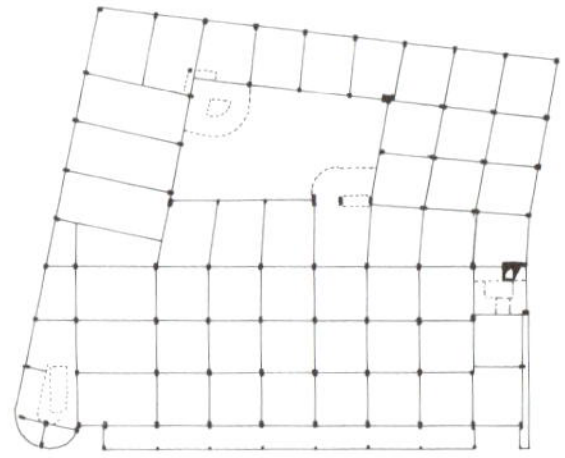

13. (left) Site plan of building in central Stuttgart. North is up, M is old market place.
14. (above) Diagram to show layering of plan.
15. (above right) Diagram showing structural grid.
16. (below) period postcard of building from main street showing the stair tower.
17. (opposite) Floor plans from basement (top left) to top floor (bottom right).

The Stuttgart store of 1926-8 came next and was for Mendelsohn a key project: a new building on a cleared site at the centre of one of Germany's leading cities. All Mendelsohn's sketches and most photographs lift it out of context, making it a separate icon, and historians have tended to read it in an equally self-contained way, but the building was very contextual: significantly, the six-line description given by Mendelsohn in his *Complete Works* of 1930 is largely to do with the site.[13] Analysis will show that he responded not only in terms of the all-important massing, but also in plan, in elevation and in section. The building occupied an important curved street just south of the city centre, once the site of the city wall and by that time an inner ring road. The store's south-west corner marked the outermost point of the curve, and here Mendelsohn placed his projecting glazed staircase for maximum visibility from both sides. In plan it also effortlessly absorbs the 10° angle shift

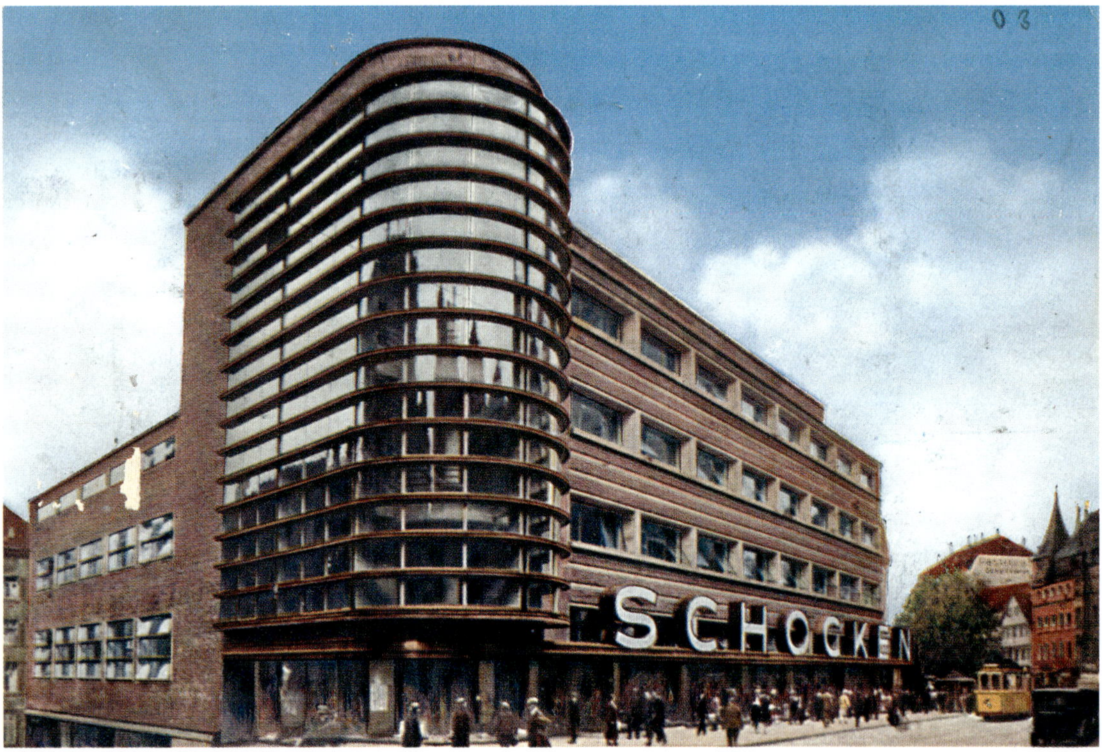

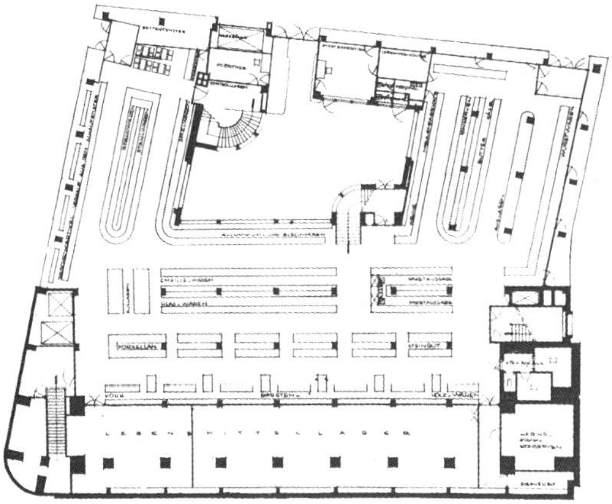

Basement

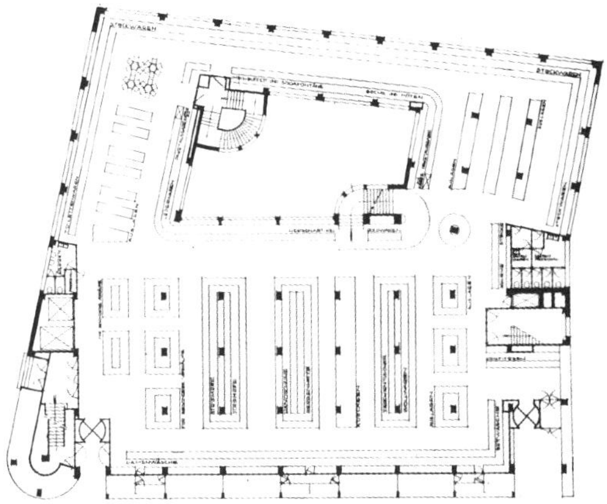

Ground floor

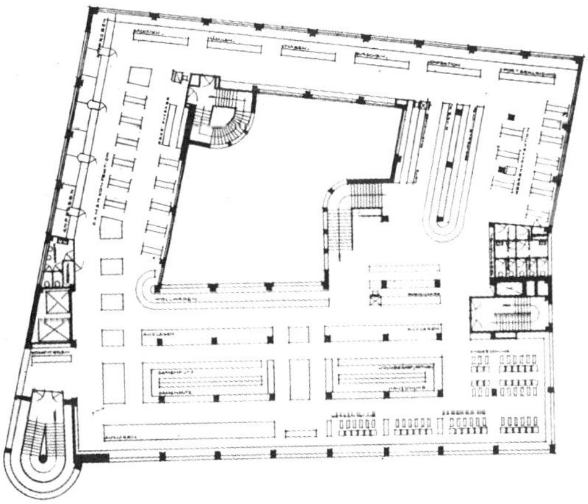

First floor

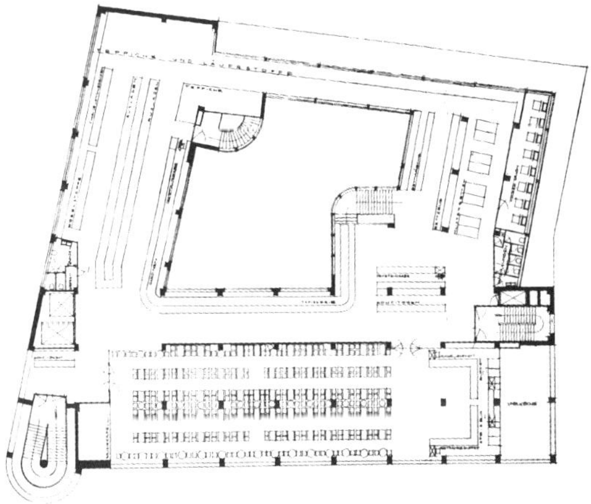

Second floor

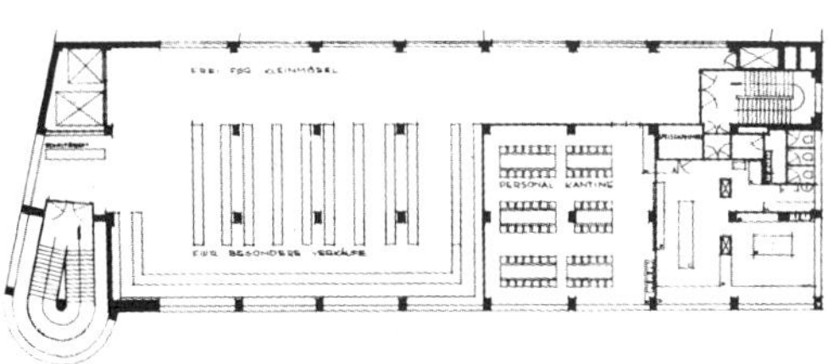

Third floor

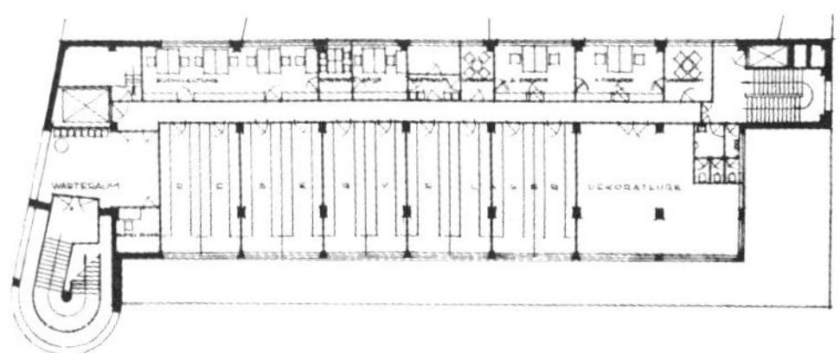

Fourth floor

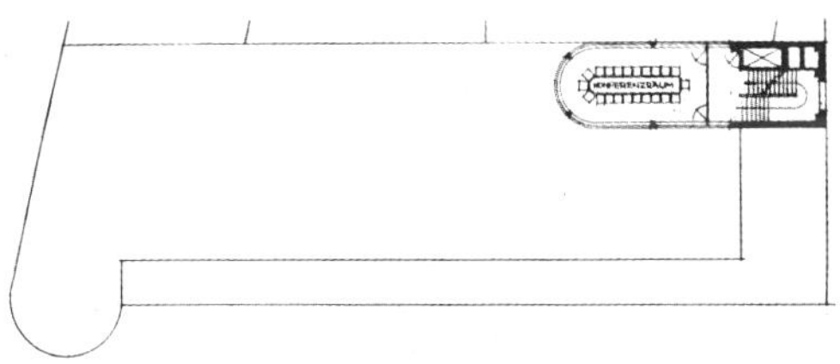

Fifth floor

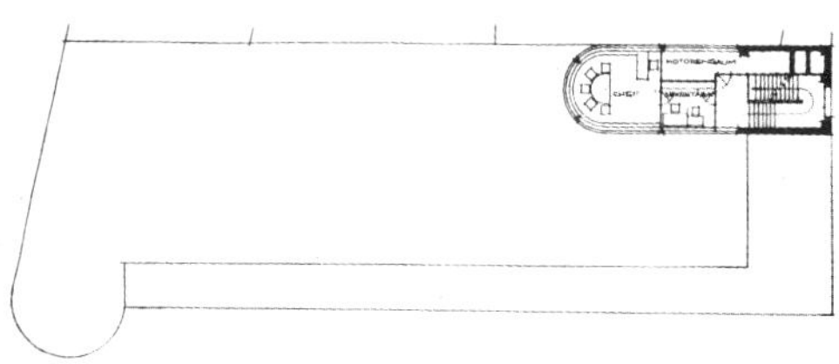

Sixth floor

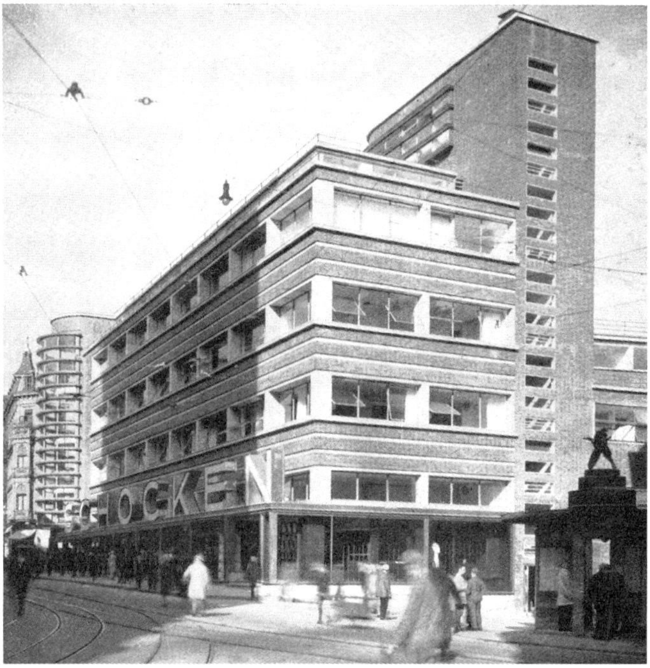

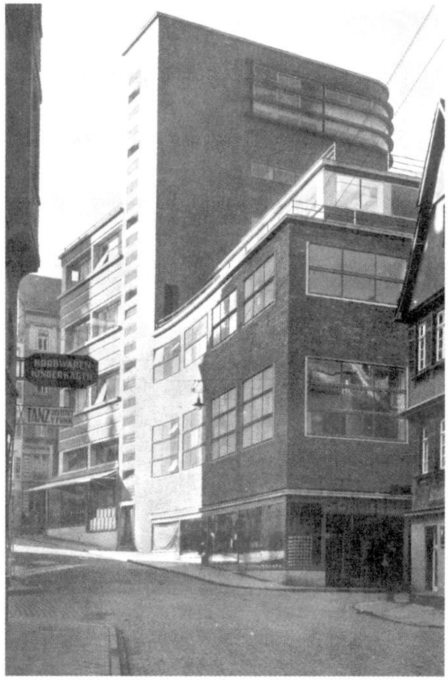

18. Main front framed by two towers. 19. (above right) Side street with tower and slope: note change to a plainer façade treatment. 20. (below) One of Mendelsohn's many study sketches for the building. 21. (below right) Mendelsohn's projection from his book on his work. 22. (opposite) View down main stair at front corner.

produced by the side street. The other main street corner to south-east met very different conditions, for it opened up visually to the street arriving axially opposite. Mendelsohn exploited this more exposed return by carrying his front facade around the corner for two bays before terminating it with his second, higher but thinner stair tower. Seen from the city behind (fig. 19), this tower with its horizontal rhythmic window slots made a dramatic termination to the narrow street linking to town hall and market place. Mendelsohn changed the elevation treatment of the south-east side at his tower: as already noted the two bays forward of it are part of the main front, but the rear part has a humbler vocabulary of blank brick and flush glazing. The side view also shows the drop in level produced by the sloping street, which allows a basement entrance at the back and a dropping cascade of display windows.

In Mendelsohn's massing sketch (fig. 20) there is a clear differentiation between the tall block at the front and the subordinate building at the back. Turning to the plans, we see that they are differently orientated, the lesser building taking the line of the back street, the geometry (and the steel framing) being reconciled in the courtyard. The disjunction is cleverly absorbed by placing two staircases - one public the other private - at opposite corners. From the preserved sketches it is clear that Mendelsohn was most exercised by the balance between the two towers which hold the building together: the larger and more prominent containing the public stair, the narrower one enclosing the staff stair but being two storeys higher. The round end of the small tower where it breaks through the roof was treated with the same glazed horizontal frame as used in the main stair

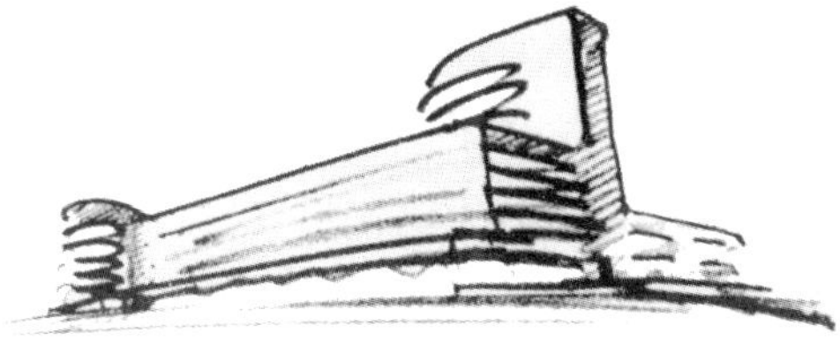

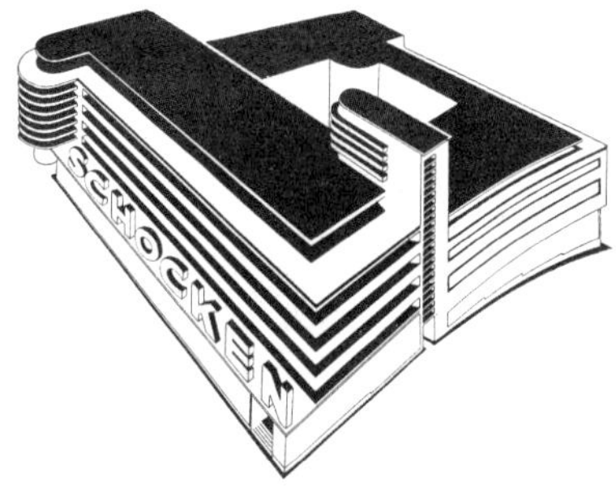

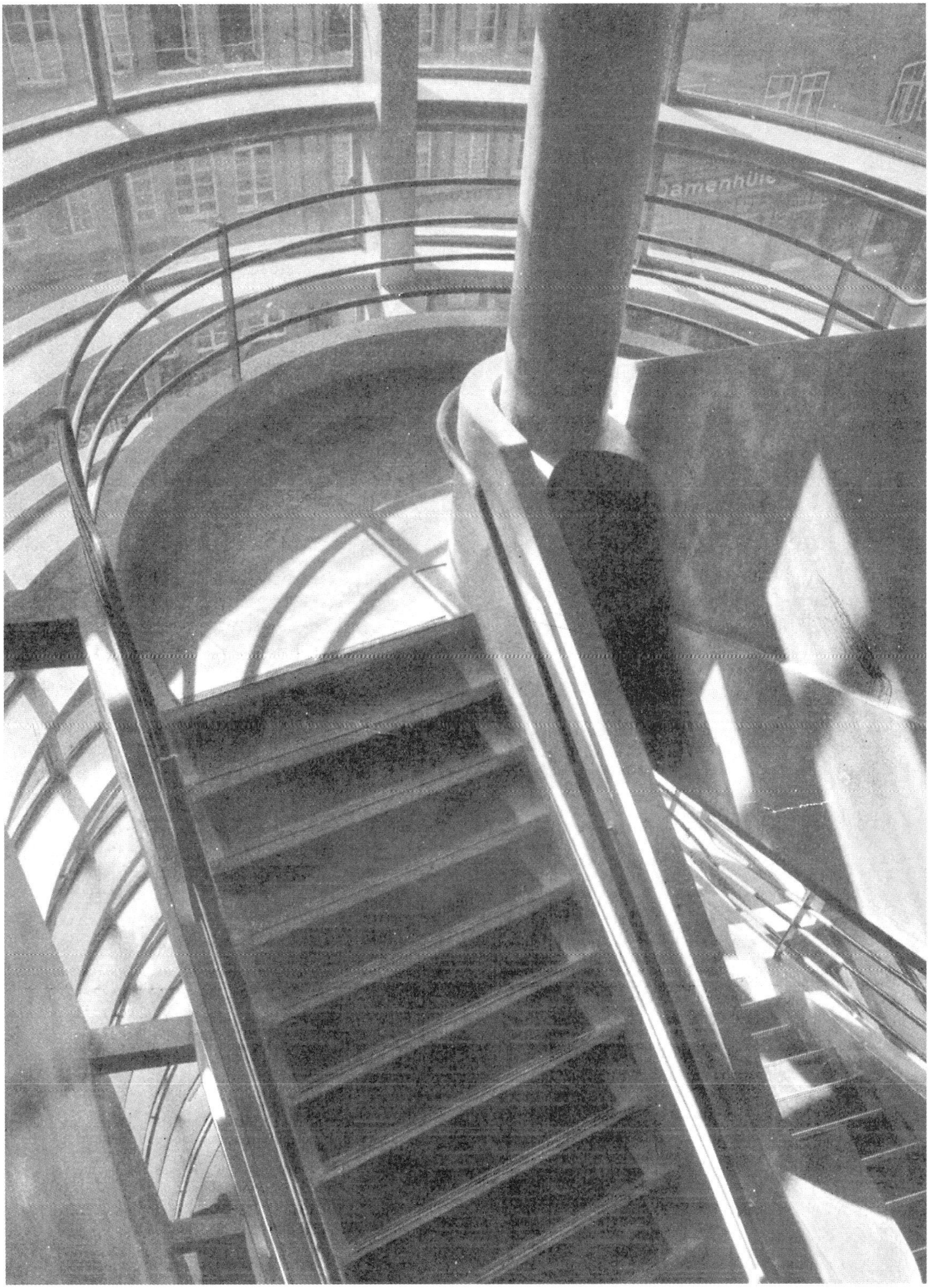

tower. He tried the lesser tower in other positions: in the end it not only defines the back corner of the front block, but partnered by the lifts at the other end, also marks the bay used for primary circulation at most levels. As noted earlier, Mendelsohn tended to work down from a geometrically pure top floor to a ground floor which fitted the contingencies of the site. In this case (fig. 14,17) the progression starts with a round-ended turret on levels seven and six. On level five the front block starts, but with a terrace to pull it back from the street. At level four the front block is completed, and at level three the rear is added, but again with a terrace around the eastern corner. Level two completes the whole outer plan figure, but level one adds an extra bay to the rear of the front block, reducing the courtyard. These changes give each floor a different character, and Mendelsohn plays up the differences with changing layouts within, a theme and variations played on the rhythm of the structural frame.

In the late 1920s, with his enthusiasm for horizontality and the dynamism of urban life noted above in relation to the *Berliner Tageblatt* building, Mendelsohn would hardly have wished to see his towers compared with those of his teacher Fischer, and if Mendelsohn ever felt sympathy for Fischer's practice of brewing a new local architectural language from an analysis of local buildings,[14] he had clearly lost it. Yet Fischer's principles are carried through at a more abstract level: the Schocken towers are undoubtedly the stabilising points of the composition, they are the vertical circulation nodes just like medieval ones, and they are placed as landmarks to tie the building into the surrounding townscape, completing views in a thoroughly Sittesque manner.[15] The drama of ascent, too, could scarcely be more marked than with the main public tower. And despite their modernity, the façades also respect Fischer's principles in their clear hierarchical differentiation between fronts and backs. The crucial issue of building height with which Fischer regulated his Munich plans was also important to Mendelsohn, who not only kept his façades low towards the narrow rear streets, but successfully fought his client against making the whole building too high.[16]

Electric light had reached most cities in Germany by the end of the 1920s, and Mendelsohn was one of the first to exploit it, considering the appearance of his buildings by night as well as by day, and dramatising them by contrast. In 1924 he visited the United States and on his return published a book of photographs: he was especially impressed by the lights of Times Square and the new potential of illuminated advertising.[17] In the Stuttgart store ground floor were set brightly illuminated display windows, and the person-high letters on the canopy above were also electrically lit. The glazed corner stair with its horizontal ribs became a beacon of light visible from afar in both directions. But despite his exploitation of lighting technology, Mendelsohn insisted on daylighting wherever possible. The courtyard was an effective lightwell penetrating to basement level, and the ground floor front was lit by clerestorys set above and behind the display windows. The main staircases all occurred in glazed towers, offering not only daylight but exciting views out as a relief when moving between floors. There was also a large rooflight at ground floor just in front of the court. All this was very different from the average department store today, where floors seem endless and the same, artificially lit from end to end, and lacking all reference to the world outside.

In his detailed planning - doubtless in collaboration with Salman Schocken - Mendelsohn was able to place the sales counters for the goods in ways that exploited the idiosyncrasies of the plan, engaging the lines of columns to prevent them becoming obtrusive, taking up changes of angle and creating corners with counters, guiding the circulation in smooth channels and exploiting more intimate backwaters for particular kinds of display. The building was a pioneering work in steel frame, reported in detail as the main example in a contemporary book on framed buildings.[18] For the most part the structure followed an even grid of about five metres both ways, but a wider span was allowed on the north-west side to create an unobstructed circulation aisle running back from the entrance corner. The sales areas on each of the lower three floors divided roughly into three: a large space at front, rear space to right of the court, and rear space to left of it. On the ground floor the front space was used for women's gloves, stockings, lingerie etc., with men's items on the long counter next to the court. Rear left held women's toiletries and at the back of the court a snackbar with soda fountain. Placed next to the lavatories were umbrellas, and opposite the south-east door a display of preserves. These must have been particularly tempting, for further display cabinets of them were set on the main stair. In the basement

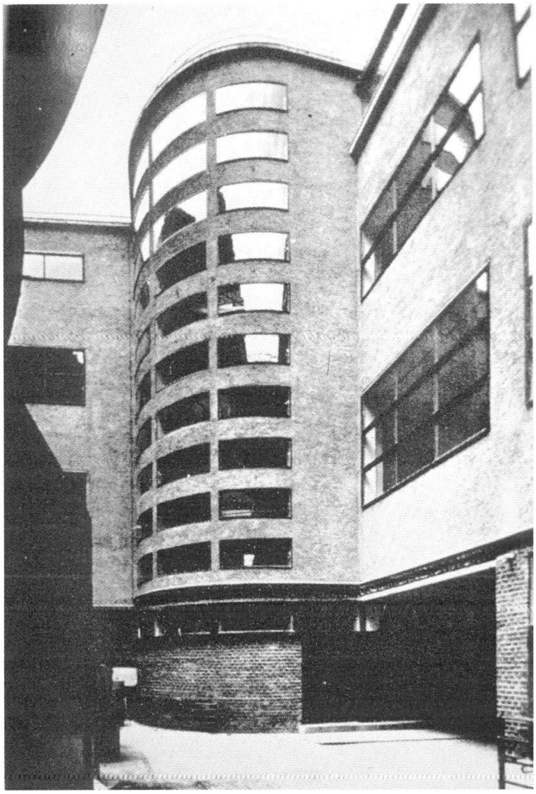

23. Corner stair in courtyard.

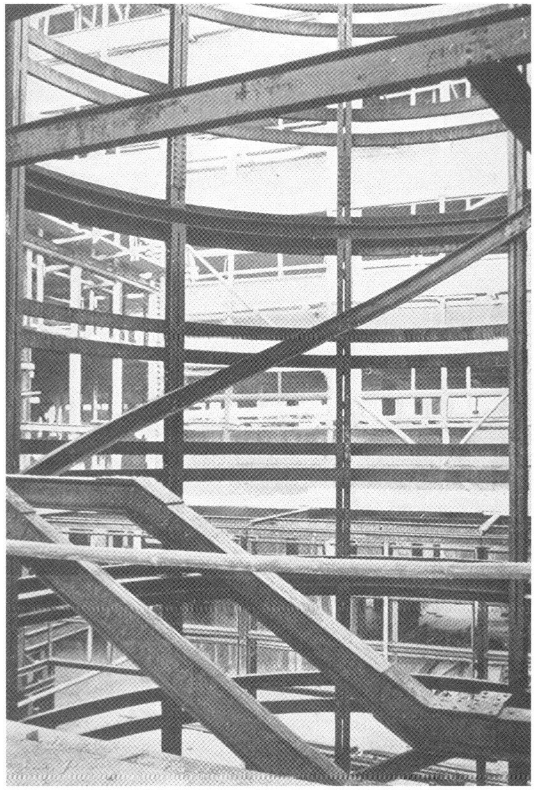

24. Main stair tower under construction.

the front space displayed porcelain, glass, stoneware etc., while rear left held games, presents, cutlery and utensils, rear right a delicatessen. First floor was devoted to clothing, with shoes front right, women's finery front left, and woollens towards the court. Rear left was ladies off-the-peg with changing rooms along the side, rear right men's off-the-peg and sportswear, again with changing rooms. While the broader ground floor had display counters running back into the plan, at first floor and basement the counters ran across it. The dominance of the ground floor was assured by a greater floor to ceiling height, and it was dramatised at the centre by the rooflight and the cantilevered semicircular landing of the internal stair set next to the corner of the court.

The second floor gained a radically different layout through the large self-service cafeteria offering views back to the street, and a 'music chapel' stood between it and the stairs, offering a contemplative moment away from the bustle of shopping. Rear areas at this level were devoted to soft furnishings such as carpets and bed linen, and to rear right a hairdressing salon. The third floor carried a 'special sales area' and a staff canteen seating no less than 78. The fourth floor housed offices and staff facilities. Appropriately hierarchical, conference room and manager's office occupied the top two floors of the tower with the best views over the city. From top to bottom all was carefully placed: despite the open frame this is no generalised type of building like those posited by Mies, but a building seeking every engagement with content and context.

Construction and detail

Stuttgart Schocken was constructed around a bolted steel frame, whose rhythm is felt right through, but nowhere did Mendelsohn leave it fully exposed, unlike for example Max Taut,[19] nor did he play with it formally like Giuseppe Terragni (see Chapter 10). As for material, it could just as well be concrete. The fenestration indicates clearly where the vertical members are, particularly at the front with its travertine claddings between the recessed windows, but the frame's horizontals are masked by even brick banding at the front which does not acknowledge any support, while at the back brick covers all. Mendelsohn liked to play in his façades with thicknesses and projections, elaborating the threshold and producing complex shadow patterns. At Schocken this helps differentiate the showy fronts from the humbler backs in a masterful way, but it makes his front construction look relatively massive, the composite brickwork within each bay being strong enough to carry the whole building. Only the back with its flush windows allows the brickwork to appear as a skin. The framing is most visible in the main stair tower, but even here the curved steel channels actually doing the work were boxed out into more solid-looking horizontal ribs, while the steel-framed stair was also rendered and painted. The tower could certainly have been much more transparent like the much earlier ones at the Werkbund model factory by Gropius and Meyer, but Mendelsohn relished the spatial effect of moving within the cage, seeing the outside world through its filter. He designed the stair as a separate free-standing structure within the glazed cylinder, leaving a substantial and somewhat vertiginous gap between the two. A new variation on this same theme was built at Bexhill, where the stair is even more the heart and focus of the building.

Conclusion

Our analysis shows that far from dreaming up some glib idea in a sketch, Mendelsohn seriously engaged all the site conditions and tried to make them work for his building. At the same time he sought to define the territories for the complex organism of the department store, finding locations for all its respective parts, differentiating between frontstage and backstage areas, and even deploying the layout of sales counters in an architectural manner. Nobody could accuse him of neglecting the plan or of failing to think about views and spatial progressions: indeed in comparison with more modern examples, his department stores are models of imaginative planning involving views and daylight, and they offer an extraordinary variety of experience between one floor and the next. On top of all this, he was experimenting with new technologies and new details on a construction programme that needed to be as fast as possible. So why did Mendelsohn cling to the sketch as a key form of representation? Perhaps because the sketch showed clearly what had become the main idea. The positions and relation of the two main towers is surely the essential gesture of the composition, for it ties together the urban concept, the structural rationale and the working of the internal spaces. Many architects might have tried to make the building symmetrical to the main street, as Mendelsohn himself did on other occasions, but the site prompts an asymmetrical response, and from this everything else follows. It had to be a balanced asymmetry, taking the form of a dialogue between the towers and contrasting the left and right internal spaces. It makes the most of the given conditions and causes the building to belong. The sketches sum up the building's virtues: they are really about the integrative nature of the architectural act, about the triumph of finding a simple way to bring a multitude of considerations harmoniously together.

Notes

1. *Wasmuths Monatshefte* no. IX 1924, pp.1-66.
2. James 1997 pp. 237-8.
3. Egon Eiermann, one of the best German architects of the post-war era, claimed that he and the owners initially wanted to keep the building, but it proved impossible to adapt to new technology such as air-conditioning and escalators; see Schirmer 1984, p. 306.
4. In some sources law, but I am taking the biographical list in the centenary exhibition catalogue as definitive (Aschenbach 1987).
5. For a general discussion of Fischer's influence on his pupils see Nerdinger 1988, pp. 86-95.
6. James 1997, p.17.
7. See Frampton 1980, pp.96-99 and Worringer 1953. The introductory chapter of *Abstraction and Empathy* contains a useful summary of German aesthetic theory up to that point.
8. James 1997, pp. 28-47.
9. Julius Posener, who worked for Mendelsohn in Palestine, told me that he was not very interested in technical issues *per se*, and clearly he relied on assistants and engineers to work out the practicalities. But he knew enough to understand the design implications. The same could be said of some of today's so-called High-tech architects.
10. From a lecture by Mendelsohn in Amsterdam of 1923, printed in English in Mendelsohn 1992, p. 28.
11. For a more detailed exposition of a later example - Mendelsohn's own house - see Woudstra, Jan and Blundell Jones, Peter, *Some Modernist Houses and their Gardens* in *Die Gartenkunst* vol. 1, 1999, pp.112-122.
12. General source for this paragraph is James 1997, pp.171-8.
13. Mendelsohn 1992, p.151.
14. For examples, see Nerdinger 1988, pp. 68-85.
15. Fischer was crucially influenced by the planning theories of Camillo Sitte, see Collins 1965.
16. James 1997, p.183.
17. Mendelsohn, Erich. *Erich Mendelsohn, Amerika, Bilderbuch eines Architekten, Mit 100 meist eigenen Aufnahmne des Verfassers*, published by Rudolf Mosse, Berlin 1926.
18. Schulze, Konrad Werner. *Der Stahl-Skelettbau* Wissenschaftlicher Verlag Dr Zaugg & Co, Stuttgart 1928.
19. I am thinking particularly of the offices of the ADGB in Berlin of 1924-6, see Akademie der Künste 1984, p. 69.

Chapter 7. Le Corbusier: Villa Savoye, Poissy near Paris, 1929

The Villa Savoye is one of the great icons of the Modern Movement, regarded by many as the masterpiece of the so-called 'Architect of the Century',[1] who was born in 1887 and died in 1965. It marks the culmination of Le Corbusier's first great period, and perhaps better than any other work shows the transfer of ideas from contemporary painting and sculpture into architecture. For in its effort to reform itself and to escape the bonds of historic styles, architecture shared with other visual arts an excursion into abstraction. This manifested itself in Dutch De Stijl, in Russian Constructivism, and slightly later in much of the work produced at the Bauhaus; but nobody made the connection quite as tantalisingly as Le Corbusier. Together with Amedée Ozenfant he led the Purist Movement in painting: they wrote the Purist manifesto *Après le Cubisme* together,[2] and started the journal *L'Esprit Nouveau*. Throughout his life Le Corbusier painted in the mornings and attended his architectural studio in the afternoons, disappointed finally that his paintings were taken less seriously than his buildings.[3] But his architecture could scarcely have had more impact. In his buildings and his drawings he demonstrated a sequence of visual styles which captivated architects across the world, providing an apparent justification for them with a series of visionary books, of which *Vers une Architecture*, published in 1923, was the most important.[4] Le Corbusier was also a gifted orator and politician, taking over the nascent CIAM (International Congresses of Modern Architecture) as soon as it started in 1928, and dominating it until the end of the 1950s.[5] He published his own work early and in detail, and he gained more attention from critics and historians than any other architect of his generation. Shelves of books testify to the diversity and subtlety of his ideas, while the wealth of interpretations seemed, at least for a while in the late 20th century, to suggest a profundity beyond that of any architect contemporary. He was a great innovator and seemed to have tried almost everything.[6]

Designed in late 1928 and built in 1929, the Villa Savoye came at the end of a line of Purist villas in which Le Corbusier had been developing his ideas and honing his compositional skills. A weekend house on a large open site at Poissy on the northern outskirts of Paris, the programme was none too pressing, the budget generous, and there was freedom from the kind of site constraints which had limited earlier villas. He responded with a house that is detached in every sense, a sculptural entity perched in the middle of its site surrounded by continuous lawn, with all significant accommodation raised to the first floor, a clear *piano nobile*. The ground floor was by contrast all about arrival, planned around the turning circle of the car which brought its owners from central Paris. For Lutyens or for Frank Lloyd Wright, let alone Scharoun[7] or Mendelsohn,[8] such a generous site would have meant an opportunity to develop a fine garden in intimate conjunction with the house, linking the two by allowing living rooms to spill onto architectural terraces, and protecting this domain from the public approach by cutting one off from the other. At the Villa Savoye the opposite happens: the garden and the damp ground are kept away,[9] the outside world reduced to a visual scene for contemplation from the upper floor. Hinting at classical sources, Le Corbusier referred to it as a 'Virgilian dream', as if the house could stand in the midst of

1. Le Corbusier's own sketch of the Villa Savoye in its setting.

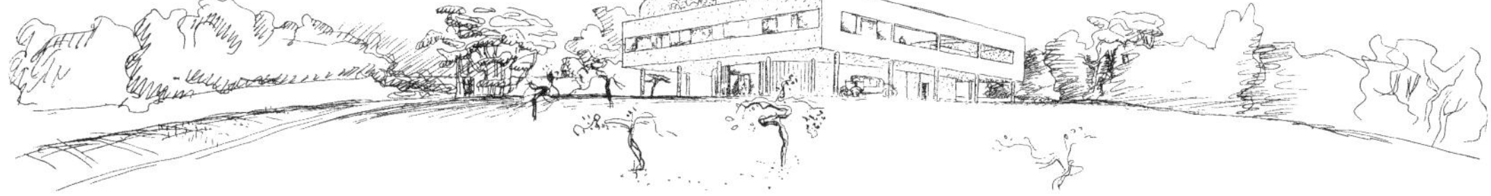

unspoiled countryside, the owners watching from their upper fastness as sheep grazed and peasants happily scythed the hay against the setting sun. In fact much money was spent on developing the garden, though it is hard now to see what was done.[10] The main job was always to cut the grass lest it develop into scrub, for the detached purity of the house depends crucially on its green border remaining undifferentiated, a *cordon sanitaire*. The house needs the clarity of its object-like status in the same way as Le Corbusier's paintings need a frame and a clear area of wall around them.

Composition

There is more than a little similarity between Le Corbusier's floor plans and his paintings. Both use the same kinds of forms and depend on the same kind of ordering procedures: perhaps unsurprisingly, since they were developed in parallel. Though unseen in execution, floor plans are the commanding devices for creating buildings, and Le Corbusier claimed repeatedly 'the plan is the generator'.[11] He drew perspectives and axonometrics, but it is the beautiful plans and sections to which the reader returns. The orthogonal treatment and regular column grid allow the spatial configuration to be imagined in a seemingly tangible way, and in the case of a building like the Villa Savoye, this projected appreciation goes a long way towards representing the space as it is experienced - it may even condition that experience. Cartesian coordinates are defined, the juxtaposition of forms is understood: one revels in the complexity of a three-dimensional interaction which is nonetheless graphically caught. The orthogonal discipline works well also for photographs, making the perspectives read as they should, with a clear contrast in forms.[12] Not the least part of Le Corbusier's genius is that he managed to produce work ideally suited to propagation in print through small line drawings and black & white photographs.[13] By purchasing his *Oeuvre Complète*, a generation of architects could feel that they possessed his work, and with the Villa Savoye he reached perhaps the ideal level of spatial complexity still transmissable via this medium.

Contemporaries must have been stunned by the extraordinary contrast between the three floor plans. Column grid, stair and ramp run through, but nearly everything else changes. Here was the most dramatic proof yet of *plan libre*, as opposed to *plan paralysé* with its loadbearing walls. It was also the best demonstration ever of the Five Points (see p. 24). Set on *pilotis*, the ground floor envelope was shaped by the flow of the arriving car. Coming from behind, it drove underneath the edge of the house, dropped the owners at the front, and was parked by its chauffeur in the garage at the far side on a dynamic diagonal, the only one in the building. The irregular entrance hall shows its in-between-ness, caught between other rooms and open to the outside though its screen of glazing, but this irregularity occurs within a symmetrical frame formed by the column grid, double drive, and centrally placed ramp. It is a subtlety of the plan that four bays require five columns with one central, yet within the house the central line of columns is

2. Le Corbusier: *Nature morte à la pile d'assiettes*, 1920, oil on canvas 81x100 cm (Oeffentliche Kunstmuseum Basel, Kunstmuseum, Gift Raoul La Roche 1963, photo Martin Bühler).

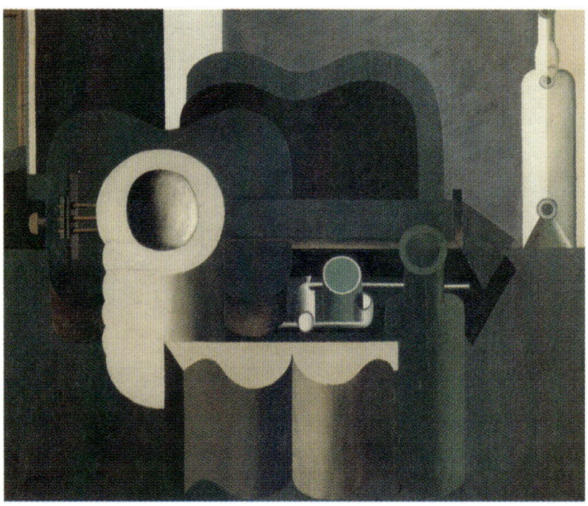

3. The same painting as published in *Le Modulor* and the geometric analysis by Le Corbusier included with it.

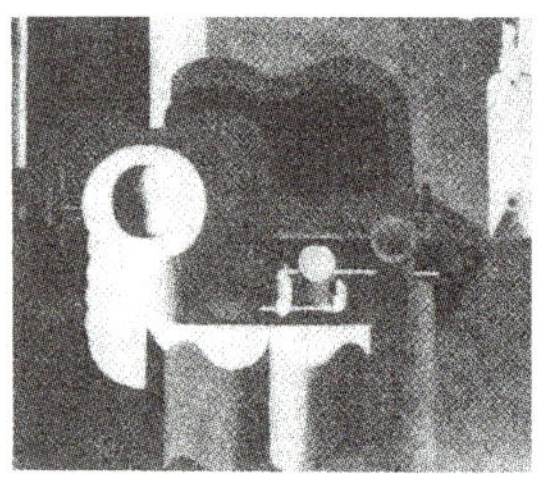

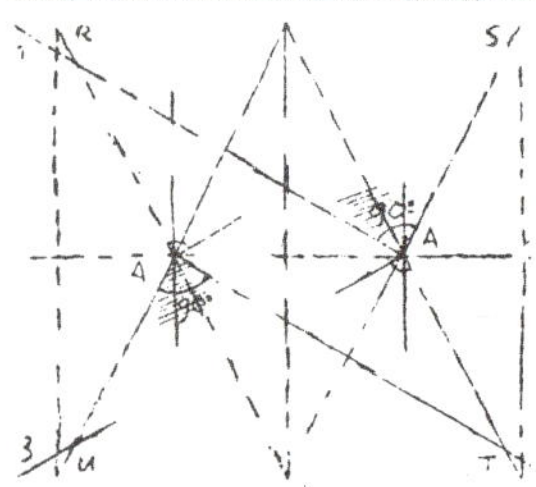

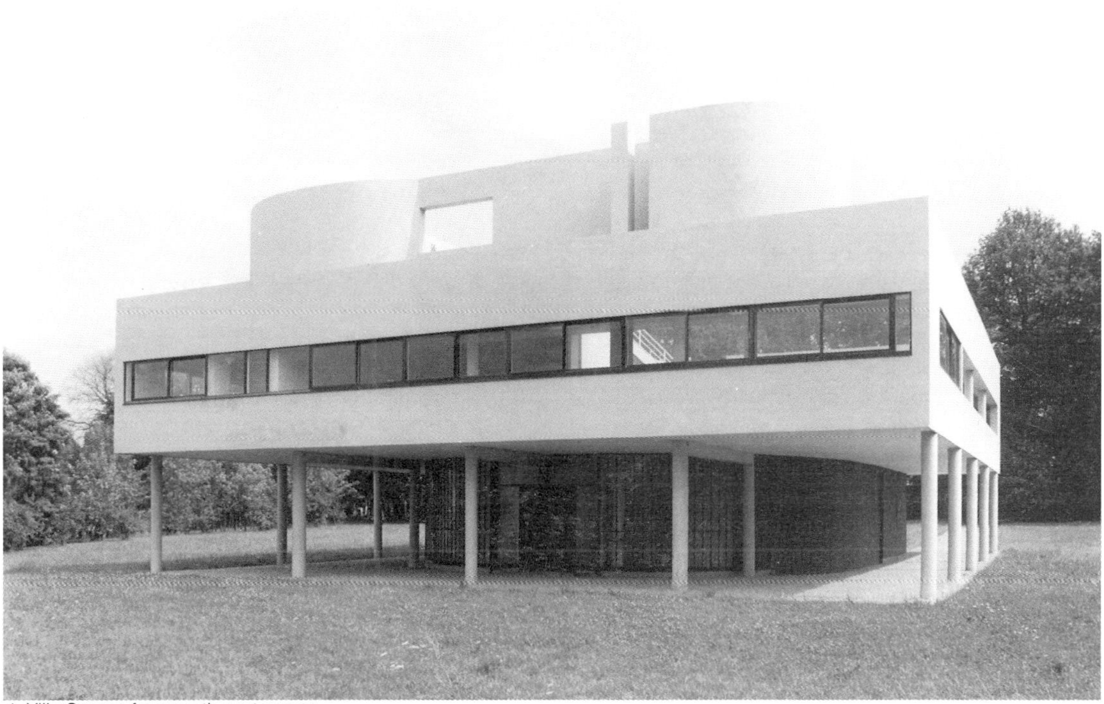

4. Villa Savoye from south-east corner.

5. Living room and first floor court.

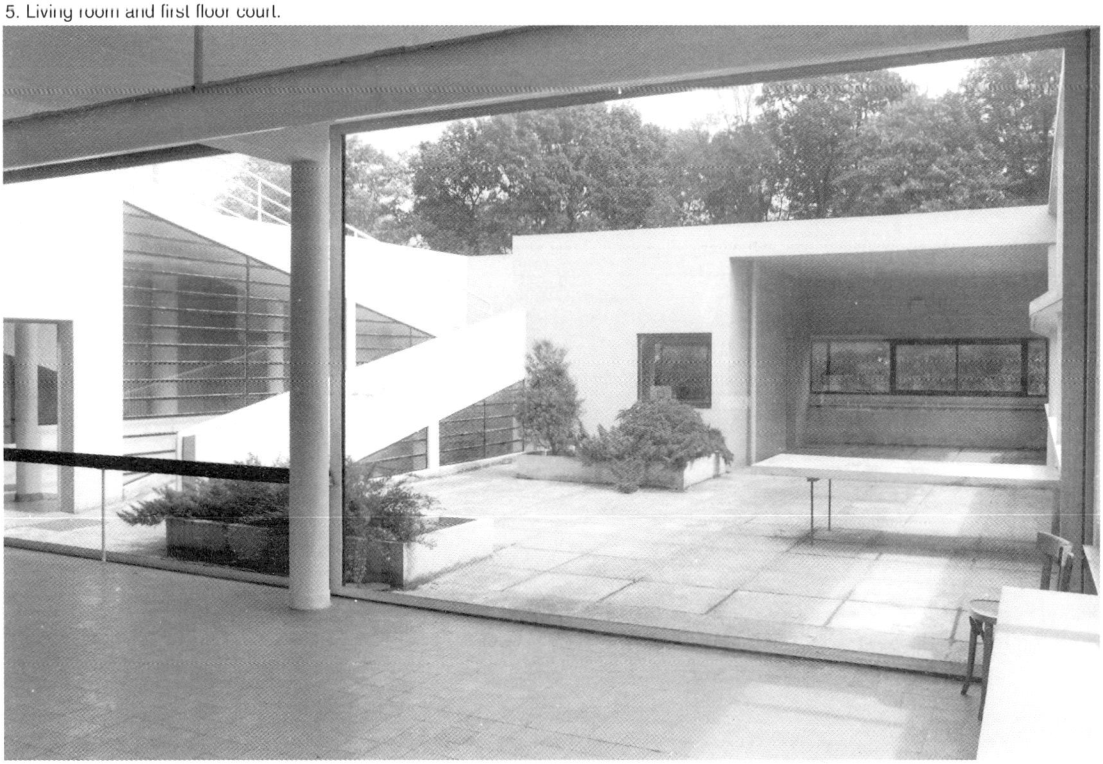

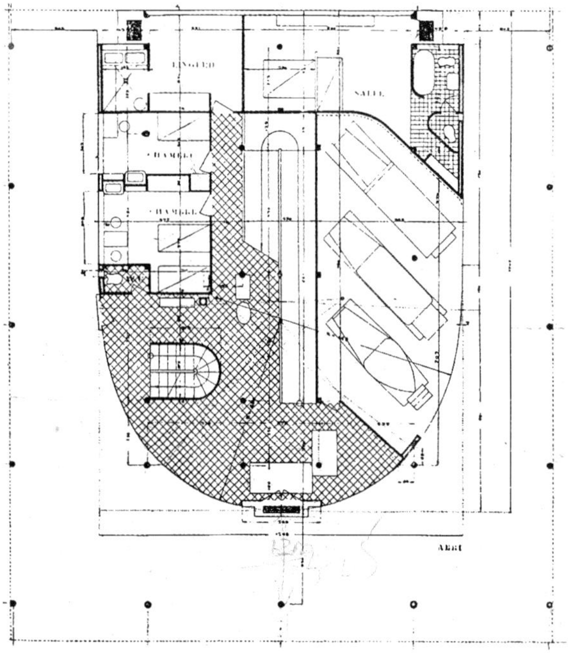

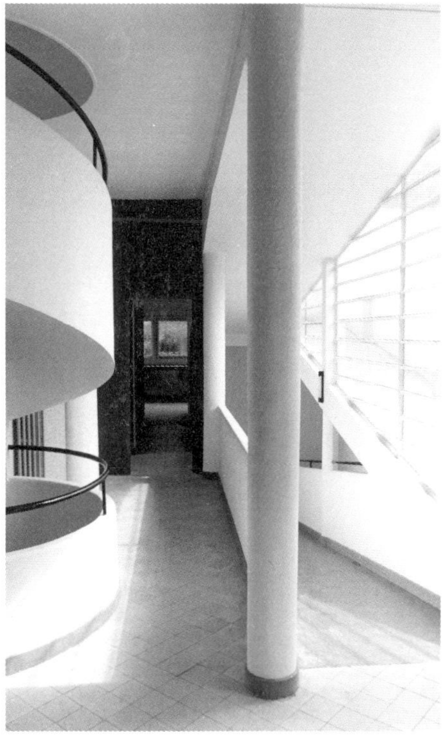

6. (above) Ground floor plan with entrance and garage.

7. Ramp arrives at first floor.

8. (below) Le Corbusier's own classification of his villas into four types: Savoye belongs to the fourth.

9. Main floor plan.

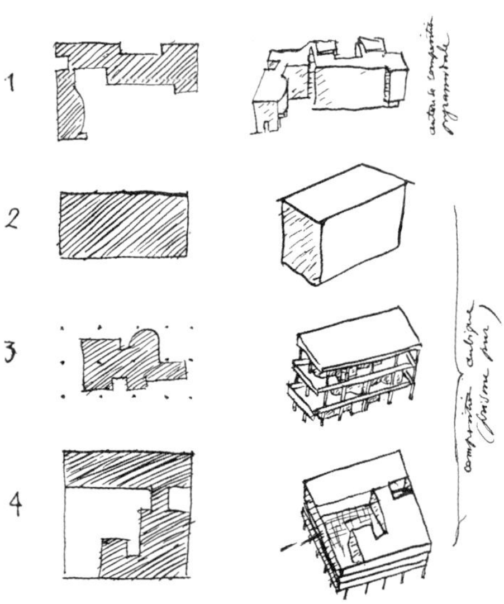

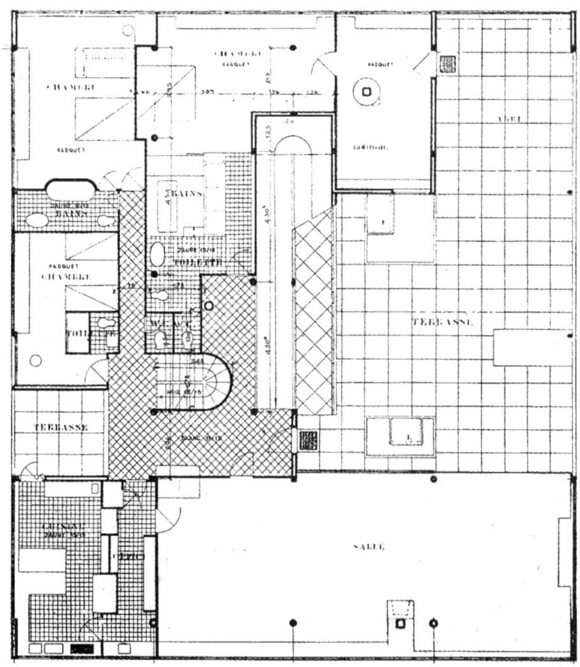

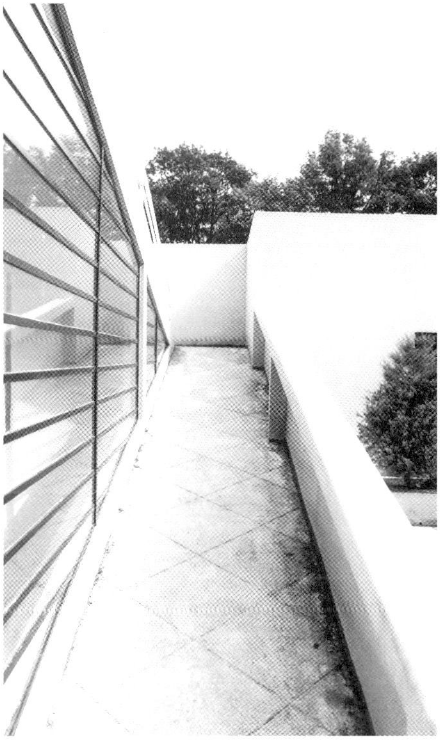

10. Beginning of the external ramp to the roof.

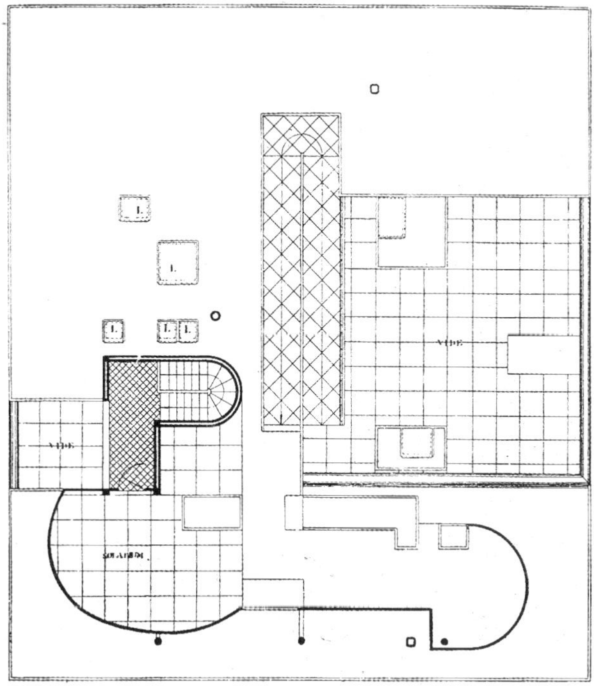

11. Roof plan.

displaced by the ramp. The outer column denies an axial approach from the garden, yet the main entrance beneath the house is back on axis. Climbing out of their car, the Savoyes would enter here, taking the centrally placed ramp to the first floor where living and sleeping rooms encircle an open courtyard.

The main floor asserts the geometry of the building as a square box, carefully proportioned and holding the composition together. The containing wall with its almost continuous horizontal window slot defines the spatial boundary more strongly than the glass envelope within its territory, and the window slot belongs to the house as a whole, denying the claims of individual rooms. On front and back the window reaches the corners, but on the sides it stops short. The other main differentiating factor between the pairs of faces is that the structure cantilevers beyond the columns at front and back, while running with it along the sides. This not only makes the sides slightly longer but also pulls the *pilotis* within the building to appear as free-standing columns in the most important room. This is the long *salon* - the main living room which occupies the south-west front enjoying the best distant view, and in preliminary versions it was given the entire width of the building.[14] Between it and the bedrooms at the rear lies a square court or hanging garden two bays wide on each axis. It ends on the centre-line of the house, taking over the upper layer of the ramp, so that both in plan and section the house is bisected between internal and external parts. That the outdoor rooms are still rooms is asserted by their definition and framing. The south-east wall, for example, continues across the court complete with a horizontal window devoid of glass, so even the open-air view is framed. At the eastern corner a lesser semi-outdoor room enjoys enclosure from above and glazed windows in the north-east side. Visually continuous with the main court, it looks across also to the *salon* beyond, maximum transparency being achieved with the largest possible glass doors. Standing in court, *salon* or eastern corner, one feels contained primarily by the outer screen-wall. On the north-west side, set between service elements, a further small court provides another glance of the screen-wall at the other side.

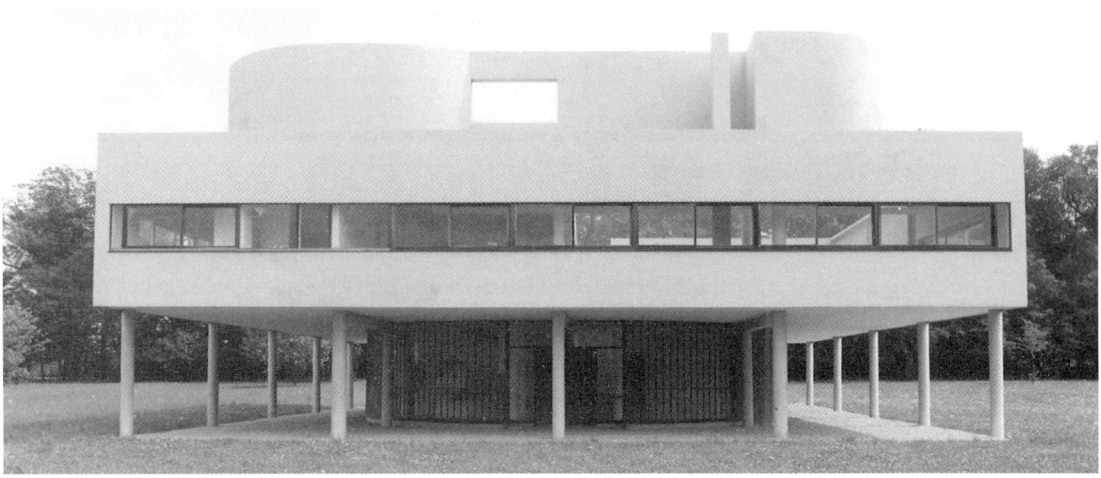

The ramp rises from the main court in the open air to arrive at the top floor, where functional elements break free of the orthogonal geometry. Initially, master bedroom and bathroom were accommodated at this level, their curved walls responding to bath and shower, but cuts reduced the accommodation to the staircase and a pair of free-standing screen-walls for the solarium. These produced the desired sculptural roofscape with an appropriate hierarchical loading towards the front. In a typically deft move, a glassless window frames the view at the top of the ramp, as a termination to the *promenade architecturale*. The need for the staircase to show itself prompted its being given a round end as the design developed, and it became increasingly sculptural, making a nice contrast with the ramp.

Rational discipline?

Without reinforced concrete (or steel) the house could not have been built. Le Corbusier had spent years dramatising the possibilities of column and slab construction, culminating in the doctrine of the Five Points, which his new house demonstrated once again. Yet for all his admiration of engineers' rationality, he was prepared to play with the new vocabulary in a cavalier way. The screen walls on the roof had to transmit their loads unevenly through the slab to columns not directly placed beneath, and an inconvenient column in the garage was simply left out. Columns next to the ramp were allowed to run out of step with the others. Comparison of the design at different stages of development shows that Le Corbusier progressively violated the formality of his column grid, even though its order was stated in each façade. He was also cavalier with technical issues, for the problems of detailing external junctions while making the building appear homogeneous were never solved. It leaked horribly, and for years the clients complained, even threatening a law suit.[15] Le Corbusier's rationalism was therefore not essentially a rationality of structure or construction, nor indeed a technically-informed acceptance of the implications of mass-production. It was more abstract: a matter of visual and aesthetic ordering linked with more fundamental ideas about reason and geometry. All this was rooted in the theory of Purism propounded a decade earlier.

The Purist aesthetic

Purism, according to le Corbusier and Ozenfant,[16] distinguishes between two kinds of aesthetic experience, primary and secondary. The primary aesthetic is supposedly universal and eternal, based on mathematical and geometrical order which is also the underlying order of nature. The secondary aesthetic is based on symbolic associations and tends to be locally specific. A dice, for example, would appear to a Papuan merely a cube with spots: he would not recognise its gaming potential which is a secondary, local meaning, even though he responded to the cube as a primary figure.[17] Because of its universality, the primary aesthetic is superior, offering the possibility of a 'universal plastic language'. *'The great works of the past are those based on primary elements, and this is the only reason why they endure'*, claim Le Corbusier and Ozenfant confidently. In *Vers une Architecture*, which continues this theorising, Le

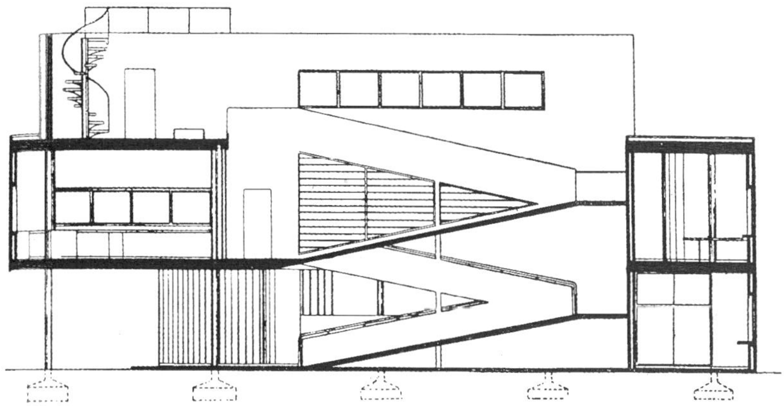

12. (opposite) South side with windows of salon.

13. (above) Section through central ramp.

Corbusier includes photographs of famous buildings with regulating lines added, such as Nôtre Dame, the Petit Trianon and Michelangelo's Capitol in Rome. He rhapsodises at length about the Parthenon, whose mouldings, he claims:

'are infallible and implacable. In severity they go far beyond our practice, or man's normal capabilities. Here, the purest witness to the physiology of sensation, and to the mathematical speculation attached to it, fixed and determined: we are riveted by our senses; we are ravished in our minds; we touch the axis of harmony.' [18]

The primary aesthetic reigns at the cost of the secondary, for he continues:

'No question of religious dogma enters in; no symbolical description, no naturalistic representation; there is nothing but pure forms in a precise relationship.' [19]

The Parthenon was shorn of specific cultural associations in the same way as the subject matter of Purist paintings; the bottles and glasses, pipes and guitars depicted within Le Corbusier's and Ozenfant's compositions (fig. 2). Associations with use and past experience were clearly not intended: instead these objects were presented for aesthetic contemplation as *objets-type*, their shapes supposedly refined by an evolutionary process towards perfection of form. And here we come to another aspect of Le Corbusier's supposed rationality: although he was unable to prove it, he claimed that the curves produced by evolutionary pressures on everyday objects, or which were honed through disciplines of performance such as aerodynamics, must have a mathematical or geometric significance as *'analagous mathematical curves of deep resonances*', thereby entering the canon of aesthetic purity.[20] One chapter of *Vers une Architecture* therefore juxtaposes Greek temples with motor cars, while another is filled with pictures of aircraft, which Le Corbusier claims are:

... 'the product of close selection. The lesson of the airplane lies in the logic which governed the statement of the problem and its realisation...The war was an insatiable "client" never satisfied, always demanding better. The orders were to succeed at all costs and death followed a mistake remorselessly. We may then affirm that the airplane mobilized invention, intelligence and daring: imagination and cold reason. It is the same spirit that built the Parthenon.' [21]

Mathematics and geometry, for Le Corbusier, had many meanings. They stood for the rational discipline of the engineer as opposed to the arbitrariness of whimsy and chance; for measure and consequent harmony; and for a procedural approach to laying out a site as with his story of the primitive temple.[22] But above all, mathematics and geometry reflected the order of everything for, as Le Corbusier consistently claimed *'geometry is the daughter of the universe'*. For him all geometries contributed to a final platonic order, a universal system whose definition became the holy grail for the rest of his life, most powerfully expressed in his book *The Modulor* written in the late 1940s.[23] The Modulor was a universal system of measures based on the golden mean, and intended to aestheticise the world. It received great publicity at the 9th Milan Triennale of 1951, where parallel attempts were made to reveal the hidden geometries of architectures across all periods and cultures.[24] The enduring monument to this cultural phase is Rudolf Wittkower's *Architectural Principles in the Age of Humanism*,[25] which analysed Renaissance systems of proportion, again implying universality.

In retrospect this phase looks like an attempt to establish an aesthetic science to accompany the other forms of scientific analysis then being applied to architecture. It was wrong on two counts. First, the geometric analysis itself was suspect, for ordered systems can be inferred that were not intended by the original authors, and even when similar ones seem to occur in different periods, they are not necessarily present for the same reasons.[26] Second, it was wrong to assume that such formal relations were necessarily the essential basis of our aesthetic experience, rather than the other effects

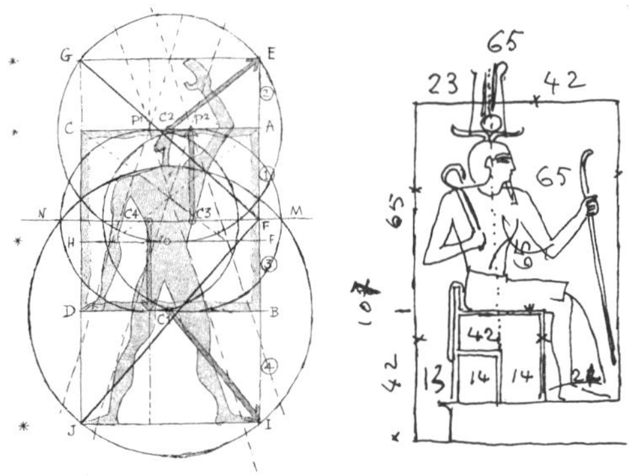

14. Modulor man, and right, Le Corbusier's drawing of ancient Egyptian proportions, suggesting universality.
15. (below) Ground floor hall and stair.

and associations experienced in relation to a building or work of art.[27] Sociological studies indicate, on the contrary, that aesthetic preferences are deeply bound up with cultural context and education.[28] To use the Purists' terms, this would mean the victory of the secondary aesthetic over the primary, even if one grants the primary aesthetic some credence. But universals are notoriously elusive, and it is not enough to point out

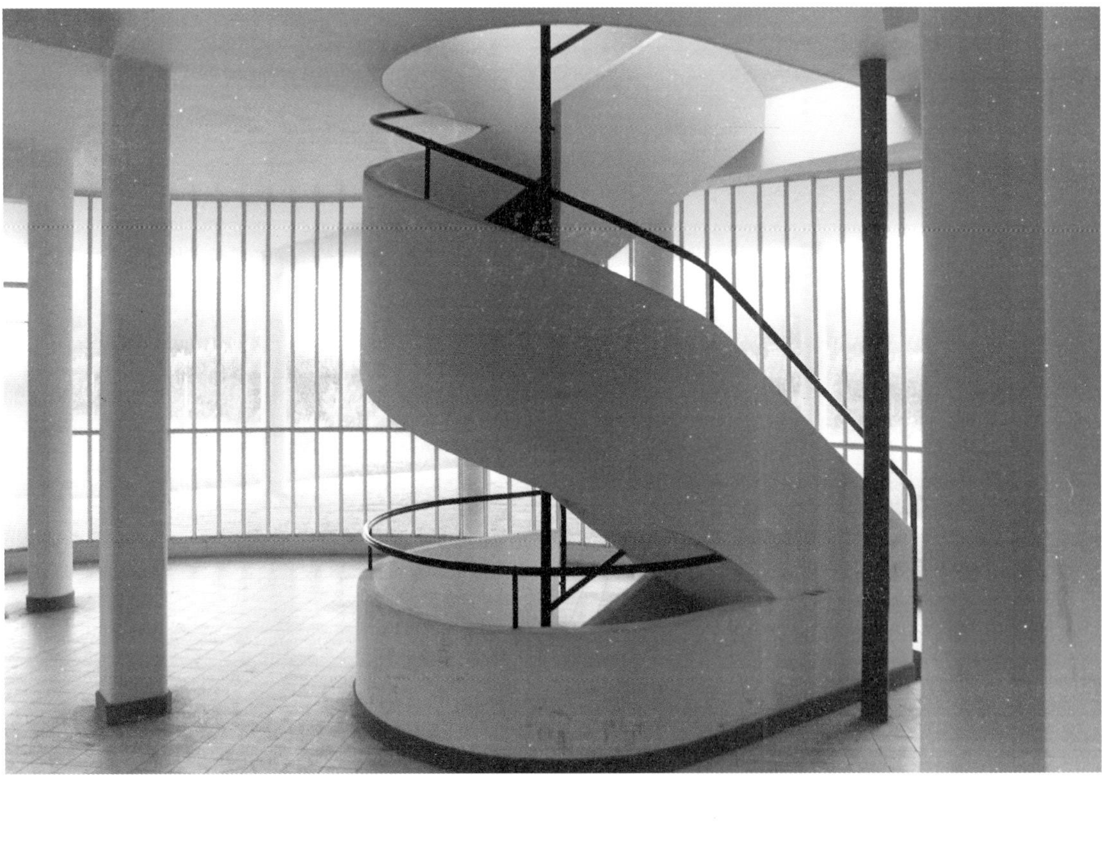

that geometry, number, order and measure are present and important in architectures across the world. They mean in different ways in different places, and even when one finds a common geometric basis, for example a square house with four columns, the local meanings attributed to it may be more significant than the common base.[29]

In setting up the Purist programme, Le Corbusier and Ozenfant sought a final solution in aesthetics. They claimed that concentration on the primary aesthetic would result in works equally valid for the Negro and the Laplander. The new housing, too, by conforming to the abstract principles of the primary aesthetic, would preclude the owner's need for sentimental association, bathing him or her in universal good taste. That this did not happen in the case of Le Corbusier's first major housing estate at Pessac is evident from Philippe Boudon's analysis.[30] The houses were taken over by their owners and subjected to all kinds of addition and *bricolage*. They proved conveniently adaptable, but at the expense of the architect's intention. The Modulor did not work either, despite a ringing endorsement from Albert Einstein.[31] The book sold several editions and is still in print. A couple of generations of architects tried to use it, but it proved too difficult and constraining, for there are many other pressures determining building dimensions, not least component sizes and safety regulations. According to Benton's analyses, Le Corbusier did not really use it himself, except as a purifying tool at the end of the design phase, as confirmation. Today interest in the Modulor is mainly historical.

Practice as opposed to theory

It would be wrong to dismiss Le Corbusier's practice because of shortcomings in his theory, and it would be a mistake also to forget how influential the theory has been. From the perspective of the 21st Century we need to understand both, and the evident gap that has emerged between them. Architects' theories often have an alibi function, both for the author and his/her clients. The myth they carry is significant for the process of realising the work even if it is not ultimately credible. But let us return to the practice and the 'plastic language' that Le Corbusier developed. In Purist painting, as in the architecture, a compositional method was developed which set in fruitful contrast two different kinds of order. First there was the canvas itself in its geometry and proportions, including the implied regulating lines defining its spatial field. Then there were the depicted shapes of the *objets-type*, usually curved and drawn by hand, certainly not mathematically defined. Both curves and compositional balance were visually executed and judged, as was the colour scheme, whose rationale is barely defined in the Purist essay. It was the first era of abstract painting, and the discoveries made in form and colour must have seemed compelling, like a form of visual music. Painting had undoubtedly gained a powerful new lease of life by breaking with established pictorial conventions, and the graphic effect was felt throughout society.

The same abstraction and purification could be applied to architecture, eliminating the clutter of historic styles: *'Culture is the flowering of the effort to select. Selection means rejection, pruning, cleansing; the clear and naked emergence of the essential'* wrote Le Corbusier.[32] Excited by developments in technology, he commended the discipline of the engineer, while always leaving himself an escape route into the realm of the 'poetic'.[33] The proportions of the canvas and the system of regulating lines had their architectural counterpart in the layout of wings and bays or the column grid. To this network could be added some pure geometric elements at a smaller scale like the rectangular ramp and half-round staircase. These lesser forms and the main form of the building might conform to the canon of *'the most beautiful forms'* by approximating to the cube, the sphere or the cylinder.[34] Within this strict system a counter-vocabulary equivalent to that of the *objets-type* could then be installed, serving visually and compositionally like the glasses and bottles, but actually suggested by functional pressures such as the flow of circulation or the embrace of a bathtub. Like the *objet-type*, the functional form was supposedly the product of Darwinian evolution, having obeyed some inner call of nature to follow the *'curve of least resistance'* or whatever. Thus could Le Corbusier convince himself of the rationality of his free forms, but they were drawn forms not unrelated to those in paintings by masters like Picasso and Braque, whom Le Corbusier greatly admired. And once drawn on the plan they were free to be used in other ways. In Villa Savoye, for example, the solarium walls as built are ghosts of earlier bedrooms, and in the Maison La Roche even the ramp originated in another place and for another purpose.[35] Engaged in his compositional games, Le Corbusier was as

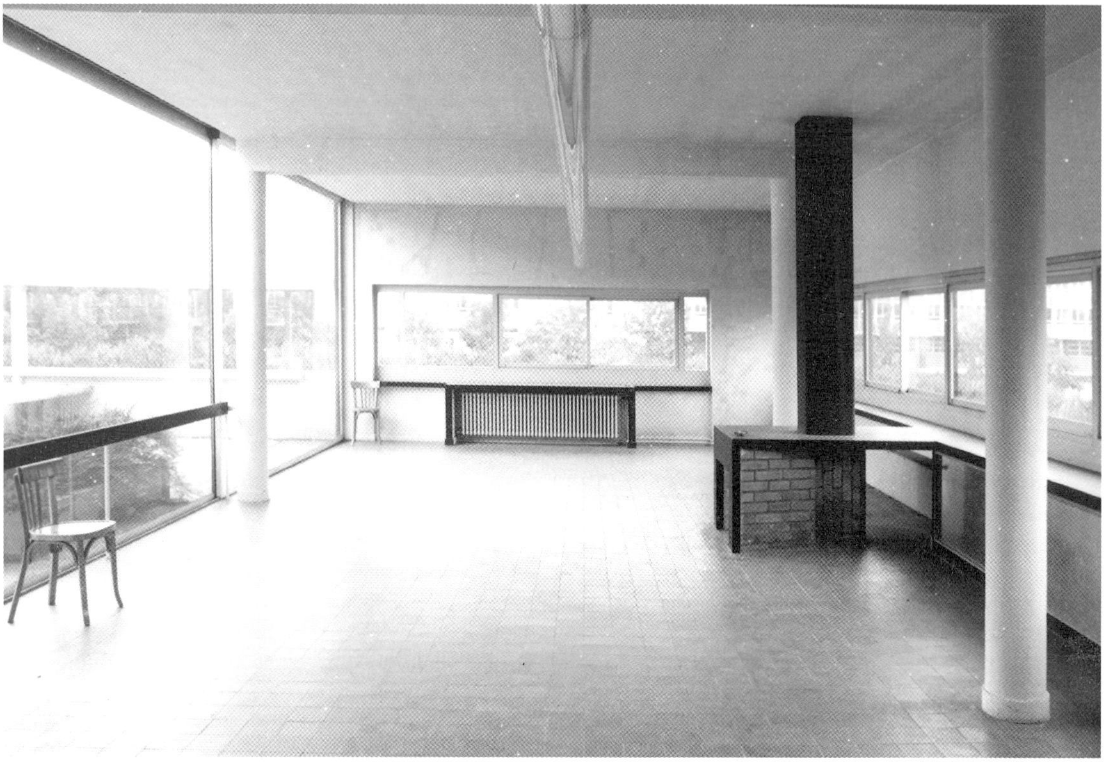

16. Interior of the *salon* and fireplace, the open court is to left.
17. Between main stair and ramp.

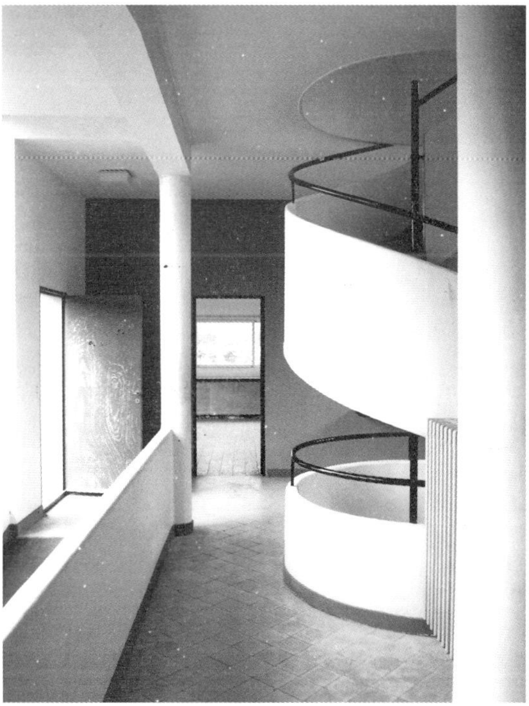

entranced as his admirers, and the making of a sculptural whole took priority over fidelity to programme, all the more so when the programme was as flexible as that of the Villa Savoye. That the composition of paintings echoes that of site plans, with similar proportional relations, is not surprising, even if the site plan can only be seen by passing aircraft pilots. For Le Corbusier, harmony at any scale was universal harmony, partaking in the order of the universe.

In the post-war period, Le Corbusier's work became increasingly sculptural and increasingly loaded with historic references. Purism gave way to a new interest in materials. In the 1950s, as the rest of the architectural world took up his more doctrinaire ideas about rationality and machine production, he shocked them by building the astonishingly irregular chapel at Ronchamp. Because of his platonic beliefs, he saw the Modulor at work here too, and it can indeed be traced in elements such as the floor pattern and main doors, but the building is so far from the straight and level and so asymmetrical that it is hard to believe that

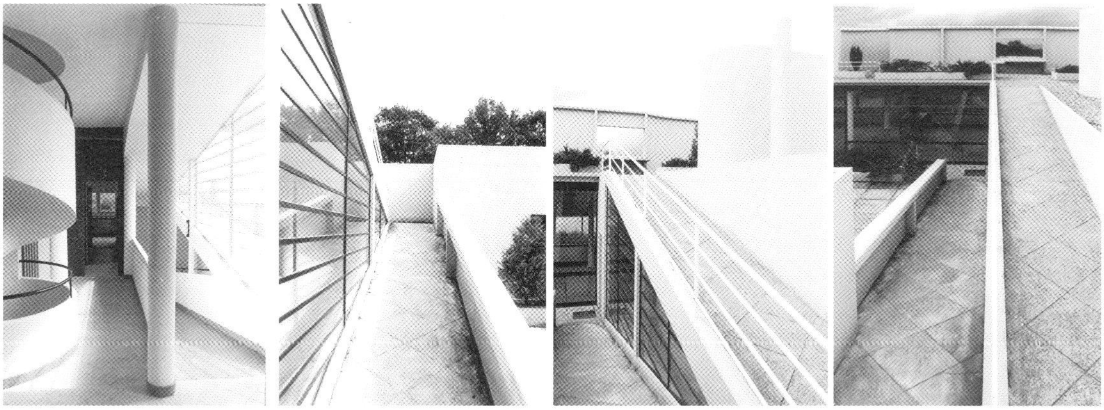

18-21. (above) Different stages of the ramp.
22-24. (below) Ramp interiors and roof garden.

the proportion system can have much effect.[36] The undoubted aesthetic power of the building must be explained in another way. Without pursuing a full analysis, we can recognise a kinship with sculptures by artists like Picasso and Miro, and note the variety and richness of interpretation proposed by the many commentators who have examined it. The building is loaded with potential references, most of them ambiguous, which makes it rich and elusive, supportive of multiple readings.[37] Whatever you call this kind of aesthetic appeal, it is plainly not that of Purism's primary aesthetic. Indeed it seems closer to the secondary aesthetic. If it can appeal to both 'Negroes' and 'Laplanders' as Le Corbusier and Ozenfant hoped in 1920, it surely appeals in different ways, evoking different associations in each case. In its rich suggestiveness, the work transcends the theory.

Conclusion

Villa Savoye provided a crucial opportunity for Le Corbusier to show what he could do with an open site, unconstraining programme and large budget. Nearly 20 metres square and three storeys high, it was a large impractical house and cost double the intended budget.[38] It suffered severe technical problems, was never much lived-in, and probably served best for summer parties, though there was nowhere for guests to stay. For most of its life it has remained an empty monument regularly patched and painted, and it now serves mainly as an architectural pilgrimage site. This unfortunate record contrasts sharply with its mythical life in photography and print, where it could hardly have gathered more fame. Prominent in every book on Modern Architecture, it dominates the cover of Hitchcock and Johnson's *The International Style*. It was the obvious choice, for it shows a formal and spatial flair beyond that of Gropius, marking a peak of artistic performance and epitomising the architecture of the period. It represents perfectly the abstraction of architecture from ornament, and also away from conventional patterns of occupation and conventional backs and fronts. Equally

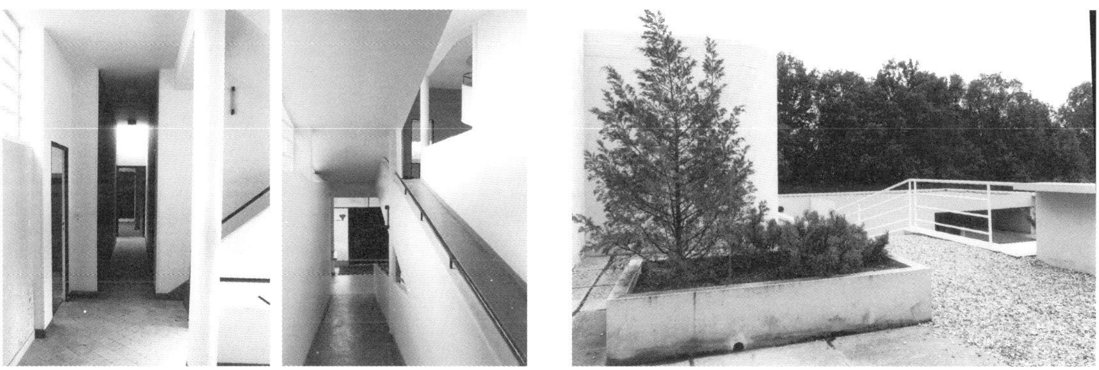

repressed are material and builderly qualities. Gone are wall and roof, cornice and gutter: perception is invited instead of pure plastic relationships.

In the dynamism of its spaces, Villa Savoye is thrillingly three-dimensional even on the page, and the *promenade architecturale* takes it into the fourth. But measured out as it is within an orthogonal frame, it could still be easily read in plans and photographs. Its simplicity made it ideal for photography in black and white. Detached from the site, it also became *the* model object-building, poised uncontaminated within the harmony of its own system, framed irrevocably within the square of its outer wall. Unsullied by context, it paved the way for generations of buildings now rightly criticised for their contextual indifference. Ironically, it seems less dated than the cars photographed alongside it to provide a 'modern' pedigree. They have long since gone to the museum or scrapyard, along with the aeroplanes and liners which also thrilled readers of *Vers une Architecture*. More timeless than the machines that inspired it, the Villa still seems strangely modern, even though it so strongly represents its period. Through sheer artistic brilliance it transcends the mistaken theories of its author, who led generations of architects astray like an architectural Pied Piper. Bruno Taut saw both the quality and the danger at the time, remarking that Le Corbusier was an architect and easel painter who tended to confuse the two.[39]

Notes

1. This was the title of the huge centenary exhibition at the Hayward Gallery in London,1987; catalogue Raeburn & Wilson 1987.
2. *After Cubism*, published Paris 1918.
3. On Le Corbusier as painter see David Green in Raeburn & Wilson 1987, pp.110-130.
4. First published in French as *Vers une Architecture*, Paris 1923, and in English translated by Frederick Etchells as *Towards a New Architecture*, John Rodker, London, 1927.
5. For more detail on the early meetings of CIAM, see Blundell Jones 1999, pp.106-109.
6. Peter Smithson once remarked that he seemed to have *'already had all one's best ideas'*.
7. See my essay *Architect and landscape architect working together: Scharoun and Mattern*, a chapter in Birksted 1999, pp.179-193.
8. See *Some Modernist houses and their gardens*, article about Erich Mendelsohn's house and garden by Wiepking written jointly by the author and Jan Woudstra, Die Gartenkunst vol. 1, 1999, pp.112-122.
9. *'Standing in a field you cannot see very far. What's more, the soil is unhealthy, damp etc...'* Le Corbusier quoted in Benton 1987, p.195. His nickname for the villa was *'les heures claires'*, suggesting a contrast with the dirty soil. As Gaston Bachelard put it in *The Poetics of Space*, *'up near the roof one's thoughts are clear'* (Bachelard 1969, p.18).
10. 48,000 Francs according to Benton: see Brooks 1987, p. 88.
11. Le Corbusier 1927, p. 8, repeated p. 44 and p. 45.
12. For a discussion of the problems of perspective failing to represent non-orthogonal space, see Chapter 15.
13. A propos the effectiveness of photographs for Le Corbusier, it is perhaps significant that after 1919 he possessed only one effective eye, and his perception was therefore monocular like that of a camera. Binocular vision allows perception of depth and layering without the convergent lines of perspective, which is why landscapes come so much more to life through stereoscopic photography.
14. For a complete set of drawings and narrative of the design development see Benton 1987, pp. 191-207.
15. See Benton in Brooks 1987, p. 93.
16. See *Purism*, first published in the fourth issue of *L'Esprit Nouveau*, pp. 369-386, reprinted complete as english translation in Herbert 1964 pp. 58-73.
17. This example is taken from the essay, Herbert 1964, p. 62.
18. Le Corbusier 1927 p. 204.
19. Ibid.
20. *Purism* as in note 16, p. 64.
21. Le Corbusier 1927, pp.100-101.
22. *'[Primitive man] has regulated his work, he has brought in order. For all around him the forest is in disorder with its creepers, its briars and its tree-trunks which impede him and paralyse his efforts.'* ibid, p. 67.
23. Le Corbusier 1961.
24. Le Corbusier, *The Modulor*, Introduction to the Second Edition, p. 5.
25. Wittkower 1949.
26. Builders of Gothic cathedrals were concerned with a specific number symbolism - three is the Trinity, for example - with different values from those used by other cultures and other periods.
27. See, for example, the chapter *How Buildings Mean* in Goodman & Elgin 1988.
28. See Bourdieu 1984, also Clifford Geertz's essay *Art as a cultural system* in Geertz 1983.
29. I concur with the anthropologist Clifford Geertz when he claims, writing of social and moral universals: *'most (conceivably all) universals are so general as to be without intellectual force or interest, are large banalities lacking either circumstantiality or surprise, precision or revelation, and are thus of precious little use ("People everywhere have views about differences between the sexes"; "All societies have systems of social ranking")...... if universals do have some degree of non-triviality, circumstantiality, and originality, if they actually assert something interesting enough to be wrong (the ubiquity of the Oedipus Complex...) they are ill-based.'* Geertz 2000 pp.134-5.
30. Boudon 1972.
31. The most thorough and elegant dismissal of the Modulor as an absolute system is the chapter *Comic Lines* in Evans 1995, pp. 273-292.
32. Le Corbusier 1927, p. 128.
33. Ibid p. 19.
34. Ibid p. 29.
35. Benton 1987, pp. 44-76.
36. See Evans 1995, pp. 289-290.
37. See Danièle Pauly particularly, but many of the Corbusian commentators have something to add, and the possibilities seem endless. Suggestive, and interesting for its theory of reconstituted memories, is Herb Greene's reading in Greene 1976, pp.1-5.
38. Benton in Brooks 1987, pp. 87, 88.
39. Taut 1929, already quoted in translation in Chapter 1, note 38.

Chapter 8. Alvar Aalto: Viipuri Library, Karelia, now Russia, 1927-35

Born in 1898, Alvar Aalto was a decade younger than most of the architects so far considered. When the Viipuri project started he was 29, but Le Corbusier was 40 and Bruno Taut 47. This meant that Aalto happened upon the Modern Movement at a later stage and that his career stretched on to reach its climax long after the Second World War, and he lived until 1976. Born and brought up in Finland, he became the figurehead of Scandinavian Modernism, his reputation eclipsing even that of his mentor Gunnar Asplund. It was not just talent: his prominent position in a small country at the northeast corner of Europe had its strengths. One was that the ideological debate in architecture polarised in the previous generation between Neoclassicism and National Romanticism provided a rich and fertile starting point. Another was that late and relatively small-scale industrialisation created opportunities for collaboration both in furniture and in architectural ironmongery and fittings. The famous bentwood chairs still manufactured by Artek needed to be developed empirically in dialogue with a manufacturer. This experience extended Aalto's sensibility and design vocabulary in a way he could scarcely have achieved on his own. Living in a relatively narrow circle, he was also lucky with clients, for as his reputation rose the jobs came thick and fast, budgets were generous, and economic conditions reasonably stable. Aalto was therefore less limited by narrow windows of opportunity than his German near-contemporaries, and he built much.

Many Aalto buildings could have graced these pages. Viipuri library - which still exists in poor condition after long neglect under Soviet rule[1] - was chosen for its key role in establishing his mature direction as a designer, but it is also of interest for its long and revealing gestation. Completed in 1935, it had started life in 1927 as a neoclassical design heavily indebted to Gunnar Asplund's Stockholm City Library. There was much intercourse between architects in Finland and Sweden, and Asplund was the architect whom Aalto most admired.[2] The transition of ideas between the two buildings - outwardly so different, yet in principle so deeply linked - provides a fascinating glimpse of the way the Modern Movement broke in Scandinavia five years later than in central Europe.

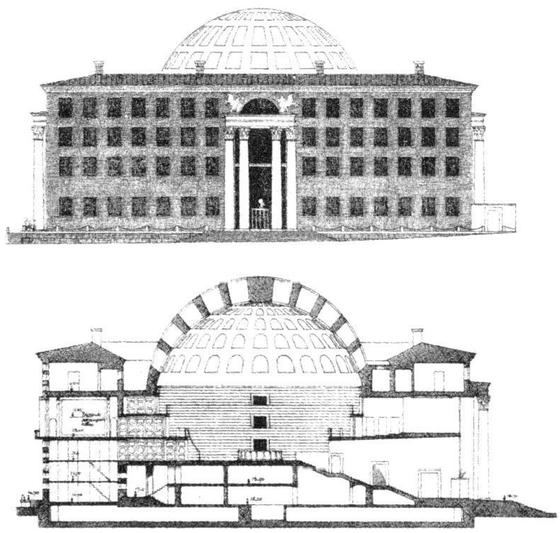

1. Gunnar Asplund, Stockholm City Library, first version 1921, elevation and section through main stair.

Asplund's library

The design of Stockholm City Library began before 1920. A library committee was convened in 1912, but it was not until 1918 that they gained the necessary funds and brought in Asplund as architect. He took the task seriously, visiting new libraries in England, Germany and the United States, and noting particularly the planning of Albert Kahn's libraries at Minnesota and Michigan, where a central lending hall was flanked with reading rooms to either side. The site was at the corner of two major streets in Stockholm, Sveavägen and Odengatan, with Observatory Hill immediately behind. As the hillside was to be left as a small park, the new library needed to stand alone, presenting itself in three directions. Asplund devised a centralised building planned as a circle within a square. Its severe geometrical form reflected the Nordic Neoclassicism of the early 1920s, also seen in such works as Tengbom's

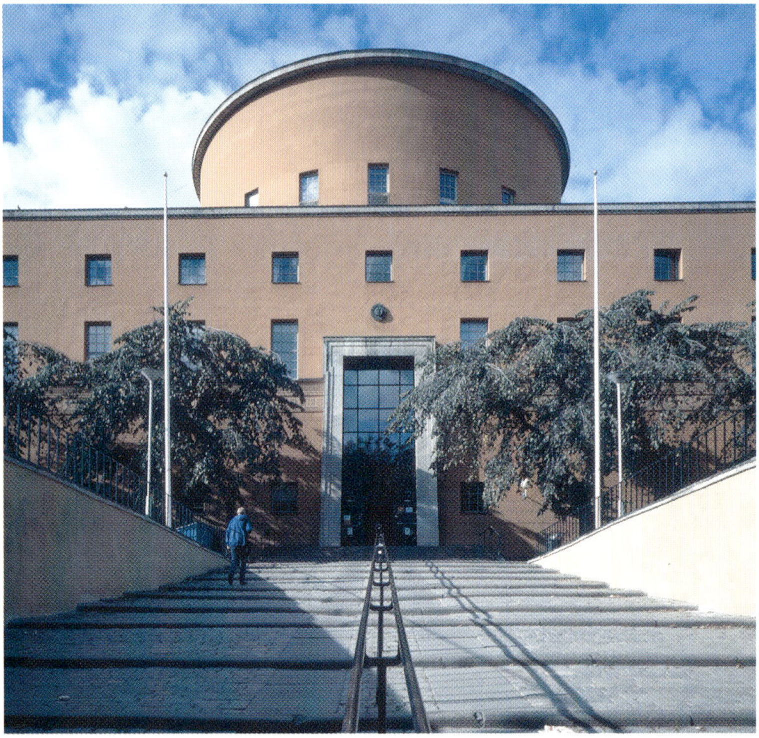

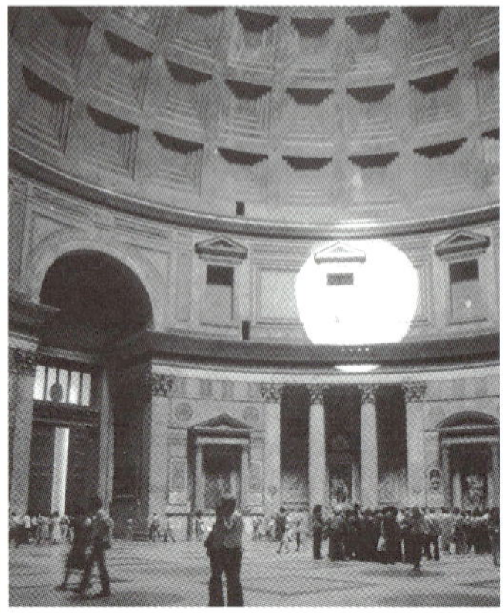

2. (left) Gunnar Asplund, Stockholm City Library as completed in 1928: main entrance.

3. (above) Interior of the Pantheon, Rome.

4. (below) Stockholm City Library site plan, with building bottom right next to major crossroads and park to left: black is water.

Stockholm Concert Hall of 1921-6. The rotunda in plan, a favourite of Asplund, was employed also in the slightly earlier Lister County Court and even for a 1919 version of the Gothenburg Lawcourts extension (see p. 167). Palladio's Villa Rotunda was a clear precedent: more doubtful is whether Asplund also knew of Ledoux's Paris Barrière, to which it is similar in form.[3] By the end of 1921 he had produced a design definitive in terms of organisation, if not of style (fig. 1).

Asplund always claimed to be concerned with the efficient implementation of the programme, and the building made it clear.[4] Entering by the door to Sveavägen, the public would rise to the main control point at the centre, arriving in a circular hall lined with three tiers of open stacks. Long rectangular side-lit reading rooms were placed to either side, leading back to a pair of shorter ones at the front for newspapers and periodicals. The ground floor of the north wing and its entrance were reserved for the children's library, ground floor south for library staff and book-handling. Main stacks, accessible to staff only, were placed beneath the central drum. The top floor housed special study rooms, with the chief librarian's office appropriately set above the main entrance in the middle of the principal façade.

Apart from the monumental presence of the building and the tricks of scale which make it unforgettable, the essential drama lies in the experience of approach and entry. Built into the hillside, the library sits on a platform of shops in which a slot is cut for a cobbled ramp (fig. 2). Ascending this, one arrives at a huge semi-Egyptian portal to enter a tall narrow hall with a

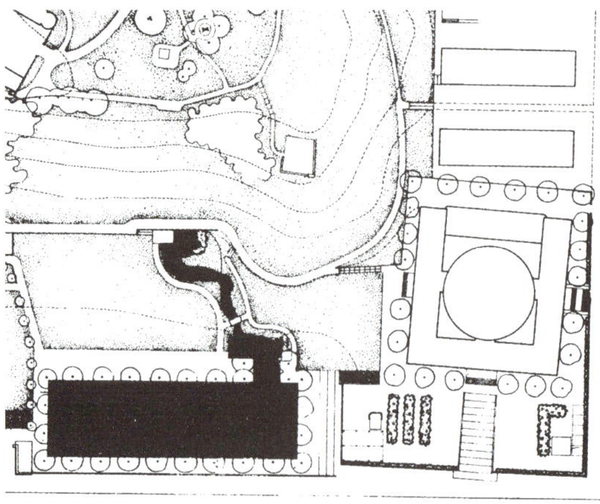

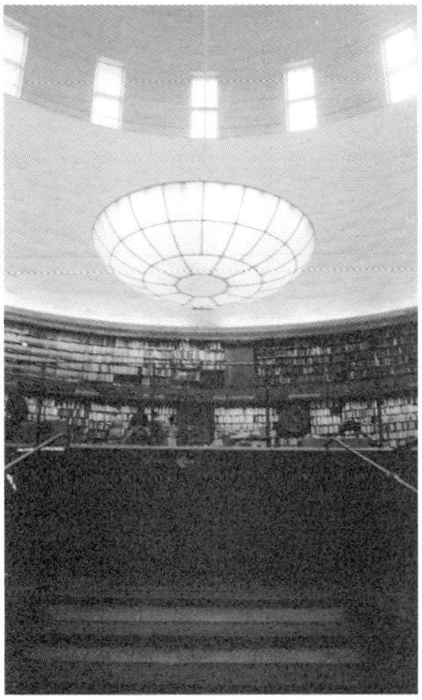

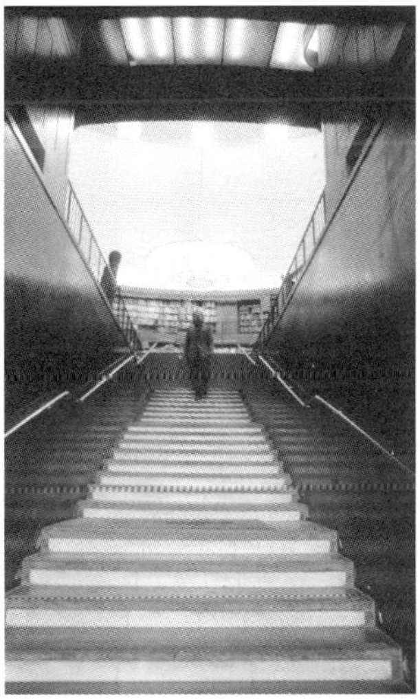

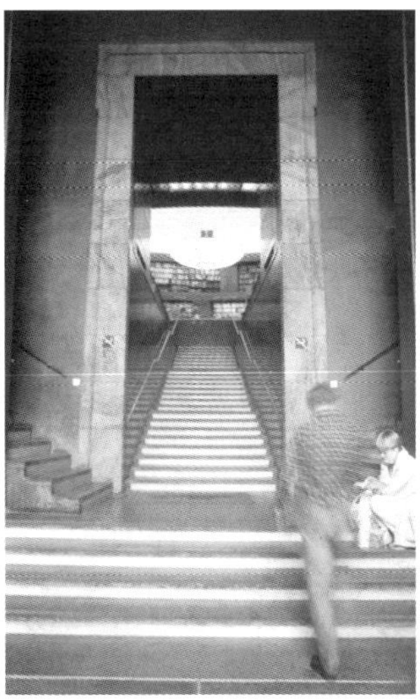

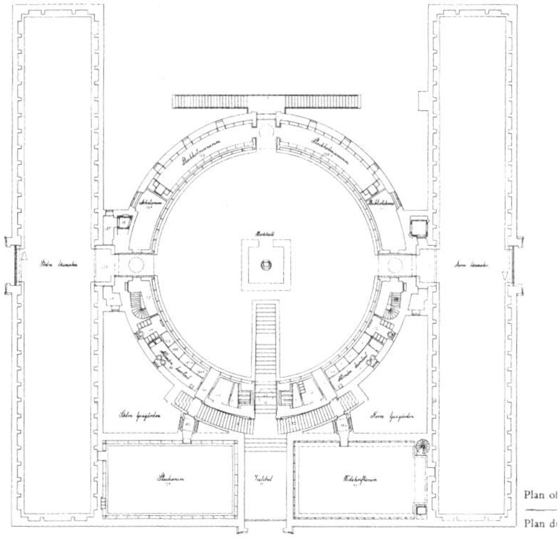

Gunnar Asplund, Stockholm City Library
5, 6, 7. (left) Progression up main stair to discover drum.
8. (above) Upper floor plan. 9. (below) Section through main stair. 10. (bottom) Lower floor plan.

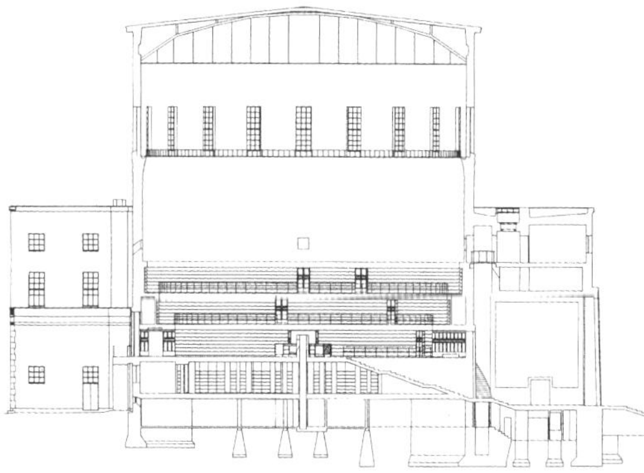

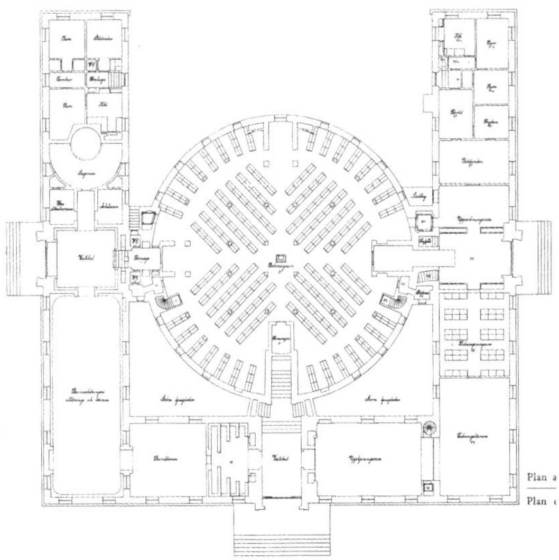

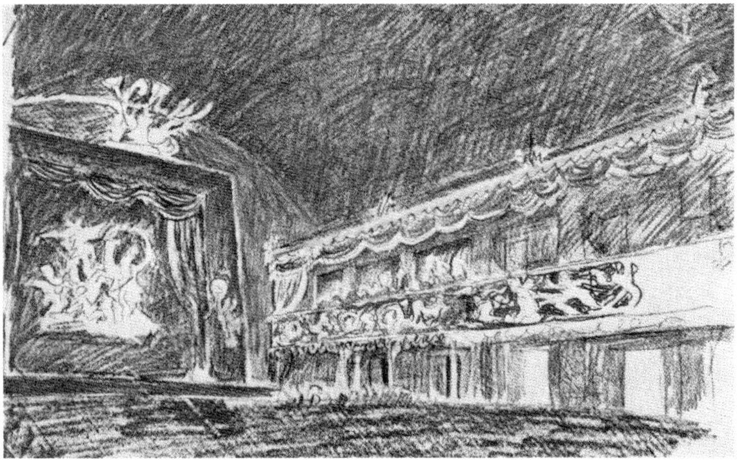

11. Asplund's sketch of his Scandia Cinema, Stockholm, 1923.

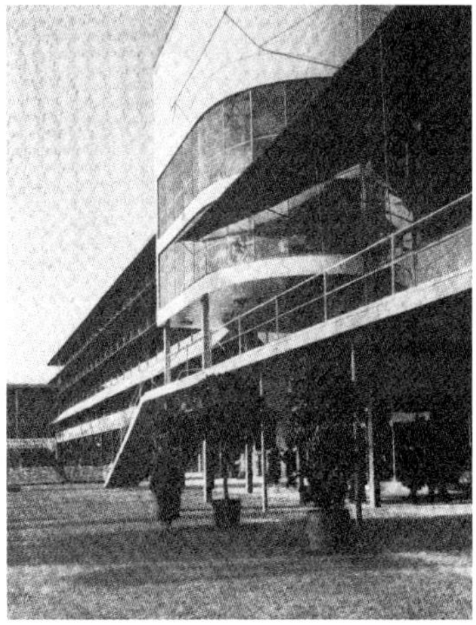

12. Asplund, Stockholm Exhibition, 1930.

great stair leading on and up (figs 5-7). As one rises, other stairs part to the side, apparently buried in the thickness of the drum-like wall, and the central space gradually unfolds. Originally conceived as a sphere lit by glazed coffering and with tiered bookstacks to define the bottom half, it was built as a drum with clerestory windows. This strongly enclosed and centralised space suggests a world in itself - a world of knowledge. Contrast between it and the outside world is enhanced by the sense of progression up and through the depth of the plan, passing a sequence of exaggerated layers. Asplund had done much the same thing at a smaller scale with Lister County Court, where similar progress to the centre suggests a larger, deeper building than in fact is present. Comparisons have been made with the Pantheon,[5] a precedent known to all traditionally educated architects,[6] which for some meant the very beginning of interior architectural space.[7] In that Roman monument, the emphasis is clearly on the interior experience (fig. 3), particularly the perceptually elusive effect of the coffered dome and its emphasised relation with the heavens through the oculus. As with Asplund's library, linear axial progression from piazza through portico and wall is suddenly arrested by the circular space, where relations are no longer axial but a matter of centre and periphery, and direction is given by the projected circle of sunlight.

Between the initial version of 1921 and the completed building of 1928, the Stockholm library plan remained much the same, but the dome became a drum, classical giant order columns gave way to the Egyptian door frame borrowed from Bindesböll,[8] and rustication on the base was surmounted by an Egyptian frieze which, instead of depicting hieroglyphs, shows modern objects including prams, toys, and locomotives. In the entrance hall, a wall-relief depicts scenes from the Iliad, and the original doorhandles were sculptural figures of Adam and Eve who, having eaten of the tree, prepare our way for the knowledge to which we aspire, and to which we quite literally ascend. This shifting iconography shows an architect struggling with questions of style, but not yet able to dispense with the notion of a symbolic or ornamental vocabulary. The instability of it, indeed the final vanity of Asplund's quest through a whole catalogue of architectural imagery, reveals the crisis which precipitated his turn to Modernism. His Stockholm Exhibition buildings of 1930 with their functional forms, generous glazing and unadorned white surfaces, decisively launched the new architecture in Scandinavia (fig. 12). Aalto wrote:

'The exhibition speaks of a happy and relaxed daily life. It propagandises consistently for a healthy and unaffected lifestyle based on economic realities. One might use a surgical metaphor and say that the appendix, where people's demands for luxuries and affected superficiality are housed, has been removed here. It is the desire for luxury that, under special circumstances, has been the point of departure for "artistic homes" but among a wider circle has resulted in silent tragedies: factory-made antique furniture and misguided values in the same vein.'[9]

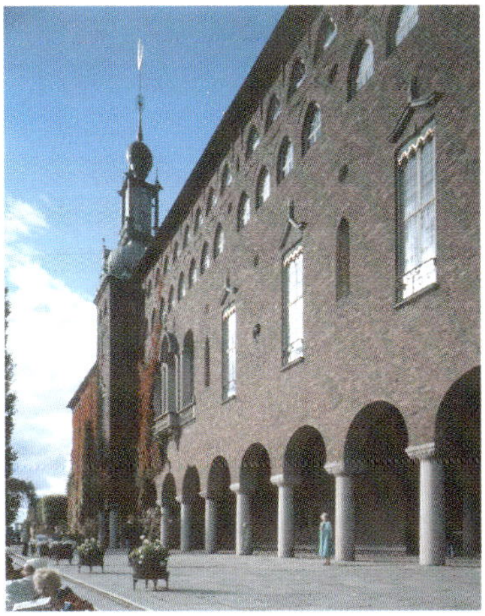

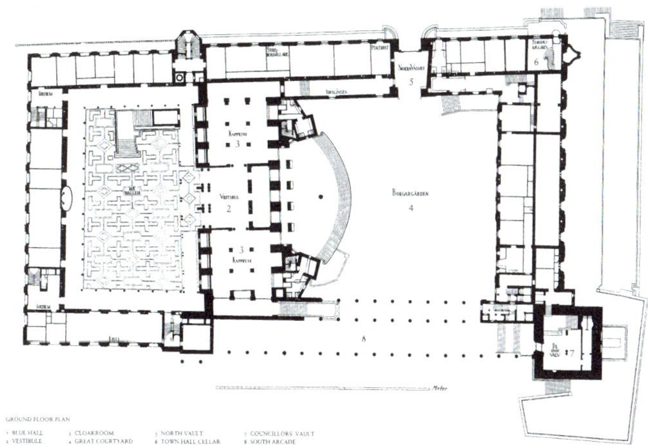

13, 14. Ragnar Östberg, Stockholm City Hall 1905-1923, main front to lagoon and ground floor plan.

Aalto was still a student when he first met Asplund in 1920, applying for a job that was not granted. Numerous reflections of Asplund's buildings in his own early work show a clear influence,[10] but Aalto was in a generally receptive state and looking everywhere. Clearly he absorbed the twin heritage of Scandinavian architecture of that time - National Romanticism and Nordic Neoclassicism - for he could soon perform confidently in either mode.[11] It is also significant that on a visit to Italy in 1924, he admired the anonymous architecture of the 'organic' hill towns quite as much as the formality of the classical monuments. In buildings such as the Workers' Club at Jyväskylä of 1924, classical formality was tempered with judicious irregularity; evidence of tricks well learned both from Asplund and Asplund's former teacher Ragnar Östberg, who produced the great masterpiece of National Romanticism, Stockholm City Hall (figs 13,14). Though planned at the turn of the century, this building was not completed until the early 1920s when it made a major impact. Inspired by the Doge's Palace in Venice and built in plain red brick, it was nicely sited to command magnificent views of and from Stockholm's principal lagoon. The interiors were contrived as a dramatic sequence, including an internal court - the Blue Hall - treated like a Nordic version of an Italian town-hall piazza. Gothic in its irregularity, it has asymmetrical facades and its windows run out of line, while plans are carefully skewed. Such irregularity seems at first absent from Asplund's library, but it shows up in the site plan as a twist of the whole building. There are studied irregularities in all Asplund's buildings: repeatedly the contrast between classical formality and local contingency is the making of them. In 1923 Aalto visited, with Asplund, the latter's most Baroque work: Scandia Cinema, with its blue-sky ceiling and seating boxes like tents at a medieval tournament. He must have noticed too how, in the foyer, the outside of the auditorium appeared like a free-standing building within a greater volume. These games of insideness and outsideness, of fantasy and illusion, reached their peak in this building. Aalto also well understood Asplund's lifelong obsession with path and progression, which was played out to perfection in collaboration with Sigurd Lewerentz at the Enskede cemetery south of Stockholm, one of the finest landscapes of the 20th century.

Viipuri - the first version

When Aalto entered the competition for the library at Viipuri in 1927, Asplund's Stockholm library was almost complete and at the height of its novelty. Aalto knew the drawings and may have visited the site: he certainly attended the opening in the following year and wrote about it.[12] The competition site in Viipuri (fig. 22) was on Alexanterinkatu, the city's main shopping street, but it lay close to the cathedral where the street traverses a park. The competition brief called for a general plan in which the library was to be balanced by a new cultural centre opposite that was to be designed in outline. Aalto proposed the library as a long thin block set back from the road but with a projecting entrance hall. Placing the cultural centre opposite and to one side, he made an open square next to the

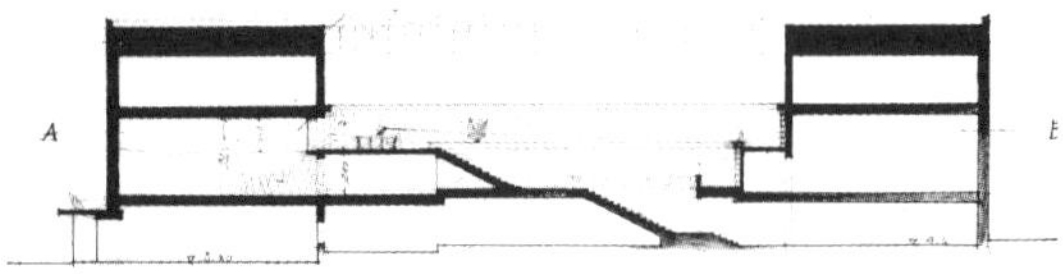

15. Viipuri library, first version 1927: section with main stair rising to control desk and skylight over.
16. (below) Plan of main library level showing asymmetrical projecting entrance, turn, and stair rising in well.

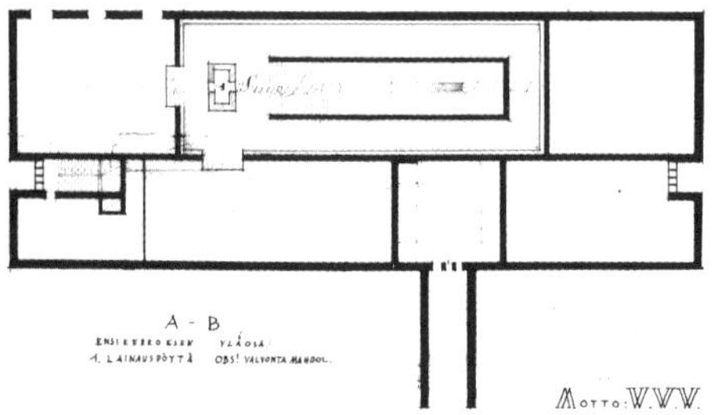

crossroads. The dividing line between cultural centre and square set the asymmetrical alignment of the library entrance not quite two thirds across the façade. Addressing the square was a relatively formal front with rustication, classical frieze and regularly spaced windows derived from Asplund (fig. 17). The decorative treatment turned the corner at each end, stopping abruptly at a cutback where, in an unexpectedly modernist manner, a vertical slot revealed a circulation zone. The rest of each side and the rear façade to the park were less formal, lacking ornament and with asymmetrical fenestration. In later versions areas of trellis were applied to increase informality and extend the greenery of the park. Formal front and informal back reflected the contrast of culture and nature, and the re-centering of the left panel of the north-east end façade with the axial door to the newspaper reading room struck a half-way point in this formal hierarchy (fig. 18).

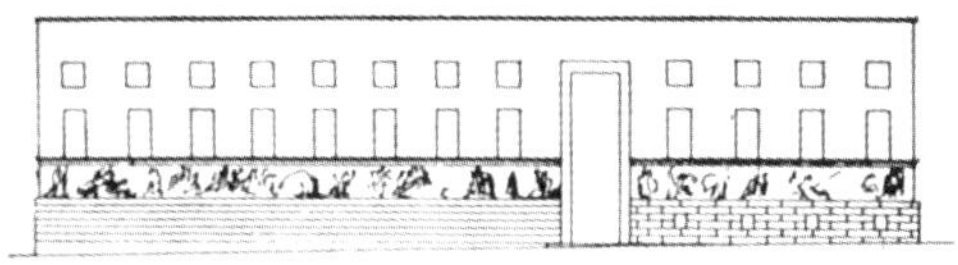

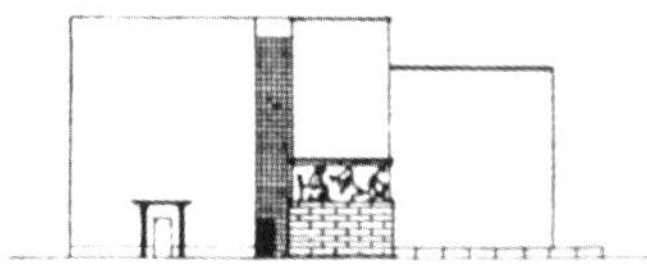

17,18. Viipuri library, first version 1927: front and end elevations.

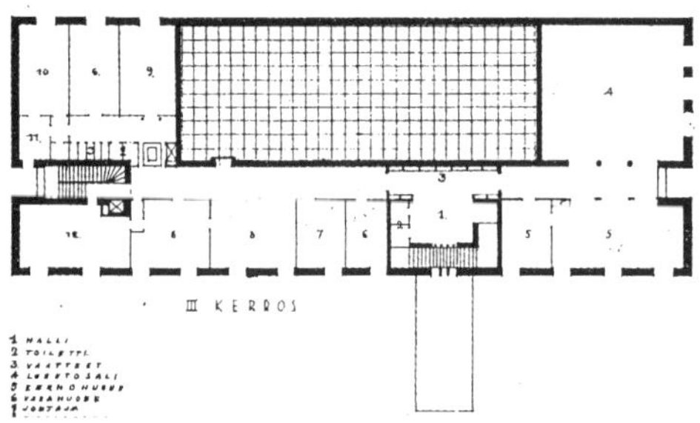

19. Viipuri library, first version 1927: plan of upper floor.
20. Plan of bottom floor showing book storage.

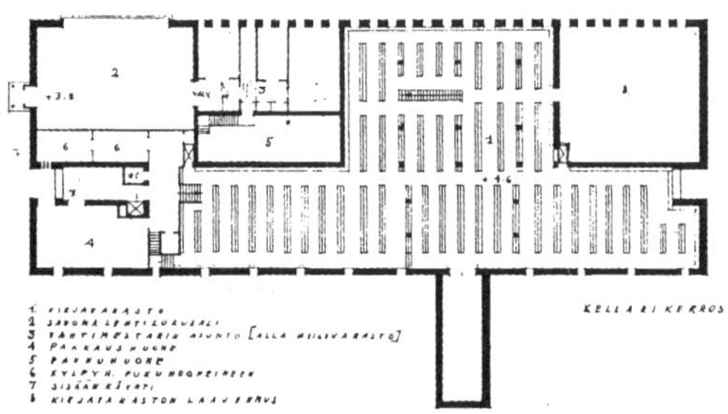

The site conditions explain the linearity of the building as opposed to the centrality of Asplund's. The route idea could still be adopted, and Aalto attempted a radical reinterpretation. He recreated the tiered lending hall in rectangular form at the back, the stairs rising leftward up a central well to arrive at the second-floor control desk. This great room was completely enclosed and surrounded by bookstacks, but lit from above by a glass roof to seem like an outside court. In section the public areas occupied the middle floors, the basement being book storage and the top floor staff offices and study rooms. To reach his *piano nobile* above the rusticated base of bookstore, Aalto proposed a main stair set within his entrance projection. Visitors would climb a storey and enter through a dark square vestibule. Before them they would see the columns of the main well, light falling mysteriously from above as in an external peristyle or atrium - an inside/outside space.[13] Turning left to climb the internal stair on axis, they would arrive at the control point, seeing the main reading room beyond. Comparison of plans at different levels suggests the lively diversity of a free-planned modern building rather than the obedient repetition of a traditional loadbearing one. Divided by a corridor linking the circulation indents, the top floor combines a narrow band of offices to front with a wider band of reading rooms behind, the glass roof of the central hall leaving a remainder of end rooms almost square and almost symmetrical. At mid level the main hall and end rooms dominate, while the circulation zone added to the front band makes a front reading room. The sideways sweep of the stair resolves the asymmetry of the front if a balance is understood between entrance hall and control point. The ground floor, whose structure carries the greatest loads, paradoxically offers the largest continuous space for the main bookstacks. A narrow stair on the axis of the main hall drops into it, so even with the public excluded, librarians would be seen descending to and ascending from this treasury of knowledge. To sum up, this first version was a hybrid. It shows Aalto's interests in route, light and the dialectic of inside and out. The asymmetry is progressive; but the architecture is theatrical and the building's visible substance still a contrivance of stucco.

The design was submitted in October 1927, and Aalto won first prize. But the jury criticised the glass roof of the main hall as impractical and did not like the dark box of the entrance hall. He produced a revised design in 1928 and a further revision in 1929 which was accepted for building, but the effects of the Wall Street crash forced postponement and the project was dropped until 1933.[14] The delay allowed disagreements about the wisdom of the choice of site to resurface, and the building was moved to a quieter position in the park, close to the cathedral. Aalto was happy to replan it for the new site, for he needed to reconcile his design with the radical changes of outlook and vocabulary that had interceded. These were due both to discoveries in his own work, notably at Paimio Sanatorium and the Turun Sanomat building, and changes in the

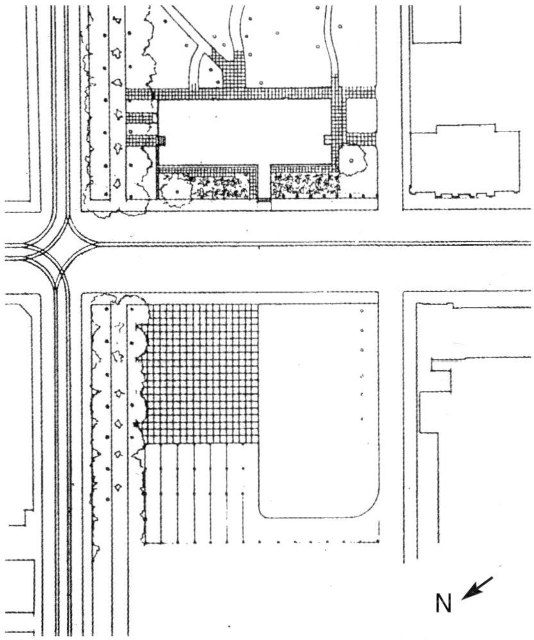

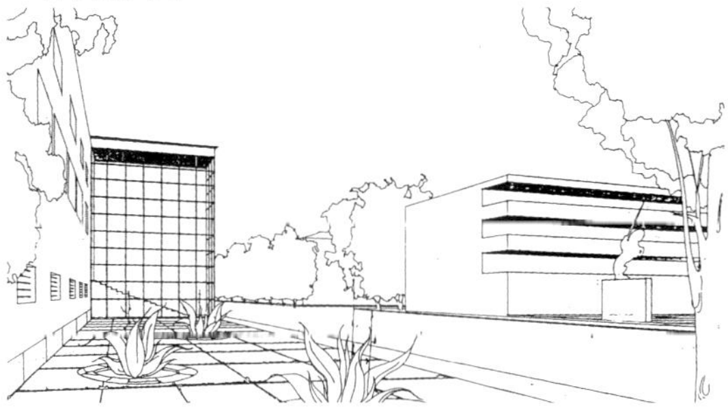

21. (below left) Viipuri library, second version 1928: perspective of main front with horizontal windows and glazed entrance stair.

22. (top) First and second version site plan, showing cultural centre opposite and intended public square.

23. (above) Perspective of second version with cultural centre.

24. (below) Second version first floor plan, 1928, showing projecting entrance stairs, arrival at central well, and stair to left. Radial planning in children's library, right, is a bold new move.

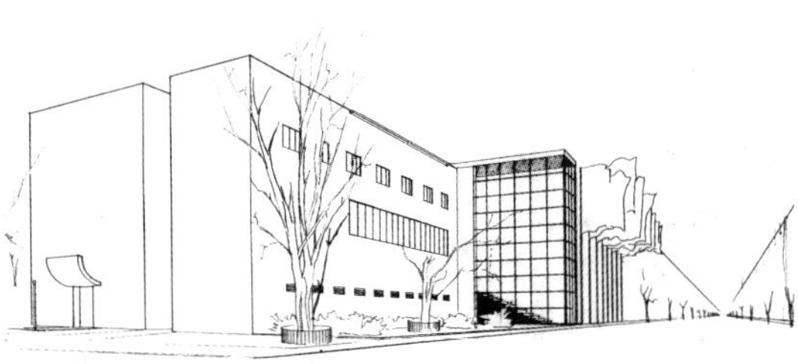

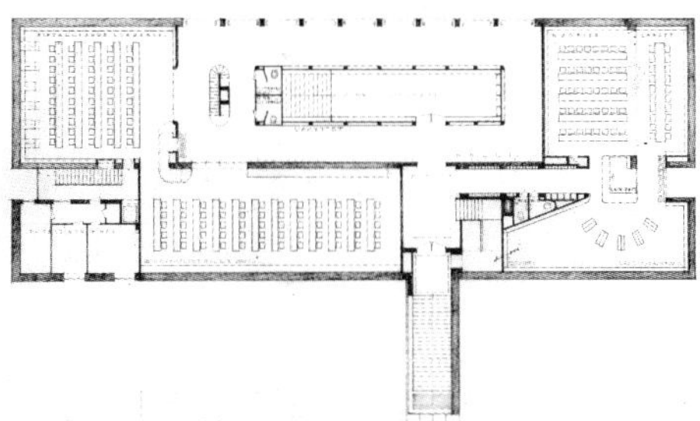

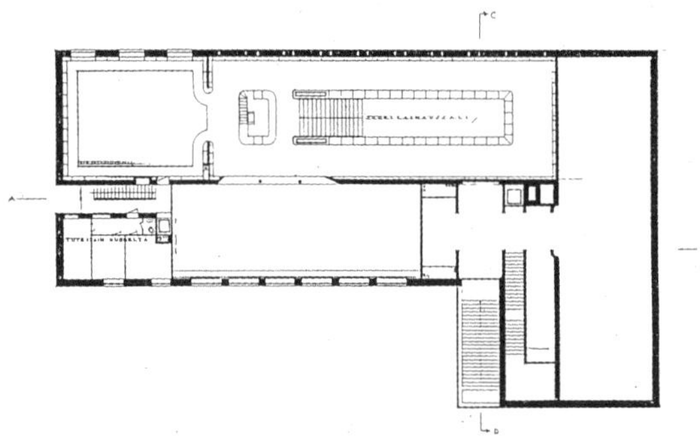

25. Viipuri library, third version 1929: upper floor plan with main stair rising to control desk: children's library has filled corner.

wider architectural world, including the arrival and acceptance of Modernism in Scandinavia.

With an eye open to the outside world and a sensibility attuned to absorbing influences, Aalto had followed events in central Europe through books and reviews, but in 1928 he visited France and Holland to witness the new work first hand. He saw some of Le Corbusier's work including the Villa Stein and visited his office, though the great man was away.[15] He also went to Holland and visited Zonnestraal, possibly meeting Duiker personally. The sanatorium had a radical influence not only on Paimio but on Aalto's functionalism more generally. As described in Chapter 4, the tuberculosis hospital combined ideas of purity and simplicity with science and health. Aalto's attempts to derive form from purpose, particularly in details like the bedroom layouts, lighting and washbasin design, seemed at Paimio to produce a social and political resonance beyond the obvious technical one, encouraging further experiments at Viipuri.

The two intermediate versions of the design show it in transition. The entrance hall became fully glazed to one side (fig. 21), and instead of the glass roof, the main library hall was lit by continuous clerestorys, modelled on Corbusian *fenêtres en longeur*. Aalto also toyed, in his second and third versions, with the idea of a Corbusian roof-garden on top of the library hall, but in the final building this frankly unnecessary feature was forgotten. The intermediate plans show advances significant for later work, such as the radial arrangement of the children's library in the first floor of the second version (fig. 24) and a half-oval auditorium on the ground floor. In the third version (fig. 25) the whole plan became L-shaped through the deployment of the children's library across the expanded south-west end, implying a new axis of symmetry. Meanwhile Aalto struggled with the elevations, drawing version after version. He wanted to modernise the fenestration while trying to decide how asymmetrical to be, or whether to differentiate the ground floor with rustication, and if so of what kind and at what level (figs 26, 27).

The final version

For Aalto's history and for that of the library, the delay and change of site proved fortunate, for they gave him a chance to rethink the building and to reintegrate it three-dimensionally in a masterly way. The new site north-east of the cathedral (fig. 35) set the building free-standing in the park, and following an interest in articulating parts that had appeared at Paimio, Aalto divided it into two blocks: the library proper as a wide box subsuming the children's section, and a narrow wing housing offices above, lecture theatre below. In a typically modernist asymmetrical manner, these two were allowed to slide past each other. They line up with lateral roads entering the site, so seem in plan to absorb a shift of grid produced by the need for space around the cathedral. The new library had four entrances: the main approach faced north-east towards Koulukatu, the most direct connection with the city centre. The children's library entrance opened behind into the park. The end entrance to north west was for staff and that to south east for the newspaper reading room.

The crucial improvement in internal planning at this late stage was to combine the lending hall with the two reading rooms in the same broad volume, while differentiating them by steps in section and a step of the end wall in plan. This unified the library space, adding power to the entry sequence, for

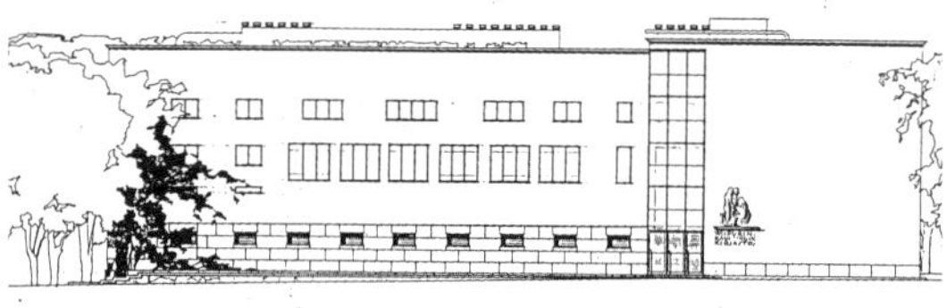

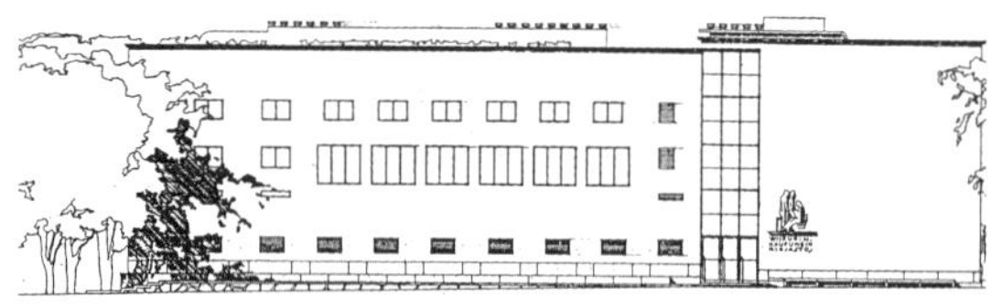

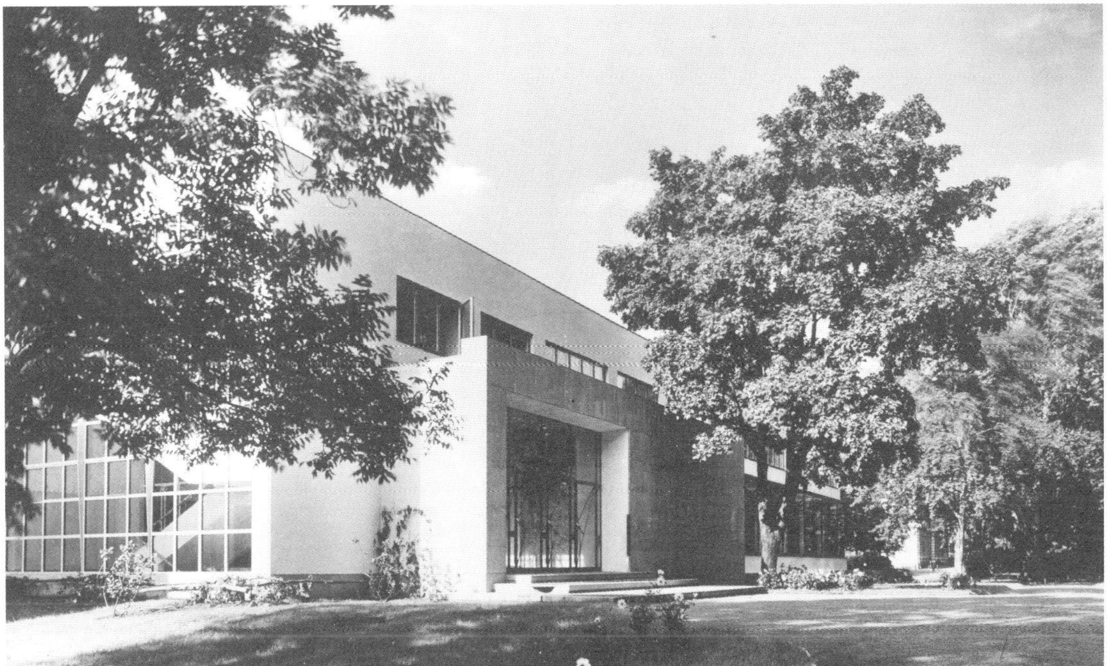

26, 27. (below opposite) Viipuri library, third version 1929, front elevation: in these alternative versions Aalto tests the effect of different heights of rustication.
28. (above) final version 1935, view of main entrance.
29. (below) library interior with sunken well and steps approaching control desk; beyond, lower set reading room and its rooflights.

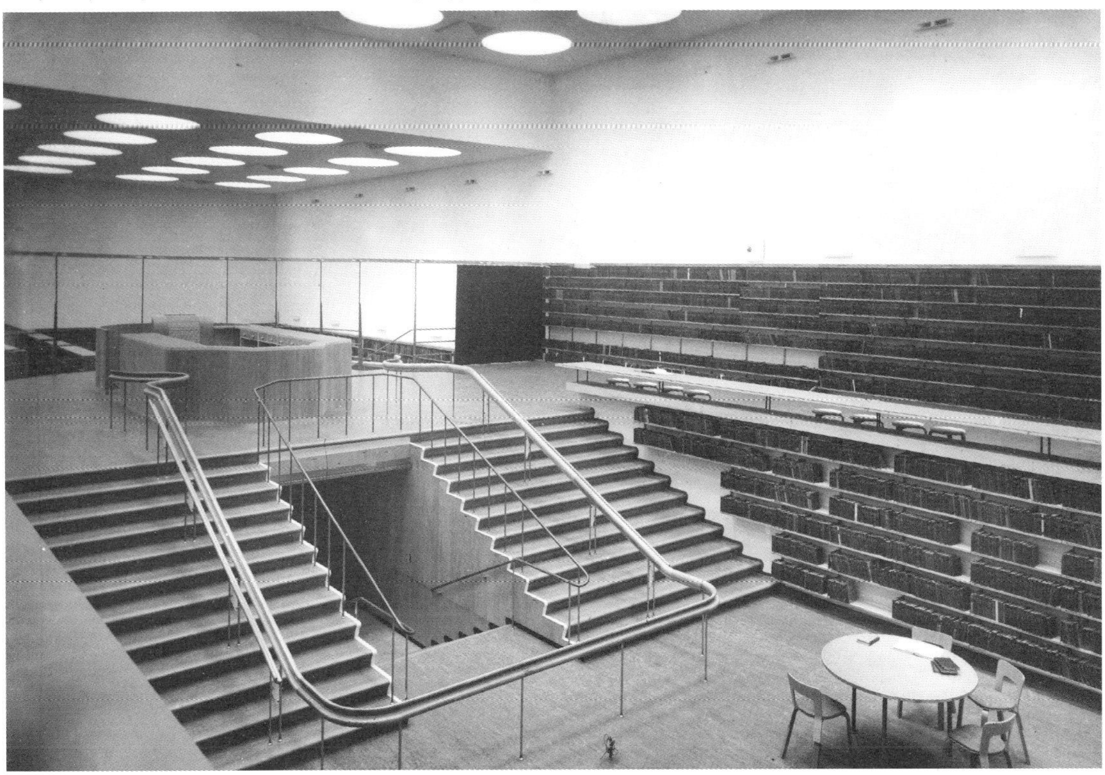

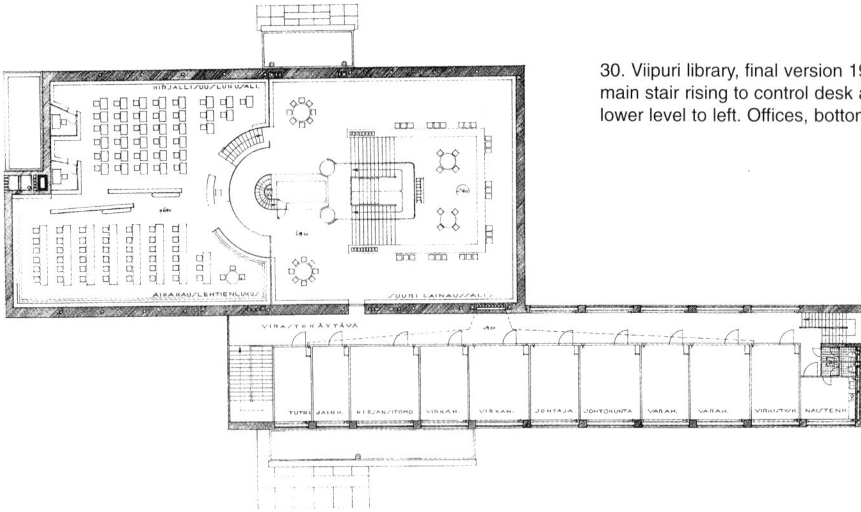

30. Viipuri library, final version 1935: upper floor with main stair rising to control desk and reading rooms at lower level to left. Offices, bottom, are for staff.

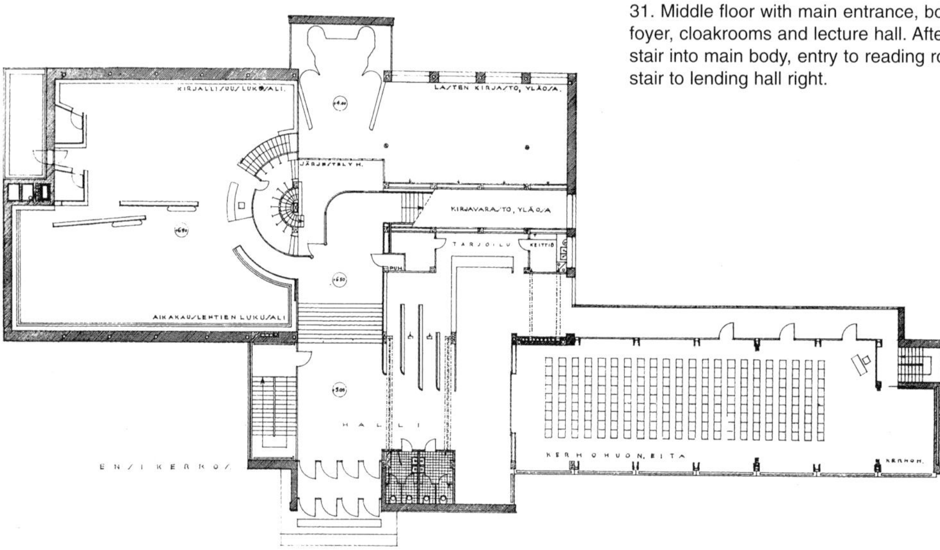

31. Middle floor with main entrance, bottom, leading to foyer, cloakrooms and lecture hall. After ascending stair into main body, entry to reading rooms is left and stair to lending hall right.

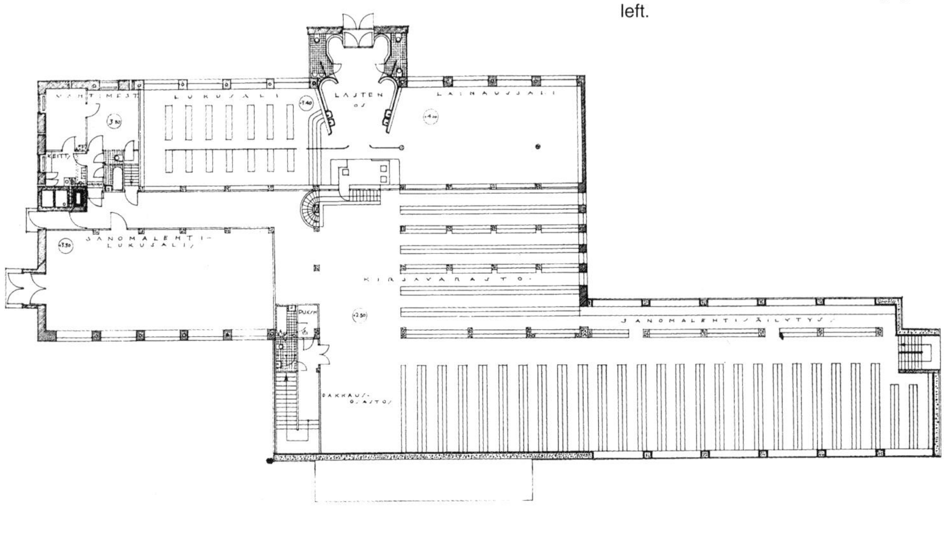

32. Lower floor with book storage. Children's library is top with own entrance and newspaper reading room left.

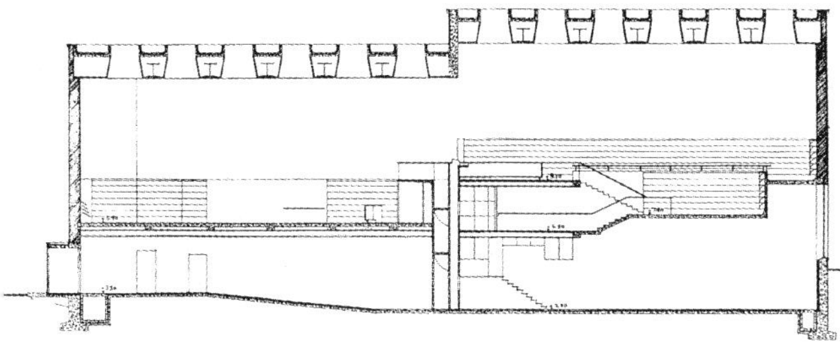
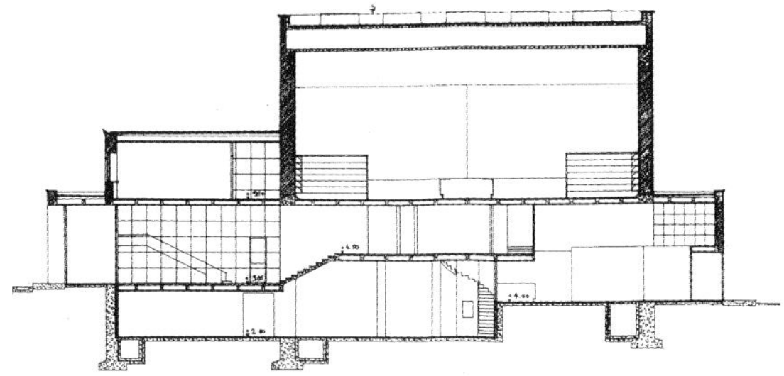

33,34. Viipuri library, final version 1935: sections through main library spaces and (right) through the two main entrances.

lenders would still ascend through the hall to arrive at the central control point, now making a full turn within a floor well. This well was an invention much afterwards repeated, by Aalto and by others. Without cumbersome and potentially dangerous ladders, publicly accessible library shelves can rise only to the height of a person, yet libraries must store as many books as possible. This is why Asplund adopted a three-tiered arrangement of bookstacks in Stockholm. Aalto played with gallery arrangements in earlier versions: now he divided the plan width almost equally between levels, linking them with stairs on both sides, a mere rail dividing those outside the control point from those within. Readers searching for books could work their way around the perimeter or down into the well, and sit to read in the upper or the lower space. The entry sequence is dramatic: the arriving reader rounds the corner to face a panorama of books and a second one beyond, the whole space bathed in generous and unexpected toplight. He or she turns to discover the control point, from which librarians supervise the whole space, a spiral stair behind the control desk allowing them to communicate with reading rooms behind and bookstore below. A curtain could divide the lower reading rooms from the lending hall as necessary, but even with the curtain drawn, the whole ceiling could be seen.

The sectional arrangement was cleverer than in the first design. Aalto dropped the bookstore into a semi-basement, using the difference in level between sides to let the two main routes slide over and under each other while sharing the same axis. Children would enter their two-room library at ground level, but readers arriving by the main entrance would mount a few steps to gain front door, foyer and lecture hall. The entrance hall was illuminated with strong sidelight from the left, for Aalto preserved the glazed staircase of earlier versions as a route to first floor offices, yet another interpretation of the inside/outside space. Having arrived in a foyer offering lavatories, cloakroom space, and access to the lecture hall, readers would ascend a half-storey stair at the threshold of the library block. At this point they would turn left into the lower reading rooms or continue and turn right into the lending hall. They would mount half a storey in the well, and a further half to the control point. They have risen not less than six metres, on short straight flights and with a goal in view.

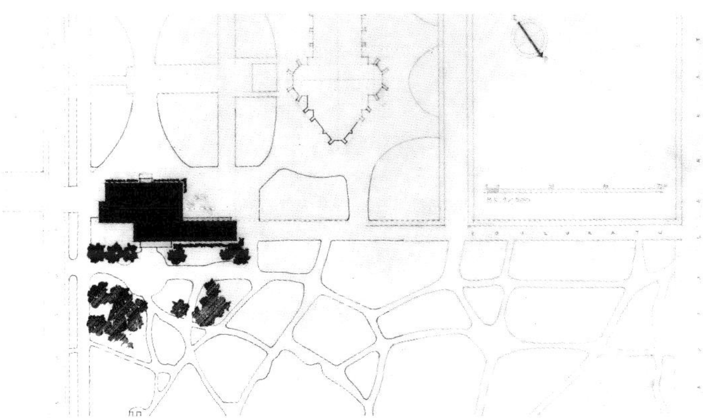

35. Viipuri library, final version 1935: site plan in new position surrounded by park. Cathedral is middle top. The two blocks of building pick up and reconcile the axes of the lateral roads.

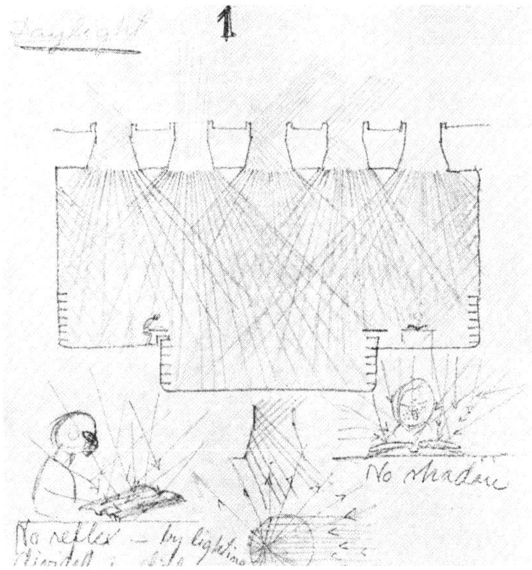

36. (above) Aalto's sketch showing the principle of the shadowless daylighting system through tubular rooflights.

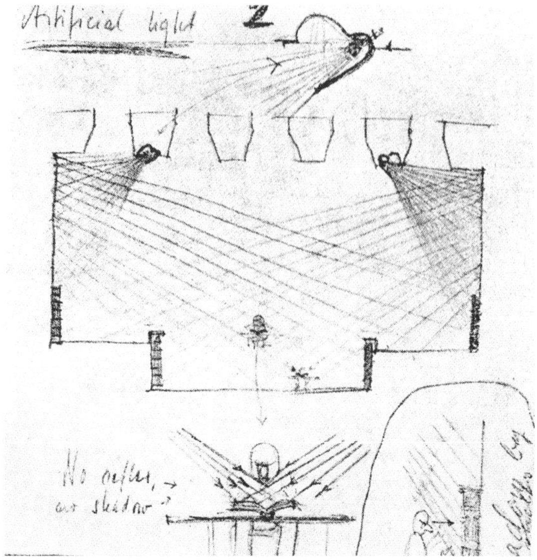

37. (above) Aalto's sketch showing the principle of the artificial lighting system.

Functionalist excursions

The intention of a glass roof in the original competition entry returned in a new form as one of Aalto's best known functionalist inventions. In a celebrated essay, he argued that in a library light should have top priority, because *'the eye is only a tiny part of the human body, but it is the most sensitive and perhaps the most important part'*.[16] The best reading light would come from all directions to preclude shadows, and needed to be bright. Aalto proposed a regular grid of circular rooflights admitting their light through deep white-painted cylinders in the thickness of the roof, so that most of it would be reflected sideways. The light cylinders are at their most spectacular when reflecting sunlight back into the room, which they can do all day while cutting off the sun's direct path, since the circular form accommodates the sun's changing angle.[17] The same system was adapted to artificial light by placing spotlights above the circular rooflights, with the added advantage of clearing snow by their heat. Aalto reused these rooflights on many later buildings and devised many other kinds of reflecting rooflight and sidelight to spectacular effect. Of all the Modernists, he was the most accomplished and inventive at daylighting, and it is surely no coincidence that he came from a country where light vanishes in the winter and is therefore highly valued. Unlike architects from Mediterranean countries, he had no need to worry about excessive solar gain, and unlike central European daylighting enthusiasts such as Hans Scharoun, he had no need to restrict himself to northlight.[18]

The deep rooflights required a thick roof plate and therefore easily allowed the necessary structural depth for steel beams spanning sideways, absorbed invisibly between them. In the side wing, with offices above, there was also a frame. Here the downstanding beams threatened to break up the lecture hall ceiling, disrupting its acoustics. This led to another famous Aalto functionalist invention: the wavy wooden acoustic ceiling. Aalto and his staff made several drawings plotting reflection paths of various ceiling shapes to discover how the sound would be bounced from speaker to audience and back (fig. 38).

There is little doubt that Aalto believed in this work and saw it as a justification for the forms chosen, but some of the reflection points are narrow, accounting for little sound energy, and the whole exercise seems to assume wrongly that reflections off the ceiling are more important than those off walls and floor. The efficacy is thus doubtful in terms of sound enhancement, though the arrangement must have helped eliminate negative acoustic effects such as standing waves between floor and ceiling or between beams.[19] But in any case, as many commentators have pointed out, Aalto only made the room long and thin to fit

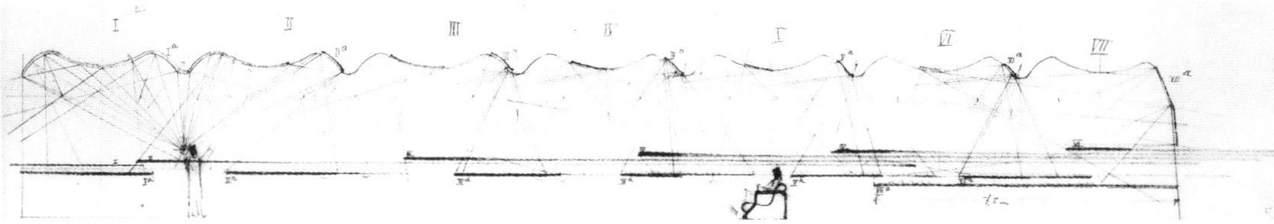

38. Aalto's drawing showing reflection paths for sounds between speaker and audience off his wavy wooden ceiling.

the wing, so he had created the very difficulty he set out to solve. Even if its physical efficacy was limited, however, the wavy ceiling was a wonderful visual metaphor for a room devoted to sound, both representing waves and shaped like a musical instrument. It became the counterpart of the toplit ceiling, devoted to the ear as the other was to the eye, setting the two in contrast. It also opened up a vocabulary of layered ceilings that Aalto was to use repeatedly, as opposed to the general modernist orthodoxy of exposed structure and expressed construction. The thickness of the void above the acoustic ceiling was actually shown to the outside world through the glazed sidewall which continued up beyond it so that the inside space could end on the curve (fig. 39). Aalto continued to explore acoustic forms, even making a light-model to test reflections in the Vuoksenniska Church of 1957-9. Certainly some of them worked, but they also fascinated the architect as part of a world of organic forms to be deployed as an alternative to the traditional box-like forms of architecture. The contrast proved fruitful, as it was in Le Corbusier's work, but in Aalto's case there was no ideal of the *objet-type*. Curved surfaces could be used to break away from the orthogonal, as for example in the Finnish Pavilion at New York World's Fair of 1939, whose slanting display screens made a kind of internal landscape. Clearly there was nothing acoustical here, just as there is nothing acoustical in Aalto's furniture, whose curves have to do with the bending of wood and the shape of the human body. A line drawn by the same hand at different scales can be used for many purposes and carry many meanings. It may also be a signature, but it is much more besides.

39. Lecture room with wavy wooden ceiling and the famous Aalto stools.

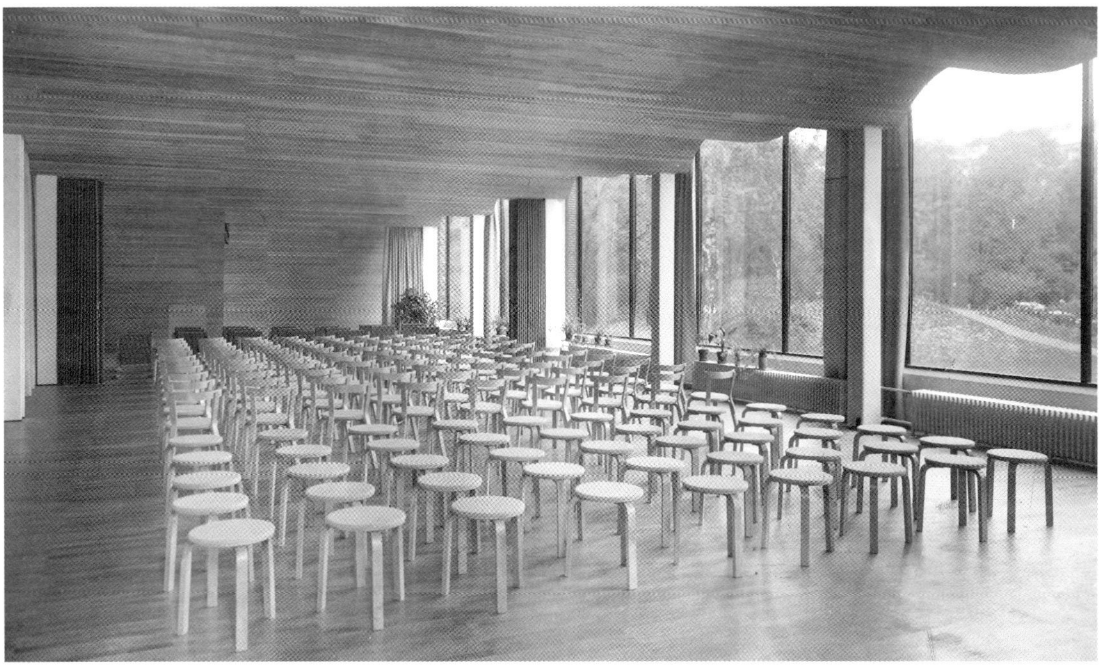

Conclusion

By the time Viipuri library was complete, Aalto had invented a range of details that he was to use for the rest of his career. The chairs, tables and three-legged stools first developed for Viipuri have become world-famous. The internal woodwork with its clever use of the latest joinery techniques, its natural finish, and its tactile appeal, brought a warmth to Modernist design as an alternative to the cold machine-art of the Bauhaus. Technical details were elegantly and thoughtfully conceived, from ergonomic doorhandles to the advanced heating system. But the most astonishing thing at Viipuri is the way old ideas combine with new. The essential drama of Asplund's library, of a journey to the centre of a new world, is fully there; yet the imagery is so different. It is no longer loaded with antique references but nakedly clear; books on open shelves, minimal furniture, the most efficient lighting; a powerhouse for scientific knowledge, direct and rational. Structure and construction are mostly concealed in unknown thicknesses behind abstract white surfaces; yet the elements on show are true. Asplund's route is present, but differently worked: even the turn marks a new departure, no longer a nodal point where axes cross, but a curving plane suggesting direction while concealing the surprise beyond. Looked at closely, Aalto's foyer too is free in shape and lighting, fragmented and in-between, an effective foil to the finite enclosure of the great white reading room beyond. For many architects the parkland view would have invited windows, yet Aalto chose an introverted space to avoid compromising his toplighting system. The introversion also helps detach the external experience from the internal, sustaining the impression of a world apart. This echoes the illusionistic tendency he admired in Asplund's cinema, where the world of film was dissociated from the city beyond.

In comparison with Aalto's later work, Viipuri's exterior may appear underplayed, but the stone cladding applied to the base is an equivalent of rustication, and the polished stone used as a luxury facing for the main entrance shows that here too the mature vocabulary was established. Aalto had been excited by the work of Le Corbusier, yet almost nothing of the Five Points survives at Viipuri: no roof garden, almost no columns, and freedom of section more than of plan. Aalto had absorbed the influences of the masters, then freed himself to set off on his own.

Notes

1. It may be restored by the time this book is published: certainly restoration has been urged. On the fate of the building see Spens 1994 and the first issue of *Acanthus* published by the Finnish Architecture Museum, Helsinki, 1990.

2. Göran Schildt describes *'a pure teacher-pupil relationship'* Schildt 1984, p. 169. Richard Weston quotes Nils Erik Wikberg: *'in the 1920s Asplund was the inspiring personality in the Nordic countries... Each new project by him was an event, and what a sensation his determined conversion to Functionalism involved.'* Weston 1995, p. 27. On Asplund's death Aalto wrote: *'Sweden... has suffered a great loss. The foremost among architects, who in a wider sense has been both pioneer and pathfinder for the living architecture of his own era, has left us.'* From *E. G. Asplund In Memoriam* in Schildt 1985, p. 66.

3. See Lars Olof Larsson's essay in Engfors 1986, p. 35.

4. See, for example, Ahlberg's reading in Ahlberg 1950, pp. 42-45.

5. Cornell, Elias *The sky as a vault* in Caldenby 1997 p. 29 (also published in Engfors 1986).

6. There had even been a competition for the building of a pantheon in Stockholm in 1791, sponsored by King Gustav III after his return from a visit to Italy. Designs by Desprez and Palmstedt are shown in Nerdinger 1990, pp. 304 & 319.

7. For a sophisticated reading and various opinions on the Pantheon see Macdonald 1965, pp.111-121.

8. Asplund scholars seem generally agreed that the source was Bindesböll's Thorvaldsen Museum, Copenhagen 1848. See Cornell, op cit. in Caldenby 1997 p. 28.

9. From *The Stockholm Exhibition 1*, published as an interview in May 1930 and printed in English in Schildt 1985, pp. 15-17.

10. See the extensive list in Schildt 1984, pp.169-176.

11. The classical examples are more numerous, but Villa Flora of 1926 is almost log cabin, see Weston 1995, p. 23.

12. Schildt 1984 pp.141,169-170.

13. On Aalto's ideas about spatial transition see his article of 1926 *From Doorstep to Living Room,* and the accompanying discussion in Schildt 1984, pp. 214-218.

14. For a detailed account see Simo Paavilainen's article about the building in the first number of *Acanthus*, see note 1.

15. Schildt 1986, p. 56.

16. Aalto's own words from his article *The Humanizing of Architecture*, 1940, reprinted in *Alvar Aalto Synopsis* (Hoesli 1970).

17. The sun in Finland (and nearby Karelia) arrives at a relatively low angle and in summer almost circles the sky, setting in the north-west and rising again soon after in the north-east.

18. In his State Library Berlin of 1964-79, Hans Scharoun went to much trouble to obtain daylight from a series of sawtooth northlight roofs, spreading it through huge diffusers. He also applied sloping glazing to the north ends of many of his late buildings in acknowledgement of the special quality of northlight. See Blundell Jones 1995, pp. 198-205.

19. Standing waves occur between flat and parallel surfaces, so the curved surface would prevent this occurring between floor and ceiling; instead it would redistribute acoustic reflections in a much more random way. Music practice rooms are often designed with sides out of parallel to avoid this problem.

Chapter 9. Pier Luigi Nervi: Aircraft Hangars Orvieto, 1935-9 (destroyed 1944)

Of all the figures whose work is examined in this book, the Italian Pier Luigi Nervi might be considered the most typical 'Modernist' as the word was understood in the immediate post-war period. Superficially, he even fits the bill as proponent of 'The Modernist Project' criticised by post-modernists, for he was interested primarily in structure and technique, and held what now seems a touching faith in the idea that the pursuit of technical and economic disciplines would drive a design automatically towards both efficiency and elegance. He vehemently denied any interest in aesthetics *per se*, considering aesthetic quality rather to be the fruit of the design process.[1] In so far as he looked at architectural history at all - he dismissed past styles as irrelevant to the conditions of modern life - he tended to take a technical view, reserving his greatest admiration for the Gothic with its structural ingenuity and efficient use of stone.[2] From his reading of Gothic vaulting came, perhaps, both a sense of structural forces shaping a building by taking the line through elements such as ribs, and ideas about prefabrication and assembly. A rash of books and lectures about his work published around 1960 established his world fame, and his work is present in every architectural dictionary and encyclopaedia. He was the only figure apart from Ove Arup to win Gold medals from both the Royal Institute of British Architects and the Institute of Structural Engineers. His buildings remain impressive and memorable, yet little has been published on him in recent years.

Trained as an engineer, Nervi is considered among architects largely because of the great formal quality of his work which, besides being technically innovative, undoubtedly ranked among the best of its time. It consistently outshines the contributions of all his architect-collaborators: few today think of the Palazzo and Palazetto of Sport built for the Rome Olympics in the mid 1950s (figs 5 & 6) as works by Piacentini and Vitellozzi, for example, since the two buildings are so completely dominated by the magnificent roof structures contributed by Nervi and controlled by him down to the smallest detail. Even his collaboration with the major architect-designer Gio Ponti on the Pirelli Tower in Milan of 1955-8 (figs 2 & 4) leaves his influence on the form of the building dominant. A great form-maker, his designs were inspired by a deep intuitive and intellectual understanding of structural forces, backed up by the most advanced calculating and modelling techniques available.

It was of crucial importance for his career, too, that he was principal in a contracting firm that executed all of his early and many of his later buildings, for his method of working was as pioneering in terms of construction techniques as in structure. His chosen material was reinforced concrete, which he used in lighter and more ingenious ways than any predecessor, combining in-situ with precast and registering many patents along the way. Even the early work was bold and innovative, with contracts often won in direct competition over price. That Nervi could have made these experiments

1. Pier Luigi Nervi, aircraft hangar under construction at Orvieto, 1939. This was one of the second batch of hangars with prefabricated components and the whole structure carried on only six legs

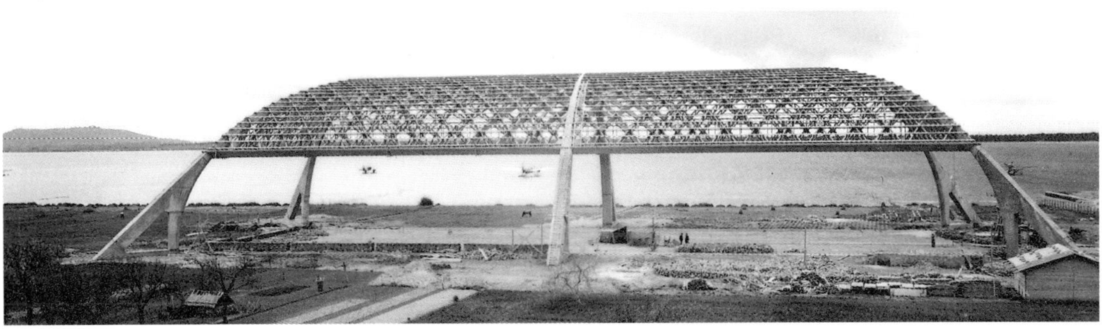

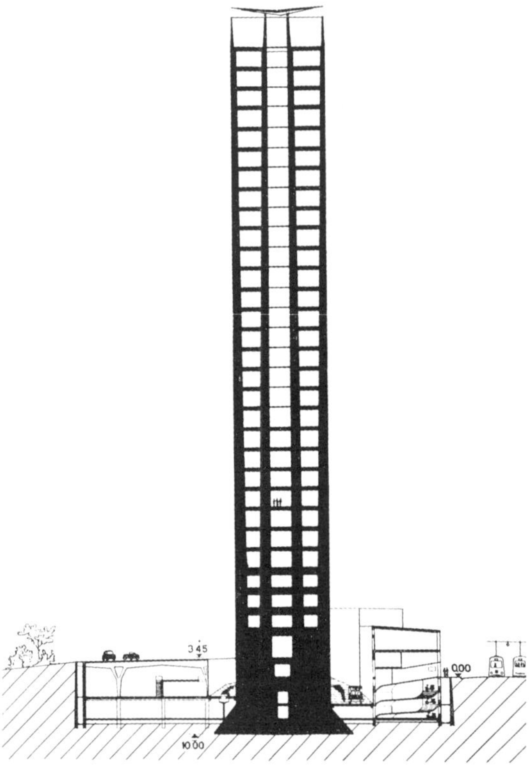

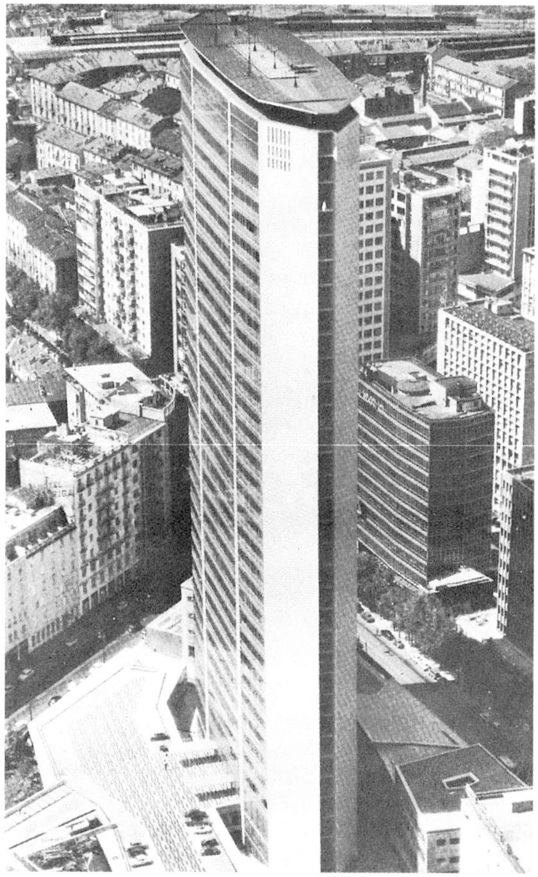

2. (above) and 4. (right) Pirelli Tower, Milan, by Gio Ponti with concrete structure engineered by Nervi, 1955-58.

3. (below) Municipal Stadium in Florence, 1928, Nervi's first major job and a pioneering work in reinforced concrete.

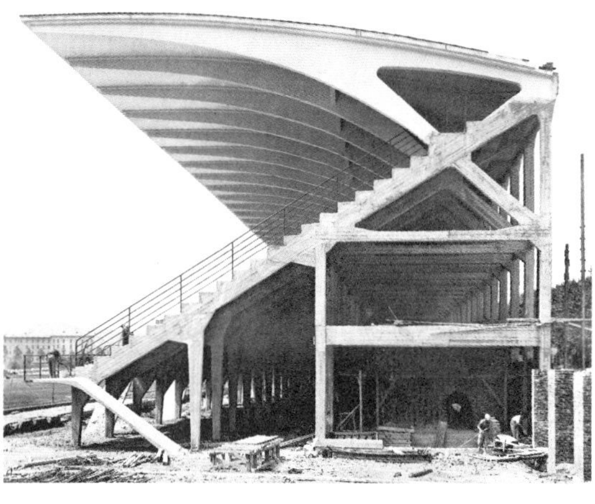

without close control of his own production firm and methods is unthinkable. A close parallel of this hands-on approach was the career of the French architect/engineer Jean Prouvé (1901-66), the blacksmith who pioneered prefabrication in metals. Just as Nervi supplied structures for buildings by other architects, so Prouvé provided doors, windows, cladding systems, lift-cars etc. for leading French Modernists of the 1930s.[3]

Early career

Nervi was born in Sondrio, Lombardy in 1891, and graduated as an engineer from the University of Bologna in 1913, after which he worked in the technical office of a large contracting firm. In 1923 he set up his own contracting firm, which in 1928 won a competitive tender for the design and construction of the municipal stadium in Florence. The 100 metre spectator stand required a cantilevered roof projecting 25 metres created in reinforced concrete. In later life Nervi claimed:-

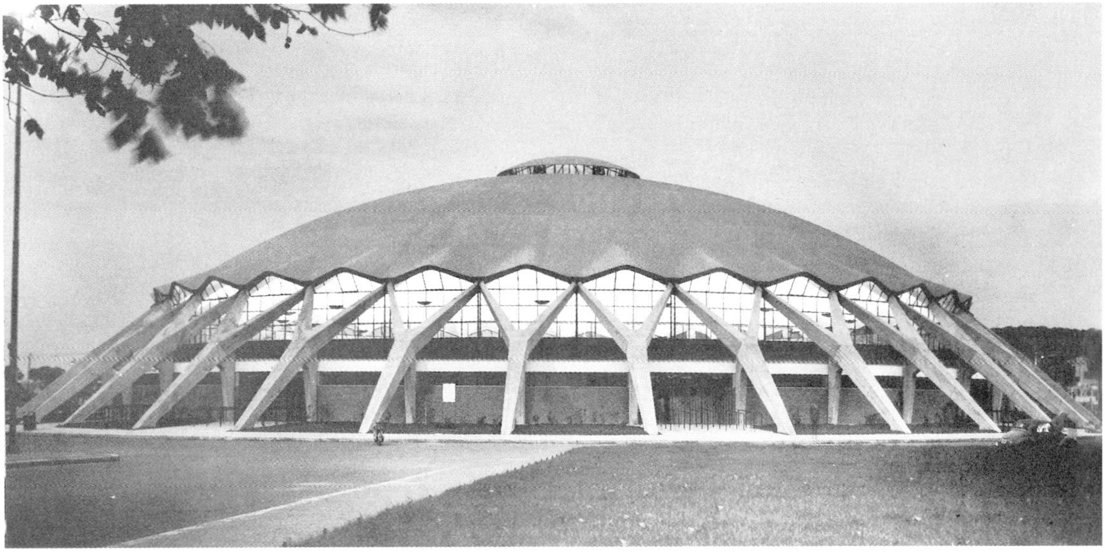

'I still remember the long and patient work to find an agreement between the static necessities which imposed a determined resisting section at the various points, and the desire to obtain something which for me would have a satisfying appearance. I must say, however, that basically this work resulted only in small refinements of shape and connections because the static guide gave suggestions which in themselves were aesthetically expressive when translated into drawings. Throughout my life I have never deviated from this method.'[4]

Work on the Florence stadium was extended with contracts for further spectator stands and continued until 1932. Nervi's firm then went on to produce designs for engineering structures such as bridges and oil storage tanks until he won his next big competition in 1935.

5. (above) and 6. (below) Palazetto of Sport, Rome 1955 by Vitellozzi, with concrete grid shell roof structure designed by Nervi mixing in-situ and precast elements, and supported entirely on the Y-shaped external legs.

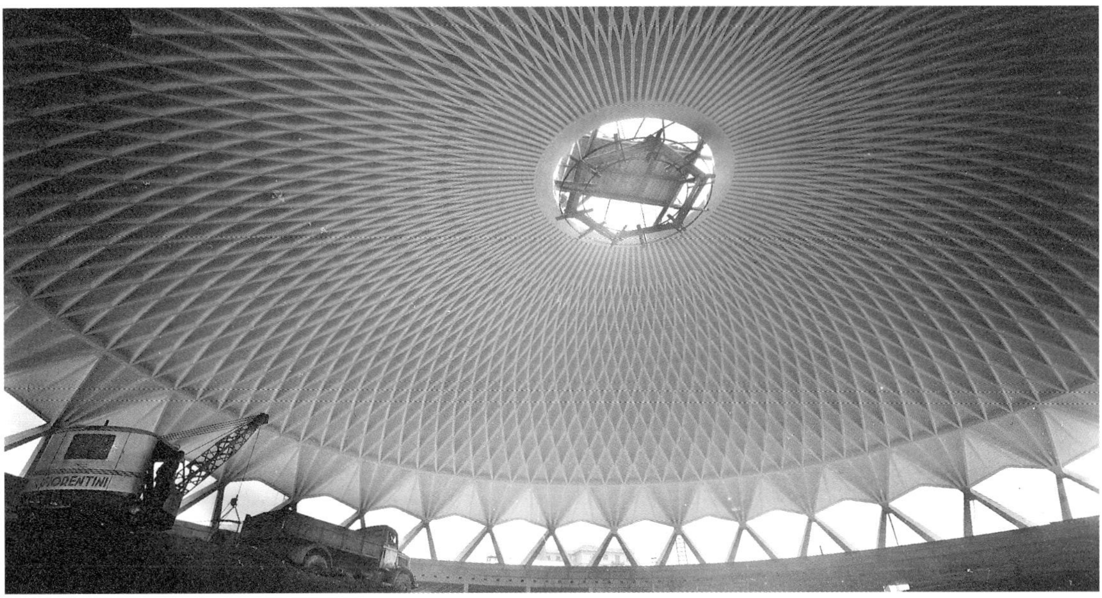

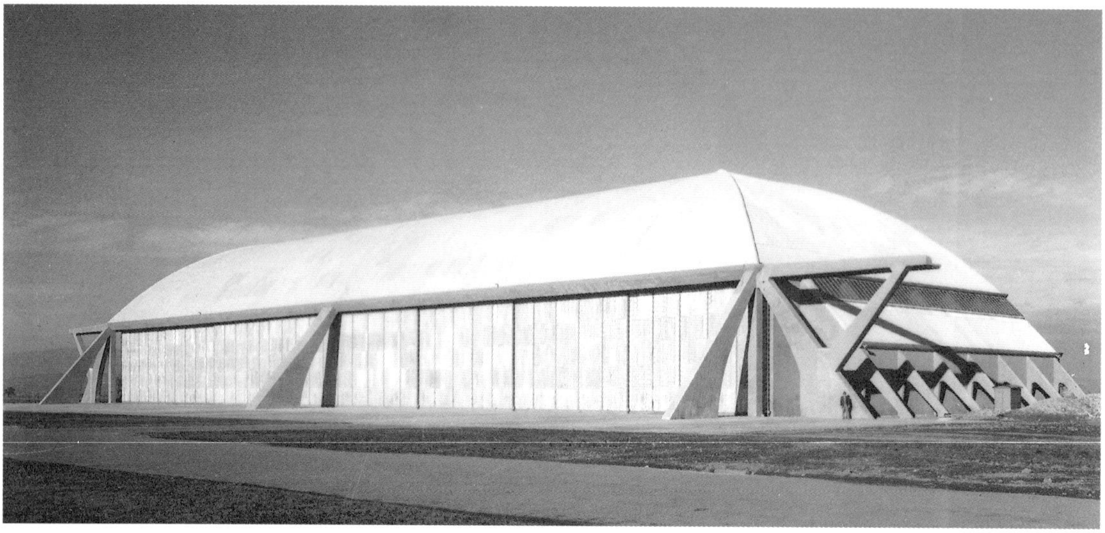

7. One of the first pair of aircraft hangars designed by Nervi and built by his firm at Orvieto in 1935. The structure was in-situ concrete, the cladding asbestos-cement sheet. 8. (opposite top) Interior of the hangar with doors open. Back and sides are supported by regular small legs, the front by a triangular truss supported at ends and centre.

The first hangars

This was again a design and construct tender against other specialist firms, this time from the Italian Air Force for aircraft hangars, two of which were built at Orvieto in the following year. Nervi reflected later that these designs were at once *'from a technical point of view the most difficult of my life'*[5] and *'the most interesting, both from a technical and constructional point of view, that I have studied during my long career'*.[6] The problem was the huge free spans required: 44.80 metres front to back and 111.50 metres in width, with one long side fully openable by movable doors 7.9 metres high, interrupted only by one central support. The type of structure was not specified, but it was clear from the competition conditions that the cheapest solution would be chosen, and complete working drawings had to be submitted as well as detailed cost estimates. Nervi tried conventional schemes with a great beam across the doors and secondary beams spanning front to back, but to no avail. Then he thought of the unified structural system of a vault:

'a single resisting organism where the stresses due to its own weight and the external forces of wind and snow could be spontaneously diffused until they reached the supports placed on the three sides and the central column on the side of the doors'.[7]

The outline of the building was rectangular and the grid of supporting ribs was laid out diagonally making squares in plan, but it curved up as a vault in section, making the shape of an inverted catenary arch and thus avoiding bending stresses.[8] The in-situ concrete ribs were 1.1 metres deep and 150 mm thick. They carried a skin of reinforced tiles supporting a weathershield of asbestos cement sheets. Along the back and across the ends, each springing point of the diagonal ribs could be carried on a leg projecting at the angle of the vault to take the line of thrust, carrying it down to a foundation.[9] The front, however, needed to be carried at only three points: two pairs of corner legs, again taking the diagonal line of thrust, and a great single central leg. To carry the load over the doors, a triangular truss was created along the edge of the great vault by adding members to the last bay of ribs, and a thick longitudinal member was added to the diagonal grid at the next intersection over. In this way the unified structure of the vault could be transferred to the larger structural order of the front legs, but as we shall see Nervi was not altogether happy and changed it in his revised version.

Daylighting was provided around the sides and rear through a glazed slot along the top of the supporting legs, thus dramatically differentiating between vault and supports. A problem was created by the need to park the large doors, which Nervi solved elegantly by adding concrete A-frames

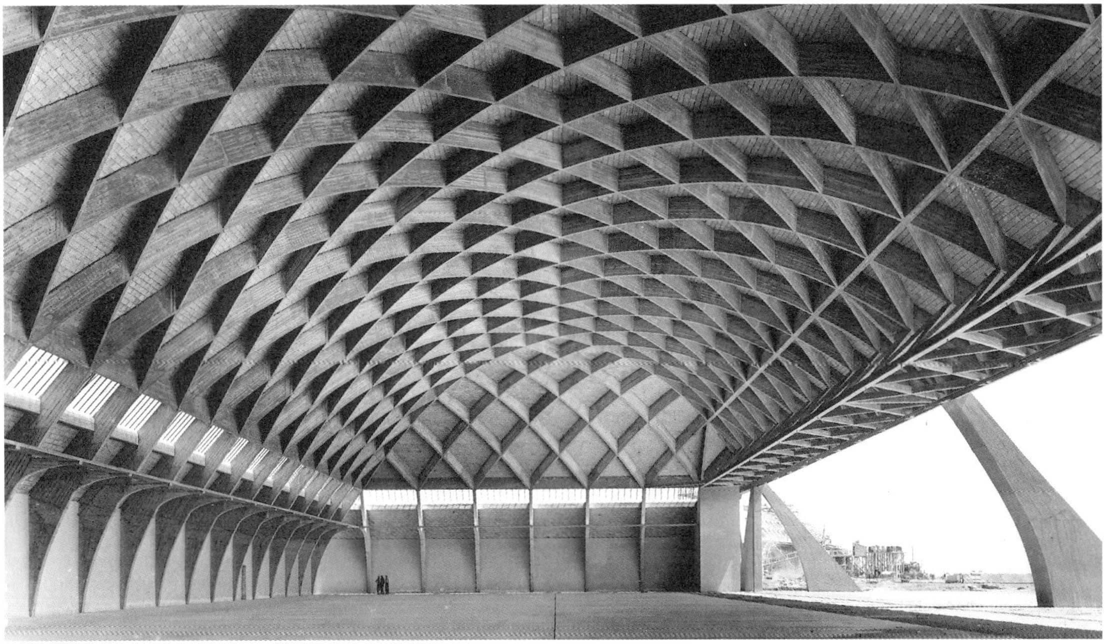

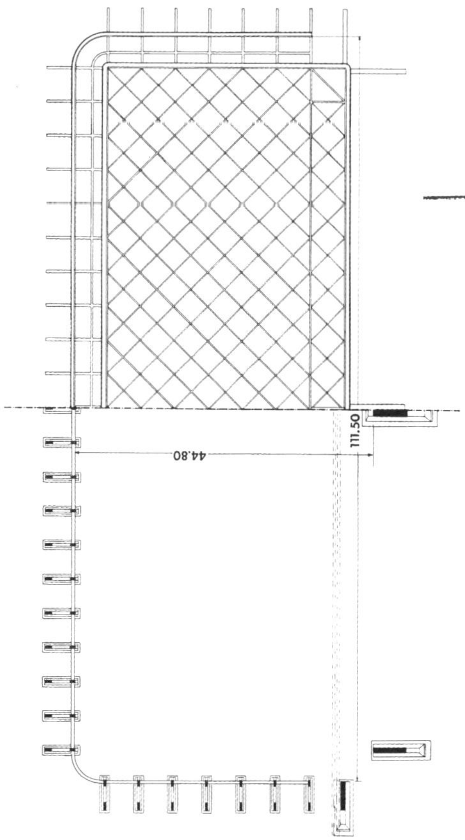

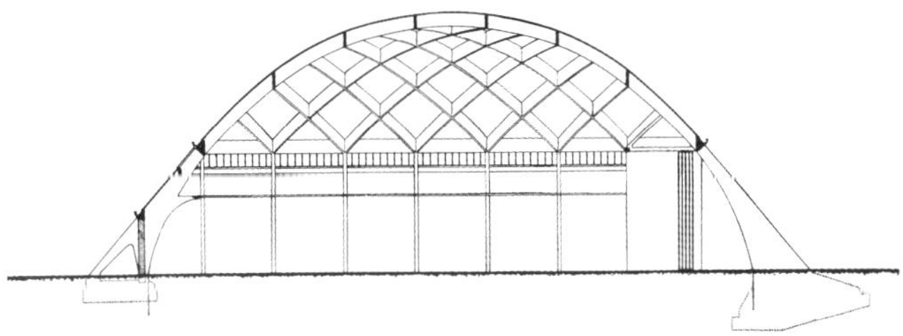

9. (left) Plan of the first hangars divided between ground level and roof structure.
10. (above) Cross-section showing the different ways by which the two sides are supported.
11. (below) Frame extending the door track at the corner: this allowed the series of doors to be stacked together outside the opening.

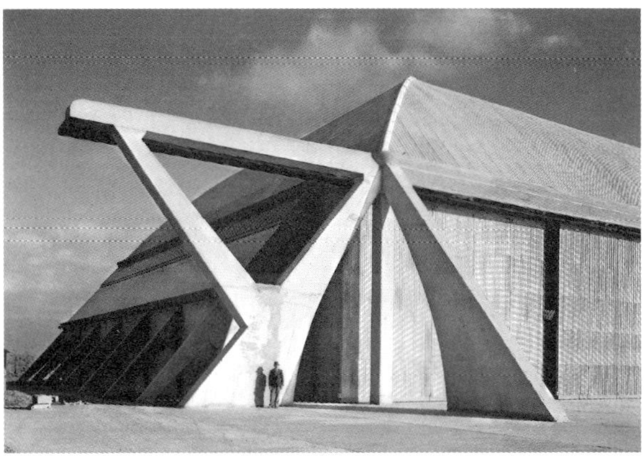

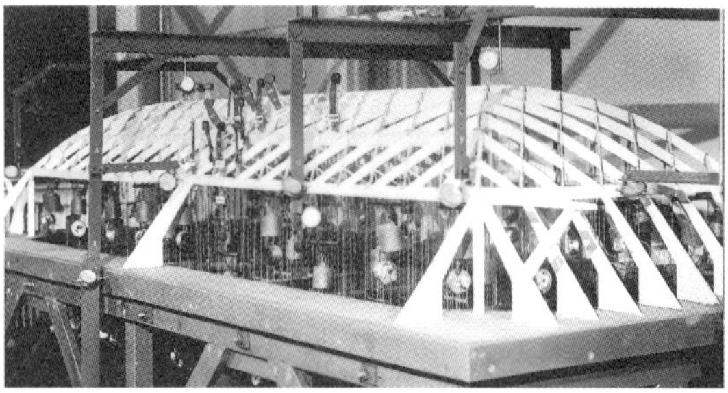

12. Since calculating all the forces was impossible, Nervi had a celluloid model made which was loaded and checked with strain gauges.

to the corner legs supporting a continuation of their hanging rails. Stacked in series, the doors were placed outside the opening when passage of aircraft was required.

Nervi admitted that with the analytical and mathematical techniques available, the loads could not be adequately calculated, for unlike a simple system of beams loading one onto the other, the members would interact in complex ways. He therefore resorted to a physical model at a scale of 1:30 in flexible celluloid. Weights were added to simulate loads, and strain gauges showed the distribution of forces. In this way the operation of the structure could be monitored, and it turned out that cooperation of the ribs made the measured forces much less than those predicted by calculation on the usual oversimplified basis.[10] The important variable in the structural design was the reinforcement, for it was easiest to build the vault with ribs of constant size and shape, while concentrating steel reinforcement invisibly at the points of highest tensile stress.[11] Nervi proudly reported that after the model tests, less steel was needed than had been predicted. The unprecedented structure represented some risk, and construction had to be carefully controlled. Nervi records his anxiety when the shuttering was struck, but the building stood firm. The only substantial problem found later was cracking of the tile skin due to excessive thermal movement. This prompted adoption of a different construction system for later hangars.

The Italian Air Force were pleased with their two hangars, whose unexpected aesthetic quality could be considered to reflect their brisk efficiency, military discipline and progressive modern stance. When Nervi later referred to the cooperation of the structural elements *'dividing their responsibilities according to their individual capabilities in a marvellous example of solidarity and justice (what a lesson for mankind!)'*[12] one cannot help remembering that he was building for a fascist state. In later life he honestly and generously acknowledged the open-mindedness of the Air Force Leaders and their readiness to experiment. They might well have wanted to hand further contracts directly to him, but were obliged again to offer competitive tender for a further set of six hangars in 1939. Nervi's firm won, and he built a variation on his former theme again at Orvieto, with further examples at Orbetello and Torre del Lago. It is instructive to observe which features remained the same and which changed.

The later hangars

The second group of six hangars were slightly smaller at 102.50 metres wide and 36.90 front to back. Rather than having the skin of tiles under the asbestos cement sheets, longitudinally running precast purlins held them directly. Nervi had noted the difficulty and expense of shuttering the ribs in-situ, and decided to try prefabrication. This meant not only that moulds could be reused, but also that the ribs, instead of being made solid, could be cast with voids to act as small trusses, considerably reducing their weight and increasing their efficiency. But he was worried about the structural continuity of the most heavily stressed members, so he cast those in-situ as before.

The most essential change was in the way the building was supported. The first hangars had been hybrid structures: the vault was even and symmetrical, but while one side was carried to the ground through numerous small legs to distribute the load evenly, on the other it was carried to only three points by the triangular truss formed along the edge. This was a valid response to the asymmetry of the programme which required only one side to be open, but Nervi felt that the structure wanted to be symmetrical. The asymmetry meant an irregular distribution of forces which to him was structurally impure and a visual compromise. He decided therefore to build the new hangars with trusses along both sides and only six points of support. If it could be done on one side, it could be done on the other, and it would allow considerable savings in legs and foundations. The corner legs were splayed at 45° rather than doubled at 90° as before, which necessitated a new solution for the extended doortrack. Also each leg, instead of following the expanding angle of load with ever more dead weight, was cast with a triangular void, which

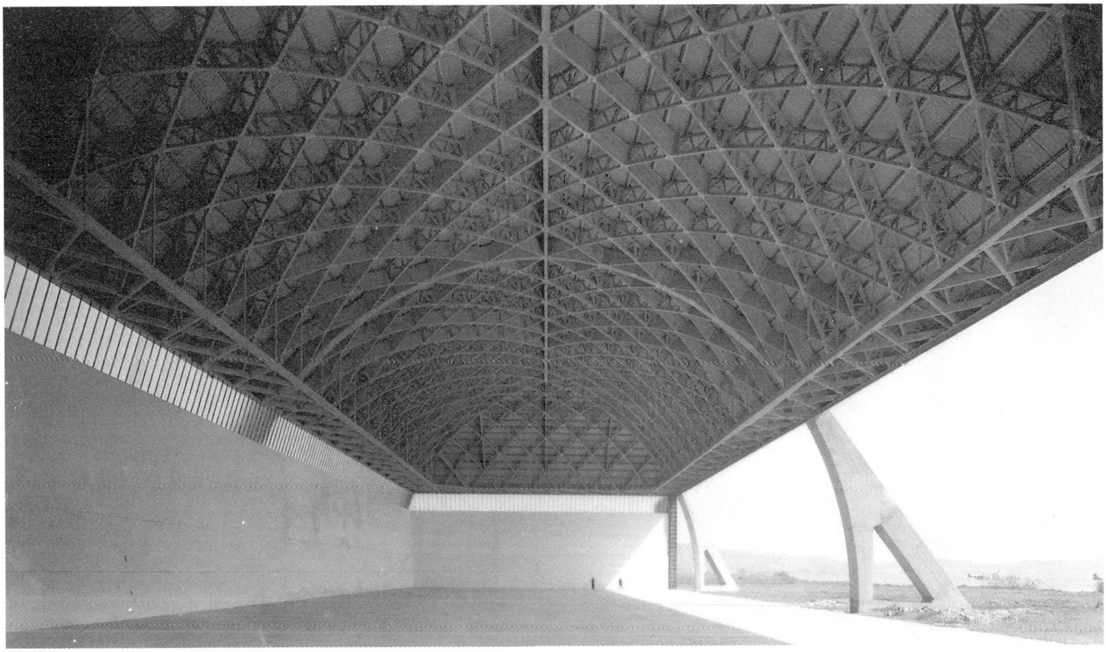

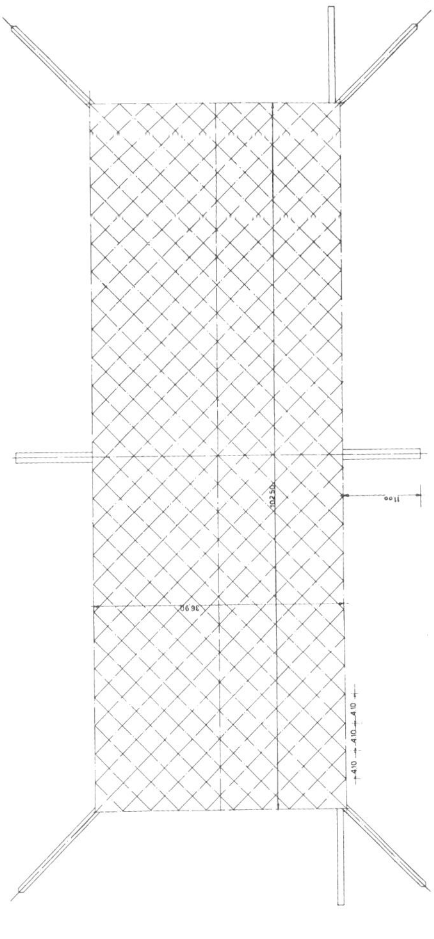

13. (above) Interior of a hangar from the second batch, designed in 1939 with some prefabricated elements. Structure is the same both sides, and the perimeter wall is added as a freestanding element.
14. (left) Plan of the second hangar type.
15. (below) Diagram of the primary loading showing how the six legs take the outward thrust (from Siegel 1961).
16. (bottom) The revised door-stacking detail and corner leg.

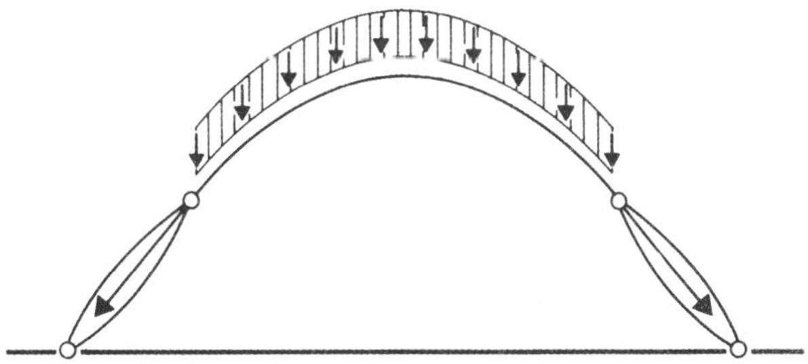

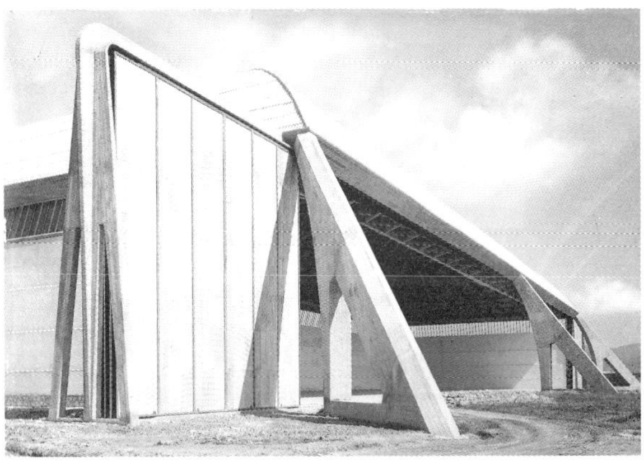

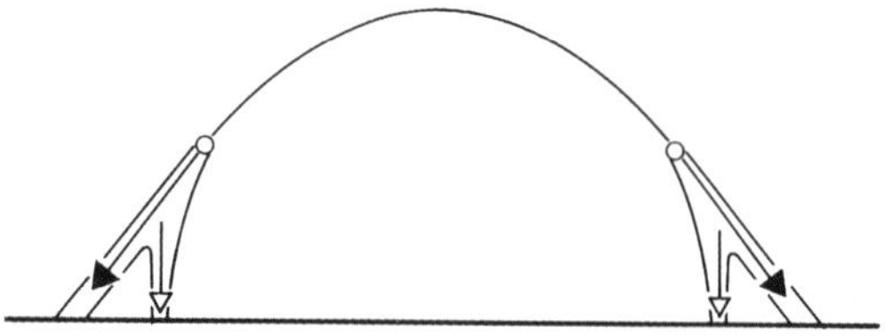

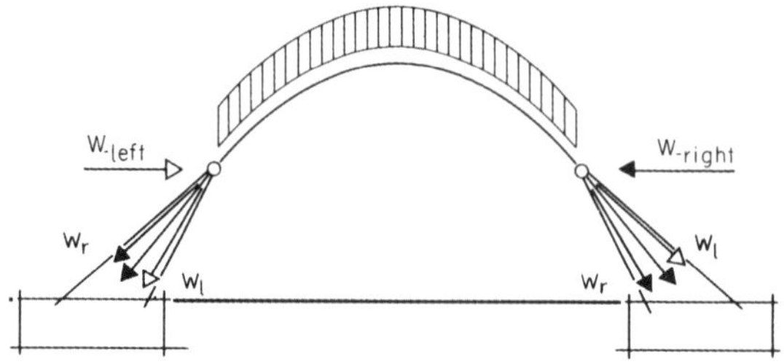

17, 18. (above) Diagrams from Siegel 1961. Left shows major forces descending at the angle of the leg, but while under construction loading is vertical. Right shows changing load path with wind pressure added to either side.
19. (below) Hangars under construction. Without walls the true span is evident. The visible difference between the open prefabricated ribs and the solid in-situ ones reveals the distribution of load.

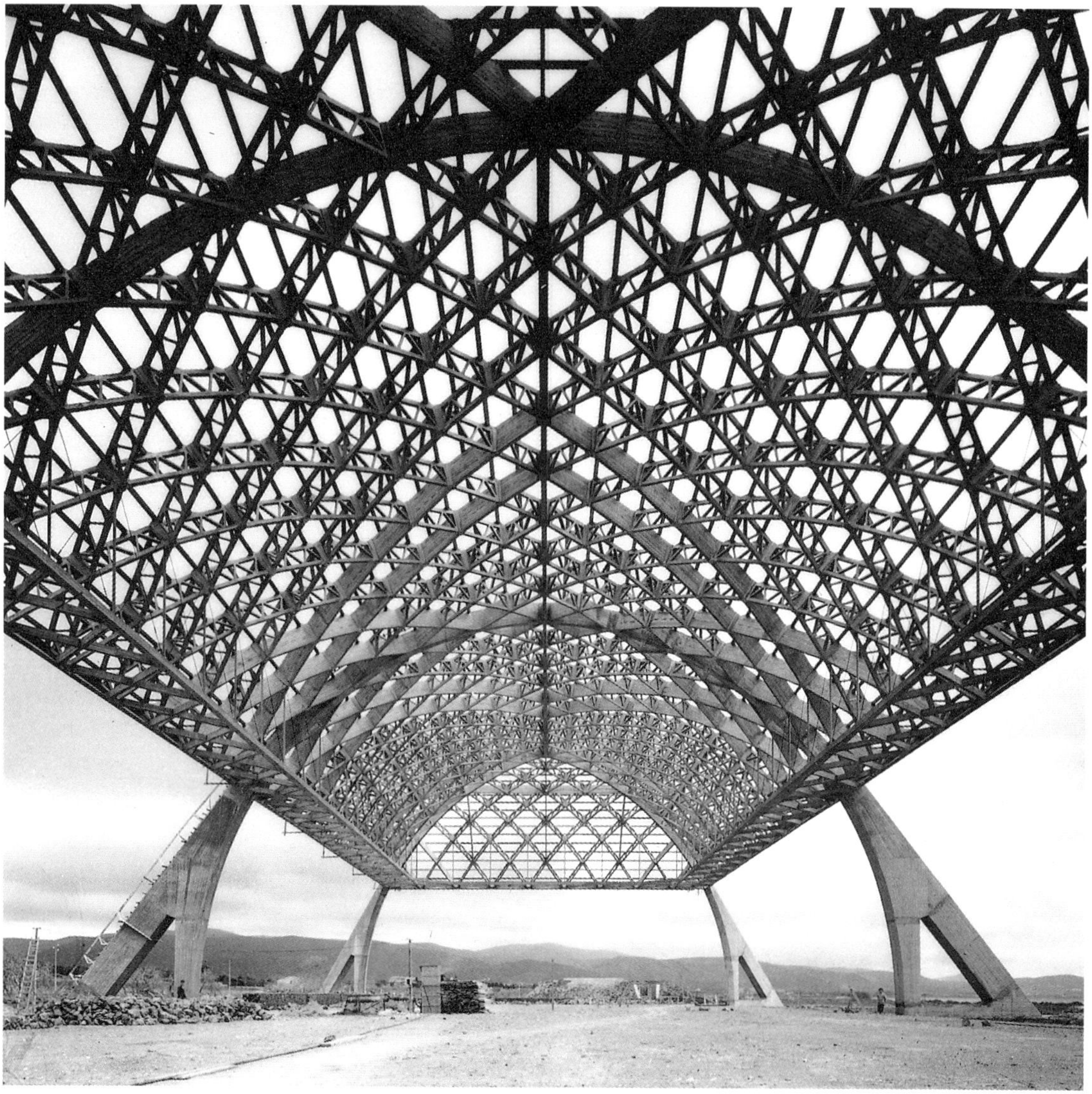

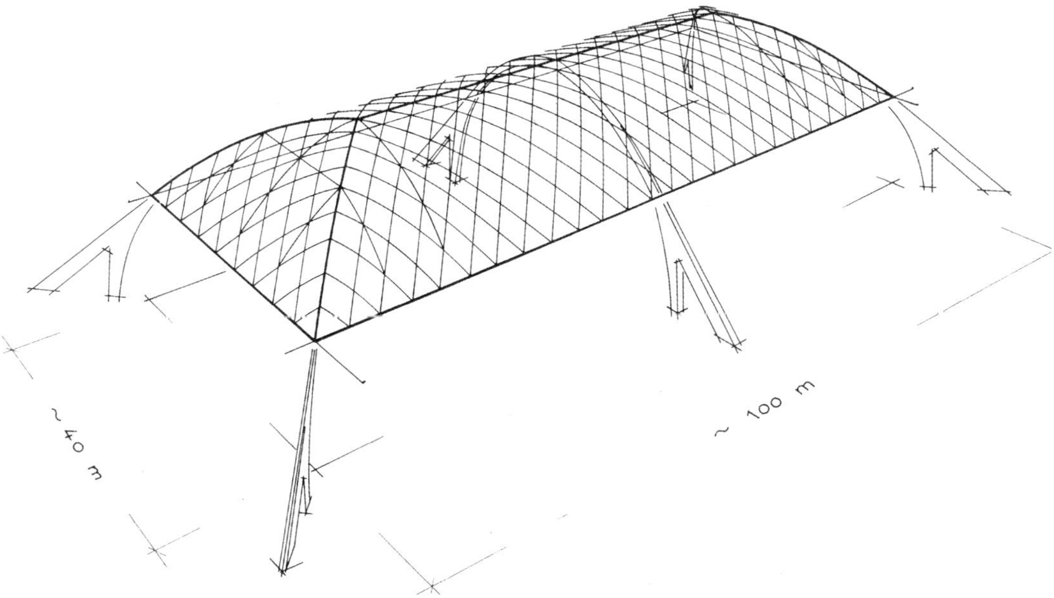

20. (above) Curt Siegel's projection of the second hangar type.

21. Triangular edge truss (first hangar type).

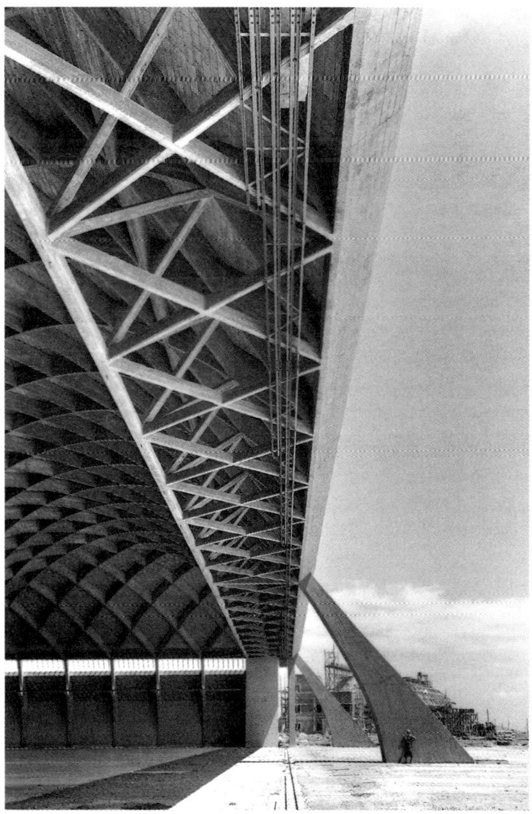

lightened it while also dramatising the spread of forces. The weather was excluded to rear and sides by an independent free-standing block wall made as plainly as possible, with a band of clerestory lighting at the top to reveal its complete detachment from the vault.

Nervi's worries about the asymmetry of loading prompted him to make careful measurements of the deformation that took place on the various hangars when the supporting formwork was removed. He was relieved to discover only minor (and acceptable) variations between the different buildings, and a maximum movement of only around 10cm. This kind of test, like the active modelling programme at the design stage, gave insight into the working of the structure and contributed in an essential way to Nervi's sense of its purity and efficiency, which for him was linked to its aesthetic value.

For others, though, it is not so clear that the later hangars are aesthetically better than the earlier ones. It is perhaps telling that the later look more impressive as skeletons than when finished, for only with the sides open does one truly register the fullness of span. Because of the way they were conceived, the roof contrasts starkly with the wall, but in the earlier hangars the multiple small legs

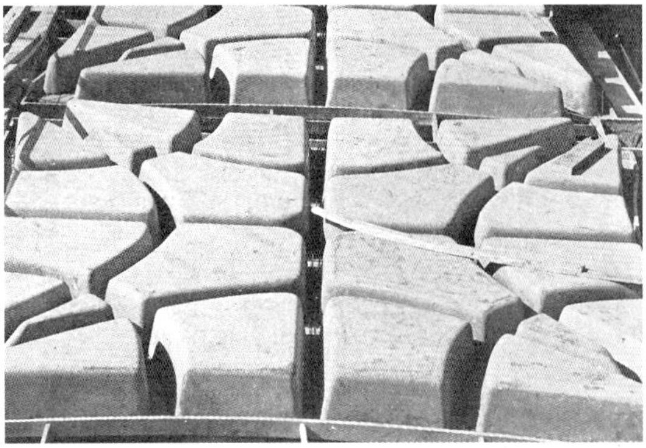

22. (above) and 23. (below) Gatti Wool Factory Rome, 1953. This column and slab structure was honed to maximum efficiency, placing the ribs to distribute the load radially from the column. The development of the easily movable and reusable moulds seen above was crucial to the economy of the process.

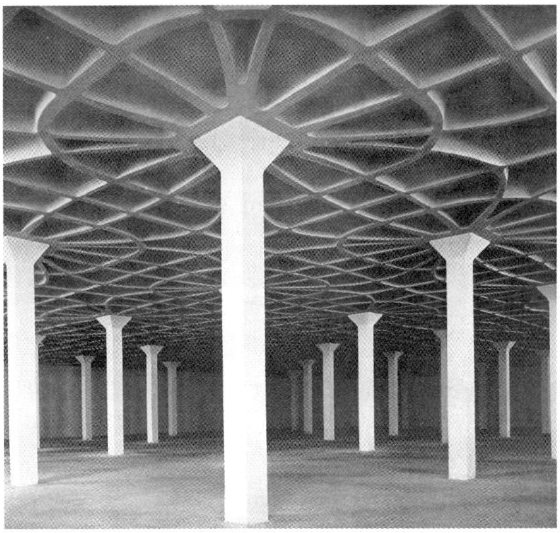

eased the transition visually, producing a comforting change of scale in contrast with the big front legs. Seen internally, the smaller legs of the earlier hangars also extended the rhythm of the vault, dramatising the effect of the clerestory. In the later ones it is less effective because less raked. But perhaps the greatest loss in the later hangars as opposed to the earlier ones is the door housing, no longer integrated with the corner structure but made into a separate element. Despite a sculptural treatment, the relationship with the corner leg at 45° remains uncomfortable, and in publications it is nearly always the corner of the earlier type of hangar that is shown. On the inside of the roof, the purlins and roofing of the later hangars also are arguably less elegant than the earlier tiling. Visible in the later hangars are the prefabricated trussed ribs, which contrast with solid in-situ ones employed at points of greatest load. In terms of structural expression this correctly differentiates strong from weak ribs, so it is arguably more honest, more informative.[13] The consistently solid ribs of the earlier version seem, though, to offer visually more sense of repose.

The advances made by Nervi cheapened his buildings and improved the production process, and it is easily overlooked that with six hangars offered at a fixed price, predictability was crucial: underbid and you lose six times over, perhaps even risking bankruptcy. As contractor as well as designer, Nervi had to give high priority to the operation of a clear and efficient construction process, and this aspect became for him part and parcel of the aesthetic outcome. That the changing conditions between the two batches of buildings entailed changes of interpretation not visually for the better, undermines Nervi's claim about economy necessarily honing a design towards the highest aesthetic quality. The changes between versions show, in fact, that it is not nearly so straightforward. They are fascinating precisely because they expose difficult choices faced by the designer over what to express or repress, how to define the relationship between large and small-scale elements, between roof and wall, and so on.

The hangars consolidated Nervi's reputation and led to a whole series of large span halls in the post-war years, starting with the vaulted Turin exhibition hall of the late 1940s which spanned 73x94 metres. The crucial advance in the later hangars of combining in-situ concrete work with precast elements became a central theme of Nervi's later practice. He developed a precise and very thin type of reinforced concrete called *ferrocemento* for elements which could make up a vault, acting as permanent shuttering while they were locked together with reinforcement and in-situ fill. Typically they formed a series of ribs to unify the structure. The assembly and bonding of elements - that is, the construction procedure - was very much part of the logic of the forms used, and Nervi was always concerned about how to assure structural integrity. After his hangars had been blown up by the retreating Germans in 1944, he visited the sites to ascertain whether the vaults of the later ones had parted at the poured joints. He was relieved to find that they had not: to the end they held as integrated units.

Form follows structure

For Nervi it seemed obvious that structural forces made formal demands that should be followed, that the pursuit of the most efficient and economical methods would lead quite naturally to the adoption of certain forms, and that these, like products of nature, would carry a certain automatic and inherent beauty. At certain moments in his lectures and writings, however, he hints at something more, and one cannot help but think of the eye-catching rib structures of his own buildings like the Palazzo of Sport when one reads his reaction to King's Chapel:

'Even in Gothic architecture one can find the evolution of the structural elements from the first achievements of purely technical inspiration, to those of greater richness, and finally to forms almost exclusively decorative. This evolution finds its greatest and most significant expression in the vault of the chapel at King's College, Cambridge where the ribs, which are reduced to pure decoration, form a pattern that suggests the isostatic lines of principal stress, invisible physical realities which modern structural analysis and the experiences in photoelasticity have revealed to us in the past few decades. It is certainly risky to imagine that the Gothic builders had a prophetic intuition, but this phenomenon remains profoundly significant.'[14]

In examining works by Nervi in detail, we saw that the structures were only achieved through struggle, and that there were many difficulties of interpretation along the way. We saw inescapably too that the form was not structural in an absolute sense, but only within the conceptual framework of the methods used to model and calculate it, and in response to the means and sequence of construction. For early Modernists like Nervi and his apologists, the simple shortcut explanation was enough by way of justification, but the work does not stand or fall thereby: each case is more complex, as are more general arguments about structural form.

Aesthetic discourse throughout history has referred back to nature as the primary example. If until the nineteenth century this was because it showed how God made things, in the twentieth it seemed to make equally significant the operation of natural law, and evolution theory only increased people's awe at the way creatures seemed so perfectly adapted in shape and size to their particular habitats.[15] Considering structure, it was evident in the skeletons of vertebrates that all was correctly sized and well-balanced. Even within the structure of a single bone such as a human femur, the shape and section changed in direct response to the loads transmitted. Our bones could thus be seen as extremely economical, piling up material where it was needed structurally close to the joint, then reducing it towards the centre. Even the hollow core was used - as a factory for blood. That an ideal building might please us by echoing the efficient operation of our own structure is an old and much reiterated idea.[16]

But of course we cannot grow a building's skeleton as we grow our bones, and until fairly recently we even lacked the means to analyse accurately how such irregular structures work. Static calculations for buildings relied for the most part on simplified assumptions, taking the members one by one, discounting interactions that in fact made the structure stronger, and generally assuming wide safety margins. We know from half-demolished houses that tiling battens help hold a roof together and that a staircase can help support a floor rather than passively loading it, but to calculate fully how a building accepts loads as its members deform in turn to absorb them, would be both complicated and difficult.

Quite apart from calculation problems, buildings are also commonly shaped by production methods. Timber and steel tend to be used straight and square because the timber emerged from a saw, and the steel was rolled in a mill. Even when used as simple beams they need maximum depth at centre span where the bending moment is greatest, so would be more efficient with a varying section, yet we generally make the section constant for ease of production and assembly.

Nervi designed some beautiful and highly efficient ribbed concrete slab structures of complex shape for a five metre span at his Gatti Wool Factory in Rome of 1953, but the idea did not catch on, though many concrete buildings of these dimensions are produced every day. Sadly, it tends to be both cheaper and quicker to use more concrete in creating a thicker and structurally cruder slab, and flat slabs are convenient for service runs requiring suspended ceilings. Cold bridges and poor quality of primary finish contribute further to the difficulty of exposing structure: usually, it is easier just to cover everything up.

It is mainly in large buildings such as bridges, halls for sport or exhibition, or aircraft hangars, that the pursuit of structure for structure's sake comes into its own. The larger the span, the more critical the structural performance, and the more money spent. This means it is worth more time and effort to design, model and calculate prior to construction, and that the parts and the process can be more complex. With bridges, structural efficiency is always a high priority, and the saving of material by clever design pays dividends. With large halls attention to detail can also produce substantial cost savings, while neglect of it can result in unwanted obtrusiveness, for large structures are obvious, and if crude or inept can poison a building irredeemably. It was on large spans, therefore, that Nervi expended his genius to greatest effect, by using a minimum of material while dramatising the forces at play. The admission of daylight was also important, both to reveal the lightness of the construction and to emphasise the rhythm of elements. As with many great engineers, calculation was backup rather than inspiration, though it was vital all the same, and in his work of the 1950s, Nervi used some of the first electronic computers for structural analysis. But design tended to proceed by a process of shape-finding in drawings and models, by careful experiment and patient refinement.

With hindsight, Nervi belongs to a noble line of experimental structuralists, starting with Antoni Gaudi's reversed hanging models in the 1890s, and continuing with the concrete bridges of Maillart and Freyssinet. Contemporaries like Felix Candela and Eduardo Torroja accomplished work parallel to that of Nervi. It was taken up again later in the hanging structures and gridshells of Frei Otto and the concrete shells of Heinz Isler, and it lives on today with Santiago Calatrava. With modern computers the possibilities of designing and testing complex three-dimensional structures have been extended. They can be built quickly and accurately with a great range of irregular and unique components, for the dimensions of each part can be precisely plotted within the computer model, the information being fed directly to robot cutting or moulding machines. Nervi's work would therefore be technically easier to emulate in the 21st century than before, given an equivalent imagination.

Notes

1. It is a general refrain in his Charles Eliot Norton Lectures (Nervi 1966). Ernesto Rogers takes exception to it in his introduction to the Nervi monograph (Joedicke 1957).
2. Nervi 1966, p. 6.
3. See Sulzer 1995 and 2000.
4. Nervi 1966, p. 25.
5. Ibid p. 25.
6. Ibid p. 99.
7. Ibid p. 26.
8. Such at least is the explanation given by Curt Siegel, see Siegel 1961.
9. The tapering form of the legs is due to variations in the static forces due to wind. Under still conditions the line of thrust should pass through the centre of the leg, but it will swing either way in relation to wind forces, see Siegel 1961, p.156.
10. I mean a system of primary, secondary and tertiary elements which assumes that each bears its load without help from the others. With the load distributed through a whole network of elements which share it between them, the basis for calculation is much more complicated.
11. Nervi 1966, pp. 26 ,27.
12. Ibid, p. 27.
13. Curt Siegel interprets the structure as lying between a shell and a barrel vault, and this difficulty of interpretation is played up by the two types of rib, see Siegel 1961.
14. Nervi 1966, pp. 6-7.
15. The pursuit of the biological analogy, its history and development, is beyond the scope of this book. Readers are referred to Steadman 1979, especially Chapter 4, *The anatomical analogy: engineering and the animal skeleton.*
16. For examples of biological analogy to structural forms in the period of Nervi's highest reputation see Siegel 1961, pp.182-3 & 212-3 and Joedicke 1962, pp. 9 &171. Taken together, these two books well illustrate the obsession at that time with structural form, of which Nervi's work was but the pinnacle.

Chapter 10. Giuseppe Terragni: Casa del Fascio, Como, 1932-36

Born in 1904, Giuseppe Terragni was the youngest of the architects considered in this book, but also the shortest lived. He was seventeen years the junior of Le Corbusier, the architect he most admired, and whom he met at the CIAM conference of 1933 which produced the Charter of Athens. He qualified as an architect in 1926, and his career was meteoric. His first major work, the Novocomum block of flats, was completed in 1928 when he was 24, and he was aged only 32 when he completed his masterpiece, the Casa del Fascio (House of the Fascists). This is widely considered the epitome of Italian Rationalism and the best Italian work of the inter-war period. He lived only to the age of 39, completing a mere 26 buildings, for his career was cut short by the Second World War. Called up in 1939, he became a captain of artillery on the Eastern Front and was caught in the carnage of Stalingrad. He suffered a nervous breakdown from which he never recovered. Sent home, he attended various hospitals, but he died a broken man in 1943 just days before the fall of Mussolini, possibly committing suicide.[1] He had not only witnessed one of the most brutal chapters of the war,[2] but had also to face the end of Fascism, to acknowledge the inherent corruption of a creed in which he had fervently if perhaps also naively believed.

Apart from the unbuilt projects of the Futurists, Modern Architecture arrived relatively late in Italy. This was partly because of poverty and late industrialisation, but mainly due to the overwhelming shadow of cultural heritage from Antiquity to the Baroque. Even in the 1920s a historicist view dominated, finding its last expression in the Novecento movement of Giovanni Muzio. So it was not until the late 1920s that a Modern Movement erupted, following the example of northern Europe and Russia. Mussolini and his Blackshirts had assumed power in 1922, so Fascism was from the start the political background for everything.

Gruppo 7, formed by Terragni and his newly graduated friends in Milan, was founded in 1926 and they immediately produced the Rationalist Manifesto.[3] Unlike Germany, where Modernism before Hitler had been associated with left-wing municipalities and building societies, in Italy it had no pre-established political colour. Indeed, it could be welcomed by the Fascists as exciting, efficient, progressive and technically innovative. But in the end, Mussolini proved to have much the same crude and monumental tastes as Hitler, so major buildings in Rome like the EUR complex went to the Neoclassicist Marcello Piacentini, who has been called Mussolini's Albert Speer and was similarly opportunistic.[4] Nevertheless, Terragni was able to enter the competition for the Palazzo Littorio, the National Party Headquarters, as late as 1937 with a thoroughly modernist project, and he almost won. Italian Fascism was for most of its duration open to the adoption of a modernist face, and not only at Como.

Local context

But the Como context was essential to Terragni's career, both for the early recognition of his talent and the gift of key commissions. Although a small place, it had a lively artistic culture and had been the home town of the Futurist Antonio Sant'Elia. It cannot have been unhelpful that Terragni's brother Attilio was mayor during the building of the Casa del Fascio, particularly as the local party boss was

1. Novocomum block of flats, Como, 1928, Terragni's first major work.

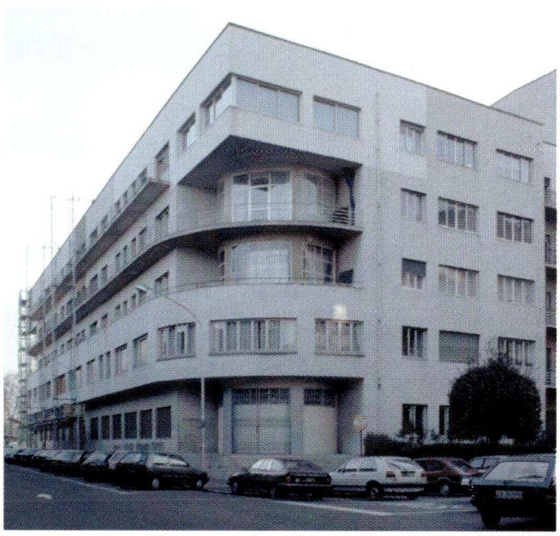

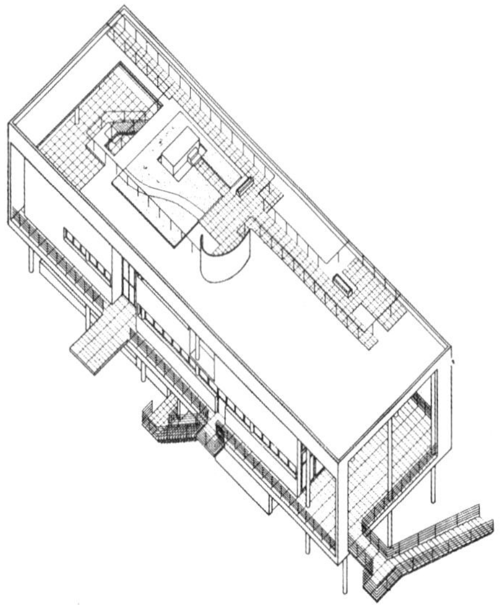

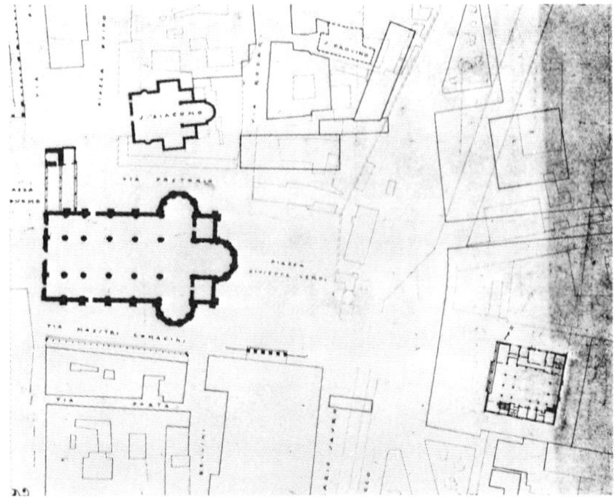

2. (left) Villa Sul Lago project, 1936, with obvious debt to Le Corbusier.
3. (above) Casa del Fascio, Como, site plan. Casa, bottom right faced east end of Cathedral, mid left, commanding the public square in between. Symmetrical balance about the Cathedral axis was applied with another square building.

not always sympathetic. Despite the need for approval in Rome, the local party branch seems to have been allowed considerable autonomy. The Unification of Italy was but decades earlier, and communications were often poor, so there were still great differences in regional culture. It was in the industrial cities of the North, Milan and Turin, that progressive art movements erupted, rather than in conservative Rome, and Como was a satellite of Milan, placed high in the lake district close to the Swiss border. This made it both the closest place in Italy to developments in Northern Europe, and a frontier city for international exchange.

Born in nearby Meda, Terragni went to school and to the Technical Institute in Como before taking up studies in architecture at Milan. Afterwards he returned to establish his career in Como before also receiving commissions in Milan for a series of blocks of flats. His father was a builder, and Como had supposedly been the centre and starting point for the Maestri Comacini, the famous Romanesque masons who worked throughout Italy.[5] This mythical notion helped perpetuate a strong local pride in craftsmanship, instilling in Terragni and his co-workers a concern for detail.[6] The Casa del Fascio was well-made, and the careful detailing of its elements contributed to its architectural success.

Although Terragni's achievements required the local context, they depended crucially also on international inspiration. He and his fellow students in Milan lived for news from the north, disseminated through books and magazines such as *Moderne Bauformen*. They followed developments in France, Holland and Germany, and also the work of the Russian Constructivists, which is reflected in several early Terragni projects.[7] But above all they were influenced by Le Corbusier, whose *Vers une Architecture* had been published in 1923. Terragni's admiration for the master was lifelong: he was still designing projects shamelessly imitative of the master in 1936,[8] he traced over published drawings,[9] and during the war, a copy of the *Oeuvre Complète* accompanied him to the front. Terragni felt a special affinity for Le Corbusier's poetic and professedly Mediterranean spirit as opposed to the cold technical rationalism of Gropius.[10] The great formal skill backed up with appeals to classical sources made the Swiss master's work seem especially relevant to Italians, who wanted to be progressive without losing their heritage. Le Corbusier's enthusiasm for pure forms such as the cube and cylinder, and proportions such as the golden mean, could also supply principles of supposed universal relevance. Terragni and his rationalist friends in Gruppo 7 stated that they did not want completely to reject the past but to work with it and reinterpret it,[11] and there is evidence throughout Terragni's *oeuvre* of reference to classical sources, not to mention overtly classical pieces such as the Stecchini tomb of 1930 and the extraordinary Danteum of 1938.

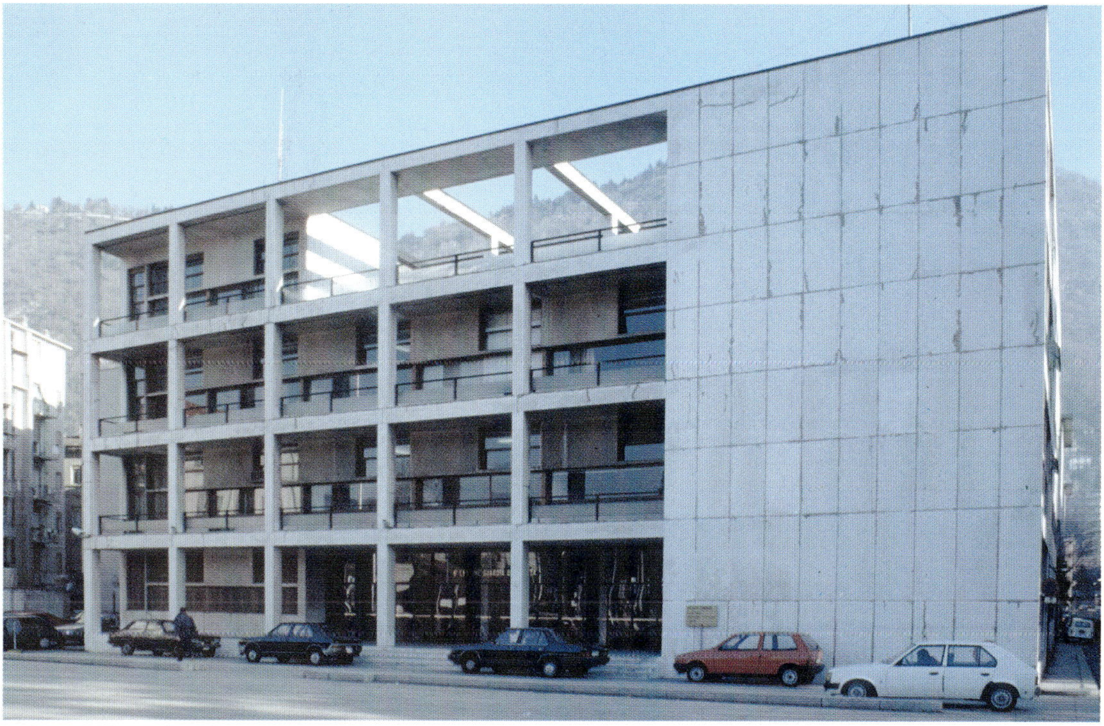

4. Casa del Fascio (now Casa del Popolo), main façade facing square.
5. (below) Casa del Fascio, perspective drawing at project stage including intended door in blank part of wall.

Terragni's greatness lay in his being neither stuck in a classical groove nor a mere imitator of Le Corbusier. The astonishing thing about the Casa del Fascio is its independence of both, for it makes classical references without being a classical building, and it hardly begins to subscribe to the Corbusian Five Points. It stands on a base, not on the ground, the columns are not *pilotis* but parts of a frame, and because of the frame, continuous horizontal windows are disallowed.

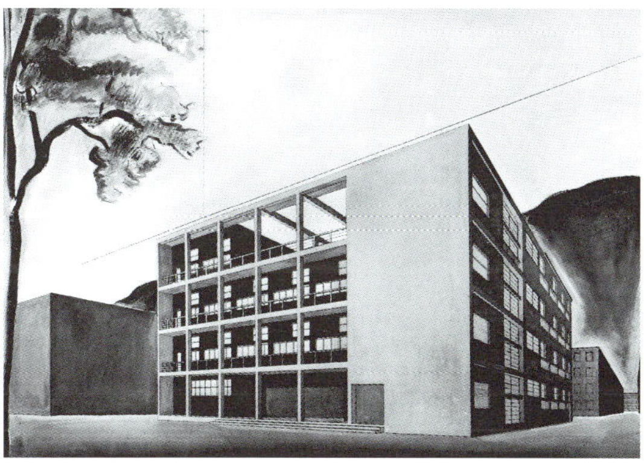

The Casa and its setting

The Casa del Fascio was the representative seat of the regime that took power when Terragni was still at school, and of which he became a party member in 1928 at the age of 24. It was his most prestigious commission and the one with the longest gestation. He saw the building as *'a House, a School, a Temple... the political and moral centre of activity of every province as testified by the miraculous dedication to their Duce'.*[12] In everyday use it provided offices for the party and subsidiary organisations such as the Veteran's Association,

6. Casa del Fascio, main façade showing proportion system. The whole figure is a double square.

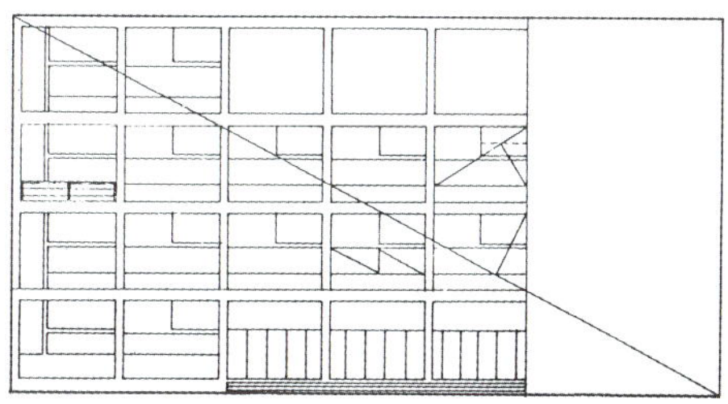

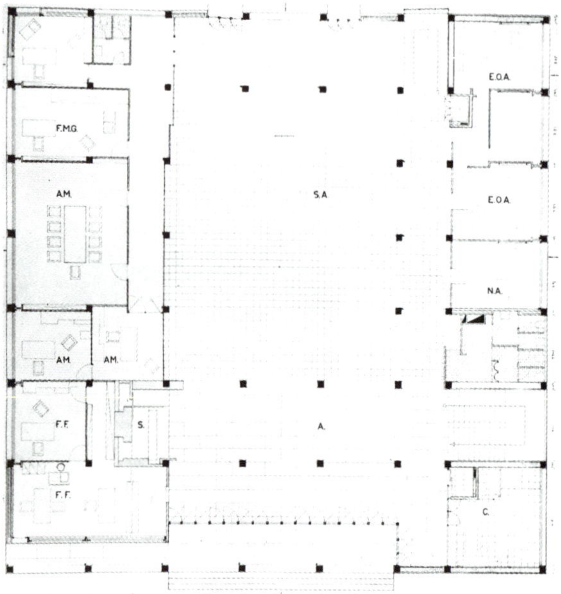

7. Casa del Fascio, Ground floor plan, north is left. Multiple doors link central hall and public square, with everyday entrance to right. Left wing is Veteran Association and Sacrarium - monument to Party Fallen is opposite main stairs.
8. Casa del Fascio, First floor plan.This is the *piano nobile* with the most important rooms: main meeting room is mid left and leader's office bottom left.

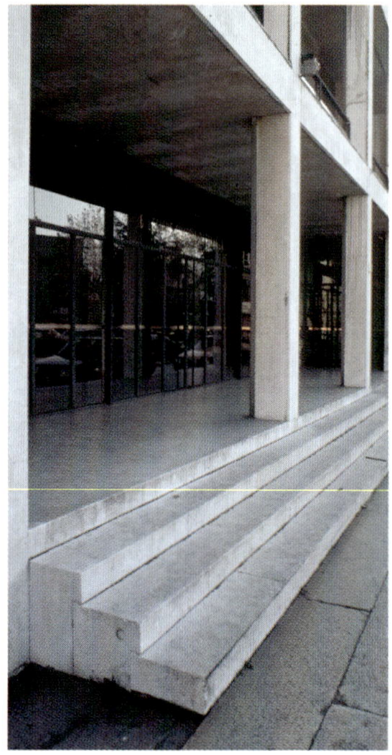

9. Front step detail.

10. Central bay of front showing balconies and frame.

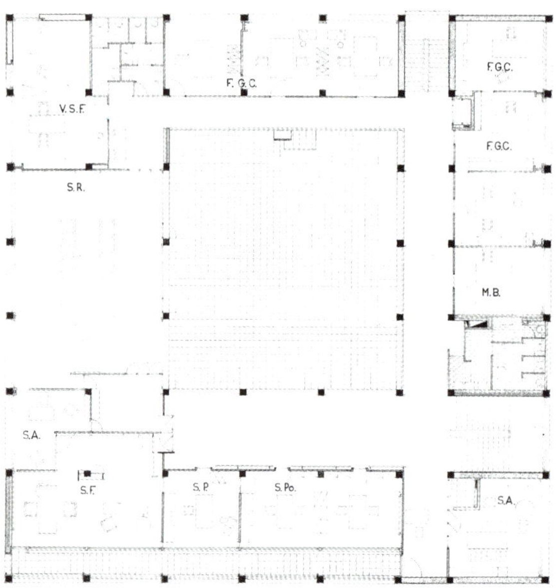

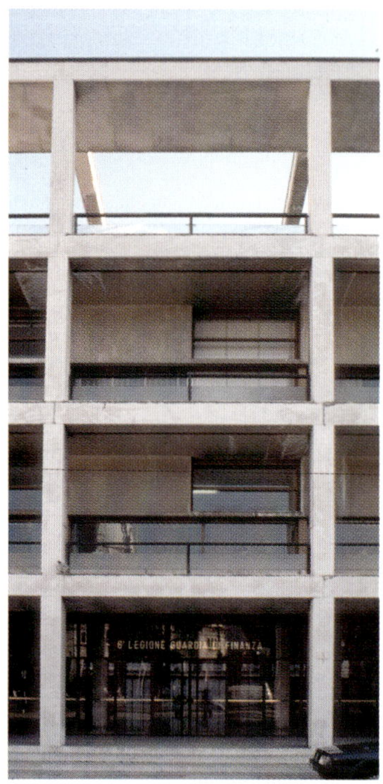

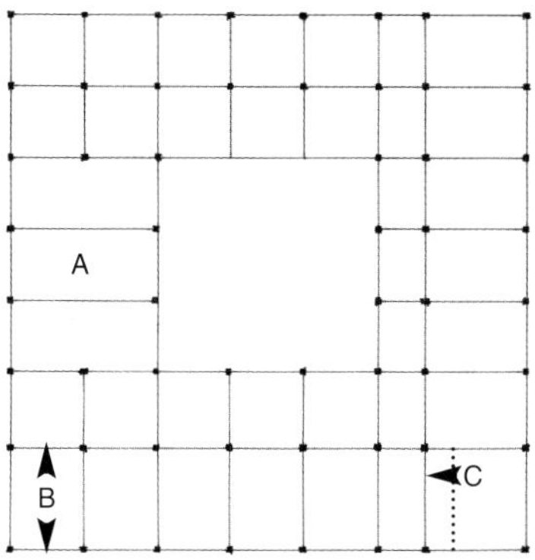

11. Casa del Fascio, column grid in plan showing the irregularities (author's drawing).
Key: A missing columns;
B wide bay;
C column line shifted to left.

The whole figure is almost precisely square, but the individual grid panels are not, due to the wide bay.

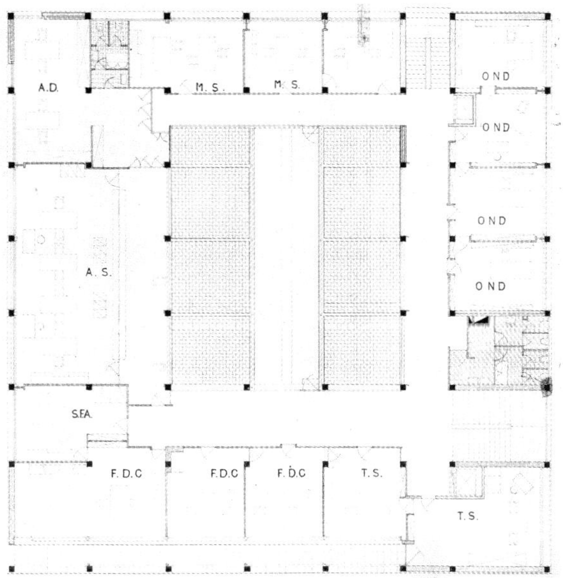

12. Casa del Fascio, second floor plan. Central hall roofed in glass blocks becomes external court. Accommodation is mainly offices.
13. Casa del Fascio, third floor plan, more offices to right, porter's flat top left. On three sides terraces leave the frame exposed, which signals to the outside world the presence of the central hall.

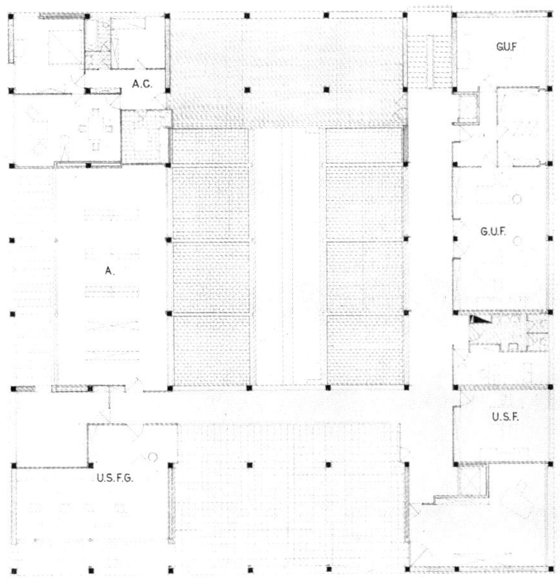

Women's front and Welfare offices. It had to allow within its walls for meetings of the local party organisers, and on special occasions it would become the focus for larger party rallies. It therefore had to be at the centre of town with a large public space where thousands could gather, and to include a speaker's platform from which the Duce could address the crowd. To gain this occasional public arena, the Casa was set behind the Cathedral with its back to the hills, taking advantage of a large square lying between it and the old heart of the town. Terragni set up a new profane piazza, leaving the Cathedral piazza outside its west doors unchallenged, for the Church retained power and respect, and it was possible to be at once Catholic and Fascist. Conceiving his building as a free-standing square block, he devised a formal plan for the new square which deferred to the axis of the cathedral. He suggested the addition of a second block of the same size placed opposite to complete the symmetry. Further political and administrative buildings were to be added to complete an intended political zone.[13] The main front of the building faces west-south-west.

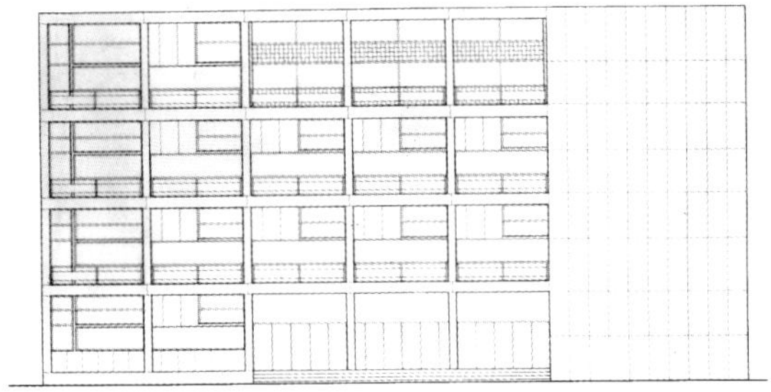

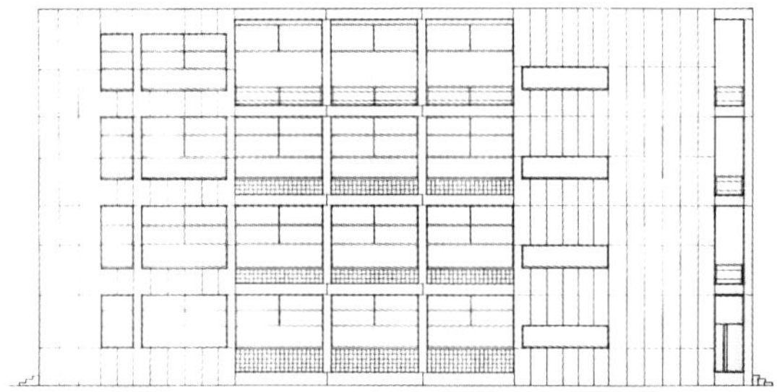

Casa del Fascio: the four façades.
14. (top) Front facing square.
15. (above) North side.
16. (below) Rear with giant order central bays.
17. (bottom) South side.

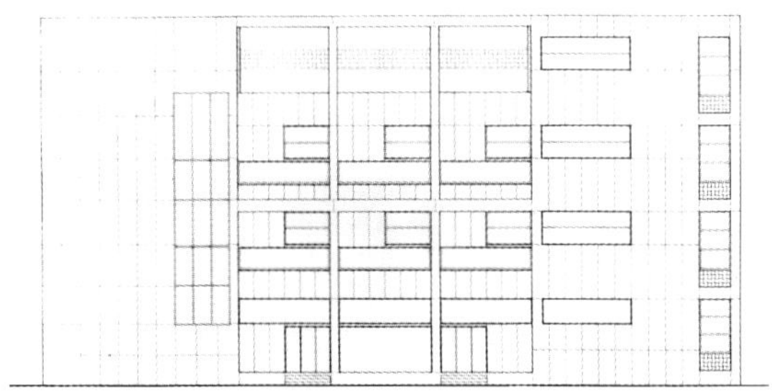

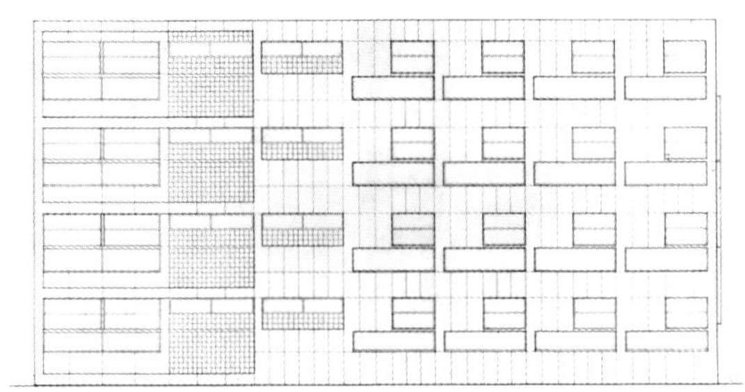

Essential geometry

Conceived as a single free-standing block, the Casa needed four storeys to achieve the required accommodation. In keeping with his rationalist beliefs in geometry and proportion, Terragni made it precisely square in plan, and half the same dimension in height, namely 33.2 x 16.6 metres.[14] The whole block is therefore half a cube, while each face is a double square. The four floors were made equal in height to continue the 2:1 system of subdivision, and each side was divided into seven bays to achieve an almost regular column grid. This of course breaks with the principle of 2:1 division which would have required eight bays, but the uneven number generates a central bay allowing movement (and arrival) on the central axis. In the middle of the building, a space three bays square each way was left column-free to form a central court. Sliced in half by a glass block floor at mid section, it was divided into a hall below and an external court above. Terragni attached particular significance to the three deep beams supporting this floor, which filled the missing centre of the grid. With their structural depth they defined the space between the ceiling and the tops of the doors, producing a horizontal line 2.1 metres above floor level to define human scale. The three beams were placed cross-wise rather than longitudinally, their rhythm counteracted by the division of the roof in the other direction. This consisted of two raised fields of glass blocks divided by a lower central section of ceiling, which centred on a glazed strip to mark the central axis.

Notice that this description so far concerns the system, not the content or the variations. It concerns a general geometry that sets the frame both literally and metaphorically. Its visible dominance as a constructive framework - present even when unneeded, for example, across the open roof terraces - is at once the statement of a modernist steel skeleton and of the more ancient and mythical idea of trabeated construction which haunts the Classical Tradition, leading back to the Greek temple and even beyond to the marriage of the first column with the first beam.[15]

Contemporaries and followers who set up such rigid ordered systems - for example Hilberseimer - too often found they had straitjacketed themselves: not so Terragni. Across the front he divided the building into seven equal bays, but he gave the sides a smaller bay-size to create an extra-deep bay at the front end. Since the added depth presents itself mostly as a balcony, it can read as an added strip of plan, but it is in fact part of the original square. This adjustment makes the sides noticeably asymmetrical in contrast with the front and back, aiding a hierarchical reading. More importantly it also affects the main entrance, exaggerating the depth of threshold through the extended column spacing. The deep front bay thickens the whole front wing in contrast with the back one, pushing the central court back into the plan. The effect is enhanced by adding a further half bay to it at first floor level.

18. Casa del Fascio seen from the north-east, showing the north and rear façades.The foreground building is a later addition.

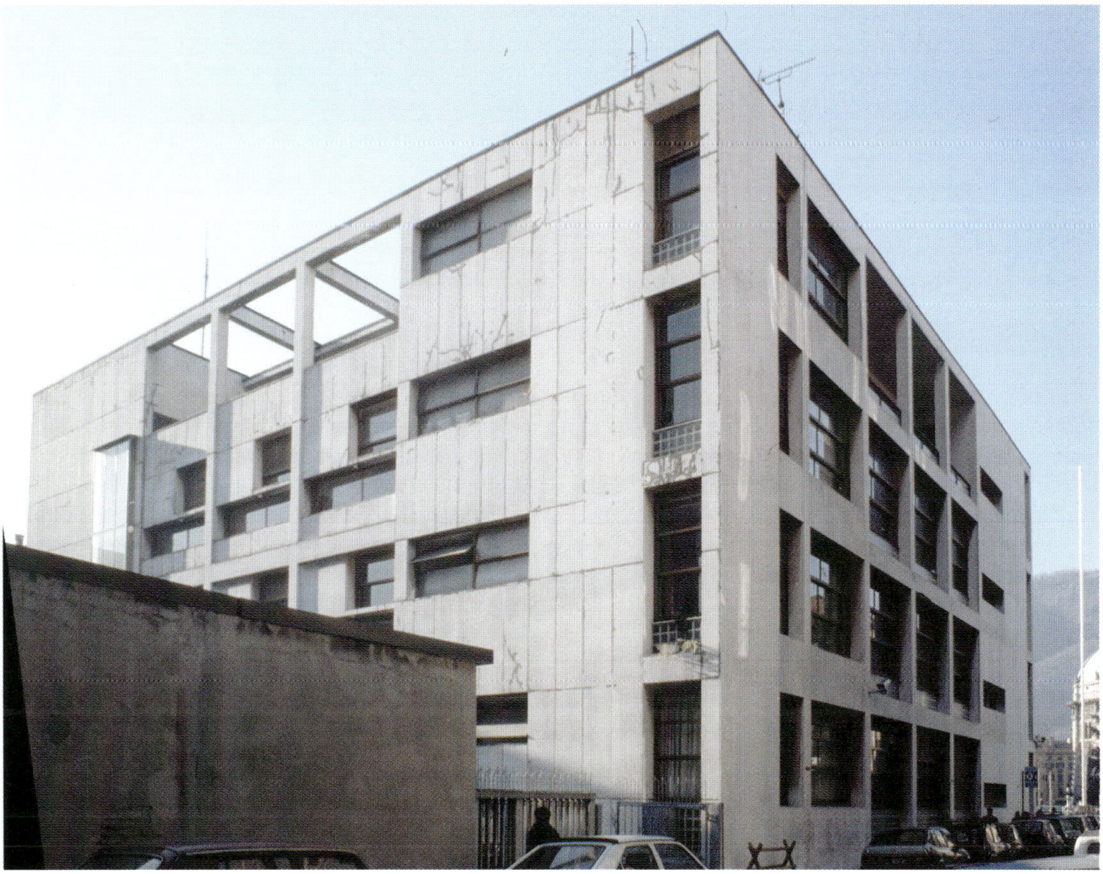

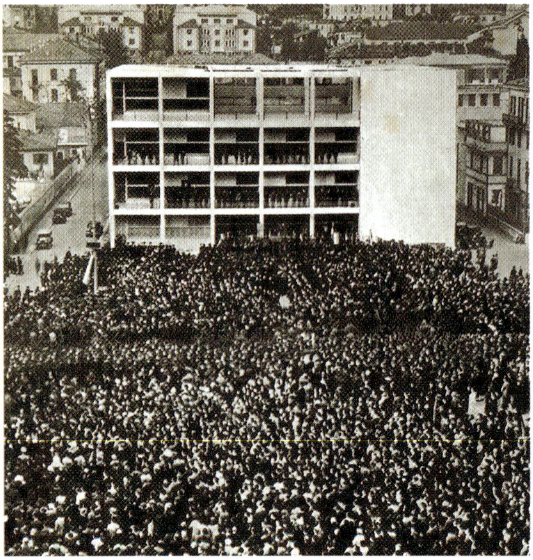

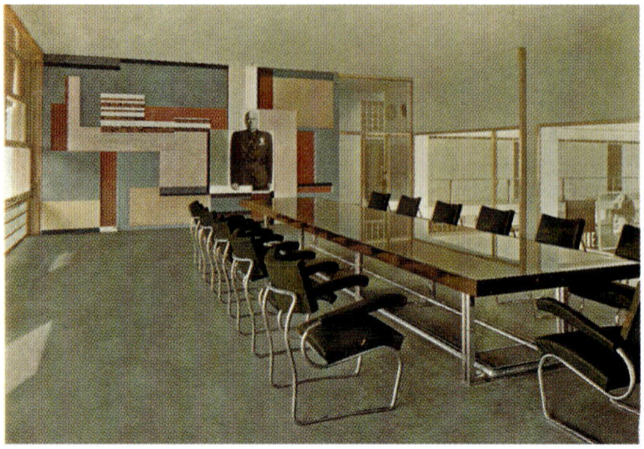

19. (left) Casa during a Fascist rally.
20. (above) First floor meeting room with abstract relief including photo of il Duce.

21. (opposite) Perspective of main façade at project stage showing intended tower and graphics on blank part of wall.

There are further irregularities: a less skillful rationalist would have retained the column-rhythm relentlessly through the building, but Terragni introduces variations. Major rooms placed to centre-left in plan involve the elimination of an expected column, while on the right a pair of even bays is redivided into large and small to accommodate offices and corridor respectively. On second and third floors, tinkering with the bay relations produces a neat expression of the circulation hierarchy, for the largest corridor/gallery is to the front, occupying a whole bay width and meshing with the main staircase; the second runs front to back, occupying the reduced lateral bay, and meshes with the rear staircase; the third at the back has only half a longitudinal bay. The fourth side has no gallery/corridor, for it contains large rooms entered from their ends. On the ground floor, though, this part gains a corridor to define the separate Veteran's Association, which has its own entrance.

Despite its largely symmetrical layout, the Casa del Fascio is determinedly asymmetrical. This asymmetry begins with the front façade, for the two bays to right are presented as solid. Schumacher sees this blank wall as the vestigial remnant of the lictor's tower in an earlier version, a kind of *campanile* with a pulpit part way up from which the leader would address the crowd.[16] Terragni certainly designed one for his later House of the Fascists at Lissone,[17] but there is no special place for the Dictator at Como, instead three layers of balconies, any of which could be used, and which photographs show were occupied during meetings by lines of uniformed officers.[18] The blank façade might alternatively be sustained by a rationalist argument. The rooms on the right side of the building are adequately lit from that side (south) and the corner need be no exception, so the blankness simply states the end of a block. This could lead to a kind of pinwheel plan arrangement as at the Bauhaus, but it only happens in a more limited way on the other corners. Comparison of all four façades shows something else: that the side to the right is by far the most solid. Rear and north façades, like the front, show an open frame across the three central bays, signalling the presence of the central court. The building might therefore be read as having a main (and more solid) wing to the right where the staircases and corridors are, to which a weaker U-shaped block is attached. Within the ground floor one finds main entry and porter's desk to the right, and one actually enters within the territory of the right wing, though the space is made visually continuous by bringing through the floor plane with its two contrasted types of paving. The spatial ambiguity here is typical of the architectural gestures which repeatedly animate the building.

Organisational hierarchies

If it is appropriate in the case of a rationalist building to emphasise the formal system before considering content (use), the triumph of Terragni's building lies in the way he reconciles the two, while

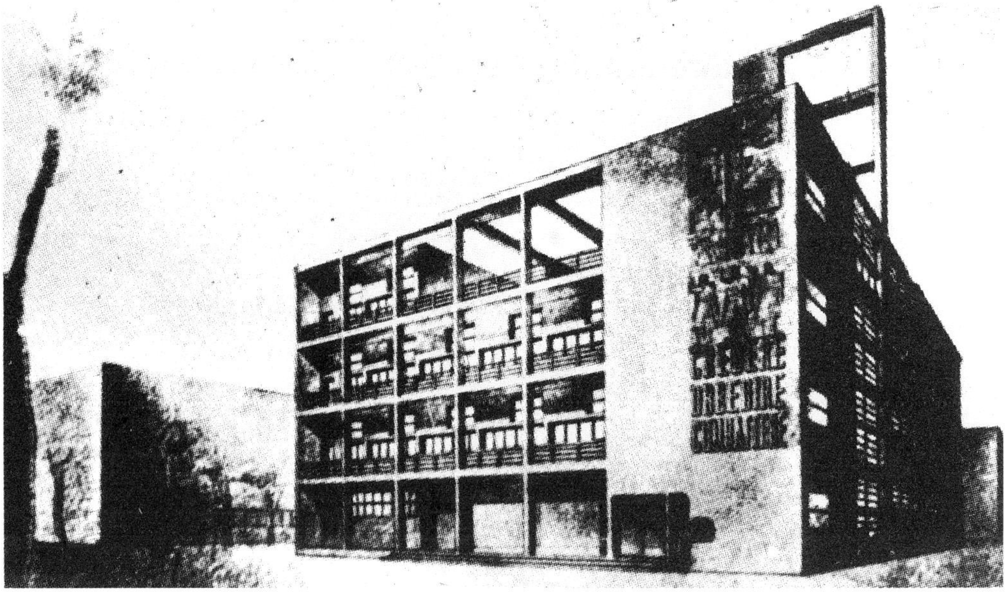

also leaving room for echoes of history. With its central void, the plan of the Casa suggests both the Roman atrium house and the Palazzo. Its circulation gallery at first floor reinforces the focal nature of the space, and though it is roofed over, the glass-block skylights and central strip of thick glass preserve its link with the heavens. The hall was used for meetings of the party faithful, and at a crucial moment the blackshirts would march out in unison through the row of glass doors which were opened simultaneously at the flick of a switch. Raised on its stone base behind a wide flight of steps, the hall thus acted as a stage for the greater public beyond, and in the first version of the plans the Leader's lectern was placed at centre rear to address both internal and external spaces.

The multiple electric doors were reserved for ceremonial occasions: everyday entrance involved a turn to the right. Terragni balanced the main staircase in plan with the Sacrarium opposite, a red granite shrine to the Fallen of the Movement. He clad the ceiling of the vestibule linking the two with funereal black marble, which by reflecting the light, added an illusory vertical dimension. Those who failed to notice this holy corner on entering would confront again it on descending the main stairs. If they knew the building they would also recognise that it occupied the same corner as the office above used by the leadership and the meeting room adjacent where important decisions were made. Terminating the widest gallery opposite the main stair, these two important rooms reiterated the dominant *piano nobile* of the Renaissance Palazzo, a model which Terragni consciously followed. As regards other rooms, mainly offices, Terragni claimed to dispose them according to hierarchies of importance and public accessibility. Front and left sides led, with lesser offices to right and the least important of all to the rear. The upper two floors, more remote from the public, housed the less visited offices, while the top back left corner - that diametrically opposite the main entrance - was reserved for the most servile function of all, the porter's flat.

The façades

Within the discipline of his gridded half cube, Terragni sought both to express the internal disposition of parts and to fenestrate according to the exigencies of the climate. The front, appropriately, became most open, with balconies at all levels. Besides allowing participation in ceremonial occasions, these provide shading and layering for the offices behind. The open frame of the three central bays at top floor level shows the position of the central hall and the penetrability of the building. This is repeated on the back and left side. In the rear elevation, the hall's presence is further emphasised by exposing the frame as a giant order, achieved by recessing façade panels and framing members at first and third floor - another disruption of the rational grid. Both on the right side and the rear, the presence of staircases is shown by vertical fenestration, in the first case using glass blocks and in the second a slightly projecting bay. Offices in the south side understandably have the smallest window areas, with a broader low sash for views and a narrow one above for light. This asymmetrical motif is also readable as the fascist emblem, but not conclusively.[19] The block of lavatories on the same façade gets high-level clear windows over translucent glass blocks, combining privacy with rhetoric. The major rooms at the centre of the left (north-facing) façade have full-size slightly recessed windows with glass-block fill at low level, though the crucial importance of the ceremonial meeting room at first floor level is in no way declared, and nor is the presence of the corner office used by the Leader. The whole series of façades including the frame was elegantly clad in finely-jointed marble panels, mostly in the same plane. On all façades the rhythm of the frame is evident, but it appears and disappears from within the putative wall as an abstract statement, never shown as the literal substance of the building's skeleton. Unlike Asplund's Lawcourts in the next chapter, there is no attempt to represent joints or a section that changes with load. The game of frame versus infill is played only in a limited way, and on the back. The game of thicknesses, of projections and set-backs, though, appears in every variation.

The rational and Rationalism

The term Rationalism was used rather generally in Italy to describe the products of the Modern Movement just as Functionalism was used in Scandinavia, and there was the same widespread suggestion that it meant a renunciation of historical styles and ornament accompanied by a new attention to logic and reasoned procedure that was implicitly if not explicitly Positivist:

'New architecture, true architecture, must emerge from a strict adherence to logic and rationality... We don't pretend to be creating a new style, but through a constant application of rationality, by letting a building meet the needs of the problem as perfectly as possible, we are certain that a style will arise by the process of selection. We must succeed in this: ennobling architecture with the indefinable, abstract perfection of pure rhythm, of simple constructiveness... We must convince ourselves that types must be created, a few fundamental types... Architecture must be partly composed of self-renunciation. We must have this courage: at the point we are now at, architecture cannot be individual, and in a coordinated effort to save it, to redirect it to a more rigid logic which stems directly from the needs of our time, we must sacrifice our very personalities. The new generation is proclaiming an architectural revolution, but it is a revolution aimed at organising and building. A longing for sincerity, for order, for logic and above all else, for great clear-mindedness - those are the real characteristics of the new spirit.'[20]

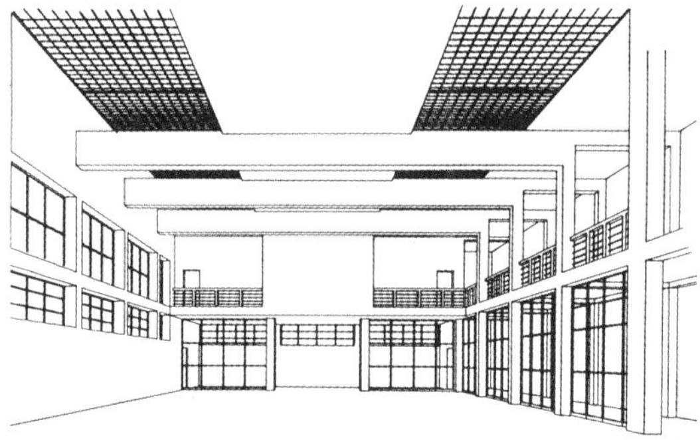

22. Casa del Fascio, perspective of central hall as seen on axis from square.

There is much reference in Terragni's account of his Casa del Fascio to logical organisation in terms of layout and disposition of parts, and to the intended exhibition of functions on the outside. In keeping with the times, and drawing on the published procedures of Neufert, he produced a series of orientation diagrams, for example, showing the path of the sun and the effects of the light.[21] It is clear, however, that the general orientation of the building was dictated by the site conditions, even if these studies affected the fenestration. Somewhat less justified are the most basic assumptions of the design, such as the decision to make the building a half cube. If such pure geometric figures are to be regarded in themselves as 'rational', they are so in a rather different way and presumably involve aesthetic assumptions of a Corbusian kind (see Chapter 7). Also questionable is the choice of a regular structural cage. Some justification is implied in remarks about difficult foundation conditions and the need for piles, but neither the engineering of the frame nor its somewhat uneven loading are discussed. In any case, structural problems on a building of this size are relatively trivial. Terragni was more interested in the frame as an abstract ordering device than as a construction system.

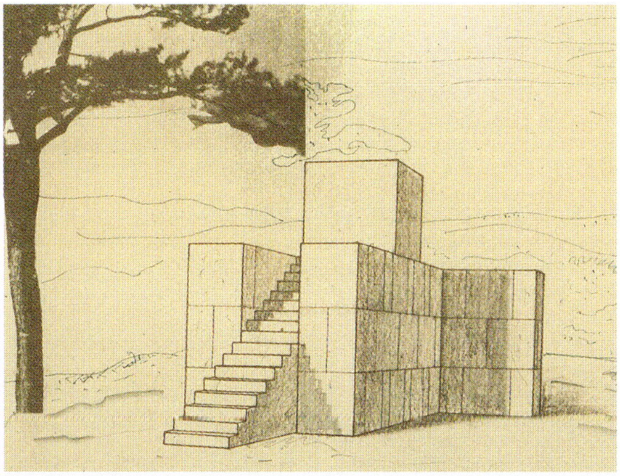

Two monuments by Terragni:
23. Sarfatti tomb, Eche Col, 1935.

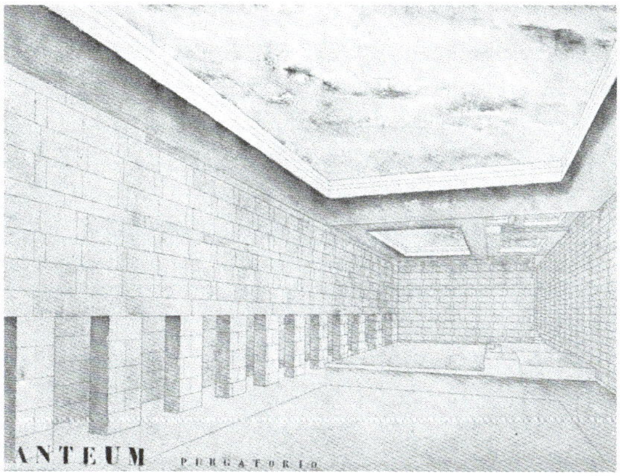

24. Purgatory hall of Danteum project 1938, a museum to Dante in Rome. Execution was prevented by the Second World War.

What is more, the exceptions are more interesting than the rule. The great glory of Terragni's Casa lies surely in his escape from the repetitive banality of a Durand or a Hilberseimer, precisely by not letting the grid dominate, but by breaking and adjusting it to accept and express local eccentricities of programme, so that in the dialogue between specific incident and the regulating system, a series of variations could be played.

A Fascist architecture?

'Our movement has no other moral consequence than to serve the revolution in hard times. We are asking for Mussolini's faith to give us a way to realise this.' So wrote the rationalists in their manifesto presented to Il Duce in March 1931, and there is no reason to suppose that they were merely being opportunistic.[22] Terragni himself leaves little doubt of his enthusiasm to serve the party, for *'the job with the most political prestige, propaganda value, and revolutionary originality remains the Casa del Fascio.'* [23] It housed *'the directors and commanders of this advanced society'*.[24] When it was finished he was thrilled by *'the thousands and thousands of black-shirted citizens amassed in front of the Casa del Fascio to hear the voice of their leader announce to Italians and foreigners the advent of the Empire'* [25] which followed the Ethiopian war. Zevi and others sometimes present Terragni as a kind of resistance figure within Fascism,[26] but this only makes sense in purely architectural terms, and in contrast with the stripped Classicism of Piacentini which in the end the Dictator preferred. Certainly Terragni's architecture was more humane, more subtle, more progressive, gentler in scale, so perhaps it can be seen as representing a softer and more ideal view of Fascism. He seems nevertheless to have been content to see party slogans like *'Ordine, Autorita, Giustizia'* displayed in it, and though in both Sacrarium and main meeting room the art was considerably abstracted, it was brought to earth with a thump by a life-size photo-portrait of Mussolini placed as if sitting at the head of the table. Terragni may have pushed the Como Fascists to the limit of their progressiveness, for during the construction he experienced opposition from the local Party Boss, and afterwards the building's exterior was judged too abstract, in need of more explicit propaganda. A proposal by M. Nizzoli for applied panels with slogans and photographs was never implemented.

Unmistakably Fascist in the building is the relation with the great Piazza and the row of electrically driven glass doors that allowed the blackshirts to march out in unison. Also Fascist is the Sacrarium, a quasi religious device celebrating the fallen heroes of the movement. Fascist dictators tended to recruit the dead not only to encourage loyalty and sacrifice, but to give their party some continuity with the past, blurring the line between those who died in political struggles and those killed for their country in earlier wars. On Sunday at the Nuremberg rallies, for example, Hitler walked the axis through silent crowds to pay homage at a temple of fallen heroes with an eternal flame, temporarily abandoning his dominant role to abase himself before these putative ancestors who gave the Third Reich an instant history. Similarly in Spain, following the Civil War, Franco gathered the fallen of both sides in his overscaled monument at the Valley of the Fallen. There, Communists and

Fascists lie in ordered ranks, while Franco's grave occupies the axis, lording it over them for eternity. The Mussolini regime also had a great liking for war memorials, and Terragni designed some good ones, starkly geometrical in form. It is not for nothing that the word 'monumental' is borrowed from the architecture of death, or that tombs made of the hardest stone in the simplest, most irreducible geometric forms are among the aptest symbols of eternity. Arguably, the strict geometric form of the Casa partakes of this monumentality. Terragni refers only to the material: *'For a representational building only a marble wall will do'*.[27]

Reading the architect's stated intentions, the idea he returns to repeatedly is that the building must be transparent. He quotes Il Duce: *'Fascism is a glass house'*,[28] and insists there should be *'no obstacles, no barriers, nothing between the political leader and his people'*.[29] The party being at one with the people in this one-party state, the Casa belonged to all, and Terragni wanted it both permeable and transparent, making the honest operations of the Party on the people's behalf visible in the street. The openness of the frame, declaring control of the space but allowing penetration to varying degrees, represented both order and generosity. The generosity of the building lay in the rich variety of ways the framework could be inhabited, played against the same background rhythm. This ideal of transparency was not exclusively a Fascist sentiment. The Marxist Hannes Meyer claimed the same qualities for his League of Nations design (fig. 3, p. 47),[30] and more recently it was the idea behind Günter Behnisch's German Parliament at Bonn, where it was the democratic process that was being exposed.[31]

Comparing the Casa del Fascio with more typically representative products of the dictatorships, such as Piacentini's University of Rome or Albert Speer's Berlin Chancellery, it seems far removed. It lacks not only the ponderous and mean style of stripped Classicism, but also the excesses of scale and repetition that characterised such buildings. The Casa has none of this: instead its spatial progressions, subtleties of organisation and quality of hand-made detail demonstrate a shared energy, common purpose and quest for perfection. If there remains a nagging doubt, it concerns the zeal for order that imposed such a unified object, for *Ordine* was a Fascist ideal.

Notes

1. Accounts differ: the alternative version is that he suffered an embolism, see Schumacher 1991 p. 48.
2. The numerous atrocities of the Eastern Front and slaughter at Stalingrad are grimly portrayed in Beevor 1998.
3. Gruppo 7 members were Sebastiano Larco, Guido Frette, Carlo Enrico Rava, Adalberto Libera, Luigi Figini, Gino Pollini, and Giuseppe Terragni.
4. For a quick summary of the political developments in Italian architecture under Fascism see Bruno Zevi's essay *Gruppo 7: the rise and fall of Italian Rationalism* in Architectural Design 51, nos 1 & 2, 1981, pp. 41-43.
5. Schumacher 1991, p. 38.
6. Particularly with his assistant Pietro Lingeri, who was a former craftsman.
7. The Novocomum block of flats was supposedly inspired by Golossov's club, the gasworks design by other Constructivist projects, see Schumacher 1991, p. 87.
8. Villa sul Lago, ibid, p. 99.
9. Ibid p. 101.
10. Ibid p. 36.
11. *'Our past and our present are not incompatible. We do not wish to ignore our traditional heritage. It is the tradition which transforms itself and assumes new aspects recognisable only to a few.'* Gruppo 7, note in *Rassegna Italiana* December 1926, quoted in English in Frampton 1980, p. 203.
12. Terragni quoted in translation in Schumacher 1991, p.152.
13. In keeping with the Charter of Athens, and a general plan made by Terragni and his Rationalist colleagues in 1934, see Terragni's statement reproduced in Schumacher 1991, p.154.
14. 16.6m is the key dimension given in Terragni's proportion diagrams published in Frampton 1980, p. 205. Schumacher reports a slight discrepancy from this module in the final plan dimensions.
15. In many indigenous cultures much is made of the bringing together of these two elements, often regarded as female and male: see for example Pierre Bourdieu's famous analysis of the Kabyle house (Bourdieu 1979).
16. Schumacher 1991, p. 25.
17. Built 1938-9, see Schumacher 1991 pp. 204-8.
18. Terragni makes it clear that the chosen spot is first floor left, outside the Federal office (Schumacher 1991, p.158), but this is in no way marked on the façade.
19. Schumacher's idea (Schumacher 1991, p.26.) The fasces, adopted as an emblem by Mussolini, was a bundle of rods containing also an axe which was carried in procession before Roman magistrates as their symbol of office. The bundle can be interpreted as a kind of column with or without the bindings, and the axe head projects forward near the top, making an L-shaped figure.
20. Extracts from the manifestoes of Gruppo 7 in *Rassegna Italiana*, December 1926 - May 1927, quoted in English by Zevi in *Gruppo 7: the rise and fall of Italian Rationalism* in *Architectural Design* 51, nos 1 & 2, 1981, p. 41.
21. Reproduced in Zevi 1989, p. 71.
22. Quoted in English as part of Zevi's article in *Architectural Design* 51, nos 1 & 2, 1981, p. 43.
23. Schumacher 1991, p.152.
24. Ibid p.143.
25. Ibid p.151.
26. For example the chapter heading *Resistance to the Fascist Involution* in Zevi 1989, p.142.
27. Schumacher 1991, p.145.
28. Ibid p.153.
29. Ibid p.143.
30. Meyer's statement about the project is included in Schnaidt 1965.
31. See Flagge & Stock 1992. Also Blundell Jones 1993.

Chapter 11. Erik Gunnar Asplund: Gothenburg Lawcourts Extension 1913-1937

As in Italy, the modernist wave broke late in Scandinavia, and not until 1930. Its arrival was marked by the Stockholm Exhibition (see p.126) at which Erik Gunnar Asplund (1885-1940) was principal architect. It took Sweden by storm, and also set the pace for adjacent Finland, as noted in Chapter 8 which introduced Asplund in relation to Aalto. Also as in Italy, Scandinavian Modernism - known simply as Functionalism - accompanied late industrialisation, but there the parallels stop, for neither political circumstances nor cultural background were similar. Far from the strutting dictators, Sweden in the 1930s saw the popular establishment of Social Democracy celebrated in the earliest full-scale welfare state in Europe. And while Italy was overwhelmed with memories of its classical past, exacerbated by Mussolini's attempts to emulate the Roman Empire, Classicism in Scandinavia meant a hint of the exotic south which might be encountered on an adventurous tour once in a lifetime. It was the style of Royalty and the aristocracy, whose Baroque palaces were part of a European network stretching from Naples to St Petersburg. This exotic, imported Classicism was balanced in Asplund's youth by the flourishing National Romantic Movement, a celebration of indigenous architecture which gave Stockholm the first open-air museum in the world, Skansen of 1891. Besides engendering a new admiration for nordic log-constructed churches and farmhouses, National Romanticism also absorbed the influence of the Gothic Revival and the Arts and Crafts Movement. It reached the height of its influence as Asplund began his career in architecture, and his teacher Ragnar Östberg was at work on its most famous monument, Stockholm City Hall (1904-1923). National Romanticism waned after the First World War, however, overtaken by a neoclassical revival known as Swedish Grace. Deeply acquainted with both ways of making architecture, Asplund combined them throughout his career, and arguably also within the modernist phase.[1]

The design of Gothenburg Lawcourts Extension began long before that of any other building in this book, for the competition was announced in 1912, but the building was not completed until 1937, a span of 25 years. This was not just any 25 years, but the crucial quarter century that saw the establishment of Modernism. We are therefore presented with a design that shows all the twists and turns of the burgeoning modernist revolution, and which contains within it the germs of earlier non-modernist versions. Asplund was deeply concerned with site and context, with making his building fit in and taking notice of history: this contextual concern and the long gestation are perhaps the reasons why the Lawcourts extension is now regarded as the prime example of a subtle relationship between new and old in the modernist work of the inter-war period.[2]

1. Gothenburg Lawcourts from canal bridge: Asplund's extension is to right of main building.

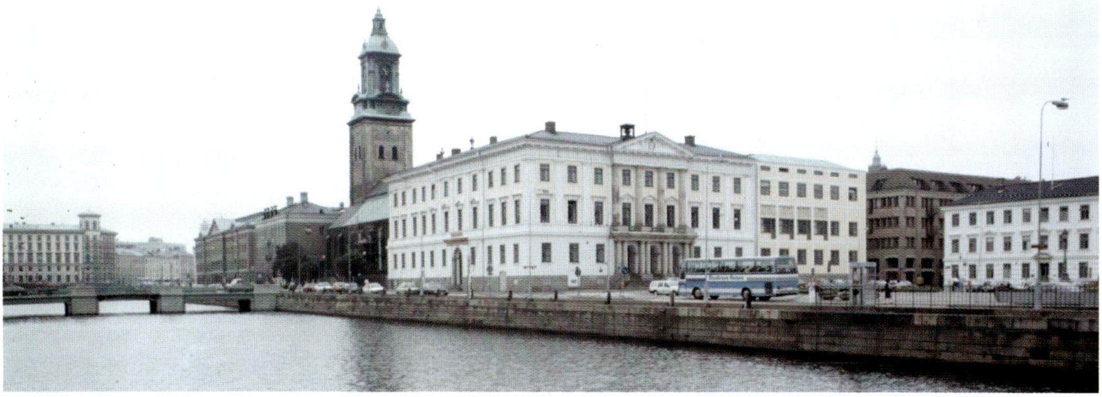

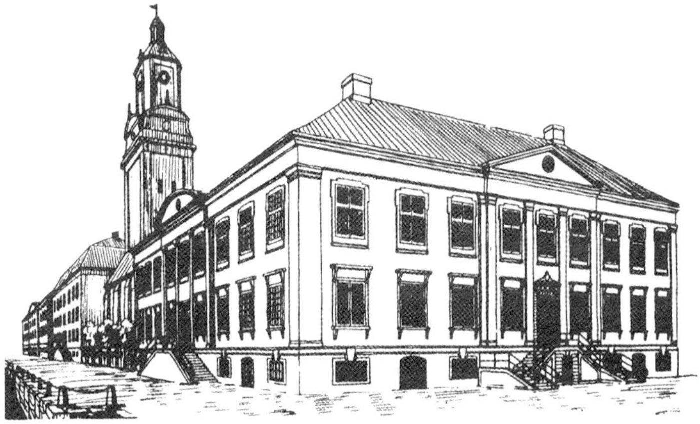

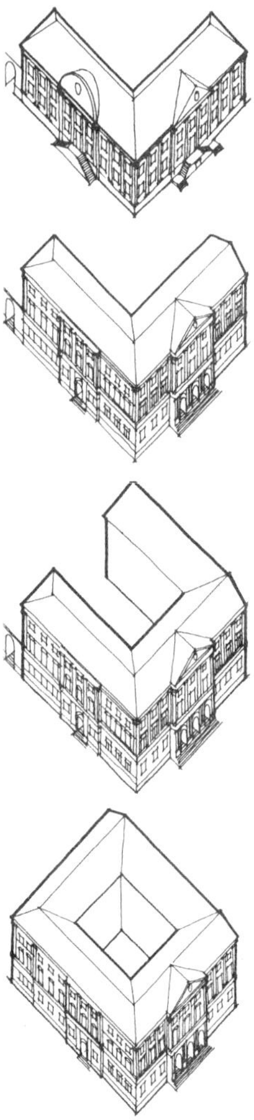

2-5. (above left) Series of projections showing growth of building as it would have appeared in 1672, 1830, 1860 and 1900 respectively.

First the L-shaped building gets raised a storey and loses its rounded pediment, then it gains a side wing and finally a back wing. The latter throws the canal-side elevation (left) out of symmetry.

6. (above right) Drawing of the building as designed by Tessin in 1672. Gustaf Adolf Square is addressed by the façade to right, canal is to left. The church tower seen behind is still present today.

The evolving project, 1912-1937.

The Gothenburg Lawcourts originated in the seventeenth century, sited from the start in Gustaf Adolf Square next to the canal at the city centre.[3] The original timber structure was replaced by a stone building of neoclassical style designed by Nicodemus Tessin in 1672, which was the basis of the building that still exists. In the early Nineteenth Century an upper storey was added and the façade reworked in the form visible today. Later that century north and west wings were added completing the central courtyard but throwing the canal-side elevation out of balance. By the century's end the functional inadequacy of the much modified building prompted the formation of a committee for rebuilding, and an architectural competition was held in May 1912, to add new accommodation on the site of the former Commandant's house to the right of the existing building. Asplund won with a drastic reworking, unifying the whole with a strongly axial plan and re-cladding the façades in National Romantic style.[4] Medieval and Renaissance elements were mixed and the rusticated base was erased, but the established bay rhythm was preserved through pilaster-like framing elements. Asplund gave prominence to the canal-side entrance and suppressed that onto the square, though its memory persisted in three filled-in arches.

The advantage of this arrangement was the clarity of plan organised around a new major axis. Starting at the canal - newly equipped with ceremonial pavilions and steps from a landing stage - one would cross the street to the entrance, rise into the existing courtyard now given a glazed

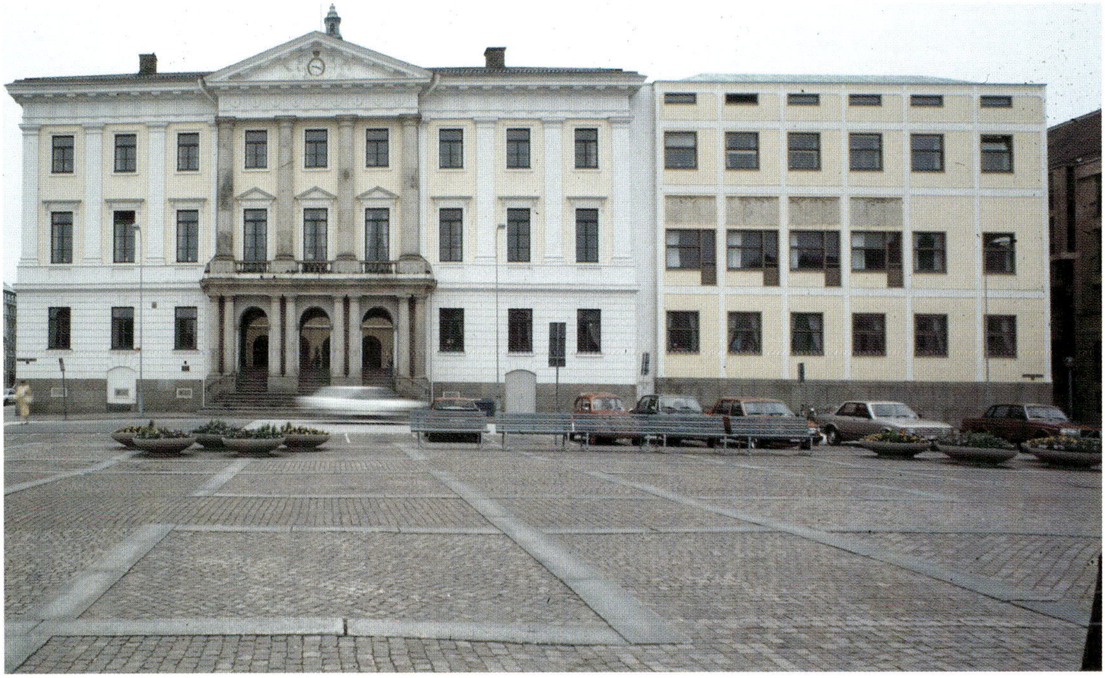

7. (above) The Lawcourts today with Asplund's 1937 extension to right.

8. (below) Courtyard with the three arches seen above coming through and Asplund's daring glass wall to his extension, left.

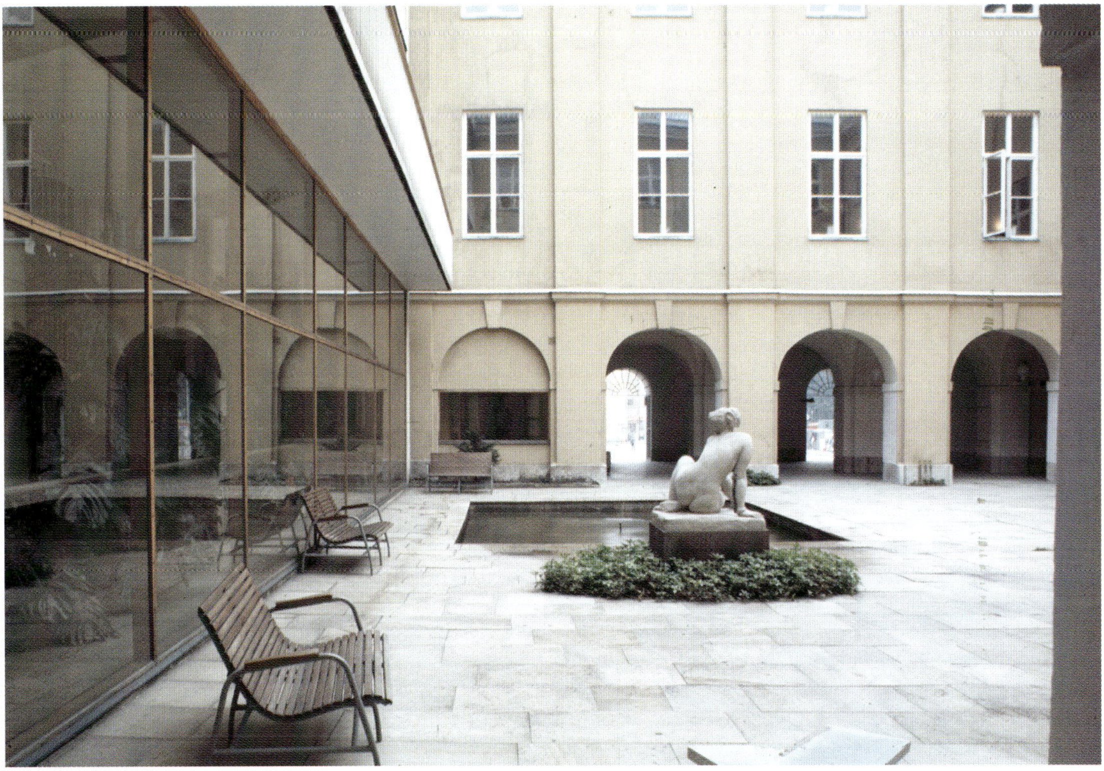

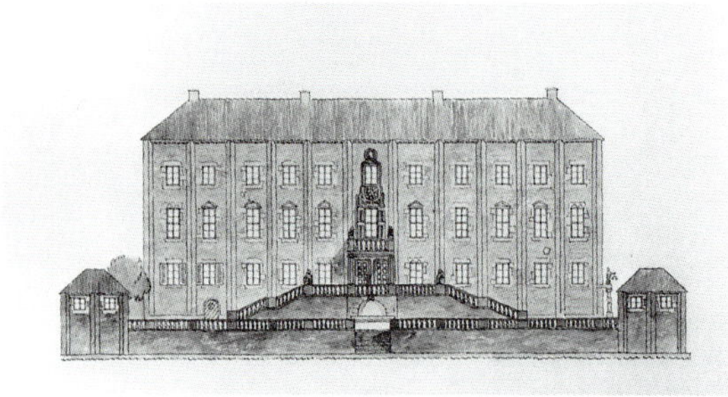

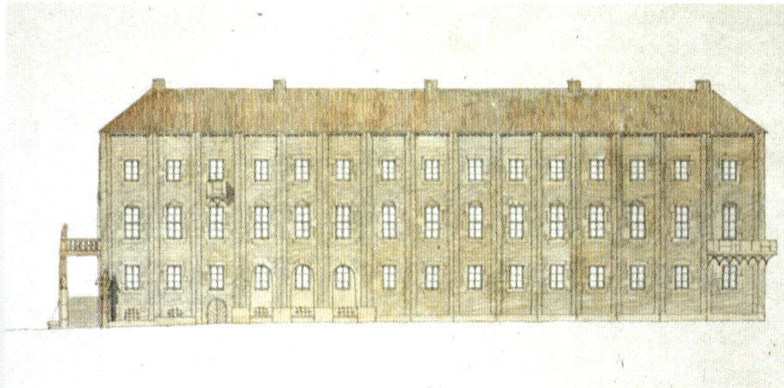

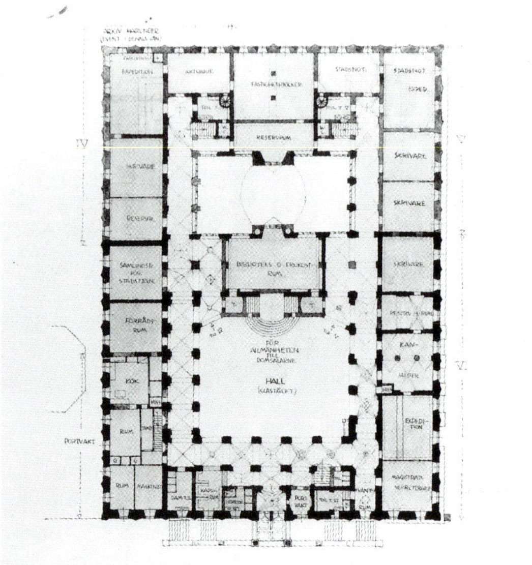

9. (top) Asplund's competition project, elevation facing canal.
11. (above) Ground floor plan.

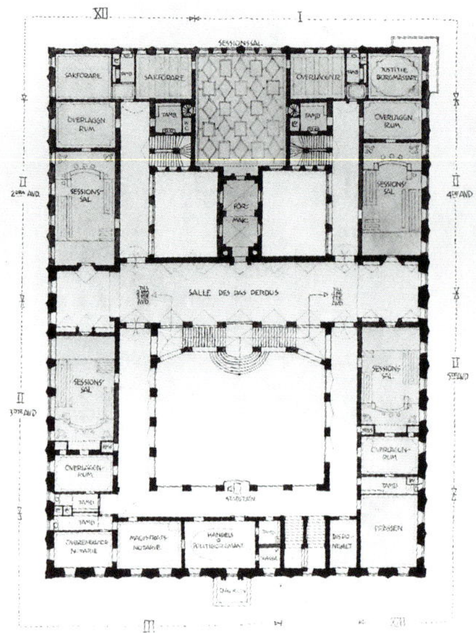

10. (top) Elevation facing square.
12. (above) First floor plan.

roof, and cross it to meet the main stair at the centre of the building. The first flight with curved treads lay on axis within the court, but gave way to paired upper flights running at right angles and arriving in a transverse gallery penetrating the building from side to side. This gallery asserted the principal cross-axis and its ends became ante-chambers to the four main courtrooms. A corridor back around the courtyard gave access to various offices, but the main axis continued beyond the stair as a bridge of sighs crossing an open court, culminating in the largest and most ceremonial room - the magistrates' meeting room - at the back end of the building. This lucid and hierarchical plan owed much to a competition design for Stockholm Lawcourts by Östberg of 1905, a preparatory scheme for his City Hall.[5] It made elegant sense of the accommodation, but the committee remained unhappy with Asplund's treatment of the existing building and the apparent negation of the square. They asked him to retain the existing portico, and invited him also to make proposals for the redevelopment of the rest of the square with further civic buildings. A plan of 1915 for the whole square shows the law courts building as before but with an added entrance to the court via the old portico. The extension consists of a series of additional bays continuing the façade without break, asymmetrically. To make a virtue of this asymmetry, Asplund set the building fronting the north side of the square askew, linking it to the law courts with a bridge to make a continuous wall of building on two sides, while the other two sides of the square were defined with street then water. This irregular arrangement reflected a general interest in skewed and picturesque organisation associated with medieval towns, which permeated the work of Asplund's teachers in the National Romantic movement.[6] By the end of the year Asplund had radically revised his ideas and produced a neo-

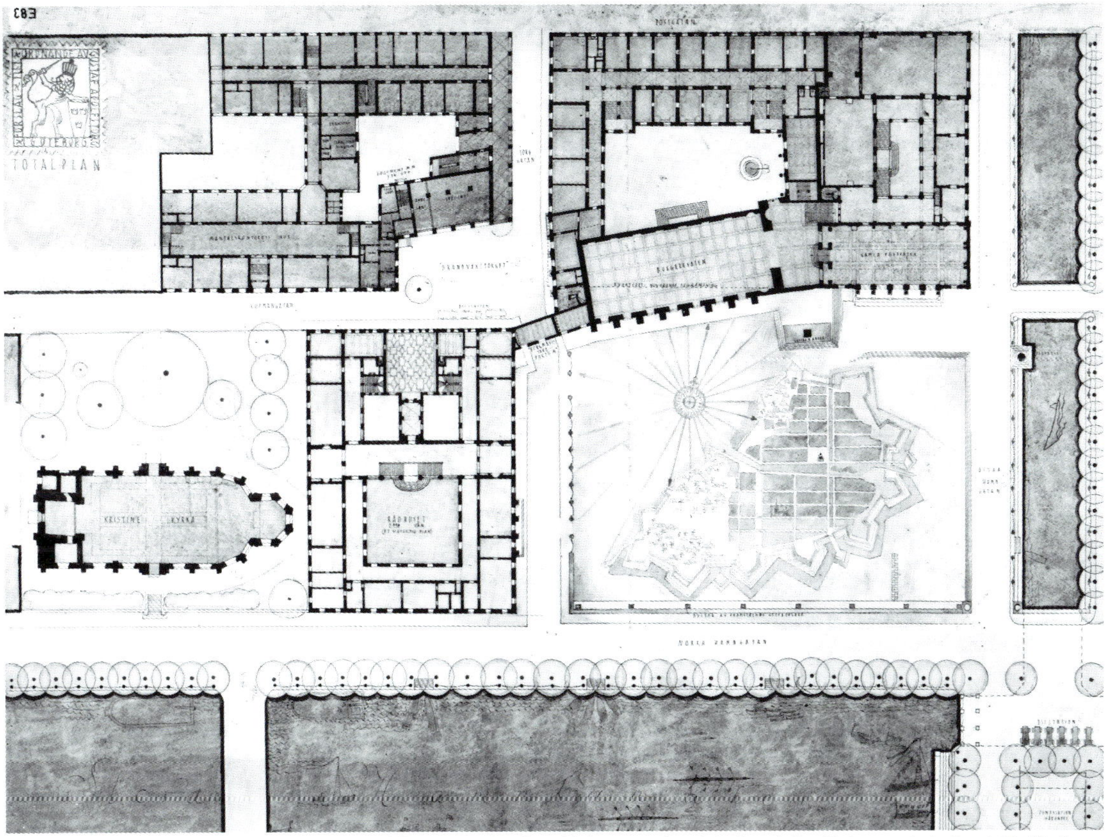

13. Asplund's plan for the whole of Gustaf Adolf Square, 1915. Canal is bottom, church bottom left, with lawcourts to the right of it, then the square with compass point and town plan depicted in paving. Asplund intended to complete the north side of the square with a new civic hall extending the existing stock-exchange (top right). Skewed hall and corner bridge link are in National Romantic mode.

classical version of the Lawcourts building. He kept his main entrance facing the canal, giving the elevation to the square two secondary entrances, thus restoring symmetry. In plan it still follows the competition scheme, but gains an asymmetrical main stair running across the plan in a single flight, now directionally related to the front facing the square instead of that facing the canal, thus neatly accommodating its hierarchical promotion.

In 1918 a competition was held for the design of the whole square, which Asplund won. Perhaps in reaction against his radical proposals of previous years, the competitors were asked to preserve the general character of the square, which limited the opportunity for spatial manipulation and resulted in concentration on façades. Asplund developed a series of self-centred elevations like separate houses, each intended to reflect its content in its stylistic treatment. For the north side he proposed an enormous and dramatic civic building behind

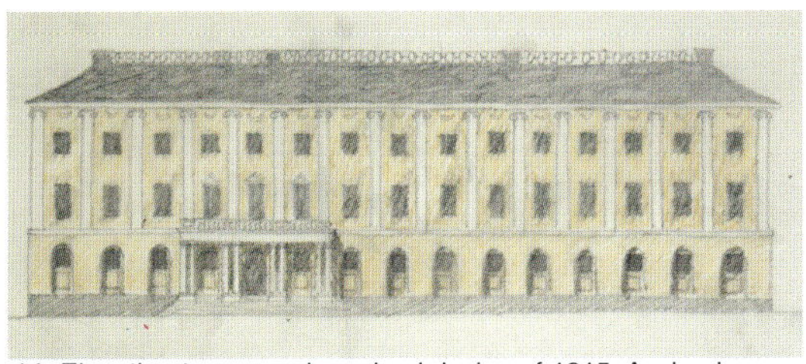

14. Elevation to square in revised design of 1915. Asplund retains existing entry, disguising extension with identical bays.

15. Symmetrical variant of 1916 with two identical portals.

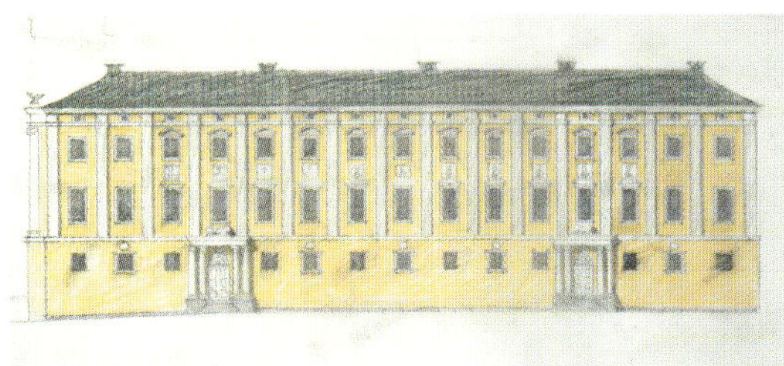

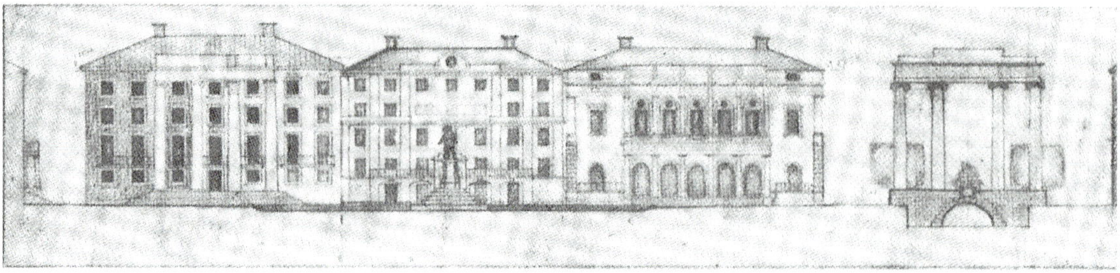

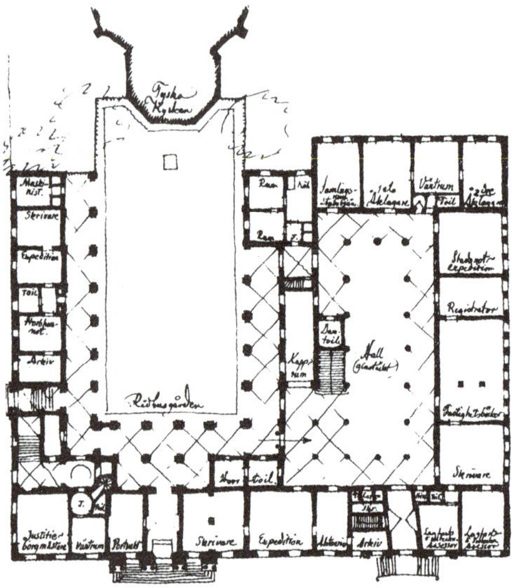

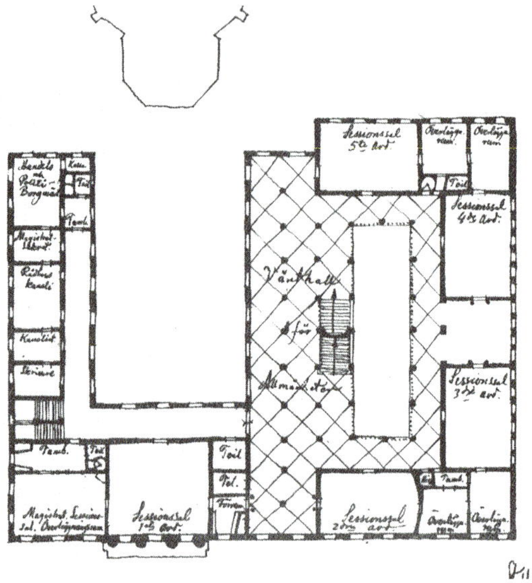

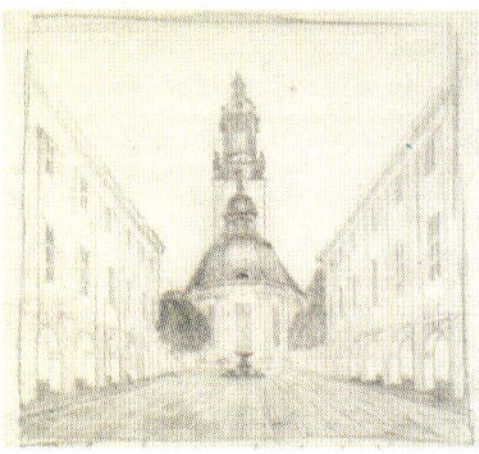

16. (top) Asplund's proposed elevation treatment for the north side of the square, including the existing stock exchange. The Lawcourts and its extension were to be treated as separate houses, as in figs 24-30.
17. (above left) Ground floor plan of 1919 with court open to church.
18. (above right) First floor plan. Courtrooms are in their final positions around glazed hall.
19. (left) Perspective of court looking towards east end of church.

three linked façades, housing council chamber with municipal offices, civic halls for concerts and banquets, and the stock-exchange. Within this general plan the existing façade of the Lawcourts building was retained, and the extension was treated as a separate 'house' with its own entrance, a recessed bay between the two disengaging them. This became the dominant pattern among the many façade variants up to 1925 (figs 24-30).

Neoclassical versions 1919-25

Asplund long clung to the essentials of his first plan, but its axial progression from the canal was not compatible with main and secondary entrances from the square, and in 1919 he radically revised it. The figure had always been double centred, a consequence of the rectangular shape, depth of plan, and the existing court at one end. The problem was how to relate the two voids and the space between them. Rejection of the axis from the canal allowed the symmetry between what had been sides, but now became front and back of the building, to be dropped. One consequence was a decision affecting all later versions: to increase the area of the extension by making it project beyond the existing building on the west side, thus displacing its centre line with respect to the court. The new freedom also prompted Asplund to

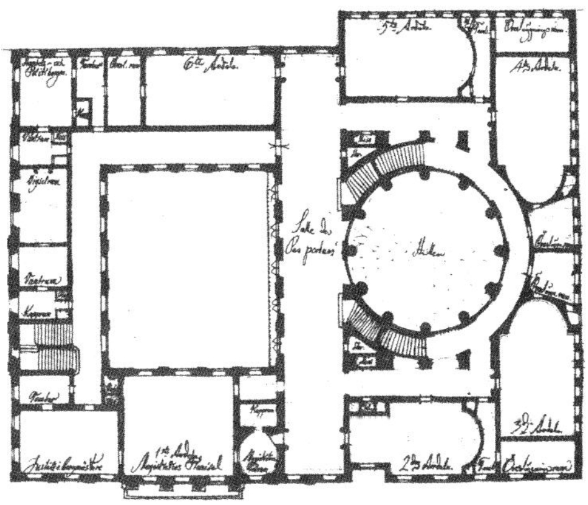

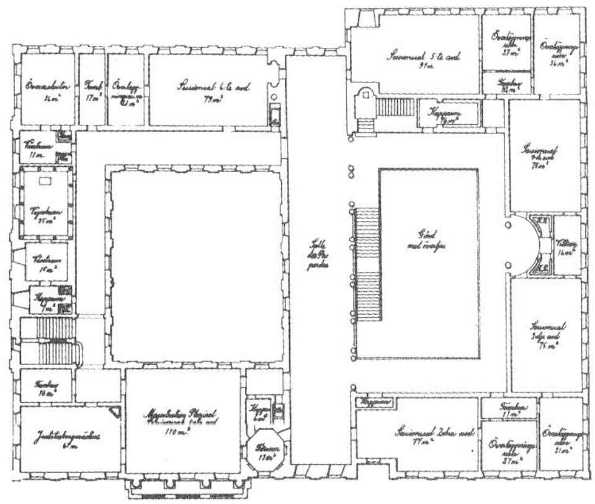

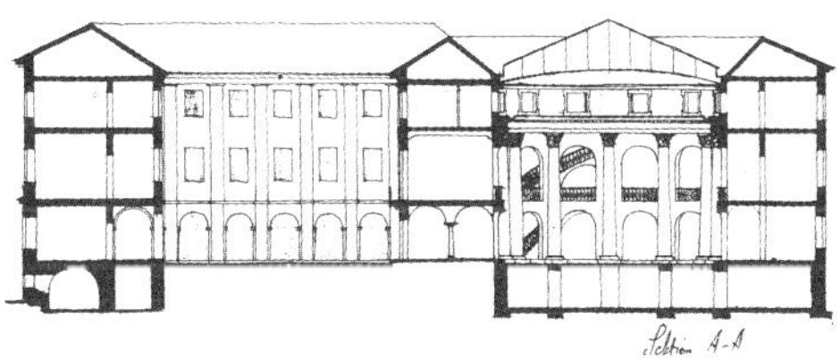

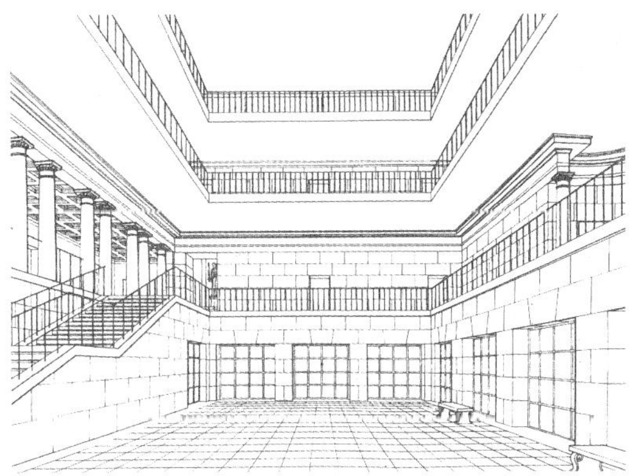

20. (top) First floor plan of rotunda version, 1919.
21. (above) Section of same version.
22. (above right) First floor plan of definitive project, 1925. In terms of organisation this is the final arrangement.
23. (right) Perspective of hall, 1925.

explore the possibility of striking up a relationship with the church behind, and a proposal of early 1919 leaves the main court incomplete as a formal garden, redimensioned to centre on the axis of the church (figs 17-19). The extension centres on a glazed hall, the principal stair running along the left-hand edge of its central well. The hall links the entrance from the court with the secondary one from the square, the stair being well placed for both. First floor courtrooms are essentially in their final positions.

Later the same year Asplund returned to the closed court, leaving it open to the sky, and he centred the extension on a large glazed rotunda. Formally this proposal relates closely to the Lister Courthouse, Woodland Chapel and Stockholm library (pp.123-5) but the focal space is employed quite differently, amounting essentially to a huge stairwell. Also the stairs, rather than hiding dramatically in the thickness of the wall, are left open. The rotunda was short-lived, but it did introduce an implication of transparency between the two focal spaces of the building which is essential to the final design. This is visible in plan in the sequence of five double doors onto the court at ground floor level. The dominant spatial sequence is as follows: the existing portico leads to the open court, linked by the double doors - presumably glazed - to the three-storey rotunda. Generous stairs lead to an upper gallery straddling the building as in the earlier designs, and this gives access to the four principal courtrooms, placed as before but given apsoidal ends - significant in view of the curves finally adopted.

By 1924, Asplund had become disenchanted with the rotunda, and returned to the glazed hall and stair of the open-courted version. The stair ran, as before, along the side of the well, turning left into the first floor gallery to overlook the old courtyard. The stair then continued to upper levels in anticlockwise rotation. This plan version improved directness and clarity, but the stair did not

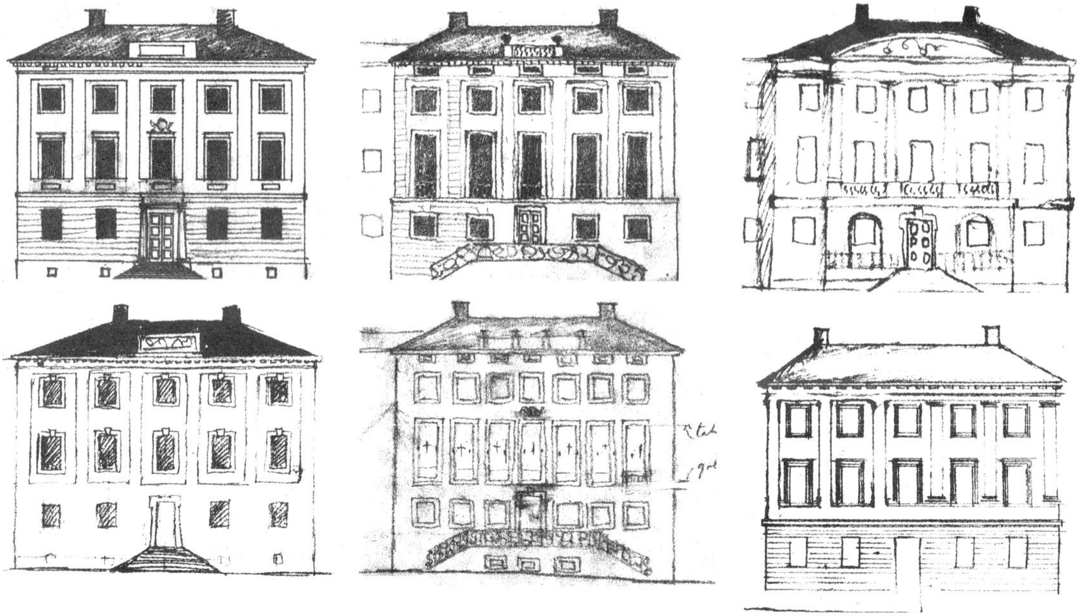

24-29. Assorted versions of the extension facade from the Asplund Archive, c. 1920-25. He tried it with 5 bays and 7, with and without columns and rustication, plain and ornate.

adequately engage the glazed hall, a fault rectified in the final neoclassical version of 1925 (figs 22, 23). Here the stair is reunited with the hall, and its implied direction of rotation is reversed by making it seem to continue in the gallery around the space. In organisation this version is very similar to the arrangement finally adopted, but the visual connection with the external court is available only through three windows at first floor level, reducing transparency in comparison with the rotunda version, and making the glazed hall seem far more contained and self-centred than in the final building.

The numerous façade versions at this stage range from a faithful extension of the existing building's vocabulary to substantial reinterpretations, but all are essentially Neoclassical. Most versions have five bays, allowing a central entrance and continuing the rhythm of the old building. All kinds of entrance were tried, from grand double-stair arrangements to an almost unadorned hole in the wall. Rustication came and went, and engaged columns could be reduced to pilasters, or even to mere framing elements without base or capital, the treatment finally adopted inside the court.

30. Final façade version of 1925, as Asplund was prepared to build it: extension is treated as a separate house with its own central entrance, served up in the style of the mother building. The two are disengaged by an area of plain wall with simple window holes.

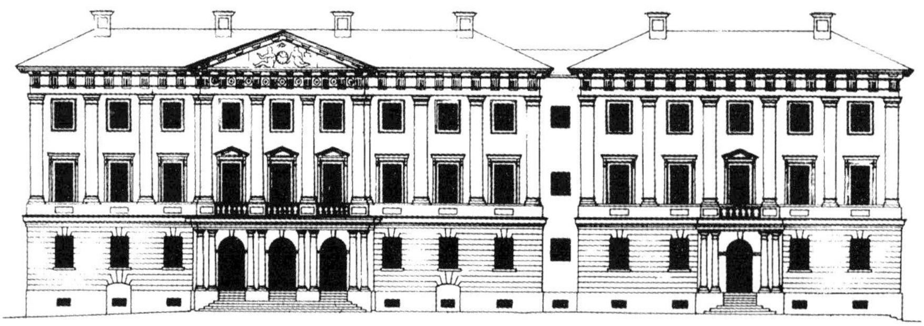

Key to both plans:

1. courtyard
2. hall
3. entrance hall
4. cloakroom
5. office
6. waiting area
7. caretaker
8. anteroom
9. magistrates
10. courtroom
11. conference room
12. burgermaster
13. court house chancery

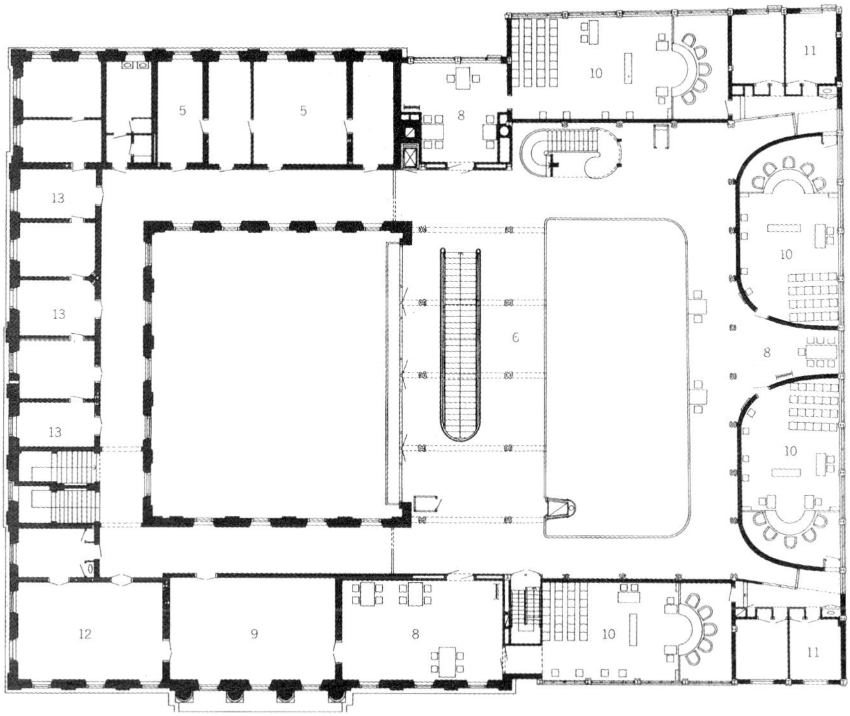

31. Final first floor plan.

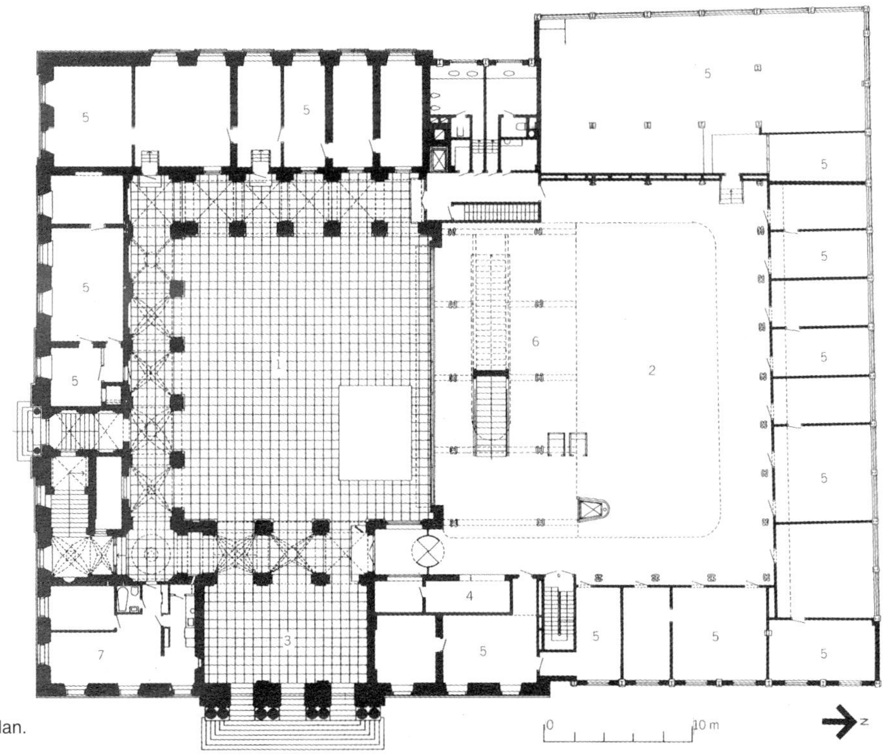

32. Final ground floor plan.

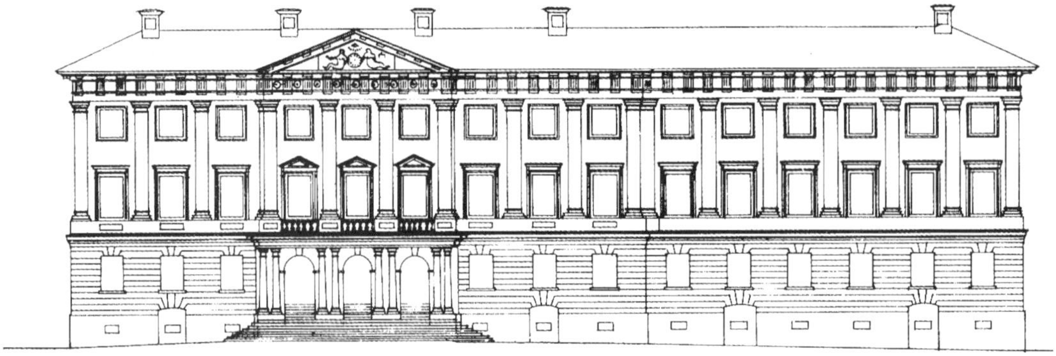

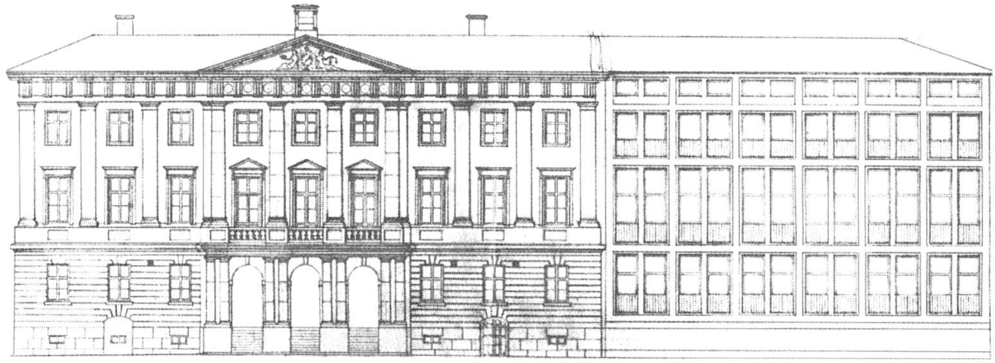

33. (top) Reconsidered façade of 1934, still in historic style. Asplund adds an even number of bays to deny entry, and disengages the extension with double columns and a slight step.
34. (above) But soon modernist versions follow, this one stating the frame most simply.

The nine year gap 1925-34

In September 1925 a set of drawings was accepted and approved by the city authorities, but for lack of funds the project was shelved until 1934. In the intervening nine years, Asplund completed his library and his buildings for the Stockholm Exhibition. He started work on the Bredenberg shop and Bacteriological laboratories, becoming the leading Swedish Modernist. Returning to the Lawcourts, he set out to rework his design of 1925 in a modern idiom. The organisation was retained, but he reversed his decision to make two entrances on the square. Banishing the new entrance, he gave the extension six bays rather than five, so that it centred on a column, denying the possibility of entrance. The whole building became subservient to the old courtyard, the new hall being inflected towards it. The wall between new and old now became a glass screen, allowing hall and courtyard to be read as a single space, and the glass roof was replaced by an angled skylight facing south towards the court to admit the low Swedish sun. Plan versions of 1934 and 35 show a gradual increase in transparency between hall and court. In December 1934 windows onto the court are still divided by substantial pieces of wall, though it is no longer the structural element of the 1925 version, being relieved by an additional line of columns. Also, offices and telephone cubicles obscure the view out at ground level. The lift, at this stage round and evidently intended to be exposed, is placed in a corner by the entrance. The main stair runs along one side of the floor well, and the upper stair continues the clockwise movement across the end of the space. Subsequent versions show the glass wall continuous, offices and telephones resited in a corner, and the lift established at the corner of the well. Even at this late stage Asplund vacillated over the position of the main stair, trying it by the well then next to the glass wall, and finally placing it mid way between the two, making it independent. The upper stair went through more drastic variations, first tried as a narrower repeat of the main one on the edge of the well, then pushed into the corner at the end of the gallery. The final version, which has such presence in the finished building, was a late development. Equally late was the adoption of curved walls for the courtrooms of the north side.

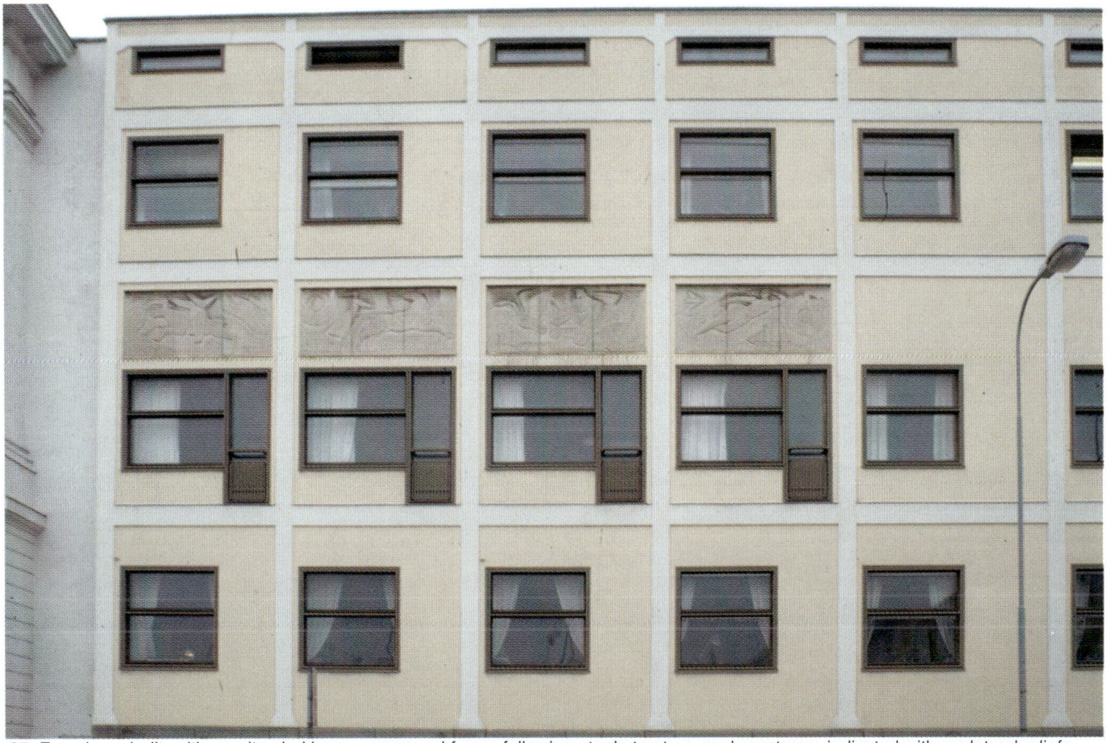

35. Facade as built, with granite-clad base, expressed frame following steel structure, and courtroom indicated with sculptural reliefs.

36. Central hall of the extension as seen at entry, with porter's kiosk to right and main stair leading to principal floor.

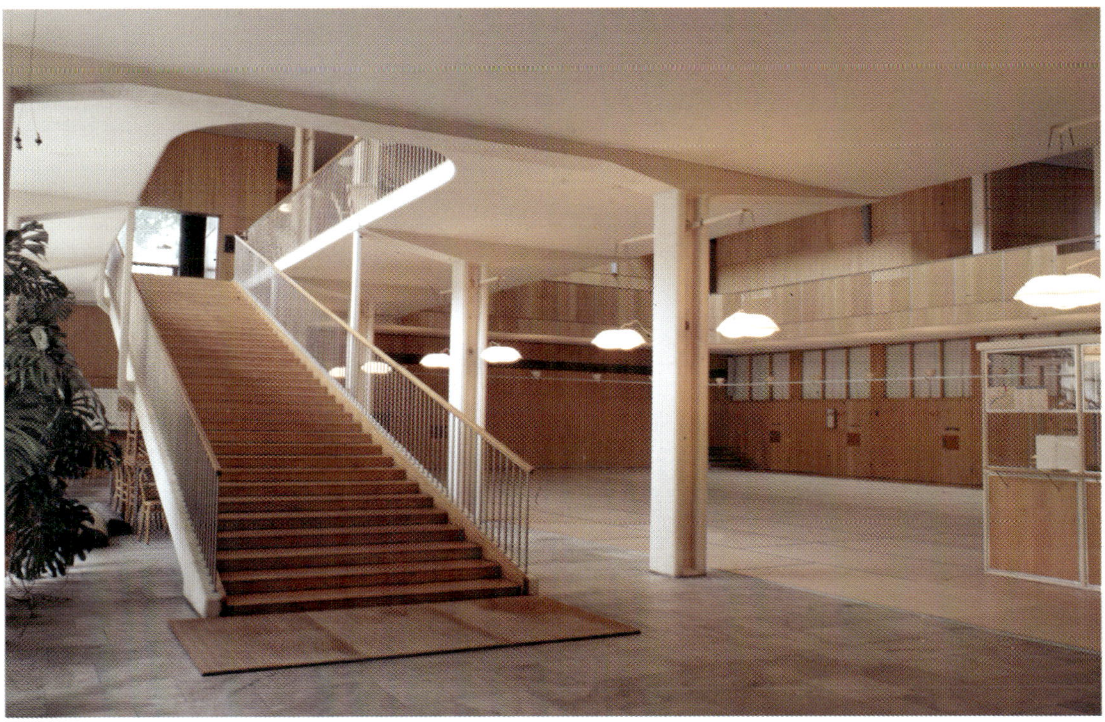

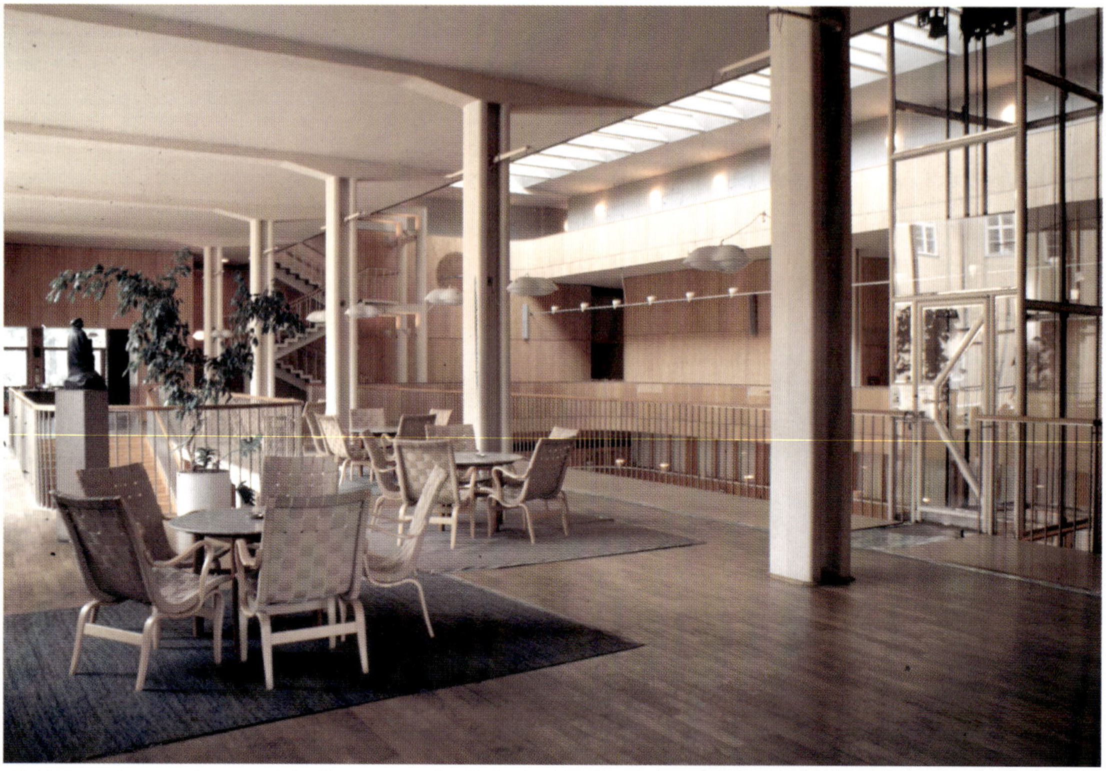

37. Hall seen from courtroom level, looking across well, with Asplund furniture in foreground.
38. (opposite) Upper stair with added clock commands end of space.

The final façade

The plan version of December 1934 relates to a traditional façade with rustication, pilasters and ornamental detail faithfully reproduced from the mother building. The roof is continuous, and there is no disengaging bay between the two parts of the façade, instead a slight step where two pilasters run together. This is a conservationists dream, the most polite possible response to the old building, but it completely conceals the story of two and a half centuries of evolution and leaves a glaring asymmetry unexplained. Had it been built, new would have been indistinguishable from old, and arguably the old building would have been de-valued by the anachronistic mix of fact and fiction. Asplund was dissatisfied, and started to explore ways of creating a sympathetic yet modern façade. He persuaded the building committee to accept this principle, and in the end they allowed his radical version, which caused outrage in the city when unveiled. It was not easily achieved: there are many drawn versions, some with exposed frame, others in plain render. Continuous balconies at one and two levels were tried, also rustication up to various levels. In the end Asplund decided on an exposed frame to follow the rhythm of the pilasters on the mother building and to continue the main horizontal divisions, while also expressing the real steel structure behind. Both buildings sit on the same kind of granite-faced base, and main floor levels run through, the string-course and cornice picked up by the first and top levels of the expressed frame. Asplund chose to emphasise the real base of the building at courtyard level in memory of the Tessin building, rather than the raised base introduced later.[7] Where the steel frame is lighter and thinner at the top, the façade steps back and the members are reduced in width. Where the steel frame meets the concrete base, each column stands on a steel plate, which is expressed externally in a pyramidal swelling.

The second level of Asplund's framing marks the common second floor level, though this is suppressed in the old building by the giant order columns and pilasters, if implied in the fenestration. The third level frame aligns itself with the capitals

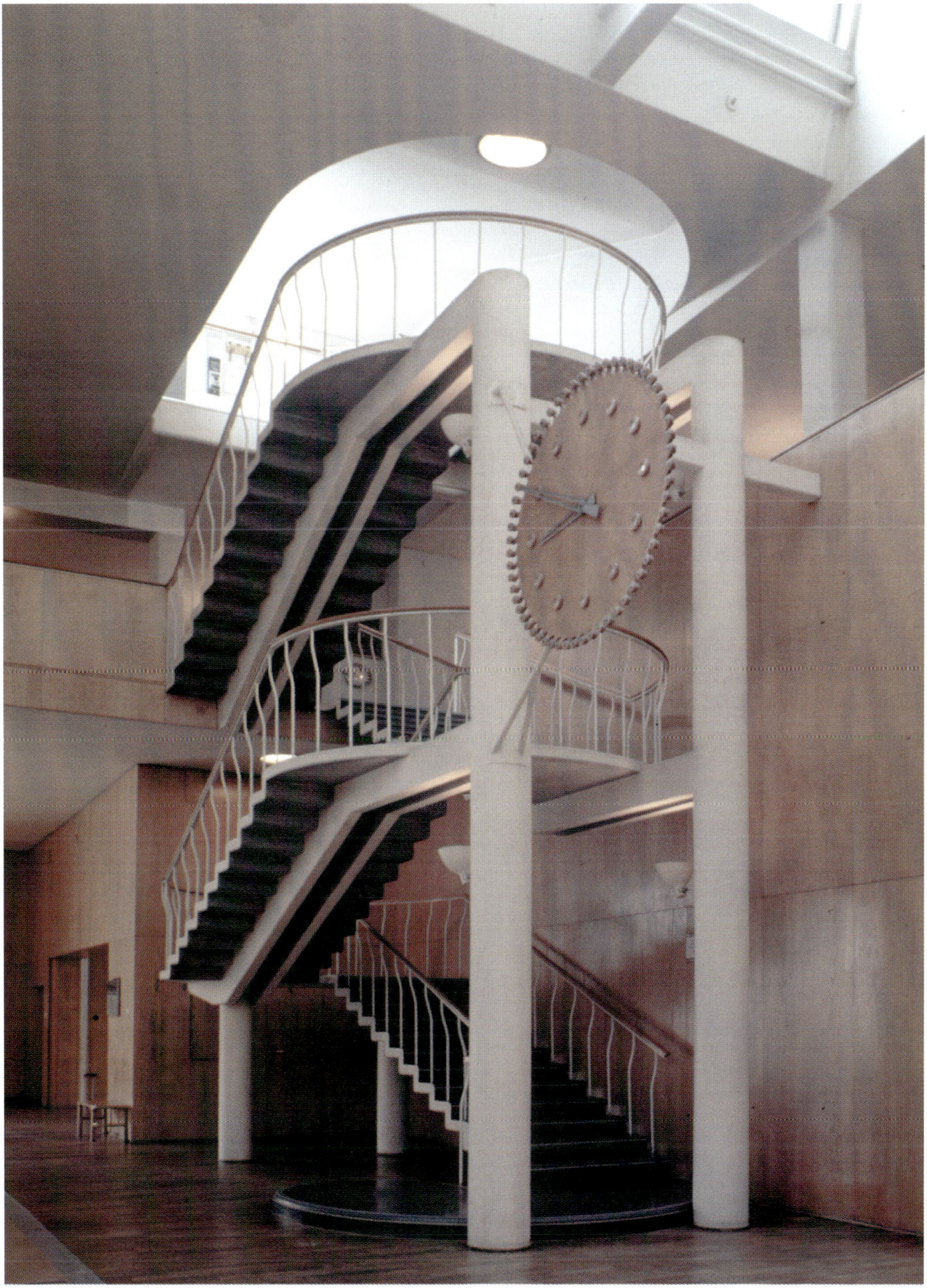

on the old façade rather than with the entablature. This reflects a reduced ceiling height in the second floor of the extension to take advantage of the roof space, the latter lit by the horizontal windows at cornice level. Construction was under way when Asplund made two final changes: first he set back the roof, forming a parapet rather than eaves. Second, he moved the windows to the left of their respective façade panels, like eyes turned toward the mother building, emphasising dependence. The colour scheme, white for implied structure and yellow for infill, is carried through. The first floor on both buildings is *piano nobile*, containing the two most important courtrooms with the highest ceilings. Windows at this level are the largest and most elaborate, and while those of the old building boast decorated heads and pediments, the four bays of the extension occupied by one of the main courtrooms are embellished with hierarchically equivalent sculpted reliefs.

The building as experienced

The entrance to the Lawcourts from the square is declared in no uncertain terms by the portico, and the open courtyard is invitingly visible at the top of the steps. Having climbed these, one finds oneself in the arcade bordering the court; and though gaining a glimpse of the court and its dramatic glass wall, one takes the door on the right, leading to the internal hall. The hall is at once foyer, circulation and waiting area. Nearby are glass lift and receptionist's kiosk, but most prominent is the main stair. Beyond one sees the toplit void, upper galleries, and curved walls of the courtrooms. Traversing the space, one encounters the great window opening onto the court. Gentle northern sunlight from glass wall and south-facing rooflight provokes a warm glow from the wood and plaster surfaces. The space is many layered with ambiguous boundaries, more like an external street or square than a traditional room. Paved in the same granite slabs as the external court, it suggests that hall and court are a single space modified by the addition of glass wall, roof, and the bridge-like gallery with stair. The shaping of the well encourages this interpretation, for its inner corners are square, not round like the outer ones, and the balustrade to the court side is open, while others are protectively solid.

One can consult offices on the ground floor, but court sessions take place on the floor above.[8] One takes the long, shallow main stair. Arriving at the first floor, one's attention is drawn to the upper stair, revealing the continuing progression of the route to second and third floors. Asplund uses this stair (fig. 38) as a focal point for the end of his hall to orientate visitors, hence a stair more sculptural than the main one, dramatically placed and detailed, rising mysteriously into the ceiling, and carrying a large clock - symbol of temporal order, and therefore of law. Beyond the head of the main stair is the antechamber to the courtroom on the west side, with desks for clerks and seats for waiting litigants, its windows opening to the churchyard behind. Although this is defined as a separate space, it is visually continuous with the main hall. Another antechamber of more generous proportions occupies the symmetrically opposite position behind the main stair, with windows onto the square. Thus the intention in the very first design to create a transverse gallery centred on the stair and looking out both ways - called by Asplund *salle des pas perdus* - persists in essence if not as a defined room. A third public antechamber is formed between the curved walls of the two north side courtrooms, while the space between courtrooms at the two corners contains private conference rooms for legal personnel.

The courtrooms

Asplund knew about courtrooms from his experiences in designing his Lister Courthouse of 1917-21, but by the time he came to design the final version of the Gothenburg Lawcourts 20 years later, he had adopted a modern idiom which precluded the overt theatricality and traditional references employed in the earlier building. In the progressive socialist Sweden of the '30s, ideals of justice were humanitarian rather than authoritarian, and offenders were treated with some leniency. The four main courtrooms display essentially the same arrangement. The Swedish system allows for juries of lay assessors who number three or five depending on the severity of the case, sharing the curved desk on the raised dais with the judge. The latter takes the central seat, which is raised very slightly above the others to give appropriate but not excessive precedence, and the shelf projecting in front is intended to bear the bible on which oaths were sworn. Asplund experimented with both semicircular and segmental arrangements for the desk before adopting the more complex curve built. The slightly skewed axis was also a late development. In the centre of the court facing the judge is the witness stand, and to either side the places for prosecution and defence: for flexibility they have free-standing chairs and tables. At the back of the room to one side are fixed ranks of seats for spectators and interested parties.

Each room has two entrances: one at the back for the public and another diagonally opposite behind the dais for those officiating. Judges and magistrates can therefore come and go without the embarrassment and compromise of encountering other participants. While in the courtroom they never leave the privileged space of the dais, underlining the independence of their role, and they are also able to effect a conspicuous and dignified entrance, essential to establish formally the opening of a session. In the curved rooms, the space behind the judicial desk expands conveniently towards the door, a typical example of functionalist planning around circulation flow which modernist architects explored in the 1920s and 30s.[9] The curved lawcourt walls are also important for their effect on the hall outside. Here was the beginning of a fluid kind of modernist space taken further in post-war years by Asplund's protégé Aalto, particularly in his libraries and foyers,[10] and paralleled in the German tradition led by Häring and Scharoun. The convexity demonstrates that the courtrooms are distinct enclosures, more important than the residual space, which gives the latter a sense of in-between-ness like a kind of internal street. Also there is an implication that the courtrooms are excised from the larger all-inclusive space of the hall.

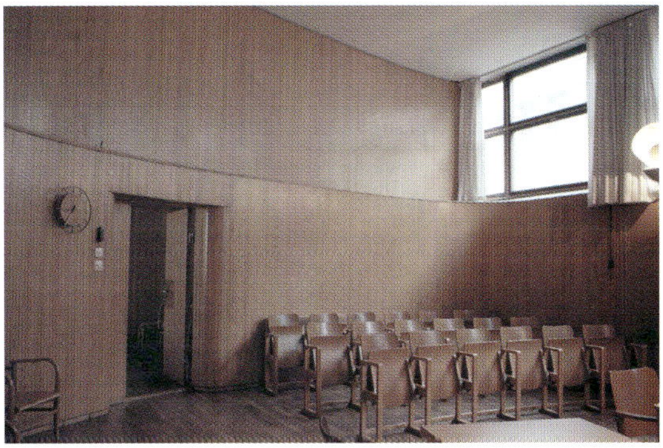

39. Courtroom on the north side, back end with public entry, curved cladding and asymmetrical seating.

40. Courtroom on the north side, front end with magistrate's desk. The magistrates' chairs and ring of lights are not original, but other furniture is.

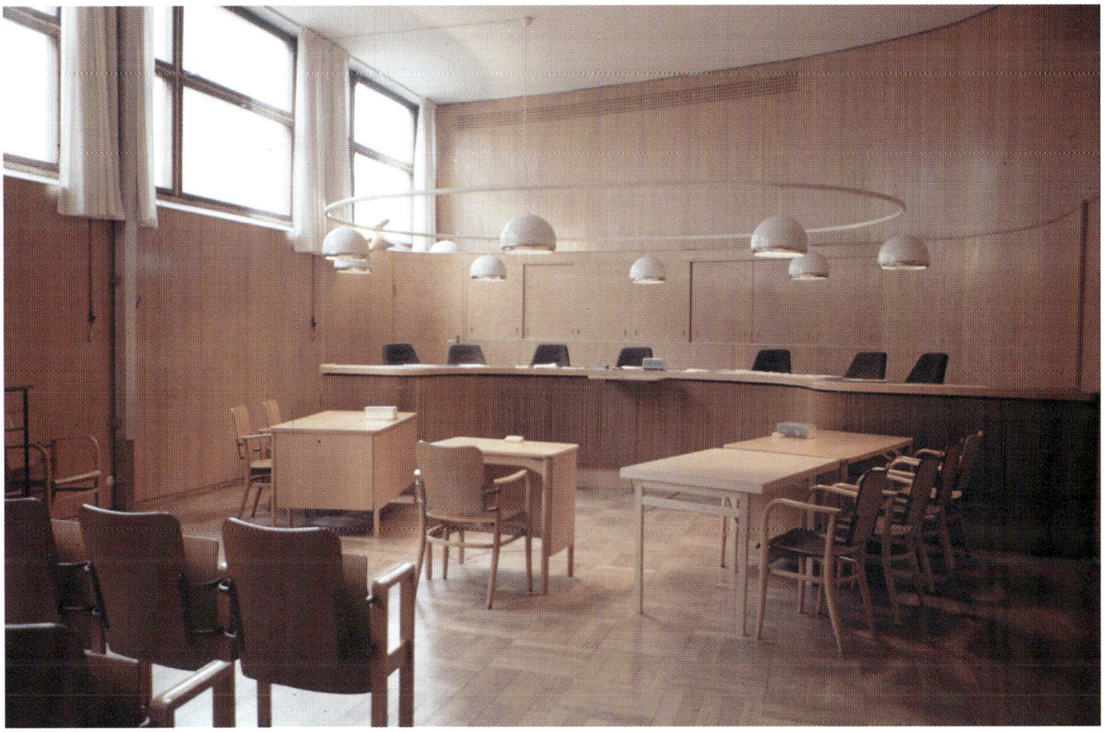

Construction

Whereas Asplund conceived his 1925 design in terms of heavy masonry construction, he finally settled for a steel frame, in keeping with his buildings at the Stockholm Exhibition and the Bredenberg shop.[11] This was the essential ingredient that allowed so much transparency in the final building, in contrast with the massiveness of earlier designs; though in basic organisation the two are very similar. Where he chooses to, Asplund makes the structure explicit; for example in the free-standing columns whose fire-proofing follows the shape of the section, in the structurally tapered beams which they carry, and in the staircases with folded risers and treads, beams and columns. The glazed lift with its exposed mechanism shows the same intention, as do smaller furnishing elements with which one has direct contact. Handrails, doorknobs, balustrades, built-in tables and drinking fountain are designed with care, elegantly revealing their materials and construction. Other elements of visual rather than tactile importance, such as suspended lamps and clocks, receive equal attention.

Despite an interest in expressed construction and services, it is not a course that Asplund pursued consistently. While some columns are displayed, others, notably within curved court room walls, are suppressed. In the ceiling of the hall, coated steel beams maintain the horizontal across the skylight, then vanish from view. The upper staircase ascends effortlessly through the plaster ceiling without revealing the detailing problems it must have caused, and the curved corners are equally mute and graceful. The use of classically derived *poché* for courtroom walls conceals rather than displays the way space is divided. Even the expression of frame in the façade was only one of many possible treatments, though carried through consistently, even accepting a discrepancy in base line to show the true line of structure behind.

Conclusion

At Gothenburg, Asplund tied together old and new in such a subtle way that each profits from the other: the old building is actually better for the experience, and the new one could not live without it. The organisation is clear and hierarchically appropriate. A respect for traditional rooms is counterpointed by the drama of modernist flowing space, and the transparency of a glass wall is exploited just once, where it counts. It opens not unprotected into the heart of the city like so much post-Miesian glazing, but into the tranquillity of a closed court, a court which would be dull without it. The long story of the building's evolution might not have been worth the telling if the end product were not such a triumph. But along the thirty-five year road down which it travelled, the design improved, and Asplund achieved a rare synthesis. The intermediate versions would be of interest had they been realised, and rejected ideas could have borne fruit. Nonetheless, the final design is an extraordinary feat. Everything has found its rightful place: the planning is so clear and logical that it unifies the building, so that evidence of its various styles and periods becomes a source of richness rather than discord. The compromise of conversion is avoided in the skill of the response.

Notes

1. The classical Enskede cemetery is counterbalanced by the lesser known but contemporary Skövde cemetery in raw stone with a roof like a primitive hut, and Asplund's late summerhouse at Stennäs follows Swedish vernacular models: see Blundell Jones *House at Stennäs* in Cruickshank 1988.

2. The text that follows is a revised and shortened version of an analysis first published by *Architects Journal* in the Masters of Building series under the editorship of Dan Cruickshank and subsequently republished as a book: *AJ* 14/10/87 and 11/11/87; Cruickshank 1988, pp. 57-96.

3. A sketch history is provided in a leaflet issued by the city of Gothenburg, from which the following paragraphs are derived.

4. The way was paved for the following analysis by a paper delivered at the Asplund conference in Stockholm and Gothenburg of 1985 by Björn Fredlund, and printed in *Asplund 1885-1940, lectures and briefings from the International Symposium on the Architecture of Erik Gunnar Asplund*, published by Swedish Museum of Architecture, Stockholm 1986.

5. On the Stockholm competitions, see Cornell 1992, pp. 31-38.

6. It had also been given definition by the Austrian Camillo Sitte with his famous book *City Planning on Artistic Principles* (Collins 1965). Sitte's ideas were spread in Germany by Theodor Fischer and in England by Garden City architect Raymond Unwin.

7. That he also considered following Hagberg is evident from late façade sketches.

8. One courtroom is now at lower level west side, but this is a recent alteration.

9. See also Chapters 1 and 13.

10. I am thinking above all of the main auditorium building at the University of Jyväskyla, where the foyers of theatre and classroom block intermingle, flowing on into waiting spaces and café. Emphasis on route and hierarchical placing of staircases, knowing use of transparency, care taken over illumination, and layering of materials both in plan and section to define space, are all inherited in some measure from Asplund.

11. At the Stockholm Exhibition the construction was somewhat hybrid, perhaps because of its temporary status. Strictly speaking, only the Paradise restaurant had a steel frame. However steel was used elsewhere for external and internal columns, contributing to the light and airy impression. Beneath asbestos slab surfaces a good deal of the remaining structure was timber. See *Gunnar Asplund and the 1930 Stockholm Exhibition* by Ake Fant, in the collection referred to in note 4.

Chapter 12. Frank Lloyd Wright: Usonian house, 1939

Born in 1867, Frank Lloyd Wright was more than a decade older than the other architects in this book, and had reached the age of sixty by the time the Weissenhofsiedlung took place. Sitting on the other side of the Atlantic he had nothing to do with it and scorned this new European fashion, but his influence had fallen across many of those taking part, even across its leader Mies, who later claimed:-

'Here finally was a master builder drawing upon the veritable fountain-head of architecture, who with true originality lifted his architectural creations into the light. Here again at last, genuine organic architecture flowered... the dynamic impulse emanating from his work invigorated a whole generation. His influence was strongly felt even when it was not actually visible.' [1]

Wright had visited Europe in 1910, exhibiting his work and publishing a portfolio of drawings with the German publisher Wasmuth. They showed the Prairie houses that he had been working on for the past decade, and which established his reputation. Radically different from anything in Europe, these buildings immediately surprised their audience with their dramatically horizontal roofs and continuous bands of windows, but even more remarkable were the flowing spaces within. Determined to 'break the box', Wright developed L,T and X-shaped plans. He made corners disappear with opening windows, and made spaces that seemed to belong to two rooms at once, their figures overlapping in plan. He dispensed both with the box-like loadbearing structures of traditional building and the Beaux-Arts rules about axial planning, instead leading the visitor through his buildings on surprising and asymmetrical routes. His early 20th century houses were ahead of anything in Europe in their freedom from historic styles, for he had already developed a remarkably refined architectural language of his own, with its own geometric and constructional principles. Wright's work was always deeply concerned with response to site and climate, though these issues could scarcely be properly understood through print. It was the planning and three dimensional assembly of forms and spaces that held European architects agog, making Wright a world leader. This could be felt in his plans as much as in his perspectives, and it opened up new, hitherto undreamed of possibilities. With his arrogant stance as self-made man,[2] his anti-institutional

1. Wright, William Martin House, Oak Park 1903, typical of the early Prairie House phase which made his name.

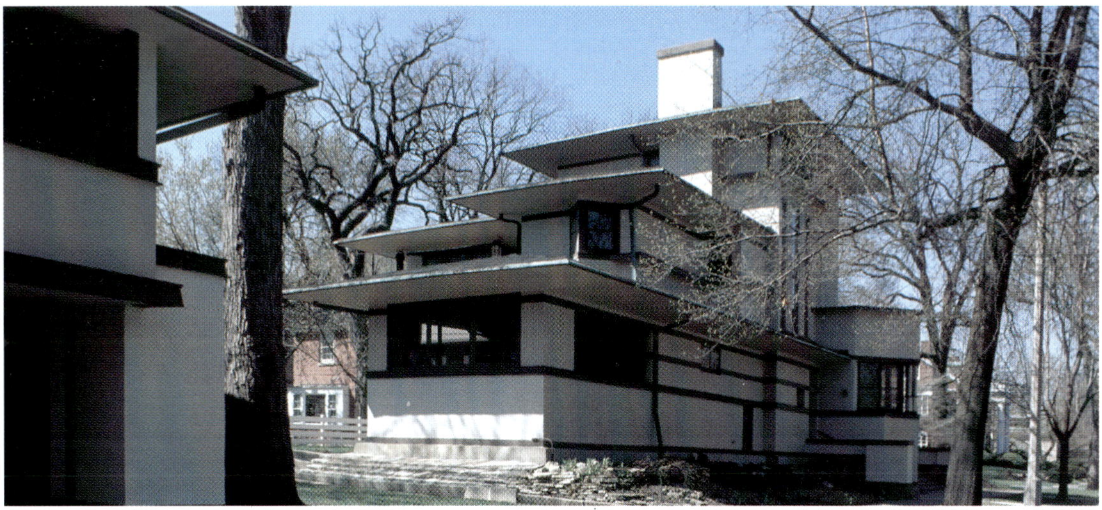

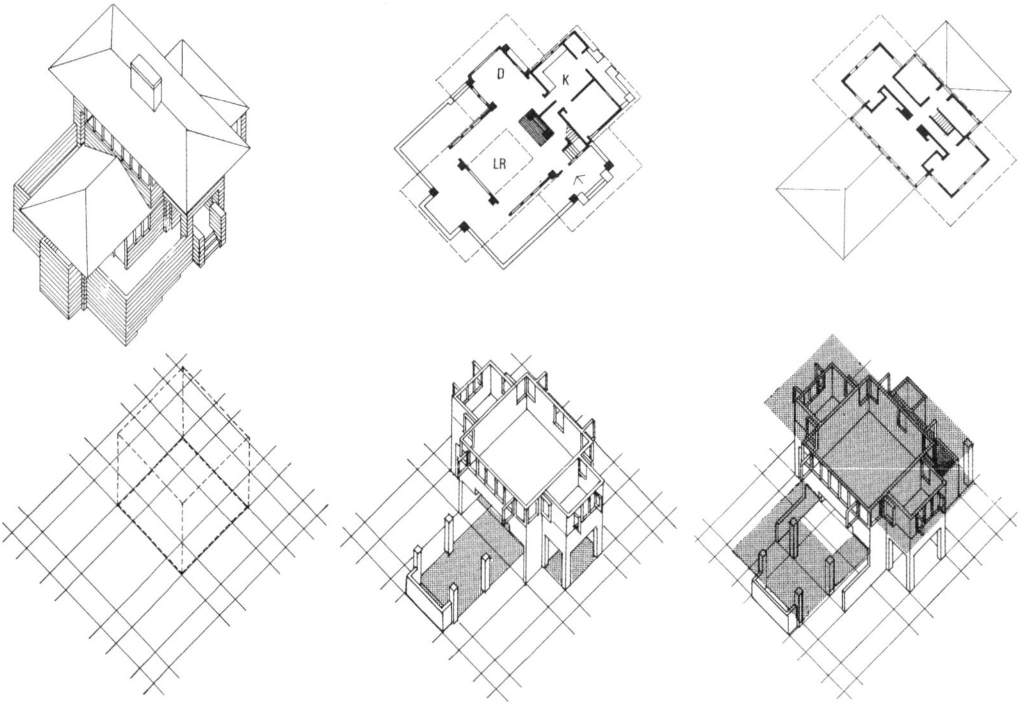

nature and his reluctance to admit influences except from his *Lieber Meister* Louis Sullivan, Wright appears more culturally isolated than in fact he was. The frontier spirit expressed in his romantic view of the farm and the prairie, in his careful juxtaposition of architecture and raw nature, and in his Utopian vision of Broadacre City as a green suburb where everybody has an acre and grows their own vegetables, also tend to mask his vital initial connection with the city. Without Chicago there could have been no Wright. This vibrant and expanding place was architecturally the most progressive in America, and Wright worked for its leading firm: Adler & Sullivan. His skill with geometry was developed and enhanced there, even if it had been founded in the Froebel games,[3] and more importantly, the search for transcendent principles behind ornament was undertaken there. While working with Sullivan, Wright must have learned much about using materials - about how they were assembled, how they could be expressed or repressed. And of course there were many other architects with whom he competed and exchanged ideas in his formative years: the whole Prairie school.[4]

The other great influence on Wright which became important in turn for Europe was Japan. He made several visits, building his Imperial Hotel in Tokyo in 1923, and he became for a time the leading importer of Japanese Prints into the United States: their effect on his drawing style is obvious.[5] In his architecture, the visible influence of Japan derives from the asymmetrical spatial progressions, the Tatami module and the open framed structure growing from a platform. He also evidently appreciated the contemplative simplicity which resides as much in the ritual of the tea ceremony as in the tea-house itself. Europeans had of course been independently influenced by imported Japanese prints, as typically seen in the architecture and furniture of E. W. Godwin, for example, but it took the progressive stance of a new-worlder, less bound by an innate sense of tradition, to ingest the Japanese sense of space.

The idea of an Organic Architecture

Wright was a prolific if sometimes undisciplined writer throughout his long life, and he produced a great deal of propaganda for his cause, sometimes even contradicting himself. He had begun to use the term 'organic' to describe his architecture by 1910. Integration with the natural setting - the house being 'of a hill, not on a hill' - was one facet. The house should grow out of its site, responding to the forms of the land and developing a series of outdoor rooms in continuity with its internal spaces.

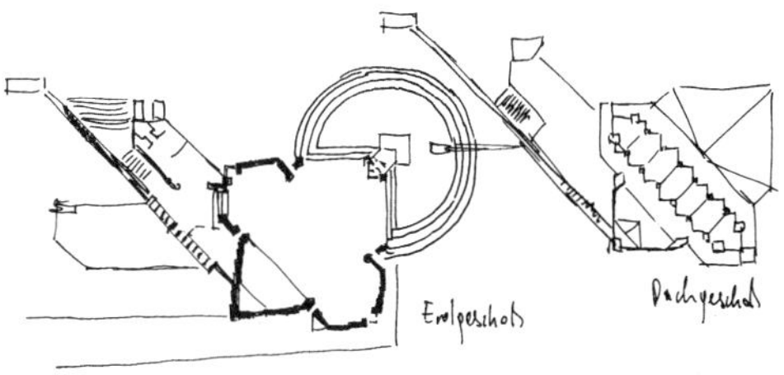

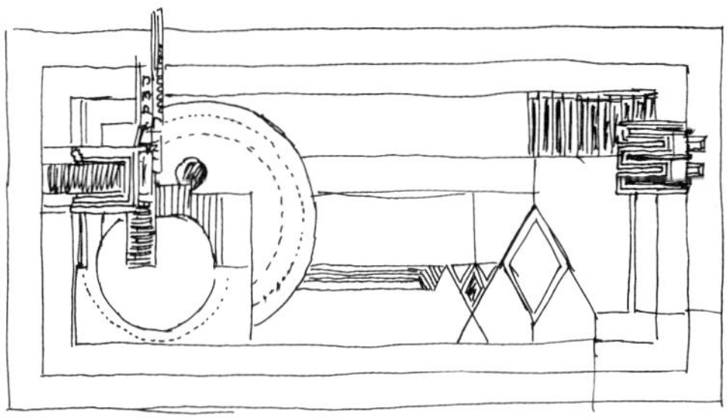

2. (opposite) Ross House 1909 as analysed and drawn by Richard MacCormac to show the grid system.

3. (above) Barnsdall House 1926, drawings by Otto Graf showing similar geometric figures in the plans for the lodge and in the fireplace relief.

Daylight and climate should also be carefully considered. Another aspect was construction: the building should be honestly and clearly built, following the logic of assembly and the nature of the materials used. Wright employed just about all available materials at one time or other, making bold experiments with many of them, and he was always acutely aware of questions of structure and assembly. The development of his ideas about interior space grew out of a conviction that furniture and fittings should as much as possible be designed for and integrated into the building. This was not just a question of getting the visual appearance of furniture to harmonise with that of the room, but of being able to design the spaces around set activities: a place to sit, a place to eat, a place to have a fire, places to store things. Because subordinate parts of rooms could start each to claim a special character: the fireplace with its seating, the dining area, a study corner by a window - it was possible to dispense with the room as rigid container and organiser of space, and fragments of rooms could slide into one another, just as an open inside corner could slide into a sheltered outside one. The sense of interconnection made the house more of an integrated whole, which was what Wright sought above all else under the name 'organic': -

'An organic-entity, this modern building as contrasted with that former insensate aggregation of parts. Surely we have here the higher ideal of unity as a more intimate working out of the expression of one's life in one's environment. One great thing instead of a quarrelling collection of so many little things.'[6]

Hugely important to this sense of integration was the geometric ordering which occurs throughout Wright's work, enabling him to keep tight control of complex three-dimensional interactions. A glance through any book on his work reveals that his plans mostly operate on a grid, which if not square or rectangular will be triangular or hexagonal. It is often a tartan grid, that is to say with small and large intervals. But there is much more. Through his drawn analyses, Otto Graf has shown how, in early Wright masterpieces such as the Dana house and Unity Temple, the same geometric forms and manipulations can be found from the scale of the site plan to that of a hanging lamp,[7] and that when Wright chose to include in a building an apparently abstract relief, as in the Barnsdall house, it contained a kind of geometric signature for the whole.[8] Wright's *Lieber Meister* Sullivan, in his bid to escape the inherited historic styles, had been much exercised by the question of reinventing ornament, seeking inspiration both in nature and in geometric construction. Owen Jones's *The Grammar of Ornament* of 1856 was essential reading. Gathering examples from around the world and across history, it almost automatically suggested underlying principles: the essence of universal ornament lying in a universal geometry.[9] The play of geometric figures in many cultures could be seen to confirm their validity as type-forms, while discoveries in sciences like crystallography could support the view of geometry underlying the structures of nature. Geometry meant universal harmony in the essence of things.

A century later, the ornament of Sullivan is as stranded on the sandbanks of history as the short-lived Art Nouveau. Wright's Prairie houses have dated less, yet still seem old-fashioned, and it is their ornamental details that are hardest to take - if daringly minimal then, too much now. The aesthetic effects of the full integration have therefore faded, but Wright's use of geometry did not end there. He developed it as second nature, as a way of working in drawings, of developing designs, of transmitting instructions to others - above all he used it to control the dimensioning and assembly of his buildings, as a vocabulary of construction as well as of design. It is most obvious in works experimenting with prefabrication, where sizes have to be driven by the repetition of the element.[10] Yet Wright never let the discipline of his geometric system overwhelm his architecture. His mastery of it was so complete, and his three-dimensional understanding so good, that he seemed to be able to do whatever he liked: the strain of keeping to the grid rarely showed.

The house as vehicle for experiment

With an *oeuvre* of over 600, Wright built more than any of the other architects discussed in this book. Most of his buildings were private houses, which was where his practice originated, and the house was more significant to him than any other building type. Although he built houses in every decade of his long career, two periods stand out as particularly important: the years 1900-1910 when he designed the Prairie houses which made his reputation, and the 1930s when he designed his most famous luxury house, Fallingwater, and his Usonian houses.

While Fallingwater - the Kaufman house at Bear Run, Pennsylvania - exploited the most romantic of sites with daring cantilevers and spaces of great complexity, the Usonian houses were modest. Repeatable and economical, they were built for middle-class clients starting in the lean years of the Depression. They stretched Wright's ingenuity in working with limited means, causing him to develop a spartan aesthetic much closer to the European Modernists. He developed the houses as a theme and variations, allowing for varying requirements and site conditions. He came to see them as a means to house Usonia, his private name for the United States,[11] and as the fabric of his imagined garden city, Broadacre.

The Rosenbaum House, built in 1939 for a college Professor and his family in Florence Alabama,[12] was one of the best: John Sergeant calls it *'the purest Usonian'*.[13] L-shaped in plan to embrace a garden space to south and west, it has two wings. The south-facing one contains the open-plan living, dining and study areas, and the west-facing the three bedrooms. Both have extensive runs of glazed doors that can be left open in summer, with overhanging eaves to provide shade and to define the threshold zone occupied by the doors when hitched open. As the street runs to the north, entry is at the north-east corner, under the shelter of a daringly cantilevered car-port, which in an aerial view makes the house T-shaped.

Although a house with so many rooms would scarcely be practical without central heating, Wright considered that the boiler should provide background heat at about 65°F (18.3°C) leaving a more essential role for the hearth. All his houses took the hearth as centre and starting point:

'I could see the necessity for one chimney only, a broad generous one, or at most two. These kept low down on gently sloping roofs or perhaps flat roofs. The big fireplace in the house below became now a place for a real fire... So the integral fireplace became an important part of the building itself in the houses I was allowed to build out there on the prairie... It comforted me to see the fire burning deep in the solid masonry of the house itself. A feeling that came to stay.'[14]

4. Rosenbaum House, view from north side and street, with cantilevered car-port. All photographs are by John Sergeant.

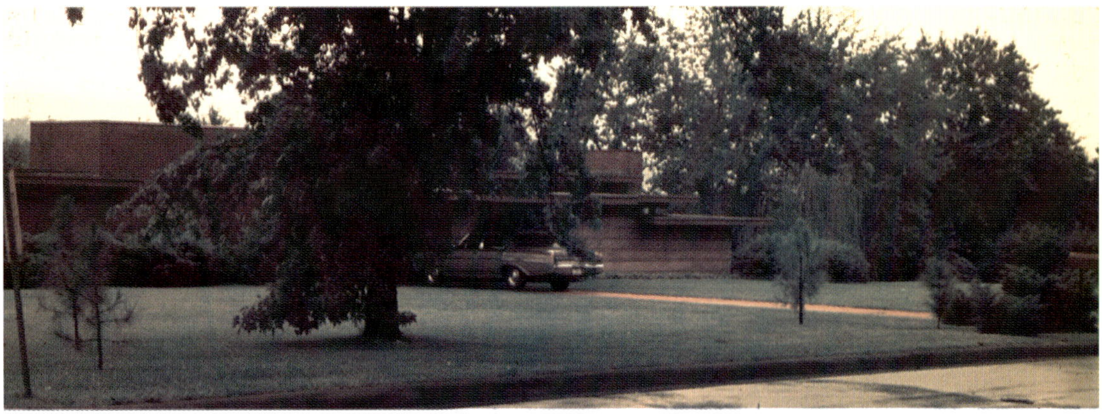

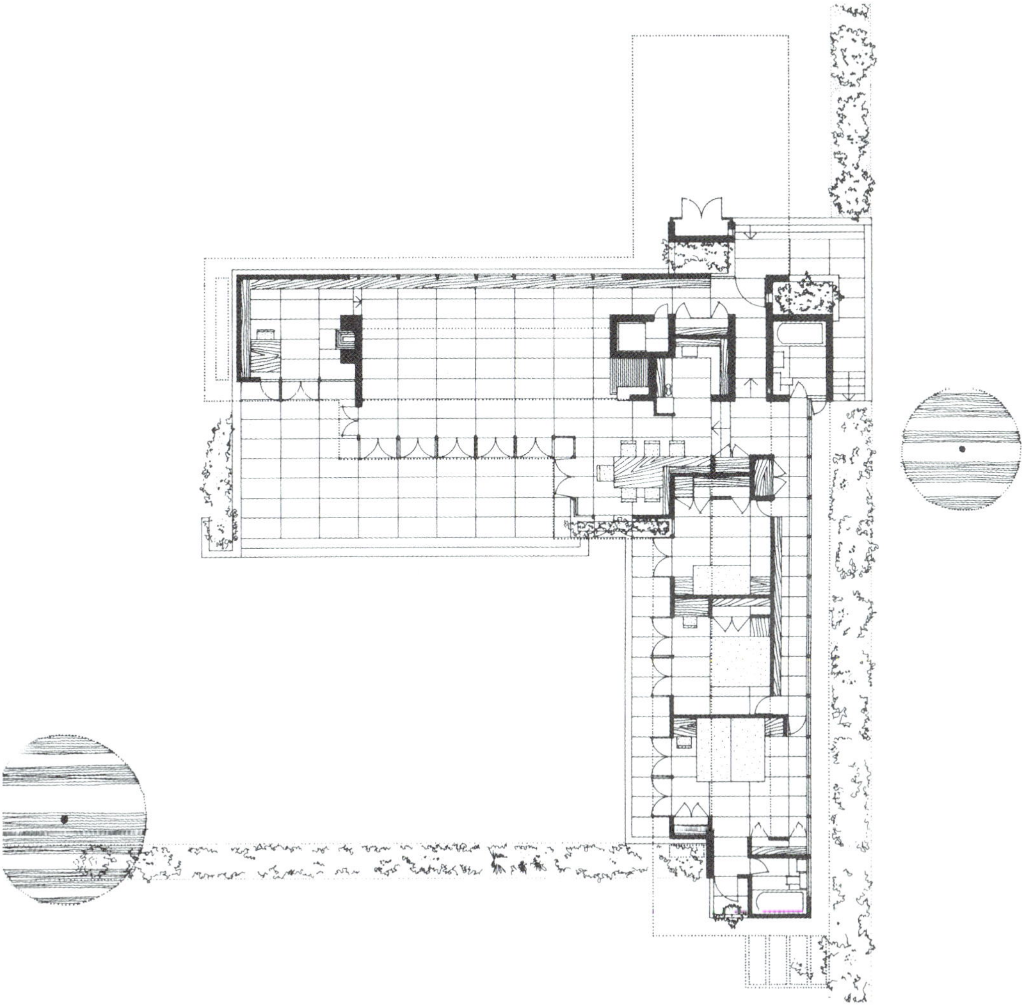

5. Rosenbaum House, ground floor plan.

6. Rosenbaum House, view from garden side.

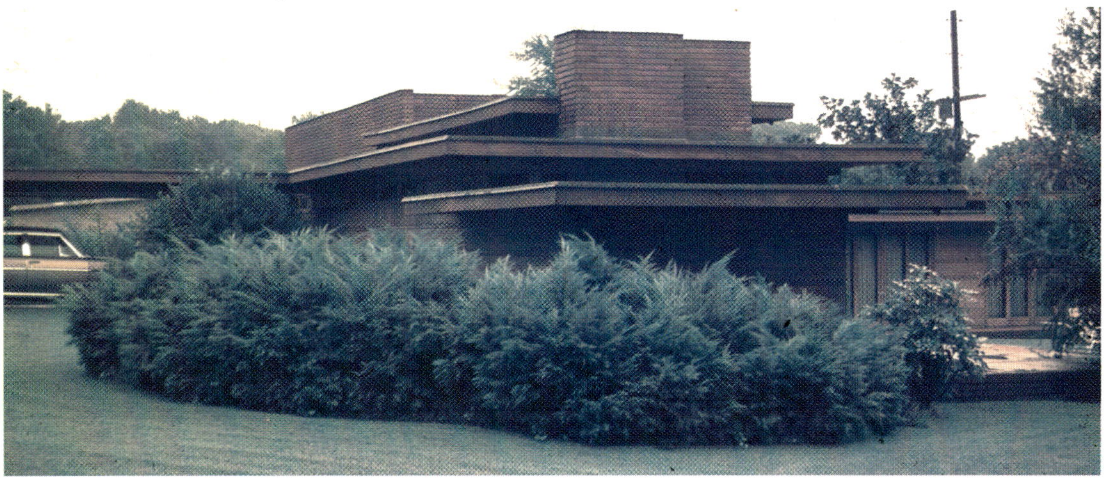

In the Rosenbaum House the great hearth is the climax of the largest and most important room, set at the end of its central axis and anchoring it to the rest of the house. Combined with it in its central role is the kitchen, placed at the hub of the dwelling to give the mother a commanding role:-

'Back in farm days there was but one big living room, a stove in it, and Ma was there cooking - looking after the children and talking to Pa - dogs and cats and tobacco smoke too - all gemütlich if all was orderly, but it seldom was: and the children were there playing around. It created a certain atmosphere of a domestic nature, which had charm and which is not, I think, a good thing to lose altogether. Consequently, in the Usonian plan the kitchen was called 'workspace' and identified largely with the living room. As a matter of fact, it became an alcove of the living room but higher for good ventilation and spaciousness.' [15]

The hearth needed to be of brick or stone both to withstand the flames and to absorb and store the heat as a thermal flywheel. From early on in Wright's work, this masonry mass became the natural centre of gravity of a house and its main structural support, a solid core in opposition to the flimsier peripheral structure. Throughout his work the fireplace takes this role, giving a sense of centre and focus to spaces that cascade outward. With the Rosenbaum, Wright added to the brick block of hearth and kitchen the boiler room and one of the bathrooms, making a service core. This was partnered in its structural role by three further brick elements: the brick fireplace of the study - a diminutive version of that in the living room even orientated the same way - a structural brick wall at the end of the bedroom wing, and the brick back of an external tool cupboard supporting the carport cantilever. Seen from the street, the naked brick projects up between the roof planes of the wooden house, revealing its layered and hybrid nature.

The living room wing sits on a broader platform which extends it into the garden, the floor surface treated the same inside as out, ending in three brick steps which descend to the lawn. Living room, dining room and study occupy only about two thirds of the platform, for the largely glazed wall steps back in characteristic Wrightian fashion to create two corners: one for a western view and exit to the living room, the other for the dining bay at the junction of the wings. At the same time the stepping is clearly hierarchical: the house gets taller and wider as it approaches its focal point. Similar stepped corners are created at the end of the bedroom, for the porch platform, and to give the main bathroom a southward view. The sidestepping in plan is also applied to the routes into and around the building. The broad steps of the north entrance platform indicate threshold, but you have to step rightward under the car-port to find the front door. Having entered, the view onward is appropriately blocked by cupboards, for the bedroom passage sidesteps to the left to maintain its privacy. Steps lead to a floor-well which is the main crossroads of the house, then to right up extra-wide steps along a route following the living room's glazed doors. This leads through end doors onto the outdoor platform, and so to the garden. The primary outdoor space is screened from the approach by the house, and is first seen by visitors from within. It intends transition to another world.

Throughout the interior there is much built-in furniture, which is not just functionally convenient but gives a role to each space-defining element. The long north wall in the living-room, for example, is beneath its clerestory a wall of books, as opposed to the wall of doors it faces. The east wall is the fireplace wall, the west one became the backdrop for a grand piano. In the bedroom passage there is again storage, but this time on the inside. Between first bedroom and kitchen/dining is a whole block of cupboards, set back to back. The bedrooms have built-in cupboards, tables and preferred bed positions. There is remarkably little naked wallspace anywhere, as opposed to the usual white boxes we live in.

The vertical dimension

The house's changes in level obey the gentle southward slope of the site, but they also provide spatial punctuation between living and bedrooms, distancing them externally also by means of their lower set terrace. Lowering the bedroom wing proved convenient for the hierarchy of massing, for it leaves it subordinate in height to the dominant living wing. The two steps down into the study at the end of the living wing also provide spatial punctuation, while creating a raised cill to the external platform as a variant connection between inside and out.

Roofs have scarcely yet been mentioned, but they are of essential importance for the character, massing, lighting and spatial flow in the house:

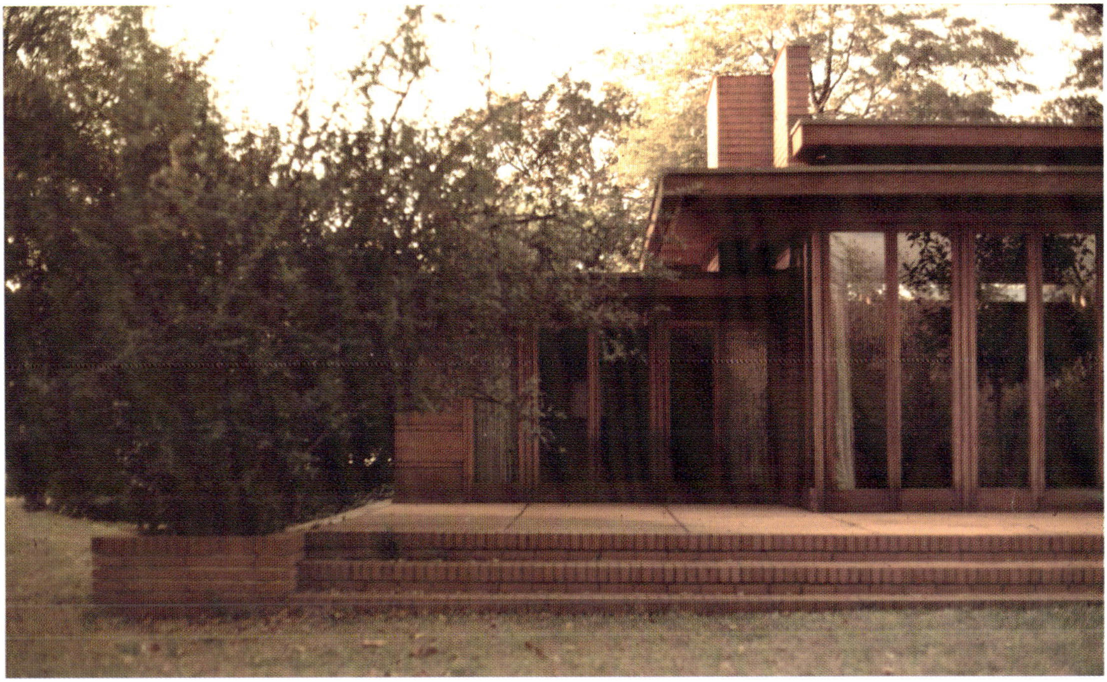

7. Rosenbaum House, terrace and junction between living room and study.

8. Rosenbaum House, fireplace and dining area.

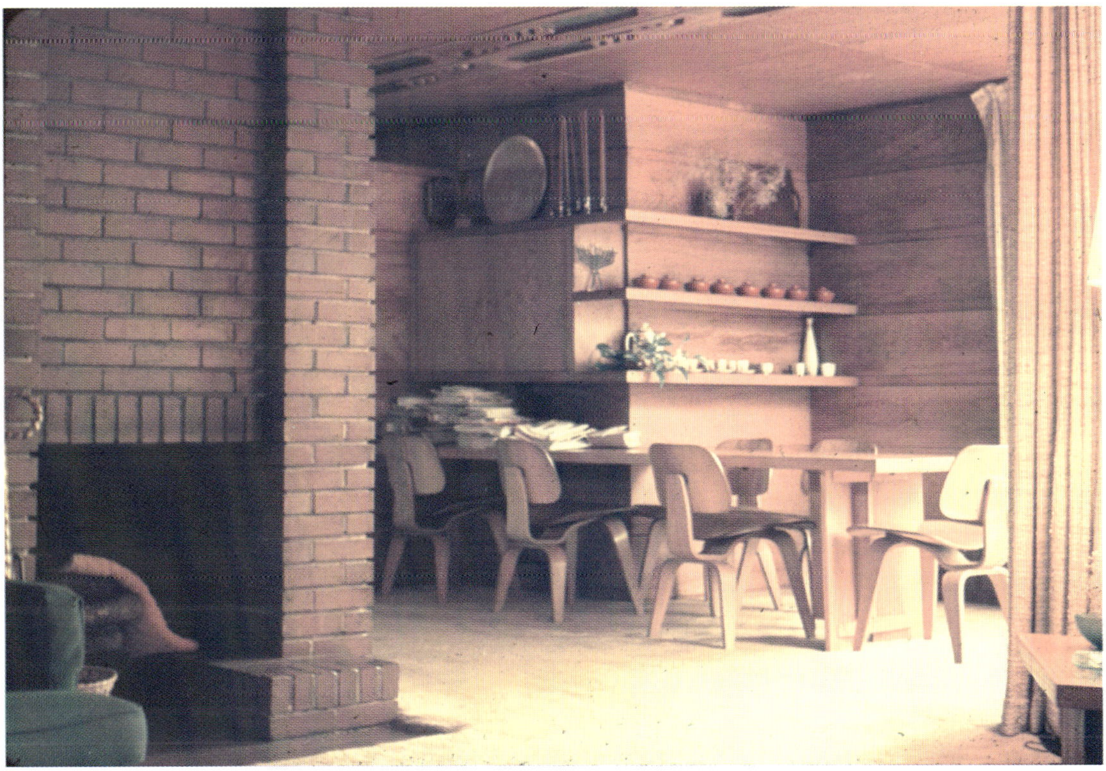

to replace their subtle layers with a single plate would wreck it. Wright had grown up as an architect when pitched roofs were obligatory and the roof-plan was as much a starting point as the ground plan, both taxing in its geometry and visually powerful in its potential form.[16] The flat roof brought freedom of plan to modern architects, but also a thoughtlessness that has become widespread. With it, the plan could be of any shape, its dark areas lit electrically, so architects needed no longer struggle over it. For Wright, in contrast, the roof never ceased to be a dominant element. Making it flat allowed him to achieve the horizontality he craved,[17] but he did not reject or forget its sheltering nature, which persisted in the form of cantilevered overhangs. At the same time the wasteful attic could be avoided, the roof structure becoming the ceiling. By layering the roofplanes, low intimate spaces and tall proud ones could be created in mutual contrast, while clerestory lighting could be introduced to the middle of the plan. Externally too, the roof layers could tell a story, made to stack up towards the centre of the building, while remaining low and gentle at the ends.

The living room ceiling divides the room into three zones: high in the middle suggests a more hall-like volume, adds clerestory light, and respects the axis of the fire, leaving a relatively static space for tables and chairs. The lower-ceilinged strips of space to either side define areas for movement. On the garden side the glass doors rise to meet the low ceiling without being unduly high or making the rest of the room too low. The study with its dropped floor can have an even lower ceiling, helping the external profile. In the bedroom wing there is also a raised central roof with clerestorys, which makes the central area of the room occupied by the bed seem more focal, and defines a working area next to the glazed doors as more intimate.

Construction

Wright was keen to eliminate all need for a basement, and in the Rosenbaum House he managed even to accommodate the boiler on the ground floor. Rather than using strip footings, he would make a gravel base on which would be cast a concrete raft, topped with a float-finished screed grooved with the regulating floor grid. A bold technical innovation of the Usonian houses was their 'Gravity' underfloor heating system, an attempt by Wright to mimic the so-called Korean rooms of Japanese houses, which had hollow floors heated by hot gases.[18] The Usonian houses had a boiler-fed hot water system using iron or copper pipes cast into the floor raft. This not only eliminated ugly radiators and their space demands, but also made use of the floor slab as thermal storage, evening out temperature fluctuations. The heavy core brick elements of kitchen and hearth just added to the thermal mass.

Brickwork elements were built up on the concrete raft, loading it over areas large enough to avoid punch-through. The remaining outside walls were made of wood on a board and batten system which ended up a mere three inches (75mm) thick. A core of vertical boards or plywood sheets was clad each side with horizontal planks of planed cypress wood just under 12 inches (300mm) wide, specially tongued into short holding battens as their only fixing. The visual effect was of regular stripes, again stressing the horizontal. The system had a module of 13 inches, which meshed with four courses of brick. Obviously this did not rhyme neatly with the floor module of two feet (600mm), which reveals the extent to which Wright's dimensioning was pragmatic as opposed to ideological. He needed to work not only with the standard brick size, but also with planks cut to a nominal 12 inches. The vertical rhythm of the boarded walls was strongly visible both inside and out, setting the scale for the stepped roofs, clerestorys, shelves and other built-in furniture.

When it came to the roof, Wright had the brilliant idea of bracketing together small sections of timber, using two pieces of four by two to make an eight inch beam and three for a twelve. Not only were the small sections cheaper because they came out of smaller trees: they also remained interchangeable on site. Interlocking joints could more easily be made, and projecting cantilevers could step back with decreasing load to allow a narrow and delicate roof edge. The internal ceilings could be panelled out in plywood, or in important rooms more nobly in cypress planking. The upper roof surface was asphalt with its own gutter and projecting rainspouts at the corners.

Spread across the United States, Wright's Usonian houses were mainly built under the control of his apprentices from Taliesin, working with local craftsmen.[19] The plans were not fully dimensioned but regulated by the grid, leaving room for adjustments of irregular details on site: and the Rosenbaum plan suggests many departures from the module due to material thicknesses.[20]

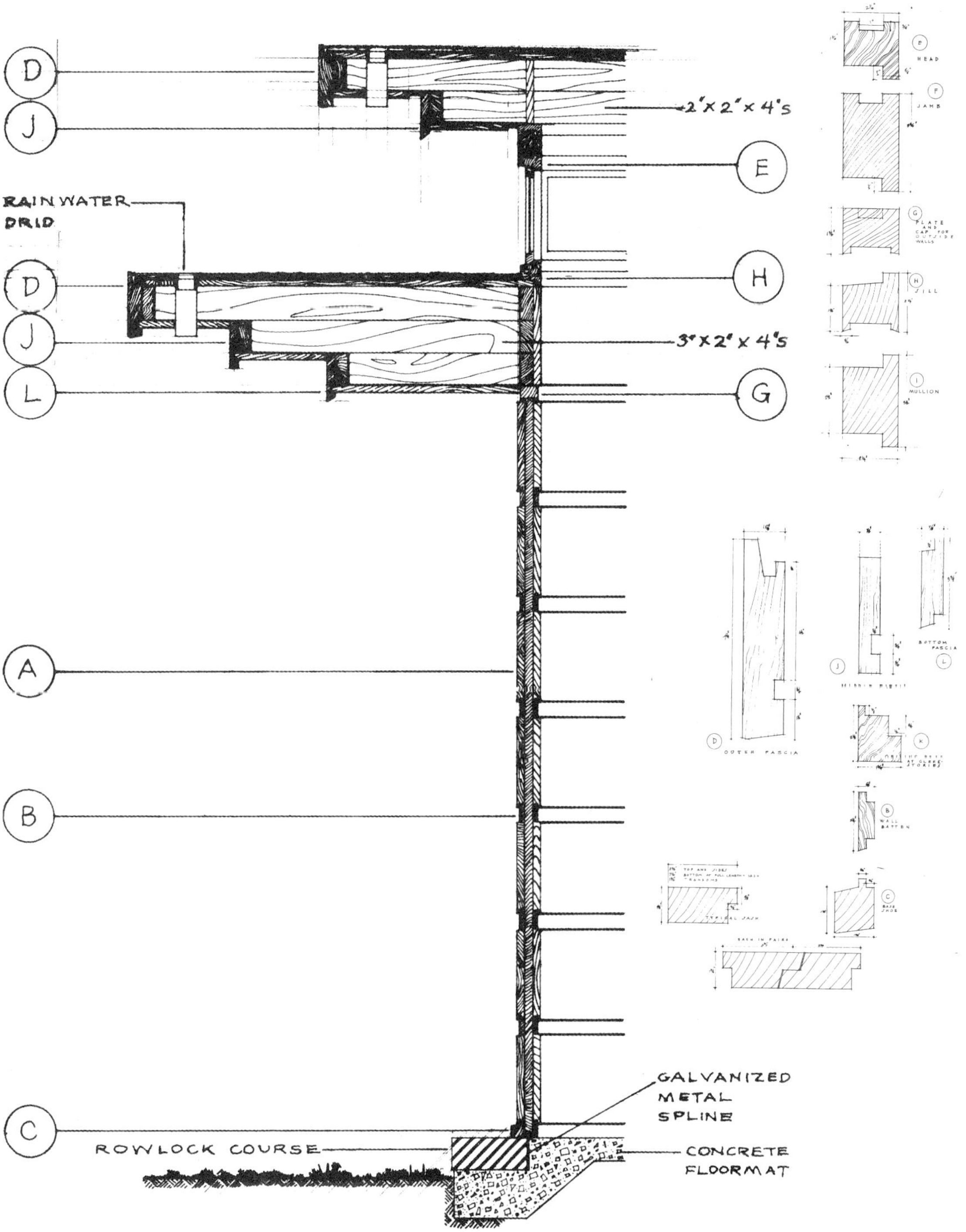

9. Usonian house generic board and batten wall: typical section and component parts.

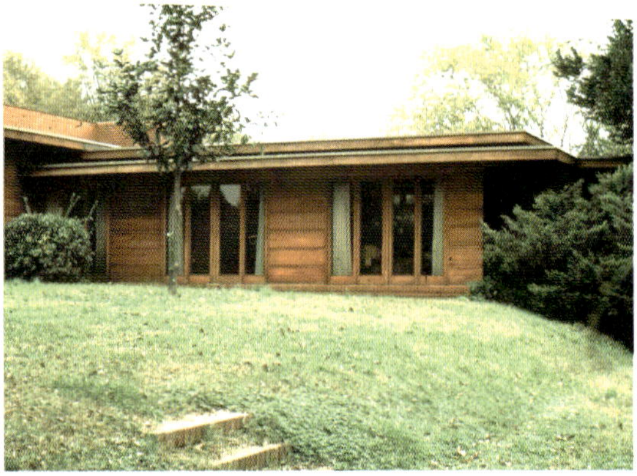

10. Rosenbaum House, the bedroom wing.

11. (below) Dining area with glass-to-glass corner, looking out on garden.

12,13,14. (right) Axonometric drawings of the house showing progressive build up of layers, by John Sergeant.

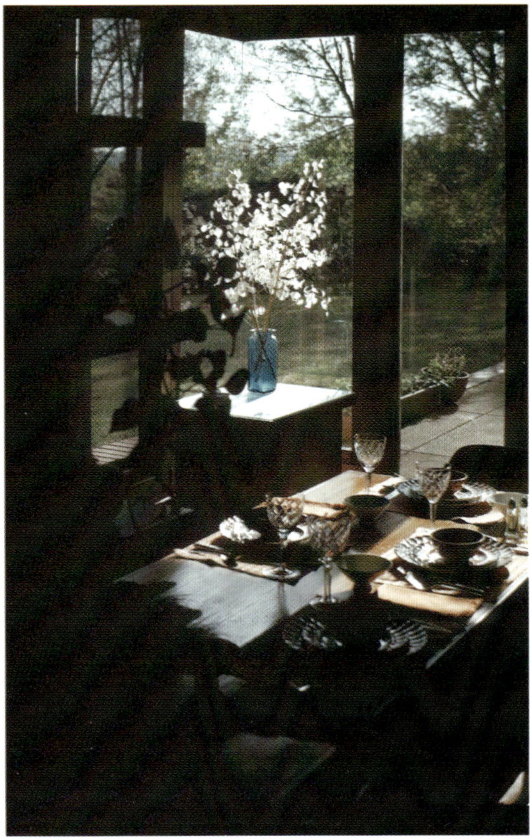

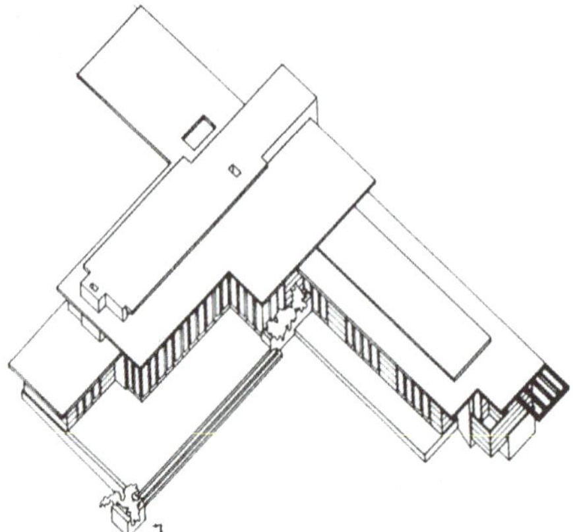

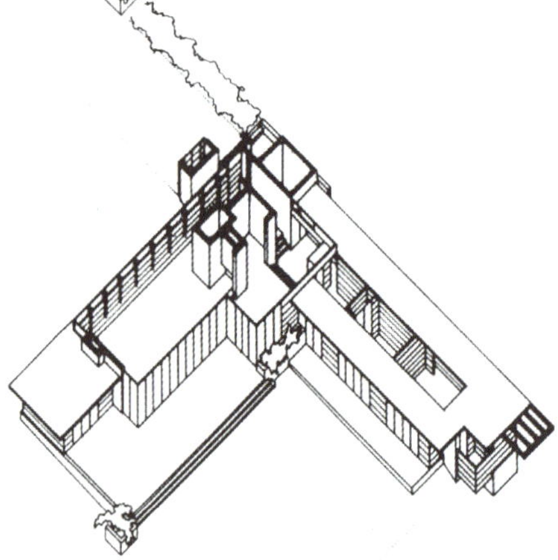

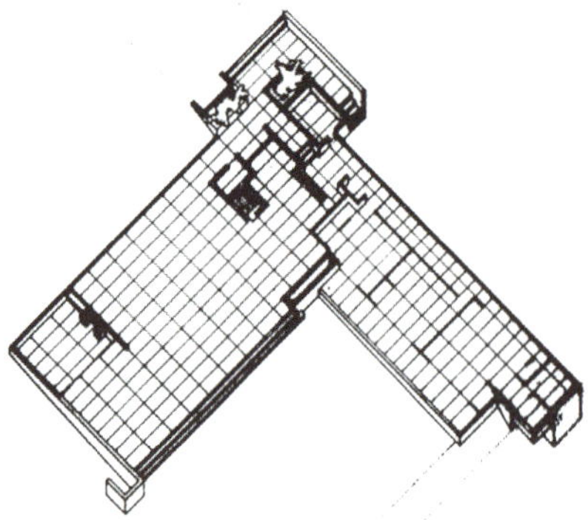

15. Wright, plan for a group of six Usonians surrounding a central farm, c.1939. North is top. The landscape treatment shows how the garden of one could lead into the next without the plot having a rigid boundary.

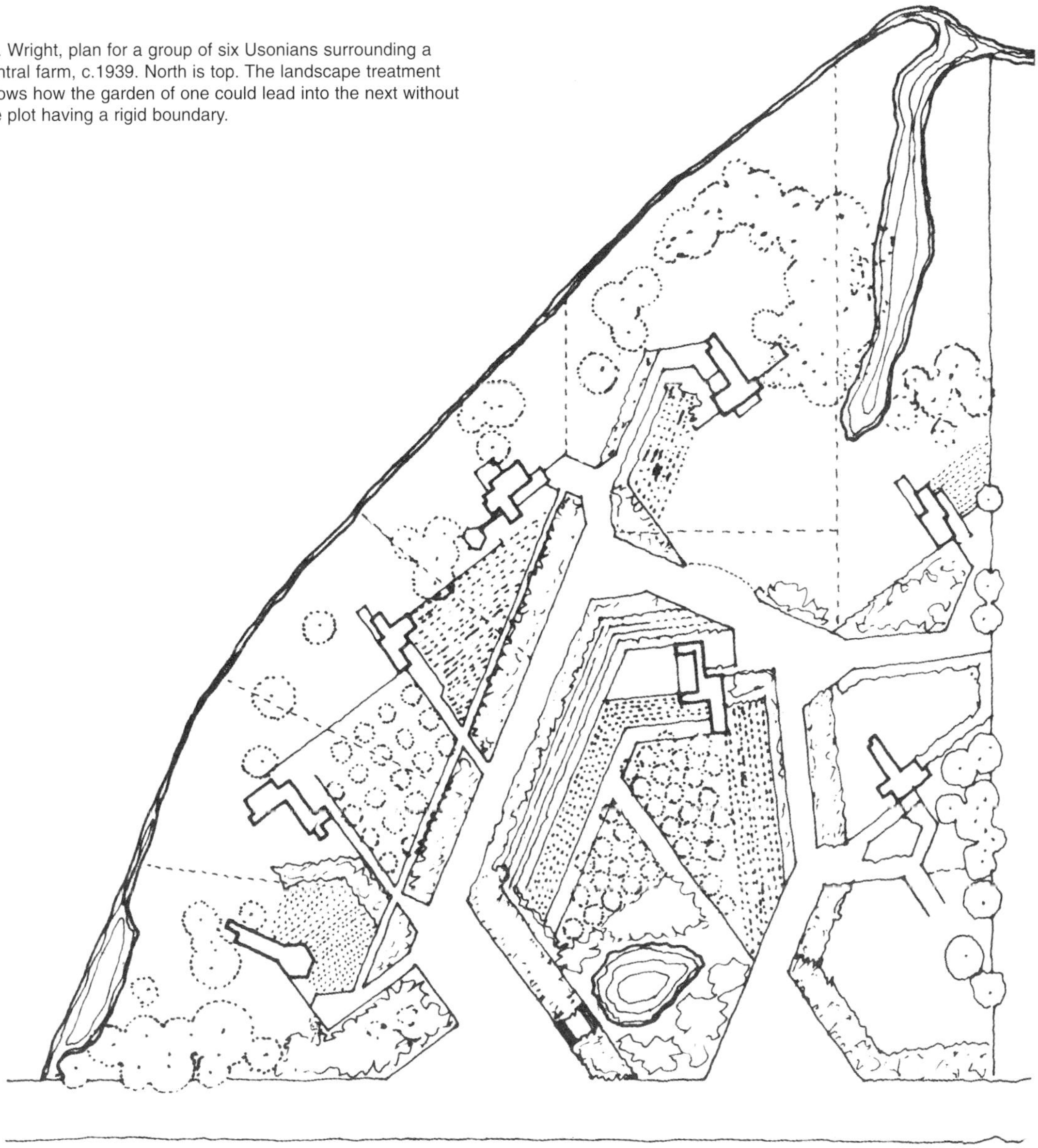

This openness of the system is what makes it so unlike the total prefabrication intended at the Gropius Weissenhof house (Chapter 1). To take another example, the 13 inch vertical module of the timber wall system had to be complied with exactly, so the timber sections processed in the mill needed to be precise, but the lengths of the boards could be crosscut on site as needed, piece by piece. There was also room for manoeuvre structurally, and Wright would even permit steel to be added when cantilevers got too long, as with the Rosenbaum car-port, and in the living room.[21] It remained protected within the timber-clad structure, quite unseen.

Repetition

Working decade after decade on houses for different clients, Wright never doubted that people's individual preferences should be reflected in their houses, and he enjoyed the varied things he was asked to do, if obstinate about anything that threatened his concept. Usonia was therefore going to be housed as a theme and variations, and a site-plan showing six Usonians gathered around a common

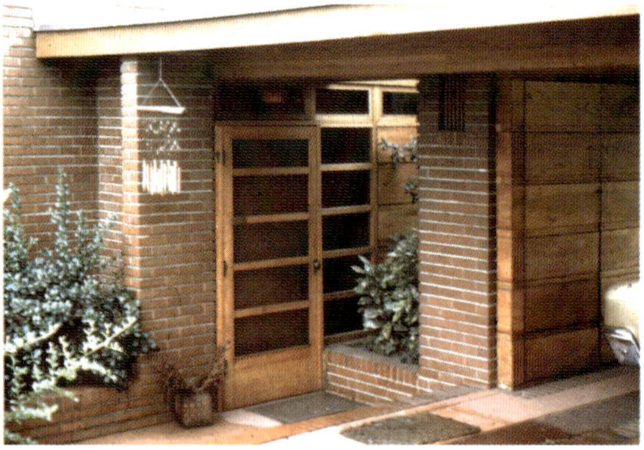

16. Rosenbaum House, entrance corner, north side.

farm makes clear both the variation in house-type and the exploitation of an irregular plot. It is of course essentially suburban and utterly dependent on the car, even if its promise of inhabitants growing their own vegetables recalls Wright's memories of his rural youth.[22] The houses are mainly of the L-shaped type and share a common orientation, but there is one hexagonal house with a tail (bottom left). John Sergeant has classified Usonian houses into five types,[23] of which the first and most ubiquitous is the Polliwog (tadpole) house with a head and tail. The Rosenbaum is this, the tail being its bedroom wing. The other types are the diagonal - with a skewed wing - the in-line, which is linear, the hexagonal which follows a tri-hex grid with everything at 60°, and the raised type, which due to site conditions occupies a raised platform or is cantilevered out of a hill. These types show at once variations in configuration, planning geometry and site response which made the Usonian concept remarkably flexible. They were also mostly expandable in order to accommodate a growing family. Wright hoped his house concept would start a general trend:-

'A natural house designed in accordance with the principles of organic architecture... may be put to work in our society and give us... "housing" which is becoming to a free society because, though standardised fully, it yet establishes the democratic ideal of variety - the sovereignty of the individual. A true architecture may evolve. As a consequence conformation does not mean stultification but with it imagination may devise and build freely for residential purposes an immensely flexible varied building in groups never lacking in grace or desirable distinction.'[24]

It held out promises for suburbia which have not been much fulfiled in the United States or, for that matter, anywhere else. Property values, large house-building companies, bureaucracy and popular taste have all intervened, and today's 'visionary' architects pursue concerns other than private housing. Nonetheless, many aspects of Wright's vision have retained their appeal, his spaces have lost none of their generosity, and his general belief in living *with* nature rather than *against* her has been given a new relevance in the era of 'sustainability'. The Usonian house remains an attractive proposition.

Notes

1. Mies *A tribute to Frank Lloyd Wright* College Art Journal 6, no. 1, 1946 pp. 41, 42. Cited in Neumeyer 1991 p.66.
2. Wright's persona was the inspiration for the film *The Fountainhead*, see Saint 1983, pp.1-18. He was a commanding personality, and defended his 'honest arrogance' by contrasting it with 'hypocritical humility'.
3. Wright's mother gave him geometrical puzzles which the educationalist Froebel had devised, and claimed this had a crucial influence, but Wright had no special memory of it.
4. See *Schooling the Prairie School: Wright's Early Style as a Communicable System* by David van Zanten in Bolon 1988, pp. 70-84.
5. See *Frank Lloyd Wright's Other Passion* by Julia Meech-Pekarik in Bolon 1988, pp.125-153.
6. Wright *Organic Architecture* 1910 quoted in Conrads 1970 p. 25.
7. Graf 1983, vol.1, pp. 149,163,193.
8. Graf 1983, vol. 2, p. 743.
9. See Frampton 1995 pp. 96-100.
10. For example in the 'Usonian Automatic' which used a concrete block system, see Wright 1970, pp. 198-205.
11. Wright attributed it (wrongly) to Samuel Butler: Wright 1970 p. 58, see also Rosenbaum 1993 p. 39.
12. For details of the family and the commissioning of the house see Rosenbaum 1993 pp. 152-166.
13. Sergeant 1976, p. 42.
14. Wright 1970, p. 32.
15. Ibid. pp. 163,164.
16. This is generally true of the architecture of the Arts and Crafts Movement, where the manipulation of roofs determines the character of the building and the plans are constrained by the limits of structural span. Philip Webb's famous Red House is typical: for an analysis see Blundell Jones 1986.
17. Wright 1970 p. 16.
18. Wright 1970 pp. 88-90.
19. Sergeant 1976, pp.112-119.
20. The west end doors of the living room are of reduced width to allow the brick pier to pick up roof loads beyond the clerestory line. The west wall of the main bathroom, being a brick in width, has to step beyond the clerestory line for its east side to line up with the narrower bedrooms partition wall. Such fine adjustments are important for the integrity of the building.
21. Wright was reluctant to admit the compromise of adding steel: see Rosenbaum 1993 pp.162-3.
22. On the car and Broadacre City see Rosenbaum 1993 pp.113-115.
23. Sergeant 1976, p. 40.
24. Wright 1970 (1954), p. 208.

Chapter 13. Hans Scharoun: National Theatre Project Mannheim 1953

A decade younger than Gropius, six years younger than Le Corbusier, Hans Scharoun (1893-1972) had barely finished his studies by the start of the First World War. He first became known for the watercolour sketches produced as a member of Bruno Taut's Gläserne Kette (Glass Chain) around 1920, which have remained among the most published icons of that movement. He was among the last architects invited to build at Weissenhof, and only because others dropped out. He emerged as a major talent around 1930, but as a Modernist was soon silenced under Hitler, obliged to work in an underground manner until after the Second World War. In 1946 at the age of 53 he briefly became Berlin City Architect, while he also started work on a series of brilliantly innovative competition designs, including that examined here. Several prize-winning projects fell through, but he completed a series of buildings in the early 1960s that made his international reputation, of which the Berlin Philharmonie concert hall completed 1963 is the best known. For the last nine years of his life he had more work than he could handle, and major buildings like the Berlin State Library, Wolfsburg Theatre and National Maritime Museum Bremerhaven were completed posthumously.[1]

The irregular nature of Scharoun's work and his enthusiastic engagement in Taut's circle have led Historians too often to dismiss him as an unrepentant hangover from the Expressionist period, but Scharoun's concern was less his own expression than the expression of the place and purpose of the building. He explicitly subscribed to Hugo Häring's theory of Organic Building, which emphasised the task not the artist (see Chapter 2).[2] Scharoun's importance is due not only to his insistence on exploiting given circumstances to make each building individual at a time when the mainstream pursued universal types and mass-production: he also pioneered a new spatial vocabulary that became highly influential in the last two decades of the 20th century. Always pushing the limits of design, he discovered as early as 1932 the advantages of deviating from the right angle in plan to differentiate territories and control movement, a new technique that opened up possibilities still being explored by architects of the current generation.[3]

Rightly regarded as Scharoun's masterpiece, the Berlin Philharmonie makes a fitting contrast with Mies's Neue Nationalgalerie which is examined in the next chapter, but we here concentrate instead on an unbuilt work, his competition design for Mannheim's National Theatre of 1953. There are three reasons: the first is that the Philharmonie - its foyer particularly - is too complicated to follow through on plans, while the simpler Mannheim project shows the same principles more clearly. The second is that while the Mannheim project pioneered the ideas of aperspectivity realised at the

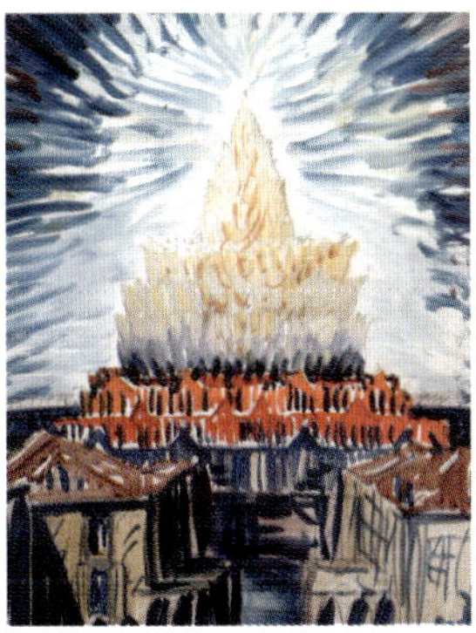

1. Expressionist watercolour c.1920.

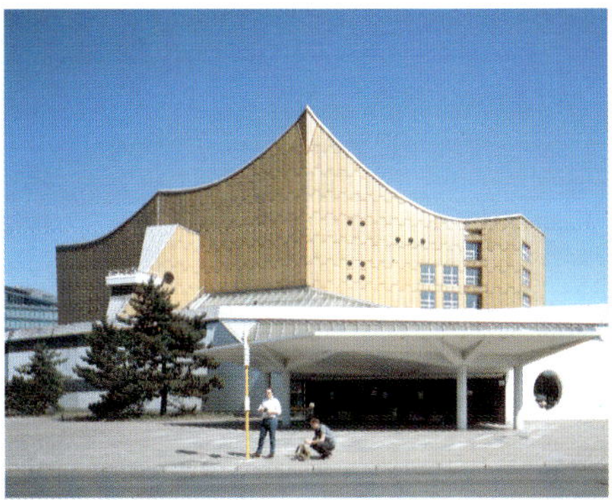

2. Philharmonie concert hall Berlin 1956-63, entrance.

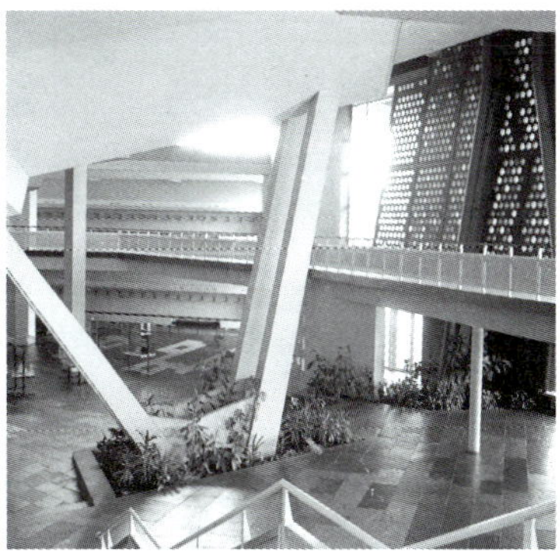

3. Philharmonie, main foyer.

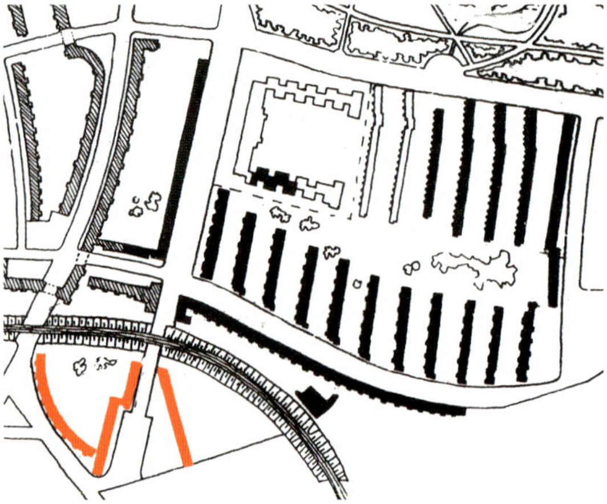

4. Site plan for Siemensstadt, 1929-30, layout by Scharoun. He chose for his own blocks those in red south of the railway.

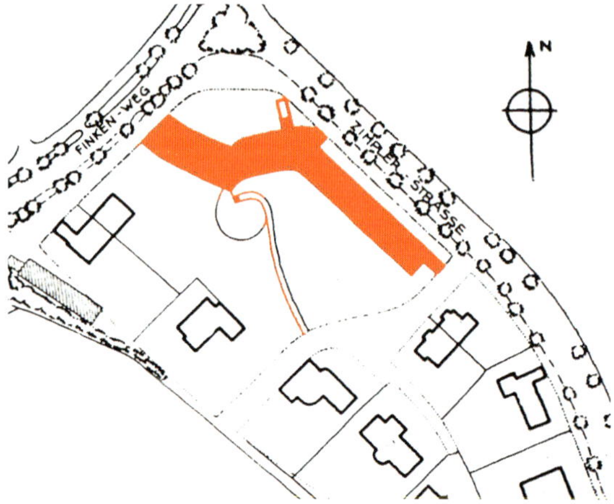

5. Werkbund Exhibition Breslau 1929, part of site plan showing Scharoun's curved and skewed building in red.

Philharmonie, its total asymmetry made it yet more radical.[4] The third and crucial reason is that the project provides better evidence of Scharoun's contextual intentions. The Philharmonie's poor site relationship is often cited as evidence against Scharoun as city-planner, in support of the idea that he was interested only in sculptural objects.[5] In fact the Philharmonie was planned for a different site, built on a wasteland, and almost every attempt by Scharoun to integrate it was compromised. The Mannheim project, in contrast, takes its whole *raison d'être* from the site and reflects the city's historical evolution.

Towards an architecture of interaction

In Chapter 1 (pp.10-46) we saw Scharoun's Weissenhof house evolve through four versions. Although orthogonally planned, it was driven by the assembly of purpose-driven spaces as well as being highly site-specific. Scharoun was already working with a broad and loose vocabulary, and though he returned in the final version to a plan dominated by an axis, he seems constantly to have been trying to liberate himself from traditional compositional conventions. From the beginning of his career he had shown an interest in responding to irregular sites, and he tended to see an odd-shaped piece of land as less a problem than an opportunity. When he won the contest for the layout of Berlin's Siemensstadt, he took for his own buildings what would have been regarded by most architects as the most awkward corner. His hostel for the Breslau Werkbund Exhibition of 1929 was even more dramatic. Two wings, one of single rooms and one of double, are joined by a central glazed hall. The hall takes the axis of the park behind, one wing follows the street, and the second bends around to meet the other street. The placing of building tracts also creates three differentiated outdoor rooms. But despite the cranked layout the internal spaces remained largely orthodox, and unlike later designs the corners of the hall where the acute or obtuse angles occur were not exploited. They are like hinges, and the building could be bent to a different shape, had the site demanded it, without much change in planning or to the spatial experience. All this changed with the Schminke house of 1932-3, Scharoun's best known private house.

Although it was set deep within the site, Scharoun chose to introduce the 26° angle change given by the site boundaries into the plan of the house. The best views were to north, so he made the living rooms a thin tract running east-west with windows on both sides, becoming increasingly transparent until it culminated in the glazed solarium at the east end. The 26° angle change was first introduced for the solarium and for the main west wall at the west end. It also skewed the external staircases in relation to the main body of the house, but until late in the deign period the main stair ran straight. Only at tendering stage, when the house had proved too expensive and needed to be reduced in area, did he discover the advantage of skewing the main staircase right, following the 26° angle. This meant that rather than facing a right angled turn at the top, the preferred direction was already established by the shallower turn.

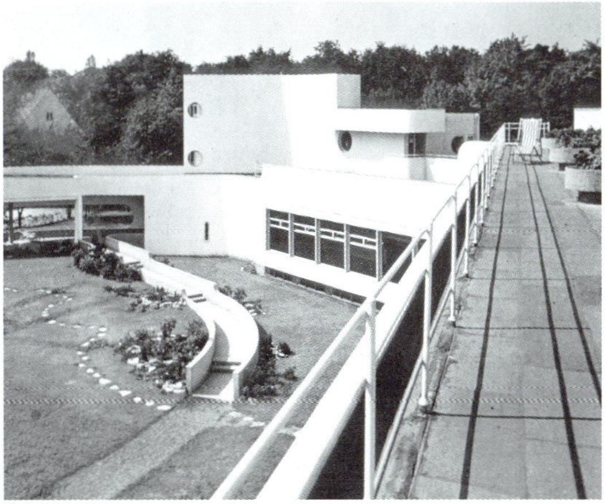

6. Werkbund Exhibition 1929, Scharoun's hostel building seen from the garden side.

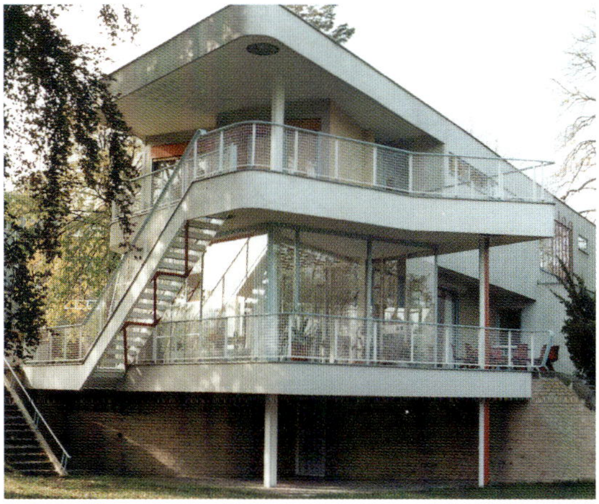

7. Schminke House, Löbau, Saxony,1932-3. Scharoun's best house and his masterpiece of the pre-war years.

Even when not climbing the stair, it still directs visitors to the right where the main rooms are. The skewed placing made the stair transitional between the house's main axes, and happily the other stairs at the east end participated in the dynamic diagonal.

This device was of crucial importance for the whole of Scharoun's later work. People could now be led through a space with small changes of angle, which operated on a hierarchy of directionality. This provided a radical alternative to the system of classical axes and intersection points which was the norm, opening the way instead to a new spatial language which he developed and perfected. This happened at first through the medium of the many private houses he built during the Nazi period, which have conventional exteriors but extraordinary flowing interiors.[6]

When he re-emerged with a public architecture after the war, it was dominated by shifts of angle, used both to articulate the different parts of a building - schools like a group of houses making up a village (p. 59, figs 26 & 28) - and to control movement through the interiors, leading the visitor through by manipulations of space and light which would indicate major and minor elements. By the time he came to work on the Mannheim project, Scharoun's architectural language was well-developed and could be deployed with great confidence, particularly as he had just spent a year developing his prize-winning design for the theatre at Kassel that unfortunately remained unbuilt.[7]

8. Schminke House, ground floor plan. Note diagonal stair opposite entrance to left.

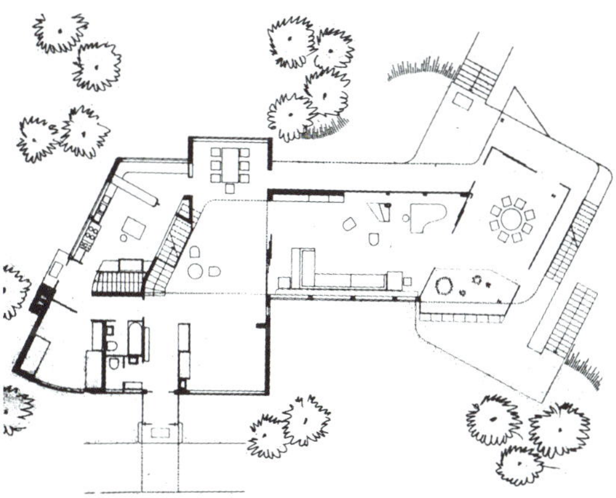

9. Schminke House site plan. Scharoun set the main body of the house east-west, but also took up the line of the east boundary.

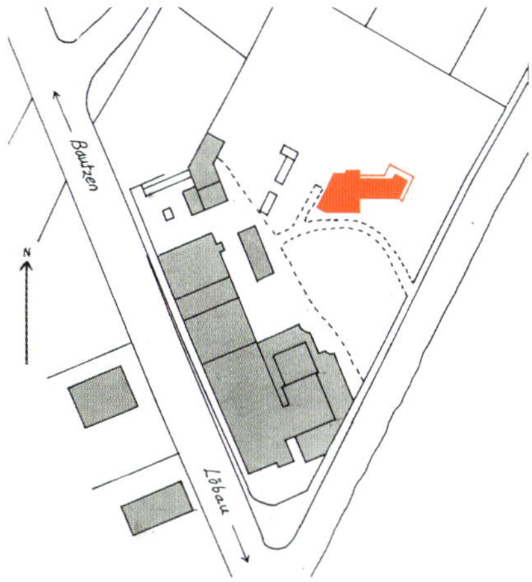

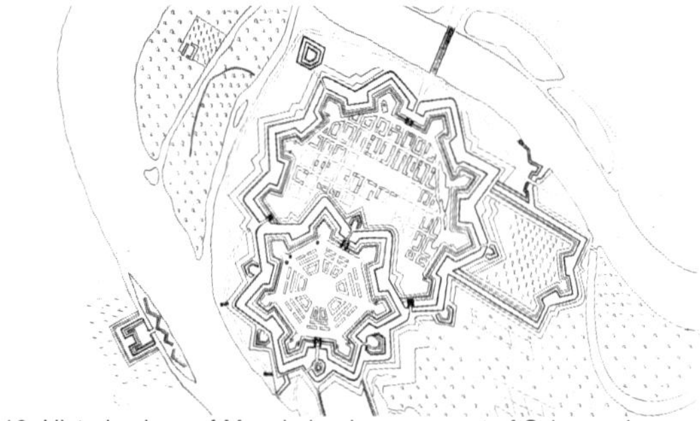

10. Historic plans of Mannheim drawn as part of Scharoun's submission. 1. Mannheim at foundation in 1606 with grid plan and fortified citadel, one bridge over the Neckar.

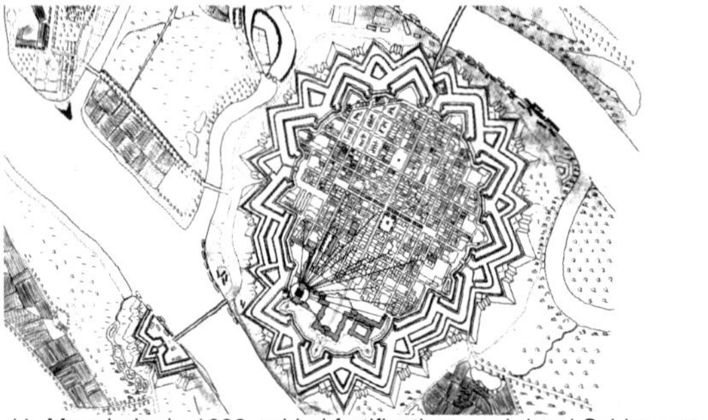

11. Mannheim in 1699, added fortifications and ducal Schloss on axis with Neckar bridge, new bridge over Rhine. Court theatre in left side of Schloss, radial lines show source of audience.

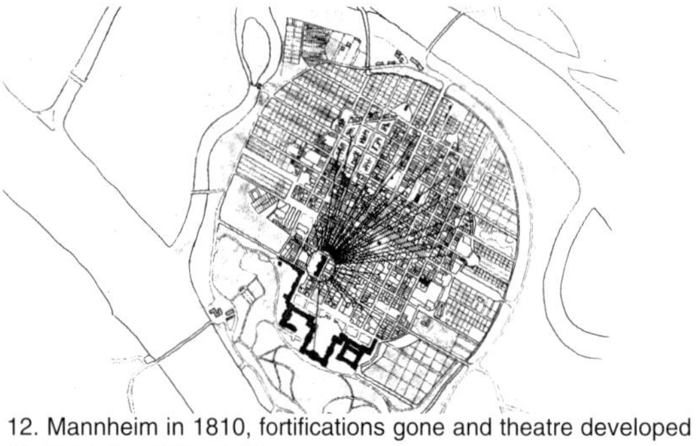

12. Mannheim in 1810, fortifications gone and theatre developed as independent institution.

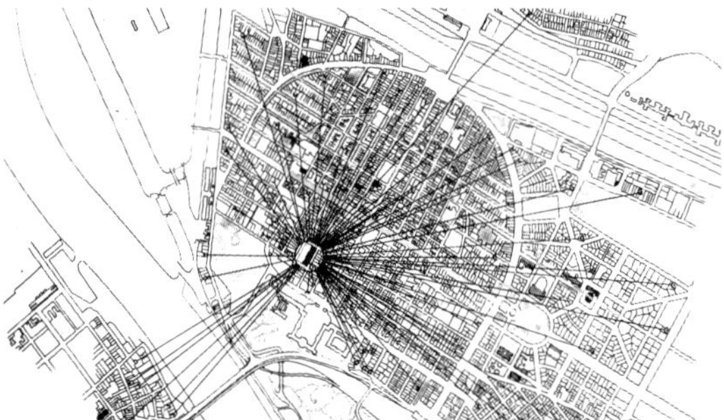

13. Mannheim in 1920, fortifications became ring road, city expanded eastward. East-west axis has taken over from north-south. Theatre draws audience from widening field.

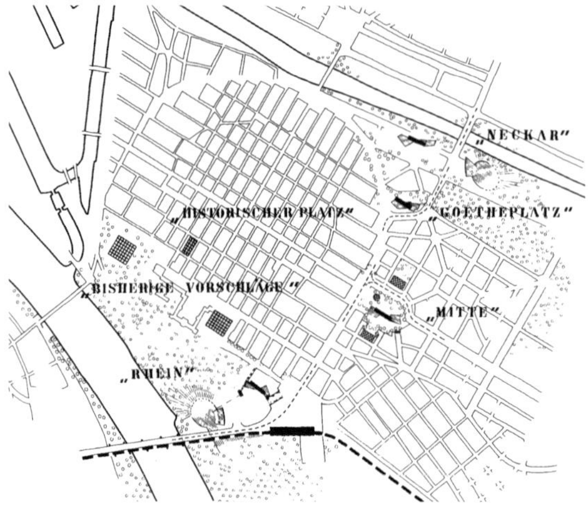

14. Scharoun's location plan, showing various possible sites and treatments for the new National Theatre. The given site for which the design was developed is Goetheplatz, set at right angles to the ring road between the gridded centre and the park next to the river Neckar. The clashes in urban geometry were the primary inspiration for Scharoun's design.

The Mannheim competition

The rebuilding of the National Theatre was one of the most important German reconstruction projects following the Second World War and the demise of the Nazis.[8] It was a chance for a new start and a celebration of returning democracy, and the competition brief called for new ideas both in relation to the siting of the building and in the development of its performance spaces. Scharoun undertook studies in both areas: on the contextual side he and his assistant Alfred Schinz made a 'structural investigation' of the growth of the city. A parallel investigation into the history and development of theatre involved discussions with Hugo Häring and culminated in a detailed paper submitted along with the project by Häring's assistant Margot Aschenbrenner, who had a literary and philosophical background.[9] The care taken over these texts and over his own description demonstrate only too clearly Scharoun's concern that the social and cultural ideas driving the project - its spiritual intentions - be properly understood.

Mannheim was founded in 1606 by Duke Friedrich IV of Pfalz at the confluence of the Rhine and the Neckar, as a grid-planned town within a radial star-like fortification system. The first bridge, over the Neckar, led to the main axial street which culminated at the Rhine in a fortified citadel. The fortifications were further elaborated, but within a century the citadel had been replaced by the ducal

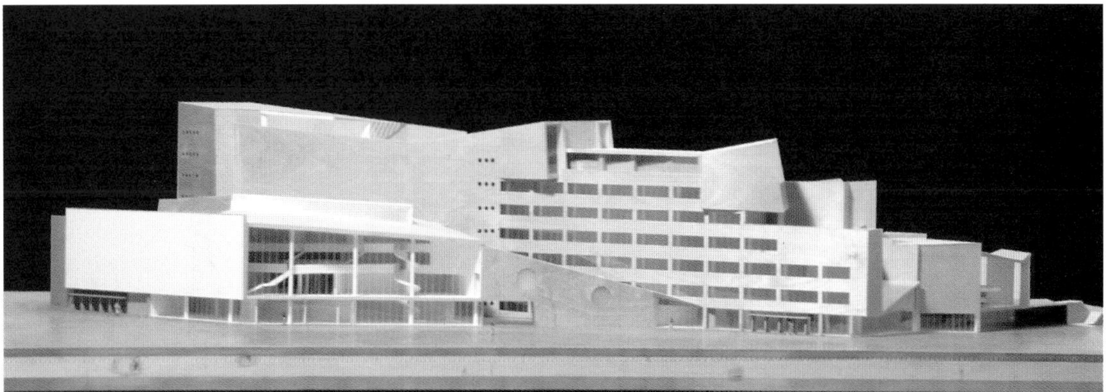

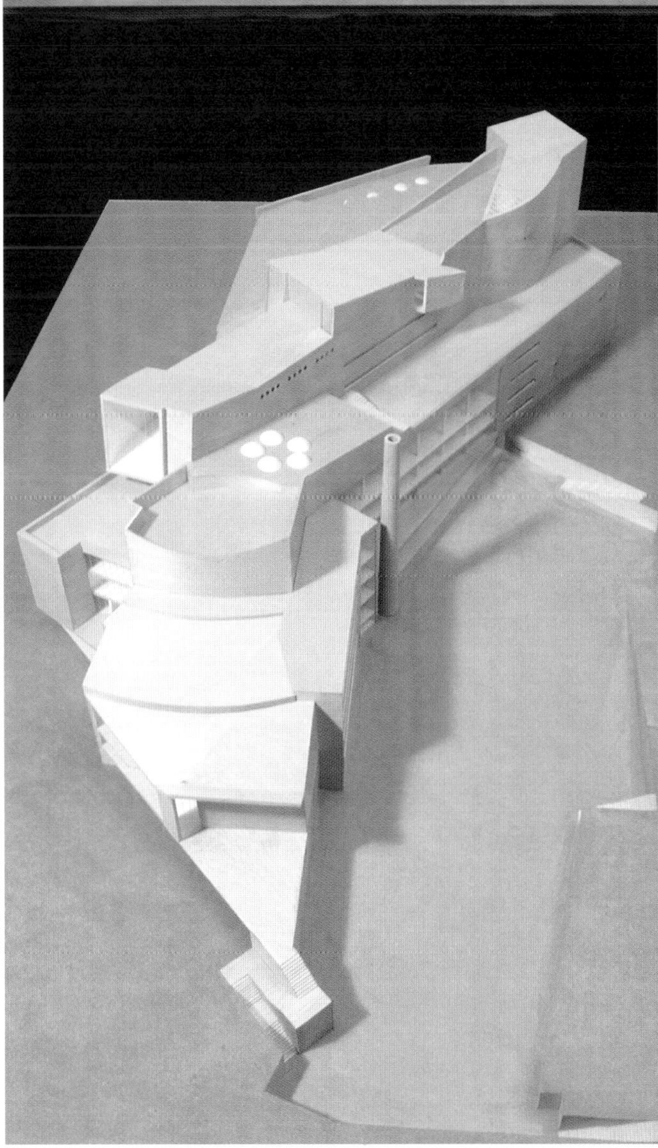

15. (above) Model of Scharoun's Mannheim Theatre Project made by students at University of Sheffield School of Architecture, 1995, front view with entrance and billboard left.

16. (left) Model seen from above and rear showing small theatre, rooftop rehearsal rooms and café terrace.

17. (below) View into model from end window showing main staircase and upper foyer.

Schloss, still on the main axis, and a Rhine bridge had appeared. By the early 19th century the fortifications were obsolete, and as so often in European cities, the wall gave way to a ring-road. Increasing river trade encouraged the building of the port and enlargement of the city. Contained to north and west by rivers, it could only expand to the south-east, where in the late 19th century a new grid was laid out, prolonging the cross-axis of the original city. So the north-west/south-east axis became dominant instead of the north-east/south-west one, an indication that power had passed from the Duke to the bourgeois merchants. This story was summed up in city plans at century intervals selectively redrawn by Alfred Schinz (figs 10-13).[10] Picked out in black are the positions first of the ducal Opera House and then of the first National Theatre, with radial lines indicating the source of the expanding audience.

The City had a preferred site, but competitors were invited to suggest alternatives, and to speculate on the appropriate place for such an important institution. Scharoun submitted a city plan showing seven possible sites (fig. 14), some with outlines of the proposed building, others as grids. The grids indicated tight sites within proposed urban blocks where the theatre might be embedded without exterior, but Scharoun felt that such placing would not give sufficient prominence to the building. He also thought it desirable for accessibility to place the building on the ring-road -

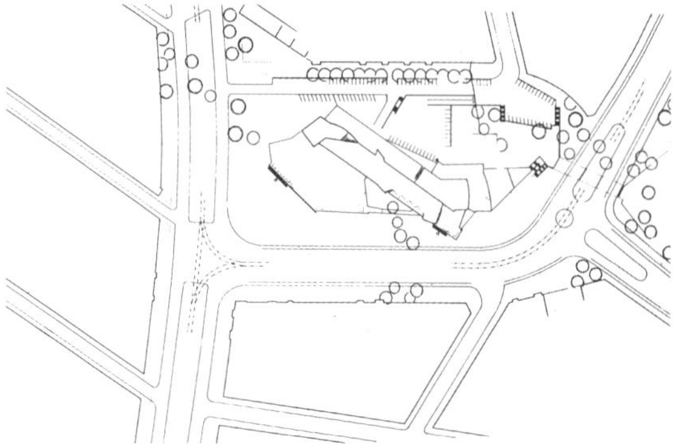

18. Site plan, old city grid to left is picked up in the diagonal dressing room/fly-tower block.
19. (below) Site model made by students at University of Sheffield School of Architecture 1995.

the border between original city and later suburbs - between Rhine and Neckar. The axial site marked 'Mitte' - middle - would have been the most prominent locally, but Scharoun felt that 'national' required connections further afield. The Neckar connected regionally to places such as Worms and Speyer, but the Rhine site would place the theatre on the historic communication axis of Germany, a truly national - and with links to France and Holland even international - setting.

Although hoping to transfer to the Rhine site if allowed to develop his proposal, Scharoun prepared his competition design for the city's preferred site on Goetheplatz, and the whole building is so subtly specific that it is hard to

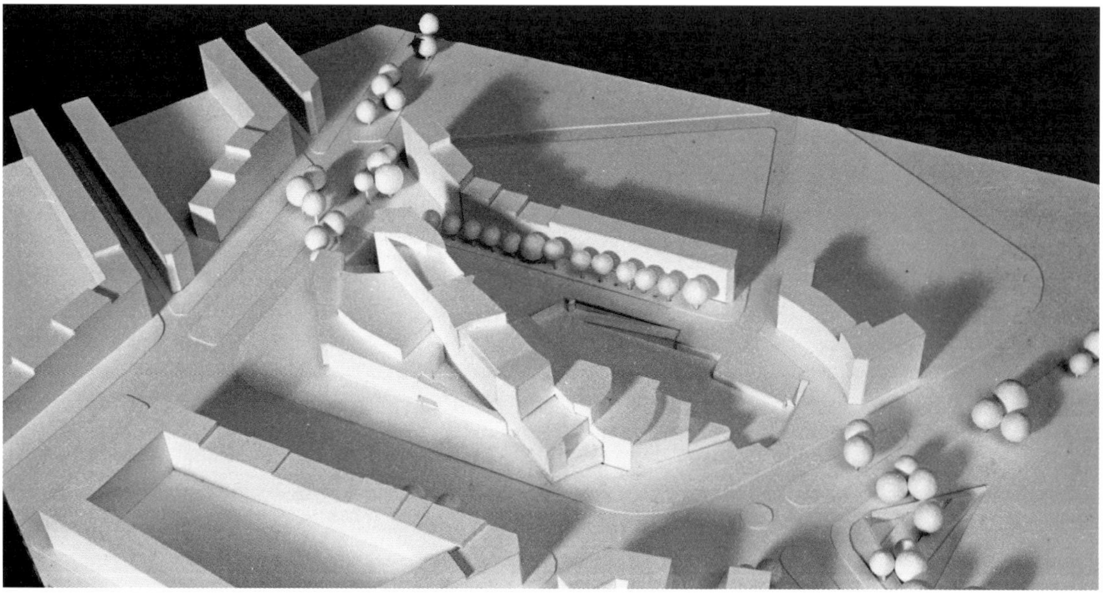

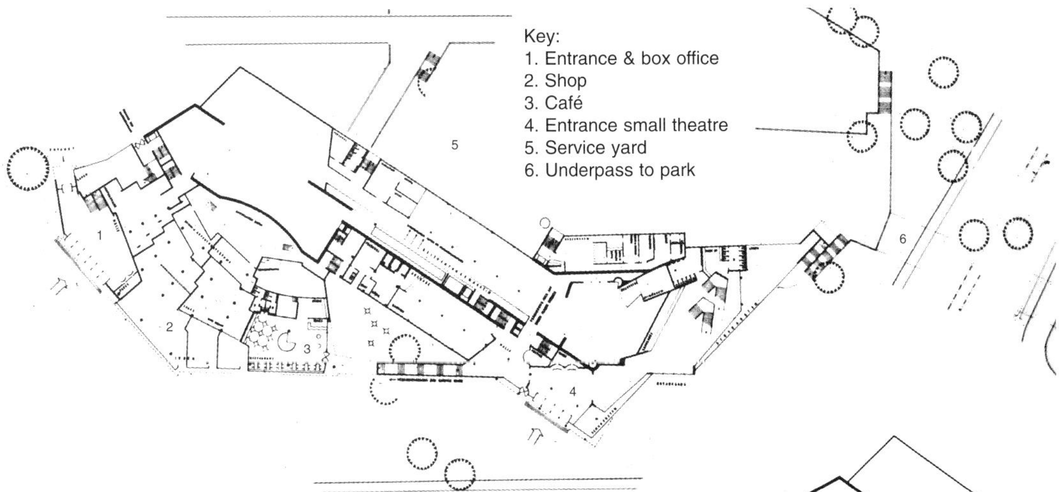

Key:
1. Entrance & box office
2. Shop
3. Café
4. Entrance small theatre
5. Service yard
6. Underpass to park

20. Ground floor plan. Entrances to theatres marked with arrows.

21. (right) Plan of large theatre at upper foyer level, main stair extreme left.

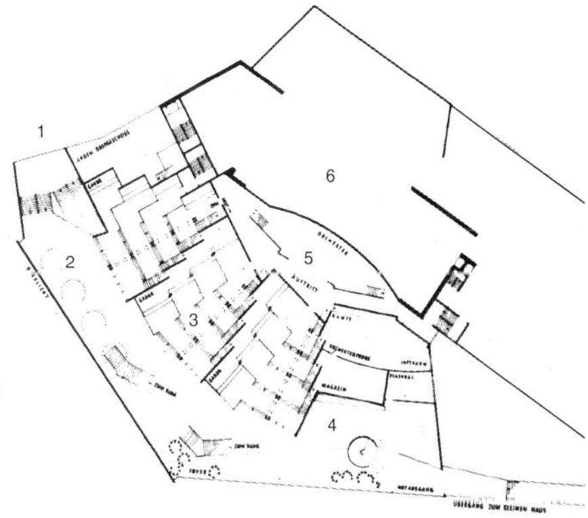

Key, right:
1. Main stair
2. Foyer
3. Coat counters
4. Bar
5. Orchestra pit
6. Stage

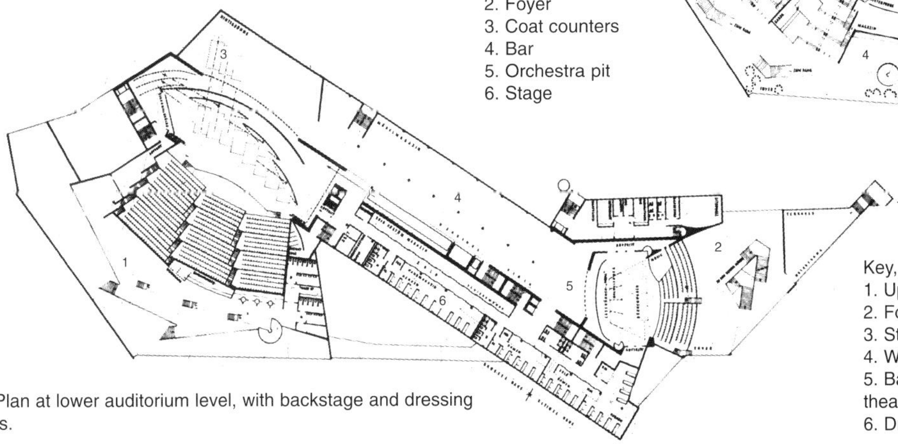

Key, left:
1. Upper foyer
2. Foyer small theatre
3. Stage machinery
4. Workshops
5. Backstage small theatre
6. Dressing rooms

22. Plan at lower auditorium level, with backstage and dressing rooms.

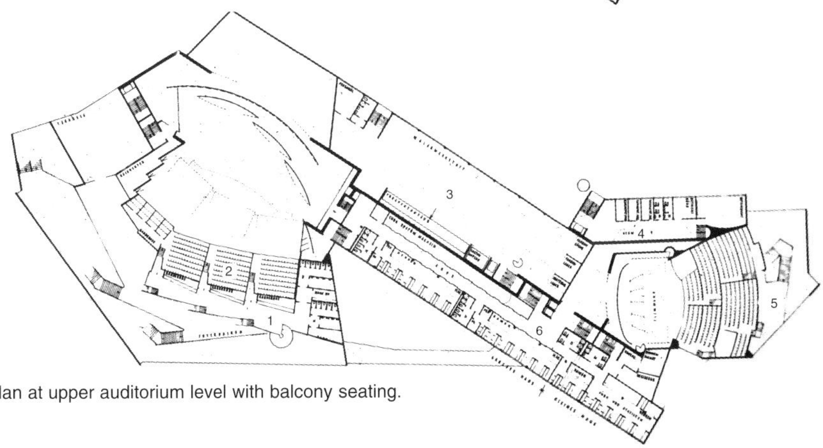

Key, left:
1. Top foyer
2. Upper seating terraces
3. Workshops
4. Administration
5. Foyer small theatre
6. Dressing rooms

23. Plan at upper auditorium level with balcony seating.

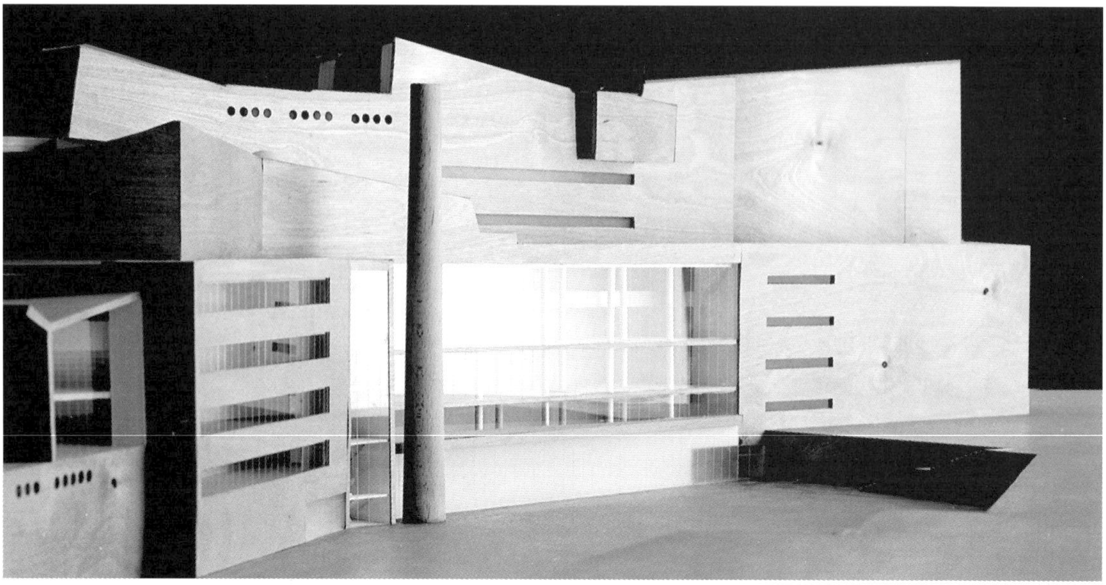

24. Rear of theatre with sunken service court, glazed workshops and heating flue.

imagine it convincingly adapted for another.[11] Goetheplatz is a square lying just outside the east corner of the original city, laid out diagonally in the nineteenth century to maintain a perpendicular relation to the ring-road. It is thus skewed by about 35° to the main grid, and Scharoun chose to exploit this angle-shift. In a stroke of genius, he set the low parts of his theatre parallel to the square, but the seven-storey block linking the two fly-towers with workshops and dressing rooms was placed diagonally in line with the adjacent grid. The border-line position on the old fortifications and the historic transition of geometry were thus dramatised in the new building form, and the transition was also ingested by the building to inform its internal spaces. The complete asymmetry which Scharoun wanted for his aperspective theatre was greatly facilitated by the angle shift.

Two theatres were required, large and small, which are placed at opposite ends and on opposite sides of the diagonal central tract. The large theatre occupies the major end of the site next to the ring-road, its corner entrance and superimposed bill-board facing south-west towards the city centre. The small theatre projects at the east end, forming a dynamic corner with the skewed road from the Neckar bridge. The south of the building is its most public side, addressing the square with both theatre entrances, a restaurant and several shops. The north side in contrast is a back, with big north light windows to its workshops and an industrial looking chimney from the underground boiler. It opens onto a sunken court for service and parking, but with an underpass to the low-lying Luisenpark beyond to the east. The building acknowledges its context in a very detailed way, and its massing is suitably assertive in the largely five-storey context. The decision to integrate offices, dressing-rooms, workshops and other such elements into a regular multi-storey block - a straight piece of Modern Architecture - provides an effective foil for the wildly irregular theatre-bodies, and gives the building an appropriately urban character.[12] This tract was to be crowned with a roof-top restaurant and a series of rehearsal rooms with projecting forms in which their internal order spills out - little theatres, special in shape like the big ones, signalling their presence across the rooftops of the city.[13]

The new concept of theatre

Although fascinated by theatres and their social and cultural role since his expressionist years, Scharoun built little during the Weimar period and Third Reich that was not house or housing. In the late 1940s he started to enter competitions, winning first prize for his unexecuted Stuttgart Liederhalle of 1949, but the hall interior was not very developed, giving little hint of what was to come with the Philharmonie. His ideas developed much further during the project for the Kassel Theatre of 1952.

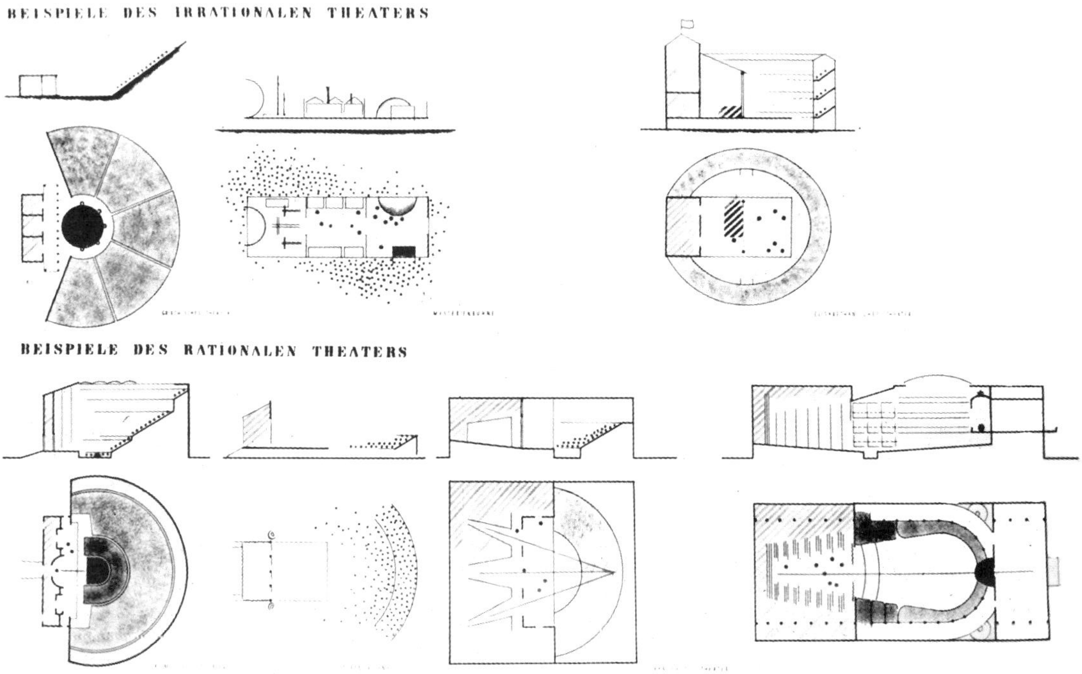

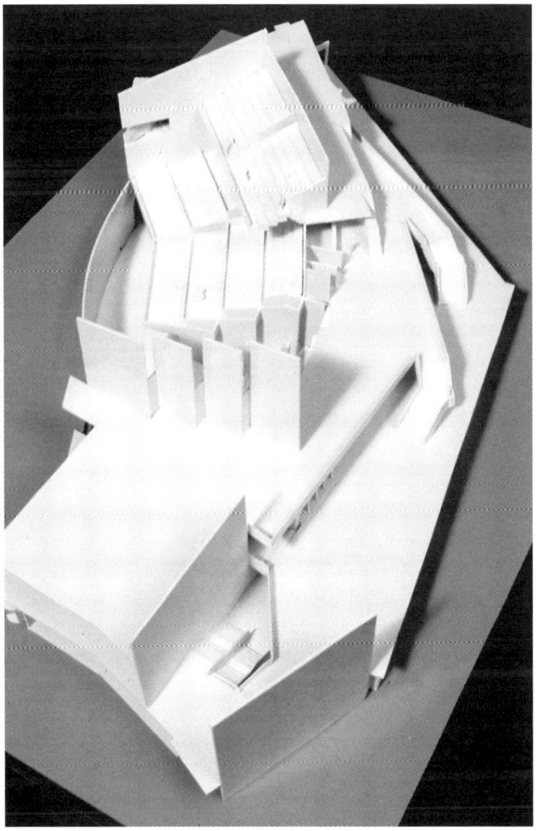

25. (above) Drawings submitted by Scharoun about the history of theatre, showing 'irrational' and 'rational' examples.
26. (left) Model of connection between foyer and main auditorium, made by students at University of Sheffield School of Architecture 1995.
27. (below) Scharoun's auditorium plan showing staging arrangements and their relation to audience seating. The 'aperspective theatre' was to have a wide deep stage to allow suspension of disbelief. Action would take place in a variety of locations as the play proceeded. There was no proscenium and orthogonal relationships were avoided.

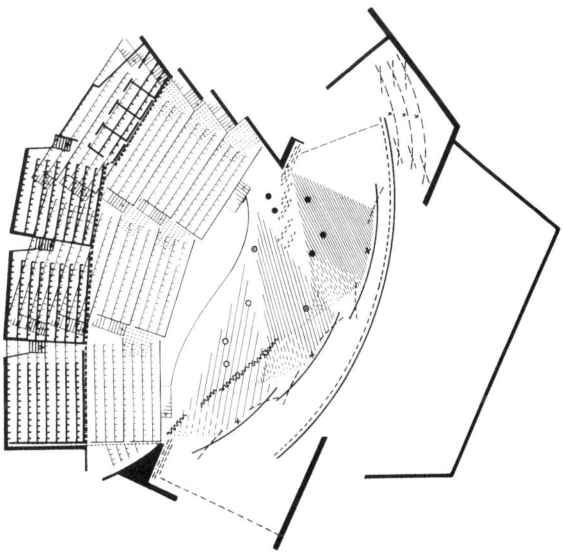

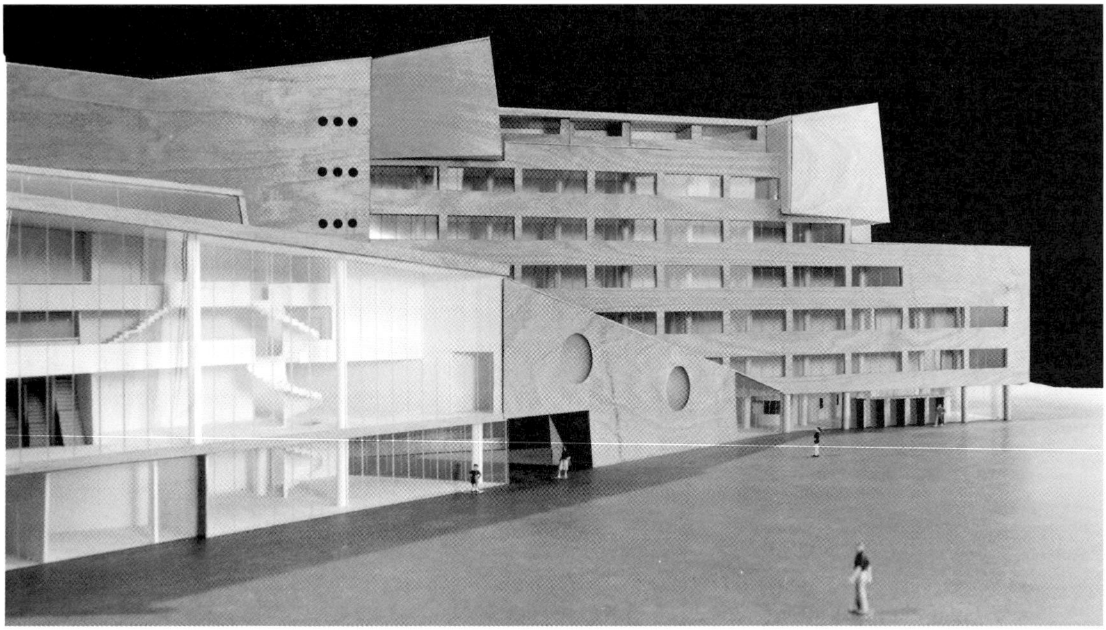

28. Model from front looking towards entrance to small theatre.

This was designed in collaboration with Hermann Mattern and theatrical consultant Wilhelm Huller. Having won first prize in September 1952, they were asked to develop the design for construction. The Mannheim project, designed during the closing months of 1952, came at just the right moment to profit from the detailed Kassel work, and its open brief seemed to invite a further exploratory step. Scharoun continued his collaboration with Huller over the staging arrangements, which became extremely radical: the first 'aperspective' theatre.

The main innovation of the Kassel project was a very wide stage, allowing flexibility of use and reducing the framing effect of the proscenium, but it remained axial to the auditorium and symmetrical, the stage/auditorium axis becoming the dorsal line for the whole building. In the Mannheim project there is no such axis, and the stage is even wider with no proscenium. The action was meant to take place in changing locations and even at different heights as the play progressed, moving out of the usual three dimensions into the fourth: scene changes were to be enacted by turning lamps on and off rather than with a curtain. Backdrops are shown as curved screens used in concave or convex positions, and in another drawing as stage wagons on a paternoster system set not perpendicular to the stage but obliquely. Placed neither axially nor symmetrically, the scenery also avoids becoming parallel with the stage opening.[14] The auditorium too is radically asymmetrical, with no symmetry between flank walls, no right and left entrances, and no central axis. Upper rows of seats run substantially askew of lower, and batteries of spotlamps occupying the left flank wall are not repeated on the right. The defining borderline between stage and orchestra pit is a shallow curve swinging from convex to concave.[15] The three banks of lower seats might suggest an axis of symmetry perpendicular to and centred on the middle row, but this would not be normal to anything on stage, and insignificant in the total plan. The conventional order of theatrical space was thus denied, and the components set in a much freer relationship.

The asymmetry was facilitated by the decision to divide up the crowd between separate seating terraces, each given its own entrance. Rather than being radial and centrally focused, the seating faces a variety of directions which may be in conflict: the angle shifts as much as 30° between lower and upper seats just left of centre. This varied orientation was partly in recognition that the action would switch from one part of the stage to another during a play, the audience turning their heads. It was also intended to stress that members of the audience were active participants with different viewpoints, metaphorically as well as literally. Scharoun spoke of 'neighbourhoods', as in town-planning.[16] The juxtaposition of the terraces would make the audience more aware of itself, reducing the contrast between spectators and action, giving instead the sense of a series of groups gathering together. The act of entering the hall was also carefully considered. Each bank of seats not only had its own entry and staircase, but also its own coats counter in the foyer beneath. This would guide people to their places and indicate the order of the auditorium externally, but the act of disrobing was also intended to help form the social group of the terrace, a moment of personal transition and revelation of the carefully groomed self to others of which Scharoun was acutely aware:

'...already with the giving up of a coat at the counter a person unclothes his or her individuality and integrates it into an ordered grouping, whose existence and identity only endures during this unique situation of experiencing the theatre space, for even in the intervals the individual rejoins the general public.' [17]

Spatial order and political order

The subdivision of the masses into recognisable groups of more or less equal status was connected with the political mood after the war, and is a powerful theme running through all Scharoun's architecture. It is found in the articulated class-rooms and differentiated grades of his schools, and in his housing with its individually planned flats, mixed in size, forming irregular blocks. Nothing could have seemed more oppressive than the events of ten years earlier, when massed ranks of obedient uniformed party members stood in silence at Nuremberg as Hitler walked Speer's great axis from the podium to the temple of fallen heroes. In the new democracy it was essential to escape all such blind obedience, to give everyone a voice and to reduce the scale of the group to manageable proportions, to forge organic links between those trusted with power and those who bestowed that trust. The hierarchy of the axis and of simple order dictated from the top had to be avoided.

Experience of Hitler only confirmed beliefs that Scharoun and his mentor Häring had already long held. Scharoun's post-war historical investigations of Berlin and other German cities showed a repeated contrast between a grown medieval centre and the later Baroque grid.[18] The grid - military based Mannheim is a clear example - was an abstract geometrical pattern reflecting single-minded political power, and was only achievable within such power. For Häring the grown town was 'organic' not just in shape, but in its complex accumulation of many gestures: it represented *Geschehensraum*, the space generated by human actions and occurrences.[19] His lifelong opposition to what he called 'geometry', which he passed on to Scharoun, was an opposition not to geometric techniques *per se* (which he certainly used) but to preconceived order of the kind found in Durand's typologies, Neufert's standards, planning and construction grids, proportion systems and other such abstract schemes. If allowed to dominate, such orderings repress *Geschehensraum*, the organic order generated by human activities and relationships, the order of route and light, of oppositions and adjacencies, of opacities and transparencies - the order understood in direct experience. Architecture must be free to develop its own *raison d'être* in relation to its place and role. Order must be discovered, not imposed.

For Scharoun and Häring, perspective was the epitome of geometrical power and control, implying orthogonality, axis and symmetry. And just as the Baroque city was a demonstration of ducal power with the Duke's residence on the central axis, so in the Baroque theatre the axis ran between his box and centre stage. The neatly framed spectacle was devised for his benefit, and optimally viewed from his central seat, with the auditorium plan a diagram of the social hierarchy. This Scharoun called the perspective theatre: it was most strongly exemplified in Palladio's Teatro Olympico, but also in the theatres devised for the French Classic.[20] Not only was this no longer socially appropriate, he argued, it also set tight bounds on theatrical performance. If suitable for types of 'rational' theatre for which it had been devised, it was unsuitable for what Scharoun and Aschenbrenner called 'irrational' theatre.[21] Greek theatre, medieval mystery plays and Shakespeare belonged to the irrational type because they dealt with metaphysical themes, themes exceeding a limited time and place. Presentation took place within the world under an open sky, often with contrasting levels for representation of different realms. The Renaissance brought the discovery of perspective and the beginning of rational theatre, which set man within the everyday world of other men, no longer

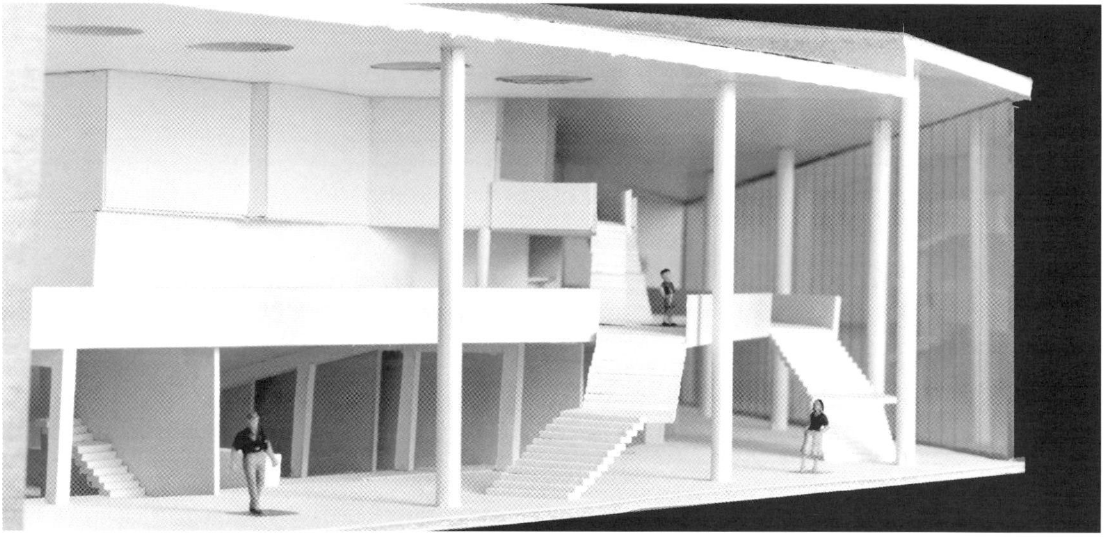

29. Main foyer in model with front billboard removed.

30. (opposite) Auditorium of the Berlin Philharmonie.

struggling with the powers of the Gods or the vicissitudes of fate. The stage was separated from the audience, creating a clear division of subject and object. Illusory sets were developed which further emphasised the division between play and everyday world. The 'aperspective' theatre[22] for Mannheim was intended to reverse all of this, and to create a new, more vital relation between action and audience:

'How can we bring stage and people together again in a convincing relationship? The form of the rational theatre with its fixed stage holds actor and spectator under the spell of the axis, allowing no escape from the force of perspective. It throws the public together in an anonymous and additive mass of individuals, grouped only by social rank. The irrational theatre, which permits dialogue between heaven and earth and vice versa, is not partnered by an audience in a cumulative mass. For in the irrational theatre the "other" dimension finds verbal expression, and brings togetherness, produces community. The audience is both saturated and divided by spiritual means, and here an important fact emerges: the irrational theatre has an educational role.... The irrational theatre instructs man in a higher knowledge of himself, and towards a higher truth and wisdom... It addresses the spiritual quality in people. It lifts them out of the perspectivist view into an aperspectivist awareness, and at the same time it delivers them from the space of the masses and of anonymous isolation, placing them in a room dedicated to emotion and feeling. The public is made a community through being moved and affected.

It is to the "affected" that the new auditorium is dedicated. They find their "place" not in an axial room, not in a piece of Formal Architecture, but in a spatial order which allows for their inner emotion and affectation. They are in the most personal way affected and not isolated. The aperspective view of things is by its nature an affected view. Under the power of its effect, the auditorium divides itself into sector-like groups which experience the events on stage from different angles, allowing each individual to interpret the same fate-like happenings in his or her own way. The place of the spectator is the place of the affected. Thus the question of communication between stage and people is solved anew in an organ-like manner.'[23]

Reinterpretation of the axis

Scharoun started his career under the spell of neoclassical ordering and remained axis-conscious, but he moved increasingly away from axial routes and axes of symmetry. Very early he discovered the potential of the switch in territories between differently orientated orthogonal systems, and by 1953 he could exploit it with great refinement.[24] By placing Mannheim's spine block diagonally, he brings the axis of the old grid into the site only to play it off against the order of the

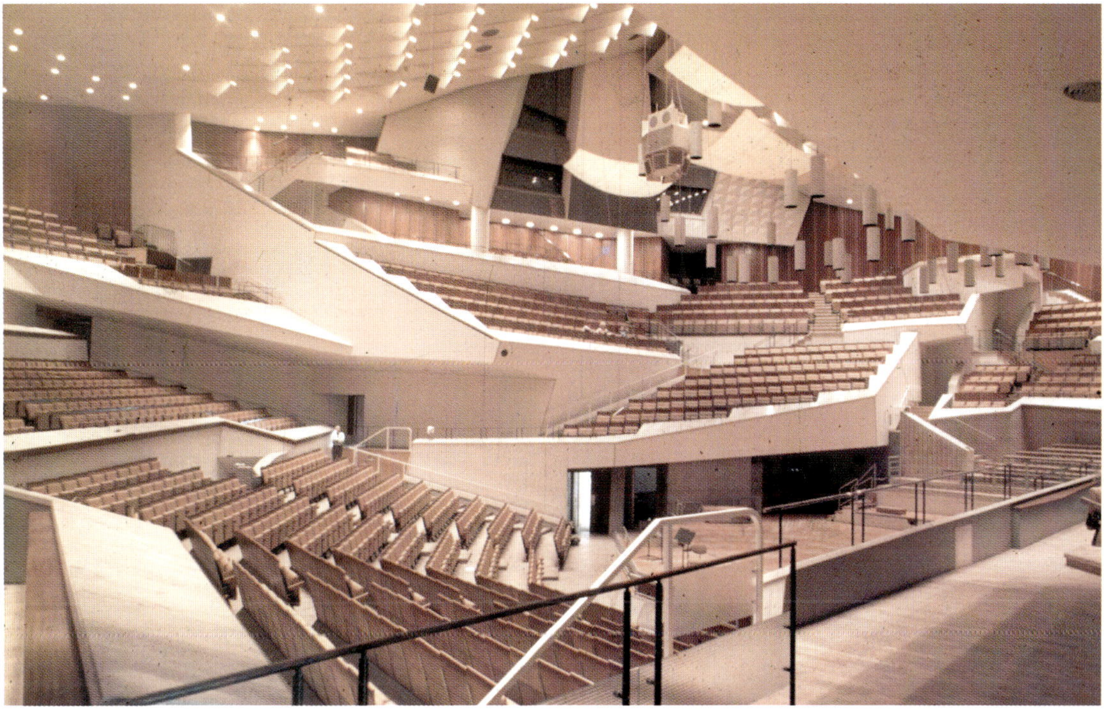

square. The building is subservient to neither order, indeed it reconciles them, showing itself to be a city-sized gesture rather than a mere local manipulation. The spine block - imagine it on its own - creates a generous space opening towards the vital south-west corner which one can imagine as a public gathering space, and here the seating banks gather against what seems from outside a great wall. It is already a kind of landscape before the foyer elements are added. Then a seemingly natural route develops, non-axial, but a compelling visual progression. The entrances lead via the box-office into the main stair at the extreme west corner. This controls a turn of almost 180°, leading all further movement anticlockwise around and in to the left, with running stairs carrying on up to visible galleries over, decreasing in size as they take less traffic. Stairs, walls and roof lights are directional devices to guide the audience, who ascend cascading levels until each finds his or her entrance. The first upper foyer behind the billboard has an urgent narrowness punctuated by regular roof lights, while the rhythmically rising stairs beyond beckon. As one moves through, the space opens out and there are places to wait on the left, a view out to the city on the right. As the running stairs finish a spiral takes over, a static stair absorbing the last of the movement into itself. One almost forgets that there was any 'problem' and hardly notices that the usual left/right entry structure has gone.

The foyer sequence of the small hall is equally assured: here again it is the pair of prominent main stairs that catches the rearward movement of the crowd, redirecting it into the back of the auditorium. The spaces are complex and irregular, yet the routes are clear and inviting. A sense of visual connections and hierarchies persists, but the neoclassical axis as route and centre of symmetry has disappeared. The logic lies in the flow and the experience of route, not in the imposing of measure on the earth (the original meaning of geometry), nor in the discipline of structure and construction.

Realisation

Unbuilt, the qualities of Mannheim might all be speculation, but we have a concert-hall version of it in the Berlin Philharmonie, designed in 1956 and completed in 1963. Its 'vineyard terraces' with their varied angles, perhaps the most important single innovation, are directly carried over. The foyer too follows and develops the principles of Mannheim with great success. Admired world-wide, the hall provides a new kind of concert experience for the late 20th century, and has been widely imitated. It would not have succeeded if it did not somehow meet the unconscious needs and expectations of its users, if they were not 'affected' emotionally when coming together to make and experience music, as Aschenbrenner's paper cited above predicts. Here is clear evidence that architecture does influence the way we think and act, not in the mechanistic or deterministic way sometimes claimed, but in the way it suggests, cajoles, reinforces, substantiates. No architecture can work without the complicity of users, and to gain that complicity it has to form a relationship with them, to persuade, to facilitate, to support and encourage, not to control and enforce. There needs to be a dialogue between architecture and life, and the magic of the Philharmonie shows that Scharoun achieved it.

Notes

1. For further information see Blundell Jones 1995.
2. On Scharoun's relationship with Häring see Blundell Jones 1999 pp. 191-194.
3. The debt has been acknowledged by Peter Wilson, Enric Miralles and Volker Giencke among others.
4. Scharoun seems not to have sought to disrupt the convention of the symmetrical orchestral podium, which Herbert von Karajan as client would presumably not have accepted. But he did propose an asymmetrical hall (unbuilt) for Saarbrücken.
5. Since the post-modernist reaction against Scharoun this misunderstanding has become so universally accepted that it even appears in the texts of those sympathetic to his work: see James-Chakraborty 2000, p. 109.
6. See Blundell Jones 1995, pp. 68-93, also Blundell Jones 1983.
7. The Kassel design, in partnership with landscape architect Hermann Mattern, won the competition of 1952 with a clear lead, and was developed for construction. Under scandalous circumstances it was cancelled after site works had begun, and the commission was handed to Paul Bode, who had developed a rival scheme. See Blundell Jones 1995, pp. 152-157.
8. *' In the architectural solution the city of Mannheim places special value on the creation of a theatre space to serve the people of our time'*, briefing document in the Scharoun Archive, Akademie der Künste, my translation.
9. Aschenbrenner (1900-1999) studied at Hamburg in the 1920s: literature under Robert Petsch and philosophy under the Neo-Kantians Ernst Cassirer and Albert Görland. She became an administrator at the art school Kunst und Werk in Berlin which Häring ran from 1935-43, and was subsequently Häring's assistant. She later edited his posthumous book *Fragmente*.
10. One of Scharoun's principal assistants at the time, and later the author of books on town-planning. He told me that these were his drawings, and clarified the content.
11. The sketches show the two theatres and spine block disposed at different angles on the various sites. Similar adaptations were later proposed for the Philharmonie on various sites in Berlin.
12. Much more urban, for example, than Scharoun's earlier and more curvaceous Kassel design which tumbled out of its square down a slope towards the river Fulda, a park-like setting.
13. The western rehearsal hall which projects both sides accommodates the staging system used in the main theatre. The eastward one has a sloping studio end window which is trying to twist around northwards.
14. A detailed report on the staging possibilities was provided by Wilhelm Huller. A copy is in the Scharoun Archive. The general principles of all the various mechanisms for introducing sets and platforms had been decided.
15. Perceptive readers may have noticed that this line is a regular curve in the general plans, and only takes this more complex form in the larger scale stage plan. This probably indicates a last minute decision furthering the bid for asymmetry.
16. *Nachbarschaftlich*: Hans Scharoun, in an undated typescript headed *Die Grundlage des Entwurfs bildet eine theoretische Unterbauung: Sie behandelt...* It was sent to Aschenbrenner in December 1952, and comes from her files.
17. Ibid. p.1, my translation.
18. For example, Darmstadt and Kassel, subjected to 'structural investigations' in relation to the Darmstadt school and the Kassel Theatre: see Blundell Jones 1995.
19. *' The given space in which the world of creatures moves, in which their life is played out, is a* Geschehensraum. *Geometry builds within the* Geschehensraum *a geometric space. This is concerned only with the space as conceived in thought, and does not engage with the* Geschehensraum. *It is a technical space-concept which gives an organisational framework to the building of a corporeal world within the* Geschehensraum. *This technical concept permitted the building up of a corporeal and material world, just as geometry provided instruction for the assembly of elements in space. But the system of coordinates has only a technical purpose: it is an instructive framework by which we control building in space. The realm of technical thinking works with a new category of space, with geometrical space... Even today temples and churches exist in* Geschehensraum, *and so do Mediterranean villages, and our Gothic towns along with their houses and castles, which we call appropriately "grown towns". Only the construction process was submitted to geometry until the geometrically planned towns challenged the form-power of the organic, and they did so only with partial success.'* From Hugo Häring *Geometrie und Organik*, 1951, reprinted Joedicke/Lauterbach Hugo Häring p. 66: my translation.
20. For example Peyre and Wailly's Théatre-Francais, Paris, of 1770.
21. A designation with which at the end of her life she was no longer happy, preferring the term multi-dimensional (letter to the author).
22. Scharoun saw the transition from perspective to aperspective as part of a profound and far reaching change of consciousness sweeping across society. The term was given definition in the book *Ursprung und Gegenwart* by Jean Gebser which appeared in 1949 and was avidly read in German intellectual circles.
23. Extract from Aschenbrenner's typescript *Über die Baustruktur des Theaters*, p. 12/13, in the Scharoun Archive, Akademie der Künste Berlin, my translation. This was written in close consultation with Scharoun, and at the end of the design period in December 1952. She commented: *'Scharoun wanted to substantiate his project with a kind of thesis-paper to clarify his idea of theatre in relation to traditional forms. He discussed this with Häring, and they decided that I should do the literary and historical research, so I received the commission. It was understood that Häring would share in the work in a supervisory way, as he was specially qualified to do.'* (Letter to the author, translated.) She was working in Biberach in daily contact with Häring, and communication with Scharoun's office was largely by post. Versions went to and fro, and included a long and apparently dictated typescript by Scharoun discussing in detail various types of theatre.
24. It was an essential innovation of the Breslau hostel in 1929, and became important for internal space with the Schminke House of 1932, see Blundell Jones 1995.

Chapter 14. Ludwig Mies van der Rohe: Neue Nationalgalerie, Berlin 1968

The National Theatre Mannheim competition of 1953 was introduced in the last chapter in relation to Scharoun's entry. The other most historically significant design was by Mies, then living in Chicago, and it is in many ways the complete opposite. While Scharoun sought to respond in detail to the site, Mies offered a general building type that could be built in any city or on any continent - truly an international style. And while Scharoun sought to reinterpret the nature of theatre for post-war democracy, Mies proposed instead a neutral, flexible building that could equally have been an exhibition space or market hall, simply a large glazed box with a wide-span roof suspended from external trusses. The stage was made as simply as possible and the auditorium seating with its staircases and landings was suspended in the void. The building's rhetoric concerned not its placing or function but its geometry and structure. Even the projecting flytower which gave the game away in the model was erased from some published photographs.[1] Mies evidently preferred the building without it.

In discussions with Hugo Häring when they shared an office in the 1920s, Mies already criticised Häring's intensely specific functionalist approach - the approach he later shared with Scharoun. Buildings change function frequently, Mies argued, so we do not know how they will be used. Rather than trying to predict, it is better to provide generous spaces which people can use however they like and adapt as they please.[2] Architecture is a kind of regulating trellis on which the plant of life can grow.[3] This generalising policy would allow some simple consistent types to be established, their materials used in a rational and efficient manner according to the disciplines of mass-production - the technology of our time, as Mies saw it. Steel must be used straight as it comes from the mill, details must be logically assembled and repetitive.

From the start of his career Mies showed a talent for simplification and reduction, boiling things down to their essentials and showing them with great clarity. This tendency was present even in his pre-modern work: the Perls House of 1911, though following models from Schinkel and Behrens, reduced classical capitals and entablature to a couple of lines. Clearing away all that is redundant, superfluous, confusing, Mies would hone what remained to perfection. The two aphorisms for which he is for ever associated are *'less is more'* and *'God is in the details'*.

We have seen how at Weissenhof he reduced the design of a block of flats to a few deft moves, leaving the floorplan as open as possible for others to complete and leaving the fenestration unspecific. Even his very first modernist projects show this essentialism. When designing his Friedrichstrasse skyscraper design of 1922, for example, he ignored

1. Mies, competition project for the National Theatre Mannheim 1953, photograph of original model as recently restored.

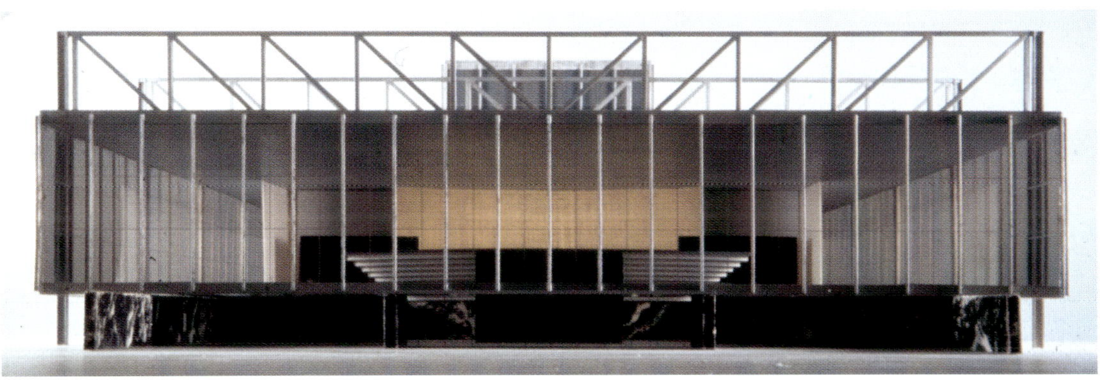

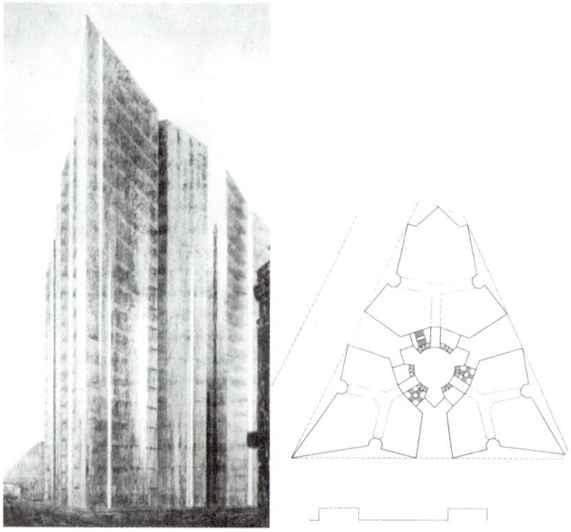

2. Mies, competition for Friedrichstrasse high-rise office building, Berlin 1922, perspective and plan.
3. (below) Mies, Apartment blocks at 850 Lakeshore Drive, Chicago 1951.

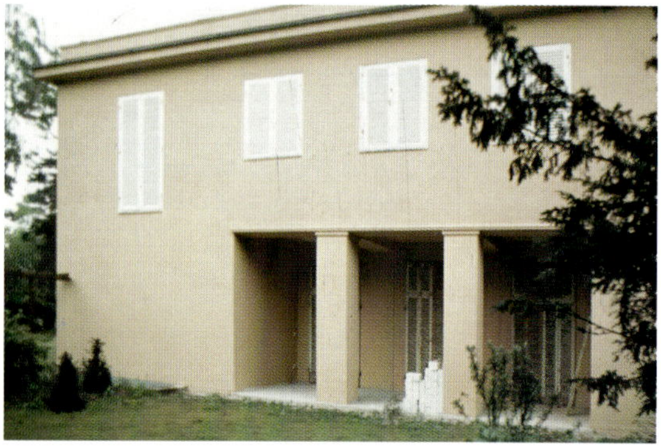

4. Mies, Perls House Berlin 1911: column capitals and entablature reduced to a few incised lines.
5. (below) Barcelona Pavilion 1929, destroyed and rebuilt in the 1980s.

6. (opposite top) Neue Nationalgalerie, Berlin, as seen from its platform.
7. (opposite bottom) Interior of the main space empty but for a few cycles, summer 2001.

much of the brief, and the only plan showed a typical upper floor.[4] As he had not made up his mind how to structure it, he omitted the supporting columns, yet his presentation of the design predicts quite brilliantly effects of transparency and reflection that architects would still be exploring half a century later. This assures its place in architectural history while other entries to that competition are forgotten.

After his later glass-box architecture (Seagram Building, Lakeshore Drive) was devalued by world-wide imitation in the 1960s, it is all too easy to undervalue the clarity Mies brought to the confused architectural scene in the 1920s, and to dismiss his originality. The failure of imitations to reach the level of the original may indicate lack of skill or persistence on the part of the imitators, but it also suggests hidden depths to Mies's work. His reputation certainly bounced back after the Barcelona Pavilion was reborn in the 1980s, and that building became a crucial example for the minimalist movement. It remains a pinnacle of modernist design, perhaps the clearest example of the new kind of space obtained by exchanging the box for a series of freestanding planes. It is all the more remarkable that despite advances in technology since 1929, nobody has yet made a work to challenge it.[5] What has gradually happened since the 1970s is that Mies has been detached from his immediate followers - the Miesians. The arguments about flexibility and technological rationality have been thrown into doubt, while on the positive side his classical heritage has been re-attached and his philosophical foundations revealed.[6] His work has

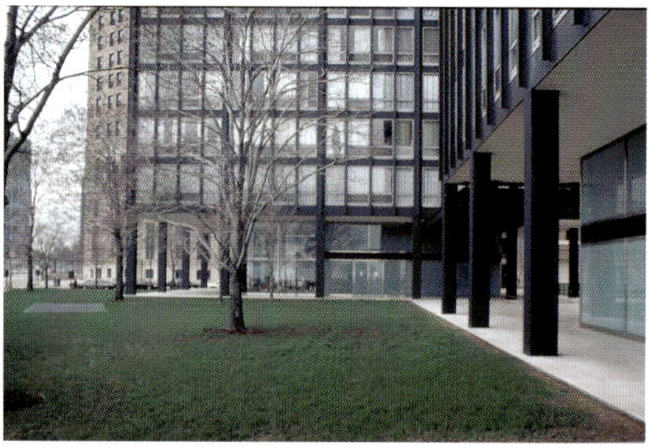

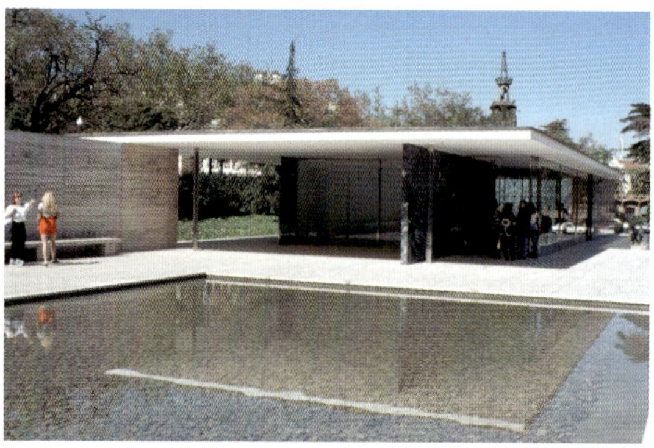

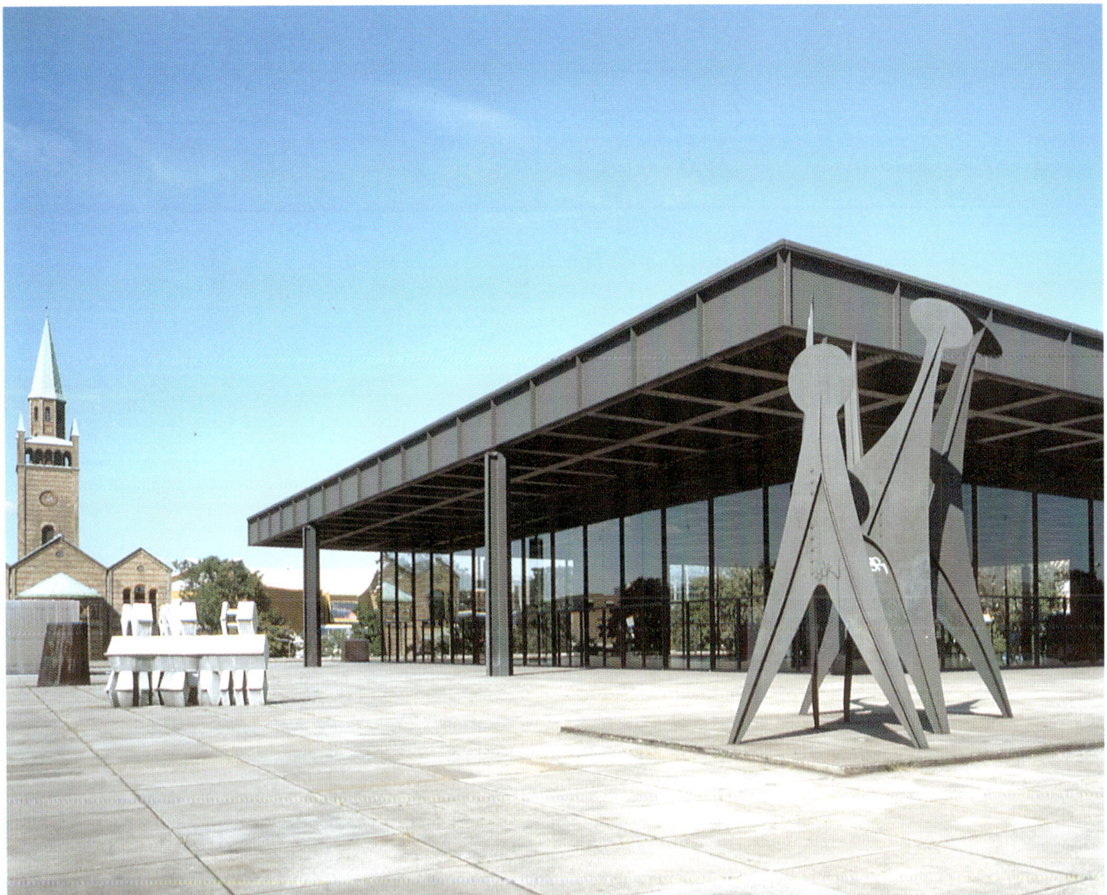

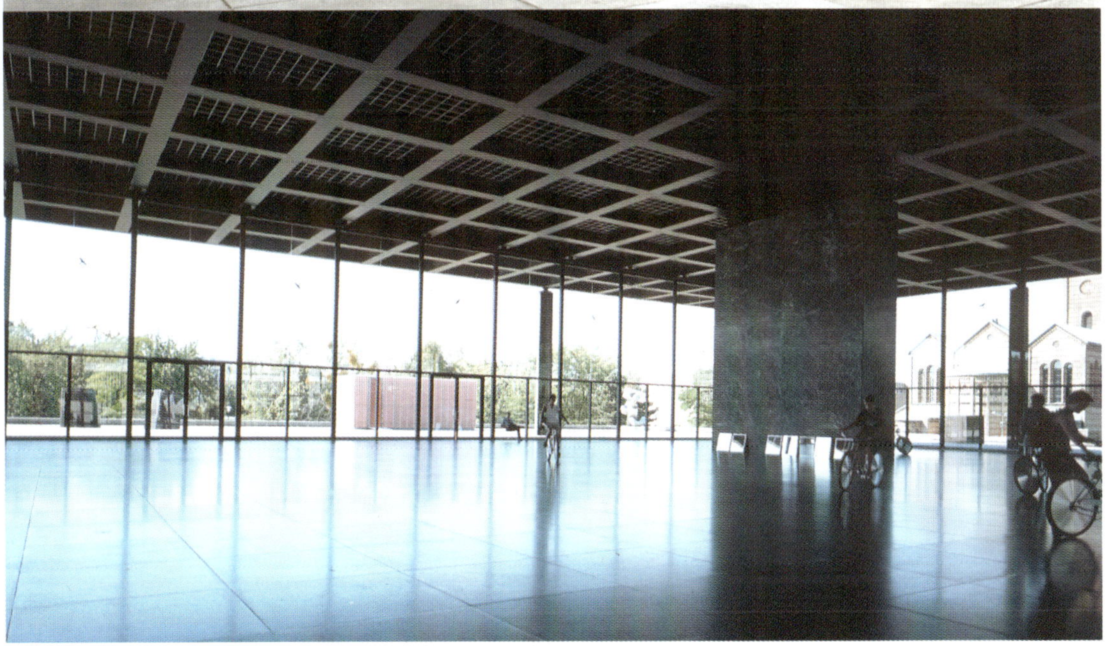

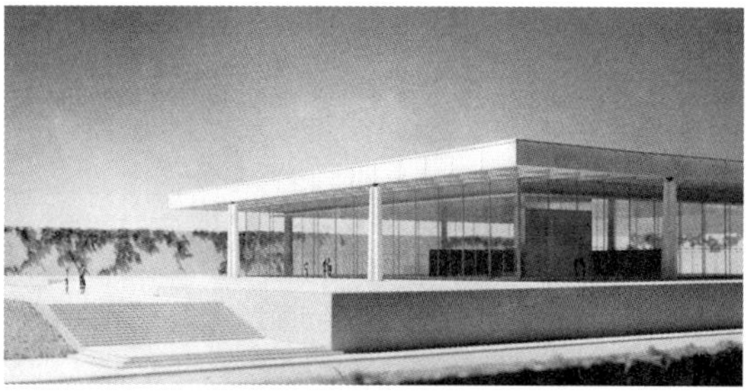

8. Mies, project for Bacardi HQ, Santiago, Cuba, 1958, first incarnation of the type to be used for the gallery; photo of model.

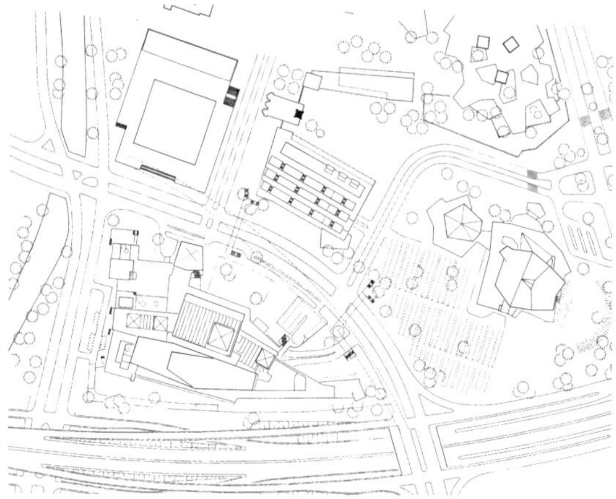

9. Plan of Kulturforum as prepared by Scharoun's office in the late 1960s: north is right. Neue Nationalgalerie is top left with Landwehrkanal passing to left of it, Scharoun's Philharmonie is mid right and State Library bottom left, setting its back to a motorway that was never built. The Senate-guest-house north of the gallery was never built and the site remains undeveloped.

become appreciated for qualities which, if intuitively felt by admirers in the 1960s, were at least not fully understood. These qualities are well demonstrated by the Neue Nationalgalerie, but it also reveals paradoxes at the heart of Mies's work.

Background to the gallery project

Mies's design for the National Theatre Mannheim was given second prize but remained unbuilt, while his reputation grew with major works in the United States. By the mid 1960s the Germans were getting embarrassed that they had no major work by this influential world master on his home soil. In West Berlin they were building the so-called Kulturforum, placed as a showcase close to the border with the East where the Wall was built in 1961.[7] It was to house cultural institutions whose pre-war buildings had stood at the old city centre but were now in the communist East.[8] Scharoun's Philharmonie, result of a competition in 1956, was the first building erected, but there were also to be a New National Gallery, State Library and other museums. In 1962 Mies was handed the commission for the gallery with a big budget and a fairly free hand. Required were a large exhibition space for the permanent collection of paintings, a temporary exhibition gallery, sculpture courts and ancillary spaces. Mies decided to rework a favourite unbuilt project developed in 1958 for the Bacardi Headquarters at Santiago in Cuba. It was a glazed hall with a square coffered roof supported on eight columns, two on each side. The glass wall was set back to free the columns and let the roof oversail. In a significantly essential drawing (below), Mies omitted the glass wall but included the pavement grid of the base, which meshes with the grid of the coffered ceiling. Visible control of space through strict geometric subdivision carried through to every detail states an ideal rational order.[9] This has nothing to do with the purpose of the building, though it necessarily dominates the construction, even though efficiency and convenience of construction were not the driving concerns.

While the Mannheim Theatre Project and many other late Mies glazed halls followed the normal convention of primary span across a rectangular space, secondary span along it, the gallery spans equally in both directions offering four identical

10. Project for Bacardi HQ, Santiago, Cuba, 1958, first incarnation of the type later used for the gallery; idealised drawing of the essential structure consisting of 8 columns and a coffered plate.

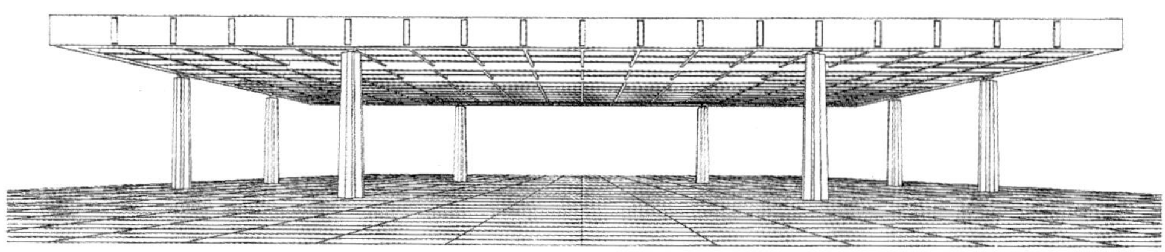

11. (right) Neue Nationalgalerie, plan of upper level, entrance right. North is top.

12. (below) plan of basement level.
Key:
1. stairs from above.
2. gallery.
3. sculpture court.
4. restaurant.
5. lavatories.
6. offices.
7. store-room.
8. delivery ramp.

N

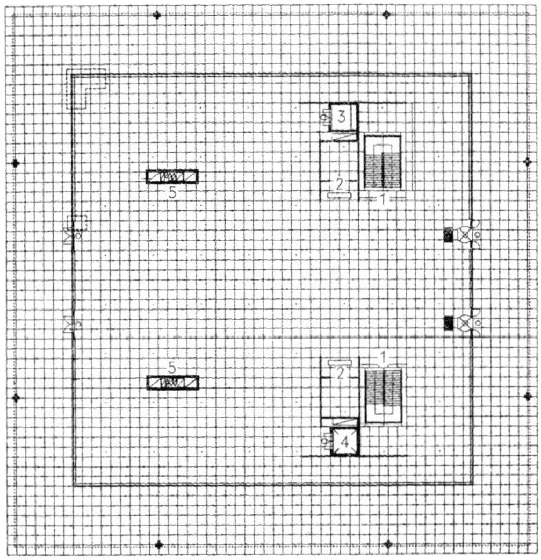

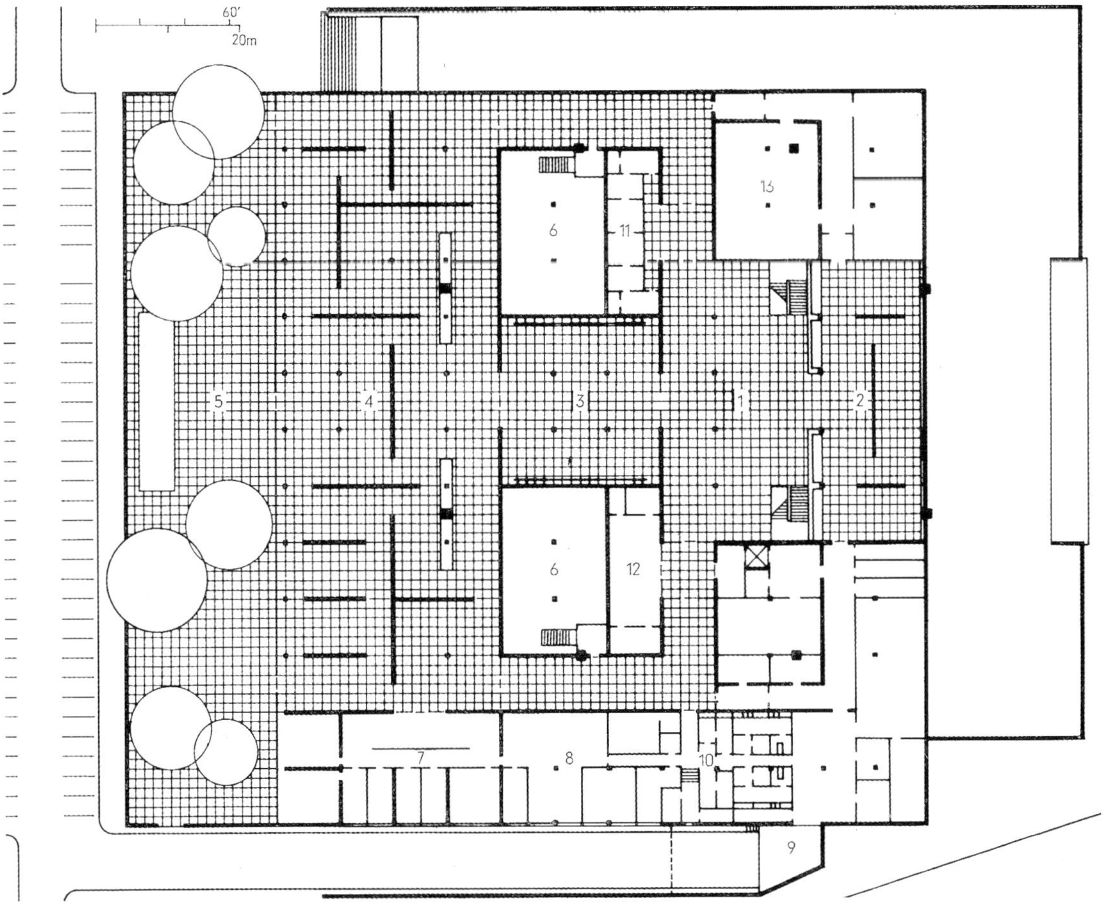

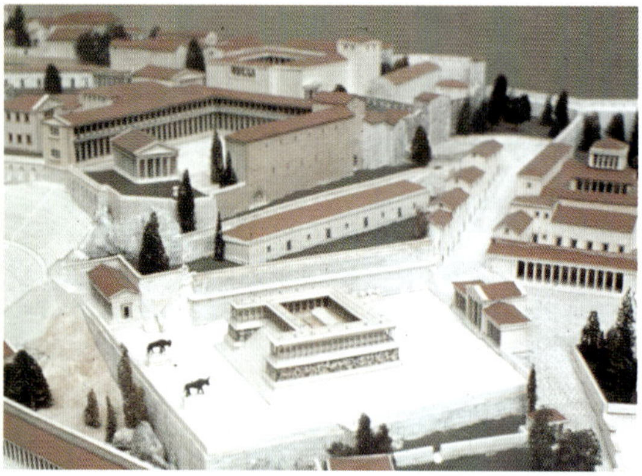

13. Model of Pergamon, Pergamon Museum Berlin. Bases absorb site irregularities leaving the temples pure.

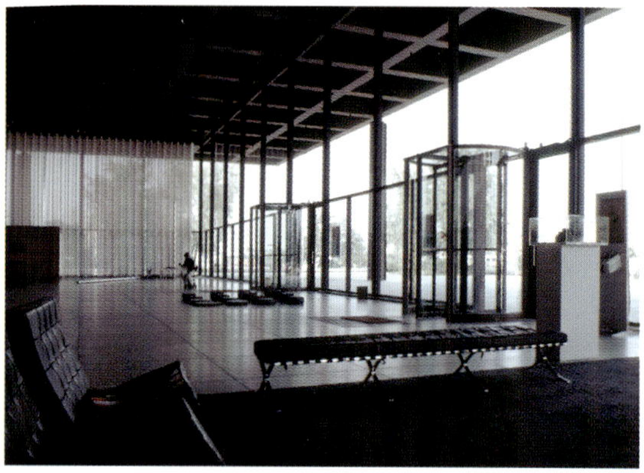

14. Gallery entrance from inside.
15. (below) Gallery, its base and steps from north-west.

façades. This is constructionally more difficult, as the members running north-south and those running east-west can no longer cross over each other, the one bearing on the other, but must occur in the same plane.[10] However, it does increase the building's purity, setting it in a special line of bi-axial centralised works of which the most famous is Palladio's Villa Rotunda. Such foursquare, four-fronted buildings are difficult practically to manage, since there are no sides and backs to absorb service functions. Their attraction is that because they address all directions they become more focal, more ideal, more obviously the centre of a world.

As first designed for Bacardi, Mies envisaged casting the building in white concrete, so the visible strips dividing the coffers of the ceiling would not have been the flanges of I beams as they ended up, but solid, and the cruciform columns would have been not crossing Is but with solid arms. Interestingly, the geometry of the entablature was to be expressed not by the vertical steel flanges finally seen, which appear structural, but instead by projecting bars of concrete cast on each beam line - a purely ornamental modern triglyph. In both versions these have the visual function of counting off the bays and asserting the building's rhythm. The change from concrete to steel may have been occasioned by different building conditions or by the impracticality of the concrete version with its heavier slab, which had to be given greater depth towards the centre where the span was widest, resulting in a slightly stepped ceiling.[11] The steel version allowed a flat ceiling, and Mies wanted the great slab to bear delicately on its eight supports,

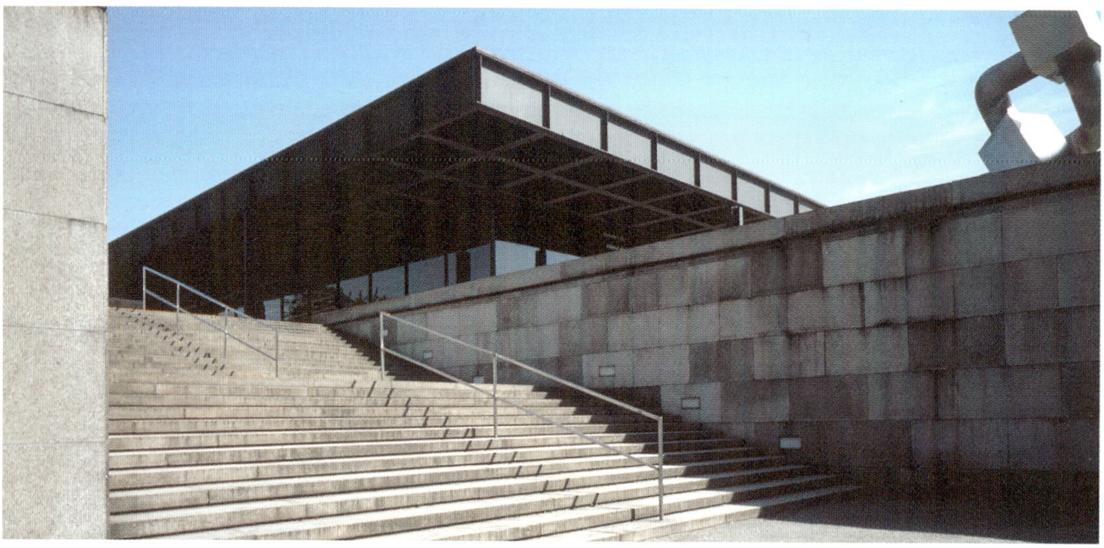

whose pin-joints are adored as a kind of modernist column capital.[12] Not only does this detail become thereby the most important in the building: it also makes the roof appear to float. Most people will never know how it was achieved, but the roof slab was welded together on the ground then jacked up one special day onto its columns, witnessed by Mies sitting in a white Mercedes. This construction ritual was for him a necessary part of the architecture. The pin-joints carry the memory of how the building was born, when it existed briefly as drawn in the ideal perspective, without the glass wall.

The presence of the building's base as a grid of lines on the perspective underlines the base's importance. In the reality of the gallery the base is also raised, creating a privileged terrace set apart from the city, from which surrounding buildings can be seen elegantly framed. It offers a perfectly flat plane against the variable ground below, and the squaring of its paving slabs asserts the building's geometry. Although completely orthogonal, the asymmetrical steps at opposite corners provide the adjustments needed to anchor the pure pavilion to the contingencies of its site, as with the temples of antiquity. The base is really roof, wall, support, and it contains most of the accommodation, but it is presented as magnificently simple, clad in polished granite slabs so large and thick that they appear to be its very substance and structure. The columns disappear into it as if into the ground, with none of the fuss of the pin-joint capitals applied to the column bases. The columns actually continue through into the basement and their stability depends crucially on this continuity,[13] but one cannot register their presence inside the building at all: two are swallowed by service ducts, four by walls and two occur randomly in storerooms. In his expression of structure, one must conclude, Mies is extremely selective.

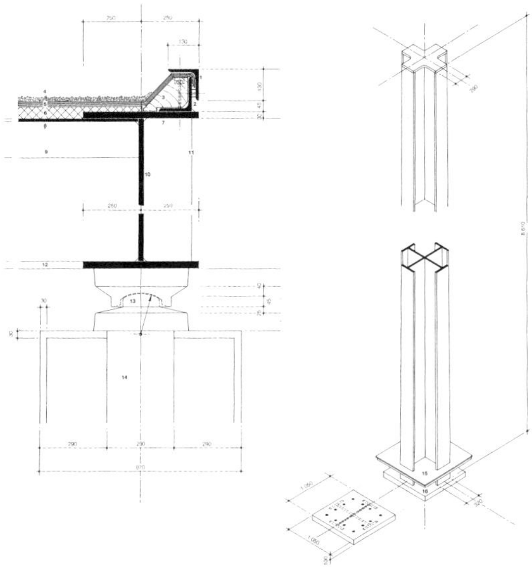

16. Details of column and pin-joint.

Beneath the surface

This whole opening description has applied to the sculpture terrace, entrance and temporary exhibition gallery. The visitor to the permanent collection ascends the base, enters by one of the paired revolving doors of the east side, then descends one of the paired dog-leg stairs to the basement. Here some of the best paintings in the city are presented in an *enfilade* of plain white air-conditioned rooms with suspended ceilings. Their symmetrical organisation acknowledges the axis of the entrance, but gives little sense of preferred route. The only daylight arrives sidewards from the sunken west sculpture court. Discreetly contained within a wall in continuation of the base, this calm rectangular outside space is one of the most impressive parts of the building, relieving the blindness of the basement. It provides a foil to the pavilion above, enclosed to the sides but open to the sky in opposition to the pavilion's open sides and closed top. Some of the minor public spaces in the basement are less inspiring: the café is completely internal, balanced by the lavatories opposite as if to underline filling and emptying as parallel services. In the early years, the café was merely a small room with seats and vending machines, though it has since been enlarged and softened in Viennese style by another designer.[14] Most of the numerous ancillary rooms are windowless apart from some offices on the south side set behind the screen wall of the delivery ramp, for it was essential to Mies not to destroy the monolithic appearance of the base.

A neoclassical monument

Impressively memorable, Mies's gallery succeeds primarily as a monument. It restates in a new way the very essence of trabeated architecture: column and entablature, the coffered ceiling. Thanks to the overhanging roof the new material glass is played

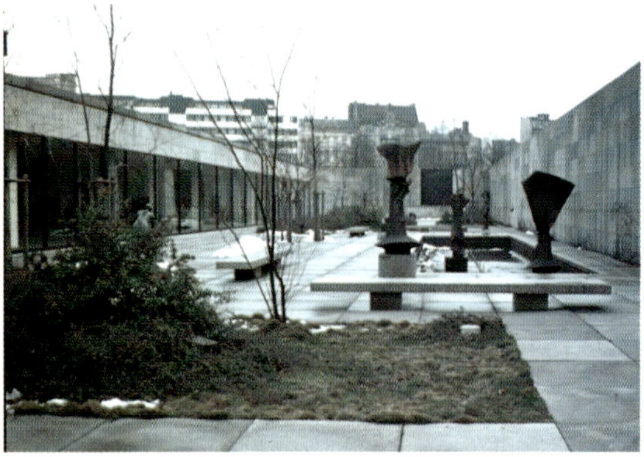

17. Sculpture court and east-facing glass wall to basement galleries.

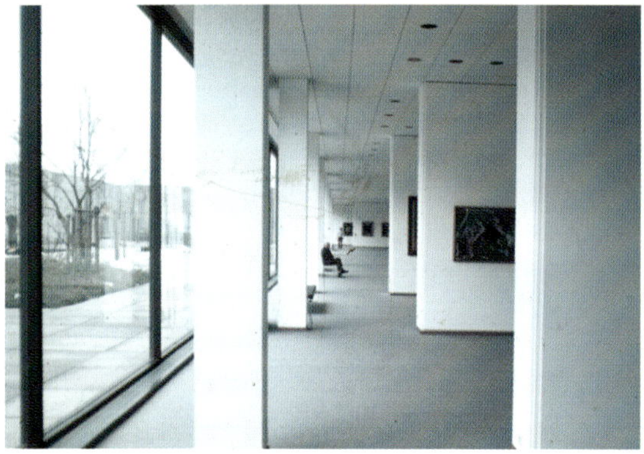

18. Sidelight in basement galleries.
19. (below) Schinkel Altes Museum, Berlin.

for its transparency as a flimsy screen, not for the reflections that would make it more solid. The gallery's temple-like form and canal-side placing refer respectfully to Karl Friedrich Schinkel's Altes Museum, not only one of Berlin's greatest monuments but also a major precedent for the building type.[15] Like Mies's gallery, Schinkel's museum puts much of its energy into approach and entry, and though in Schinkel's case progress is frontal, arrival is equally centralised. Mies knew it well. He had worked for Behrens during the neoclassical revival just before the First World War, as job architect for the St Petersburg Embassy[16] and was probably involved in the peristyle house for the archaeologist Wiegand.[17] Behrens was obsessed with Schinkel, urging his assistants to visit the architect's work.[18] The formality and sense of geometric control seem particularly to have influenced Mies, for both architects show the same desire for consistency between general plan and detail. Recently, for example, one test bay of Schinkel's rigorous Bauakademie has been rebuilt in Berlin, and one can already sense the whole from the part.[19] With Mies too, the ordering of dimensions is of extreme importance, so that everything fits and every corner turns, there is always the right number of bays, and the visible thicknesses add up. The building must be a finite geometric entity marching to its own rhythm.[20] Kinship with Schinkel is deep, and Mies's gallery is essentially neoclassical, yet its forms, spaces, materials and technology belong unmistakably to the mid twentieth century. This marriage of novelty and tradition is its greatest triumph.

Success as a monument was bought at a price, for the building does not work well as a gallery. Its artificially-lit basement spaces disappoint less in an age when curators fearing daylight are everywhere tending to dim galleries down, but in the 1960s architects like Aalto and Kahn took daylighting as the driving consideration in their art galleries with very inspiring results (see Chapter 16). Where Mies does allow daylight to enter from the court, it comes

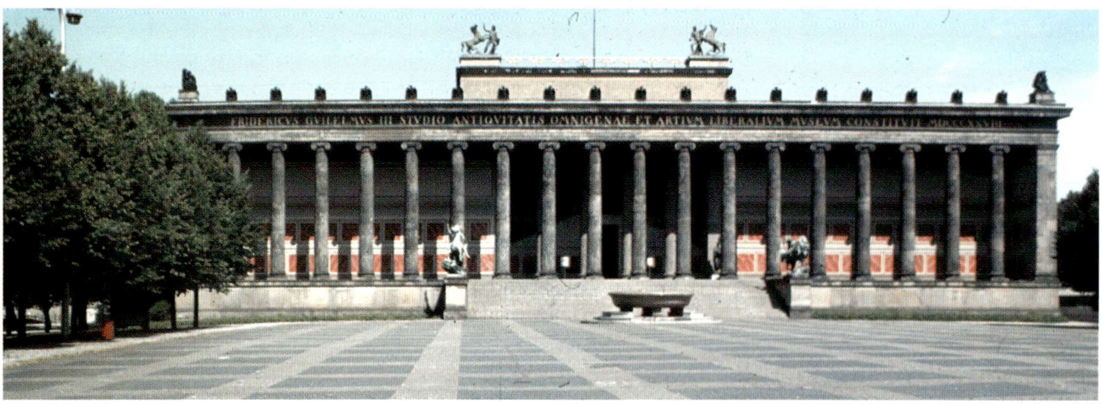

sideways, falling off in intensity across the pictures, and initially even the sun would enter at certain times. The temporary exhibition pavilion above is worse. Mies made tempting collages of paintings standing in front of glazed walls with views beyond, promoting the idea that the architecture - sketched in a few lines - would retreat into the background to allow concentration on the work. In practice the illumination of the works cannot compete with the glare behind. The effect is less disastrous with sculpture, but even then the building dominates. Recently an artist had the idea to bring in a few bicycles and let people ride around in the empty space (fig. 7): this 'artwork' gives in completely to the building.

Practice and theory

How does this late work of Mies stand up to the theories which he taught and claimed to subscribe to? With such an influential architect this is a vital question, and important for an understanding of Modernism. To propose essentially the same building for a company headquarters in Cuba and for an art gallery in Berlin suggests an independence from all local considerations: place, culture, context, climate, and purpose. Let us take these one by one. The building is almost certainly more appropriate to Berlin where Mies spent his formative years than it would have been to Cuba, but Mies's great success depended, surely, on his ability to cross global boundaries and make architectural statements that seem absolute. As a result of this success, many of his buildings could even be considered to be located more in a world of images than in any real place. The original Barcelona Pavilion was destroyed within months, so has been known for most of its mythical life only through drawings and photographs. Even the revived version belongs, arguably, to an international audience rather than to Barcelona or its otherwise forgotten exhibition. The recreation allowed new photographs (in colour) and created a site of architectural pilgrimage, often as confirmation of the building's existence in print rather than as the primary experience. Mies could not have foreseen this in the 1920s, and certainly the 'Bilbao effect' was nowhere in sight,[21] yet his work took to print immediately and would perhaps not have done so if more decisively located.

In discussing the relation of the building to the immediate context, though, it must be admitted that as usual Mies adapted his ideal building rather well. The steps to the bridge which erode the podium, the opposite ones leading to the cultural forum's proposed centre, the axial ones which declare entrance, the sunken court and relation with the canal: all are knowingly handled and tie the building to its site. Yet the design of the building itself owes nothing to the site. Mies juxtaposes it with the context, creating new relationships. It could as easily be placed in any other city, not just Santiago, unlike Scharoun's more essentially rooted proposals. Their Mannheim Theatre projects prompt direct comparison. Mies chose a rectangular type (fig. 1) to fit the site, and he set the larger theatre at the major end, but his figure remained symmetrical and avoided engaging the sides, unlike Scharoun's proposed shops and café to south, delivery and workshops to north, and entrance addressing the busiest corner. And of course, Mies did nothing with the site's history or street angles; that the plan was a precise double square demonstrated, rather, the operation of its own private geometry.

As regards climate, Mies is notorious for having promoted the type of glass tower in which the same kind of wall faces north as south, and whose windshape produces turbulence.[22] Most of his buildings have deep enough plans to depend on electric light if not also on air-conditioning, and many habitable rooms have no windows.[23] His later works - mostly in the United States - belong to a time of cheap and abundant energy, with no oil-crisis yet in sight and global warming yet unsuspected. Mies had good reason to believe that all climatic problems could be solved mechanically, and he designed buildings on this assumption. The upper gallery at Berlin is air-conditioned through a maze of pipes in the ceiling, which are connected to the basement plant by a pair of marble-clad ducts. This servicing provision was kept as invisible as possible: for Mies it is simply not part of the architecture.[24]

The matter of purpose is perhaps the most crucial one: Mies's main argument was about flexibility - yet how flexible does a national gallery need to be? It is hardly likely to get turned into a police station or a hotel, and if so might better be rebuilt. The displays of paintings are likely to change, but his basement areas offer only limited opportunities for repartitioning, while the pavilion above seems violated when used like a hangar and invaded by an independent box. Ironically, the main way in which national galleries do often need to be flexible is not anticipated by Mies at all: there is no provision for expansion, and it is hard to imagine a

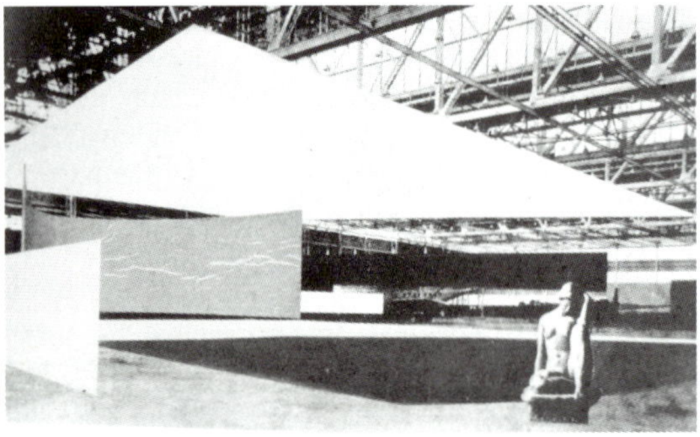

20. Mies's collage proposal for a concert hall, 1942.

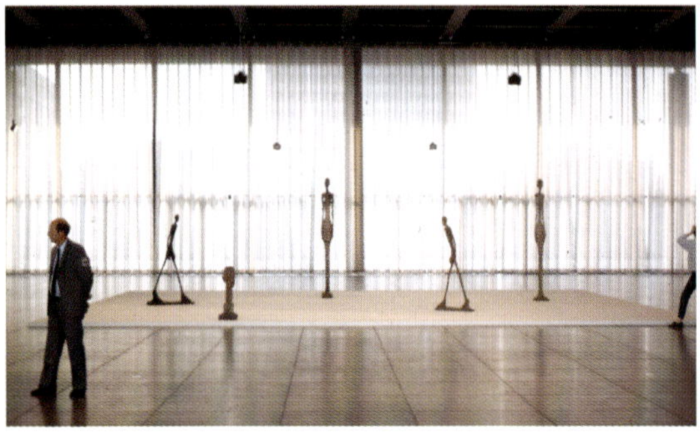

21. The Neue Nationalgalerie pavilion during a Giacometti exhibition.

suitable strategy. All in all, the flexibility argument does not hold, and it is equally dubious for many other Mies works. With nothing between its freely suspended auditorium and glass skin, for example, his Mannheim Theatre promised insuperable problems in terms of both lighting and acoustics, which is perhaps why it was not taken up. Mies's seductive collage about making a concert hall in an empty factory by throwing up a few free-standing partitions (above) was equally unrealistic. Unlike Scharoun and Häring, whose design philosophy demanded that a building be shaped by place and purpose, so that these became the inescapable raw ingredients of design, Mies tried as far as possible to ignore such shaping agents and pushed towards the opposite extreme. He tried to free himself from all functional considerations, to concentrate on perfecting his ideal types and their rules of assembly. The flexibility argument provided the perfect alibi.

Rational construction?

The gallery also poses difficulties for the Miesian arguments about rational production and use of materials. His apologists often refer to his appropriate use of materials, and there is no denying his sensitivity to their qualities and textures,[25] yet if the same building can be designed in concrete as in steel, it can hardly be regarded as bound to either. The changes between the two versions are remarkably subtle, but the message is that form transcends material. While undermining Mies's modernist arguments, this reflects interestingly an earlier debate about Gothic cathedrals and Greek temples. While the Gothic Revivalists - notably Pugin, Ruskin and Viollet-le-Duc - interpreted Gothic arches and buttresses as an appropriate use of stone, ridiculing classical trabeated construction as primitive, the classicist Konrad Fiedler argued back the other way. Accepting that temples were derived from timber prototypes and built in stone, he claimed that this showed the primacy of form. Stone made them more enduring, the all-important form being retained.[26] Form transcended material, as it does with Mies. This primacy of form also explains why the structure, though impressive in its way, was no elegant engineering solution like those of Nervi (Chapter 9). In no way minimal for span and load, its constant depth denies all sense of the play of structural forces. Furthermore, a constructional headstand had to be performed to prevent the real structure deviating from the ideal form: it was predicted to deflect by around 100mm. This was counteracted by building it to an upward slope towards the centre, so that it settled precisely flat when hung on its columns. Geometry conquers nature, the ideal conquers the real.

The gallery was a relatively expensive building for its size, despite its apparent simplicity, because of the relatively large pieces of costly materials and the precise assembly required. Sizes were dictated by the design rather than accepted from the market, and the steel was certainly not used as it came from the mill. The tapered columns must have required hours of welding along their length, let alone the great plate roof with its endlessly intersecting members. Furthermore, Mies insisted that all visible welds be ground off and painted over: all painstaking work by hand to give the impersonal look of the machine.[27] Believing that he needed to discover an appropriate spirit for the age, Mies developed a machine aesthetic of great power that was made, with difficulty, by hand. Convinced that the future lay with serial production, he distilled poetry from its supposed disciplines,

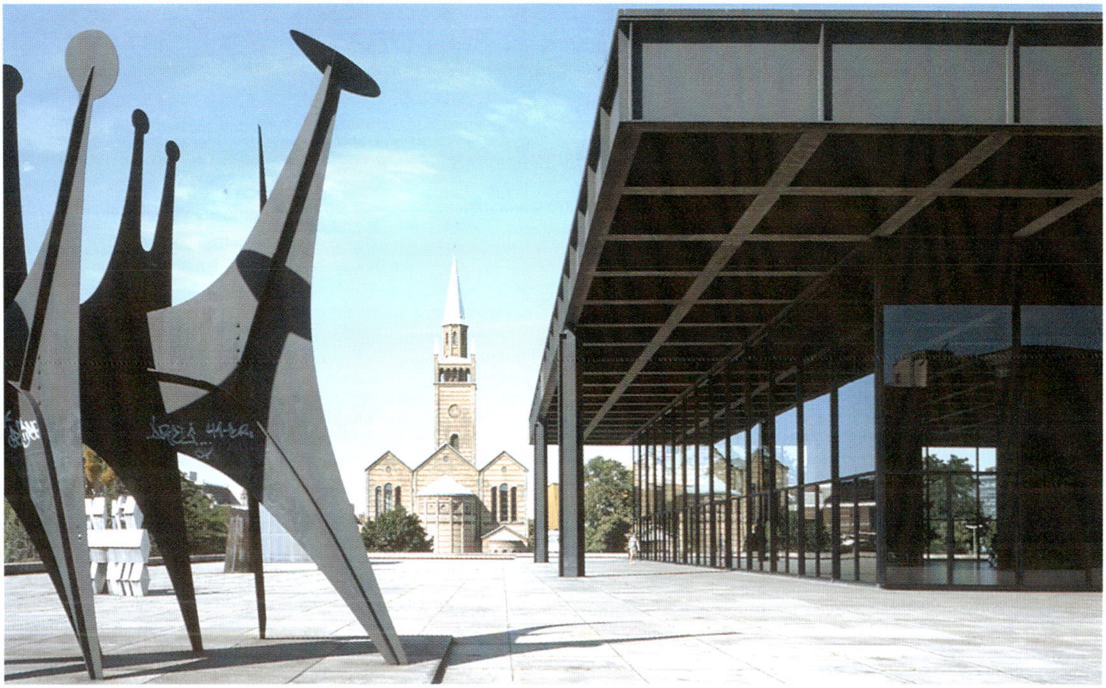

22. East side with St Matthew's Church beyond - the only surviving pre-war building on the site.

and he refined prototypes without worrying about the realities of economic production or the implications of repetition.

Finally it has to be admitted that the gallery was a one-off, expensive, hand-made building, like other prestigious cultural projects before and since. One would hardly expect a national gallery to be done in any other way, yet Mies and his apologists claimed to be producing repeatable universal types. Taking them at their word you could imagine a line of national galleries with the first as museum, the second as corporate head-quarters (as formerly intended), the third as a bank, the fourth as a furniture showroom, etc. The building might adapt to these uses, but repetition would devalue it, and use for varied purposes would also destroy any specific associations. The point need hardly be laboured: the building as a monument needs to be unique, and flexibility was never really the issue. But the *idea* of flexibility provided the excuse for abdication from functional issues that allowed Mies to pursue his ideal types, to produce his absolute architecture. He once admitted to *'trying to bring a little order into the desperate confusion of our time'* and in the clamour of contemporary Berlin, retreat into his gallery as a haven of calm can be appealing. The purity, the reduction, the *beinahe Nichts* (almost nothing) of which he often spoke was an ideal tidy world with nothing out of place, perfect order in a perfectly ordered system.[28] This is perhaps why Mies's buildings are at their best when empty, and why the Barcelona Pavilion proved such a perfect task for him. Such escape from dirty reality also motivates today's Minimalists and is perhaps why Mies has become their patron saint. It requires the drawing of boundaries, both physical and metaphorical, to keep the pollution out. To expose the ideal, much must be excised: purity in its sheer exclusiveness is both a strength and a weakness.

The building's failure to engage with life save as a very loose frame is also what makes it seem so fascinatingly timeless. It is abstraction, not empathy.[29] The celebration of perfect geometry - a square is a square is a square - evokes a platonic world untouched by the ravages of time and nature. If a building can be detached enough from use to remain aloof to change, it is perhaps not so much in a state of open flux as totally still, not so much built for change as altogether to avoid it, becoming the only constant. One can imagine the Neue Nationalgalerie filmed by time-lapse camera over decades, over centuries even. Days and nights, summers and winters come and go; exhibitions change; adjacent buildings rise and fall; uses and meanings change; strange people arrive speaking strange new languages: yet the one constant is Mies's building, periodically repaired and repainted but always there in its pristine purity.

Notes

1. Photos of the Mannheim model are in some Mies books printed complete with fly tower, but in the double page photo in Blaser 1965 pp. 104-5, it is excised.
2. In German on the gramophone record of an interview with Mies published by *Bauwelt*, reported verbally to the author and in his writings and lectures by Julius Posener, also cited in Neumeyer 1991.
3. Julius Posener's metaphor, verbal communication.
4. Compare with Häring's entry, where great attention is given to the ground floor containing cinema and shopping arcade: see Blundell Jones 1999 pp. 40-41.
5. It has even recently been used in the UK in television advertisements for Renault cars, as a symbol of the most chic modernity.
6. Particularly Neumeyer 1991.
7. The Berlin Wall was not anticipated, but the antipathy of the cold war was already present, and while the original centre and east part of Berlin had been in Russian hands at the end of the Second World War and became capital of the DDR (East Germany), West Berlin was controlled by England, France and USA, becoming an island of intentionally visible liberalism within the Eastern block. The Kulturforum was built at the edge of the Western sector to be as close as possible to the centre after reunification.
8. The original National Gallery on Museum Island at the old centre is under restoration at the time of writing.
9. There are 18 bays of 12 feet / 3.60 metres in each direction, and the columns are placed 5 bays in, with 8 bays between them. The latter number of bays being even, the centre-line falls on a bay division and cannot permit entrance, so there have to be paired doors. Mies revised the dimensions in relation to the Bacardi proposal, whose bay size was around 10 feet 5 inches.
10. In structural terms it becomes a space frame, and Mies showed his interest in this for its structural as opposed to purely formal character with a larger version, his Chicago Convention Hall project of 1953.
11. The section is given in Frampton 1995, p. 204.
12. *'Ornament is the adoration of the joint'* Louis Kahn (Ronner & Jhaveri 1987, p. 345). The pin-joints are inevitably reminiscent of those at the bases of the portals in Behrens's Turbine Factory of 1909, iconic images of early modernism.
13. They have to take all lateral pressures, particularly wind-loading, through a relatively narrow section, and so must be seriously stiff, unlike stone classical columns which merely bear downward.
14. The vending machines were in place when I first visited it in 1972. This was long before the era of the *'nice café with a museum attached'*, but Mies's apparent indifference to the ritual of hospitality was still surprising. The current Viennese café works well, a happy example of Mies's work completed by others.
15. It was one of the first public museums, built in 1823-30, with antiquities below and paintings above, see Pevsner 1976, pp. 126-128.
16. Mies worked in Behrens's studio from October 1908 until January 1912 (Anderson 2000 p.166); on his participation in the Embassy, ibid p. 313, note 45.
17. Neumeyer 1991 p. 46.
18. Anderson 2000 p. 170.
19. *'Schinkel strove in all his buildings to combine the rationalistic order with the poesis of construction... This romantic synthesis was facilitated by the precise articulation of components... A similar elementarism is detectable in the work of Mies...(who acknowledged the debt , remarking) in 1959 "In the Altes Museum he (Schinkel) separated the elements, the columns and the walls and the ceiling, and I think that this is still visible in my later buildings".'* Frampton 1995, pp. 203-4.
20. At IIT Mies claimed that *'the eternal laws of architecture (were) Order, Space, Proportion'* (Frampton 1995 p.186 after Carter), but his approach was very different from the mathematical abstractions of Le Corbusier, and grounded rather in a builderly sense of how things fit together. Mies tended to work in modules of whole numbers in metres or feet, and with simple whole-number ratios. Typically, the Mannheim project was a double square in plan 80 metres by 160 metres, with window panels between the main mullions 4 metres wide and 12 metres high. Each of these consisted of 6 glass sheets 4 metres by 2, following the same module as the floor slabs.
21. Joseph Rykwert comments that Frank Gehry's Guggenheim Museum in Bilbao has *'focused attention on the city in a way no other building has done, and emphasised the fact that the institution of the museum can create a new kind of public ambience.'* Rykwert 2000 p. 238.
22. Working in Sheffield University Arts Tower, a 20 storey homage to Mies by Gollins Melvin & Ward completed in the late 1960s, I have first-hand experience of this type. The excessive glazing brings solar gain in summer and cold in winter, and in high winds it can be difficult to enter without being blown about. The rectangular box-like form of that period, following the rational assembly of the frame, completely ignored the question of aerodynamics.
23. Internal rooms in the gallery can be seen on the lower floor plan. Most of the offices and dressing rooms in the basement of Mies's Mannheim Theatre Project were completely internal, and at Crown Hall, IIT, several offices have no connection with the outside world.
24. In notable contrast with the work of Louis Kahn, see Chapter 16 (pp. 229-240).
25. In choice and treatment of materials Mies was extremely fastidious: the Barcelona Pavilion was planned around the dimension of a chosen onyx block, and bricks for his houses were sorted for firing variations, see Frampton 1995, pp.169-171.
26. Herbert Read, *The Aesthetics of Architecture*, Architectural Association 125th anniversary publication, London 1972.
27. The elegant scissor-like joint of the famous Barcelona Chair was particularly difficult to achieve. A considerable mass of material had to be built up by the welder only to be ground off again to create the curve. The result, of course, is wonderful (verbal information from Thomas Stevens).
28. We hardly need the stories of Mies's legendary neatness - putting disturbed chairs back to axial positions, reluctant to allow Mrs Farnsworth a wardrobe - to make the connection with pollution-avoiding behaviour. In her classic *Purity and Danger*, anthropologist Mary Douglas makes the point that dirt is not so much a question of hygiene as of *'matter out of place'*: it has to do with ordering and classifying the world (Douglas 1966).
29. The terms are those of Wilhelm Worringer, aesthetic theorist at the turn of the 20th century. His reading of abstraction - applied to the 'primitive' and Gothic - was that geometric patterns reassure us because of their unchanging nature, as opposed to the confusing flux of everything else in life. While the interpretation of the material to which he applied it is now completely outdated, the polarity empathy/ abstraction is still suggestive (Worringer 1953).

Chapter 15. Sigurd Lewerentz: Church of St Peter, Klippan, Sweden, 1963-6

The wall is rough brick, very rough with unusually wide joints. The pointing is not raked or trowelled as usual but 'bagged off', crudely wiped with an old sack, causing the bricks to be smeared. From time to time this texture is relieved by another in acute contrast: a pure semi-reflective plane of glass with a perfect silver edge, evidently applied to the outside of the wall. Its delicate form is held in position by the crudest means: a bracket in each corner secured with two screws. This window in St Peter's Church Klippan, by Sigurd Lewerentz, is a favourite with architects, for once seen it is never forgotten; but it is only imitated by the brave. First a brick hole is formed, a pure rectangular void surrounded by a pure brick edge. A thick layer of mastic is then applied to the outside face of the hole, and a sealed double-glazing unit a few centimetres larger is pressed into place, the brackets screwed on to retain it. From inside there seems hardly a window at all, for the glass remains invisible and frameless, simply a brick hole in a thick brick wall. On the outside the precision and fragility of the glass contrast poignantly with the brutality of the brickwork. It is of course a fixed window, ventilation being supplied by other means.

This arresting detail is typical of numerous instances at St Peter's when assumptions about building methods and 'good practice' are apparently thrown into question. It produced a new and unexpected architectural vocabulary, but it can also be read as a commentary on the significance of expressed construction, on deriving a building's identity from its tectonic nature. St Peter's was Lewerentz's last major work, begun when he was 78 years old, and carried through with great fastidiousness and constant site-supervision. It is as extreme a statement in its different way as Mies's gallery described in the last chapter. The two buildings were conceived and built at more or less the same time, and the two architects were almost precise contemporaries, Mies born in 1886 and Lewerentz in 1885. Arguably, they were equally obsessive in their pursuit of materials and detailing, and equally indebted to the Classical Tradition, but Lewerentz's work moved in quite a different direction from Mies's. From the beginning of his career, he was interested in irregularity and conflicting orders rather than in the calm finality sought by Mies. And far from purifying a building's appearance by erasing every mark left by the hand, Lewerentz asked his workers to refrain from tidying up, making the marks of the process more obvious. In complete contrast with Mies, for example, he had them leave the welded and soldered joints with irregular pimples of melted metal protruding. At times the rawness is shocking, a dirty architecture

1. Church of St Peter, Klippan, mirror-like windows of parish rooms at outer south-east corner.

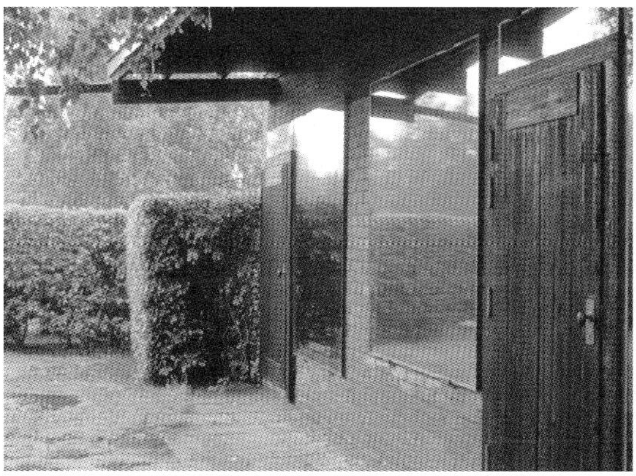

2. Fixing detail of windows showing brick hole, mastic bed and metal bracket. Note also the 'bagged-off' pointing.

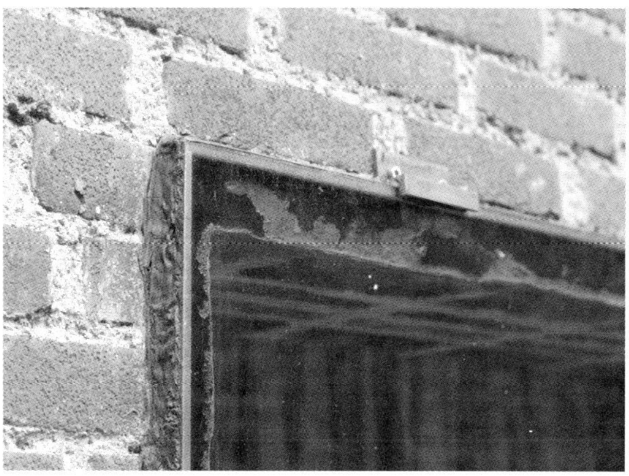

as opposed to Mies's obsessively clean one. And if, like Mies, Lewerentz still held to a concern for geometry and proportion visible in the completely orthogonal plan with its square within a square and carefully modulated dimensions, the three-dimensional composition of St Peter's is untidy, asymmetrical, contextual, contingent; its irregularities are not repressed but relished. Despite the classical rigour of an early masterpiece like his Chapel of the Resurrection of 1926, Lewerentz seems in his late work to have returned increasingly to the National Romanticism of his youth, reworking it in an entirely new form.

The Scandinavian background

That this symphony of the raw and the rough should have occurred in Scandinavia is no accident. Cites were small, industrialisation late, and in the extreme northern climate the powers of nature were more directly felt. Classicism, romantically linked with the distant Mediterranean sun, was opposed by the raw Nordic farmhouse of rough-hewn logs set on granite boulders, celebrated at the time of Lewerentz's architectural education by the National Romantic movement, for he and Asplund were taught by two of its Swedish leaders, Ragnar Östberg and Carl Westman.[1] For both these architects, however, the classical example was also ever-present and they struggled to achieve a synthesis between these opposite poles. So while Östberg's masterpiece Stockholm City Hall (see p.127) drew on the irregular Venetian Gothic of the Doge's Palace, his Stockholm patent office boasted a symmetrical and classical front. Even so, the patent office has the rawest and roughest brickwork, as if waiting for a coat of render that was never applied.

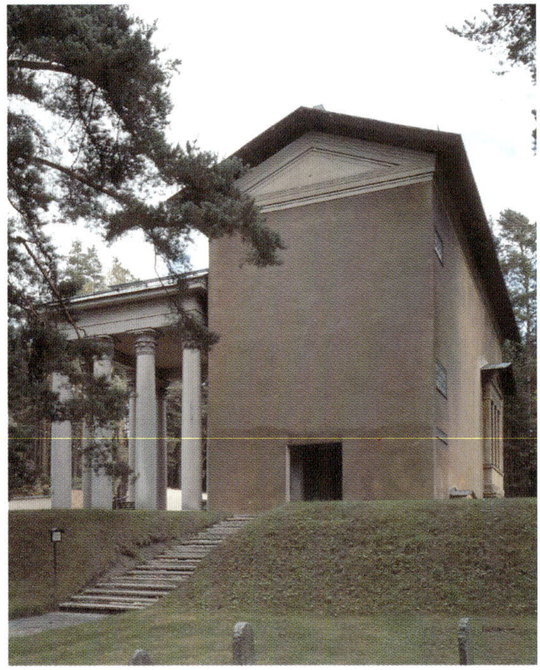

3. (above) Lewerentz, Chapel of the Resurrection, Enskede Cemetery Stockholm 1926, west side.

4, 5. (below) The double heritage of Swedish Architecture summed up in two images from the Skansen open-air museum: left the rough farmstead in logs and granite, right imported Classicism in painted wood.

6. (above opposite) West side of the church showing vaults and reflecting pool, with the 'street' leading to parish rooms and offices to right.

7. (below opposite) South side of the outer wing showing the heroic chimney of the social hall and further mirror-like windows. Note the brickwork of the chimney shaped for the flow of hot gases but built without cutting bricks.

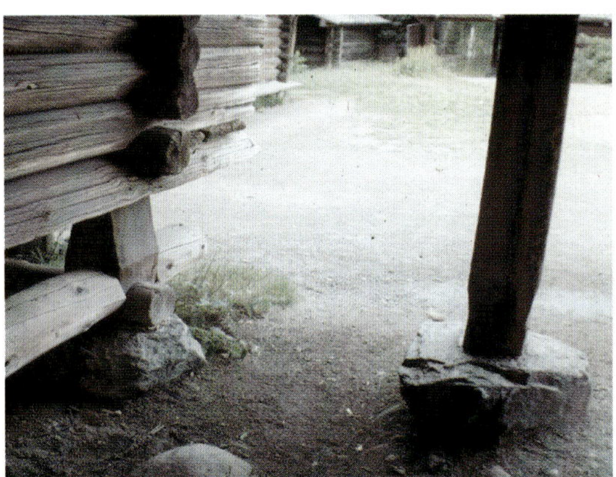

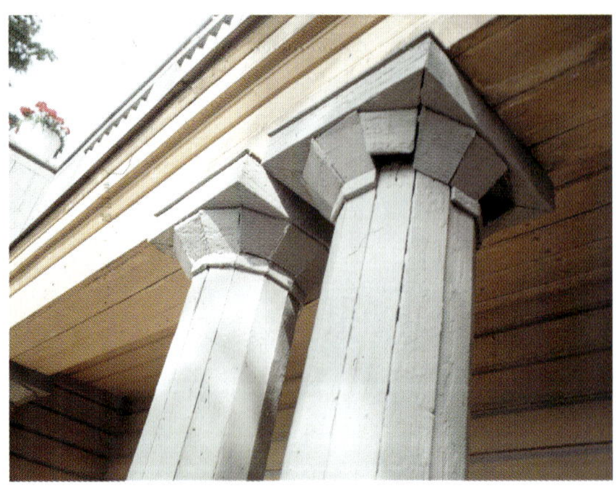

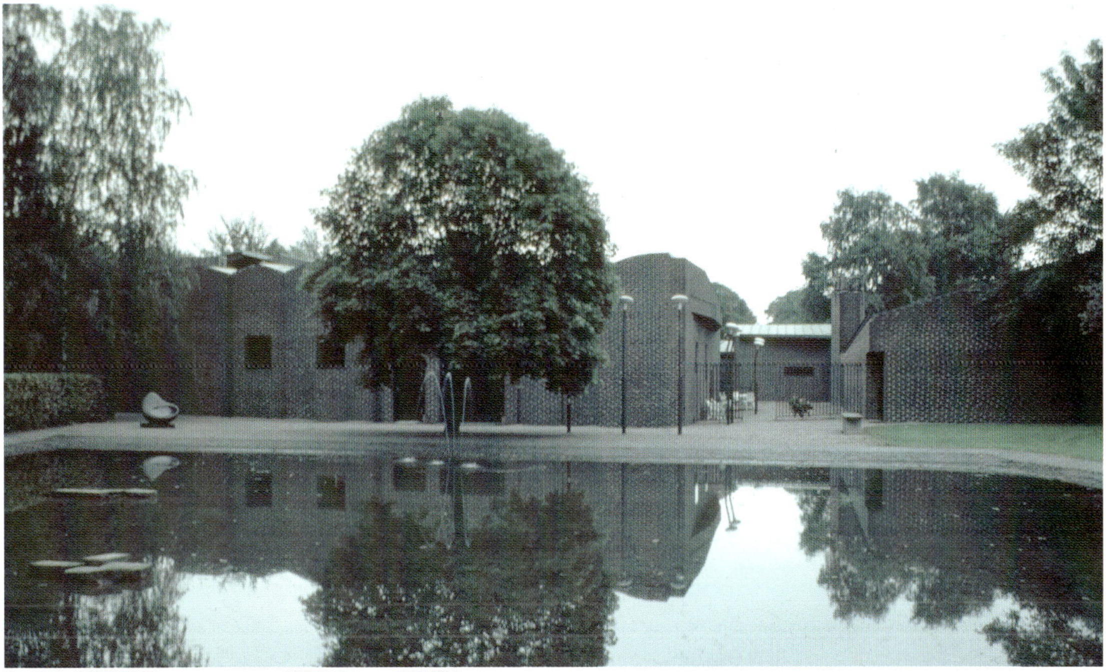

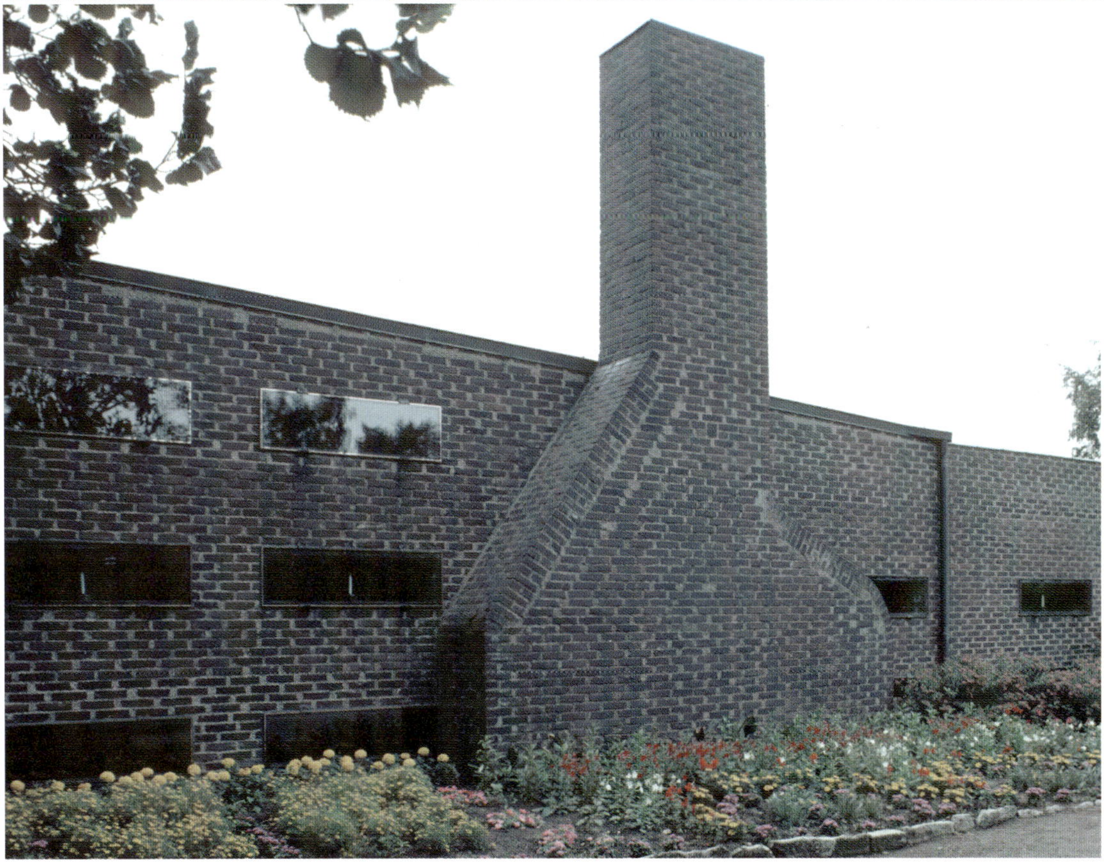

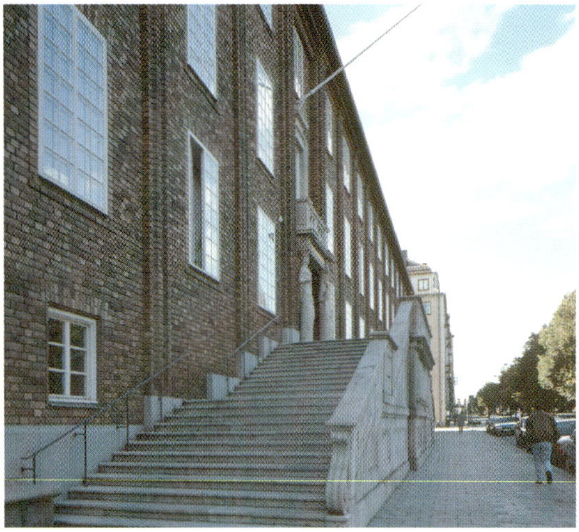

8. Ragnar Östberg, Stockholm Patent Office, main front.

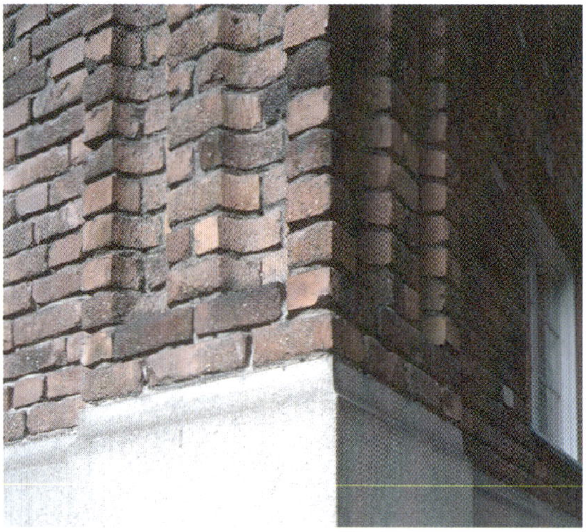

9. Stockholm Patent Office, main front, corner detail showing rough brickwork.

National Romanticism, which exploded in the 1890s across Europe from Finland to Hungary, was a complex phenomenon. The celebration of local culture and identity that seems to lie at its heart was already artificial and self-conscious, performed on an international stage.[2] Its ubiquitous half-round arches, for example, derive from H. H. Richardson in the United States, learned through publications. Even the most apparently local manifestations were part of this larger debate: the quintessentially Catalan Gaudi is unthinkable without the example of Viollet-le-Duc, just as the Glaswegian Mackintosh depends on Pugin and the Arts and Crafts Movement. Even the intense regionalist Theodor Fischer, for whom Lewerentz briefly worked on a visit to Germany around 1910, was not tied to one place. He thought respecting a context meant learning the local architectural language, and he built contrasting Bavarian, Swabian and Tyrolean buildings not from the viewpoint of the artless local, but as visiting professor. What he relished in the task - quite legitimately - was the discovery of and dialogue with the place, the participation in *genius loci*.[3]

Behind the pan-European National Romantic movement the Gothic was a powerful inspiration - the Gothic, that is, as understood through the simple polemic of Pugin, the sophisticated aesthetic stance of Ruskin and the scholarly analysis of Viollet.[4] It was relished for its honest and direct use of materials, but also for its complex, irregular and articulated forms. Understandably, it was taken as a refreshment for the architectural debate in counterpoint to various forms of tired academic classicism. It could be seen as a design philosophy of responsiveness to local need as opposed to the imposition of an ideal order, and of returning to naked building as opposed to the grafting on of borrowed iconographies like icing on a cake. The adoption of local vernacular building traditions as manifestations of a 'Gothic' spirit makes sense for both of these oppositions, however nonsensical it may seem in relation to Gothic as a style.[5] The classical heritage within the Gothic could, of course, be ignored.

Lewerentz and Erik Gunnar Asplund (Chapter 11) were both students of the breakaway Klara School. Their careers developed in parallel and they worked together for 18 years on their mutual masterpiece, Enskede Cemetery in southern Stockholm.[6] Having absorbed the lessons of National Romanticism, they both passed through an intensely neoclassical period in the late teens and 1920s, when they not only applied classical decorative forms but could adopt the most formal of schematic plans and build in ways that were not just constructionally deceptive but positively scenographic (see pages 165-168).[7] The faked façade of high culture with its references to Greece and Rome remained as much a possibility as the primitive hut or log-cabin, and they could switch from one precedent to the other even within a single project.[8] This meant that expressing construction - to isolate one issue - was not so

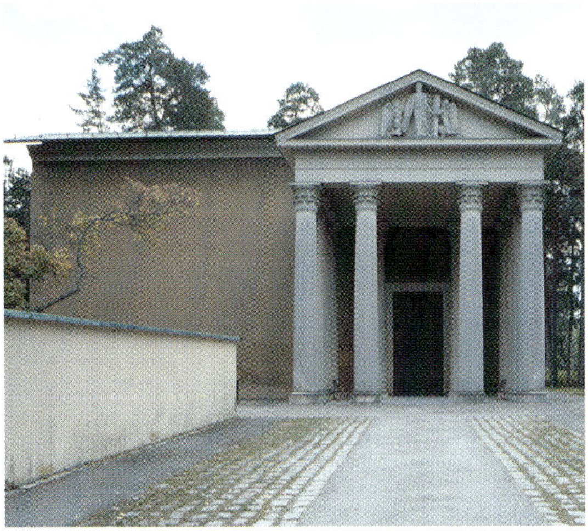

10. Lewerentz, Chapel of the Resurrection, Enskede Cemetery Stockholm, axial view of portico.

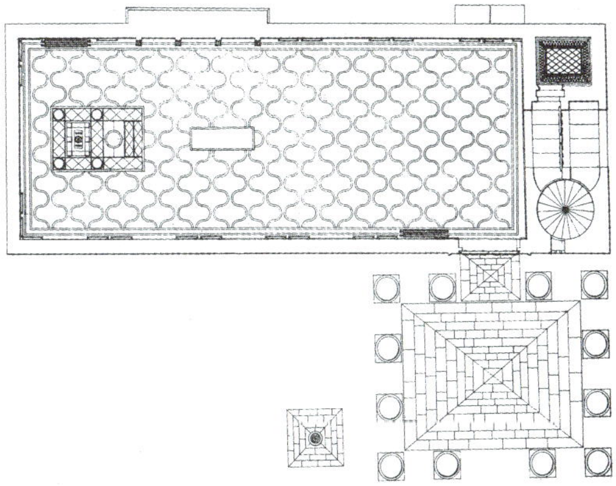

11. Chapel of the Resurrection, floor plan. Note the slight discrepancy in angle between portico and chapel.

much a rule as a perpetual option, always involving the question of what to express and how. For both architects, the advent of white Modernism around 1930 was extremely short-lived, for almost immediately questions of constructional expression re-emerged. For Asplund this meant that by the late 30s he was again polarising his work between a sophisticated and a primitive vocabulary[9] For Lewerentz the soul-searching led to an immersion in technical detail rivalled among Modernists only by Jean Prouvé, for he founded a firm called Idesta which produced high-quality door and window frames and allied ironmongery.[10]

Necessary irregularities

Just as the question of how to express or repress the substance of the building remained in debate throughout the two architects' careers, so their National Romantic background also gave them a special interest in the specifics of sites and the handling of irregularities. They won the competition for the Enskede Cemetery mainly for the sensitive handling of the forest site, and although their development plan was for a while much more formal, the final triumph lies in the subtle interaction of given and imposed orders.[11] Lewerentz's Chapel of the Resurrection, added to the cemetery in 1926, is his most severely formal classical building, yet its asymmetry is the making of it. The noble portico, set on the axis of the Way of Seven Wells, the longest straight route on the site, is detached from the chapel, whose orientation follows the axis of the sunken west garden. The two axes are not normal but 2° out, and rather than concealing this fact like most architects, Lewerenz played it up through the skewed disjunction of the two buildings. This gesture makes all the difference, for it shows that the parts are separate entities, their relationship not self-contained but given by the place. This would be quite alien to Mies, incomprehensible even. Parallel examples are legion in Lewerentz's work, and are found also in Asplund's.

Lewerentz and Asplund developed the cem etery until 1933, taking turns to build its various parts. Together they developed preparatory designs for the main crematorium, but after some difficulties with the clients Asplund was asked to continue alone, and Lewerentz broke off all contact until Asplund's early death in 1940. Lewerentz lived on: discouraged by this and other disappointments he built little and became something of a recluse, but he ran his firm. An elaborate and ingenious restoration programme for Uppsala Cathedral was not taken up.[12] He faded into obscurity as far as the profession was concerned, only to re-emerge quite suddenly with a handful of remarkable late works, twenty years after the death of his rival.

St Peter's is the best of these. Its architectural language was a development of that employed at the slightly earlier church of St Mark at Skarpnäck near Stockholm which also had rough brickwork, vaults, and much expressed construction. At Klippan, however, the language is more refined and even more austere.

The church and its setting

Klippan is a small town on the West side of Sweden. St Peter's stands just east of the town centre, between a pair of converging roads which lead out towards suburbs. Beyond is a park, and the site initially suggested for the building was nearer the middle of it, further to the east. However Lewerentz chose to anchor his church against the northern road from which it is approached, turning the area to the west - i.e. between it and the road junction, and facing the town - into a garden. This garden is the principal outdoor room of the complex, celebrating the west and main façade of the church, that with the largest and most ceremonial doors, from which couples emerge together for the first time after marriage. The space boasts the only piece of added sculpture, and also a large brick-lined pool - a still nordic lake for reflection and reflectiveness, rather than the cooling fountain of the south.

The church is correctly orientated, so the altar stands opposite the west doors. It is square in shape, suggesting a more intimate ritual in the tradition of *circonstantes* (standing in a circle) in place of the more usual linear progression. This marks an attempt to return to origins: to the early Christianity of secret meetings in the catacombs.[13] This was the religious equivalent of the search for the essential and the primitive that runs so poignantly through the architecture. The church is entered via a side chapel off a tiny alleyway to the north, deliberately intimate and informal, for people arrive for religious observance one by one: it is only at the end of the service that, united by the experience, they process out together through the west doors. The bells are placed to one side of this alleyway above the sacristy, so one is summoned by their music directly to the point of entry.

Behind the church to south and east is a lower L-shaped block of parish offices and meeting rooms, placed to make a larger square in plan with the church, set on the same diagonal. This element

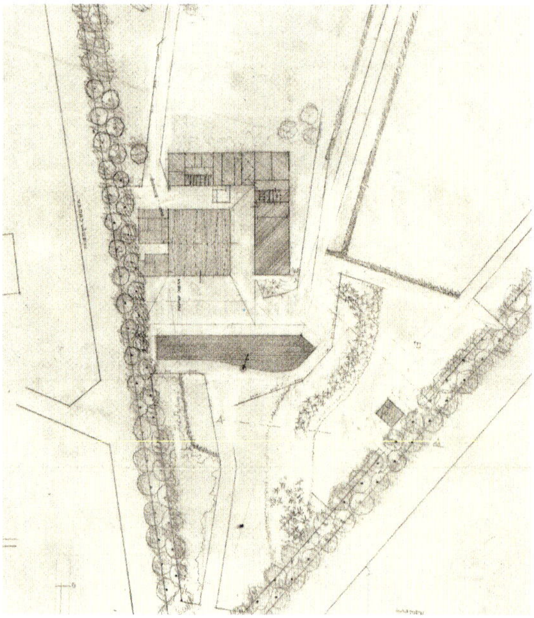

12. St Peter's Klippan, site plan, north is left, centre of town bottom and park top.The building is approached from the road on the north side. Rounded body to west is pond.
13. (below) View from the park to east.

is separated from the church by another outdoor room, a narrow street-like space onto which doors of the various facilities open, and which is closed at night by iron gates. It appears at first sight to be of constant width, but the minor branch south of the church is slightly narrower. At the north end, where it gives onto the main road, the entry is partly screened by a skewed free-standing wall. The only other departure from the right-angle in plan is the stage of the meeting room. The façades facing the park to south and east are the most subdued and informal, but they also boast the largest windows - belonging to the corner confirmation rooms; and also the most domestic element - the expressed fireplace and chimney of the meeting room, an original 'foyer'.[14] The organisation of the complex is clearly hierarchical, focusing on the church as

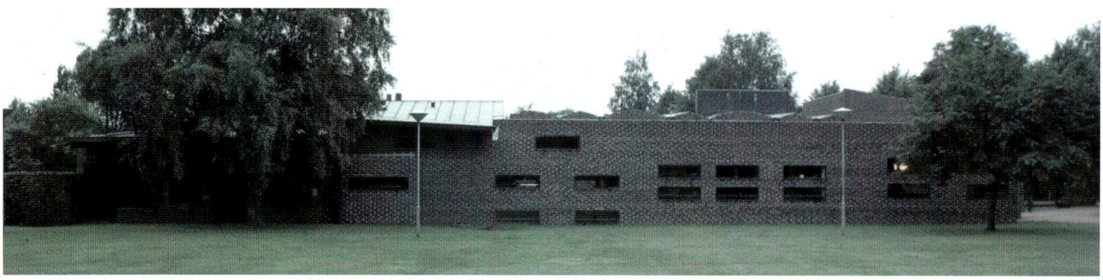

Key:
1. church
2. font
3. altar
4. vestibule & wedding chapel
5. entrance passage
6. organist
7. sacristy
8. offices
9. priest
10. archive
11. council room
12. confirmation room
13. meeting room

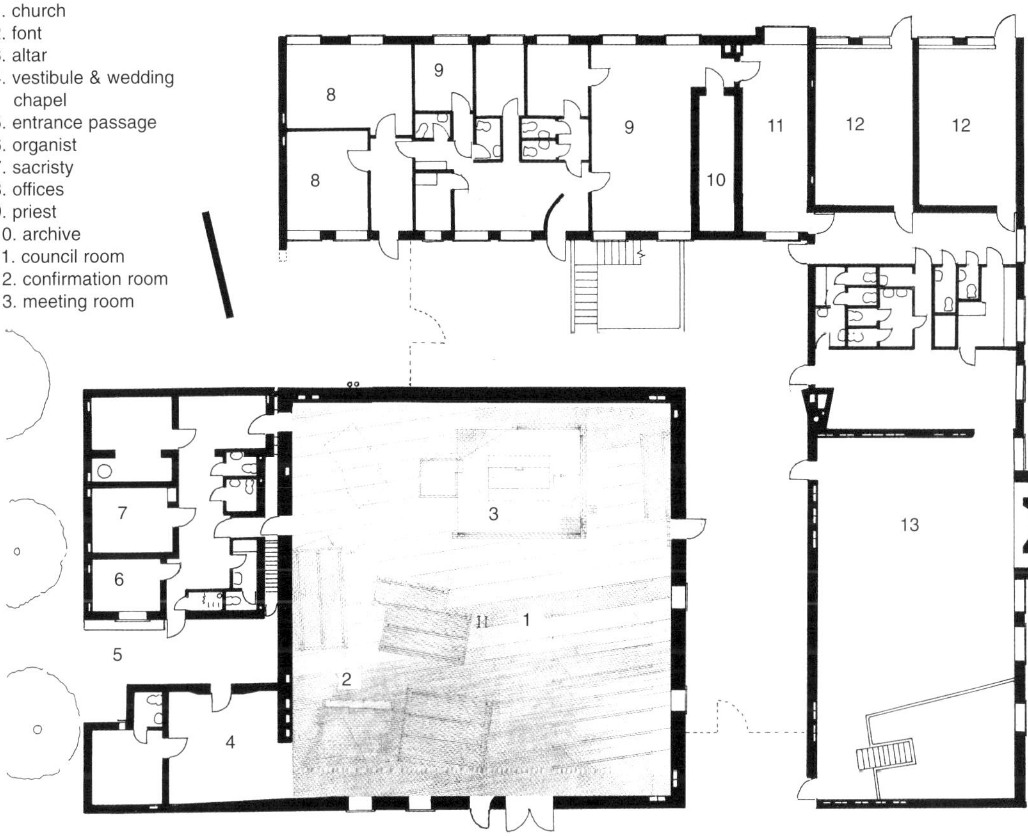

14. St Peter's Klippan, main floor plan, north is left. The square church is surrounded to south and east by wings containing social rooms and parish offices respectively. Entry is via the narrow passageway to left, which runs between the sacristy to east and the wedding chapel/vestibule to west.

15. (below) West-east section through church, gated street and parish offices. Note cross supporting vaults and sloping floor.
16. (bottom) North-south section through sacristy, church and meeting room. Note light tubes, vaulting and great chimney.

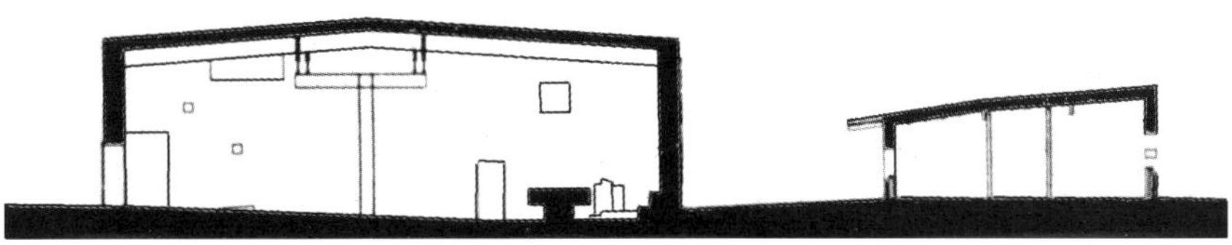

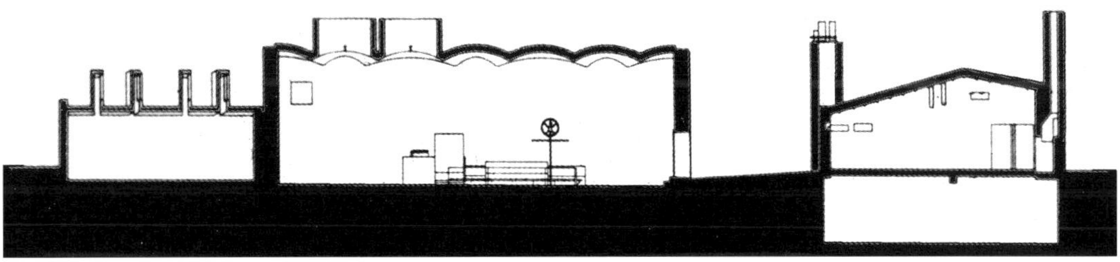

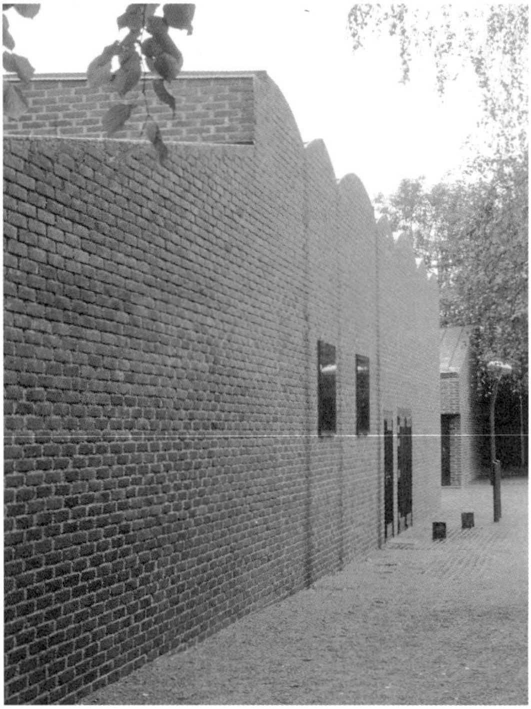

17. West front seen from its north end.

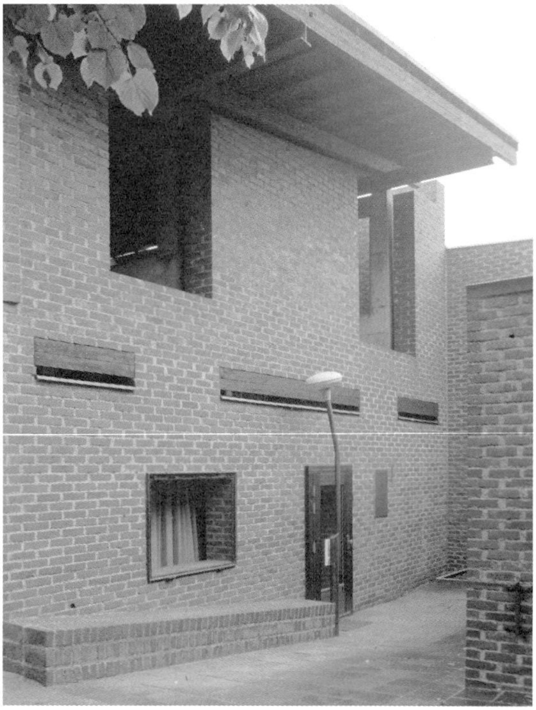

19. Entrance alleyway with sacristy window and bell chamber.

18. (below) Central part of west front with main doors.

20. (opposite) Church interior seen from entry with shell font and floor fissure in foreground.

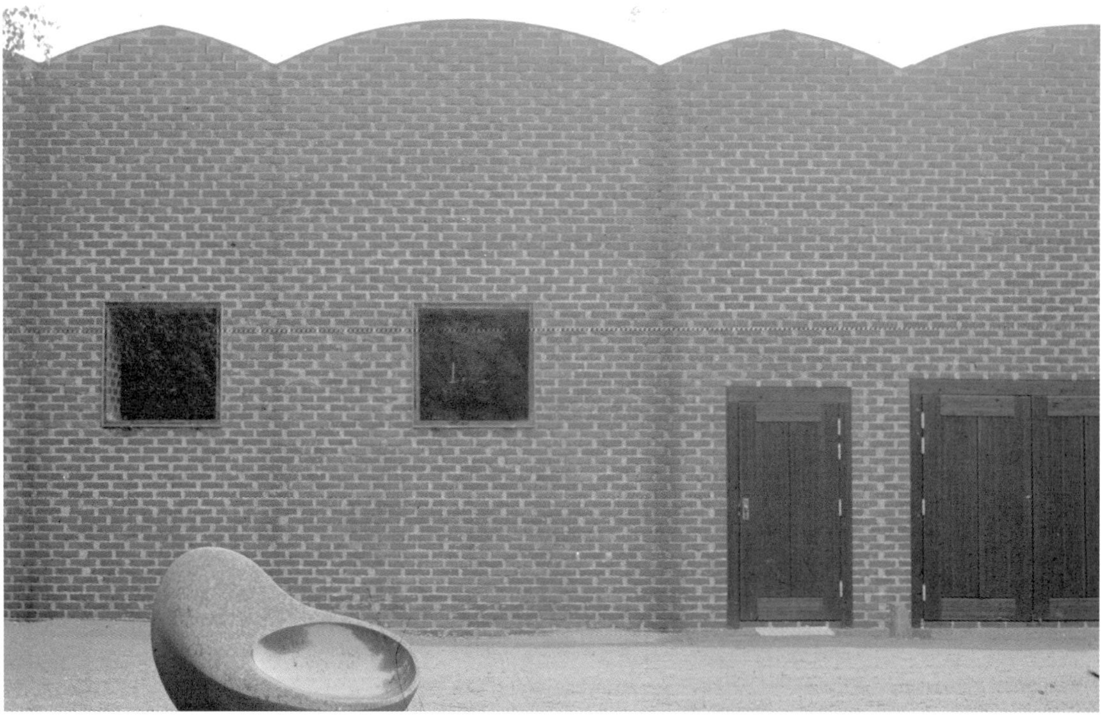

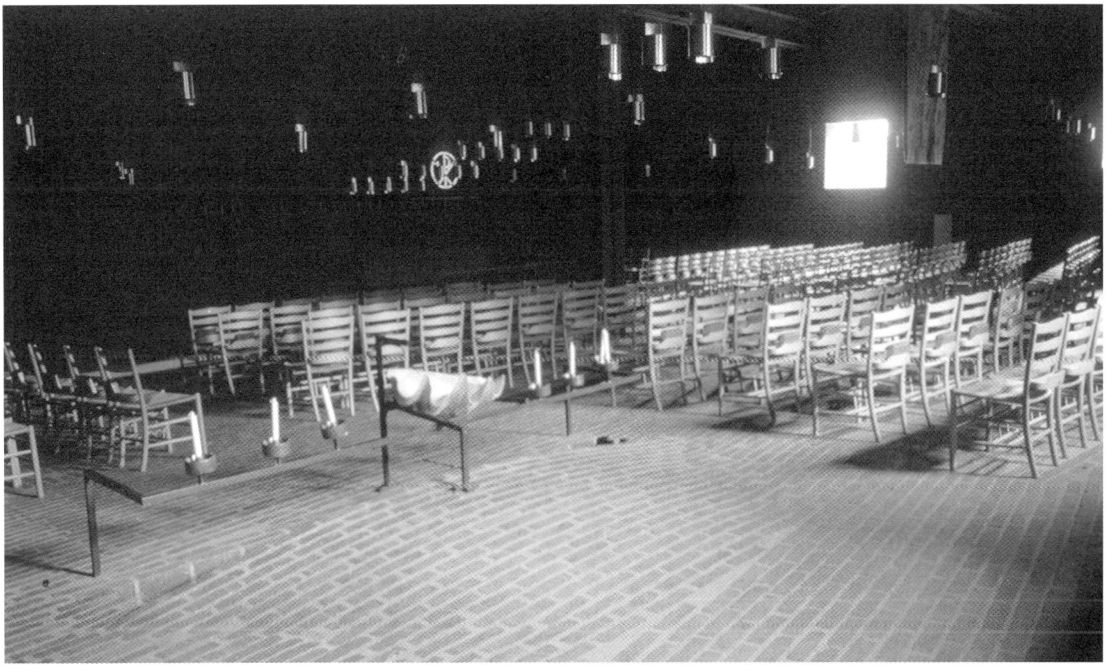

centre. The profane elements are separated from it by the internal street, while it is touched to north by the semi-holy elements of sacristy and vestibule, the latter also serving as a wedding chapel.

Sacredness of vaults

Vaults have long been associated with religious architecture. They are essential not only to the Gothic, but also to Romanesque and Byzantine building, and to Mosques. They make a skyscape (we also speak of 'the heavenly vault'), they confer some order and rhythm on the plan, and they demonstrate inspiringly how the hardest and heaviest materials are persuaded to defy gravity. Their use in the second half of the 20th century is unusual and could seem archaic, were they not reinterpreted in a wholly modern manner. Lewerentz uses brick vaults, but what he does with them is only possible with the strength of iron, for they are laid between rolled steel joists. They are expressed externally by following their form directly with a copper skin, unlike the secondary roof of Gothic churches - another instance of the desire to return to essentials. The church vaulting runs on the axis of the altar, so it is seen externally on the most important west and east ends. It rises towards the centre, both to provide a spatial climax and to drain the rainwater to the sides, while it is lifted above the supporting structure by a series of minimal steel posts. This gives the impression that the vaults are floating above, rather than loading onto, the supporting structure. They are in fact hold up on a pair of great transverse beams carried by a cross-shaped central column. That this element has a more than structural, utilitarian, profane role, is underlined by it being asymmetrical when structural logic would demand symmetry. The shorter arm is found, as one might expect, in the direction of the altar. Although clearly symbolic, it remains T-shaped, without the upper arm of a true cross: for its meaning is evident enough, and must not be overstressed. The steelwork is not painted but left raw and rusty, ageing, and therefore a symbol of suffering, but in a way more felt than analysed.[15] The welded joints, as throughout the building, are left unground, so the welder's work appears in its naked simplicity.

This kind of vault was first tried at St Mark's Skarpnäck (1960), where vaults were used for all parts of the complex. At St Peter's they occur more hierarchically: they serve only for the church, the side chapel, and the council chamber in the corner of the L-shaped block. Furthermore, only the church vaults are left visible externally, for the other parts of the complex have more profane low-pitched copper-covered timber roofs. And while the

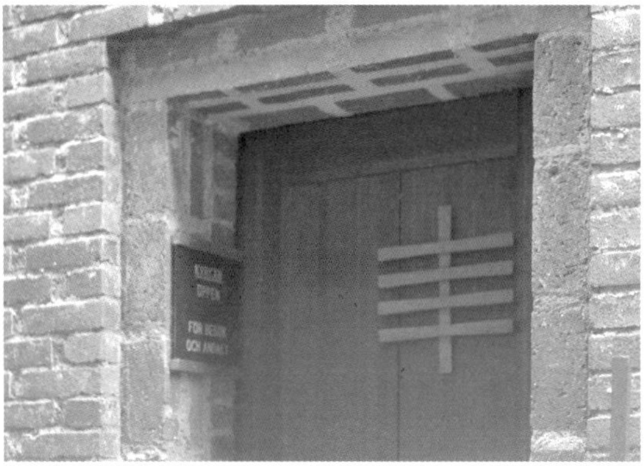

21. Main entrance: the only door in the whole complex which is set at the back of its reveal.

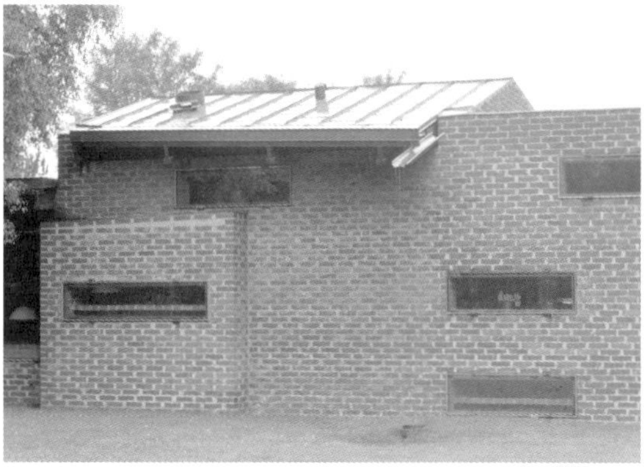

22. East side of outer wing: projecting bay belonging to council chamber and pitched roof over vaulted ceiling.

roof edges of vaults are finished as flush as possible, the profane buildings have overhanging eaves which project, displaying their timber structure and the way it is strapped down to the walls. These roof projections are pulled out obliquely in several places, exaggerating the practical and profane need to bring the rainwater to an outlet at the lowest point, but also providing additional protection over doors. The general effect of the building in three dimensions is a lively profile quite unpredicted by the orthodox and laconic looking plan.[16]

Crazy brickwork

Brick is used everywhere at St Peter's, a rough dark brick, between brown and purple in colour. In the church it forms the walls, the vaulted roof, the altar and pulpit, and of course the floor. This is broken only by the baptismal trough at the corner where one enters, a primeval slot, a water-filled fissure, the edge of which swells up mysteriously. The effect of all this brick is dark and hard and earthy: it generates a space almost invisible until one's eyes adapt to the gloom. It echoes with the quiet drip of water from the tropical shell, set by Lewerentz on a steel frame, which serves as font. Baptism is the resounding theme: the space of the church is cave-like and intimate, more sanctuary than celebration, a place of deep mystery rather than stark protestant clarity.

In the external brickwork there is much play with different bonding patterns, notably at the end of the street-like space to the east of the church, where alternating vertical and horizontal coursing suggests a huge chequerboard, reminding one also of the decorative games played with brick infill on old timber-framed houses. Lewerentz seems to have imposed one unorthodox rule at the start: a brick should never be cut. This is not in the interests of time-saving and modular construction, far from it: indeed it is almost an ironic comment on that idea - made at a time when it was everywhere

23. Copper rainpipes with visibly soldered straps.

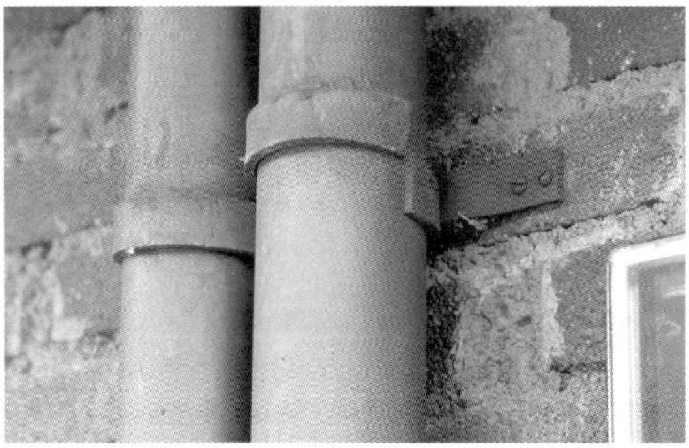

24. Brick infill at south end of street between church and parish offices.

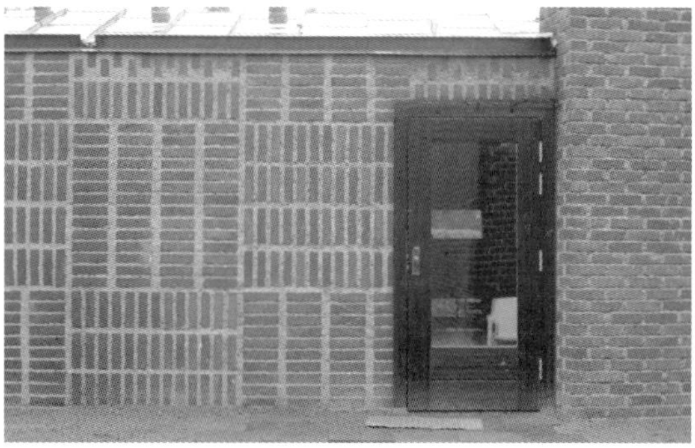

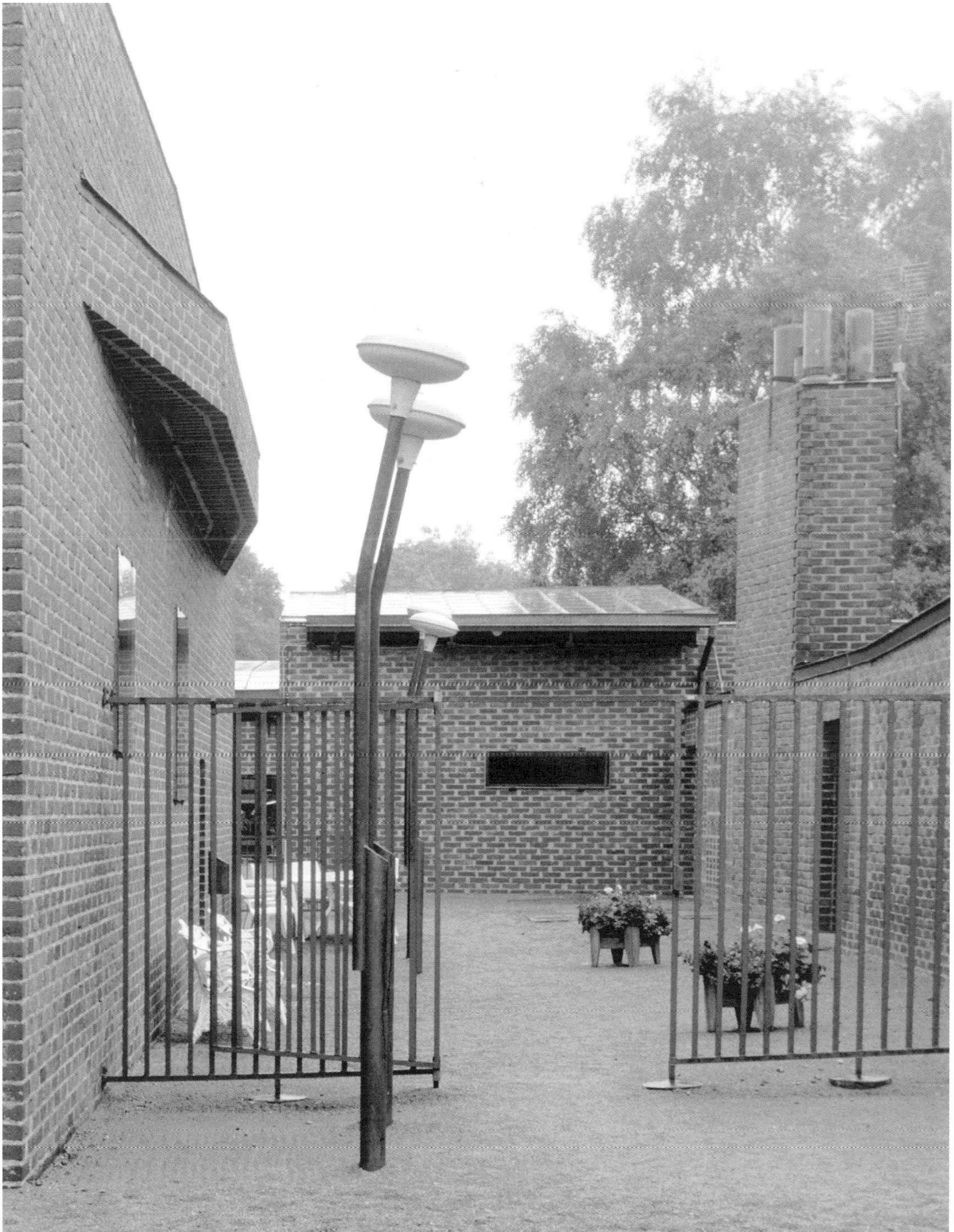

25. View of gated street space between south side of church and parish rooms. The projecting structure top left is an expressed ring beam to tie in the ends of the north-south running structural joists.

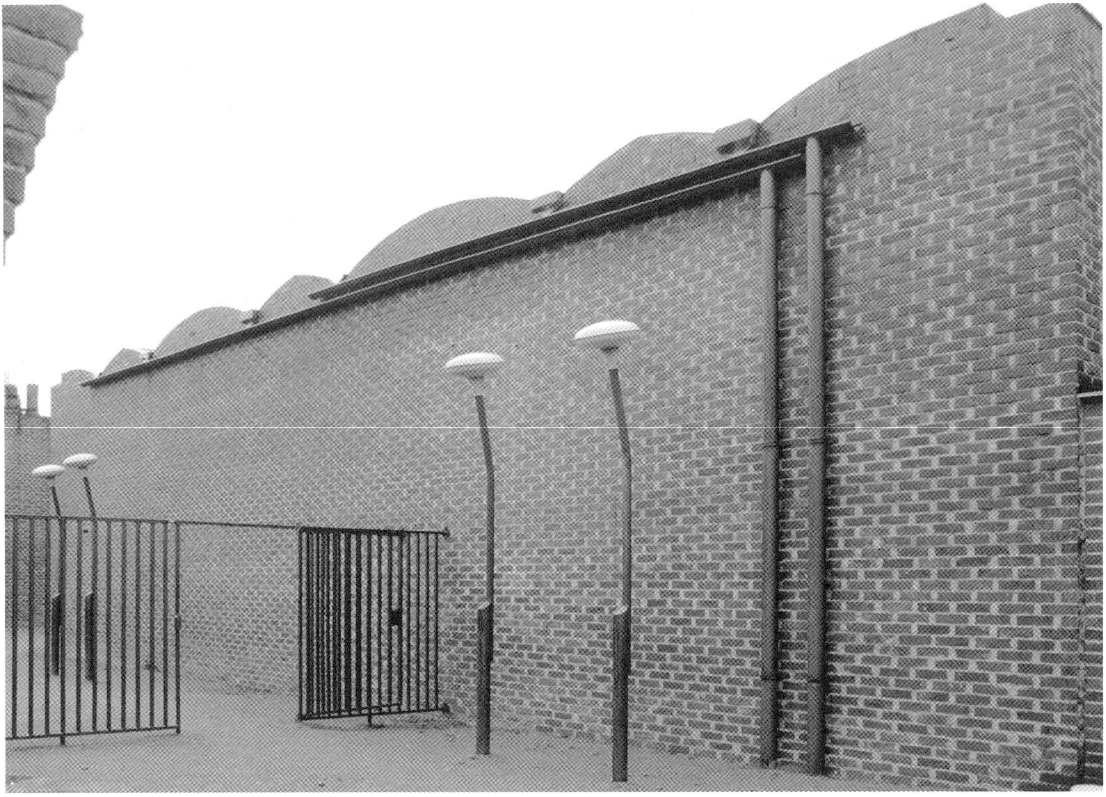

26. East side of church showing vault ends, rainwater disposal, and gated entry to street with parish offices. Note also corbel, left.

in force. For Lewerentz does so many difficult irregular things with his bricks that his rule creates more problems than it solves. So why? Is it out of respect for the brick and what it *'wants to be'*, as Louis Kahn put it? (next chapter) Or is to create a discipline of construction which will inform the design - an aesthetic derived from and founded in technique? Perhaps both.

To avoid cutting bricks there are wide joints. At the edges of sloping roofs are triangular wedges of mortar as deep as a brick, achieved only by bulking out the mortar with ground slate to make it concrete-like. The effect is often crude and messy, almost shockingly so in places, and carried through with utter ruthlessness. In dimensioning the plan, brick sizes had often to be the determining factor, and brick thicknesses had to be accommodated at corners and junctions, requiring some unexpected manipulations. Internal floor tiles too were laid uncut, size adjustments being taken up within the pattern rather than at the edges, producing some unusual and ingenious arrangements.[17]

Joinery

We began with the windows. The doors too, with notable exceptions, are applied to the front of a brick hole, bolted on and sealed with mastic. The exceptions are the most sacred, most hierarchically important doors. One is the main entrance down the side alley, the only door in the complex to be placed at the back of its - specially thickened - brick hole rather than on the face, and with its iron cross, the only one decorated with a symbol of any kind. Also exceptional are the two doors of the west front, which are placed flush within their façade rather than onto its face. Normally it would make no sense to change the principle of a construction detail in this way: that Lewerentz takes the trouble to do so leaves us in no doubt that this was his way of indicating the doors' superior status. The larger double door is also taller than others in the building, declaring its role as ceremonial exit.

It would only be too easy, in concentrating on traditions and crafts, to produce an olde worlde and sentimental image. This Lewerentz avoids entirely

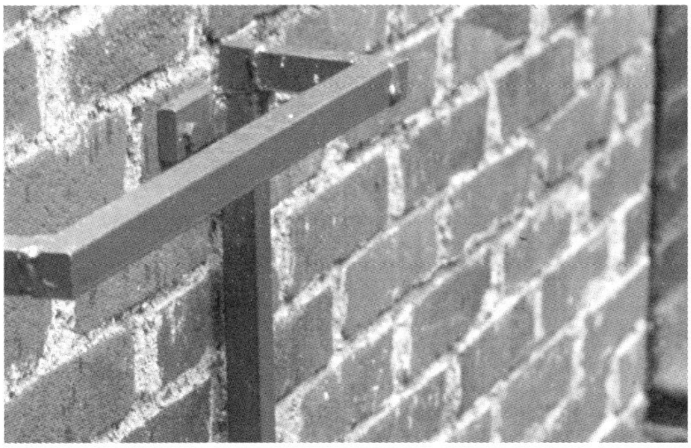

27. Welded handrail with welds left unground.

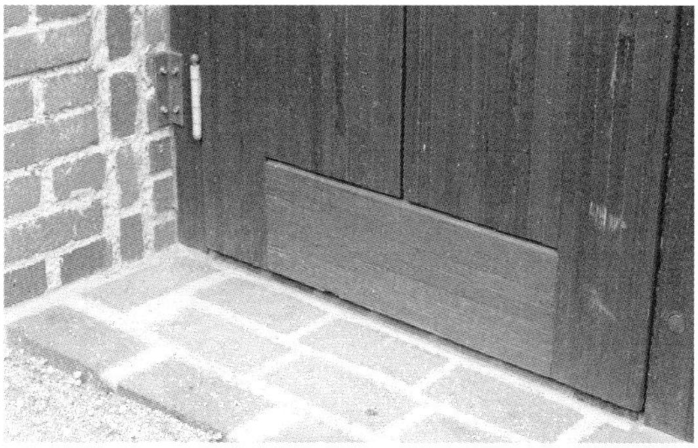

28. Door at corner of outer wings: laminated construction, central expansion slot and sliding joint with bottom rail.

by reinterpreting ancient techniques, yet combining them with what was then the latest technology. The doors and their frames are made of laminated timber, with glued joints left visible. Externally they remain as sawn, with the slight ridges produced when the separate strips of wood did not quite lie flat in the glueing clamp, but internally they are sanded off to give a smooth surface, though the grain is visible beneath the varnish. This slight difference of texture is the only concession to the increase in civilisation between front and rear faces of the door,[18] for both are finished in the same dark stain. The construction of the doors is stated in a somewhat minimal way, for though they are essentially formed of frame and panel elements, the panel is made flush and continuous with the side pieces of the frame, while only a simple groove and change in direction of grain reveals the joints with the top and bottom members. Running vertically down the centre of each door is an expansion slot between the two sides of the panel, producing a clear vertical stripe.

Expressed construction - or something more?

At first sight it seems that all materials and techniques are exposed and expressed: brick and its bonding, timber and its assembly, the fragility of glass, the unground welds of steel. Yet on further reflection it becomes obvious that this expression is neither wholly consistent nor complete. Comparison with the expressive brickwork of the 19th century, with that of Butterfield or Berlage for example, reveals a big difference. The openings are treated quite differently. For while an architect like Butterfield[19] would give considerable attention to arches over doors and windows, and to restraining arches in the wall above, Lewerentz takes bricks across the head of an opening apparently unsupported. This allows his brick holes to be treated in the same way on every edge, asserting their geometric purity, but it denies all expression of the way the forces of gravity make a head fundamentally different to a cill. The construction was achieved, presumably, by laying steel reinforcing bars between the brick courses where tension forces are felt. But all this is completely concealed. It is certainly not brick construction in the traditional sense, indeed it could almost be interpreted as a concrete building, with the bricks acting as aggregate.[20]

The expression of functional requirements can be equally selective. The building had to be heated, a very necessary provision in cold Sweden, and there is a basement boiler which somehow delivers hot air to cavities in the walls. It then enters the church through cills of window openings and a peppering of open joints in the inner brickwork. Apart from the pattern of openings, all is suppressed. But perhaps the most interesting example of Lewerentz's selectivity is the treatment of rainwater. All the way around the subordinate buildings its disposal is made highly conspicuous with projecting roof edges, and on the back of the church - the east face (fig. 26) - is an elaborate arrangement of copper gutters and downpipes draining the vaults.[21] On the west front however (figs 17, 18), there is no visible apparatus of this kind, although the roof must discharge just as much water. It disappears, apparently, into a series of downpipes concealed in the thickness of the walls. This was the right decision - a poignant decision - for it liberates the sacred face from profane considerations and helps differentiate it from the hierarchically less important east face.

In terms of pure construction or convenience, however, it makes no sense - again a change of principle in a detail - and in terms of functional expression it might be even called downright dishonest.

From fact to fiction

But dishonest in whose terms? After a lifetime of thought and experiment, Lewerentz knew exactly what he was doing. He knew that pure use and pure construction as architectural determinants are a chimera, that they are always. open to interpretation. Use and construction are nonetheless the fundamental themes of architecture, for by their spatial relations and formal articulation, buildings show how they might be used, and encourage certain kinds of use. They have to be made, and tell us (or lie to us) about how they were made, if we can so read them. Functionalism and Constructivism might thus be considered less pedantic principles than fictional themes: the building telling stories about itself, relating to its ancestors and retelling its myth of origins. That is what St Peter's is about: it reveals the latent poetry that lay at the heart of Modernism before it became prosaic; and as distilled by one of the original pioneers.

Lewerentz spent much time on site developing the details, and it is in the details that the building lives most profoundly. The crudeness, almost clumsy or ugly in places, is not only deliberate but poetic. It is an old man's building, and the weight of a lifetime's experience is somehow encapsulated, which can be as much by renunciation as by quotation. Lewerentz had shown a propensity for classical ordering, yet St Peter's has no orders, no clear axial progressions, little symmetry, and little in the way of an evident proportioning system.[22] In middle age, Lewerentz had given his whole attention and energy to designing door and window frames made by Idesta and prized by his colleagues, yet the windows at Klippan have no frame whatsoever: indeed they use the most advanced technology of their time - sealed units and mastic - expressly to avoid it. It was perhaps typical of Lewerentz that in the age of Brutalism he should have produced what now seems the last word in that manner.

Notes

1. For the architectural education of Lewerentz and Asplund see Claes Caldenby *Beginnings* in Engfors 1986, pp. 8-10.
2. For an analysis of National Romanticism see Lane 2000.
3. For information on Fischer see Nerdinger 1988.
4. Until the early 19th century, the Gothic had not been systematically studied, and it rapidly progressed through several interpretations, moving from the romantic picturesque view embraced by the Gothic novel to the constructive rationalism of Viollet, which influenced the Modern Movement. The triumvirate Pugin, Ruskin and Viollet had complementary talents: Pugin produced short and exaggerated polemics with satirical drawings like his *True Principles* (Pugin 1853), Ruskin produced sophisticated aesthetic theory (*The Stones of Venice*: Ruskin 1903-12) and Viollet made an encyclopaedic study of surviving Gothic buildings in France (Viollet 1873). For a history of the Gothic Revival on the continent see Germann 1972.
5. The Gothic Revival and Kentish vernacular meet at Philip Webb's Red House, particularly in relation to the planned half-timbered and tile-hung extension (Blundell Jones 1986).
6. The best and most detailed source on the design and construction of the Woodland Cemetery is Constant 1994.
7. The most extreme example is the extraordinary group of buildings planned by Asplund for the north side of Gustav Adolf Square in Gothenburg (p.166, fig. 16, but see also plans).
8. Asplund's Woodland Chapel was conceived in a classical version before it was built in a rustic manner with steeply pitched shingle roof and tree-trunk ridge pole. Lewerentz played the same game: his Chapel of the Resurrection is like Asplund's first project, while his primitive version was built at Kvarnsveden.
9. The Woodland Crematorium is unmistakably classical, while the contemporary but less known Skövde Crematorium returned to the primitive model. Asplund also showed his affection for the vernacular again in his summer house at Stennäs of 1937.
10. Ahlin 1987, pp. 138-141.
11. Constant 1994. pp. 29-47.
12. Ahlin 1987, pp. 147-148.
13. Colin St John Wilson has commented on this: see Architectural Association 1988 p. 21. On Lewerentz more generally, see also Wilson 1992 pp. 111-139.
14. The word in French originally meant a hearth.
15. Often in the 1970s and 80s Post-modernists produced deliberate symbols to be read, for example Terry Farrell's eggcups on TVAM and Charles Jencks's endless encoded symbols in his own house. If you need a written programme to undertake the intellectual 'decoding', the thing is surely already too far removed. Lewerentz's rusty column is suffering visible degradation, and the effect is felt.
16. It is the same with St Mark's Skarpnäck: the plan has subtlety but is not in itself rhetorical, and could have given rise to a very different building.
17. For example, where the tiled floor of a passage narrows by a few centimetres, all the tiles in that section are laid with tighter joints, and thus out of step with those of the wider part.
18. It seems to be a widely accepted convention that buildings be smooth inside, rough without, like a coconut, expressing internally an increased degree of control and refinement, a transition from the raw to the cooked, from nature to artifice.
19. William Butterfield was a Gothic Revival architect working in the middle of the 19th century, and known particularly for his bold use of polychromatic brickwork. Famous works are All Saints Margaret Street, London, and Keble College Oxford.
20. I owe this reading to Florian Beigel.
21. Ahlin reported (1987) that the apparatus of rainwater collection was important in his restoration plans for Uppsala cathedral, but the drawings have not been published.
22. There is a limited geometrical system in the plan, but it does not seem to run through consistently in three dimensions, whereas the Chapel of the Resurrection has a clear proportional system both visible in the drawings and confirmed by analysis.

Chapter 16. Louis Kahn: Kimbell Museum, Fort Worth, Texas 1966-72

Born in 1904, Louis Kahn is the youngest of the architects considered in this book and his Kimbell Museum is the most recent building. Estonian in origin, Kahn grew up in the United States, receiving his architectural education within the American version of the Beaux Arts system. As a designer he was a late developer, and it took him a long time to find his voice, perhaps because it was difficult to fuse all his interests together in the kind of synthesis he wanted. But he died as arguably the best Modernist in the United States apart from Frank Lloyd Wright, applauded for the range and thoroughness of his late work. As has been illustrated by the examples in this book, there are many issues which architects may choose to address in a design project. They can decide to relate the building to a local context, an historical precedent, or the social order implied in a brief. Alternatively, they might concentrate on the appropriate use of technology, pursuing rationally or more fictionally the tectonic issues of construction, structure, and detail. They might expend their energies on a flexible type-solution for more general application, or concentrate on the efficient and expressive provision of services, including control of the way the building envelope filters day- and sun-light. They might have loftier, more spiritual aims, such as an ordering geometry which resonates through the building, or the orchestration of route and spatial progression to control the visual experience enjoyed by a visitor. Or they might simply settle for a striking and meaningful external image. Looking back over the architecture of the last fifty years, one can find excellent examples of each of these things, for with the expansion of the modernist ethic after the Second World War, all avenues were explored, even if many of the issues listed can also be seen as perennial themes of architecture. However, the weakness of many if not most examples is that they are monothematic: some buildings manage to address three or four of these issues at once, but most address only one or two at the expense of the others.[1] Architects tend to be good at strategy *or* detail, plan *or* section, interior spaces *or* external form, space *or* construction, but seldom both, and very rarely all. Kahn's Kimbell Museum not only addresses all the issues, but breaks new ground on many of them. This breadth of concerns has few rivals this century: Wright, Aalto and Asplund come to mind, and Le Corbusier in late works like La Tourette.

City, site and context

Fort Worth is a substantial city in Texas with a relatively long history, a university and other cultural pretensions, though it is commercially overshadowed by nearby Dallas. Once an attractive place, its centre has been half gutted in favour of overscaled office towers, whole blocks

1. Kimbell Museum from the north side, showing level change and six vaults, the end one left open as a portico.

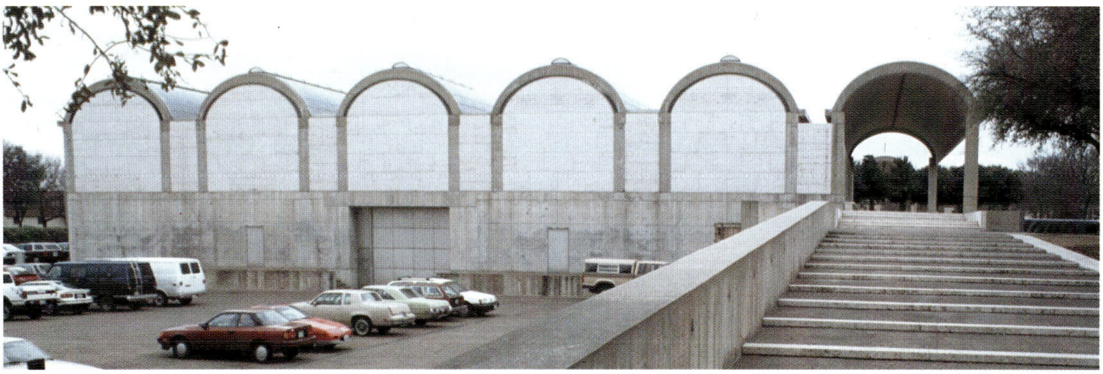

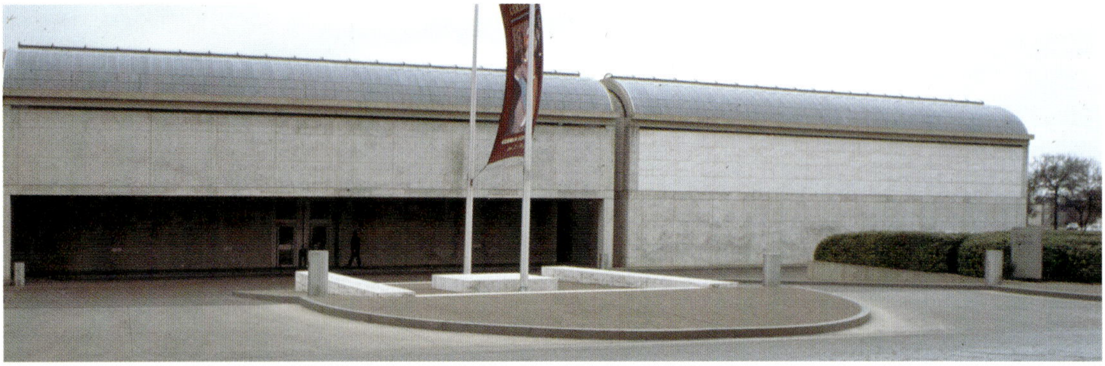

2. Vehicle entrance and drop-off point at lower level on the east side. Only two of the three long bays are visible.
3. (below) Inner portico with grove of trees left and glass wall right.
4. (opposite top) Northern portico and pond, with grove of trees behind announcing entrance.
5. (opposite bottom) Vault and its side bays seen from sunken sculpture garden to south.

being left vacant for parking, the bomb sites of some imaginary war. The explosion which the city has suffered is a real one in another sense, for life sucked out of its centre has been sprayed around the periphery. Complete domination by the private car, a ready availability of cheap land, and a lack of planning restrictions, has produced suburban sprawl stretching to Dallas and beyond.[2] The Kimbell Museum is set in a kind of cultural zone with the University and other museums, on a gentle hillside some three miles west of the old centre. It is not an attractive place by European standards, for there is little sense of enclosure, only wide boulevards lined with parked cars and a series of free-standing buildings in a weak park. Kahn was given a relatively large site, a rectangular block in the north-south orientated grid but with the north-west corner lopped off by a major avenue. There could have been no question of completing a street or creating a square, for the density is too low, nor do neighbouring buildings provide a consistent stylistic context. The building thus needed to be free-standing, developing its own identity and immediate context. The difficulty is easily under-estimated, particularly as the finished building seems so effortless. Open sites are often wrongly presumed to be easier than tight ones, because they seem to allow more freedom; but they also make connections more difficult. The skill of Kahn's response is threefold: first, in his ability to create a sufficiently imposing structure despite the large site and the necessarily low profile due to top-lighting.

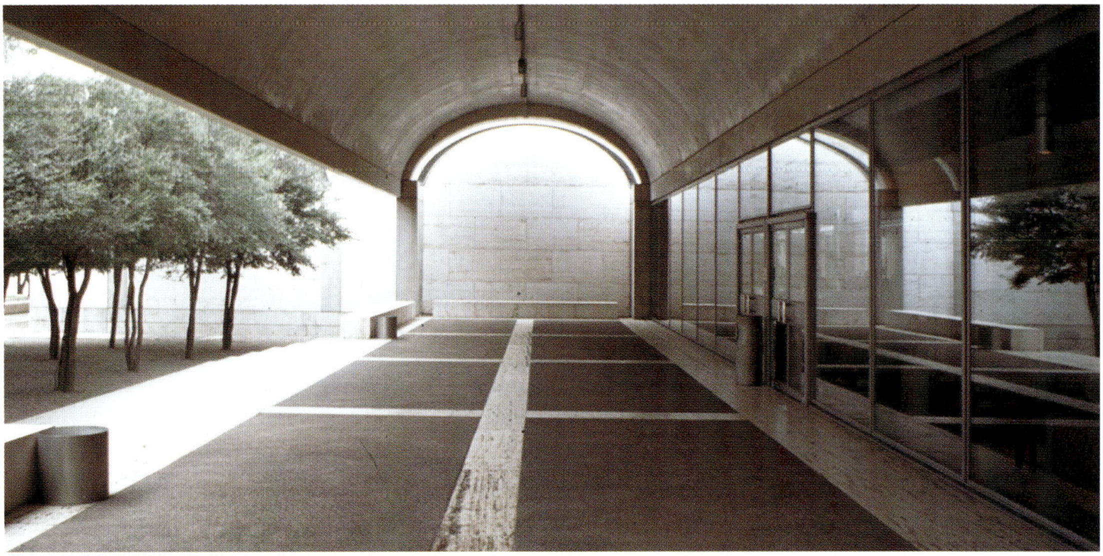

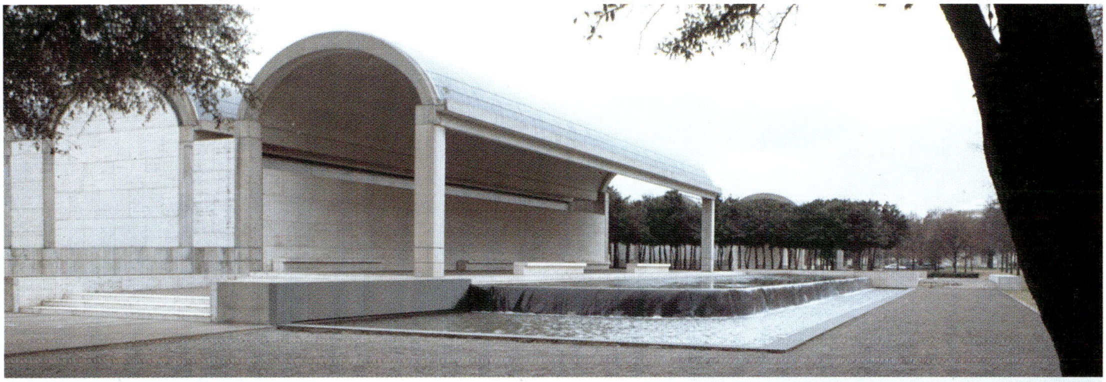

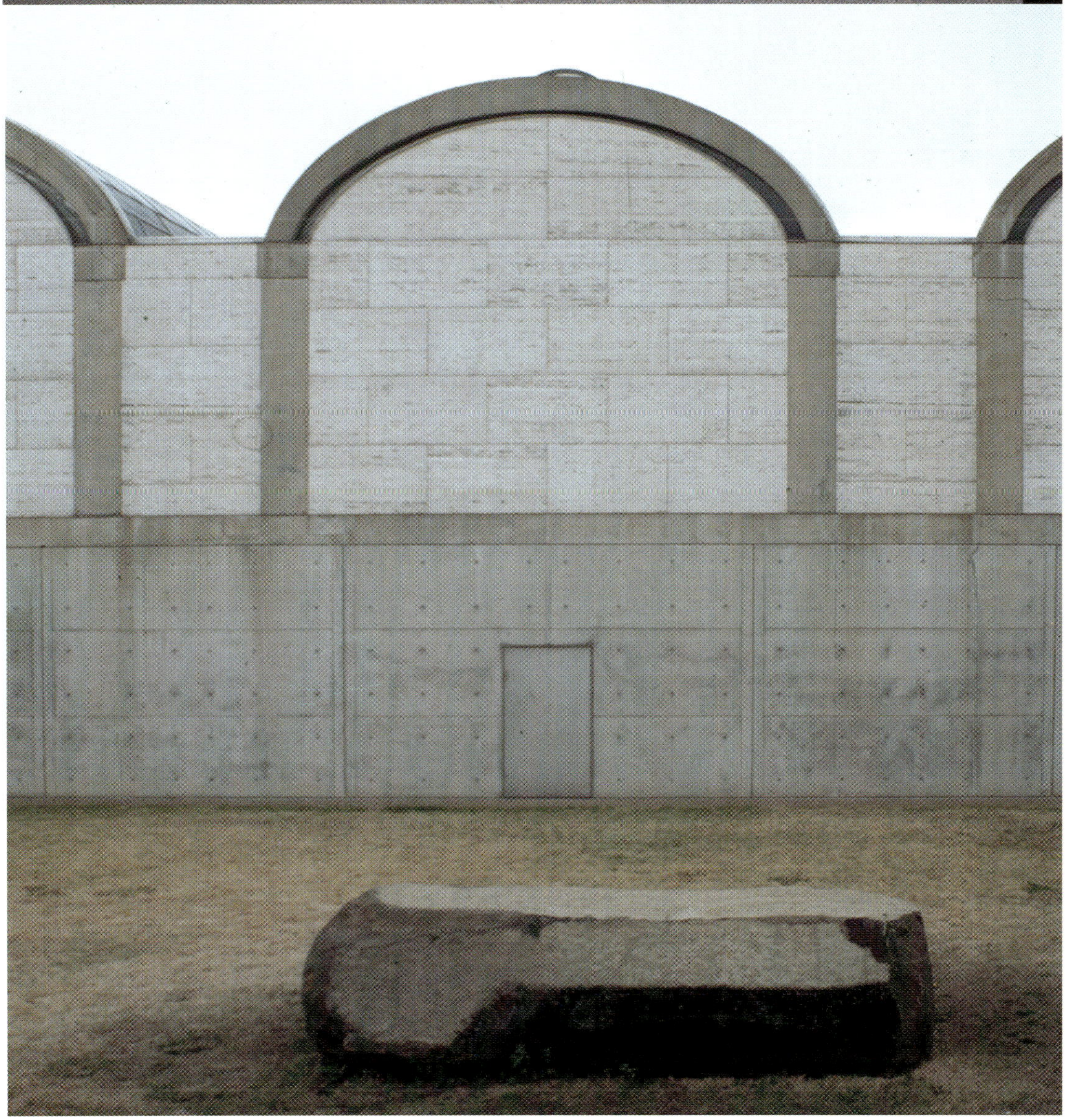

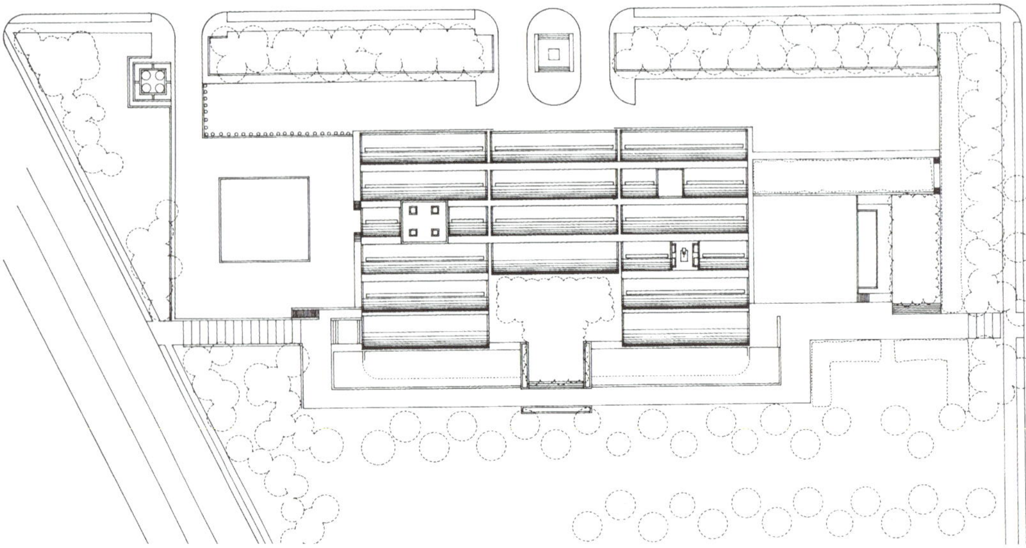

Second, he manages to make sense of the large unbuilt site area with a series of outdoor rooms as gardens and sculpture-courts, which serve to introduce the building. Third, he accepts and exploits edge conditions and level changes across the site. There are contrasted fronts for pedestrians and vehicles at different levels, each facing one of the quiet avenues bordering the site to east and west (as opposed to the busy ones to north and south). These fronts, the longer faces, show lead roofs over the vaults. Each is symmetrical with central entrance, though neither is approached axially.[3] The vehicle entrance to east is the more severe and imposing in scale with its two storeys, but there is no doubting the supremacy of the western front, with its more elaborate treatment, its triple porticos, extensive lawn and basins. This is the main front, leading to the main floor, the *piano nobile*. It is the best façade, but it is approached mainly via the corners, for the majority of pedestrians arrive from north and south. These sides display their vault ends like a series of gables to the busy roads. Six vaults deny the possibility of central entrance,[4] while the open vault to west in each case introduces a radical asymmetry, leading visitors through to the west front.

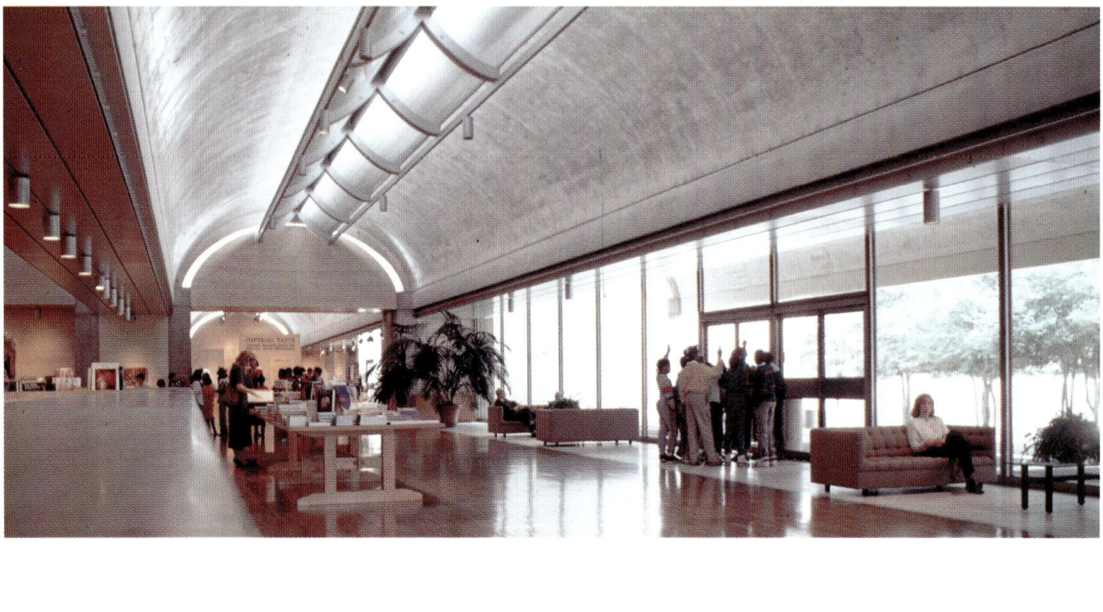

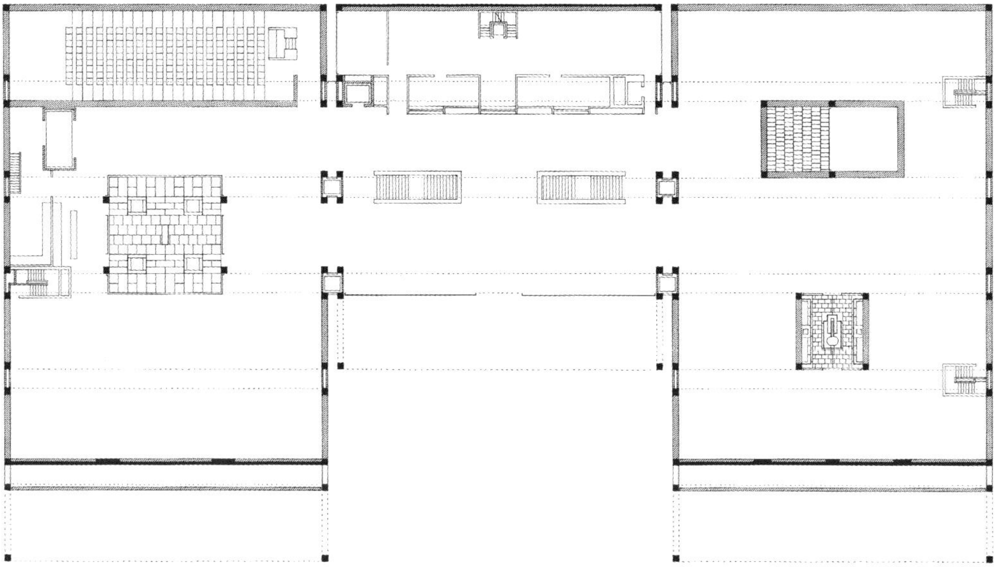

6. (opposite) Site plan, north is left and main entrance bottom.

7. (below opposite) Main entrance hall.

8. (above) Main floor plan, orientated as site plan.

Key: 1 outer portico,
2 grove of trees,
3 inner portico,
4 entrance hall,
5 gallery,
6 inner court,
7 restaurant,
8 lecture hall,
9 main stairs.

9. (right) Constructional axonometric (from Frampton 1995).

10. (below) South-north section through the six vaults, with portico to right and double-height lecture hall to left.

6, 8, 10, 14, 18 Original Kahn drawings © 1977 Louis I. Kahn Collection, University of Pennsylvania and Pennsylvania Historical and Museum Commission.

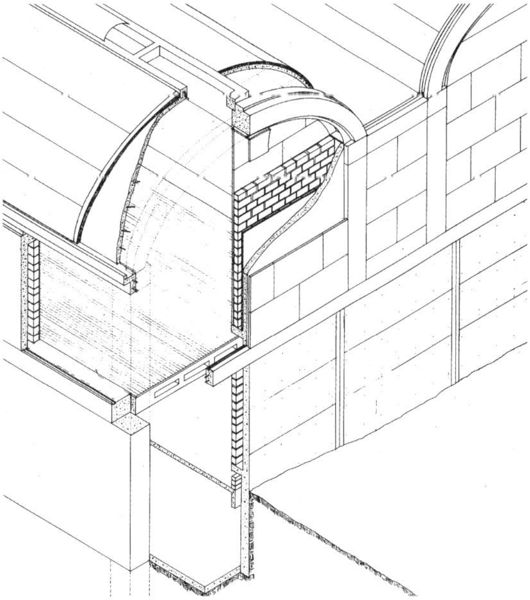

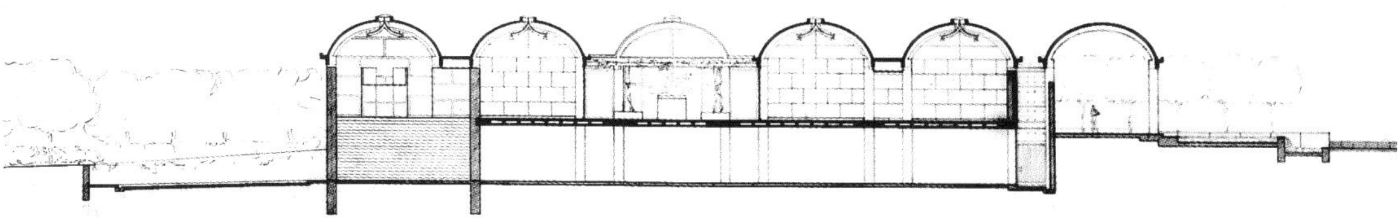

North and south approaches are treated in contrasting ways, with car-park and sunken garden respectively. The path in each case leads to the long cool vault which acts as first portico, with a stone seat on the inside and a cooling basin of water opposite. A second route in front of each basin provides an alternative path more external to the building, arriving at a central flight of steps. These steps and the outer porticos meet at a central square on the building's east-west axis, which is also the axis of entry. Here it is a surprise to discover not a bombastic focal court as envisaged in some of Kahn's earlier plan versions,[5] but a grid of trees, whose low canopy creates a second, natural portico, reminiscent of the orange tree court at the Great Mosque of Cordoba. Having turned onto the axis, one discovers beyond the trees another vault, identical in shape and dimensions to the outer ones except that one crosses it transversely, and it has closed ends.[6] A few steps lead into the shade of this third portico, and a glass wall beyond leads to the interior.

11. One of the small courts interrupting the vault system.

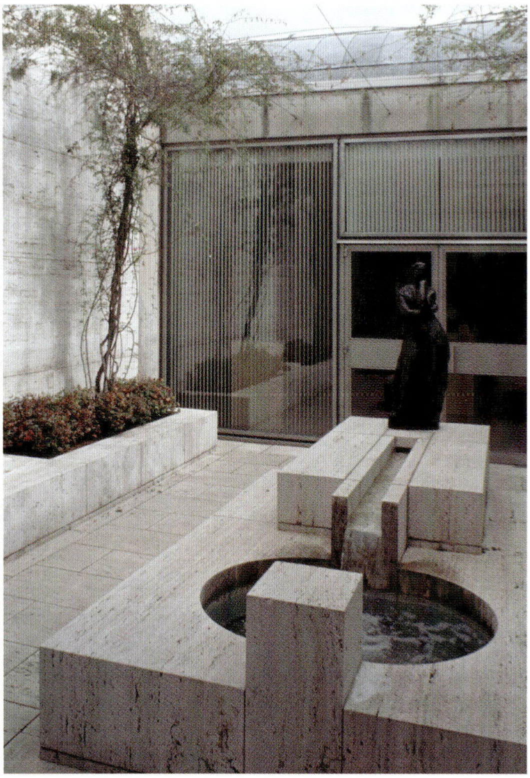

A glass door in the glass wall opens onto a vaulted entrance hall. The structure is the same shape and size as before, but instead of being solid, the vault has a slot at its apex and daylighting reflectors, the system used throughout the exhibition galleries. The light is of a radically different character, but seems comparable in intensity to that of the adjacent portico. External and internal vaulted spaces stand in a tense and fascinating contrast right at the centre of the plan, for the glass wall divides third from fourth bay in a total sequence of six. If the sixth bay is excluded, however, as not being part of the internal experience of the building, the inner vaulted space is the third bay of five transversely, and the second of three longitudinally - the central one in both directions: it is thus the focal space of the museum.

Almost immediately on entry, one is expected to turn left or right onto the main north-south axis of the building. Such a shallow turn is usually a tricky thing for an architect to do,[7] but it works here because of the dominance of the vault and the long vistas opened up in both directions. The paired longitudinal staircases help too, their strong concrete containing walls creating a barrier to the next vault eastward, which contains the gallery shop. What could be an uncomfortable symmetry in the main routes is avoided by a long view of the major galleries to south, while the view north is shorter, broken by an open court on axis. The court divides between temporary exhibition space to west, restaurant and lecture hall to east. At the south end of the building both sides are given to the main gallery, where the fine collection of paintings is hung. Some smaller lightcourts relieve the repetition of the plan with glimpses out. The two sizes of court derive from the bay system running through the building, with additional columns added where the spans of vaults are broken. It is evident from views of the models produced at the various design stages, that the breaking of the vault structure with these courts was one of the principal ways in which variety was introduced into the composition, preventing excessive repetition.[8]

The system, daylighting and the vault

With all its subtleties and contrasts of spatial sequence, one easily forgets what a systematic and repetitive building the Kimbell is, how strict in its geometry. For although in execution the building responds to specificities of many kinds, the essential idea is typological, growing from one

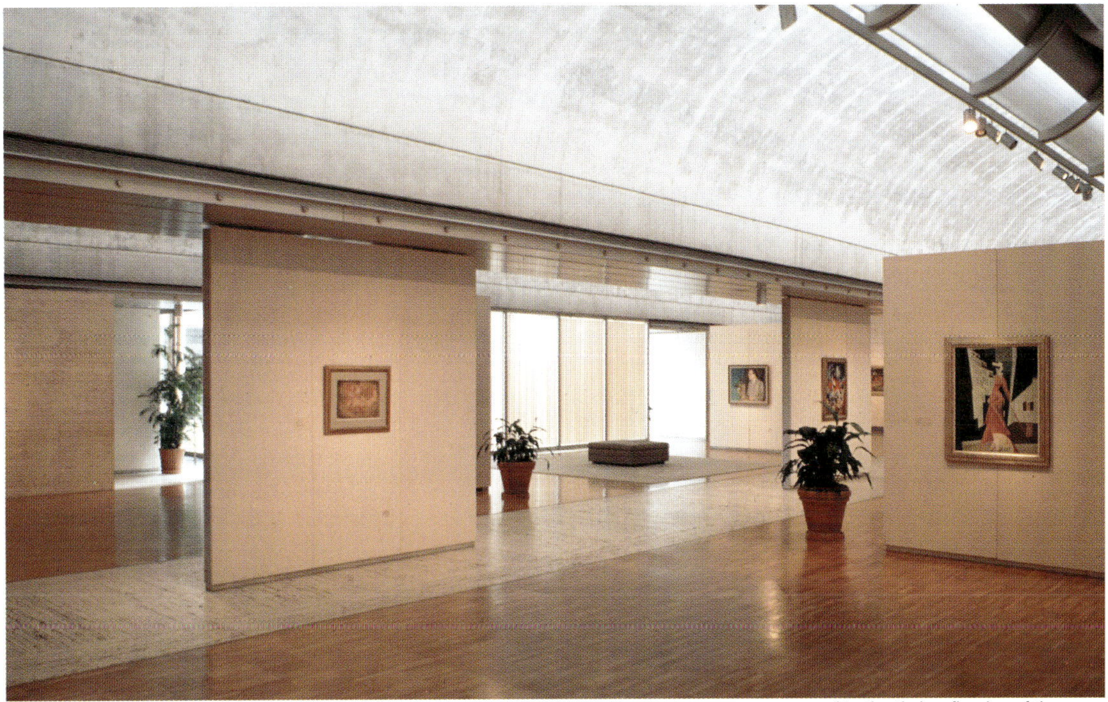

12. Typical gallery space with flexible partitions. Travertine floor marks the 'serving' spaces as opposed to the timber flooring of the 'served'.

13. Main stairs from basement entrance occupying a serving space between vaults

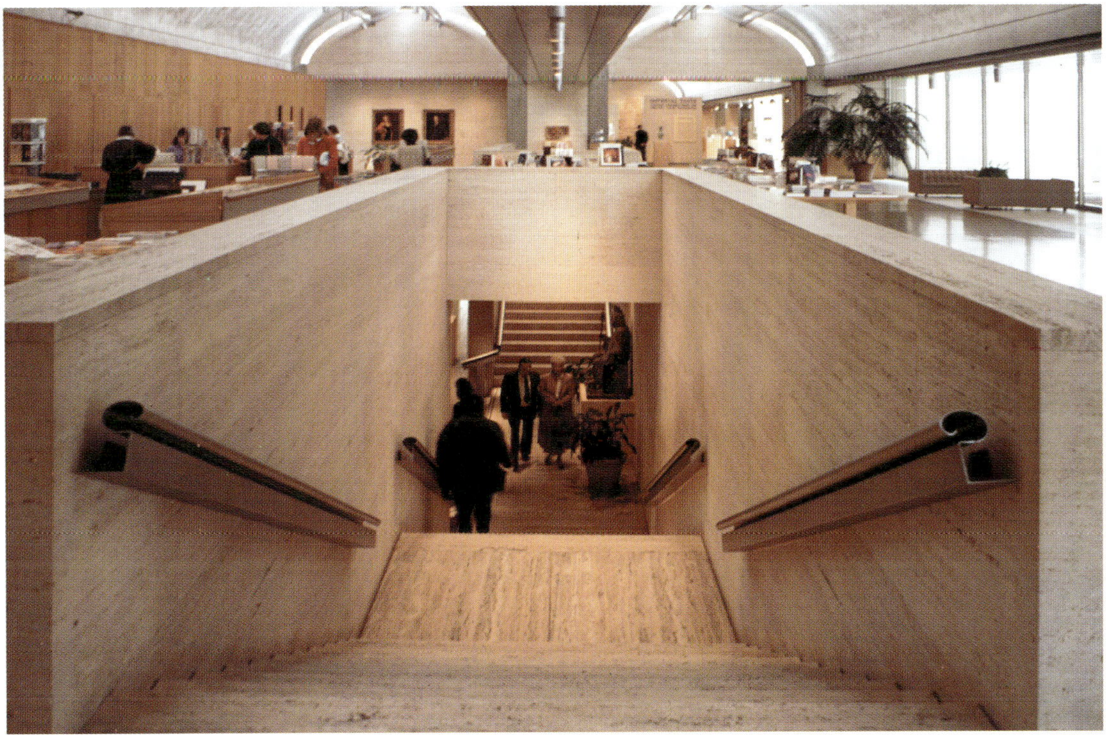

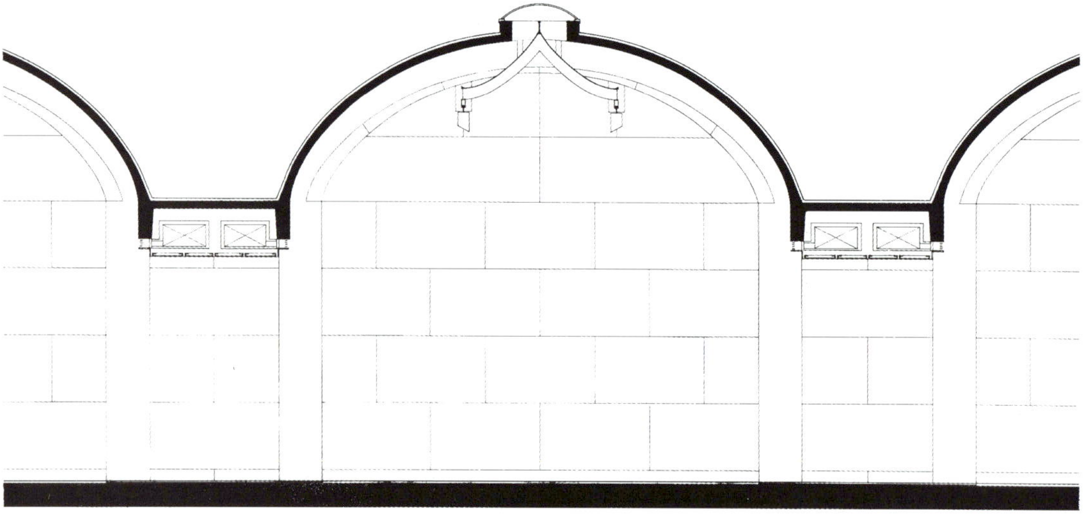

14. Vault section showing reflecting daylighting device and service provision.

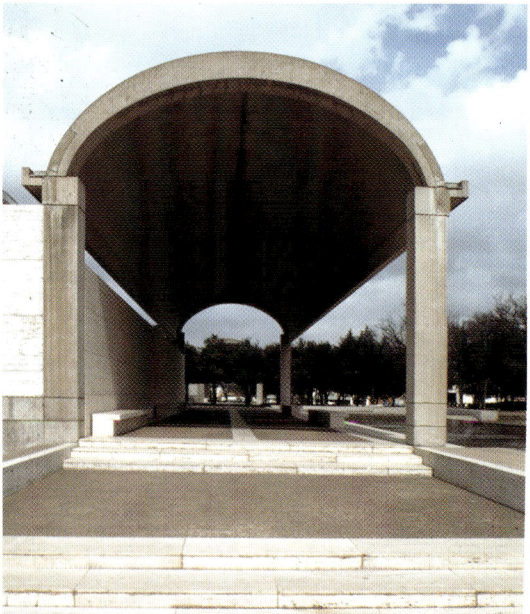

15. The vault presented as a free-standing element in the outer portico, making its structure clear.

16. Cycloid geometry of the vault, rolling a circle along a line.

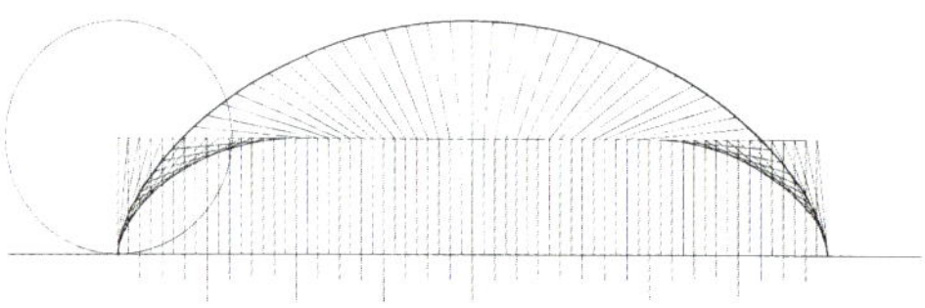

element: a rectangular vault with columns at its corners, its section inspired by daylighting requirements. Daylighting has always been a major concern in galleries, but as deterioration of paintings became better understood, conservationists imposed more and more restrictive limits. Directly sunlit or brightly daylit galleries are no longer considered acceptable, and light at the permitted level can seem very dim, particularly for fragile works like watercolours. Where daylight is allowed, the obsession with quantification has led designers to tortuous arrangements of mobile louvres and filters to even out the fluctuations, but ironically it is the very variability of daylight that is also its most inspiring quality.

As we saw in Chapter 14, Mies was quite prepared to put a magnificent national collection of paintings into basement rooms devoid of daylight, and also in many of his buildings to make inhabited rooms without windows. It has become quite normal in deep-plan buildings to rely on artificial light and forced ventilation, leading all too often to oppressive and placeless environments, where people do not know if it is day or night - a perceptual deprivation of measurable psychological effect. Kahn instinctively rebelled against this tendency, claiming that daylight was essential to the experience of architecture:-

'We were born of light. The seasons are felt through light. We only know the world as it is evoked by light, and from this comes the thought that material

is spent light. To me, natural light is the only light, because it has mood - it provides a ground of common agreement for man - it puts us in touch with the eternal. Natural light is the only light that makes architecture.' [9]

Throughout his work Kahn strove to bring daylight into his buildings and to every possible room. He was determined that the Kimbell museum, like his other museums and galleries, should be daylit, but in this case the difficulty was exaggerated by the strength of the outdoor light in relation to what was allowable for conservation of the paintings. At latitude 35°, Fort Worth is roughly comparable with Athens and Casablanca, hot in summer, and very bright. To reduce the intensity, Kahn devised a double reflection system: daylight and sunlight pass through a transparent rooflight along a slot at the apex of the vault, falling on a curved reflector of perforated metal.[10] Some light passes through the perforations, so the rooflight is visible and the metal element has a glow of its own, but the majority of the light is reflected onto the underside of the concrete vault, and from there reflected again onto the paintings. As Kahn put it:

'The vault is a kind of surface that can receive light. The measure of an interior space is its sense of position to light, and in what way the light confirms the chosen shape of the room.' [11]

The concrete is grey, thus only moderately reflective, but the colour of the light reaching the paintings seems natural. The vaults run strictly north-south, so the most even light is at midday, and the bias shifts from side to side between morning and afternoon. When clouds pass, the change in light flickers dramatically down the length of the building. Because of the way the light from the narrow slot is spread, the whole building feels lighter and more transparent. But the real stroke of genius is in the transition of the lighting, from the solid but side-lit vaults of the portico to the illuminated ones within. An astonishing degree of attenuation goes quite unremarked.

The glowing vault is a skyscape, a new artificial version of the heavenly vault. It is also, as noted in discussion of Lewerentz, a form associated with religious buildings throughout the ages. Few have managed to use it in the twentieth century without it seeming archaic,[12] but Kahn's vault is in no way anachronistic, for it makes structural sense, and the organisation of the whole building grows around it. At about seven metres across, the vaults are convenient in scale and height, and when cast as structural shells, allow a span along their axis of some 30 metres. They look deceptively simple, but in fact were the result of long development and discussion with engineers. Several curved forms were tried before arriving at the final cycloid section, and the upstand and downstand edges at support and apex were thickened for structural strength. In order to achieve the long span without deflection, post-tensioning also had to be employed, with cables that are completely concealed.[13] As with Lewerentz in the last chapter, the structural expression is very selective.

The vault form appears at its most naked in the portico, visibly supported only at the corners, but it persists throughout the building, even stretching out and becoming double height for the lecture hall.[14] The unusual structure gives an exceptional ratio between longitudinal and lateral spans of more than 4:1. It is this stark contrast between bay sizes in the two plan axes that makes the axial progressions described earlier workable, and it is one of the major innovations of the building.

The room, served and serving

As an axially entered building with a symmetrical frontage, the Kimbell might be considered classical, and its formality certainly reflects Kahn's Beaux Arts training. Throughout his career he used geometry in a precise and obsessive way, and it is typical that he ignored the skewed site boundary, precisely the element that Hans Scharoun would have taken as a main opportunity. Kahn never permitted himself such geometric freedom. For him, as for Wright or Mies, the controlling geometry not only rolled out a regular rhythm but also regulated the way in which the parts would fit together, their various material thicknesses being absorbed. But unlike the other architects, it also allowed Kahn in the age of infinite flowing space, to hang on to the idea of the room as a finite self-centred entity and a meeting place:-

'Architecture comes from the making of a room... The room is the place of the mind. In a small room one does not say what one would in a large room. In a room with only one other person...the vectors of each meet. A room is not a room without natural light. Natural light gives the time of day and [allows] the mood of the seasons to enter.' [15]

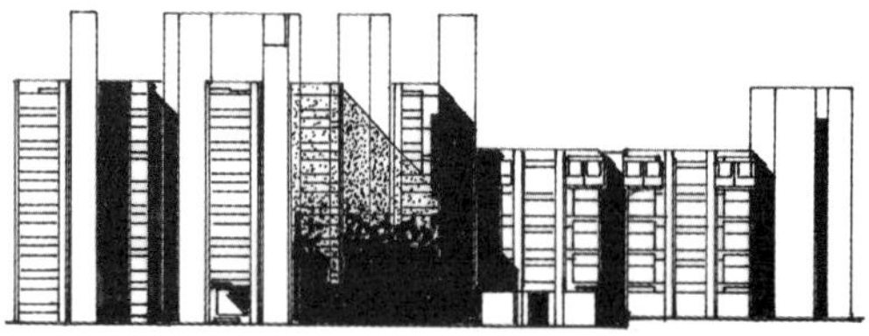

17. Kahn: Richards Medical Laboratories at the University of Pennsylvania of 1957-61, elevation showing the narrow service towers and larger served blocks.

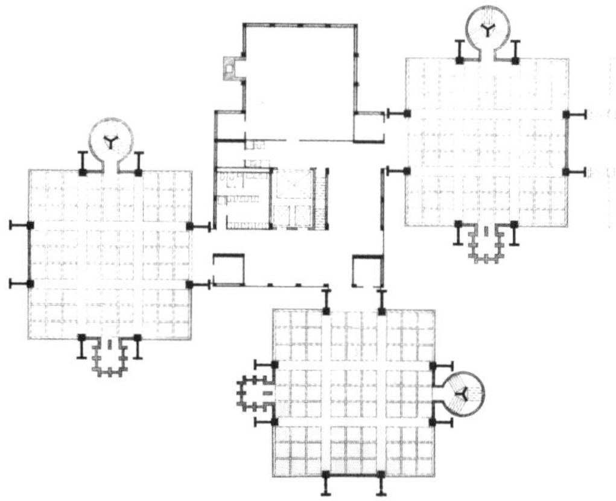

18. Richards Laboratories, typical floor plan.

19. (opposite) Kimbell: the inner portico and grove of trees.

The nobility of the room requires a certain completeness and detachment from other rooms, giving rise to in-between spaces, zones of negotiation which gradually became a set of secondary areas not conceived as rooms but as a serving apparatus. Here could be put all the clutter not wanted in the noble rooms: the pipes and wires, heating and ventilating, even the ways to get in and out. This gradually became a key theme of Kahn's work, reaching its most extreme expression in the served and serving towers of the Richards Medical Laboratories at the University of Pennsylvania of 1957-61. Kahn's way of making architecture out of the discipline of servicing, now widely regarded as his main contribution to the history of architecture, grows precisely out of his respect for 'the room'. At Kimbell the notion of served and serving seems less obvious, perhaps because it is so perfectly integrated. The vaults are the 'rooms' and the low-ceilinged bands of space between them are the servants. Kahn was very pleased that the forms of the vaults proved strong enough to always to retain their roomness:-

'Even when partitioned, the room remains a room. You might say that the nature of the room is that it always has the character of completeness.' [16]

Adjacent vaults could easily have shared a column, but Kahn wanted the structural entity defining his room - the vault with four columns - to have some autonomy, and having decided on two columns at each junction, it was possible to space them apart to produce a 2 metre gap. Turned into bands of servicing, these gaps allow rainwater collection channels on the roof above, and introduce air-conditioning and electrical services at ceiling level. Creating a banded plan with an ababababa rhythm, they provide locations for lavatories, lifts and stairs including the main ones. The bay rhythm is further underlined by a floor treatment of wood under the vaults and travertine between. In the gallery spaces, the low soffits in the servant areas provide opportunities to fix temporary screens, subdividing the space and increasing the hanging surface. Thus a measure of flexibility is incorporated. The screens can be fixed in the centre of the servant area or closer to either edge.

There are gaps of another kind between the three 30m bays in the other plan axis, though these do not have a servicing role and are relatively narrow. Pragmatically they must provide a neat thermal expansion joint, but their main significance is certainly conceptual, giving the 'rooms' autonomy and producing a differentiation between the central body of the building and its two side wings. They exaggerate the threshold, and one registers, through dramatic glimpses of the outside world at the end of the open slots, that one is leaving one territory and entering the next. Most crucially, however, the longitudinal gaps allow daylight to enter the eyebrow-like glazed apertures where each vault meets its end wall, a device intended to enhance the floating impression of the vault, as well as demonstrating that the end wall is not structural. Kahn commented: *'I put the glass between the*

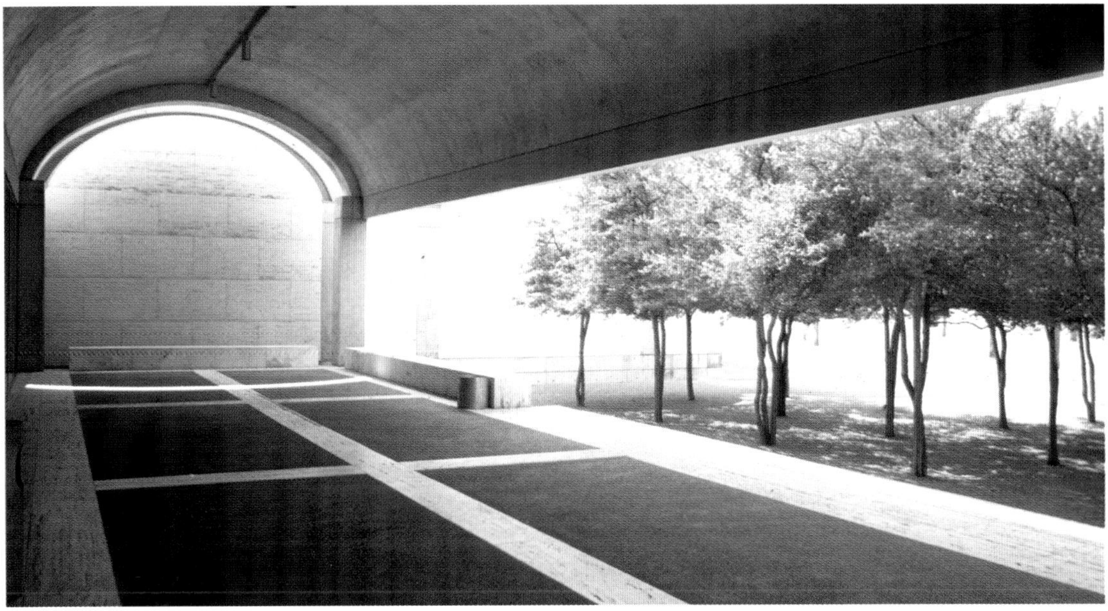

structure members and the members which are not of structure because the joint is the beginning of ornament. And that must be distinguished from decoration which is simply applied. Ornament is the adoration of the joint.' [17]

Construction and detail

Kahn is known for his interest in the appropriate use of materials, and his line about asking a brick what it wants to be is often quoted. The following statement puts the case very directly:

'I believe the artist instinctively leaves indications of the process by which an object was created, in architecture as in the other arts. The tendency to embellish the exteriors of buildings derives from the custom of hiding their component parts and the manner of their creation. The structures we build should meet all the technical requirements of the spaces they define. False ceilings which conceal the elements of construction tend to destroy the proportion. We need to design in the same way as we build: from the bottom up. The building ought to reveal the materials of which it is made and the way it was put together. In this way architecture will have the expressive power which comes from method rather than superficial ornamentation. The result of this is that it will not be necessary to doctor the construction with acoustic partitions or artificial lighting, or conceal the ducting, pipes and wiring.' [18]

Most materials used at Kimbell exhibit their natural form and texture, and a very conscious contrast is made between structural concrete and travertine infill. On the side walls, for example (fig. 5), the basement level is in-situ reinforced concrete with lead-filled bolt-holes. The placing of shuttering boards is fastidiously designed and plainly shown, a modern rustication. Above appears the vault end with its columns, also in exposed concrete, but given a continuous base and minimal capitals between columns and vault. Both vaults and interstitial bays are filled with travertine slabs, an expensive material appropriate to a *piano nobile*, but also clearly an applied material, expressing a degree of openness as opposed to the solidity beneath. Laid in a bonded pattern, the travertine reflects the tradition of stone work and its nature as wall,[19] while the monolithic concrete beneath is treated more mechanically, in accordance with shuttering procedure.

Travertine is also used as a flooring material both inside and out, framing panels of gravel or asphalt on the approach, and panels of fine wood within. In each case it states the regulating geometry of the whole design and controls the transition of spaces. What lies beneath one never knows, for the main floor is presented as if solid, with only a relatively small area on the east side around the lower vehicle entrance open and available to the public. The very considerable mechanical servicing that must be present in the rest of that basement is rendered as invisible as possible.

Quality of detailing at Kimbell is impressive: even in the lavatories, the position of every tap and switch is accommodated, with tiles and stainless steel panels meshing at every junction. A particularly representative detail is the handrail of the main stair (fig. 13), curved in a continuous section of stainless steel. Shaped to welcome the hand, it reveals at each end how it is made, and what it is made of. Also it seems to comment on the vault theme above, for the vault is likewise an extruded section, and so much in the building has to do with whether you are confronted with its length or its cross-section.

Conclusion

As with the Beaux Arts tradition that inspired him, there is always a danger with Kahn that the geometry of a building can become too dominant, the schematic idea of a repeated element too insistent. Yet at Kimbell, thanks perhaps to a relatively protracted gestation involving no less than nine design stages, the balance between the general and the particular comes off to perfection. It operates as a theme and variations. The use of essentially the same vault for portico and gallery, for example, introduces the theme of the building to approaching visitors and prepares them for the attenuated light. That the external vault is solid, thus completely different in character to that inside, is essential. It might seem a bit much to experience the gallery vault again over the restaurant, but the strong side-light from the largest of the open courts produces another different experience. The vault appears again in a blindable form over the lecture hall, which seems almost forced into the long, thin volume, but the space is made special by the raking floor which sinks into the basement - and note the way the steps fall within the minor bay. Both within and without, there are many subtle variations which break symmetries and reinterpret the stated relationship between major and minor bays. But the most inspired invention of all was the lighting device, about which Kahn was not immodest to claim: *'I made a natural light fixture in place of electric fixtures, to filter the injurious rays and diffuse the light into the rooms. This could lead others now to do it better. It should edge itself into the realm of availabilities.'* [20] Nobody else has yet surpassed it.

Notes

1. Of course all buildings have sites and functions, involve structure, construction, services etc., have routes through them and present some kind of external image. I am not concerned here with mere practical fulfilment of these conditions, but their elevation to architectural themes.

2. The nature of such American cities is well explained by Thomas Colbert with the example of Houston, also in Texas. See *Space and Society* no. 40, Oct/Dec 1987, pp. 94-101.

3. This is a crucial point, dividing Kahn from his Beaux Arts inheritance and bringing him closer to the Organic Modernist tradition. The use of axes is not dissimilar to that of Asplund, whose famous portico at the Enskede crematorium is never approached on its axis of symmetry. For further reflections on this theme see *The Architectural Review* March 88, *From the neoclassical axis to aperspective space*.

4. Five or seven would have left a central vault, whereas with six the centre is solid. The same principle was observed by Asplund at the Gothenburg law-courts extension, where facade versions with an entrance have five or seven bays, and the built version without has six.

5. See the site plan of the eighth version, numbered KAM 31 in Ronner & Jhaveri 1987, p. 346.

6. The gap at roof level which throws daylight onto the end walls is of course vital.

7. It is generally easier to control movement into the depth of the plan, and in earlier versions Kahn spread out the building much more in an east-west direction, with as many as 14 bays as opposed to the final six, using up much of the lawn space that now lies at the west front. See second and fifth plan versions, KAM 18 and 21 in Ronner & Jhaveri 1987 pp. 344-5.

8. See model photos and plans in Ronner & Jhaveri 1987, pp. 340, 341, 344, 346.

9. Ibid p. 345.

10. For the story of the lighting system's tortuous development see Meyers *Making the Kimbell: a brief memoir* in Belinelli 1997, pp. 17-23.

11. Ronner & Jhaveri 1987, p. 345.

12. Some notable examples are Auguste Perret's church at Le Raincy, 1923, Erich Mendelsohn's synagogue at Cleveland, Ohio, 1952, Le Corbusier's Maisons Jaoul from the late 50s, and of course Lewerentz's St Mark's Björkhagen and St Peter's Klippan.

13. See Frampton 1995, p. 244.

14. Kahn evidently struggled with this, preferring at one stage a two-bay wide version (Ronner 1987 p. 346.) but the audience would have felt divided.

15. From Giurgola and Mehta *Louis I. Kahn* p.187, cited in Frampton 1995, p. 226.

16. Ronner & Jhaveri 1987, p.345.

17. Ibid.

18. Quoted in *Louis I Kahn, works and projects*, Romando Giurgola 1979.

19. Tectonic fiction as opposed to tectonic fact, but the top two courses which lie within the vault volume have a straight central joint, perhaps to remind us that it is not really bonded.

20. Ronner & Jhaveri 1987, p. 345.

Conclusion

'If the history books were illustrated, they gave the impression that the world had been moving steadily forward in the past thousands of years, from the vague to the defined, the crude to the scientific, the unfamiliar to the known. It was as though the nineteenth century had been a machine absorbing into itself at one end humanity dressed in fancy dress, unwashed, fierce and immoral, and emitting at the other modern men in their utilitarian clothes with their hygienic houses, their zeal for reform, their air of having triumphed by mechanical, economic and scientific means over the passionate, superstitious, cruel and poetic past.'

Stephen Spender, 1951.[1]

The poet captures the optimistic thrust of the modernist revolution, its worship of science and rejection of superstition, its arrogant assumption of having achieved a final enlightenment. But already at mid-century there is a touch of irony and more than a hint of disbelief.[2] Fifty years later the modernist style is gone, or at least is seen as only one style among others. The Bauhaus, to take a key example, seems both less and more than Nikolaus Pevsner claimed: less in the sense that it marked no final style and was not really about science and technology - only an *idea* of technology; more in the sense that it was an aesthetic *tour de force* and the crucial embodiment of a key institution, completing a now obvious symbolic role that was not always acknowledged. Most of the other works considered in this book are also both less and more than originally accounted, but the impression given by the whole series must surely be one of richness and diversity, not only of different concepts explored within different buildings, but even of multiple concerns within the same building. Not all the experiments can be regarded as successful, but there can equally be no blanket accusation of general failure or of a completely 'mistaken' direction.

If the buildings live on, many of the terms used to describe them seem bankrupt, or at least in need of redefinition. 'Functionalism', 'Rationalism', 'Expressionism', 'International Style', 'Organic Architecture' all have such tortuous histories that they have lost all clarity, and most of the works described in these pages transcend all such labelling systems.[3] 'Isms' can be either a gift or a curse, for they allow quick reification of a perceived style or movement in one decade, only to turn into a term of opprobrium the next. Increasingly they have become the weapons of influential critics and museum curators as the means to identify styles as commodities.[4]

The notion of a style to end styles and the conviction of arrival at a final plateau of enlightenment - both no longer tenable - made necessary a further revolutionary notion: the *tabula rasa*, the supposed cutting off of history, which has also since been questioned. Clearly, Modernists were happy to rebel against the increasingly meaningless proliferation of historical examples and the dead weight of academic tradition, but this did not mean that they could really start again from scratch. Even the youngest had a traditional training, and mostly they designed buildings in classical or other historic styles in their early years. This experience was carried over tacitly into their modernist work in nearly every case. With the hindsight of the Twenty-first Century, for example, Mies's gestures to Schinkel in his Berlin Gallery give it a moving historical depth. Le Corbusier's recycling of history in his post-war work, if not covered here, is also well known.[5] Kahn and Lewerentz's brave readoption of archaic vaults has been noted, but the skill required to manage this without kitsch was perhaps inadequately emphasised.

The most poignant example in these pages of a dialogue with history is surely Asplund's twenty-five year struggle at Gothenburg to retain the history of the context while yet being modern at the same time. Its many versions reveal the exceptionally broad vocabulary available to him and the sophistication of its roots. This utterly site-based project has unexpected parallels with those of Mendelsohn and Scharoun, both of which take their unique shape and massing from their urban surroundings.[6]

There are many ways in which works of architecture can succeed and fail, and it is the sign of a skillful architect that he or she addresses not just one but several at once. The complexity of doing so is belied by many of the theoretical shortcuts to which Modernists paid lip service, such as 'form follows function', but these mottoes were not so much wrong as too narrowly construed. There are clearly functional limits to the design of a knife and fork, for example, when the knife no longer cuts, the fork fails to retain the food, or the handle can no longer be grasped by the hand. This is equally true of a door handle, but with the added complication that it must indicate how the door is opened before providing the means. Whole buildings are yet more complicated, because their functions are several and less well-defined. Most activities could occur in a variety of settings, but some degree of spatial organisation is usually needed; which starts first to determine, and later to reflect, social rituals and habits of use, making them readable.[7] Dining may require table and chairs, for example, raising the question of how many places, in which order or hierarchy - round or rectangular table - and how the setting is related to the source of the food.

Prisons excepted, buildings are seldom coercive, but they can, and often do, imply use in a particular manner, reinforcing particular social customs. If mother habitually sits at head of table distributing the food, it becomes 'her place', reflecting her power and status.[8] This is a question of meanings read rather than of sheer physical fit, but the two are not readily separable: the felt softness of the bed confirms to the body the reading of softness that its appearance suggests to the eye. We move in our daily lives neither in a realm of pure utility (which would be difficult if not impossible to isolate) nor in a realm of pure signs and symbols. If a building is less than a text because the conventions of meaning are less securely established, it is at the same time much more than a text because we inhabit it, and because it gains its meaning in relation to experience of use.[9]

Most examples in the book explore this issue in some way. With their different wings for living and sleeping, their set positions for storage and furniture, their hierarchical culmination in the hearth and variable progressions of enclosure, Wright's Usonian houses (Chapter 12) have much to say about the way of life intended and the frontier spirit that inspired it. Taut's Berlin housing (Chapter 5) tries to be as efficient as possible in the use of space but also implies social reform, offering a dignified and well-ordered life for the low paid. Häring's farm (Chapter 2), with its pear-shaped cowshed plan, reflects not only the processes involved in feeding and caring for cattle, but the very relations between the cattle themselves: cows and bull, calves and heifers are all set in a hierarchical arrangement.[10] This is, of course, an ordering of the farmer's world for *his* sake more than for that of the cattle, whatever they might or might not be able to perceive. The Scharoun school mentioned at the close of Chapter 2 applies the same principle to a human situation. It shows how classes and other rooms can be articulated like separate houses in a village, at once confirming each class's identity and reducing the scale of the whole institution.[11] In the same architect's Mannheim Theatre Project (Chapter 13) the same kind of articulation confirms the identities of small and large theatres along with their flowing foyers, while the less public functions are subordinated into a more anonymous urban block.

Lewerentz's Klippan church (Chapter 15) seems less rhetorical in plan, but it is clearly hierarchical, with a sense of centre and periphery as well as axial routes. Seen in three dimensions, there is no mistaking the culminative presence of the vaulted church in relation to the lower and profanely roofed peripheral parish offices, and the whole burden of the vaulted roof is carried both literally and symbolically on a centrally placed steel cross. In all these examples, choices had to be made about what to articulate and by how much. It was not so much a question, then, of *whether* to articulate the programme as of *how*. The one big exception to all this is of course Mies, who chose to consider the programme unpredictable, and to design his architecture to be independent of it. Interestingly, this is by no means the mere practical matter it first appears to be, for the aesthetic power of Mies's approach depends quite as much on its deliberate aloofness as Häring's and Scharoun's does on its intended engagedness.[12]

The notion 'form follows construction' is a parallel case, difficult to fulfil in a definite and final way because so much interpretation is always required. It is inseparable, if different in emphasis, from alternative versions such as 'form follows material' or 'form follows structure'. Nervi's aircraft hangars (Chapter 9) took us about as near to the latter as anyone has yet managed to get, but the subtle differences in interpretation between the two hangar versions show that even so close to the structural limit there is much room for manoeuvre. That the change was largely procedural, i.e. concerned with the means of production, reveals just how much forms can be tied to construction processes, not just to structure and material. Häring, Wright, Mies, Lewerentz and Kahn all showed intense interest in expressed construction, yet each can be accused of selectivity, of being 'dishonest' in certain ways.[13] Häring switches from frame to loadbearing wall when it suits him, and plays games with brick bonding; Wright puts in secret steel for his cantilevers; Mies plays up his column capital but denies its base and hides his basement structure; Lewerentz exposes primary workmanship, yet suppresses how loads are carried over openings; Kahn worries over subtle differences between in-situ and precast concrete, contrasting them poetically with stone, yet he suppresses the very necessary tension cables needed to secure his 'archetypal' vault. As in the case of function, it is not so much a question of *whether* to express structure and construction, as of *how* or *how much*.

It can, at times, be equally important to suppress them, as with Le Corbusier's Villa Savoye (Chapter 7), whose dematerialised surfaces were intended to focus interest on form and proportion; or in Scharoun's Philharmonie interior where the 'aperspective' space enhances the experience of the music, making it mysterious and ethereal. To be reminded of the construction here could bring you down to earth with a bump.[14]

Whether form was to follow function or construction, the damaging shortcut was to take the issue too literally, too pragmatically. For with the rejection of the so-called historic styles came a rejection of ornament and symbolism, of the whole issue of meaning. In exaggerating the purely 'objective' and technical aspects, and in discovering the beauty of the unadorned, the rhetorical and mnemonic functions of architecture tended to be ignored, even if, in works such as those considered in this book, they remained tacitly present.[15]

But these, it must be said, were the works of the best pioneers. In sad contrast were thousands of dull utilitarian buildings made especially in the post-war era, that followed the modernist programme at its most literal, basic level. The enthusiasm for expressing the production process opened the floodgates to system building of the most crass and unpoetic kind, and the ethos of economy of means gave way, all too easily, to economy pure and simple.[16] By the end of the 1960s a 'Crisis in Architecture' was being declared,[17] and the so-called Post-modernist revolution was soon launched. It provoked a healthy new interest in meaning in architecture and a long-overdue reconsideration of the city, but it also encouraged a return to history, which led to a fresh pillaging and mixing of historic styles. Some traditionalists, with royal encouragement, even suggested dispensing with Modernism altogether, intending to return instead to the tried and tested old ways of building. Certainly there was an echo of approval from the general public, but the way we build and the way we live have changed so much in the past century that such attempts to put the clock back have ended up as mere stage-sets.[18]

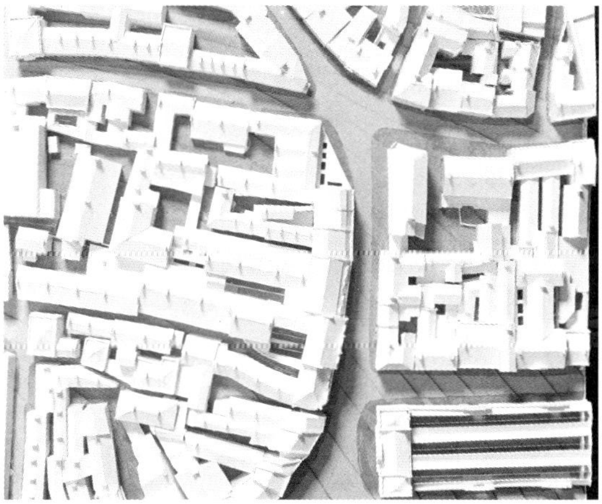

Model of a part of central Sheffield in 1900, built by students at the University of Sheffield School of Architecture.

Look at almost any city as it existed around 1900 and you see numerous narrow pitched-roof buildings huddled together around tight streets and courts. The city was dense because everything had to be within walking distance, and the buildings were narrow partly because of the limitations of span with wooden construction, partly for need of daylight and air in every room. The use of stone or brick walls and slate or tile roofs on timber structures reflected the limited availability of materials. The proliferation of chimneys revealed that coal and wood were the only sources of heat.

A century later, the city has spread far and wide, its workforce living in the suburbs and commuting by car or train. Great holes have been cut into its fabric to provide the ever expanding space for car parking. Its buildings can be both high - thanks to steel frame and lifts - and deep - thanks to electric light and air-conditioning. The materials used in construction are international, their choice driven largely by economic decisions. The institutions housed are larger and operate internationally, connected by telephone and computer. Shops are no longer local, serving across the counter, but huge international self-service stores offering stuff from across the world. The whole programme for most kinds of building has changed almost beyond recognition. Modernity is definitely here to stay.

But Modernism in architecture has reached a difficult point of development, at least in its humdrum everyday manifestation. The crisis of the late 1960s about the quality of the built environment has not abated, and even if there have been cosmetic improvements, the underlying situation has in many ways worsened. Mass production has become cheaper, handwork relatively more expensive, so that economic pressure to do things in standard ways has increased. Building materials are produced and distributed internationally, making local and traditional techniques a scarce luxury. It has become easier than ever before in history to wipe out whole areas of cities, their archaeology included, using mechanical excavators, and to rebuild them in a form quite unrelated to what was there before, destroying all sense of place. The growth of large inter-city design offices means that all too often the designer has no knowledge of the place and no interest in local history. The relentless proliferation of rules and regulations not only restricts the designer's scope but also determines increasingly where the money must be spent, yet neither the cost of implementing them nor their real effectiveness in preventing accidents seem to be much questioned.[19] Planning mechanisms, if clearly needed to prevent overdevelopment, also include an aesthetic component whose main effect is to bend all new buildings towards an innocuous norm, a sort of lowest common denominator of public taste.[20]

Buildings are increasingly built for profit rather than performance, and when envisaged by those in control firstly as financial assets, their perceived resale value becomes the driving consideration. For the sake of adaptability, generic, relatively anonymous forms and floor-plans are preferred, rather than ones designed around particular and specialised uses, and this flight from particularity is gently eroding the identity of every city. The generalised type of building is also often repeated from plans already in the drawer, which is as good for profit as it is bad for place. On larger buildings, a higher proportion of the budget is now spent on pipes, wires and allied services than ever before, often over 30% of total building costs.[21] This means that the money cannot be spent elsewhere, and that service engineers take a more dominant role in the design.

Added together, these factors make the design of buildings increasingly complex, difficult and hard to manage. The people who use the building hardly get a look in, and are unable to design for themselves any more, for even in the case of a modest family house, a trained specialist is required just to draw the drawings and run the gauntlet of the bureaucracies. The architect, as a result of it all, is heavy laden, but the ground is being cut away from beneath his or her feet, as power is handed over to a legion of specialists in techniques, costing, site management etc. Each wishes, consciously or not, to steer the project towards advantages seen from his or her viewpoint alone. It is too often only the architect, fighting an ever smaller corner, who owns up to a more general responsibility towards human culture and history.[22]

As the technical side of building and servicing has become more complicated, there has also been a tendency to separate the surface layer that is seen by the eye from the underlying substance, destroying the kind of integrity prized by most of the architects in this book. Implicit in much of the practice of Interior Design, this tendency has moved increasingly also into the realm of façades - Exterior Design - leaving the real substance of the building marooned somewhere between as a mere frame and servicing system, an anonymous and purely technical provision. Artificial lighting and ventilation are too often taken for granted, as are the deep plan and multiple floors, and economic considerations compel their use.[23] As the visible parts of buildings increasingly adopt the character of a stage set, they can of course quickly be changed for the next scene - the coming of the next business or the next fashion. Whether it be a shop, a restaurant, or the latest fashionable apartment, the fantasy of 'the look' has become the dominant force in the visual media, with ever more spectacular trade in virtual realities of every kind.[24]

While computer video projections may cost little and allow all kinds of exciting possibilities, such fantasy worlds exist in contrast with a real world in which we eat and sleep, make love, and lead our everyday lives.[25] The artificial place that is here today and gone tomorrow allows little opportunity for relationships to mature and memories to accrue: it hardly gets a chance to become a place at all.[26]

A real place needs a measure of stability if it is to retain the power to frame our lives and sustain our memories, but the extent to which shared memories are still carried by buildings remains unrecognised and undervalued. Because of this failure of understanding, the frenetic building and rebuilding of life-like stage-sets, often in luxury materials, has become self-defeating. It is also expensive and needlessly consumptive of energy, both that used during building, and that embodied in materials. To save the planet we need to build more carefully, for the long-term, with low energy, and in an integrated manner. It would help to rediscover the promise of responsive architecture made by the early Modern Movement. The emphasis would have to be on habitability rather than image, and we would need to attend less to style, more to the underlying processes that bring buildings about.

Finally, architecture continues to be about Place, Use and Construction. It is not just a matter of the pragmatic and literal provision of this triad, but a continuing commentary on their meaning and on their ever developing possibilities.

Notes

1. Stephen Spender, *World Within World*, Faber & Faber, London 1951, p. 1.
2. Spender's statement makes a fascinating contrast with that by Nikolaus Pevsner quoted on page 61, which is apparently lacking in any form of irony. It was, presumably written as much as eight years later than Spender's (Pevsner 1960, p. 217).
3. Inevitably we keep arguing about the uses of these terms (see, for example, Baumeister 5/2001 on *Expressionism*) because they are labels we have been brought up with. Even using them strictly within the limits of the original context in which they were coined does not work, because so many associations have been applied to them since. Some, like *Functionalism* and *Organic Architecture*, have gained negative connotations in some quarters and therefore arouse prejudices which make them a liability to use, but others such as *Rationalism*, still in general use as terms of approval, can be equally misleading.
4. *International Style, Post-Modernism* and *Deconstruction* were all launched with major exhibitions at the Museum of Modern Art, New York. This institution is clearly a powerful cultural legitimator.
5. The books on Le Corbusier are almost endless: for a useful range of views see the catalogue of the London Centenary Exhibition (Raeburn & Wilson 1987).
6. A good test of this is to imagine the building moved to another site: how well would it work, how much would it have to be adapted? In both cases cited here, not only are the irregular shape of the building and the section of the ground used to advantage, there has also been careful control of the massing and views from surrounding streets, none of which would work if it was summarily transplanted.
7. For a good general summary see Parker Pearson & Richards 1994, pp. 1-37.
8. It is often the father, of course, as in the example of the Swiss farmhouse reported in Rapoport 1969, p. 54. See also Visser 1993, pp. 121-136.
9. There was a vogue for referring to buildings *as* texts, see for example Blier 1994, the introduction.
10. See Blundell Jones 1999, pp.56-67, pp. 160-162.
11. See Blundell Jones 1995, pp. 136-151.
12. This argument is developed in Blundell Jones 1999, pp. 156-8.
13. The only perfect example I can think of is the French Provencale shepherd's hut where vaulted stone walls turn into vaulted stone roof so that only one material is used and it is left completely visible inside and out.
14. The abstraction of white plastered surfaces has remained an important part of many architects' vocabularies, allowing them to hide parts they do not want to expose, even if materials and construction are strongly expressed elsewhere in the same building.
15. On the Mnemonic functions of architecture see Blundell Jones 2000 (2).
16. The ills of system building were epitomised in the UK by the Ronan Point disaster of 1968. A searing critique and photographic record of the period can be found in Keller 1973.
17. Title of an issue of the *RIBA Journal* (London) by Malcolm McEwan 1969.
18. Epitomised by Quinlan Terry's Richmond Riverside, see Blundell Jones 1988.
19. Provision for fire safety often destroys quality of space and freedom of movement, as well as adding cost. Few dare challenge safety issues, but we should perhaps reflect on the wisdom of designing for something we hope will never happen rather than for things which will. Differences of view on what is safe are evident in the variations in building regulations for different countries, which suggest that in some cases we may be overdoing it.
20. In the UK, brick walls and slate roof have become a universally accepted vocabulary, even when the building is really a frame and most of the roof really flat.
21. Frampton 1995, p. 381.
22. There is clearly an aesthetic of good plumbing if that is your concern, or equally of good financial management: these do not necessarily support the architectural quality or habitability of the building.
23. For many building types concerned with display such as shops, daylight and sunlight have come to be regarded as dangerously unpredictable, if not destructive for goods: they are therefore considered better eliminated.
24. I mean restaurants and holiday homes as well as computer games!
25. I side with Joseph Rykwert on this; see Rykwert 2000, pp.156-159.
26. On when a place is not a place, see Augé 1995. A telling early critique of placelessness in orthodox Modernism of the 1960s was Jacques Tati's film *Playtime*, for which he built a series of special sets playing up the repetition, anonymity and confusion of purpose in the modern city.

Bibliography

Achenbach, Sigrid, ed. *Erich Mendelsohn,* exhibition catalogue of the Kunstbibliothek Berlin, 1987.

Ahlberg, Hakon ed. *Gunnar Asplund Architect*, Ab Tidskriften Byggmästaren Stockholm 1950 (reprint of English language edition 1981).

Ahlin, Janne. *Sigurd Lewerentz Architect*, MIT Press Cambridge Mass & London 1987.

Akademie de Künste. *Bruno Taut 1880-1938*, exhibition catalogue no. 128 from the centenary exhibition of 1980.

Akademie der Künste. *Max Taut 1884-1967*, exhibition catalogue no. 142, from the centenary exhibition of 1984.

Akademie der Künste. *Poelzig Endell Moll und die Breslauer Kunstakademie 1911-32*, exhibition catalogue, Berlin 1965.

Anderson, Stanford. *Peter Behrens and a New Architecture for the Twentieth Century,* MIT Press, Cambridge Mass 2000.

Architectural Association. *Sigurd Lewerentz 1885-1975: The Dilemma of Classicism*, Architectural Association Publications, London 1988.

Architectural Design 51. *From Futurism to Rationalism: The Origins of Modern Italian Architecture*, No. 51, 1/2 1981, Papadakis, London.

Augé, Marc. *Non-places: introduction to an anthropology of supermodernity*, Verso, London & New York 1995.

Bachelard, Gaston. *The poetics of Space*, Beacon Press, Boston 1969.

Banham, Reyner. *The New Brutalism*, Architectural Press, London, 1966.

Banham, Reyner. *Theory and Design in the First Machine Age*, Architectural Press, London, 1960.

Barbieri, Umberto. *J.J.P. Oud*, Artemis Verlag Studio Paperback, Zurich 1989. (German text, Italian original 1986).

Bauhaus Dessau Foundation & **Kentgens-Craig**, Margret, eds. *The Dessau Bauhaus Building 1926-1999*, Birkhäuser, Basel/Berlin/ Boston 1998.

Beevor, Antony. *Stalingrad*, Penguin Books, Harmondsworth 1999.

Behne, Adolf. *Der Moderne Zweckbau*, München 1926. (Modern edition Ullstein, Frankfurt / Main & Berlin 1964).

Belinelli, Luca ed. et al. *Louis I Kahn: the construction of the Kimbell Museum*, Exhibition catalogue of the Accademia di architettura dell' Universita della Svizzera Italiana, Skira, Milan 1997.

Benton, Tim. *The Villas of Le Corbusier*, Yale University Press, New Haven and London 1987.

Birksted, Jan ed. *Relating Architecture to Landscape*, E&F Spon, London 1999.

Blake, Peter. *Mies van der Rohe: Architecture and Structure*, Pelican Harmondsworth 1960.

Blaser, Werner. *Mies van der Rohe: the Art of Structure*, Thames & Hudson, London 1965.

Blundell Jones, Peter. *Red House, Architects Journal* (London) 15th January 1986, pp. 36-56. (Webb's house for Morris).

Blundell Jones, Peter. *From the Neo-classical Axis to Aperspective Space*, *The Architectural Review* March 1988, pp. 19-27. (An essay tracing parallel isues in the development of architecture by Aalto, Asplund, Häring, and Scharoun).

Blundell Jones, Peter. *Richmond Riverside: sugaring the pill, The Architectural Review* November 1988 (2), pp. 86-90. (Criticism of office development by Quinlan Terry).

Blundell Jones, Peter. *Der Bundestag, The Architectural Review* March 1993, pp. 20-33. (Analytical article on Bonn Parliament by Behnisch and Partners).

Blundell Jones, Peter. *Scharoun at Weissenhof, The Architectural Review* September 1993 (2), pp. 78-84.

Blundell Jones, Peter. *Hans Scharoun*, Phaidon Press, London 1995.

Blundell Jones, Peter. *Dialogues in Time: New Graz Architecture*, Haus der Architektur, Graz 1998.

Blundell Jones, Peter. *Hugo Häring: the Organic versus the Geometric*, Edition Axel Menges, Stuttgart 1999.

Blundell Jones, Peter. *Günter Behnisch,* Studio Paperback series, Birkhäuser Basle/ Boston/ Berlin 2000.

Blundell Jones, Peter. *Architecture as Mnemonic: The Accumulation of Memories around Morris's Red House*, Nineteenth Century Contexts, 2000 (2); Vol 21, pp. 513-540.

Blier, Suzanne Preston. *The anatomy of architecture, ontology and metaphor in Batammaliba architectural expression*, Cambridge University Press 1987 (2nd edition University of Chicago Press 1994).

Bolon, Carol R. Nelson, Robert S.& Seidel, Linda. *The Nature of Frank Lloyd Wright* The University of Chicago Press, Chicago & London 1988.

Boudon, Philippe. *Lived-in Architecture*, Lund Humphries, London 1972.

Bourdieu, Pierre. *Outline of a Theory of Practice*, Cambridge University Press 1977.

Bourdieu, Pierre. *Algeria 1960*, Cambridge University Press, Cambridge 1979.

Bourdieu, Pierre. *Distinction: a Social Critique of the Judgement of Taste*, Routledge and Kegan Paul, London & New York 1984.

Brooks, H Allen, ed. *Le Corbusier*, Princeton Univ. Press 1987.

Bullock, Nicholas. *Housing in Frankfurt 1925-1931 and the new Wohnkultur, The Architectural Review* June 1978, pp. 335-344.

Caldenby, Claes & Hultin, Olof. *Asplund,* Ginkgo Press California 1997.

Collins, George R. *Camillo Sitte and the birth of modern city planning*, London 1965.

Conrads, Ulrich. *Programmes and Manifestoes on 20th Century Architecture*, Lund Humphries, London 1970.

Constant, Caroline. *The Woodland Cemetery: Toward a Spiritual Landscape,* Byggförlaget, Stockholm 1994.

Cornell, Elias. *Stockholm Town Hall*, Byggförlaget, Stockholm 1992.

Cruickshank, Dan, ed. *Erik Gunnar Asplund* published by *The Architects Journal*, 1988. (Essays on Gothenburg Law Courts parts 1 and 2, by Peter Blundell Jones on pp. 57-96.)

De Zurko, Edward. *Origins of Functionalist Theory*, Columbia University Press New York 1957.

Denis, Marie-noele and Groshens, Marie-Claude. *Alsace* volume of *L'Architecture Rurale Francaise*, Paris 1978 (french text).

Douglas, Mary. *Purity and Danger*, Routledge and Kegan Paul London, 1966.

Durand, J. N. L. *Précis des lecons d'Architecture données à l'Ecole Royale Polytechnique*, Paris 1819. (Facsimile edition Verlag Dr. Alfons Uhl, Nördlingen 1985).

Dymling, Claes, ed. *Architect Sigurd Lewerentz, Drawings and Photographs*, Byggförlaget, Stockholm 1997.

Engfors, Christina. ed. *Lectures and briefings from the internatonal symposium on the architecture of Erik Gunnar Asplund* 14th-17th October 1985 in Stockholm and Gothenburg, Swedish Museum of Architecture, Stockholm 1986.

Evans, Robin. *The Projective Cast: Architecture and its Three Geometries*, MIT Press, London & Cambridge Mass 1995.

Flagge, Ingeborg & **Stock**, Wolfgang Jean. *Architektur und Demokratie*, Hatje, Stuttgart 1992.

Ford, Edward R. *The Details of Modern Architecture, Volume 2, 1928-98* MIT Press, Cambridge Mass, 1996.

Frampton, Kenneth. *Modern Architecture: a Critical History*, Thames & Hudson, London 1980.

Frampton, Kenneth. *Studies in Tectonic Culture: the Poetics of Construction in Nineteenth and Twentieth Century Architecture*, MIT Press, Cambridge Mass & London 1995.

Frank, Josef, ed. *Die Internationale Werkbundsiedlung Wien 1932*, volume VI of the series *Neues Bauen in der Welt*, Verlag von Anton Schroll & Co, Vienna 1932.

Gebser, Jean. *The Ever-Present Origin*, authorized translation by Noel Barstad with Algis. Ohio University Press, Ohio 1991.

Geertz, Clifford. *Local Knowledge*, Basic Books, New York 1983.

Geertz, Clifford. *Available Light: Anthropological Reflections on Philosophical Topics*, Princeton, New Jersey 2000.

Germann, Georg. *Gothic Revival in Europe and Britain: Sources, Influences and Ideas*, Lund Humphries with the Architectural Association, London 1972.

Giedion, Sigfried. *Mechanisation Takes Command*, MIT Press, Cambridge Mass & London 1950.

Giedion, Sigfried. *Space, Time and Architecture*, MIT Press, Cambridge Mass & London 1941.

Goodman, Nelson. *Languages of Art*, Hackett, Indianapolis 1976.

Goodman, Nelson, & **Elgin**, Catherine. *Reconceptions in Philosophy & Other Arts & Sciences*, Routledge, London 1988.

Graf, Otto Antonia. *Die Kunst des Quadrats zum Werk von Frank Lloyd Wright* Verlag Böhlau, Vienna 1983 (2 vols).

Greene, Herb. *Mind and Image*, Granada, London 1976.

Gropius, Walter. *The New Architecture and the Bauhaus*, Faber and Faber, London 1935.

Herbert, Gilbert. *The Dream of the Factory-made House*, MIT Press, Cambridge Mass 1984.

Herbert, Robert L. ed. *Modern Artists on Art*, Prentice Hall, New Jersey 1964. (Reprinted and translated essays by Le Corbusier and Ozenfant, Malevich, Mondrian, and Gabo among others).

Hertzberger, Herman. *Lessons for Students in Architecture*, Uitgeverij 010 Publishers, Rotterdam 1991.

Hoesli, Bernhard, ed. *Alvar Aalto Synopsis,* Birkhäuser, Zurich 1970 in association with Swiss Federal Institute of Technology Zurich.

Hilberseimer, Ludwig. *Internationale neue Baukunst*, Verlag Julius Hoffmann, Stuttgart 1927.

Hitchcock, Henry Russell, and **Johnson**, Philip. *The International Style, Architecture since 1922*, Norton, New York 1932.

Hitchcock, Henry Russell. *Modern Architecture: Romanticism and Reintegration*, Payson and Clarke, New York 192. Reprint Hacker, New York 1970.

Hugh-Jones, Stephen, and **Carsten**, Janet, eds. *About the House*, Cambridge University Press 1995.

Huizinga, John. *Homo Ludens: a Study of the Play-Element in Culture*, Routledge and Kegan Paul, London 1949.

Issacs, Reginald. *Gropius: an Illustrated Biography of the Creator of the Bauhaus*, Bullfinch Press, USA 1991.

Jaeggi, Annemarie. *Fagus: Industrial Culture from Werkbund to Bauhaus*, Princeton Architectural Press, New York 2000.

James, Kathleen. *Erich Mendelsohn and the Architecture of German Modernism*, Cambridge University Press 1997.

James-Chakraborty, Kathleen. *German Architecture for a Mass Audience*, Routledge, London 2000.

Joedicke, Jürgen, and **Lauterbach**, Heinrich. *Hugo Häring, Schriften, Entwurfe, Bauten*, Karl Krämer Verlag Stuttgart, 1965. (General documentation with drawings, photos, and 24 of Häring's essays written between 1925 and 1954).

Joedicke, Jürgen, ed. *The Works of Pier Luigi Nervi*, Architectural Press, London 1957.

Joedicke, Jürgen. *Shell Architecture*, Tiranti, London 1962.

Joedicke, Jürgen & **Plath**, Christian. *die weissenhofsiedlung stuttgart,* Karl Krämer Verlag Stuttgart 1977.

Johnson, Philip. *Mies van der Rohe*, Secker & Warburg, London 1978.

Jones, Owen. *The Grammar of Ornament,* Dorling Kindersley London 2001. (Original edition Day & Son London 1856).

Junghanns, Kurt. *Bruno Taut 1880-1938*, Henschelverlag Berlin 1970 (German text).

Keller, Rolf. *Bauen als Umweltzerstörung*, Artemis, Zürich 1973.

Kirsch, Karin. *Die Weissenhofsiedlung: Werkbund-Austellung "Die Wohnung", Stuttgart 1927*, Deutsche Verlags-Anstalt, Stuttgart 1987 (English edition Rizzoli 1989). References taken from the German Edition, which may differ over page numbers.

Kirschenmann, Jörg C; and **Syring**, Eberhard. *Hans Scharoun: die Forderung des Unvollendeten*, Deutsche Verlags-Anstalt Stuttgart 1993.

Kremer, Sabine. *Hugo Häring (1882-1958) - Wohnungsbau: Theorie und Praxis*, Karl Krämer Verlag, Stuttgart, 1984.

Kroll, Lucien. *The Architecture of Complexity*, Batsford, London 1986.

Lane, Barbara Miller. *Architecture and Politics in Germany 1918-1945*, Harvard University Press, Cambridge Mass 1968.

Lane, Barbara Miller. *National Romanticism and Modern Architecture in Germany and the Scandinavian Countries*, Cambridge University Press, Cambridge 2000.

Le Corbusier. *The Modulor*, translated by Peter de Francia and Anna Bostock, Faber, London 1961 (French edition 1951).

Le Corbusier. *Towards a New Architecture,* published in French as *Vers une Architecture*, Paris 1923, and in English translated by Frederick Etchells, John Rodker, London 1927.

Lethaby, William Richard. *Form in Civilisation*, (selected essays) London 1922.

Loos, Adolf. *Spoken into the Void: Collected Essays 1897-1900*, MIT Press, Massachusetts & London 1982.

Macdonald, Wiliam L. *The Architecture of the Roman Empire*, Yale University Press, New Haven & London 1965.

Markus, Thomas A. *Buildings and Power*, Routledge, London & New York 1993.

Mehlau-Wiebking, Friederike. *Richard Döcker: ein Architekt im Aufbruch zur Moderne*, Vieweg Braunschweig/Wiesbaden 1989.

Mendelsohn, Erich. *Erich Mendelsohn, Complete Works of the Architect*, first published Mosse Berlin 1930, english edition Triangle Publishing, London 1992.

Molema, Jan. *Jan Duiker*, Spanish/English edition by Uitgeverij 010, Rotterdam 1989.

Nerdinger, Winfried. *Theodor Fischer: Architekt und Städtebauer 1862-1938*, Ernst & Sohn, Berlin 1988.

Nerdinger, Winfried. *Walter Gropius*, Bauhaus Archive, Berlin 1985.

Nerdinger, Winfried. *Revolutionsarchitektur*, Hirmer, Munich, 1990.

Nervi, Pier Luigi. *Aesthetics and Technology in Building*, Harvard University Press, Cambridge Mass 1966.

Neumeyer, Fritz. *The Artless Word: Mies van der Rohe on the Building Art*, MIT press 1991. (German original *Das kunstlose Wort*, Berlin 1986).

Paavilainen, Simo, ed. *Nordic Classicism 1910-1930*, exhibition catalogue by Museum of Finnish Architecture, Helsinki 1982.

Parker Pearson, Michael & **Richards**, Colin. *Architecture and Order: Approaches to Social Space*, Routledge, London 1994.

Pearson, Paul David. *Alvar Aalto and the International Style*, Mitchell, New York, 1978.

Pehnt, Wolfgang. *Expressionist Architecture*, Thames & Hudson, London 1973, original German edition Hatje, Stuttgart 1973.

Pehnt, Wolfgang. *German Architecture 1960-1970*, Architectural Press, London 1970, original German edition Hatje, Stuttgart 1970.

Pevsner, Nikolaus. *Pioneers of the Modern Movement*, Faber and Faber, London 1936. Revised edition used here *Pioneers of Modern Design*, Penguin, Harmondsworth 1960.

Pevsner, Nikolaus. *A History of Building Types*, Thames & Hudson, London 1976.

Pfankuch, Peter, ed. *Adolf Rading, Bauten, Entwürfe und Erläuterungen*, Schriftenreihe der Akademie der Künste vol. 3, Berlin 1970. (German text).

Pfankuch, Peter, ed. *Hans Scharoun: Bauten, Entwürfe, Texte*, Akademie der Künste Berlin 1974, revised edition with updated worklist 1993. (Primary documentation on Scharoun).

Pitz, Helge & **Brenne**, Winfried, eds. *Die Bauwerke und Kunstdenkmäler von Berlin: Siedlung Onkel Tom Zehlendorf 1929 Architekt Bruno Taut*, Gebr. Mann, Berlin / Il Punto Editrice, Rome 1980. (German / Italian / English parallel texts).

Pommer, Richard, and **Otto**, Christian. F. *Weissenhof 1927 and the Modern Movement in Architecture*, University of Chicago Press, 1991.

Pommer, Richard; **Spaeth**, David; and **Harrington**, Kevin. *In the Shadow of Mies: Ludwig Hilberseimer, Architect, Educator and Urban Planner*, Rizzoli, New York 1988.

Porphyrios, Demetri. *Sources of Modern Eclecticism*, Academy Editions, London 1982.

Posener, Julius. *From Schinkel to the Bauhaus*, A.A. Paper number no. 5, Lund Humphries, London 1972.

Posener, Julius. *Hans Poelzig, Reflections on his Life and Work*, MIT Press, Cambridge Mass, 1992.

Posener, Julius. *Hans Poelzig*, Schriftenreihe der Akademie der Künste Berlin, Band 6, Gebr. Mann, Berlin 1970.

Pugin, Augustus Welby Northmore. *The True Principles of Pointed or Christian Architecture*, London 1853. (Various modern facsimiles).

Raeburn, Michael, and **Wilson**, Victoria, eds. *Le Corbusier, Architect of the Century*, Arts Council Catalogue, London 1987.

Rapoport, Amos. *House Form and Culture*, Prentice Hall, Englewood Cliffs, N.J. 1969.

Risselada, Max, ed. *Raumplan Versus Plan Libre*, Delft University Press 1988.

Ronner, Heinz and **Jhaveri**, Sharad, eds. *Louis I. Kahn: Complete Work 1935-74.* Birkhäuser, Basel 1987. (First ed. ETH, Zurich 1977).

Rosenbaum, Alvin. *Usonia: Frank Lloyd Wright's Design for America*, The Preservation Press, Washington 1993.

Rowe, Colin, and **Koetter**, Fred. *Collage City*, MIT Press, Cambridge Mass & London 1978.

Ruskin, John. *The Complete Works of John Ruskin*, eds E.T. Cook and A. Wedderburn, 13 vols, London 1903-12.

Ryan, Frank. *Tuberculosis: the Greatest Story Never Told, the Human Story of the Search*, Swift, Bromsgrove 1992.

Rykwert, Joseph. *The Seduction of Place,* Weidenfeld and Nicholson, London 2000.

Saint, Andrew. *Towards a Social Architecture: the Role of School Building in Post-War England*, Yale University Press, New Haven & London 1987.

Schildt, Göran. *Alvar Aalto: the Early Years*, Rizzoli, New York 1984.

Schildt, Göran. *Alvar Aalto: the Decisive Years*, Rizzoli, New York 1986.

Schildt, Göran. *Sketches: Alvar Aalto* MIT Press, Cambridge Mass 1985.

Schnaidt, Claude. *Hannes Meyer: Bauten, Projekte und Schriften*, Tiranti, London 1965.

Schulze, Frank. *Mies van der Rohe: a Critical Biography*, University of Chicago Press 1985.

Schulze, Konrad Werner, *Der Stahl-Skelettbau*, Wissenschaftlicher Verlag Dr Zaugg & Co, Stuttgart 1928.

Schumacher, Thomas L. *Surface and Symbol: Guiseppe Terragni and the Architecture of Italian Rationalism*, ADT Press, London 1991.

Sergeant, John. *Frank Lloyd Wright's Usonian Houses: the Case for Organic Architecture,* Whitney, New York 1976.

Siegel, Kurt. *Structure and Form in Modern Architecture*, Crosby Lockwood & Son, London 1961.

Spalt, Johannes, ed. *Josef Frank 1885-1967*, exhibition catalogue, Hochschule für angewandte Kunst, Vienna 1981.

Speidel, Manfred, ed. *Bruno Taut: Natur und Fantasie*, Ernst & Sohn, Berlin 1995. (German text).

Spens, Michael. *Viipuri Library 1927-35,* Academy Editions, London 1994.

Starr, S. Frederick. *Melnikov: Solo Architect in a Mass Society*, Princeton University Press 1978.

Steadman, Philip. *The Evolution of Designs: Biological Analogy in Architecture and the Applied Arts*, Cambridge University Press, Cambridge 1979.

Sulzer, Peter. *Jean Prouvé, Complete Works, Volume 1: 1917-33,* Wassmuth, Tübingen / Berlin 1995.

Sulzer, Peter. Jean Prouvé, *Complete Works, Volume 2: 1934-44*, Birkhäuser, Basel / Berlin 2000.

Taut, Bruno. *Die neue Wohnung; die Frau als Schöpferin*, von Klinkhardt & Biermann, Leipzig 1924. (German text).

Taut, Bruno. *Die neue Baukunst in Europa und Amerika*, Berlin 1929. Modern edition Julius Hoffmann Verlag, Stuttgart,1979.

Thiekötter, Angelika, ed. *Kristallisationen, Splitterungen: Bruno Tauts Glashaus*, Birkhäuser Basel / Berlin / Boston 1994. (German text).

Vandenberg, Maritz. *New National Gallery Berlin, Ludwig Mies van Der Rohe:* Architecture in Detail, Phaidon, London 1998.

Viollet-le-Duc, Eugene. *Dictionnaire Raisonné de l'Architecture Francaise du XI au XV1 siècle*, Morel & Cie, Paris 1873.

Visser, Margaret. *The Rituals of Dinner*, Penguin, Harmondsworth 1993.

Wendschuh, Achim, ed. *Hans Scharoun, Zeichnungen, Aquarelle, Texte*, Akademie der Künste, Berlin 1993.

Weston, Richard. *Alvar Aalto*, Phaidon, London 1995.

Whitford, Frank. *Bauhaus*, Thames and Hudson, London 1984.

Whyte, Iain Boyd. *Bruno Taut and the Architecture of Activism*, Cambridge University Press, Cambridge 1982.

Whyte, Iain Boyd ed. *Crystal Chain Letters*, MIT Press, Cambridge Mass 1985.

Wilson, Colin St John. *Architectural Reflections*, Butterworth Oxford 1992.

Wilson, Colin St John. *The Other Tradition of Modern Architecture: the Uncompleted Project*, Academy Editions, London 1995.

Windsor, Alan. *Peter Behrens, Architect and Designer*, Architectural Press, London 1981.

Wittkower, Rudolf. *Architectural Principles in the Age of Humanism*, London 1949, 1952.

Worringer, Wilhelm. *Abstraction and Empathy*, International Universities Press, New York 1953. (First German edition 1908)

Worringer, Wilhelm. *Form in Gothic*, Tiranti, London 1957. (First German edition 1910).

Wright, Frank Lloyd. *The Natural House*, Meridian Press 1970. (Original ed. Horizon Press, New York 1954).

Zevi, Bruno. *Giuseppe Terragni*, Triangle Architectural Publishing, London, 1989. (Italian edition 1980).

Zevi, Bruno. *Erich Mendelsohn Opera Completa*, Etas Kompass, Milan, 1970.

Zevi, Bruno. *Towards an Organic Architecture*, Faber and Faber, London 1950. (Original edition *Verso un' Architettura Organica*, Einaudi, Turin 1945).

Zoetbrood, Ronald. *Jan Duiker en het sanatorium Zonnestraal*, Van Gennep, Amsterdam 1985.

Sources of illustrations

Chapter 1
1,6,7,12,18,32,33,39,40,41,44,47, 57,68,82 88: author's photographs.
2: Landesmedienzentrum Baden-Württemberg.
5,11,13, 22,30,35 42,43,78,87: from Joedicke1977.
3,4,19, 24,25,26,29,67,69,70,71,75,76,79: from Kirsch 1987.
8: from Moderne Bauformen 1934.
9,10,20,21,23,36,65,66,74,81,83,84,85,86: versions modified by the author of drawings by Gerhard Kirsch in Karin Kirsch's *Die Weissenhofsiedlung* 1987. Based on the architects' final plans, these redrawn versions do not necessarily document the work precisely as built or as renovated. Copyright of the drawings remains with Gerhard Kirsch.
14,15: courtesy of Bauhaus Archive, Berlin.
16,17: from F.R.S. Yorke, *The Modern House*, with English annotations.
27,28: drawings by the author.
31,34: courtesy of Beeldrecht Foundation, Amsterdam.
37,38,45,46: courtesy of Fondation Le Corbusier, Paris.
48: models by Teresa Jiryes, School of Architecture, University of the South Bank 1993, author's photograph.
49,50,51,52,53,54,55,56: courtesy of Scharoun Archive, Akademie der Künste, Berlin.
58,59,60,61: courtesy of Rading Archive, Akademie der Künste, Berlin.
62,63: from Pfankuch 1970, original source & photographer unspecified.
64: Stadtarchiv Stuttgart.
72,73: courtesy of Max Taut Archive, Akademie der Künste, Berlin.
77,80: courtesy of The J Paul Getty Trust, Los Angeles, Hans & Lily Hildebrandt Collection.

Chapter 2
1,7,8,9,10,11,13,14,19,20,21,26: author's photographs.
2: from Starr 1978.
3: courtesy of Bauhaus Archive, Berlin.
4,5,27: author's photographs of originals in Häring Archive, Akademie der Künste, Berlin.
6,12: from Joedicke/ Lauterbach 1964.
15,22: photographs by Peter Lathey, University of Sheffield.
16: from Die Form 1925.
17: from Bauwelt 1960.
18,23: author's redrawing after originals in Häring Archive, Akademie der Künste, Berlin.
24,25: from Pugin 1853.
28: courtesy of Scharoun Archive, Akademie der Künste, Berlin.

Chapter 3
1,7,8,9,11,12,13: courtesy of Bauhaus Archive, Berlin.
2,4,5,6,16,17,18,19: author's photographs.
3: Hinnerk Scheper 1926, Bauhaus Archive: © Scheper Family, Berlin.
10: author's drawing.
14: photo © Albert Renger-Patsch, Bauhaus Archive, Berlin.
15: photo Hugo Schmölz, Bauhaus Archive, Berlin.

Chapter 4
1,6,8,9,10,11,12,13,16: courtesy of Netherlands Architecture Institute.
2,3,4,5,14,17: author's photographs.
7: from the collections of the IISH, Amsterdam.
15: from Molema 1989.

Chapter 5
1,4,5: from Pehnt 1973.
2,3: from Taut catalogue, Akademie der Künste 1980.
6,7,8,9: from Taut 1924.
10,12: courtesy of Bruno Taut Archive, Akademie der Künste, Berlin.
11,14,15,16,21,22: author's photographs.
13,17,20: from Pitz & Brenne 1980.
18,19: from Pitz & Brenne 1980, modified by the author.

Chapter 6
1,3,4,6,7,9,10,11,12,,21,22: courtesy of Mendelsohn Archive, Staatliche Museen zu Berlin, Kunstbibliothek.
2, 8: author's photograph.
5: from Dekorative Kunst XXII 1914.
13,14,15: author's drawings.
16: 1950s postcard lent by Karin Kirsch, date & photographer unknown.
17: from Bauwelt 1930.
18,19,20: from Mendelsohn *Das Gesamtshaffen des Architekten* Mosse, Berlin 1930.
23: from Schulze 1928.

Chapter 7
1,6,8,9,11,13: Le Corbusier drawings from *Oeuvre complète*, courtesy of Fondation Le Corbusier, Paris.
2: Oeffentliche Kunstsammlung Basel, Kunstmuseum: photograph Martin Bühler.
3,14: from *Le Modulor*, courtesy of Fondation Le Corbusier, Paris.
4, 5, 7,10,12,15,16,17,18,19,20,21,22,23,24: author's photographs.

Chapter 8
1,4,8,9,10,11,12: courtesy of Swedish Architecture Museum, Stockholm.
2,3,5,6,7,13: author's photographs.
14: from Cornell 1992.
15,16,17,18,19,20,21,22,23,24,25,26,27,30,31,32,33,34,35,36,37: courtesy of Alvar Aalto Foundation, Helsinki.
28,29,39: photographs by Gustaf Welin, courtesy of Alvar Aalto Foundation.

Chapter 9
1,6,7,8,9,10,11,12,13,14,16,19,21: Centro Studi Pier Luigi Nervi, Parma
2: from Nervi 1957.
3,23: from Nervi 1957, Photo Vasari.
4,6: from Nervi 1966.
5: from Nervi 1966, Photo Savio.
15,17,18,20 Curt Siegel's drawings from Siegel 1961.

22: from Nervi 1957, Photo Savio.

Chapter 10
1,4,9,10,18: author's photographs.
2,3,5,6,7,8,12,13,14,15,16,17,19,20,22,23: courtesy of Centro Studi Giuseppe Terragni, Como. The plan and elevation drawings are from photos of the Terragni originals.
11: author's drawing.
21,24: from Zevi 1980.

Chapter 11
1, 7,8,35,36,37,38,39,40: author's photographs.
2,3,4,5,6: drawings from guide leaflet to building.
9,13,14,15,16,17,18,19,20,21,22,23,24,25,26,27,28,29,30,33,34: Courtesy of Swedish Architecture Museum, Stockholm.
31,32: plans redrawn for author's article, *Architects Journal*, 1987.

Chapter 12
1: author's photograph.
2: drawings by Richard MacCormac, as printed in Segeant 1976.
3: drawings by Otto Graf from Graf 1983.
4,5,6,7,8,9,10,11,16: photographs by John Sergeant.
5, 9,15: from Sergeant 1976, courtesy of Frank Lloyd Wright Foundation.
12,13,14: drawings by John Sergeant from his article 'Woof and Warp'.

Chapter 13
1,3,4,5,6, 8,10,11,12,13,14,18,20,21,22,23,24,25,27: courtesy of Scharoun Archive, Akademie der Künste, Berlin.
2,30: author's photographs.
7: photo by Hilmar Reuter.
9: author's drawing after original in Scharoun Archive.
15,16,17,19,26,28,29: photos by Peter Lathey, University of Sheffield.
The models of the Mannheim Theatre Project were built by Maurice Friel, Jo Witchell, Richard Bradbury, Jonathan Brent, Andy Groarke, Mark Hancock, Chris Milan, Graham Ovenden and Guy Smith while Diploma students in the School of Architecture, University of Sheffield, 1994-5, in a programme supervised by Peter Blundell Jones and Prue Chiles.

Chapter 14
1: photograph by Robert Häusser, Mannheim, following the restoration of the model organised in 2000 by Helmut Striffler. The model is owned by the City of Mannheim.
2: courtesy of Akademie der Künste, Berlin.
3,4,5,6,7,13,14,15,17,18,19,21,22: author's photographs.
8: photograph by Hedrich Blessing (from Johnson 1978)
9: courtesy of Scharoun Archive, Akademie der Künste, Berlin.
10,11,12: from Pehnt 1970.
16: from Vandenberg 1998.
20: from Johnson 1978
Mies images are used courtesy of Mies's heir Dirk Lohan.

Chapter 15
1,2,3,4,5,6,7,8,9,10,13,17,18,19,20,21,22,23,24,25,26,27,28: author's photographs.
11,12: courtesy of Swedish Architecture Museum, Stockholm.
14,15: composite redrawing by the author of plans in Dymling 1997.

Chapter 16
1,2,3,4,5,7,11,12,13,15,19: author's photographs.
6, 8,10,14,16,18: courtesy of Louis I. Kahn Collection, University of Pennsylvania and Pennsylvania Historical and Museum Commission.
9: from Frampton 1995 p. 244.
17: redrawn by the author after UPL 32 in Ronner & Jhaveri, 1987, p. 108.

Chapter 17
1: Photograph by Peter Lathey, University of Sheffield.

While every attempt has been made to trace the source and copyright of images used, the circumstances surrounding some of the older images are obscure. The author and publishers apologise for any copyrights unknowingly infringed, and invite owners to identify themselves so that appropriate acknowledgement can be made in subsequent editions.

Index

(Page references in italic are to illustrations)